W9-DCL-011

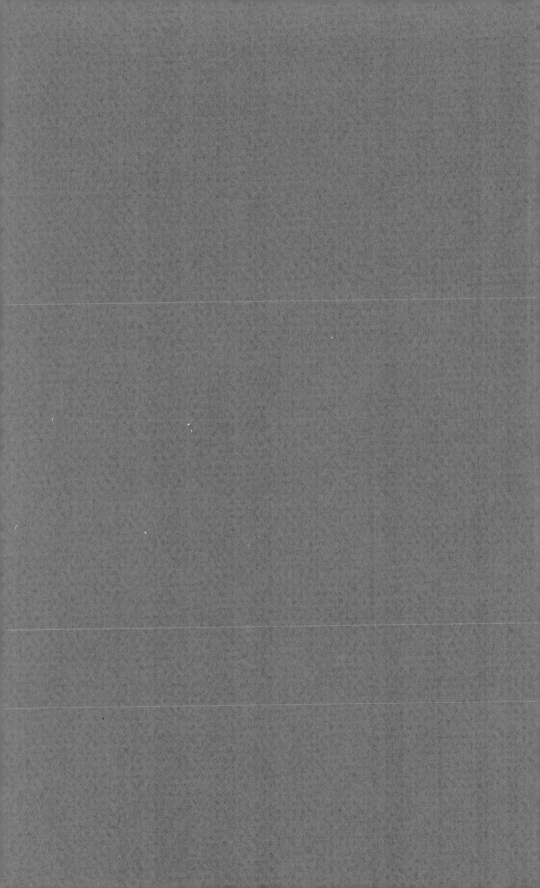

The Writings of Herman Melville

The Northwestern-Newberry Edition

VOLUME FIFTEEN

Journals

Texts revised
with Historical Note
and annotations
by
HOWARD C. HORSFORD
with
LYNN HORTH

Series Editors
HARRISON HAYFORD
G. THOMAS TANSELLE

Editorial Coordinator
ALMA A. MACDOUGALL

Associates
RICHARD COLLES JOHNSON
ROBERT C. RYAN
BRIAN HIGGINS
R. D. MADISON

Journals

HERMAN MELVILLE

NORTHWESTERN UNIVERSITY PRESS
and
THE NEWBERRY LIBRARY
Evanston and Chicago
1989

PUBLICATION OF *this edition of* THE WRITINGS OF HERMAN MELVILLE *has been made possible through the financial support of Northwestern University and its Research Committee and The Newberry Library. The research necessary to establish the text was initially undertaken under the Cooperative Research Program of the Office of Education, and preparation of this volume has been supported by the National Endowment for the Humanities, a federal agency which supports the study of such fields as history, philosophy, literature, and languages. Northwestern University Press produced and published this edition and reserves all rights.*

LIBRARY OF CONGRESS CATALOG CARD NUMBER 88–63305

PRINTED IN THE UNITED STATES OF AMERICA

Cloth Edition, ISBN 0–8101–0822–4
Paper Edition, ISBN 0–8101–0823–2

Contents

ILLUSTRATIONS

Journals

Journal 1849–50

Journal Of a Voyage from New York to London 1849

Thursday Oct 11th After a detention of three or four days, owing to wind & weather, with the rest of the passengers I went on board the tug-boat Goliath about 12½ P.M. during a cold violent storm from the West. The "Southampton" (a regular London liner) lay in the North river. We transfered ourselves aboard with some confusion, hove up our anchor, & were off. Our pilot, a large, beefy looking fellow resembled an oyster-man more than a sailor. We got outside the "Narrows" about 2 O'clock; shortly after, the "tug" left us & the Pilot. At half past 5.PM, saw the last of the land, with our yards square, & in half a gale. As the ship dashed on, under double-reefed topsails, I walked the deck, thinking of what they might be doing at home, & of the last familiar faces I saw on the wharf — Allan was there, & George Duyckinck, and a Mr McCurdy, a rich merchant of New York, who had seemed somewhat interested in the prospect of his son (a sickly youth of twenty bound for the grand tour) being my roommate. But to my great delight, the promise that the Captain had given me at an early day, he now made good; & I find my self in the undevided occupancy of a large state-room. It is as big almost as my own room at home; it has a spacious birth, a large wash-stand, a sofa, glass &c &c. I am the only person on board who is thus honored with a room to himself. I have plenty of light, & a little thick glass window in the side, which in fine weather I may open to the air. I have looked out upon the sea from it, often, tho not yet 24 hours on board.

Friday Oct 12th Walked the deck last night till about eight o'clock; then made up a whist party & played till one of the number had to visit his room from sickness. Retired early & had a sound sleep. Was up betimes, & aloft, to recall the old emotions of being at the mast-head. Found that the ocean looked the same as ever. Have tried to read, but found it hard work. However, there are some very plasant passengers on board, with whom to converse. Chief among these is a Mr Adler, a German scholar, to whom Duyckinck introduced me. He is author of a formidable lexicon, (German & English); in compiling which he almost ruined his health. He was almost crazy, he tells me, for a time. He is full of the German metaphysics, & discourses of Kant, Swedenborg &c. He has been my principal companion thus far. There is also a Mr Taylor among the passengers, cousin to James Bayard Taylor the pedestrian traveller. He is full of fun — or rather *was* full of it. —Just at this moment I hear his mysterious noises from the state-room next to mine. Poor fellow! he is sea-sick. As yet there have been but few thus troubled, owing to pleasant weather. There is a Scotch artist on board, a painter, with a most unpoetical looking only child, a young-one all cheecks & forhead, the former preponderating. Young McCurdy I find to be a lisping youth of genteel capacity, but quite disposed to be sociable. We have several Frenchmen & Englishmen. One of the latter has been hunting, & carries over with him two glorious pairs of antlers (moose) as trophies of his prowess in the woods of Maine. We have also, a middle-aged English woman, who sturdily walks the deck, & prides herself upon her sea-legs, & being an old tar.

Saturday Oct 13 Last evening was very pleasant. Walked the deck with the German, Mr Adler till a late hour, talking of "Fixed Fate, Free-will, foreknowledge absolute" &c. His philosophy is *Colredegian:* he accepts the Scriptures as divine, & yet leaves himself free to inquire into Nature. He does not take it, that the Bible is absolutely infallible, & that anything opposed to it in Science must be wrong.

He beleives that there are things *out* of God and independant of him, — things that would have existed were there no God: — such as that two & two make four; for it is not that God so decrees mathematically, but that in the very nature of things, the fact is thus. —— — Rose early this morning, opened my bull's eye window, & looked out to the East. The sun was just rising, the horizon was red; — a familiar sight to me, reminding me of old times. Before breakfast went up to the mast-head, by way of gymnastics. About 10 o'clock A.M. the wind rose, the rain fell, & the deck looked dismally enough. By dinner time, it blew half a gale, & the passengers mostly retired to their rooms, sea sick. After dinner, the rain ceased, but it still blew stiffly, & we were slowly forging along under close-reefed topsails — mainsail furled. I was walking the deck, when I perceived one of the steerage passengers looking over the side; I looked too, & saw a man in the water, his head completely lifted above the waves, — about twelve feet from the ship, right abreast the gangway. For an instant, I thought I was dreaming; for no one else seemed to see what I did. Next moment, I shouted "Man overboard!" & turned to go aft. The Captain ran forward, greatly confused. I dropped overboard the tackle-fall of the quarter-boat, & swung it towards the man, who was now drifting close to the ship. He did not get hold of it, & I got over the side, within a foot or two of the sea, & again swung the rope towards him. He now got hold of it. By this time, a crowd of people — sailors & others — were clustering about the bulwarks; but none seemed very anxious to save him. They warned *me* however, not to fall overboard. After holding on to the rope, about a quarter of a minute the man let go of it, & drifted astern under the mizzen chains. Four or five of the seamen jumped over into the chains & swung him more ropes. But his conduct was unaccountable; he could have saved himself, had he been so minded. I was struck by the expression of his face in the water. It was merry. At last he drifted off under the ship's counter, & all hands cried "He's gone!" Running to the taffrail, we saw him again, floating off — saw a few bubbles, & never saw him again. No boat was lowered, no sail was shortened, hardly any noise was made. The man drowned like a bullock. It afterwards turned out, that he was crazy, & had jumped overboard. He had declared he would do so several times; & just before he *did* jump, he had tried to get possession of his child, in order to jump into the sea, with the child in his arms. His wife was miserably sick in her berth. The

Captain said that this was the fourth or fifth instance he had known of people jumping overboard. He told a story of a man who did so, with his wife on deck at the time. As they were trying to save him, the wife said it was no use; & when he was drowned, she said "there were plenty more men to be had." —— Amiable creature! — By night, it blew a terrific gale, & we hove to. Miserable time! nearly every one sick, & the ship rolling, & pitching in an amazing manner. About midnight, I rose & went on deck. It was blowing horribly — pitch dark, & raining. The Captain was in the cuddy, & directed my attention "to those fellows" as he called them, — meaning several "Corposant balls" on the yard arms & mast heads. They were the first I had ever seen, & resembled large, dim stars in the sky.

Sunday Oct 14 A regular blue devel day. A gale of wind, & every one sick. Saloons deserted, & all sorts of nausea noise heard from the state-rooms. Taylor, M^c^Curdy, & Adler all in their berths — & I alone am left to tell the tale of their misery. Read a little in Mrs Kirkland's European tour. Like it. She is a spirited, sensible, fine woman. Managed to get thro' the day somehow, by reading & walking the deck, tho' the last was almost as much as my neck was worth. I forgot to say that shortly after the loss of the crazy man (a Dutchman by the way) some of the steerage passengers came aft & told the Captain that there was another crazy man, an Englishman in the steerage. This morning, coming on deck, I saw a man leaning against the bulwarks, whom I immediately took for a steerage passenger. He stopped me, & told me to look off & *see the steamers*. So I looked for about five minutes, — straining my eyes very hard, but saw nothing. — I asked the 2^d^ Mate whether *he* could see the steamers; when he told me that my informant was the crazy Englishman. All the morning this poor fellow was on deck, crying out at steamers, boats, &c &c. I thought that his mad feelings found something congenial in the riot of the raging sea. In the evening, he forced his way into the dining saloon, & struck the Steward, who knocked him down, & dragged him forward. We have made no progress for the last 36 hours; wind ahead, from the Eastward. The crazy man turns out to be afflicted with delirium tremens, consequent upon keeping drunk for the last two months. He is very earnest in his enquiries after a certain *Dr Dobbs*. Saw a lady with a copy of "Omoo" in her hand two days ago. Now & then she would look up at me, as if comparing notes. She turns out to be the wife of a young Scotchman, an artist, going out to Scotland to sketch scenes for his patrons in Albany, including Dr Armsby. He introduced himself to me by mentioning the name of Mr Twitchell who painted my portrait gratis. He is a very unpretending young man, & looks more like a tailor than an artist. But appearances are &c. ——

Monday Oct 15 The gale has gone down, & we have fine weather. By noon the passengers were pretty nearly all on deck, convalescent. They seem to regard me as a hero, proof against wind & weather. My occasional feats in the rigging are regarded as a species of tight-rope dancing. Poor Adler, however, is hardly himself again. He is an exceedingly amiable man, & a fine scholar whose society is improving in a high degree. This afternoon Dr Taylor & I sketched a plan for going down the Danube from Vienna to Constantinople; thence to Athens in the steamer; to Beyroot & Jerusalem — Alexandia & the Pyramids. From what I learn, I have no doubt this can be done at a comparitivly trifling expence. Taylor has had a good deal of experience in cheap European travel, & from his knowledge of German is well fitted for a travelling companion thro Austria & Turkey. I am full (just now) of this glorious *Eastern* jaunt. Think of it! — Jerusalem & the Pyramids — Constantinople, the Egean, & old Athens! —— The wind is not fair yet, & there is much growling consequently. Drank a small bottle of London Stout to day for dinner, & think it did me good. I wonder how much they charge for it? I must find out; & not go thro' the sad experience that "Powell" did (as he says)

Tuesday Oct 16 Beautiful weather, but wind against us. Passengers all better, & quite lively; excepting young McCurdy with a touch of the ague, and a lady, who seems quite ill. Read little or nothing, but lounged about. The sea has produced a temporary effect upon me, which makes me for the time incapable of any thing but vegetating. What's little Barney about? Where's Orianna?

Wednesday Oct 17 Fine weather, quite warm & sunny. The decks lively, the ladies lively, the Captain lively, & the ship now going her course. Spent a good part of the day aloft with Adler, in conversation. In the evening had a sort of concert. An Irish lady, an opera singer they say, leading off with a guitar & her voice.

Thursday Oct 18 Delightful day, & the ship getting on famously. Spent the entire morning in the main-top with Adler & Dr Taylor, discussing our plans for the grand circuit of Europe & the East. Taylor, however, has communicated to me a circumstance, that may prevent him from accompanying us — something of a pecuniary nature. He reckons our expenses at $400.

Friday Oct 19 No events; spent the morning in lounging & reading; and after a hand at cards, retired.

Saturday Oct 20 Newfoundland weather — foggy, rainy &c. Read account of Venice in Murray. Cleared up in the afternoon — passengers played shuffle-board on the quarter-deck. For the first time promenaded with some of the ladies — a Mrs ——— of Monmouthshire, England, & a Miss Wilbur (I think) of New York. The former is flat: the latter is of a marriagable age, keeps a diary & talks about "winning souls to Christ." — In the evening for the first time went into the Ladies' Saloon, & heard Mrs Gould the opera lady sing. There was quite a party — the saloon is guilt & brilliant, & as the ship was going on quietly, it seemed as if I were ashore in a little parlor or cabinet. — Where's Orianna? How's little Barney? — Read a chapter in Pickwick & retired pretty early. Towards morning was annoyed by a crying baby adjoining.

Sunday Oct 21 Rainy — near the Banks. Can not remember what happened to day. It came to an end somehow.

Monday Oct 22 Clear & cold; wind not favorable. I forgot to mention, that *last night* about 9½ P.M. Adler & Taylor came into my room, & it was proposed to have whiskey punches, which we *did* have, accordingly. Adler drank about three table spoons full — Taylor 4 or five tumblers &c. We had an extraordinary time & did not break up till after two in the morning. We talked metaphysics continually, & Hegel, Schlegel, Kant &c were discussed under the influence of the whiskey. I shall not forget Adler's look when he quoted La Place the French astronomer — "It is not necessary, gentlemen, to account for these worlds by the hypothesis" &c. After Adler retired Taylor & I went out on the bowsprit — splendid spectacle. —— It came on calm in the evening, & we await a favorable shift of wind.

Tuesday Oct 23 On gaining the deck this morning was delighted to find a fair wind. It soon blew stiff, & we scudded before it under double-reefed topsails, & mainsail hauled up. Running about 14 knots all day. Every one in high spirits. Captain told a rum story about a *short skipper* and a *long mate* in a little brig, & throwing overboard the barrels of beef & turpentine &c.

Wednesday Oct 24 Fair wind still holds on; at 12 M. supposed to be half way over. Saw several land birds — very tame, lighted on deck — caught one.

Thursday Oct 25 A fair wind — good deal of rain — About noon saw a ship on the other tack. She showed her colors & proved a Yankee. The first vessel that we had seen so near. She excited much interest. By evening blew a very stiff breeze, & we dashed on in magnificent style. Fine moonlight night, & we rushed on thro' snow-banks of foam. McCurdy invited Adler the Doctor & I into his room & ordered champagne. Went on deck again, & remained till near midnight. The scene was indiscribable. I never saw such sailing before.

Friday Oct 26 Fair wind still. Towards noon came on calm, with a gawky sea. The ship rolled violantly, & many comical scenes ensued among the passengers. Breezed up again in the afternoon, & we went on finely. For a few days passed, Adler & I have had some "sober second thoughts" about our grand Oriental & Spanish tour with Taylor. But tonight, the sight of "Bradshaw's Railway & Steamer Guide" showing the marvellous ease with which the most distant voyages may now be accomplished has revived — at least in *my* mind, — all my original enthusiasm. Talked the whole thing over again with Taylor. Shall not be able to decide till we get to London.

Saturday Oct 27. Steered our course on a wind. I played Shuffle board for the first time. Ran about aloft a good deal. McCurdy invited Adler Taylor & I to partake of some *mulled wine* with him, which we did, in my room. Got — all of us — riding on the German horse again — Taylor has not been in Germany in vain. After another curious discussion between the Swede & the Frenchman about Lamertine & Corinne, we sat down to whist, & separated at about 3 in the morning.

Sunday Oct 28 Came on a strong breeze & lasted all day. Ship going about 12 miles an hour — begin to talk of port. Decks very wet, & hard work to take exercise ("Where dat old man"?) Read a little, dozed a little & to bed early.

Monday Oct 29 Wet & foggy, but a fair fresh breeze — 12 knots an hour. Some of the passengers sick again. In the afternoon tried to create some amusement by arraigning Adler before the Captain on a criminal charge. In the evening put the Captain in the Chair, & argued the question "which was best, a monarchy or a republic?" — Had some good sport during the debate — the Englishmen would'nt take part in it tho'. — After chat & Stout with Monsieur Moran & Taylor went on deck, & found it a moonlight midnight. Wind astern. Retired at 1 A.M. ———

Tuesday Oct 30 Glorious day — Capital cakes for breakfast. — ("Where dat old man"?) Saw a land bird. Weather beautifully clear. For the first time in five days got our observation. Find ourselves heading right into the middle of the Channel" — the Scilly Island out of sight to the North. Played Shuffle Board with Taylor & the ladies. Had a superb dinner, which we all relished amazingly. Drawing near port with a fine fair wind makes passengers feel generous. A good deal of wine & porter on table. A magnificent night — but turned in very early.

Wednesday Oct 31 Fair, fresh wind still holds. Coming on deck in the morning saw a brig close to — & two or three ships. If the wind holds we shall make the Lizzard Light this evening, probably. May be in Portsmouth tomorrow night. All hands in high spirits. Had some mulled Sherry in the evening from M^c^Curdy. Up late, expecting it to be the last night.

*Thursday. Nov 1st* Just three weeks from home, and made the land — Start Point — about 3 P.M. — well up Channel — passed the Lizzard. Very fine day — great number of ships in sight. Thro' these waters Blake's & Nelson's ships once sailed. Taylor suggested that he & I should return M^c^Curdy's civilities. We did, and Captain Griswold joined and ordered a pitcher of his own. The Captain is a very intelligent & gentlemanly man — converses well & understands himself. I never was more deceived in a person than I was in him. Retired about midnight. Taylor played a rare joke upon McCurdy this evening, passing himself off as Miss Wilbur, having borrowed her cloak &c. They walked together. Shall see Portsmouth tomorrow morning.

Friday Nov 2d Wind from the East — ahead. Clear & beautiful day — but every one greivously disappointed. I think I shall get off at Portsmouth, instead of going round. May be in to night, after all. Spoke a Portsmouth Pilot boat, but took no pilot. Made the Bill of Portland — from which the Portland stone is got. Melancholy looking voyage, white cliffs indeed! In the evening played chess, & talked metaphysics my learned friend till midnight.

Saturday Nov 3d Woke about 6 o'clock with an insane idea that we were going before the wind, & would be in Portsmouth in an hour's time. Soon found out my mistake. About eight o'clock took a pilot, who brought some papers two weeks old. Made the Isle of Wight about 10 A.M. High land — The Needles. Wind ahead &, tacking. Get in to night or to morrow — or next week or year. Develish dull, & too bad altogether. X X X X Continued tacking all day with a light wind from West. Isle of Wight in sight all day & numerous ships. One of our steerage passengers left in the Pilot Boat. Rum scene alongside with the boat. In the evening all hands in high spirits — Played chess in the ladies' saloon — another party at cards; good deal of singing in the gentlemen's cabin & drinking — very hilarious & noisy — Last night every one thought. Determined to go ashore at Portsmouth. Therefore prepared for it — arranged my trunk to be left behind — put up a shirt or two in Adler's carpet bag & retired pretty early.

Sunday Nov 4 Looked out of my window, first thing upon rising & saw the Isle of Wight again — very near — ploughed feilds &c. Light head wind — expected to be in a little after breakfast time. About 10, A.M rounded the Eastern end of the Isle, when it fell flat calm. The town in sight by telescope. Were becalmed about three or four hours. Foggy, drizzly; long faces at dinner — no porter bottles. Wind came from the West at last. Squared the yards & struck away for Dover — distant 60 miles. At 6 o'clock (evening) passed Dungeness — then saw the Beachy Head light. Close reefed the topsails so as not to run too fast. Expect now to go ashore tomorrow morning early at Dover

— & get to London via Canterbury Cathedral. Mysterious hint dropped me about my green coat. Talked with the Pilot about the perils of the Channel. He told a story of running down a brig in a steamer &c. —— It is now eight o'clock in the evening. I am alone in my state-room — lamp in tumbler. Spite of past dissappointments I *feel* that this is my last night aboard the Southampton. This time tomorrow I shall be on land, & press English earth after the lapse of ten years — *then* a sailor, *now* H.M. author of "Peedee" "Hullabaloo" & "Pog-Dog".

—— For the last time I lay aside my *"log,"* to add a line or two to Lizzie's letter — the last I shall write onboard. — ("Where dat old man?" — "Where books?)"

I commence this Journal at 25 Craven Street, Strand, at 6½ P.M. on Wednesday Nov 7th 1849 — being just arrived from dinner at a Chop House, and feeling like it.

Mon: Nov: 6th 1849. Having at the invitation of McCurdy cracked some Champaign with him, I retired about midnight to my state-room; and at 5 in the morning was wakened by the Captain in person, saying we were off Dover. Dressed in a hurry, ran on deck, & saw the lights ashore. A cutter was alongside, and after some confusion in the dark, we got off in her for the shore. A comical scene ensued. The boatmen saying we could not land at Dover, but only at Deal. So to Deal we went, & were beached there just at break of day. Some centuries ago a person called Julius Caesar jumped ashore about in this place, & took possession. It was Guy Fawke's Day also. Having left our baggage (that is Taylor, Adler & self) to go round by ship to London, we were wholly unincumbered; & I proposed walking to Canterburry — distant 18 miles, for an appetite to breakfast. So, we strode thro' this quaint old town of Deal — one of the Cinque Ports, I beleive, and soon were in the open country. A fine autumnal morning & the change from ship to shore was delightful. Reached Sandwich (6 miles) and breakfasted at a tumble down old inn. Finished with ale & pipes. Visited "Richboro' Castle" — so called — a Roman fortification near the sea shore. An imposing ruin; the interior was planted with cabbages. The walls some 10 feet thick, grown over with ivy. Walked to where they were digging — and saw defined by a trench, the exterior wall of a circus. Met the proprietor — an antiquary — who regaled us with the history of the place. Strolled about the town, on our return, and found it full of interest as a fine specimen of the old Elizabethan architecture. Kent abounds in such towns. —— At one o'clock took the 2[d] class (no 3[d]) cars for Canterbury. The Cathedral is on many accounts the most remarkable in England. Henry II, his wife, & the Black Prince are here — & Becket. Ugly place where they killed him. Fine cloisters. There is a fine thought expressed in one of the inscriptions on a tomb in the nave.

Visited the Dane John in the afternoon, rather evening. Beautiful view of the city & its numerous old churches. The old wall forms a fine promenade. Dined at the "Falstaff" Inn near the Westgate. Went to the theater in the evening, & were greatly amused at the performance: more people on the stage than in the boxes. Ineffably funny, the whole affair. All three of us slept in one room at the inn — odd hole.

Tuesday Nov 6th. Swallowed a glass of ale, & away for the R.R. Station, & off for London, distant some 80 miles. Took the third class cars — exposed to the air — develish cold riding against the wind. Fine day — people sociable. Passed thro' Penshurst (P.S.'s place) & Tunbridge (fine old ruin there). Arrived at London Bridge at noon — crossed at once over into the city, & dinner at a chop-house in the Poulterey —— having eaten nothing since the previous afternoon dinner. Went on passed St Paul's to the Strand to find our house. They referred us elsewhere, being full. Secured rooms at last (one for each) at a guinea & a half per week. Very cheap. — Went down to the Queen's Hotel to inquire after our ship friends — (on the way green coat attracted attention) — not in. Went to Drury Lane at Julien's Promenade Concerts. (Admittance 1.S.) A great crowd, & fine music. In the reading room happened to see "Bentley's Miscellany" with something about Redburn. (By the way, stopped at a store in the Row, & inquired for the book, to see whether it had been published. They offered it to me at a guinea). At Julien's also saw Blackwood's long story about a short book. It's very comical — seemed so, at least, as I had to hurry over it — in treating the thing as real. But the wonder is that the old Tory should waste so many pages upon a thing, which I, the author, know to be trash, & wrote it to buy some tobacco with. —— On the way home, stopped at the American Bowling Saloon in the Strand. A good wash & turned in early.

Wednesday Nov 7th Rose at eight, & away we went down into the city & breakfasted at a "hole in the wall." Then to the Blackwall R.R. Station for the East India Docks, after our trunks. After infinite trouble with the cursed Customs, we managed to get them thro'. (Two disconsolates on board the ship) At five PM. arrived home, & dined, & went to see Madam Vestriss & Charles Mathews at the Royal Lycceum Theater, Strand. Went into the Gallery (one shilling) Quite decent people there — fellow going round with a coffee pot & mugs — crying "Porter, gents, porter!"

Thursday Nov 8th Dressed, after breakfast at a Coffee house, & went to Mr Bentley's. He was out of town, at Brighton. The notices of "Redburn" were shown me, — laughable. Staid awhile, & then to Mr Murray's, — Out of town. Strolled about, & went into the National Gallery. Dined with the Doctor & Adler, & after a dark ramble thro' Chancery Lane & Lincoln's Inn Feilds, we turned into Holborn, & so to the Princess's Theatere in Oxford Street. Went into the pit at the half price — one shilling. The part of a Frenchman was very well played. So also, skaters on the ice.

Friday Nov 9th Breakfasted late, & went down to Queen's hotel — saw McCurdy there & Mulligan. Parted from the Doctor & Adler near the Post Office, & went into Cheapside to see the "Lord Mayor's Show" it being the day of the great civic feast & festivities. A most bloated pomp, to be sure. Went down to the bridges to see the people crowding there. Crossed by Westminster, thro' the Parks to the Edgeware Road, & found the walk delightful — the sun coming out a little, & the air not cold. —— While on one of the Bridges, the thought struck me again that a fine thing might be written about a Blue Monday in November London — a city of Dis (Dante's) clouds of smoke — the damned &c — coal barges — coaly waters, cast iron Duke &c its marks are left upon you, &c &c &c

Stopped in at the Gallery of the Adelphi Theater, Strand, — horribly hot & crowded — good peice tho' — was in bed by ten' o'clock.

Saturday Nov 10th. At breakfast received a note from Mr Bentley in reply to mine, saying he would come up from Brighton at any time convenient to me. Wrote him, "Monday noon, in New Burlington

St:" — After breakfast at a Coffee room, Adler went off to Hampton Court & the Dr: to the Botanic Gardens, Regent's Park. For me, I lounged away the day — sauntering thro' the Temple courts & gardens, Lincoln's Inn, The New Hall, Gray's Inn, down Holborn Hill thro' Cock Lane (Dr Johnson's Ghost) to Smithfield (West). And so on to the Charter House, where I had a sociable chat with an old pensioner who guided me thro some fine old cloisters, kitchens, chapels. Lord Ellenborough lies buried hard by the founder. They bury all their dead on their own premises. Duke of Norfolk was confined here in Elizabeth's time for treason. From the Charter House thro' the Goswell Street Road to Barbican towards London Wall. Asked an officer of the Fire Department where lay St Swithin's — He was very civil & polite & offered to show me the way in person. "Perhaps you would like to see the way to the house where Whittington was born? Many Londoners never saw it" — "Lead on," said I — & on we went — thro squalid lanes, alleis, & closes, till we got to a dirty blind lane; & there it was with a slab inserted in the wall. Thence, thro' the influence of the Fire Officer, I pushed my way thro cellars & anti-lanes into the rear of Guildhall, with a crowd of beggars who were going to receive the broken meats & pies from yesterday's grand banquet (Lord Mayor's Day). — Within the hall, the scene was comical. Under the flaming banners & devices, were old broken tables set out with heaps of fowls hams &c &c pastry in profusion — cut in all directions — I could tell who had cut into this duck, or that goose. Some of the legs were gone — some of the wings, &c. (A good thing might be made of this) Read the account of the banquet — the foreign ministers & many of the nobility were present. From the Guildhall, strolled thro' the Poultery to the Bank & New Exchange — thence, down King William Street to Fish Street Hill, & thro Eastcheap to Tower Hill. Saw some fine Turkish armor (chain) every ring bearing a device. a supurb cannon, cut & bored from one peice of brass — belonged to the Knights of Malta. The headsman's block, upon which Kilmarnock & the Scotch lords were beheaded in the Pretender's time. The marks of the axe were very plain — like a butcher's board. —— Lounged on by St: Katherine's & London Docks & Ratcliffe-High Way, & within the dock walls to Wapping to the Tunnel. Crossed, to Rotherhithe, & back by boat — flinging a fourpenny peice to "Poor Jack" in the mud. Took a steamer, & returned to the Temple landing & off to the Adelphi to dinner at five

P.M. — dark. After dinner, Adler & I strolled over to Holborn & it being Saturday night, entertained ourselves by vagabonding thro' the courts & lanes, & looking in at the windows. Stopped in at a Penny Theater. — Very comical — Adler afraid. To bed early.

Sunday Nov: 11th. A beautiful autumnal day. Breakfasted about 10, & down to the Temple Church to hear the music. Saw the 10 Crusaders — those who had been to the Holy Land, with their legs crossed. Heads of the damned, fine. Then down to St Pauls — looked in a moment — then took a buss for Hampton Court with the Doctor. Thro' the Strand to Piccadilly & Hyde Park, past Kensington Gardens, Kensington, Hammersmith, Chiswick, Turnham Green, Kew, & across the Thames to Richmond Hill. — The royal gardens at Kew very splendid — past the Pagoda built by Chambers. From Richmond Hill, the prospect was ineffably fine. The place is justly renowned for its beauty. The day was one in a million for England, too. Here the poet Thompson dwelt. I was on top of the coach. Pope lived near here, at Twickenham, over the way. Arrived at Hampton Court about 2 P.M. — distant some 20 miles, I think, from St Paul's. —— The place is full of pictures. — Lely' & Vandique's — the Beauties — are lovely — the Dutchess of Cleveland. — Ignatius by Guido(?) — A Venus by Titian. — The Cartoons are not well disposed for light. — Oak work very rich dyed. — Rembrandt's Jew. — State Beds — Walked thro' the parks with the Doctor till after sundown — then to a road side inn, & drank a glass of ale. Returned to town by RR & dined at the Adelphi — then stopped in at St Martin's-In-the-Feilds, & to bed early.

Monday Nov 12th. Received another note from Mr Bentley saying he would be in town this morning, according to my suggestion, at 12. A.M. Stopped in at the National Gallery on my way to New Burlington Street. Saw Bentley. Very polite. Gave me his note for £100 at 60 days for "Redburn" — Could'nt do better, he said. He expressed much anxiety & vexation at the state of the Copyright question. Proposed my new book — "White Jacket" — to him & showed him the Table of Contents. He was much pleased with it. And notwithstanding the vexatious & uncertain state of the Copyright matter, he made me the following offer: — To pay me £200 for the first 1000 copies of the book (the privilege of publishing that number). And as we might afterwards arrange, concerning subsequent editions. A liberal offer. But he could make no advance. — Left him, & called upon M[r] Murray in Albemarl Street. Not in — out of town. Strolled down St James into the Park; took a buss & got out at the Cigar Divan in the Strand. Cheerlessly splendid. Walked to St Paul's, & sat an hour in a dozing state listening to the chaunting in the choir. Felt homesick & sentimentally unhappy. Rallied again, & down Ludgate Hill to the London Coffee House to dine according to appointment with Captain Griswold. Met Joseph Harper casually. He goes home in the Southampton. A regular Yankee. — Had a noble dinner of turtle soup, pheasant &c: with glorious wine. At 10 o'clock, left with the Captain & the rest of the company (Doctor, Adler, Mulligan, M[c]Curdy, "Stetson") for the "Judge & Jury" Bow Street. Exceedingly diverting but not superlatively moral. Nicholson is a naturally able man — so was one of the barristers. Was in bed before 1 o'clock.

Tuesday Nov 13th. According to arrangement overnight, the Doctor & I sallied out at seven o'clock (A.M.) & walked over Hungerford Bridge to Horsemonger Lane, Borough, to see the last end of the Mannings. Paid half a crown each for a stand on the roof of a house adjoining. An inimitable crowd in all the streets. Police by hundreds. Men & women fainting. — The man & wife were hung side by side — still unreconciled to each other — What a change from the time they stood up to be married, together! The mob was brutish. All in all, a most wonderful, horrible, & unspeakable scene. — Breakfasted about 11.A.M. & went to the Zoological Gardens, Regent's Park. Very pretty. Fine giraffes. Dreary & rainy day. Returned home at 4.P.M. & wrote up Journal. M[c]Curdy called in about six o'clock, at the house, & bored me terribly. But I wrote a letter home meantime.

Wednesday Nov 14th After a very sound night's sleep rose much refreshed. Breakfasted at the old place in the Strand. Taylor on his last legs; some one loaned him a sovereign. But he said — "Never say die". His designs upon the two ladies (awkward expression, but perfectly harmless) have failed completely. Adler & I started for the Abbey & Westminster Hall. Wandered about there awhile — went thro' the chapels — a knight with one wife on his right side, & a vacant space on the left — the vacant lady refusing to be put there. A serio-comico moment about Death. Up the river in a penny steamer as far as Vauxhall, passing Lambeth Palace. Began to rain hard, & arrived home drenched. Rigged up again, & in my *green* jacket called upon M[r] Murray in Albemarle St: —— He was very civil — much vexed about copyright matter. — I proposed *"White Jacket"* to him — he seemed decidedly pleased — & has since sent for the proof sheets, according to agreement. —— Went down to the Exchange in an omnibus — & tried to thrust my way in "Loyd's" — but it was no go. Sauntered away the two hours to dinner by lounging by the shops. Opposite Somerset house in the Strand, happened to see a copy of Beaumont & Fletcher — stepped in — & found the shopman to be an old acquaintance of young Duyckinck's — M[r] Stibbs. I bought a folio of "B & F" also one of Ben Johnson. And shall purchase more. He showed me a Chapman's Homer. —— Dined with the Dr: M[c]Curdy & Adler — the Dr paying the bill. Tomorrow he starts with M[c]C for the East — Jerusalem, &c. — Went to the New Strand Theater. A capital peace, excellently played — "The Clandestine Marriage" by Coleman. All the parts admirably sustained. Mrs Glover (an old veteran & great favorite) as Mrs Hidleburgh. Leigh Murray as Melvil — the finest leg I ever saw on a man — a develishly well turned out man, upon my soul. Old Farren was Lord Ogleby. ——

Thursday Nov: 15th. Special Thanksgiving day appointed by the Queen. All the shops shut as if it were Sunday, & all the churches open. Went down to the Queen's Hotel to bid good bye to M[c]Curdy & the Dr: Thence took a 'buss with Adler down Newgate Street thro' Holborn & Oxford Street to Paddington & Edgeware Road to St John's Wood & so round Regent's Park to Primrose Hill. The view was curious. Towards Hampstead the open country looked green, & the air was pretty clear; but cityward it was like a view of hell from Abraham's bosom. Clouds of smoke, as tho' you looked down from M[t] Washington in a mist. Crossed Regent's park to New Road & got into a buss — outside — passed King's Cross & the famous Angel Inn, thro' City Road into Moorgate & so to the Bank. Lunched in a hole in Leadenhall Street — dismal lunch enough — & took a buss across London Bridge to the Elephant & Castle, Borough. Thence walked over Westminster Bridge to the Abbey & attended service there at 3 o'clock P.M. A vast crowd present & no seats. Walked home & wrote up journal &c. At half past 5 (P.M.) went with Adler to the "Edingburgh Castle" a noted place for its fine Scotch ale, the best I ever drank. Had a glorious chop & a pancake a pint & a half of ale, a cigar & a pipe, & talked high German metaphysics meanwhile. Home & to bed by 10'o'clock. The "Castle" is the beau ideal of a tavern — dark walled, & like a beef-steak in color, polite waiters &c.

Friday 16th Nov. After breakfast at the old place in the Strand, went to the British Museum — big arm & foot — Rosetta stone — Ninevah sculptures — &c. From thence to Albemarle Street — Mr Murray was not in. Home, & wrote to Allan by the "Canada". Walked thro' Seven Dials to Oxford Street & so to Murray's again. Found him in — was very polite, but "would not be in his line to publish my book". Offered to give me some of his "Hand Books" as I was going on the Continant. So he sent me to the house his Book of the Continant & for France. Met Adler by appointment at the "Mitre Tavern", Mitre Court, Fleet Street — the place where Dr Johnson used to dine. His bust by Nollekins is there. Had a "stewed rump steak" — very fine, & bread & cheese, & ale (of course). Then up stairs & smoked a cigar. Cosy, & comfortable place enough. No cursed white walls. Stopped in at the "Dr Johnson Tavern" over the way & drank a glass of ale. Bust of him there, also. Go to the place thro' a court, where the Dr used to live. Some rivalry between the two places. The last the *darkest*. Thence walked down to the Queen's Hotel, St Martin's Le Grand to see Timpson & get some more money for the fund to purchase the book for Cap: Griswold. P. was just off for Paris by Express. From thence took buss for Sadler's Wells Theater, Islington. Pit. One of Colley Cibber's comedies — "She would, & she would not" — Don Manuel, Mr A Younge — an oldish man — seemed a favorite with the audience — not a bad comic actor. — The women (stage) were not peculiarly lovely. — After the first farce (a new one, "The First of May" "by A Younge") we walked to the Angel Inn, & took a buss across to Holborn & thro' Chancery Lane to Temple Bar. — Stopped at the "Cock Tavern" adjoining — (Tennyson's) — and drank two glasses of Stout, for which the place is famous — & sells no ales. — Dark & cosy — something Like the "Edinboro' ". Smoked a pipe also, & home with Adler & to bed.

Saturday 17th Nov: Adler proposed a visit to the Dulwich gallery, distant five miles, southwards. So, went to the "Kings & Key" Fleet Street, and mounted a buss there. Crossed Blackfriars to Elephant &

Castle — & thro' Newington, Walworth, Camberwell, & Denmark-Hill to the beautiful hamlet of Dulwich — A most sequestered, quiet, charming spot indeed. — The gallery is full of gems — Titians, Claudes, Salvators, Murillos. — The Peasant Boys — The Venus — The Peasant Girl — Cardinal Beaufort — The mottled horse of Wouvermans — St John — The Assumption — The old man & pipe — Mrs Siddons as Tragic Muse. Curious old clock & tables. Met Yankee there. Left gallery, & took a little ramble round the country. Profound Calm — the green meadows & woodlands steeped in haze — strikingly English. — Rode back to town on top of buss. Adler & the Yankee carrying on a spirited discussion concerning the merits of the various paintings. —— Walked towards home from the Kings & Key & concluded the affair of the present of the book to Cap: Griswold — Adler & I, however, have to pay down the most; it so happens. — Upon my arrival in Craven Street, & found the letter which I expected, from Mr Colbourn. — I should have put it down yesterday, that after leaving Mr Murray's in the afternoon — (by his instigation) I went to Mr Colbourn's in Great Marlborough Street — was ushered up into a suite of drawing-rooms & received by Mr C, who said, at last, I would hear from him, by the next day at 3.P.M. —— The letter simply declines my proposition (£200 for 1st 1000 copies) & on the ground, principally, of the cursed state of the copyright matter. —— Bad news enough — I shall not see Rome — I'm floored — appetite unimpaired however — so down to the Edingburgh Castle & paid my compliments to a chop. Smoked a long pipe — & then into the adjoining book store — & turned over some noble old works, & chatted with the bookseller — a very civil, intelligent young man. Bought a quarto of Davenant, & a little copy of Hudibras. — Thence walked up to St Martin's Lane, thro' Seven Dials — St: Giles — to Holborn & down Regent St: home & to bed.

Sunday 18th Nov: Rose & wrote up journal till nine o'clock. Then with the Professor down to a cheap chop house near Temple bar — & had a villainous cup of coffee, a large dirty roll, & a strip of fried bacon for 4 pence. — Then to the Temple Church — not open — so walked the cloisters awhile. Church opened & went in & walked round a half hour. Then out, & across the street to St: Dunstans. Then down Fleet Street & Ludgate hill (detour thro White-Friars) and parted with Adler at Black Friars. Took his umbrella for my cane.

Went down street alone — looked in at St Paul's — and at last entered Bow Church, Cheapside. Was shown to a seat like a pit & sat out the entire service. Curious old church indeed. Returning home, left St Paul's Church Yard, thro' a court towards Doctors Commons, & wandered among a labyrinth of blind allis & courts to Apothecaries Hall & Printing House Square. Then crossed Fleet Street near Temple Bar, towards the North & threaded more allies, lanes, & courts & so home at 3. PM of a dismal drizzling day. Read a little about the Mannings murder — guide books &c — wrote Lizzie. — Dined with Adler at the Adelphi — then to the Rainbow tavern — (Tennyson's) & smoked a cigar in a room inhabited by a melancholy man. Splendid dining room at the Rainbow. Terrific bumper of Stout. famous for Stout. — Walked off alone down Fleet Street & went to St: Bride's Church. Woman showed me to a big pew — almost unasked — blushed a good deal, what with Stout, jam, heat, & modesty. Excited vast deal of gazing somehow. good sermon — a charity one. gave sixpence. Home & to bed.

Monday 19th Rose & wrote. After breakfast with Adler went down to the city & presented my letters to Thomas Delf (Duyckinck's). Not in. — Then to David Davidson (Young D's) Paternoster Row — Wiley's Agent. Not in. Then to J. M. Langford P. Row — (Mrs Welford's) — Very civil reception — invited me to go to hear McCready same night — also to sup with him & meet Albert Smith, the comic writer who has just returned from the East & purposes writing something "funny" about it. Leaving Mr Langford, went to the Longmans in the Row & proposed "the book". Saw Mr Longman himself — very polite — promised to send me a note by evening. Took a buss up to Mr Bentley's to see if there should be any letters. Found two budgets from home — much delighted me — also other letters. On first entering the place, a "clark" steps up — "Lord John Manners has been here for you, sir!" — The devel he has "And left this letter, Sir" — Shove it along then. His Lordship's note was very kind indeed, — he enclosed two letters to Monckton Miles & Lady E. Drummond. Went into B's private room & read my home letters. All well thank God — & Barney a bouncer. Went to Mr Murray's. Told him, that people here having anticipated me, I should stay awhile now, & make some social calls &c. He took me up stairs to see his gallery of literary portraits. Fine head of Byron, Moore, Campbell,

Borrow &c &c. — (Among other letters from the U.S. I received one from Willis, enclosing a letter to Lord J. Manners & M F Tupper. The letter to L. J. Manners is from his sister in New York.) Went home & answered Manners' note, saying I would call tomorrow. Having no one to send it by took it myself to the Albany, & handing it to the beadle to be delivered was told that Lord J. M. had that morning left town.

Wrote him therefore at Belvoir Castle. Also sent off letter to Lizzy by the Herman. Dined with Adler at the Adelphi. Then home. Mr Langford called, & bidding poor Adler good bye (he is off for Paris at midnight by the steamer) went to the Haymarket. Full house. Went into the critics' boxes. "Times" & "Herald" men there. Mcready painted hideously. Did'nt like him very much upon the whole — bad voice, it seemed. James Wallack, Iago. very good. Miss Reynolds Desdemona — very pretty. Horrible Roderigo. Stayed out the first farce — "Alarming Sacrifice" by Buckstone the great commedian, who played the principal part — Bob Ticket. Very funny. Home & to bed at 12. Found a note from Murray inviting me to dine & meet Lockhart on Friday. Also note from Capt Griswold acknowledging volume.

Tuesday 20th Opened the door & found a note on top of my blackened boots. It was from the Longmans, saying they abided by their original terms. — Breakfasted alone at the old place — capital coffee that — a nice neat place indeed & the morning papers delightfully *fresh*. The old lady too very nice. Returned home & read & wrote till 12 o'clock. Then got out some of my letters & resolved to go at it, like a regular job, which it is, this presenting letters of introduction. First went to Mr Rogers in St James' Place — very quiet & death-like; — not in — left letter & card. Then across the Park to Upper Belgrave Street to the American minister. Found both him & Davis the Secretary. Mr Lawrence received me very kindly, said that the Duke of Rutland (father of L J Manners & L Emmeline) had been seeking my address from him. The D left town yesterday. Mr L invited me to call same evening at the Clarendon Hotel to see his wife &c. Learning from him that Lady E Drummond was in town, I went home, rigged up & jumped into an omnibus for Oxford Street. Walked from thence to Bryanston Square — out of town — would'nt return till after Christmas. Left letter & card. Then walked to Upper Harley

Street (devel of a walk, too) and left letter & card for Russell Sturgis. Also walked to Portman Square & left same for Joshua Bates. Then walked down street, stopped & learnt the address of Moxon the Publisher. Found him in — sitting alone in a back room — he was at first very stiff, cold, clammy, & clumsy. Managed to bring him to, tho', by clever speeches. Talked of Charles Lamb — he warmed up & ended by saying he would send me a copy of his works. He said he had often put Lamb to bed — drunk. He spoke of Dana — he published D's book here. — Thence, down to the Adelphi by buss & dined alone. — fried sole. Then home, & read & wrote. At 7 P.M. called at the Clarendon Hotel, Bond Street, upon Mr & Mrs Lawrence. Found them in a noble drawing room. M[r] Lawrence was very kind, unaffected & agreeable. I like him much. He is a very fine looking benevolent-seeming man. But his wife! Such a sour, scrawny, scare crow was never seen till she first saw herself in the glass. I do not fly out at her for her person — no, but her whole air & manner — God deliver me from such horrors as Mrs. Lawrence possesses for me. — Her skinny scrawny arms were bare — She talked of Lady Bulwer — said that — but there is no telling how she managed so well her veiled & disgusted air, without being at all uncivil or meaning any incivility. She belongs to that category of the female sex, there are no words to express my abhorrence of. I hate her not — I only class her among the persons made of reptiles & crawling things. Coming home stopped at a place in the Haymarket — singular interview there for a moment. Home early & to bed by 9½.

Wednesday Nov 21st. Breakfasted & took a ha'penny steamer at the Adelphi and down to London bridge — thence another steamer for Greenwich Hospital. Crowds of pensioners. Went into the Painted Hall — sea peices & portraits of naval heroes, coats of Nelson in glass cases. Fine ceiling. Was shown about the wards by a machine. Visited the Chapel. Fine painting by West of St Paul. Saw the Pensioners at dinner. over 1500. Remarkable sight. The negro. — Hat off! — Hat on! — Married men & unmarried — mess apart. 2 & 2. Pensioners in palaces! Story of Charles II. Walked in Greenwich Park. Observatory. Fine view from a hill — talk with an old pensioner there. Home by railway. From London Bridge walked to Delf's — not in. Thence to Davidson's in Paternoster Row. Had a talk with him — invited me to dine — went to Queen's Hotel. (Previously I stopped in at the

Longmans about the book) Dined on ox-tail soup — chops — ale — port wine. Good dinner & David a good fellow. Strolled thro' Fleet Market — butchering under hatches — blubber rooms. Walked with Davidson to American Bowling Saloon. Made me go in. Rolled one game & beat him. Then home & dressed for Mr Langford's. On the way, bought Lavater's Phisiognomy in Holborn, for 10 shillings (sterling). Found Langford & a young fellow, in his lodgings. Snug place enough. At last there came in four or five young fellows — sociable chaps. And in the end, Albert Smith the comic writer & Tom Taylor the Punch man & Punch poet. Smith was just from the East, & sported a blazing beard. A rattling, guffaw, cockney — full of fun & a little malice perhaps. — Nice plain supper — no stiffness. Porter passed round in tankards. Round table, potatoes in a napkin. Afterwards, Gin, brandy, whiskey & cigars. Smith told funny stories about his adventures in the East, &c. Gave me his address &c. Came away about 2.AM. & thro' Oxford Street home, & turned flukes. Found Moxon had sent me his copies of Charles Lamb — also found a card from Russel Sturgis & a note from Joshua Bates inviting me to dine & spend Sunday with him at East Sheen. Accepted.

Thursday Nov 22 Rose late — headache — breakfasted & off on top of omnibus to Great Western Rail Road for Windsor. Had to wait an hour. Pleasant day. Round Tower — fine view. Long Walk. Went thro' the state apartments. Cheerlessly damnatory fine. Mast of the Victory & bust of Nelson. Shield of Cellini. Gobelin tapestry is miraculous. Made the acquaintance of an Englishman — viewed the royal stables with him. On the way down from the tower, met the Queen coming from visiting the sick Queen Dowager. Carriage & four, going past with outriders. The Prince with her. My English friend bowed & so did I, — salute returned by the Q but not by the P. I would commend to the Q Rowland's Kalydore for clarifying the complexion. She is an amiable domestic woman tho' I doubt not & God bless her, say I, & long live the "prince of whales" — The Stables were splendid. Endless carriages &c. — Walked in the Great Park with the Englishman talking about America. Arrived in London about 5 P.M. Dined & home. Found my book (Lavater & ½ sovereign, on top of it) in my room, also note from Mr & Mrs Lawrence inviting me to dinner, which, had to decline owing to prior engagement with Mr Murray. Went & left my reply in person at the Clarendon Hotel. Then to Bentley's — not in. Home & wrote up journal.

Friday Nov 23 A long nights rest — having turned in at 9½ & rising at about the same hour this morning. Must have caught cold last evening on top of the omnibuss from R.R. Station. Felt feverish & chilly by turns. Light breakfast, & down the Strand. Called on Capt: Griswold — — not in. Then to the Aldine Chambers, & saw Davidson. Took me up stairs, & had a chat. He said he thought he could get my note (Bentley's) cashed for me — by which, felt much releived. Talked to him concerning White Jacket & Copyright. He said I must keep pushing & mentioned the names of some more publishers whom I ought to try. At his instance, he went with me to Bogue's (Strand) & introduced me. I stated my business. B. was all ears. Gave him an idea of the book. He finally said he would send me his answer by six o'clock this evening. It is now 3½ P.M.; & I predict that he declines. We shall see. — After leaving Bogue, walked in the Temple courts & gardens. Then, went musing along thro' Drury Lane to Holborn, & came home with a fit of the Blues. On my way, bought a pound & a half of figs & brought them home to make lunches of. Wrote Lizzie & Allan by the Steamer which goes to Boston this time. ———

Friday Nov: 23ᵈ, Continued ¼ to 11.PM. I have just returned from Mʳ Murray's where I dined agreeably to invitation. It was a most amusing affair. Mʳ Murray was there in a short vest & dress-coat, looking quizzical enough; — his footman was there also, habited in small clothes & breeches, revealing a despicable pair of sheepshanks. The impudence of the fellow in showing his legs — & such a pair of legs too! — in public, I thought extraordinary. The ladies should have blushed, one would have thought — but they did not; — Lockhart was there, also, in a prodigious white cravat, (made from Walter Scott's shroud, I suppose) He stalked about like a half galvinized ghost — gave me the tips of two skinny fingers, when introduced to me — or rather, I to him. Then, there was a round faced chap by the name of Cook — who seemed to be Murray's factotum. His duty consisted in pointing out the portraits on the wall, & saying that this or that one was esteemed a good likeness by the high & mighty ghost Lockhart. There were four or five others present — nameless, fifth rate looking varlets — & four lean women. One of them proved agreeable in the end. She had resided some time in China — I talked with her some time. Besides these, there was a duodecimo footman, or boy in a tight jacket with bell-buttons. —— At dinner the stiffness, formality, & coldness of the party was wonderful. I felt like knocking all their heads together. I managed to get thro' with it, however, somehow, by conversing with Dr Holland, a very eminent physician, it seems — & a very affable, intelligent man, who has travelled immensely. After the ladies withdrew, the three decanters — Port, Sherry & Claret — were kept going the rounds with great regularity. I sat next to Lockhart, and seeing that he was a customer, who was full of himself & expected great homage; & knowing him to be a thorough going Tory & fish-blooded Churchman & conservative, & withall, Editor of the Quarterly — I refrained from playing the snob to him, like the rest — & the consequence was he grinned at me his ghastly smiles. — After returning to the drawing room, coffee & tea were served, & I soon after came away. Such is a publisher's dinner. A comical volume might be written upon it. — Oh Conventionalism, what a ninny, thou art, to be sure. And now, I must turn in. But first, let me add, that upon coming home, I found a note for me from Bogue, the publisher. I knew its contents at once — there seemed little use in opening it. — He declined; alleging among other reasons, the state of the copyright question. — So we go.

Saturday Nov 24 Upon sallying out this morning encountered the oldfashioned pea-soup London fog — of a gamboge color. It was lifted, however, from the ground & floated in mid-air. When lower, it is worse. Lamps lighted, as it was in the old lady's room where I took my usual breakfast — two small rolls, a bit of butter the size of a dollar, & about the thickness, — & two cups of incomparable coffee. After digesting the "Times" & the rolls, went down street & stopped in at Chapman & Hall's the publishers. Saw Mr Chapman, a very gentlemanly man. Proposed the book. He at once threw the copyright matter at me. No go. Then went to the Aldine Chambers & saw Davidson who very kindly said he would get my note cashed. Left it with him, & went to H. G. Bohn's, York Street, Covent Garden. A florid fellow in a crimson vest. Proposed the book. No go. Walked thro the market, home.

Saturday Nov: 24th Continued. Midnight. Just returned from East Sheen with an indefinite quantity of Champaigne Sherry, Old Port,

Hock, Madeira, & Claret in me. But first to bring down my chronicle. After seeing Bohn (as above) & coming home, I was called upon by M[r] Stevens, who travelled all the way up to my room here in the 4th story. He proves to be a very fine fellow, and I was the more pleased with him, & in some sort loved him, from the circumstance that he told me had been acquainted with "my wife" that is to say with Dolly. He stayed so long, however, that little time was left me to dress for M[r] Bates'. Being rigged at last, tho', I sallied out, jumped into a buss & down to St: Paul's — there, took a Richmond stage, & away to East Sheen — 9 miles. The buss was crowded. Alighted in a dark foggy lane, & picked my way towards a distant illumination which proved M[r] Bates'. Upon entering the vestibule, some dozen footmen in small clothes & gold lace received me, and I was ushered into a sumptuous chamber up stairs. Descending into a parlor, M[r] Bates gave me a courteous welcome. Shortly after, a mustache entered the room & sat down in a chair opposite — a Vienna man. The company gradually all appeared, & we went into dinner. On my left was a nephew of Lord Ashburton, & the Baroness de Somebody I don't know who. On my right was M[r] Peabody, an American for many years resident in London, a merchant, & a very fine old fellow of fifty or thereabouts. There was a Baron opposite me, and a most lovely young girl, a daughter of Captain Chamier the sea novelist. Half the company were foreigners. The dinner was supurb — the table was circular — the service very rich. I ate of sundry mysterious French dishes. Every body was free, easy & in good humor — all talkative & well-bred — a strong contrast to the miserable stiffness, reserve, & absurd formality of M[r] Murray's, the tradesman's, dinner last night. Mrs Bates is a fat, ugly, good-natured, amiable woman of sixty. The Baroness is a pretty vivacious woman of thirty. Her husband, a round, sleek man, who said little, but ate his dinner with a relish. Mr Russel Sturgis was there. Somehow he reminded me of Murray's man, Cook, last night. Mrs Sturgiss is a fine looking lady. The wine went round freely after the ladies withdrew. Upon entering the drawing room, coffee & tea were served. The house is a large & noble one — the rooms immense — the decorations brilliant — statuary, vases, & all sorts of costly ornaments. I saw a copy of Typee on a table. M[r] Bates seemed to be quite a jolly old blade. — I had intended to remain over night agreeably to invitation, but Peabody inviting me to accompany him to town in his carriage, I went with him, along with Davis the Secretary of Legation. —— By the way, Mr: Stevens invites me to dinner to morrow (Sunday) at Morley's. — Mr Peabody was well acquainted with Gansevoort when he was here. He saw him not long before his end. He told me that Gansevoort rather shunned society when here. He spoke of him with much feeling. No doubt, two years ago, or three, Gansevoort was writing here in London, about the same hour as this — alone in his chamber, in profound silence — as I am now. This silence is a strange thing. No wonder, the old Greeks deemed it the vestibule to the higher mysteries.

Sunday Nov 25th. Passed a most extraordinary night — one continuous nightmare till daylight. Hereafter if I should be condemned to Purgatory, I shall plead the night of Nov: 25th 1849 in extenuation of the sentance. I impute the nightmare to a cup of prodigiously strong coffee & another of tea, which I took at Mr Bates' just previous to leaving. At daylight turned over & had a nap till about 10 o'clock. Dressed and emerged into a fog — quite thick. As my old coffee haunt in the Strand is closed on Sundays, I steered my way up St: Martin's Lane, intending to breakfast at the Hotel de   commended to me by George Duyckinck, as "good & cheap". Lost my way in the fog, & stopped at an atrocious hole where I got coffee & roll for the sum of four pence — including a thimble-full of sugar. Drunken fellow there. Came at last upon Leicester Square, & as my breakfast had been most meagre & mean, proposed to myself a cup of French Coffee at the Hotel de   Stepped in & called for it. & very good it was. Place full of Frenchmen. Charged me 18 pence for the coffee & small roll. — Thence to the Abbey & attended service. Abbey full of fog. Thence walked in St: James' Park. Saw the sentries (mounted) at the Horse Guards releived. Thence down to Edinboro' Castle and read the Sunday Times & Despatch. Thence down to Queen's Hotel to see Davidson. Not in. Thence, down street further yet, & wandered about Threadneedle, Throgmorton, Leadenhall Streets &c, passed Aldgate Pump into White Chapel Road (where Bayard Taylor stopped) Passed Moses & Son establishment. Thence took buss to St: Pauls to service. Thence by buss home at 5 P.M. And thus closes a most foggy, melancholy, sepulchral day. But in half an hour's time from now I go to Morley's to dine with Stevens & Davis

— & there I hope to recover myself in the companionship & conversation of mortals. — "Oh Solitude! where are the charms" &c. —

Tuesday Nov 27th. Dined at Morley's & had a very pleasant time, on Sunday. Mr Davis and a Mr Newton (Chaplain in the Navy) were there. Newton is a fair sample of an idle man. He seems a good natured, well disposed sort of a liver upon Uncle Sam, however. —— No more. I am on board the steamer "Emerald" bound for Boulogne — we are just in the Nore, and the jar & motion are so great that writing is too hard work. I must defer bringing up my journal till I reach terra-firma. X X X X X X After the lapse of a few days, I find myself this Thursday night, snugly *roomed* in the fifth story of a lodging house No 12 & 14 Rue di Bussy, Paris. It is the first night that I have taken possession, & the "Bonne" or chambermaid has lighted a fire of wood, lit the candle, & left me alone, at 11 o'clock, P.M. On first gazing round, I am struck by the apparition of a bottle containing a dark fluid, a glass, a decanter of water, & a paper package of sugar (loaf) with a glass basin next to it. — I protest all this was not in the bond. — But tho' if I use these things they will doubtless be charged to me, yet let us be charitable, — so I ascribe all this to the benevolence of Madam Capelle my most polite, pleasant, and Frenchified landlady below. I shall try the brandy before writing more.

—— And now to resume my Journal. — To go back to Sunday afternoon, Nov: 25th. After dining with Mr Stevens agreeably to invitation at Morley's, I smoked a cigar with Davis, & then we went to the Clarendon Hotel & called upon Mrs Lawrence. Found the lady & the Minister in. Mrs. Lawrence was so very pleasant this evening that I must take back the bitter things I said of her before. They have taken the Earl Cadogan's house in Piccadilly, to reside in. — Coming home with Davis I was struck with his expressions concerning the poverty & misery of so large a portion of the London population. He revealed a heart. Next day — Monday, Nov 26 — after breakfast went to Davidson's to see about my note's getting cashed. Waited some time. At last, he came in, gave me a checque on his bankers, & off I went to Livingston & Wells down Lombard Street, & deposited £40 for Allan to draw in New York. When I went to the bankers, they shoveled the sovereigns over to me in curious style. At 2. P.M. called for Stevens at Morley's, & went with him & Newton to the library of the British

Museum. Endless galleries & three-deckers of books. Saw many rareities. — Maps of London (before & after the Great Fire), Magna Charta — Charlemagne's bible — Shakespere's autograph (in Montaigne) &c &c &c. Went into the Manuscript room — saw the famous Alexandrian Manuscript & many Saxon M.S.S. of great value. Comical librarian. — Dined at the "Mitre" Fleet Street with Davidson, & paid the joint bill myself. Then to the "Blue Posts" Cork Street & took some of their renowned punch. Wrote Allan from thence. Then home & to bed, after packing my little portmanteau, which I had bought in London for travelling on the continent. On Tuesday — the 27th Nov: — rose early, paid my bill — 3 guineas — & into a cab, & down to London Bridge stairs for the Bologne boat. Took a fore cabin passage (8 shillings — (saloon 12)). Fine run down the river, & fine cold morning. Passed Gravesend, Tilbury Fort (mid way to the sea) passed Sheerness near the mouth, & Margate. Great number of ships running out. Passed by the Goodwin Sands, Deal, South Foreland, Dover, & then across the Channel to Bologne. A shocking accident occurred to one of the hands of the boat. His foot was ruined in the machinery. All the passengers sea sick, but three or four. Young Frenchman consoling them. Arrived in Bologne about 8½ P.M. Marched off to the Custom House & surrendered Passport. Then to the Bedford Hotel & took some tea & cold beef. Then to a cold bed. Rose early & took the 7 o'clock train for Paris, — distant 160 miles or more. Took "third class" train (fare about 15 francs) Fine day & rode thro' a charming country. Did not stop at Amiens to see the Cathedral there — no time. Arrived in Paris (Rue Lazare) at 4 P.M. Took a cab with the young Frenchman & off to N° 3 Rue de la Convention to find Adler. Could hear nothing of him. So went to "Meurice's" Rue Rivoli & took a room. Dined at table d'hote at a little after 5 P.M. Splendid table — French dishes — ate I know not what. Talked with two Englishmen at table. After dinner went to Galignani's — Adler's address not there. Subscribed to the reading room. Then walked to the Palais Royal. Gorgeous cafes there & shops — capital of Paris. Turned in early.

To day — *Thursday 29th Nov* — rose early — breakfasted at a cafe in the Rue Rivoli & walked to the Place Concorde — magnificent. Crossed the Seine towards the Chamber of Deputies. Returned & met great numbers of troops marching all about. Like a garrisoned town. Wrote two letters to Adler. Went to the "Latin Quarter" in search of Madam Capelle — found her, engaged a room & recrossed the river. Visited the Bourse — great hum round a mystic circle — & Livingston & Wells's. Dined in the Rue Viviene for two francs — several courses including a bottle of Bordeaux. Then went to "Meurice's" — paid my bill (15 francs for a dinner, a bed & a sheet of paper) and drove to my present quarters on the other side of the Seine. Then walked to the Palais Royal (National now) & went into the pit of a theater there (Admittance 25 sous) Three comical comedies — plenty of babies & wet napkins &c. Came away early & home — smoked & to bed.

Next day, *Friday*. Breakfasted over the way at the "Cafe Francais". Very good place. Then down street with a blue nose (so cold it was) & visited Notre Dame. They are repairing it. A noble old pile. Then walked about the old city & crossed to Rue St Antone, to the Place de la Bastile, where now stands the column of July. Cafe la Bastile & villianous hole there. Then in a buss (roundabout way) to the Louvre, & spent three hours in the Museum. Heaps of treasures of art of all sorts. Admirable collection of antique statuary. Beats the British Museum. Then to the Bourse & dined at the "Rosbeef" Restaurant. Then to Galignani's & read the papers. Late arrival from New York. Great excitement again about California. Saw that the thing called "Redburn" had just been published. Extract from "Lit World" notice &c. Having received a note from Adler (to my great joy) who said he would be at his rooms at ¼ past 7 this evening I called accordingly — Not in — so sat & jabbered as well as I could with Madam till he arrived. Was rejoiced to see him — we went together to his room — he brought out tobacco & we related our mutual experiences. Left him at nine o'clock & came home. Fire made & try to be comfortable. But this is not home & — but no repinings.

Saturday Dec 1st. Coffee & roll at 10½ at Cafe over the way. At 11 A.M. Adler called & we started for the Hotel de Cluny. Stumbled upon the Sorbonne, & entered the court. Saw notices of Lectures — Cousin &c. — Hotel de Cluny proved closed. Took buss & went to Pere le Chaise. Fine monument of Abelard & Heloise. tombs of generals &c. Returning, visited Abattoir of Popincourt. Noteworthy place, founded by Napoleon. Old woman &c. Thence to the Boulevards & thro them to Rue Viviene to the Bourse & Livingston &

Wells'. Dined with Adler at the "Rosbeef" & thence to his room in Rue de la Convention. At 7½ p.m. left for the Palais Royal to see Rachel in Phedre. Formed in the "cue" in the arcade — stood an hour or two & were cut off. Returned bitterly disappointed to Adler's room, — bought a bottle of Bordeaux (price 8 sous) & drank half a glass of it. Home at 11 & to bed.

Sunday Dec 2d. Rose about 10, & walked over to Palais Royal, where breakfasted at Cafe d' Orleans. Then to Adler's rooms & with him to the church of St Roche — noble interior — ladies' chapel — paintings &c. Singularly eloquent preacher — funeral. Thence to the Madeline — went in. Supurbe exterior. Thence thro Place Vendome, across Place de la Concorde over the river to Hotel des Invalids. In the Chapel saw the Austerliz flags &c. Algiers &c. Dining rooms. silver plate of officers. gallery of paintings. Thence thro' out-of-the way streets to the Luxemburgh. Fine gallery of modern French school. Large park, gardens. Chamber of Peers. Thence to the Sorbonne. Got into the church, & saw tomb or rather monument of Cardinal Richelieu. Good sculpture. Adler here left me. Went to the Panthenon — still building. Thence into an old church near by, & thro Middle-Age courts & lanes to the river & thro' Place de la Carousel, to Adler's. At 5. P.M. dined at his table' d'hote. Two members of the Chamber there. Several Yankees. Any quantity of Bordeaux. Cold room & chilly wine. A lady talking about *"Flemish"* things. After dinner Hotchkiss (A's friend) joined us in A's room; & we had a talk, with some Eau de vie & cigars. At 10, sallied out into a dark, rainy night, & made my melancholy way across the Pont (within a biscuit's toss of the Morgue) to my sixth story apartment. I dont like that mystic door (tapestry) leading out of the closet.

Monday Dec 3d 1849. Went to Galignani's after breakfast to get Continental Guide. Returning met Adler in the Rue de la Fontane Moleire. Thence walked thro Champs Elysee to the Triumphal arch de l'Etoile. Ascended it — splendid view of Paris. Bought little medal of old woman. Took buss to the Pont Neuef. Got my original passport at the Police. Looked in at the Morgue. Dined at the "Rosbeuf". Called on Adler about five (P.M.) Smoked a cigar till his return from dinner. Then, went with him to the "Opera Comique" Boulevard des Italeans. Two peices, house crowded. Splendid orchestra. Home

& to bed, after stopping with Adler at the Cafe de Foy for a cup of "chocholat," which was exquisite.

Tuesday Dec 4th 1849. Met Adler at the "Bibliotheque Royale" (Cardinal Mazarin's) Looked over plates of Albert Durer, & Holbein. Walked thro' the halls of books. Saw autographs, Persian M.S.S. &c Coptic &c. Franklin's letter. Parnassus. Museum. Left Adler at his room & walked to the American Minister about passport. Thence to the Prefecture of Police &c. Develish nuisance, the whole of it. Bought two pair of gloves, one pair of shoes for Lizzie. Bought a copy of Telemachus for self near the Louvre. Called on Adler at his room & invited him to dinner. Went to the Italian Boulevard and dined at the Cafe Anglais. Thence to Cafe de Cardinal for chocolate. Thence to his room and talked high German metaphysics till ten o'clock. Then home & wrote up journal, as above. And now to bed. ———

Wednesday Dec 5th. Breakfasted at a cheap place in the Place de Carousel. Wandered about the stalls along the quays & bridges. Went to the Museum Dupryten. Pathological. Rows of cracked skulls. Skeletons & things without a name. Thence to the Hotel de Cluny. A most unique collection. The house is just the house I should like to live in. Glorious old cabinets — ebony, ivory carving. — Beautiful chapel. Tapestry, old keys. Leda & the Swan. Descended into the vaults of the old Roman palace of Thermis. Baths &c. Thence lounged along the quays to the Palace of the Deputies. Sauntered in past the guards. And would have gained admittance to the Chamber but for the unlucky absence of my passport, which I had left to get the "visas" of the Belgian & Prussian ministers. Thence to Adler's. He invited me to dine with him. Went to the N° 3 Rue de la Convention and dined with three Americans. Thence to the Theatre Francais, to hear Madam Rachel. Formed in the *"queue"* but gave it up at last. Back to Adler's, smoked a cigar & crossed the river home, & to bed early.

Thursday Dec 6th Took my last breakfast in Paris at The Cafe Francais, Rue de Bussy. Thence to Galignani's, & read the papers. Thence took buss for the R.R. Depot & off to Versailles. Old man for guide thro' the gardens. A most magnificent & incredible affair altogether. Splendid paintings of battles. Grand suite of rooms of Louis Le

Grand. Titan overthrown by thunderbolts &c. Apollo & the horses on the fountain. Back to Paris by dusk. Took a cab & went to Meurice's & got my passport. Thence to my rooms in Rue di Busy— paid my bill &c — took a last adieu of Madam Capelle & went to Adler's. Dined at a Restaurant near Palais Royale & with Adler went to his rooms — where I now write up my last Parisian journal. — Selah!.

Friday Dec 7th 1849. Brussels. Sat up conversing with Adler till pretty late, —(Topic—as usual—metaphysics.) Then turned in, in a room below him with orders to be roused at 6½ A.M. Rose accordingly & dressed in the dark — taking my usual bath. Off to the R.R. Station in a cab — Fare to Brussels, something like 27 francs — 2d class cars. A dull dreary ride all day over an interminable flat pancake of a country. Passed thro' Amiens, (second time; could'nt see the cathedral) — Arras (where were an immense number of windmills) & several fortified towns—Doual, Valenciennes (renowned for lace) At Quievrain passports were demanded. At Valenciennes we entered the Netherlands or Belgium — Low Countries indeed. — And so thro' Mons & Soignies to Brussels. Drove a prodigious ways up a long narrow ravine of a street to the Hotel de France, where I arrived about 7½ P.M. in the dark. Was accompanied by a fellow passenger from the R.R. — a phlegmatic impracticable North of England man. He conversed however, a little upon America. Took tea with him — then a short stroll & here I am in a fine chamber, all alone, in the capital of Belgium.

> —— "There was a sound of revelry by night,
> And Belgium's capital had gathered then her beauty
> and her chivalry"

But no sound of "revelry" now, heaven knows. A more dull, humdrum place I never saw — tho' it seems a fine built place. Waterloo is some 8 miles off. Can not visit it — & care not about it. To morrow I am off for Cologne. It is a chance whether I can get up the Rhine, or not — owing to the ice. Must try it tho'.

Saturday Dec 8th 1849 Breakfasted *tete a tete* with the English phlegmatic — he said nothing & I ditto. Having determined to travel into Germany entirely unincumbered, I left my carpet bag — or rather portmanteau at the hotel, and after a short stroll (during which, I walked thro the Palace Park & by the Palace, & past the Botanic Gardens of the King, & along the miniature Boulevards) I went to the R.R. Station & took my seat for Cologne. I took a second class car, which was as pleasant as the 1st class in America & incomparably better than the corresponding class in England. For fellow "voyagers" I had a cocked-hatted priest & several dark eyed young women in crape hoods. One of them looked mysterious. For the first 60 miles or so our way lay thro' the same flat, dead country, as from Paris to Brussels. But at Liege (the gun place) the scenery changed. It was all hill & valley & we wound thro' the most romantic defiles imaginable — by old ruined mills & farm houses of the Middle Ages. At the Prussian frontier my passport was demanded & taken. In the car was a young Frenchman — a genuine blade, who carried a flask of Belgian Gin in his pocket with a glass, & he frequently invited me to drink. He had been in America. At Aix-la-Chapelle he & party left us, & there only remained in the car, with me, a young Berlin man, who talked a little English. About 9 o'clock we arrived at Cologne, in the dark, and taking a "buss" drove to a Hotel — I supposed that it was the Hotel de Cologne, having been advised to go thither by the Guide Book. The place proved to be a great, cold, vacant palace (half stable) I took tea (a la Francais) and retired early into a German bed, with a pillow at my feet.

I intended taking the boat at 10¼ in the morning, & so slept sweetly dreaming of the Rhine.

Sunday Dec 9th 1849 Cologne Sallied out before breakfast, and found my way to the famous cathedral, where the everlasting "crane" stands on the tower. While inside was accosted by a polite worthy who was very civil pointing out the "curios". He proved a *"valet de place"*. He tormented me home to the Hotel & got a franc out of me. Upon going to the Steamer Office I learned that no boat would leave that morning. So I had to spend the day in Cologne. But it was not altogether unpleasant for me so to do. In this antiquated gable-ended old town — full of Middle-Age, Charlemaigne associations, — — where Rubens was born & Mary De Medeci died — there is much to interest a pondering man like me. ——

But now to tell how at last I found that I had not put up at the "Hotel de Cologne", but at the "Hotel de Rhin" — where my bill for a bed, a tea, & a breakfast amounted to some $2, in their unknowable German currency. — Having learnt about the Steamer, I went to the veritable Hotel de Cologne, (on the river) & there engaged the services of a *valet de place* to show me the sights of the town for 2 francs. We went to the Cathedral, during service — saw the tomb of the *Three Kings of Cologne* — their skulls. The choir of the church is splendid. The structure itself is one of the most singular in the world. One transept is nearly complete — in new stone, and strangely contrasts with the ruinous condition of the vast unfinished tower on one side. From the Cathedral we went to the Jesuits' Church, where service was being performed. Thence to the Museum & saw some odd old paintings; & one splendid one (a sinking ship, with the Captain at the mast-head — defying his foe) by *Schefferen*(?). Thence, to St Peter's Church, & saw the celebrated *Descent from the Cross* by Rubens. Paid 2 francs to see the original picture turned round by the Sacristan. Thence home. Went into a book store & purchased some books (Views & Panorama of the Rhine) & then to the Hotel. At one' o'clock dinner was served (Table d'hote). A regular German dinner & a good one, "I tell you". Innumerable courses — & an apple-pudding was served between the courses of meat & poultry. I drank some yellow Rhenish wine which was capital, looking out on the storied Rhine as I dined. After dinner sallied out & roamed about the town — going into churches, buying cigar of pretty cigar girls, & stopping people in the streets to light my cigar. I drank in the very vital spirit & soul of old Charlemagne, as I turned the quaint old corners of this quaint old town. Crossed the bridge of boats, & visited the fortifications on the thither side. At dusk stopped at a beer shop — & took a glass of *black ale* in a comical flagon of glass. Then home. And here I am writing up my journal for the last two days. At nine o'clock (3 hours from now) I start for Coblentz — 60 miles from hence. — I feel homesick to be sure — being all alone with not a soul to talk to — but then the Rhine, is before me, & I must on. The sky is overcast, but it harmonizes with the spirit of the place.

Monday Dec: 10th 1849. Coblentz. Embarked last night about 9½ PM. for Coblentz. But before so doing went out after tea to take a final stroll thro' old Cologne. Upon returning to the hotel, found a large party assembled, filling up all the tables in the Dining Saloon. Every man had his bottle of Rhenish, and his cigar. It was a curious scene. I took the tall spires of glasses for castles & towers, and fancied the

Rhine flowed between. I drank a bottle of *Rudenshimer*(?). When the boat pushed off it was very dark, & I made my way into the 2[d] cabin. There I encountered a German, who was just from St: Louis in Missouri. I had a talk with him. From 9½ P.M. till 5. A.M, I laid down & got up, shivering by turns with the cold. Thrice I went on deck, & found the boat gliding between tall black cliffs & crags. — A grand sight. At last arrived at Coblentz in the dark, & got into a bed at the *"Giant Hoff"* near the quay. At ten o'clock in the morning descended to breakfast, & after that took a *valet de place* & crossed the Bridge of Boats to the famous Quebec fortress of Ehrbrincedstein. A magnificent object, truly. The view from the summit is superb. Far away winds the Rhine between its castellated mountains. Crossed the river again, & walked about the town — entering the curious old churches — half Gothic, half Italian — and crossed the Moselle at the stone bridge — near where Prince Metternich was born. —— Singular that he was born so near the great fortress of Germany — Still more curious that the finest wine of all the Rhine, is grown right under the guns of Erhbreistien. At one'o'clock dined at "The Giant" at the table d'hote. There were some six or eight English present — two or three ladies & many German officers. The dinner was very similar to the dinner at the Hotel de Cologne yesterday. After dinner, walked out to the lower walls & into the country along the battlements. The town is walled entirely. At dinner I drank nothing but Moselle wine — thus keeping the counsel of the "Governor of Coney Island" whose maxim it is, "to drink the wine of the country in which you may be travelling." Thus at Cologne on the banks of the Rhine, & looking at the river thro' the window opposite me — what could I imbibe but Rhenish? And *now,* at Coblentz — at the precise junction of the Moselle — what regale myself with but Moselle? — The wine is blueish — at least *tinged* with blue — and seems a part of the river after which it is called. At dusk I found myself standing in the silence at the point where the two storied old rivers meet. Opposite was the frowning fortress —— & some 4000 miles was America & Lizzie. — Tomorrow, I am *homeward-bound!* Hurrah & three cheers!

X X X I last wrote in my Journal on the banks of the Rhine — & now after the lapse of a few days, I resume it on the banks of the Thames, in my old chamber that overlooks it, on Saturday the 15th of Dec: '49.

—— I broke off at Coblentz on *Monday night, Dec: 10th*. That same night I fell in with a young Englishman at a cigar shop & had a long talk with him. He had been in America, & was related to Cunard of the Steamers. Next morning, *Tuesday Dec 11th*, I again rambled about the town — saw the artillery-men & infantry exercise on the parade ground. Very amusing indeed. Saw a squadron of drumers. Walked down & up the river, & while waiting for the Cologne boat spent at least two hours standing on a stone peir, at the precise junction of the Rhine & Moselle. At 3 o'clock started for Cologne on a Dusseldorf boat. It was intensely cold. Dined at the table d'hote in the cabin. Fine dinner & wine. Drank Rhenish on the Rhine. Saw Drachenfells & the Seven Mountains, & Rolandseck, & the Isle of Nuns. The old ruins & arch are glorious — but the river Rhine is not the Hudson. In the evening arrived at my old place — Hotel de Cologne. Recognized Drachenfells in a large painting on the wall. Drank a bottle of Steinberger with the landlord, a Rhinelander & a very gentlemanly well-informed man, learned in wines. At ½ past 6 P.M went to the Theatre. Three vaudevilles acted. Audience smoking & drinking & looking on. Stopped in a shop on my way home & made some purchases for presents, & was insidiously cheated in the matter of a breast-pin, as I found out after getting to London, & not before. God forgive the girl — she was not very pretty, either — which makes it the more aggravating. *At 5. A.M. Wednesday Dec 12* was called & took a chilly breakfast in a vast saloon & paid my bill. The "garcon" who had proved exceedingly polite & attentive to me during my whole in the house, endeavored in the blandest manner imaginable to cheat me out of one "thaler" in giving me my change. I brought him up however & the villian — the smiling, civil, attentive villian seemed to be sorry that he had forever forfeited my good-will, & in vain!

Drove to the R.R. thro' an old antique gate-way in the city wall. A very cold ride & a very doleful one, all the way to Brussels, where we got at 5. PM, after stopping a while at Aix la Chapelle. I saw the old Cathedral & the town-house — but that was all. At Brussels, went instanter to my hotel there, to get my shirts I had left to be washed. The insidious landlady & the rascally waiters wanted me to stop & dine — & so the peices "were not come home yet" —— Had a few comical scenes with the landlady & started off in a pet & went dodging about town to get a cheap dinner. Swallowed a little beer here &

ate a bit of cake there, & at last got to the Station house. — A horrible long dreary cold ride to Ostend on the coast. In a fit of the nightmare was going to stop at a way-place, taking it for the place of my destination. Arrived at Ostend at 11½ P.M. The boat was at the wharf — took a 2^d class passage, & went down into a dog-hole in the bow, & there sat & smoked, & shivered, & pitched about in the roll of the sea from midnight till *5 o'clock in the morning, Thursday 13th Dec* when we arrived at Dover. Disembarked in the dark in a small boat & went to The Sign of "The Gun". Breakfasted, & took myself off to the Custom House to get my luggage thro'. They seized my fine copy of "Anastasius" which I had bought at the Palais Royale & told me it was food for fire. Was much enraged therat. Took 2^d class train for London at 6½ A.M. A fat Frenchman in the car with whom I conversed a little. A burly farmer in small clothes & high boots sat opposite me. Another long dismal ride thro' Kent, on a raw dismal morning — & at 12. M. arrived at London Bridge — after posting all the way from Coblentz, without cessation. Took buss for Craven Street. On getting there found that Mr Rogers had called — "a gentleman from St: James who came in his coach" — as the chambermaid expressed it. Also was handed — with a meaning flourish — a note sealed with a coronet. It was from Mr Rutland — The Duke of Rutland I mean — inviting me to visit Belvoir Castle at any time after a certain day in January. Can not go — I am homeward-bound, & Malcolm is growing all the time. — I was in a villians garb with travel — had not shaved in a week — dirty shirt &c — So, dressed, & went to Bentley's after letters. Found one from Lizzie, & Allan. Most welcome but gave me the blues most terribly — Felt like chartering a small-boat & starting down the Thames instanter for New York. Dined at the "Blue Posts" & took some punch to cheer me. Came home, had a fire made, & wrote to Lizzie & Allan. While so employed the girl knocked & brought me a package of letters. They were from the Legation, & were from Lizzie & Allan — a week later than those I got in the morning. I read them, & felt raised at once. Both were written in fine spirits — & that was catching. Walked out & read them over again — with the "Powell Papers" at the "Edingburgh Castle". Home early & to bed.

Friday Dec 14 '49. Breakfasted at my old place. Then went & bought a Paletot in the Strand, so as to look decent — for I find my green coat plays the devel with my respectability here. Then went & got my hair cut, which was as long as a wild Indian's. Then dressed, & went to M[r] Rogers' — out of town — left card. Thence to Lincoln's Inn Feilds & left letter & card for M[r] Foster of the "Examiner". Thence to the College of Surgeons, & called on Mrs: Daniel. Spent a half hour there very pleasantly. Two fine girls her daughters. (Invited me to tea at 8 o'clock, Saturday.) Thence in a buss to the Bank, & stopped to inquire of the agents about the packet ships. I shall go on the "Independence", if nothing happens. Thence home & wrote further to Lizzie & Allan & put up the "Times" for Judge Shaw. Wrote Willis, Duyckinck, & the Judge. Then at 6. P.M. dined at the old place — The Adelphi — & treated myself to a cut of turkey. Thence to the Haymarket & saw Mr & Mrs Charles Kean & Buckstone, & Wallack in "The Housekeeper" a drama by Douglas Jerrold. The same thing we saw murdered at Canterbury. Left the theater at 9'o'clock & bought a pair of pantaloons for one pound five. Then home & to bed after a cigar — one of the Secretary's bunch.

Saturday Dec 15th 49 After breakfast went among the book stores & stalls about Holywell Street. At last succeeded in getting the much desired copy of Rosseau's Confessions" for eleven shillings. Walked down Fleet Street after a copy of "Knight's London" Could not get it — but, returning, found a copy in the Strand. Bought it for £1.10. Then home & rigged for Bentley's — whom I expected to meet at 1. PM. about "White Jacket." Called, but he had not yet arrived from Brighton. Walked about a little & bought a cigar case for Allan in Burlington Arcade. Saw many pretty things for presents — but could not afford to buy. Bought a bread trencher & bread knife near Charing Cross. "The University bread trencher" used of old at Commons, now restored. Very generally used here. A fine thing, & English — Saxon: — Home & wrote up journal. At 4. PM. am to call again at Bentley's. He does not know I am in town — I earnestly hope I shall be able to see him & that I can do something about that "pesky" book. ——

6 O'clock P.M. Hurrah & three cheers! I have just returned from M[r] Bentley's, & have concluded an arrangement with him that gives me tomorrow his note for £200. It is to be at 6 months — and I am almost certain I shall be able to get it cashed at once. This takes a load off my heart. The £200 is in anticipation — for the book is not to be

published till the 1st of March next. Hence the long time of the note. The aforementioned sum is for the 1st 1000 copies. Subsequent editions (if any) to be jointly divided between us. — I also spoke to him about Liut: Wise's book, & he is to send for it. At eight to night I am going to Mrs Daniel's. What sort of an evening is it going to be? Mr Bentley invited me to dinner for Tuesday at 6. P.M. This will do for a memorandum of the engagement. I have just read over the Duke of Rutland's note, which I have not fairly perused before. It seems very cordial. I wish the invitation was for next week, instead of being so long ahead — but this I beleive is the mode here for these sort of invitations into the country. — (Mem: at 1.P.M on Monday am to call at Mr Bentley's)

Sunday Dec 16 '49. Last night went in a cab to Lincoln's Inn Feilds, & found Mrs Daniel & "daughts:" very cordial. The elder "daught" remarkably sprightly & the mother as nice an old body as any one could desire. Presently there came in several "young gents" of various complexions. We had some coffee, music, dancing & after an agreeable evening I came away at 11 o'clock, & walking to The Cock near Temple Bar drank a glass of Stout & home & to bed, after reading a few chapters in Tristam Shandy, which I have never yet read. This morning breakfasted at 10, at the Hotel de Sabloneire (very nice cheap little snuggery being closed on Sundays) Had a "sweet ommelette" which was delicious. Thence walked to St: Thomas's Church, Charter House, Goswell Street to hear my famed namesake (almost) "The Reverend H Melvill." I had seen him placarded as to deliver a Charity Sermon. The church was crowded — the sermon was admirable (granting the Rev: gentleman's premises). Indeed he deserves his reputation. I do not think that I hardly ever heard so good a discourse before — that is from an "orthodox" divine. It is now 3. P.M. I have had a fire made & am smoking a cigar. Would that One I know were here. Would that the Little One too were here. —— I am in a very painful state of uncertainty. I am all eagerness to get home — I ought to be home — my absence occasions uneasiness in a quarter where I must beseech heaven to grant repose. Yet here I have before me an open prospect to get some curious ideas of a style of life, which in all probability I shall never have again. I should much like to know what the highest English aristocracy really & practically is. And the Duke of Rutland's cordial invitation to visit him at his

Castle furnishes me with just the thing I want. If I do not go, I am confident that hereafter I shall upbraid myself for neglecting such an opportunity of procuring *"material."* And Allan & others will account me a ninny. — I would not debate the matter a moment, were it not that at least three whole weeks must elapse ere I start for Belvoir Castle — three weeks! If I could but get over *them!* And if the two images would only *down* for that space of time. —— I must light a second cigar & revolve it over again.

½ past 6. P.M. My mind is made; rather, is irrevocably resolved upon my first determination. A visit into Leicester would be very agreeable — at least very valuable, in one respect, to me — but the Three Weeks are intolerable. Tomorrow I shall go down to London Dock & book myself for a state-room on board the good ship Independence. I have just returned from a lonely dinner at the Adelphi, where I read the Sunday papers. An article upon The "Sunday School Union" particularly struck me. In an hour's time I must go to Morley's & call upon Stevens & Davis. — Would that I could go home in a Steamer — but it would take an extra $100 out of my pocket. Well, its only 30 days — one month — and I can weather it somehow.

Monday Dec 17th 1849. Was delighted & exhilerated this morning by a view of the sun — a rare sight here — looking into my river window. Upon sallying out, I found a fine day. Last night after writing my journal (as above) I called on Stevens & sat a while. He spoke of Powell, & that certain persons had called upon him denouncing Powell as a rogue — Poor fellow — poor devel — poor Powell! Took my breakfast as usual at the old place & walked down to London Dock. The "Independence" proves to be an old ship — she looks small — & smells ancient. Only two or three passengers engaged. I liked Captain Fletcher, however. He enquired whether I was a relation of Gansevt Melville, & of Herman Melville. I told him I was. I engaged my passage & paid £10 down. Took a buss & rode to Mr Bentley's according to appointment at 1 o'clock. We concluded the arrangement of "White Jacket" & he gave me his note for £200 at 6 mos: From thence went to Mr Murray's. Had a talk with him about sundry things. On going away his cousin invited me to dine with him on Wednesday at his chambers in the Temple. Accepted. Thence to the National Gallery & spent an hour looking at Rembrandt's Jew & the Saints of Taddeo Gaddi, & Guido's Murder of the Innocents. Looked in at the Vernon Gallery. Thence walked down the Strand & stopped at a book auction in Wellington Street. Gruff chap had no "catalogues." Thence to Adelphi & dined. Thence to Davidson's — not in. Thence down Newgate St: looking in at the book stores. Saw many books I should like to buy — but can not. Then thro' Farrington Street (where I bought pocket Shakspeare &c) to the Strand (a little this side of the Bar) & had a long chat with a tobacconist of whom I bought ¾ pound of very fine Cuba Cigars at about 2 cents & a half (our money) a peice. Thence home; & out again, & took a letter for a Duke to the Post office & a pair of pants to be altered to a tailor. Drank a pint of ale & by the Haymarket, & so home & wrote Journal.

Tuesday Dec 18th 1849 Miserable rainy day. Treated myself to a sugar omelette, at the old place, for breakfast. Thence went to the British Museum — closed. Thence among the old book stores about Great Queen Street & Lincoln's Inn. Looked over a lot of ancient maps of London. Bought one (A.D. 1766) for 3 & 6 pence. I want to use it in case I serve up the Revolutionary narrative of the beggar. Thence into Chancery Lane, into a horrible hole & bought a fine copy of Chatterton & a 3. Vol: ed: of Guzman. (Chatterton was 5 Shillings — Guzman 2) Left them to be bound. Thence to Paternoster Row & saw Davidson. Saw the Literary World's review of "Redburn". Also the Publisher's Advertisements in the New York "Courier". Gave Davidson my £200 note to get discounted, if possible, at his banker's. I have no receipt to show — so if he dies to night, I am minus $1000. Ditto if he decamps. But he is a very fine, good-hearted fellow — & I hope he wont see this. Upon getting home at 2. P.M. found my copy of "Knight's London" & a note from Mr Rogers, inviting me to breakfast for Thursday next. Accepted. Putting my reply in the office, I stopped at a silversmith's (corner of Craven St & Strand) & bought a solid spoon for the boy Malcolm — a *fork,* I mean. When he arrives to years of mastication I shall invest him with this fork — as of yore they did a young knight, with his good sword. Spent an hour or so looking over "White Jacket" preparatory to sending it finally to Bentley — who, tho' he has paid his money has not received his wares. At 6 I dine with him.

Wednesday Dec 19, '49 Last night dined with Mr Bentley, and had a very pleasant time indeed. I begin to like him much. He seems a very fine frank off-handed old gentleman. We sat down in a fine old room hung round with paintings (dark walls) A party of fourteen or so. There was a Mr Bell there — connected with Literature in some way or other. At all events an entertaining man and a scholar — but looks as if he loved old Port. Also Alfred Henry Forrester ("Alfred Crowquill") the comic man. He proved a good fellow — free & easy — & no damned nonsense, as there is about so many of these English. Mr Bentley has one daughter a fine woman of 25 & married, and 4 sons — young men. They were all at table. — Some time after 11. went hence with Crowquill, who invites me to go with him Thursday & see the Pantomime rehearsal at the Surrey Theater. — After breakfast this morning called in at Stibbs' the bookseller & coming across a fine old copy of Sir T. Browne — bought him, for 16 Shillings (sterling) — about $4, also, nice edition of Boswell's Johnson — for 21 Shillings. Thence went to the British Museum — & wandered about for a couple of hours there. Thence to Gordon Square and left letter & card for Mr Atkinson. Thence thro' the New Road to Tottenham Court Road into Oxford Street & so to St: James's. Stopped in Arlington Street to see Mr Moore the apothecary. Was out of town. Thence to N° 1 St James's place where I remained about 20 minutes. Thence home & made up a fire at 3. P.M. To night at 6. I dine with Mr Cook

Thursday Dec: 20 '49. Last night dined in Elm Court, Temple, and had a glorious time till noon of night. A set of fine fellows indeed. It recalled poor Lamb's "Old Benchers". Cunningham the author of Murray's London Guide was there & was very friendly. A comical Mr Rainbow also, & a grandson of Woodfall the printer of Junius, and a brother-in-law of Leslie the painter. Leslie was prevented from coming. Up in the 5th story we dined. The Paradise of Batchelors. Home & to bed at 12. This morning breakfasted with Mr Rogers at 10. A remarkable looking old man truly. Supurb paintings. No one but he & I to gether. At leaving he invited me to breakfast with him again on Sunday & meet some ladies. Accepted. Thence went to Bentley's — saw him — got some books out of him. Thence to Mr Murray's & saw him. With Mr Cooke I then went to the Erechtheum Club House in St: James Square, where I dine to night with Cooke's brother, a barrister with a quizzical eye. Thence looked in at the Reform Club House. Thence down Whitehall St & in thro' the Privy Gardens, & Sir Robert Peels to the New Houses of Parliament. After much trouble & waiting got into the House of Lords to see the frescoes. An artist a friend of Murray's, Mr John Tenniel, was our "open sesamie" Went all over the place — & spent two hours there — much against my will. A finished frescoe by "Herbert" is very fine in the Poets Hall — representing Cordelia & Lear. Cope is another of the artists. Tenniel's painting is St: Cecilia from Dryden. — Thence crossed the river to the Surrey Theater to keep appointment with "Crowquill". Too late. But went in behind the scenes, a little. Thence to Blackfriar's bridge, & took steamer for home. Made a fire & here I am. *Stone,* I beleive, is the name of the brother-in-law of Leslie. He was extremely urgent for me to spend Christmas with him & Leslie in St: John's Wood. I could barely resist him. But I sail on Monday. Last night — just on the eve of my going to the Temple — a letter was left for me — from home! — All well & Barney more bouncing than ever, thank heaven. — In a few days now my letter will be received announcing my sailing. — When at Bentley's this morning he said Mr Miller wanted to see me. Spoke to B—— about the time of bringing out White Jacket. And we mutually appointed the 23d day of January next (Wednesday) as the day for publishing *here*.

Friday Dec 21, 1849 Last night dined at the Erechtheum Club St: James's with Mr Cooke (he with the eye) — nine sat down — fine dinner — Rainbow & others were there. Mr Cleaves is a fine fellow. An exceedingly agreeable company. The *"Mull"* after dinner, looked at some billiard playing awhile, & left. After breakfast this morning called on Mr Cleaves at his rooms in the Temple, & we visited the Library — Hall of the Benchers — Kitchen — rooms — Dessert room & *table*. Portraits of the Benchers. In the Library saw some fine old M.S.S — of the Kings & Queens & Chancellors hundreds of years ago. Thence to Lincoln's Inn, & visited the New Hall, Kitchen, Library &c — Very fine. Sublime Kitchen — *chimney place*. Also visited the courts in the Inn — 2 Vice Chancellors courts, — and the Lord High Chancellor Cottenham — an old fellow, nearly asleep on the bench. Thence to the Court of the Master of the Rolls — Rolls' Court — a very handsome man — Lord Something, I forget what — Strange story about him. Thence, left Mr Cleaves & went to London Dock, thro' the Wharves to see about the ship's sailing. Saw Captain Fletcher. —— Sails 3 P.M. tomorrow. Thence walked to Davidson's

Paternoster Row — invited him to dine with me tonight. Thence towards home & bought a large carpet bag for my traps — price 14 Shillings. —— Found a note from Mr Foster of the Examiner inviting me to breakfast Sunday morning — declined being engaged at Mr Rogers.

Saturday Dec 22, '49. Dined last night with Mr Davidson at the Blue Posts. Sat there in very pleasant conversation till 11 o'clock — then home. This morning breakfasted at the old place — then returned to my room & packed up. Cabbed it to London Docks & put my luggage aboard to go round to Portsmouth. Ship Sailed at 3 P.M. to day. Thence to Davidson's to see about my money. While waiting for him, ran out, & at last got hold of "The Opium Eater" & began it in the office. A wonderful thing, that book. — Davidsons checque I got cashed, & went with the *"funds"* to Baring Brothers &c in Bishopgate St: & got a letter of credit on America for £180. Thence walked home — cold dry day — & made fire at ½ past 3. PM. To night at 6 I dine again at the club in St: James's Square. On this account I declined the invitation from Mrs Daniel to tea &c. Cooke sent me a note inclosing an order for me to visit the Reform Club House. He is very obliging.

Sunday Dec 23^d^ '49 Last night dined at the Erechtheum Club — a party of eight — Charles Knight the author of London Illustrated &c & the Publisher of the Penny Cyclopedia & concerned in most of the great popular publications of the day; — Ford the Spanish Traveller & Editor of the Guide Book — Leslie the painter — Cunningham the London Antiquarian & author of the London Guide published by Murray; — & Mr Murray the Albemarl Street man — together with Cooke & a youth whose name I forget. — We had a glorious time & parted at about midnight. This morning breakfasted with Mr Rogers again. And there met "Barry Cornwall" otherwise Mr Procter; & his wife — and Mr Kinglake (author of Eothen?) A very pleasant morning we had, and I went away at ¼ past one o'clock. Thence walked thro St: James's Park & came home & made a fire. 3. P.M. — While sitting in my room reading the "Opium Eater" by the fire I am handed Mr George Atkinson's card — the girl (pursuant to my directions) having told him at the door that I was *"not in"*. I am obliged to employ this fashionable shift of evasion of visitors — for I have not a decent room to show them — but (& which is *the* cause) I can not in conscience ask them to labor their way up to the 4th story of a house. —— ½ past 3 P.M. Have just this moment finished the "Opium Eater". A most wondrous book.

Portsmouth Monday Dec 24th 1849 Coffee Room of the Quebec Hotel. After finishing the marvellous book *yesterday* sallied out for a walk about dusk, & encountered Capt: Fletcher who was on the point of calling upon me. Walked down the Strand with him & left him at the London Coffee House. He seems a very fine fellow. Dined at Morley's at six PM yesterday with Parker (a little chap) & Somerby my future fellow passenger in the ship. Home by 11 o'clock & to bed. This morning (Monday) breakfasted for the last time at "the old place" and took an affectionate & melancholy adieu of my two ladies there. Thence to Mr Bentley's — saw him — exchanged my odd volume of the thing; — and thence went to the "Reform Club". — Supurb hall of pillars &c. Kitchen — pastry room — meat room — cutlets arranged like cravats — "butters" &c. Bathing & Dressing rooms — boot-pullers. Thence strolled about & bought some books — & a bread trencher & knife for Mrs Shaw, (£3.10.) — Thence to dinner at "the old place" & bid that also an adieu. Bought some things at the Bazaar in the Strand. Bid good bye to my room in Craven Street — drove to the Waterloo Station in a cab — after a five hours ride — here I am waiting the ship in Portsmouth. Mr Somerby came with me.

Tuesday Dec 26. 1849

Christmas.

Rose from a right comfortable English bed and took a short stroll into the town — passed the famous "North Corner". Saw the "Victory", Nelson's ship, at anchor. While at breakfast with Captain Fletcher a messenger arrived saying that our ship was off the harbor. Instantly the coffee cups were capsized, & every thing got ready for our departure. Jumped into a small boat with the Captain, Somerby, an Englishman (Mr Jones) and his little girl — & pulled off for the ship about a mile & a half distant. Upon boarding her, we at once set sail with a fair wind, & in less than 24 hours passed the Land's End & the Scilly Isles — & standing boldly out on the ocean, stretched away for

New York. —— Five days have elapsed — the wind has still continued favorable, & the weather delightfull. —— No events happen — & therefore I shall keep no further diary. — I here close it, with my departure from England, and my pointing for home. ——

At sea, Dec 29. 1849.

——— " ———

Wednesday, Jan: 30th 1850 Got sight of a pilot boat, this morning about 12.M.

Journal 1856–57

Sailed from New York Oct 11th, Saturday, 1856 in the screw-steamer Glasglow bound for Glasglow. In 15 days made the north of Ireland, — Rathlin isle — passed Arran Ailsa Crag &c (see map) Ailsa looming up in the mist. Got to Greenoch 10 at night, lay there at anchor, next morning, Sunday, went up the Clyde to Glasglow. Great excitement all along. Banks like tow-pathes — narrow channel — immense steamer — green heights — received by acclamation — Lord Blantyre's place — opposite mud cottage — cattle tenders — women — pace like cattle — places for building iron steamers.

Next morning went to old cathedral, — tombs, defaced inscriptions — others worn in flagging — some letters traced in moss — back of cathedral gorge & stream — Acropolis — John Knox in Geneva cap frowning down on the cathedral — dimness of atmosphere in keeping — all looked like picture of one of the old masters smoked by Time —

Old buildings about the hill stone walls & thatch roof — solid & fragile — miserable poverty — look of the Middle Ages — west end & fine houses — the moderns — contemporary. — The University. The park — the promenade (Seychill street) — at night population in the middle of the street. High Street.

Next morning took steamer down the Clyde to Loch Lomond — R.R. part of the way — thick mist, just saw the outline of Ben Lomond — like lake George — came back & stopped at Dumbarton Castle — isolated rock, like Ailsa — promontory at the juncture of the Clyde & Levern — covered with sod & moss — a cleft between — stone stairs & terraces — W. Wallace's broadsword — great cleaver — soldiers in red coats about the Rock like flamingoes among the cliffs — some rams with smoky fleeces — grenadiers — smoked by the high chimnies of furnaces in Dumbarton village —

Memorandum of stay in Liverpool

Saturday, Nov 8th 1856. Arrived from York, through Lancaster, at 1. P.M, having passed through an interesting country of manufactures. A rainy day. Put up at "White Bear Hotel" Dale St:. Dined there at ordinary. Before sitting down, asked bar-maid, "How much?" Curious to observe the shrinking expression, as if shocked at the idea of anything mercenary having part in the pure hospitality of an ordinary. Host & hostess at table. Comical affectation of a private dinner party. All thought of the public house banished. Entertaining his friends. "Will you have some ale?" — But charged in the bill. — Affectation of the unstinted bounty of a Christmas party, but great economy. — Capital bed. — After dinner went to Exchange. Looked at Nelson's statue, with peculiar emotion, mindful of 20 years ago. — Stayed at hotel during the evening. Rain. Made acquaintance with an agreeable young Scotchman going to the East in steamer "Damascus" on Monday. Wanted me to accompany him. Sorry that circumstance prevented me.

Sunday, Nov 9th Rain. Stayed home till dinner. After dinner took steamboat for Rock Ferry to find Mr Hawthorne. On getting to R. F, learned he had removed thence 18 months previous, & was residing out of town. — Spent evening at home.

Monday Nov 10th Went among docks to see the Meditteranean steamers. Explored the new docks "Huskisson" &c. Saw Mr Hawthorne at the Consulate. Invited me to stay with him during my sojourn at Liverpool. — Dined at "Anderson's" a very nice place, & charges moderate.

Tuesday Nov 11 Went among the steamers in the morning. Took afternoon train with Mr Hawthorne for Southport, 20 miles distant on the sea-shore, a watering place. Found Mrs. Hawthorne & the rest awaiting tea for us.

Wednesday Nov 12 At Southport. An agreeable day. Took a long walk by the sea. Sands & grass. Wild & desolate. A strong wind. Good talk. In the evening Stout & Fox & Geese. —Julian grown into a fine lad; Una taller than her mother. Mrs Hawthorne not in good health. Mr H. stayed home for me.

Thursday Nov 13. At Southport till noon. M^{r}. H. & I took train then for Liverpool. Spent rest of day pressing inquiries among steamers, & writing letters, & addressing papers &c.

Friday Nov 14 Took 'buss for London Road, — "Old Swan" Passed quarry. Returning, called at Mr Hawthornes. Met a Mr Bright. Took me to his club & lunched there. Then to view Unitarian church, & Free Library & Cemetery.

Saturday Nov 15 Rode in the omnibuss. Went out to Toxhete Park &c — Grand organ at St. George's Hall.

Sunday Nov 16 In the morning packed trunk. To church in the afternoon, & evening.

Monday Nov 17. Was to sail to day in "Egyptian" Captain Tate, but put off till tomorrow. Great disappointment. Tired of Liverpool.

Tuesday Nov 18 — Sailed about three o'clock. Fine sight going out of harbor.

Voyage From Liverpool to Constantinople.

Nov 19th. Saw Tusca Rock, on Irish Coast.

Nov 20, 21, 22^{d} Fair wind & fine weather. Passed Cape Finnistere.

Sunday 23[d] Passed within a third of a mile of Cape St: Vincent. Light house & monastery on bold cliff. Cross. Cave underneath light house. The whole Atlantic breaks here. Lovely afternoon. Great procession of ships bound to Crimea must have been descried from this point.

Monday 24th Strong wind ahead. Sighted Cape Trafalgar. Entered the Straits of Gibralter at 4. P.M. Mountainous & wild-looking coast of Africa — forsaken barbarous. "Apes Mountain" nearly opposite Gibralter. "Pillars of Hercules". Tarifa, small village, — white. Insular Rock. Sunset. Rock strongly lit, all the rest in shade. England throwing the rest of the world in shade. Vast heighth. Red sky. Sunset in the Straights. Gate of the East. Many ships. — Looks insular as Bass Rock or Ailsa. — Calm within Straits. Long swell took us. The Mediterranean.

Tuesday 25. Nov Beautiful morning. Blue sea & sky. Warm as May. Spanish coast in sight. Mountains, snow capped, always so Captain says. Mate comes out with straw hat. Shirt sleeves. Threw open my coat. — Such weather as one might have in Paridise. Pacific. November too! Like sailing on a lake.

Wednesday 26. At sunrise close to African Coast. Mountains, in parts crested with snow. Peeps of villages, wild looking. At noon, off Algiers. In the vicinity beautiful residences among the hills. White house among gardens. Reminded one of passages in Don Quixotte, "Story of the Morisco." Saw the Mole & lighthouse — the town built up a hill — latteen boats in view. The sun hot. High mountains all around. Fine bay. Piratical corsair look. — Leaving it in the distance the town looked like a sloping rock, covered with bird lime — the houses all white. — In the afternoon passed a detached group of very high mountains covered a long way down with snow — Alpine heigths. The most solitary & dreariest imaginable.

Thursday 27th Same glorious weather. In the evening passed Isle Galita — uninhabited. Clear nights, stars shining with brilliancy.

Friday 29th Bright & blue as usual. At noon passed close to Pantalaria, an isle 150 ms from Malta, & 200 from Africa. Cultivated slopes & plain all round a mass of lofty rock. Beautiful landscapes inland. A town & scattered houses. A large castle. Belongs to Naples. Convicts here. — Went to bed at 8. P.M and at 1. A.M. dressed & went on deck, the ship about entering Malta harbor. To bed again when anchor was down.

Saturday. 29th Lying in the harbor of Malta. Ashore all day. At 6. P.M. got under weigh, with two passengers in cabin, a Greek & Austrian, very gentlemanly men.

Sunday 30. Cross sea, ship rolling very bad. G & A quite sick. Rather dismal day. At night had to secure myself in berth against being rolled out.

Monday Dec 1. Sea less cross. At 12. M. pleasant, & made the coast of Greece, the Morea. Passed through the straits, & Cape Matapan.

Tuesday Dec 2. At daylight in the midst of Archplago; 12 or 15 islands about. Came to anchor at Syra about 8 A.M. Port of the archilpalgo. Much alarmed lest we should have a quarantine of eleven days. Saw the quarantine house — lonely place among bare hills; opposite the shipping. At the Custom house with the Captain & his papers; at a grating, took the ship's papers with pair of wooden tongs. Meantime an officer off to the ship to muster the crew; if one was dead, or missing, — quarantine! All right, though. — Went ashore. New & old Town. Animated appearance of the quay. Take all the actors of operas in a night from the theaters of London, & set them to work in their fancy dresses, weighing bales, counting codfish, sitting at tables on the dock, smoking, talking, sauntering, — sitting in boats &c — picking up rags, carrying water casks, bemired &c — will give some notion of Greek port. Picturesqueness of the whole. Variety of it. Greek trousers, sort of cross between petticoat & pantaloons. Some with white petticoats & embroidered jackets. Fine forms, noble faces. Mustache &c. — Went to Old Town. From the water looks like colossal sugarloaf. white houses. Divided from New Town by open lots. Climbed up. Complete warren of stone houses or rather huts, built without the least plan. Zig-zag. little courts in front of each, sometimes overhead, crossing the track. Paved with stone, roofs flat & m'cadamized. Up & up, only guide was *to mount*. At last got to the top, a church, from court of which,

fine view of archilpago & islands (name them) — Looks very old; — probably place of defence. Poor people live here. Picturesque. Some old men looked like Pericles reduced to a chiffonier — such a union of picturesque & poverty stricken. — Streets of stairs up the Old Town. As if made for goats. The donkeys climb them. All round barren tawny hills, here & there terraced with stone. Saw a man ploughing with a peice of old root. — Some roofs planted. Very dirty. Terrible nest for the plague. — View of the islands — little hamlets, white, half way up mountains. — The azure of the sea, & ermine of the clouds, the Greek flag (blue & white) seems suggested by the azure of her sky & ermine of her clouds.
The wharf, a kind of semicircle, coinciding with the ampitheater of hills. — In December tables & chairs out of doors, coffee & water pipes. —— Carpenters & blacksmiths working in the theatrical costumes — Scavenger in his opera costume going about with dust pan & brush through the streets, & emptying his pan into panniers of an ass. — No horses or carriages — streets merely made for foot-passengers. — The crowds on the quays all with red caps, looking like flamingos. Long tassells — laborers wear them, & carry great bundles of codfish on their heads. — Few seem to have anything to do. All lounge. Greek signs over a pieman's.

*Wednesday & Thursday 3^d^ & 4th* still at Syra. On the last day I did not go ashore. Several steamers arrived. Got my sovereigns back from Loyd's. Other two passengers sailed for Athens.

*Friday 5th* At 2 A.M got under weigh for Salonica. Passed various islands. First bad weather encountered since leaving England. Rain & wind About sunset passed through very narrow passage into the Gulf of Salonica. In the cabin had a Greek gentleman & wife for passengers; with 12 or 15 Greeks for deck passengers. Steamed slowly during the night, so as to make the harbor at a proper time in the morning.

*Saturday 6th* At day break roused by the Captain to come on deck. Did so. Saw Mount Olympus, covered with snow at the summit, & looking most magestic in the dawn. Ossa & Pelion to the South. Olympus 10,000 feet high, according to the Captain's chart. O & P about 4 or 5000. Long ranges of hills along the Thessalain shore.

Mount Athos (rather conical) on the opposite shore. About nine o'clock came to anchor before Salonica. A walled town on a hill side. Wall built by Genoese. Minarets & cyprus trees the most conspicuous objects. The Turkish men of war in harbor. Olympus over against the town far across the water, in plain sight. Went with Captain with papers to the quarantine. All right & shook hands. (Usual ceremony of welcome). Went to the Abbots, ship's agents. Politely received. One of their employees took me a stroll through the town. Went into the mosques. Tomb of an old Greek saint shown in a cellar. Several of the mosques formerly Greek churches, but upon the conquest of the Turks turned into their present character. One of them circular & of immense strength. The ceiling mosaic. Glass. Peices continually falling upon the floor. Brought away several. — Saw Roman remains of a triumphal arch across a street. Fine sculpture at the base representing battle scenes. Roman eagle conspicuous. About the arch, miserable buildings of wood. A Turkish cafe near one pier. Also saw remains of a noble Greek edifice. 3 columns &c. used as gateway & support to outhouse of a Jew's abode. Went into the Bazaar. Quite large, but filthy. Streets all narrow, like cow lanes, & smelling like barn-yards. Very silent. Women muffled about the face. All old. No young. Great numbers of Jews walking in long robes & pelisses. Also Greeks mixed with the Turks. Aspect of streets like those of Five Points Rotten houses. Smell of rotten wood. Three months ago a great fire, overrunning several acres. Not yet rebuilt. 60 persons killed by explosion of powder in a Greek warehouse, — powder not known to have been there.

Sunday Dec 7th Purposed going with Captain Tate to the Protestant missionaries, but learned they were absent at Cassandra. Duckworth, the English resident, came off early. Talked with him. Said he had been *a day's shooting in the Vale of Tempe* — Ye Gods! whortleberrying on Olympus, &c. —— Went ashore with Captain. Started from Abbots' on horseback with a guide & guard to the Abbotts place three miles inland. On emerging from gate met the first troop of camels. Passed an immense cemetery. Turbanded tomb stones. Rode over bleak hills — no verdure — here & there an old sycamore. A shade with fountain, & inscription from the Koran. Passed some vineyards. Abbots place enclosed by high thick stone wall. On knocking, after a good time, gate was opened, & we were repulsed. But presented letter. Guards came running with muskets. Letter read at last by a handsome, polite Greek, who then led us through the grounds. Oriental style. Very beautiful. Hot houses & fountains & trellises & arbors innumerable. Old sycamores. Served with sweetmeats & liqueurs & coffee. Bath rooms Thick dome perforated — light but no heat. — Returned at 3 P.M. & dined aboard. — Saw several flocks of sheep & shepherds on the hills. Met donkeys a plenty. Surprising loads they carry. Long timbers, bales &c. Scene in the Gate. — In the evening Captain told a story about the heap of arms affecting the compass. Beautiful weather all day, & gloriously clear night.

Monday Dec 8th. Lovely day. Ashore & visited the walls. Was repulsed from a tower by a soldier who refused money. Went through the bazarrs. At the landing watched for an hour or two a vast crowd & tumult. An Austrian steamer from Constantinople just in, with a great host of poor deck passengers, Turks, Greeks, Jews &c. Came ashore in boats, piled up with old dusty traps from which the Plaige seemed shaken. Great uproar of the porters & contention for luggage. — Imagine an immense accumulation of the rags of all nations, & all colors rained down on a dense mob, all strugling for huge bales & bundles of rags, gesturing with all gestures & wrangling in all tongues. Splashing into the water from the grounded boats. — After dinner on board, several deck passengers came off to us to go to Constan^{ople}. Turkish women among others. Went right aft on deck & spred their carpets. One prayed, bowing her head. Two negreses, faces covered, to conceal their beauty. Arms all taken down into the cabin after being discharged. — Upon the uproar at the landing Olympus looked from afar cold & snowy. Surprising the Gods took no interest in the thing. Might at least have moved their sympathy. — Heard a rumor by way of Trieste that Louis Napoleon had been assassinated. — Forgot to mention the pulpit of St. Paul in the court of a mosque. Beautiful sculpture — all one stone. Steps &c. The chief lion of Salonica, is this.

Tuesday Dec 9th Remained on board, observing the arrival of deck passengers for Constanto^{ple}. A large number in all costumes. Among others two "beys effendi" in long furred robes of yellow, looking like Tom cats. They had their harems with them. All on deck. At 1½ P.M got under weigh. Lovely day. A calm. Ship steady as a house. Like a day in May. A moonlight night followed. Passed Olympus glittering at top with ice. When it was far astern, its snow line showed in the moonlight like a strip of white cloud. Looked unreal — but still was there. Passed Ossa & Pelion. Rounded Athos. Got up tents for the two harems. Guard set over them. Fine old effendi wounded at Sinope. Some very pretty women of the harem. "Ashmacks" worn by them. Very lazy.

Wednesday Dec 10th. Up early, fine morning, off "Lemnos, the Ægean isle." Passed to the north of it, between it & Imbros. About 11 A.M. entered the Helespont. Gentle wind from the north. Clear & fine. The new castles of Europe & Asia on either hand. Little difference in the aspect of the continents. Only Asia looked a sort of used up — superannuated. Shores moderately lofty. A sober yellow the prevalent colour. Passed a good many vessels bound down before a gentle wind with all sail set. Among others a Turkish steam friggate. Passed the New Castles at the Dardeneles, proper; then Point Nagara; then Cape Sestos & Abydos — a long swim had Leander & Byron; then Gallipoli, where the French & English first landed during the War. Then entered the Sea of Marmora, when we were suddenly met by a dense fog. It cleared up soon however; but was followed by other mists. The weather changed. — The sail up the Helespont is upon the whole a very fine one. But I could not get up much enthusiasm; though passing Xerxes' bridge-piers (or the site of them) & the mouth of the Granicus, &c &c &c. Still, I thought what a sublime approach has the Sultan to his capital. Antichambers of seas & lakes, & corridors of glorious straits. *8½ P.M.* Tomorrow morning I must rise betimes to behold Constantinople, where it remains to be seen how long I shall sojourn. N.B. Cap. T. has not yet accounted for the piastres.

Thursday Dec 11th Thick fog during the night. Steamed very slowly, ringing the bell. Ere daylight came to anchor in the Sea of Marmora, as near as the Captain could determine, within but three miles or less of Constantinople. All day the fog held on. Very thick, & damp & raw. Very miserable for the Turks & their harrems; particularly when they were doused out by the deck-washing. Some sick & came below to the fire; off with their "ashmacks" &c. Several steamers at anchor around us, but invisable; heard the scream (alarms) of their pipes &

ringing of bells. — During the second night, heard the Constantp[le] dogs bark & bells ring. Old Turk ("Old Sinope") I said to him "This is very bad" he answered "God's will is good, & smoked his pipe in cheerful resignation.

Friday Dec 12th. About noon fog slowly cleared away before a gentle breeze. At last, as it opened around us, we found ourselves lying, as in enchantment, among the Prince Islands, scores of vessels in our own predicament around us. Invisable confounds. (Forgot to note that during the fog several "kyacks" came alongside, attracted by our bell. They had lost their way in the fog. They were Constanople boats. One of them owned by a boy, who moored under our quarter & there went to sleep in the fog. Specimen of an oriental news boy. The self-possession & easy ways. The first appearance of Constanople from the sea is described as magnificent. See "Anastasius" But one lost this. The fog only lifted from about the skirts of the city, which being built upon a promontory, left the crown of it hidden wrapped in vapor. Could see the base & wall of St. Sophia but not the dome. It was a coy disclosure, a kind of coquetting, leaving room for imagination & heigthing the scene. Constantinople, like her Sultanas, was thus seen veiled in her "ashmack". Magic effect of the lifting up of the fog disclosing such a city as Constan[ple]. — At last rounded Seraglio Point & came to anchor at 2 PM in the Golden Horn. Crossed over to Tophanna in a caique (like a canoe, but one end pointed out like a knife, covered with quaint carving, like old furniture) No demand made for passport nor any examination of luggage. Got a guide to Hotel du Globe in Pera. Wandered about a little before dinner. Dined at 6 P.M. 10 F per day for 5th story room without a carpet &c. Staid in all night. Dangerous going out, owing to footpads & assassins. The curse of these places. Cant' go out at night, & no places to go to, if you could. *Burnt Districts*

Saturday Dec 13th. Up early; went out; saw cemeteries, where they dumped garbage. sawing wood over a tomb. Forrests of cemeteries. Intricacy of the streets. Started alone for Constan[ple] and after a terrible long walk, found myself back where I started. Just like getting lost in a wood. No plan to streets. Pocket-compass. Perfect labryth. Narrow. Close, shut in. If one could but get *up* aloft, it would be easy to see one's way out. If you could get up into tree. Soar out of the maze.

But no. No names to the streets no more than to natural allies among the groves. No numbers. No anything. — Breakfast at 10 A.M. Took guide ($1.25 per day) and started for a tour. Took caique for Seraglio. Holy ground. Crossed some extensive grounds & gardens. Fine buildings of the Saracenic style. Saw the Mosque of St Sophia. Went in. Rascally priests demanding "bakshesh". Fleeced me out of ½ dollar; following me round, selling the fallen mosaics. Ascended a kind of horse way leading up, round & round. Came out into a gallery fifty feet above the floor. Supurb interior. Precious marbles Porphyry & Verd antique. Immense magnitude of the building. Names of the prophets in great letters. Roman Catholic air to the whole. — To the Hippodrome, near which stands the six towered mosque of Sultan Achmet; soaring up with its snowy spires into the pure blue sky. Nothing finer. In the hippodrome saw the obleisk with Roman inscription upon the base. Also a broken monument of bronze, representing three twisted serpents erect upon the tails. Heads broken off. Also a square monument of masoned blocks. Leaning over & frittered away — like an old chimney stack. A Greek inscription shows it to of the time of Theodosius. Sculpture about the base of the obelisk, representing Constantine, wife & sons, &c. Then saw the "Burnt Column". Black & grimy enough & hooped about with iron. Stands soaring up from among a huddle of old wooden rookeries. A more striking fire monument than that of London. Then to the Cistern of 1001 columns. You see a rounded knoll covered with close herbage. Then a kind of broken cellar way, you go down, & find yourself on a wooden, rickety platform, looking down into a grove of marble pillars, fading away into utter darkness. A palatial sort of Tartarus. Two tiers of pillars one standing on t'other; lower tier half buried. Here & there a little light percolates through from breaks in the keys of the arches; where bits of green straggle down. Used to be a resivoir. Now full of boys twisting silk. Great hubbub. Flit about like imps. Whir of the spinning jennies. In going down, (as into a ship's hold) and wandering about, have to beware the invisable skeins of silk. Terrible place to be robbed or murdered in. At whatever point you look, you see lines of pillars, like trees in an orchard arranged in the quincus style. — Came out. Overhead looks like a mere shabby common, or worn out sheep pasture. — To the Bazarr. A wilderness of traffic. Furniture, arms, silks, confectionery, shoes, saddles — everything. Covered overhead with stone arches, with side openings. Immense crowds. Georgians Armeanians, Greeks, Jews & Turks are the merchants. Magnificent embroidered silks & gilt sabres & caparisons for horses. You loose yourself & are bewildered & confounded with the labyrinth, the din, the barbaric confusion of the whole. — Went to the Watch Tower within a kind of arsenal. (immense arsenal.) The Tower of vast girth & heigth in the Saracenic style — a column. From the top, my God, what a view! Surpasses everything. The Propontis, the Bosphorous, the Golden Horn, the domes the minarets, the bridges, the men of war, the cypruss. — Indescribable. — Went to the Pigeon Mosque. In its court, the pigeons covered the pavement as thick as in the West they fly in hosts. A man feeding them. Some perched upon the roof of the collonades, & upon the fountain in the middle & on the cypresses. — Took off my shoes, & went in. Pigeons inside, flying round in the dome, in & out the lofty windows. — Went to Mosque of Sultan Sulyman. The third one in point of size & splendor. — The Mosque is a sort of marble marquee of which the minarets (four or six) are the stakes. In fact when inside it struck me that the idea of this kind of edifice was borrowed from the tent. Though it would make a noble ball room. — Off shoes & went in. This custom more sensible than taking off hat. Muddy shoes; but never muddy heads. Floor covered with mats & over them beautiful rugs of great size & square. Fine light coming through side slits below the dome. Blind dome. Many Turks at prayer; bowing head to the floor towards a kind of alter. Chanting going on. In a gallery saw lot of portmanteaus chests & bags; as in a R.R. baggage car, put there for safe-keeping by men who leave home, or afraid of robbers & taxation. "Lay not up your treasures where moth & rust do corrupt" &c. Fountains (a row of them) outside along the sides of the mosque for bathing the feet & hands of worshippers before going in. Natural rock. — Instead of going in in stockings (as I did) the Turks wear over shoes & doff them outside the mosque. — The tent like form of the mosque broken up & diversified with infinite number of arches, buttresses, small domes, collanades &c &c &c. — Went down to Golden Horn. Crossed bridge of pontoons. Stood in the middle & not a cloud in the sky. Deep blue & clear. Delightful elastic atmosphere, altho December. A kind of English June cooled & tempered sherbet-like with an American October; the serenity & beauty of summer without the heat. — Came home through the vast suburbs of Galata &c. Great crowds of all nations — money changers — coins of all nations circulate — Placards in four or five languages; [(Turkish, French, Greek, Armenian) Lottery.] advertisements of boats the same. You feel you are among the nations. Sultan's ships in colors — no atmosphere like this for flags. — No wonder poor homes. Dont want them. Open air. Chairs in the streets — crowds &c. Great curse that of Babel; not being able to talk to a fellow being, &c. *(Ruffians of Galata)* — Have to beware of your pockets. My guide went with his hands to his. — The horrible grimy tragic air of these streets. The rotten & wicked looking houses. So gloomy & grimy seems as if a suicide hung from every rafter within. — No open space — no squares or parks. You suffocate for room. — You pass close together. The cafes of the Turks. Dingy holes, faded splendor, moth eaten, on both sides wide seats or divans where the old musty Turks sit smoking like conjurers. — Saw in certain kiosks (pavilions) the crowns of the late Sultans. You look through gilt gratings & between many curtains of lace, at the sparkling things. Near the mosque of Sultan Solyman saw the cemetery of his family — big as that of a small village, all his wives & children & servants. All gilt & carved. The women's tombs carved without heads (women no souls) The Sultan Solyman's tomb & that of his three brothers in a kiosk. Gilded like mantle ornaments.

Sunday Dec. 14. Three Sundays a week in Constan^{ple}. Friday, Turks; Sat, Jews; Sunday, Romanists, Greeks, & Armenians. — At 8. AM crossed over the 2^{d} bridge to Stamboul to ride round the Walls. Passed between wall & Golden Horn through Greek & Jew quarters, and came outside the land wall in view of Sweet Waters, which run inland & end in beautiful glades. Rode along the land wall. By this wall Constan^{ple} was taken by the Turks & the last of the Constantines fell in their defence. Four miles of massiness, with huge square towers — a Tower of London — every 150 yards or so. In many parts rent by earthquakes. The towers especially. Great cracks & fissures. In one tower you see a jaw of light opening; the riven parts stand toppling like inverted pyramids. Evergreen vines mantling them. 4 walls parallel — added defences. The strength of the masonry shows, that when by earthquake the summit of a tower has been thrown down, it has slid off retaining its integrity — not separating, but rubbing like a rock-slide. In the wide tracks, they cultivate them — garden spots — very rich & loamy — here fell the soldiers of Constantine — sowed in corruption & raised in potatoes. — These walls skirted by forrests of cemetery — the cyprus growing thick as firs in a Scotch plantation. Very old — a primal look — weird. The walls seem the inexorable bar between the mansions of the living & the dungeons of the dead. —— Outside the wall here is a Greek Church (for name see G.B.) Very beautiful, new upon an ancient site. (The miraculous fish here) Decorated with banners of the virgin &c. A beautiful cave chapel — a fountain of holy water — Greeks come here & wash & burn a candle. All round under the trees people smoking narguiles, drinking & eating, & riding. Gay crowds. Greek Sunday. Rode to the wall-end at Sea of Marmora. The water dashes up against the foundation here for 6 miles to the Seraglio. Went into the Seven Towers. 200 feet high. 2 overthrown. Immense thickness. Top of walls a soil & sod. Like walking on a terrace. Seven-sided enclosure, towers at angles. Superb view of the city & sea. Dungeons — inscriptions. — Soldiers — A mosque. Immensely long ride back within the walls. Lonely streets. Passed under an arch of the acqueduct of Valens(?) In these lofty arches, ivied & weatherbeaten, & still grand, the ghost of Rome seems to stride with disdain of the hovels of this part of Stamboul. — Overtopping houses & trees &c. — Recrossed the 2^{d} bridge to Pera. Too late for the Dancing Dervishes. Saw their convent. Reminded me of the Shakers. — Went towards the cemeteries of Pera. Great resort in summer evenings. Bank of the Bosphorus — like Brooklyn heights. From one point a superb view of Sea of Marmora & Prince Isles & Scutari. — Armenian funerals winding through the streets. Coffin covered with flowers borne on a bier. Wax candles borne on each side in daylight. Boys & men chanting alternately. Striking effect, winding through the narrow lanes. — Saw a burial. Armenian. Juggling & incantations of the priests — making signs &c. — Nearby, saw a woman over a new grave — no grass on it yet. Such abandonment of misery! Called to the dead, put her head down as close to it as possible; as if calling down a hatchway or cellar; besought — "Why dont you speak to me? My God! — It is I! — Ah, speak — but one word! — All deaf. — So much for consolation. — This woman & her cries haunt me horribly. ———

¶ *Street sights.* — The beauty of the human countenance. Among the women ugly faces rare. — Singular these races so exceed ours in this respect. Out of every other window look faces (Jew, Greek, Armenian) which in England or America would be a cynosure in a ball room. — Wretched looking houses & filthy streets. Tokens of pauperism without the paupers. Out of old shanties peep lovely girls. like lillies & roses growing in cracked flower-pots. Very shy & coy looking. Many houses walled. Lower story no windows. Great gates like fortresses. Sign of barberism. Robbers. Lattices to Turkish houses — little windows. Confusion of the streets — no leading one. No clue. Hopelessly lost. — Immense loads carried by porters. — Camels, donkeys mules, horses. &c. — These Consto^{ple} bridges exceed London bridges for picturesqueness. Contrast between London Bridge & these. Kayacks darting under the wooden arches. Spread about like swarm of ants, when their hill is invaded. On either side rows of Turkish craft of uniform build & heigth, stand like troops presenting arms. Mass of black English steamers. Guide boys on the bridge. Greeks. beautiful faces. Lively, loquacious. Never wearied leaning over the balustrade & talking with them. — Viewed from bridge, the great mosques are shown to be build most judiciously on the domed hills of the city. Fine effect. Seems a spreading, still further, of the tent.

Monday Dec 15. Utterly used up last night. This morning felt as if broken on the wheel. — At eleven o clock went out without guide. Mounted the Genoese Tower. A prodigious structure. 60 feet in diameter. 200 or more high. Walls 12 feet thick. Stair in wall instead of at the tower's axis. Peculiar plan of the stairs. "Bakshesh." Terminates in a funnel-shaped affair, like a minaret. The highest loft nest of pigeons. From the gallery without, all round, another glorious view. (Three great views of Consto^{ple}) All important to one desirous to learn something of the bearings of Pera &c. After much study succeeded in understanding the way to the two great bridges. Came down, & crossed the first bridge. There took a boy-guide to the bazar. (All the way from the G. Tower down steep hill to bridge, a steady stream of people) Immense crowds on the Consto^{ple} side. Way led up steps into large court surrounding mosque. There clothes bazar. Most busy scene; all the way to the Bazar by this route — crowds, crowds, crowds — From the Fez caps, the way seemed paved with tiles. — The Baazr is formed of countless narrow aisles, overarched; and along the sides looks like rows of show-cases, a sort of sofa-counter before them (where lady customers recline) and a man in each. Persian bazzarr, superb. Pawnbrokers here, money changers, fellows with a bushel or two of coins of all nations, handling there change like pedlers of nuts. — Rug merchants, (Angora wool) P. 10 for small one. — After dismissing my boy, was followed for two or three hours by an infernal Greek, & confederates. Dogged me; in & out & through the Bazaar. I could neither intimidate or elude them. Began to feel nervous; remembered that much of the fearful interest of Schiller's Ghost-seer hangs upon being followed in Venice by an Armenian. The mere mysterious, persistant, silent following. At last escaped them. Went to the Aga Janizzary's. Tower of Fire Watchman. An immense column of the Saracenic order. Colossal Saracens. Saw drill of Turk troops here. Disciplining the barbarians. — Looked at the burnt Column again. Base bedded in humus. It leans, is split & chipped & cracked. Of a smoky purple color. Is garlanded round with laurel (chissled) at distances. (Croton water pipes on end) — Street scenes. Gilded carriages of style of Hogarths carriages. Yellow boots daintily worn by the ladies in the mud — Intricacy of the place. No way to get along the water-side — but by labryths of back lanes. — Strange books in the Mosque bazaar. — Englishman at dinner. Invited me to Buyakderre — give me a shake down &c. Said nothing would tempt him to go by night through Galata. Assassinations every night. — His cottage on Bosphorous attacked by robbers. &c.

Tuesday Dec 16th At 8½ A.M took steamer up the Bospherous to Buyukdereh. — Magnificent! The whole scene one pomp of art & Nature. Europe & Asia here show their best. A challenge of contrasts, where by the successively alternate sweeps of the shores both sides seem to retire from every new proffer of beauty, again in some grand prudery to advance with a bolder bid, and thereupon again & again retiring, neither willing to retreat from the contest of beauty. — Myrtle, Cyprus, Cedar — evergreens. — Catch glimpse of Euxine from Buy^{akd}

The water clear as Ontario — the banks natural quays, shelving off like those of a canal. Large vessels go close along shore. — The palaces of the Sultan — the pleasure-houses — palaces of embassadors — The white foam breaks on these white steps as on long lines of coral reefs. One peculiarity is the introduction of ocean into inland recesses. Ships anchor at the foot of ravines, deep among green basins, where the only canvass you would look for would be tents. — A gallery of ports & harbors, formed by the interchange of promontory & bay. Many parts like the Highlands of the Hudson, magnified. Porpoises sport in the blue; & large flights of pigeons overhead go through evolutions like those of armies. The sun shining on the palaces. View from the heights of Buuydereh. "Royal Albert" Euxine in sight from Buuyckdereh. A chain of Lake Georges. No wonder the Czars have always coveted the capital of the Sultans. No wonder the Russian among his firs sighs for these myrtles. — Cedar & Cyprus the only trees about the capital. — The Cyprus a green minaret, & blends with the stone ones. Minaret perhaps derived from cyprus shape. The intermingling of the dark tree with the bright spire expressive of the intermingling of life & death.——

— Holyday aspect of the Bospherous — The daisies are tipped with a crimson dawn, the very soil from they spring has a ruddy hue. — Kiosks & fountains. One is amazed to see quite such a filigree, such delicate & fairy-like structures out of doors. One would think the elements would visit them too rudely; that they would melt away like castle of confectionery. Profuse sculpture & gilding & painting. — The bays sweep round in great ampitheatres. — Coming back from Bospherous, stood on the First Bridge

[[Curious to stand amid these millions of fellow beings, some of whom seem not unwilling to accept our civilization, but with one consent rejecting much of our morality & all of our religion. — Aspect of the Bridge like that of a Grand Fancy Ball. (An immense Persian Rug.) 1500000 men the actors. Banvard should paint a few hundred miles of this pageant of moving procession. Pedlers of all sorts & hawkers. Confectionery carried on head. A chain of malefactors with iron rings about their necks — Indian file. Porters immense burdens, brains doing the office of sinews. Others carrying burdens with poles, hands resting on each others shoulders. Military officers followed by running footmen. Ladies in yellow slippers. "Arabas." Horses, whose docility & gentleness is much as harmless as any other foot passengers. — Taking toll on the bridge (Three or four men) Splendid barges of the Pashas darting under the arches. A gentleman followed by his Greek servants on horseback. An officer conversing with his confidential servant. A Black eunuch followed by white servants in great state. Sherbet sellers on bridge-side. An Arab wandering. Or a Georgian. The soldiers. The droves of sheep

— shepherds marching in sheep clothing in advance. A file of loaded horses — sacks of flour. A drove of donkeys — everybody giving them a poke. — You hear names of Yusef, Hassan, Hamet (Arabian Nights) bandied on all sides. A Mosque at end of bridge. The Bazarr Mosque. Shaving heads in its court &c. Road to Bazarr leads through this court.

Visited Mosque of Achmet (6 towers) Forecourt like a huge conservatory. 20 small cupolas or domes. A double gallery. A Verandah without, and a collonade within. A fountain in the middle. Columns of variously colored marbles & mosaic. Heaps of old traps, old capotes being cut up by beggars. bales, with marks. Pile of old hoops rusting. Pile of old haversacks and belts & spoons & kettles. [Grated windows look between the double galleries. Beautiful effect. Outside, under gallery, rows of penstocks, with stone footstool below, for worshippers to wash feet &c. Within, four vast pillars supports to the dome, like towers (white marble) Most perfect specimen of the mosque. Regular square, inside. Small domes & half domes. — In the "towers" are fountains. Birds perched among the chandeliers, flying about

Constantinople Tuesday, Dec 16

Wandered about in vicinity of Hippodrome till nearly dusk; lost myself, & finally came out at a gate on the Sea of Marmora. Returned to Tophanna by kayack. Interesting appearance of the walls here. Owing to the heighth of the shore above the sea, the fortifications here present a wall on the water side, but only a parapet on the land. Hence, from the sea, the houses look immensely lofty; they are of all shapes; in some parts their windows are formed by the open spaces of the battlements. In some parts, there are balconies. Several gates & archways are to be seen walled up. Collonades are disclosed, closed up. Pilasters. The fall, or rather crumbling away of the wall at one angle discloses a solitary column of white marble, looking strange as the resurection of a body masoned up in a tomb. Reminded me of the Abbotsford walls — only, on a grand scale. Where huge masses of the masonry have fallen, they lie like rocks, in confused heaps, the mortar as hard as the tile & stone. — At dinner to day the French attache estimated the population of Consta[ple], suburbs, & banks of Bospherous at 1,500,000. A moderate estimate, judging from the swarms. — The fortress of Mamud II. on Bospherous built in the likeness of the Arabic letters of his name. Conveys an idea of his spirit. Plenty who with a flourish skate their names on ice, but few who solidly build them up in walls upon the enduring rocks. — Extraordinary aspect of this fortress from the sea.

Wednesday Dec 17 Spent the day revisiting the Seraglio &c. — Owing to its peculiar form St: Sophia viewed near to, looks as partly underground; as if you saw but the superstructure of some immense temple, yet to be disinterred. You step *down* to enter The dome has a kind of dented appearance, like crown of old hat. Must inevitably cave in one of these days. Within dome has appearance (from its flatness) of an immense sounding board. A firmament of masonry. It rests on 4 arches, two of which are blind. The others open. Seems to rest here on cobweb. (Massy buttresses.) (Entrance in them, like caves) The interior a positive appropriation of space. The precious marbles. of the interior. The worshipping — head prostration. — In the part of the town near Old Seraglio — silent appearance of the streets. Strange houses. Rows of quaint old sideboards, cupboards, beauforts, tall Nuremberg clocks. Lanes & allies of them. Seraglio. Many prohibited spots. The Seraglio (proper) seems to be a quadrangle, on the hill, where buildings present blank walls, buttressed, outside; but within open. Cyprus overpeer the walls in some parts. Grand view from Seraglio Point — Marmora, Bospherous, Scutari. —— The courts & grounds of Seraglio have a strange, enchanted sort of look. (Silence of Seraglio as house of prayer.) — *The dogs.* roam about in bands like prarie wolves. No masters. No Turk seems to have a dog. None domesticated. Nomadic Against religion to kill them. Scavengers of the city. Terrible outcries at times. At night. Fighting of the dogs. Strange to come up on pack of them in some lonely lane. Mostly yellow, with long sharp noses. Some much scarred, others mangey. See them lying amidst refuse, hardly tell them from it. — Same color. See them over a dead horse on the beach. — Wandering about came across Black Hole in the street. Did not enter far. — Harem (sacred) on board steam boats. Lattice division. Ladies pale, straight noses, regular features, fine busts. Look like nuns in their plaine dress, but with a roundness of bust not belonging to that character. Perfect decorum between sexes. No ogling. No pertness. No looking for admiration. No Cyprians. No drunkards. Saw not a single one, though liquor is sold. — Industry. — Beauty of fountain near St: Sophia. Gilding. Grapes & foliage.

Thursday Dec 18 In morning took caique, & crossed the Bospherous to Scutari. Luxurious sailing. Cushioned like ottoman. You lie in the boat's bottom. Body beneath the surface. A boat bed. Kauck a sort of carved trencher or tray. — Fleet of fishermen at mouth of Golden Horn. Calm of water. Tide-rips. Sun shining on Sultan's Palaces. Sunrise opposite the Seraglio. As Constan^{ple} is finest site for capital, so Seraglio for pleasure-grounds, in the world. — Great barracks at Scutari. Noble view of Constantinople & up Bospherous. Cemeteries like Black Forrest. Thuringian look. Roads passing through it. Beautiful daises. The quays. The water mosque. The hills & beach. —— *General thoughts about Consta*^{ple}. As for its mud, mere wet pollen of a flower. — Tenedos Wine on table — The Negro Mussleman. Unlike other dispersed nations (Jews, Armenians, Gypsies) who proof against proslytism adhere to the faith first delivered to their fathers. Negro is indifferent to forms as horse to caparisons. —— At 4. P.M. sailed in steamer Acadia for Alexandria, via Smyrna. It was sunset ere we rounded Seraglio Point. Glorious sight. Scutari & its heights, glowed like sapphire. Wonderful clearness of air. As a promontory is covered with trees, terraced up clear to its top, so Consa^{tople} with houses. Long line of walls. — Out into Sea of Marmora.

Friday Dec 19 Passed through Dardenells at daybreak. Showers of rain. Cleared off. Passed Plain of Troy. Mount Ida beyond. Passed The Tumuli of Achilles &c. Steered in between Tenedos & the main. Passed a town & harbor of Tenedos; a promontory in the midst of the harbor covered with massive fortifications, — the work of the old Genoese. Passed Cape Bàba crowned with a fort protecting a town on high land. The Asiatic coast all along lofty with ranges of mountains in the background — a yellow look. Steered in between Mytelene & the main. A large & lovely island, covered with olive trees. They make much wine. The whole island green from beach to hill-top — a dark rich bronzy green, in marked contrast with the yellow & parched aspect of most other isles of the Archipelago. — Asia looks in color like those Asiatic lions one sees in menageries — lazy & torpid. — Many beautiful hamlets seen on Mytelene. It has one fine landlocked harbor in the middle of the isle. Near sunset came to anchor for the night in a little bay of Mytelene, so as to have the benefit of daylight for getting into Smyrna, a tickelish harbor. Sent a boat off to get soundings. A boat came from shore; bought olives & figs. According to a chart of "Mouth of Dardenelles & Plain of Troy" in the Captain's posession, I see that the whole coast hereabouts & for some ways inland is covered with ruins of great antiquity. [Sailed through Besika Bay partly sheltered by Isle Tenedos, where the E & F fleets first joined in 1853.]

Saturday Dec 20. At two in the morning up anchor at Mytelene, and by daylight were entering the bay of Smyrna. A very spacious one, thirty miles deep & 7 or 8 wide, with villages nestling in the hill sides, and lofty mountains all round. The town is at the end of the bay, and where for a little it stretches along a declivity, it looks, from the lowness of the houses, their flat roofs red-tiled like a feild of broken potterey. On Mount Pagus behind the town is an old castle, conspicuous from the sea. — Met the steamer Egyptian in port; saw Cap. Tate. A steamer grounded & one towing her off. Went ashore & called up American Consul, a Greek. Spent an hour conversing with him & his brother. Got a guide (a grave ceremonious man with a frogged coat carrying a silver mounted sword in a velvet scabbard in one hand, and a heavy silver mounted cowhide in the other) and went to Bazarr, to see the slaves. Failed. Went up Mt Pagus. A large circuit. The interior strewn over with fragments of stones, looking like a barren moor. Commands a supurb view of bay & town of Smyrna. An old ruinous mosque within. A Boston name written there. Descended, & went to the Caravan Bridge, a great resort on holydays, and country gate of the town. Here passed a constant succession of trains of camels, horses, mules, & donkeys. Sometimes a horse leading a camel-train, sometimes a donkey, sometimes a donkey also following. Horsemen with arms. Buffalo. — The camel a most ungainly creature From his long curved and crain-like neck, (which he carries stiffly like a clergyman in a stiff caravat) his feathery-looking forelegs, & his long lank hind ones, he seems a cross between an ostrich & a gigantic grasshopper. His hoof is spongey, & covered with hair to the ground, so that walking through these muddy lanes, he seems stalking along on four mops. Carries his neck out like a tortoise. Tail like long eel, driver holds it & steers him. Has a way of turning his head so that his face & tail face you together. Camel seems built by nature with special precautions against man's use. The hump in way of saddle, but man outwits nature here. [A sort of saw-buck. — Swaying of the rider — heigth. [Motion increases as on mast of ship. [Camel dung like pancakes stuck against houses, to dry. Loads of them on women's heads. Coals.

— The cemeteries very interesting, broken columns & capitals of great antiquity strewn among the broken tomb-stones; sometimes a dilapidated tomb-stone is seen composed of an old column — a double ruin. Cyprus very high & pillar-like.

Sunday Dec 21 Called with Captain Tate upon his Agent, living in a handsome house upon the Marina. Married to a Greek lady, with a child that speaks as yet only Greek, her father a Scotchman. With reference to the American Mission here the Agent said it was about discontinued; a hopeless affair; all the converts made, mercenary ones. Attended chapel at the English Consulate. Very flat affair, the chaplain, however, a curiosity. — There dined to day on board "Arcadia" C. Orpheus, C Tate, C. Eustace & self. Much talk of India voyages.

Monday Dec 22 Went ashore in the morning, interested in the curious appearance of strings of loaded camels passing through the narrow and crowded covered ways of the Bazaar. Heard a good deal about the commerce of England with Turkey. The Turkish manufactures almost at an end. The people of Manchester imitate exactly every fabric in the world. Cotton & silk imported from Turkey & returned in the form of Turkish manufactures, being retailed in the Bazars as such, & as such articles are sometimes taken home as curiosities to England & America by travelers. Copper is found in Turkey & quanities are sent to England to be made into coin for the Sultan. The English manufacturers alloy it, & return a base metal for the pure, charging for the process. In the "Egyptian" there were several casks of unstamped copper coin for Constan^{ple}. — Altho' it was a little rainy the morning of our arrival here, yet ever since, the weather has been very beautiful, like fine Spring days at home. — This evening an odd affair between C Orpheus & his first officer, to which I was an unavoidable listener.

Tuesday Dec 23^{d} Expect to sail to day for Syra, so did not go ashore. Two passengers came off to day, one a Greek officer, a comical looking fellow. — Got under weigh for Syra about 3. P.M. Fine sail down the bay. Came on blowing a gale outside, but by morning pleasant weather. Strong winds of short continuance here. Approached Syra by Myconi Passage between the islands of Myconi & Tinos. Many other isles scattered about. Among others, Delos, of a most barren aspect, however flowery in fable. I heard it was peculiarly sterile. Patmos, too, not remote; another disenchanting isle. Tinos is a large island, with numerous small hamlets (60 of them I was told) no trees, but they cultivate the grape. Each little village has its little church. They are Catholics on Tinos, wholly agricultural people. Said to be 365 isles in the Archipelogoe, one for every day in the year. Entering Syra harbor, I was again struck by the appearance of the town on the hill. The houses seemed clinging round its top, as if desperate for security, like shipwrecked men about a rock beaten by billows. A Greek on board tells me that, escaped from the massacres of Scio & Mytelene, certain Greeks escaped here in 1821, & founded the town. Syra is the most considerable place in the Archipelago, &, for commerce, perhaps in all Greece. Came to anchor at 12.M. Put us in quarantine for 24 hours (to begin from time of leaving Smyrna) tho' no case of illness on board. C. storms at the nuisance.

Wednesday, Dec 24th Included in preceding day.

Thursday Dec 25 Christmas. To day appears to be no holy day among the Greeks. Or theirs is the old style of almanack; people are so busy here I can not learn which. — Went ashore to renew my impressions of the previous visit. The Greek, of any class, seems a natural dandy. His dress, though a laborer, is that of a gentleman of leisure. This flowing & graceful costume, with so much of pure ornament about it & so little fitted for labor, must needs have been devised in some Golden Age. But surviving in the present, is most picturesquely out of keeping with the utilities. — Some of the poorest sort present curious examples of what may be called the decayed picturesque. The Greeks have a great partiality for the tassel. This seems emblematic. You see one going about the quay displaying in every tempting mode, a long graceful tassel, — holding it up admiringly. — On the Custom House quay lie bales of tobacco, jars of oil, and what you would call rows of dead goats, but which prove to be goat skins, filled, not with the flesh of goats, but the blood of the grape. — In the cafes, much card playing, all through the day. Syra is the depot for the Archipelago. They export, sponges, raisins, tobacco, fruit, olive oil &c. Their imports are hardware, & cloths, all from England. They have quite a ship-yard here. Two Greek men-of-war lie here; little fellows, yawls-of-war one might call them. — One motive for building the old town on the hill was fear of pirates, & as a defence from them as well as the Turks. After things became more favorable, they descended, & built the new town along the water. — In the afternoon some Greek ladies came off, passengers for Alexandria. At five P.M. got under weigh — Farewell to Syra and the Greeks, & away for Egypt & the Arabs.

Friday Dec 26. Last night, the Captain mildly celebrated the day with a glass of Champagne. — Contrast between the Greek isles & those of the Polynesan archipelago. The former have lost their virginity. The latter are fresh as at their first creation. The former look worn, and are meagre, like life after enthusiasm is gone. The aspect of all of them is sterile & dry. Even Delos whose flowers rose by miracle in the sea, is now a barren moor, & to look upon the bleak yellow of Patmos, who would ever think that a god had been there. — No shoals in the Archiplago; you may sail close to any of the isles, which makes easy navigation. Many of islands composed of pure white marble. Islanders retain expression of ancient statues. — This morning was invited by Chief Engineer to inspect his department. The furnaces were a fearful scene. A hell in the hull. All day a head wind & bad sea. Passengers mostly laid up. The Greeks invisable. [Passed pretty close to Scarpanti, — rugged & barren — Rhodes in sight.]

Saturday Dec 27. Sea gone down with the wind. Towards noon fine weather, transparent air & a Syrian sun, rather scortching to the cheek. Expect to reach Alexandia tomorrow early. Saw in "Sailing Directions" brief account of Jaffa. Oldest sea port in the world (some say it was a port before Noah) rocks & sands, barren & dreary look. —

Sunday Dec 28 At early morning came in sight of Alexandria Light house, and shortly after, saw Pompey's Pillar. Landed at 10. AM. Donkey to hotel, near which garden of the date palm. Pompey's pillar looks like huge stick of candy after having been long sucked. Cleopatra's Needles — one of them down & covered over. Rode along banks of Canal of Mahmoud, and to Garden of the Pasha.

Monday Dec 29th Called at Consul's for my passport. M[r] De Leon formerly political literary man at Washington. Met officers of U.S.F. Constellation. Went to the Catacombs on the sea.

Tuesday Dec 30. To Cairo, arrived there at 4 P.M. put up at Shepherd's. Walked about the square with Dr Lockwood.

Wednesday Dec 31. To the Pyramids; through the town to the Citadel & back to Shepherd's at night fall. — Never shall forget this day. It racks me, that I can only spend one day in Cairo, owing to steamer.

Thursday Jan 1st 1857. From Cairo to Alexandia. Put up at Victoria Hotel.

Friday Jan 2d Expected to have sailed to day for Jaffa. But steamer not arrived. Spent day reading a book on Palestine.

Saturday Jan 3d. Steamer for Jaffa will not sail till tomorrow, so that I am wearied to death with two days in Alexandria which might have been delightfully spent in Cairo. But travellers must expect these things. — I will now without any order jot down my impressions of Cairo, ere they grow dim. — It seems one booth and Bartholomew Fair — a grand masquerade of mortality. — Several of the thoroughfare covered at vast heigth with old planks & matting, so that the street has the light of a closed verandah. In one case this matting extends from mosque to mosque, where they are opposite. The houses seem a collection of old orchestras, organs, proscenium boxes, — or like masses of old furniture (grotesque) lumbering a garret & covered with dust. Lattice-work of the projecting windows. With little square hole, just large enough to contain the head. Curious aspect of women's faces peeping out. Most of the house built of stone of a brownish white. Some of the streets of private houses are like tunnels from meeting overhead of projecting windows &c. Like night at noon. Sometimes high blank walls — mysterious passages, — dim peeps at courts & wells in shadow. [Streets leading through arch of abandoned mosque. [The gates dividing one part of town from another. Jew Quarters] Great number of uninhabited houses in the lonelier parts of the city. Their dusty, cadaverous ogerish look. Ghostly, & suggestive of all that is weird. Haunted houses & Cock Lanes. Ruined mosques, domes knocked in like stoven boats. Others, upper part empty & desolate with broken rafters & dismantled windows; (rubbish) below, the dirty rites of religion. Aspect of the thoroughfares like London streets on Saturday night. All the world gossipping & marketing, — but in picturesque costumes. Crookedness of the streets — multitudes of blind men — worst city in the world for them. [Flies on the eyes at noon. Nature feeding on man. Contiguity of desert & verdure, splendor & squalor, gloom & gayety; numerous blind men going about led. Children opthalmick. Too much light & no defence against it. — Animated appearance of the population. Turks in carriages, with Osmanli drivers & footmen; sitting back proudly & gazing round on the people still with the air of conquerors. Footmen running ahead with silver tipped bamboos. Rapid driving, shouts of the driver. Camels carrying water in panniers of leather, carrying straw in bags — donkey loads of green grass, — of stones — of pottery — of garden stuff — of chickens in wicker panniers — of babies in panniers — Long strings of them. Turk on donkey, resting his pipe vertically before him on pommel. Grave & tranquil. — The antiquity of Egypt stamped upon individuals. [Streets great place for studying the beard. — Appearance of the women. Thing for the face. Black crape hanging like trunk of elephant. Profusion of jewelry. Brass on face. Staining the eyes (black) & finger nails. (yellow) — Some in fine silks & on donkeys.

View from Citadel. Built by Saladin. Cairo nipped between two deserts — the one leading to Suez & the Red Sea, the other the Lybian Desert. — Dust colored city. The dust of ages. The Nile — the green — desert — pyramids. Minarets unlike those of Constan^{ple} which gleam like lighthouses, — but of an ashy color, and wonderfully venerable. Citadel perched on solid rock. Within, wall of decayed fortresses. You stand at base of forecourt of Mosque to get the view, looking sheer down some 200 feet on tops of deserted houses, to immense square full of people, and near the spot where the Memlook saved himself by leaping his horse. Mosque (new) splendid court & collonade. Within, green & gold. Square, with four half-domes. Superb pillars. Alabaster. Could make brooches of them. Mosque of Hassan on the square below citadel. Finest in Cairo.

Pyramids. Scamper to them with officers on donkeys. Rapid passing of crowds upon the road; following of the donkey-boys &c. [In hey-day holyday spirits arrived at the eternal sorrows of the pyramids. Cross Nile in boats. Isle Roda, pavilions & kiosks & gardens. Donkeys crossing, rapid current, muddy banks. Pyramids from distance purple like mountains. Seem high & pointed, but flatten & depress as you approach. Vapors below summits. Kites sweeping & soaring around, hovering right over apex. At angles, like broken cliffs. Table-rock overhanging, adhering solely by morter. Sidelong look when midway up. Pyramids on a great ridge of sand. You leave the angle, and ascend hillock of sand & ashes & broken morter & pottery to a point, & then go along a ledge to a path &c. Zig-zag routes. As many routes as to cross the Alps — The Simplon, Great St: Bernard &c. Mules on Andes. Caves — platforms. Looks larger midway than from top or bottom. Precipice on precipice, cliff on cliff. Nothing in Nature gives such an idea of vastness. A balloon to ascend them. View of persons ascending, Arab guides in flowing white mantles. Conducted as by angels up to heaven. Guides so tender. Resting. Pain in the chest. Exhaustion. Must hurry. None but the phlegmatic go deliberately. Old man with the spirits of youth — long looked for this chance — tried the ascent, half way — fainted — brought down. Tried to go into the interior — fainted — brought out — leaned against the pyramid by the entrance — pale as death. Nothing so pathetic. Too much for him; oppressed by the massiveness & mystery of the pyramids. I myself too. A feeling of awe & terror came over me. Dread of the Arabs. Offering to lead me into a side-hole. The Dust. Long arched way, — then down as in a coal shaft. [At one moment seeming in the Mammoth Cave. [Subterranean gorges, &c. Then as in mines, under the sea. The stooping & doubling. I shudder at idea of ancient Egyptians. It was in these pyramids that was conceived the idea of Jehovah. Terrible mixture of the cunning and awful. Moses learned in all the lore of the Egyptians. The idea of Jehovah born here. — [When I was at top, thought it not so high — sat down on edge, looked below — gradual nervousness & final giddiness & terror. [Entrance of pyramids like shoot for coal or timber. Horrible place for assassination. As long as earth endures some vestige will remain of the pyramids. Nought but earthquake or geological revolution can obliterate them. Only people who made their mark, both in their masonry & their religion (through Moses) [*Color of pyramids same as desert.* Some of the stone (but few) friable; most of them hard as ever. The climate favors them. Pyramids not in line. Between, like Notch of White Mountains. *No vestige of moss upon them. Not the least. Other ruins ivied. Dry as tinder. No speck of green.* Arabs climb them like goats, or any other animal. Down one & up the other. Pyramids still loom before me — something vast, indefinite, incomprehensible, and awful. These the steps Jacob lay at. Line of desert & verdure, plain as line between good & evil. An instant collision of the two elements. A long billow of desert forever hovers as in act of breaking, upon the verdure of Egypt. Grass near the pyramids, but will not touch them — as if in fear or awe of them. Desert more fearful to look at than ocean. Theory of design of pyramids. Defence against desert. A Line of them. Absurd. Might have been created with the creation. *The Sphynx.* back to desert & face to verdure. Solid rock. — You ride through palms to the pyramids. You are carried across the mire &c by Arabs. The two black Shieks in black robes. —— *The ride to the pyramids.* Passed succession of suburbs & villages — high walls with date palms behind or heavy vines overhanging the walls. Across bridges, the party condensing & then expanding in disorderly dispersion. The acqueduct. The gates. Passed groves of palms, like temple of 1001 columns. [Beauty of the suburbs of Cairo. Long avenues of acacais; locusts &c

Road to Shoobra. Processions of people.

Life at hotel. Magnitude of Shepherds, lofty ceilings, stone floors, iron beds, no carpets, thin mattress, no feathers, blinds, moscho curtain. — All showing the tropics. And that you are in the East is shown by fresh dates on table for desert, water in stone jars — (cool) waited on by Arabs — dragomen — clap your hands for servants. — Brilliant scene at late dinner — hard to beleive you are near the pyramids. Yet some repose in fastidiousness.

— *Appearance of the great square.* Upon entering Cairo, saw the crescent & star — arms of Sultan in the sky. Large extent of square. Canal about it. Lower level than walks around. Avenues of acacas & other trees. Shrubs. Seems country. No fences. The booths & cafes. Leapers, tumblers, jugglers, smokers, dancers, horses, swings, (with bells) sherbert, &c. Lovely at evening. In morning, golden sun through foliage. Soft luxurious splendor of mornings Dewy. Paridise melted & poured into the air. Soft intoxication; no wonder these people never drink wine. Wondered at the men in hotel drinking it here.

Account of donkey & donkey boys. Wonderful endurance of both. Runs like deer (the boy). stick in hand, barefooted & barelegged. pounds the donkey, talks to him, remonstrates, advises. Donkey says nothing. [☞ See Constantinople] Every one pushes him. Donkey is one of the best fellows in the world. It is the patience & honesty of the donkey that makes him so abused & despised. He is so useful & indispensable, that he is contemned. He is so unresisting. Tipe of honesty. &c. As for his bray, that is the original Egyptian. Run about like rats. Their saddles very curious. High balled pommel. Thrown by donkeys. A great love for them. Hacks.

[Climate of Egypt in winter is the reign of spring upon earth, & summer in the air, and tranquility in the heat.

Ride to Cairo from Alexandria. The Delta. Like Mohawk Flats in spring. Soil like moist pulverised manure. Seems spaded over. Barnyard. 4 crops a year. Sugar, wheat, cotton. — Villages of unbaked brick. Wasps nests & mud pies. beaver-dams. Pigeon houses, on dwellings. roofs covered with piles of husks & straw. — [No fences.] Cattle tethered in lines & eat clean on straight march. Buffalo, camel, donkey. Palms. Villages like sand banks at distance. Approaching Cairo long avenues (raised above level) processions of people, crossing & recrossing at long distances. Encampment of troops, white soldiers. Cavalry in long strings. Canal. boats, latteen (long) yard like well sweep. Canal flowing between sand-hills. Canal in ditch of R.R. irrigation. Dipping & machines. 3^{d} class passengers. On top of cars. Noise & confusion of troops. Extra roof to cars. Turk squatting in baggage car on rug with his pipe. 2^{d} class passengers. Turk & Egyptian. Jingle of scimitars & flash of silks. Smoking. Cross the Nile. Machines From the car (1st class) you seem in England. All else Egypt. Seems unreal & a panorama, beginning with Pompey's Pillar & ending with Cheops.

Alexandia. Seems M^{c}adamed with the pulverised ruins of thousand cities. Every shovel full of earth dug over. The soil, deep loam, looks historical. The Grand Square. Lively aspect. Arabs looking in at windows. The sea is the principal point. Catacombs by it. R.R. extension driven right through. Acres. Wonderful appearance of the sea at noon. Sea & sky molten into each other. Pompey's Pillar like long stick of candy, well sucked. Cleopatras needles close by hovels. One down & covered. Sighing of the wave. Cries of watchmen at night. Lanterns. Assassins. Sun strokes.

The Pyramids. The lines of stone do not seem like courses of masonry, but like strata of rocks. The long slope of crags & precipices. The vast plane. No wall, no roof. In other buildings, however vast, the eye is gradually innured to the sense of magnitude, by passing from part to part. But here there is no stay or stage. It is all or nothing. It is not the sense of heigth but the sense of immensity, that is stirred. After seeing the pyramid, all other architecture seems but pastry. Though I had but so short a time to view the pyramid, yet I doubt whether any time spent upon it, would tend to a more precise impression of it. As with the ocean, you learn as much of its vastness by the first five minutes glance as you would in a month, so with the pyramid. Its simplicity confounds you. Finding it vain to take in its vastness man has taken to sounding it & weighing its density; so with the pyramid, he measures the base, & computes the size of individual stones. It refuses to be studied or adequately comprehended. It still looms in my imagination, dim & indefinite. The tearing away of the casing, though it removed enough stone to build a walled-town, has not one whit subtracted from the apparent magnitude of the pyramid. It has had just the contrary effect. When the pyramid presented a smooth plane, it must have lost as much in impressiveness as the ocean does when unfurrowed. A dead calm of masonry. But now the ridges magestically diversyfy it. It has been said in panegyric of some extraordinary works of man, that they affect the imagination like the works of Nature. But the pyramid affects one in neither way exactly. Man seems to have had as little to do with it as Nature. It was that supernatural creature, the priest. They must needs have been terrible inventors, those Egyptian wise men. And one seems to see that as out of the crude forms of the natural earth they could evoke by art the transcendent mass & symmetry & unity of the pyramid so out of the rude elements of the insignificant thoughts that are in all men, they could rear the transcendent conception of a God. But for no holy purpose was the pyramid founded.

January 4th 1857. Sailed from Alexandria for Jaffa. 2d class passage. Many deck passengers Turks &c.

Jan 5th. Fine day & warm. On deck all the time.

Jan 6th. Early in the morning came in sight of Jaffa. A swell rolling, and saw the breakers before the town. Landed, not without some danger, — boatmen (Arabs) trying to play upon my supposed fears. Cunning dogs! — Employed a Jew dragoman to take me to Jerusalem. — Crossed the plain of Sharon in sight of mountains of Ephraim. Arrived at Ramla & put up at alleged (hotel). At supper over broken crockery & cold meat, pestered by moschits & fleas, dragoman said, "Dese Arab no know how to keep hotel" I fully assented. After horrible night, at 2 in the morning in saddle for Jerusalem. The three shadows stalking on the plain by moonlight. Moon set, all dark. At day-break found ourselves just entering the mountains. Pale olive of morning. Withered & desert country. Breakfast by ruined mosque — Cave. Hot & wearisome ride over the arid hills. — Got to Jerusalem about 2 P.M. Put up at Meditterranean hotel. Kept by a German converted Jew, by name, *Hauser.* Hotel overlooks on one side Pool of Hezekiah (balconies) is near the Coptic Convent, is on the Street called Street of the Patriarchs leading out of Street of David. From platform in front of my chamber, command view of battered dome of Church of Sepulchre & Mount Olivet. Opposite house is open space, ruin of old Latin Convent, destroyed by some enemy centuries ago & never since rebuilt. Landlord pointed out the damaged dome, as beginning of the war with Russia. Still in same state as then. Walked out to the North of the city, but my eyes so affected by the long days ride in the glare of the light of arid hills, had to come back to hotel.

Jan 7th All day with dragoman roaming over the hills.

Jan 8th The same.

Jan 9th. Thought I should have been the only stranger in Jerusalem, but this afternoon came over from Jaffa, a Mr Frederick Cunningham of Boston, a very prepossessing young man who seemed rejoiced to meet a companion & countryman.

Jan 10th (Some mistake in my dates, but which I cant now rectify.) Spent the remaining days till Jan. 18th in roaming about city & visiting Jordan & Dead Sea.

Jan 19th. Quitted Jerusalem with Mr Cunningham & his dragoman — The Druse, Abdallah — Stayed at Greek convent at Ramlah. No sleep. Old monk like rat. Scurvy treatment. Letter from Greek Patriarch. Countess staying there. — Before going to convent visited the ruined mosque(?) & tower of Ramlah. A curious sight.

Jan 20th Rode from Ramlah to Lydda. A robbery of a village near by, by party of Arabs, alarms the whole country. People travel in bands. We rode to Lydda in train of the Governor's son. A mounted escort of some 30 men, all armed. Fine riding. Musket-shooting. Curvetting & caracoling of the horsemen. Outriders. Horsemen riding to one side, scorning the perils. Riding up to hedges of cactus, interrogating & firing their pistols into them. Entering Lydda, Governor's son discharged all his barrel (Revolver) into a puddle — & we went to see the ruined church of Lydda. Evidently of the time of the Crusaders. A delightful ride across Plain of Sharon to Jaffa. Quanities of red poppies. (Rose of Sharon?) Found the *Petra Party* at Jaffa. In the afternoon had a bath in the Meditterranean. Inspected some old ruins of walls, by & in, the sea.

Jan 22d Mr Cunningham & the Petra party left this afternoon in the French steamer for Alexandria. Very rough getting off. After their departure, returned to the place called "The hotel", and ascended to the top of the house — the only promenade in the town. — Jaffa is situated upon a hill rising steeply from the sea, & sloping away inland towards the Plain of Sharon. It is walled & garrisoned. The houses, old, dark, arched & vaulted, and of stone. The house I sojourn in crowns the summit of the hill, & is the highest from the ground of any. From the top of it, I see the Meditterranean, the Plain, the mountains of Ephraim. A lovely landscape. To the North the nearest spot is Beyroot; to the South, Gaza — that Philistine city the gates of which Sampson shouldered. — I am the only traveller sojourning in Joppa. I am emphatically alone, & begin to feel like Jonah. The wind is rising, the swell of the sea increasing, & dashing in breakers upon the reef of rocks within a biscuit's toss of the sea-wall. The surf shows a great sheet of yeast along the beach — N & S, far as eye can reach.

Jan 23[d] Could not sleep last night for the fleas. Rose early & to top of the house. The wind & sea still high. No boat could get off in this weather. Wrote in this diary (Jerusalem) to day. In the afternoon called upon Mr & Mrs Saunders, outside the wall, the American Missionary. — Dismal story of their experiments. Might as well attempt to convert bricks into bride-cake as the Orientals into Christians. It is against the will of God that the East should be Christianized. Mrs S, an interesting woman, not without beauty, and of the heroine stamp, or desires to be. A book lying on her table, entitled "Book of Female Heroines," I took to be the exponent of her aspirations. She talked to me, alone, for two hours; I doing nothing but listen. M[r] S. came in. A man feeble by Nature, & feebler by sickness; but worthy. A Seventh Day Baptist — — God help him! A Miss Williams, an elderly English woman, a kind of religious teacher, joined us in a walk through the orange groves.

Jan 24th No sleep last night — only resource to cut tobacco, & watch the six windows of my room, which is like a light-house — & hear the surf & wind. The genuine Jonah feeling, in Joppa too, is worth experiencing in the same sense that, according to Byron, the murderer sensation were worth a trial. — Joppa is certainly antidiluvian — a port before the Flood. It has no antiquities worth speaking of — It is too ancient. Yet I have been to the alleged house of Simon the Tanner — "by the sea" & with a well. It is now the site of a mosque & shrine. I have such a feeling in this lonely old Joppa, with the prospect of a prolonged detention here, owing to the surf — that it is only by stern self-control & grim defiance that I contrive to keep cool & patient. — The main beam crossing my chamber overhead, is evidently taken from a wreck — the trenail holes proving it. In the right lintel of the door is a vial masoned in, & visable, containing some text of Jewish scripture — a charm. The keeper of the place is a Jew. All of which provides the old — genuine, old Jonah feeling.

Jan 25th *[Friday]* Thank God got some sleep last night. Wind & sea subsided. Lovely day, but wet underfoot. The showers yesterday toward evening were like our June showers. — Walked on top of the house. Read Dumas's "Diamond Necklace" — Excellent, Cagliostro's talk in opening chapter. — Walked out & looked at rocks before town. After dinner went with M[r] Saunders to Mr Dickson's.

Jan 26th (Saturday) — Bravo! — This moment, sitting down to jot awhile, hear that the Austrian steamer is in sight, & going to the window, behold her. —— Thus then will end nearly six days in Joppa. — This morning very clear, & from the house-top I think I see Leabanon — M[t] Hermon, it may be — for its summit is covered with snow. — 11. A.M. Just returned from stroll. Steamer drawing nigh. Was again pleased with the queer school kept in chicken-coop under dim arches nigh Gate. Old Turk schoolmaster, smoking away solemn as ever. ☞(Jonah's pier) — Took boat & rowed off to rocks off harbor. They bear no appearance, as some affirm, of being ruins of an ancient pier, or any ruins of any work of art. It is the remnant of a rocky ledge, worn away into *seeming* ruins of old piers, by continual wear of the sea. At a little distance, the rock looks to be mere dirt-heaps, being of same color. But in fact are excessively hard & tough. Some look igneous. While by the water saw men emptying sacks of rubbish into the harbor, such as it is. Vastly improving, this. — Amused with the autographs & confessions of people who have stayed at this hotel. "I have *existed* at this hotel &c &c". Something comical could be made out of all this. Let the confessions being of a religious, penitential resigned & ambiguous turn, apparently flattering to the host, but really derogatory to the place. — Bright sun & sea. You seem to look through a vaccum at every thing. The sea is like a great daub of Prussian Blue.

From Jerusalem to Dead Sea &c

Over Olivet by St: Stephens Gate to Bethany — on a hill — wretched Arab village — fine view — Tomb of Lazarus, a mere cave or cell — On down into vallies & over hills — all barren — Brook Kedron — immense depth — black & funereal — Valley of Jehosophat, grows more diabolical as approaches Dead Sea — Plain of Jericho — looks green, an orchard, but only trees of apple of Sodom — P. of J. corresponds to P. of S. on other side of mountains. Mount of Temptation — a black, arid mount — nought to be seen but Dead Sea, mouth of Kedron — very tempting — foolish feind — but it was a display in vision — then why take him up to Mount? — the *thing itself* was in vision. — Where Kedron opens into Plain of Jericho looks like Gate of Hell. — Tower with sheiks smoking & huts on top — thick walls — village of Jericho — ruins on hill-side — tent — fine dinner — jolly time — sitting at door of tent looking at mountains of Moab. — tent the charmed circle, keeping off the curse. Marsada. — Rain at night — Thunder in mountains of Moab — Lightning — cry of jackall & wolf. — Broke up camp — rain — wet — rode out on mouldy plain — nought grows but wiry, prickly bush — muddy — every creature *in human form* seen ahead — escort alarmed & galloped on to learn something — salutes — every man understands it — shows native dignity — worthy of salute — Arabs on hills over Jordan — alarm — scampering ahead of escort — after rain, turbid & yellow stream — foliaged banks — beyond, arid hills. — Arabs crossing the river — lance — old crusaders — pistols — menacing cries — tobacco. — Robbers — rob Jericho annually — &c — Ride over mouldy plain to Dead Sea — Mountains on tother side — Lake George — all but verdure. — foam on beach & pebbles like slaver of mad dog — smarting bitter of the water, — carried the bitter in my mouth all day — bitterness of life — thought of all bitter things — Bitter is it to be poor & bitter, to be reviled, & Oh bitter are these waters of Death, thought I. — Rainbow over Dead Sea — heaven, after all, has no malice against it. — Old boughs tossed up by water — relics of pick-nick — nought to eat but bitumen & ashes with desert of Sodom apples washed down with water of Dead Sea. Must bring your own provisions, as well, too, for mind as body — for all is barren. Drank of brook, but brackish. — Ascended among the mountains again — barren. ——

Barrenness of Judea

Whitish mildew pervading whole tracts of landscape — bleached — leprosy — encrustation of curses — old cheese — bones of rocks, — crunched, knawed, & mumbled — mere refuse & rubbish of creation — like that laying outside of Jaffa Gate — all Judea seems to have been accumulations of this rubbish. So rubbishy, that no chiffonier could find any thing all over it. — — You see the anatomy — compares with ordinary regions as skeleton with living & rosy man. — No moss as in other ruins — no grace of decay — no ivy — The unleavened nakedness of desolation — whitish ashes — lime-kilns

Crossed elevated plains, with snails, that tracks of slime, all over — shut in by ashy hills — wretched sheep & black goats. — Arab-Bedouin encampment in hollow of high hills — oval — like two rows of hearses — Brook Kedron — two branches — *St. Saba* — zig-zag along Kedron, sepulchral ravine, smoked as by fire, caves & cells — immense depth — all rock — enigma of the depth — rain only two or 3 days a year — wall of stone on ravine edge — Monastery (Greek) rode on with letter — hauled up in basket into hole — small door of massive iron in high wall — knocking — opened — salaam of monks — Place for pilgrims — divans — St Saba wine — *"racka"* — comfortable. — At dusk went down by many stone steps & through mysterious passages to cave & trap doors & hole in wall — ladder — ledge after ledge — winding — to bottom of Brook Kedron — sides of ravine all caves of recluses — Monastery a congregation of stone eyries, enclosed with wall — Good bed & night's rest — Went into chapel &c — little hermitages in rock — balustrade of iron — lonely monks. black-birds — feeding with bread — numerous terraces, balconies — solitary Date Palm mid-way in precipice —— Good bye — Over lofty hills to Bethalem. — on a hill — old chapel of Helena — (Passed over Bethalem hills — where shepherds were watching their flocks, (as of old) but a Moslem with back to Jerusalem (face to Mecca) praying. — In chapel, monk (Latin) took us down into cave after cave, — tomb of saints — lights burning (with olive oil) till came to place of Nativity (many lamps) & manger with lights. View from roof of chapel &c. — Ride to Jerusalem — pressing forward to save the rain. — On way to Bethelam saw Jerusalem from distance — unless knew it, could not have recognized it — looked exactly like arid rocks.

Jerusalem
— " —

Village of Lepers — houses facing the wall — Zion. Their park, a dung-heap. — They sit by the gates asking alms, — their whine — avoidance of them & horror.

Ghostliness of the names — Jehosophat — Hinnom &c.

Thoughts in the Via Dolorosa — women panting under burdens — men with melancholy faces.

Wandering among the tombs — till I began to think myself one of the possessed with devels.

Variety of the tombs — with stairs like pulpit &c. "Multitudes, Multitudes" in the Valley of Hinnom. (tradition authorized by scripture) Stones about Absalom's tomb — grave-stones about Zachariah's. *Church of Holy Sepulchre.* Broken dome — Anointing stone lamps — dingy, — queer smell — irregular — caves — grots — Chapel of Finding of the Cross. Pilgrims — chatting — poor — resting *Armenian Convent* — Large — pilgrims.

Hill-side view of Zion — loose stones & gravel as if shot down from carts.

[The mind can not but be sadly & suggestively affected with the indifference of Nature & Man to all that makes the spot sacred to the Christian. Weeds grow upon Mount Zion; side by side in impartial equality appear the shadows of church & mosque, and on Olivet every morning the sun indifferently ascends over the Chapel of the Ascension.

[The South East angle of wall. Mosque of Omar — Solomon's Temple. Here the wall of Omar rises upon the foundation stones of Solomon, triumphing over that which sustains it, an emblem of the Moslem religion, which at once spurns that deeper faith which fathered it & preceded it. &c.

[How it affects one to be cheated in Jerusalem.

[The old Connecticut man wandering about with tracts &c — knew not the language — hopelessness of it — his lonely batchelor rooms — he maintained that the expression "Oh Jerusalem!" was an argument proving that Jerusalem was a byeword &c.

[Warder Crisson of Philadelphia — An American turned Jew — divorced from former wife — married a Jewess &c — Sad.

[The strange arches, cisterns, &c you come upon about Jerusalem — every day discovered something new in this way.

[Siloam — pool, hill, village. (Here, at narrow gorge begins Vale of Kedron &c. Village, occupying the successive terraces of tombs excavated in the perpendicular faces of living rock. Living occupants of the tombs — household arrangements. One used for an oven. Others for granaries. —

[In Jehosophat, Jew grave stones lie as if indiscriminately flung abroad by a blast in a quarry. So thick, a warren of the dead — so old, the Hebrew inscriptions can hardly be distinguished from the wrinkles formed by Time. Shapeless stone &c. — (See over leaf) Side by side here tombs of Absolom, Zachariah & St: James. Cut out of live rock in Petra style. St: James a stone verandah overlooking the gorge — pillars. — Jehosophat, shows seams of natural rock — capitals of pilasters rubbed off by Time. — Large hole in front — full of stones inside, heap of stones (cart loads) before it — The maledictory contribution of the pilgrim, one of the melancholy amusements of Jerusalem. (See Bible for origin of Tomb) To be stoned is his memorial. — The grave stones project *out* from the side-hill, as if already in act of resurrection. At distance hardly tell them from natural rock which lies profusely around. The stones climb midway up Olivet. Opposite, the cemetery of the Turks — close up to walls of the city, & barring the way of the closed arches of the Beautiful Gate. — both Jew & Turk sleeping in another faith than that of Him who ascended from the nigh Olivet. — The city besieged by army of the dead. — cemeteries all round. —

[The Beautiful, or Golden, Gate — two arches, highly ornamental sculpture, undoubtedly old, Herod's Time — the Gate from which Christ would go to Bethany & Olivet — & also that in which he made his entry (with palms) into the city. Turks walled it up because of tradition that through this Gate the city would be taken. — One of the most interesting things in Jerusalem — seems expressive of the finality of Christianity, as if this was the last religion of the world, — no other, possible.

[In pursuance of my object, the saturation of my mind with the atmosphere of Jerusalem, offering myself up a passive subject, and no unwilling one, to its weird impressions, I always rose at dawn & walked without the walls. Nor so far as escaping the pent-up air within was concerned was I singular here. For daily I could not but be struck with the clusters of the townspeople reposing along the arches near the Jaffa Gate where it looks down into the vale of Gihon, and the groups always haunting the neighboring fountains, vales & hills. They too seemed to feel the insalubriousness of so small a city pent in by lofty walls obstructing ventilation, postponing the morning & hasting the unwholesome twilight. And they too seemed to share my impatience were it only at this arbitrary limitation & prescription of things. — I would stroll to Mount Zion, along the terraced walks, & survey the tomb stones of the hostile Armenians, Latins, Greeks, all sleeping together. — I looked along the hill side of Gihon over against me, and watched the precipitation of the solemn shadows of the city towers flung far down to the haunted bottom of the hid pool of Gihon, and higher up the darkened valley my eye rested on the cliff-girt basin, haggard with riven old olives, where the angel of the Lord smote the army of Sennacherib. And smote by the morning, I saw the reddish soil of Aceldema, confessing its inexpiable guilt by deeper dyes. On the Hill of Evil Counsel, I saw the ruined villa of the High Priest where tradition says the death of Christ was plotted, and the feild where when all was over the traitor Judas hung himself.

[And in the afternoon, I would stand out by St: Stephen's Gate, nigh the pool likewise named after him, occupying the spot where he was stoned, and watch the shadows slowly sliding (sled-like) down the hills of Bezetha & Zion into the valley of Jehosaphat, then after resting awhile in the bottom of the ravine, slowly begin creeping up the opposite side of Olivet, entering tomb after tomb & cave after cave. &c. —— Pilgrims, their serious expressions, wandering about the hills &c. —

[The Holy Sepulchre — ruined dome — confused & half-ruinous pile. — Laberithys & terraces of mouldy grottos, tombs, & shrines. Smells like a dead-house, dingy light. — At the entrance, in a sort of grotto in the wall a divan for Turkish policemen, where they sit crosslegged & smoking, scornfully observing the continuous troops of pilgrims entering & prostrating themselves before the anointing-stone of Christ, which veined with streaks of a mouldy red looks like a butcher's slab. — Near by is a blind stair of worn marble, ascending to the reputed Calvary where among other things the showman point you by the smoky light of old pawnbrokers lamps of dirty gold, the hole in which the cross was fixed and through a narrow grating as over a cole-cellar, point out the rent in the rock! On the same level, near by is a kind of gallery, railed with marble, overlooking the entrance of the church; and here almost every day I would hang, looking down upon the spectacle of the scornful Turks on the divan, & the scorned pilgrims kissing the stone of the anointing. — The door of the church is like that of a jail — a grated window in it. — The main body of the church is that overhung by the lofty & ruinous dome whose fallen plastering reveals the meagre skeleton of beams & laths — a sort of plague-stricken splendor reigns in the painted & mildewed walls around. In the midst of all, stands the Sepulchre; a church in a church. It is of marbles, richly sculpted in parts & bearing the faded aspect of age. From its porch, issues a garish stream of light, upon the faces of the pilgrims who crowd for admittance into a space which will hold but four or five at a time. First passing a wee vestibule where is shown the stone on which the angel sat, you enter the tomb. It is like entering a lighted lanthorn. Wedged & half-dazzled, you stare for a moment on the ineloquence of the bedizened slab, and glad to come out, wipe your brow glad to escape as from the heat & jam of a show-box. All is glitter & nothing is gold. A sickening cheat. The countenances of the poorest & most ignorant pilgrims would seem tacitly to confess it as well as your own. After being but a little while in the church, going the rapid round of the chapels & shrines, they either stand still in listless disappointment, or seat themselves in huddles about the numerous stairways, indifferently exchanging the sectarian gossip of the day. The Church of the Sepulchre is the thronged news-room & theological exchange of Jerusalem, and still the more appears so, from various little chapels, the special property of the minor sects of the Copts, the Syrians & others, which here & there beneath the dome meet the eye, much like those boxes of the stock-auctioneers, which one sees in commercial Exchanges. — — The Chapel of the Finding of the Cross. — wine cellar. &c.

— If you approach the church from the squalid alley leading towards it from the Via Dolorosa, you pass a long old wall, lofty & dingy, in every corner of whose massive buttresses, at their base, lies in open exposure an accumulation of the last & least nameable filth of a city. But at the time you are far from imagining that the wall treated with such apparent contumely (by the Turks, only, it is to be hoped) is a main wall of the fabric containing the supposed tomb of one of the persons of the Godhead. This wall passed, you dive into a steep wynd, like those in Edinburgh, and presently come to a space less confined, where you are met by a thick wall peirced by a gateway with an old wooden gate, low enough & grimy enough to be the entrance to a stye. This admits you to the immediate, masonry-locked court of the church. A considerable area, flagged with venerable stones, upon which are seated a multitude of hawkers & pedlers of rosaries, crucifixes, toys of olive wood and Dead Sea stone, & various other amulets & charms. The front of the church is made very irregular, by the careless lapping over of subsequent erections upon the original one. To the left is a high & venerable tower, which like an aged pine, is barked at bottom, & all decay at top. Much elaborate sculpture once graced what is now visable of the original facade; but Time has nibbled it away, till it now looks like so much spoiled pastry at which the mice have been at work.

Interior of Jerusalem. Leads from St. Stephens Gate up towards Calvary. Silence & solitude of it. The arch — the stone he leaned against — the stone of Lazarus &c. City like a quarry — all stone. — Vaulted ways — buttresses (flying) Arch (Ecce Homo), some one has built a little batchelor's abode on top.

Talk of the guides "Here is the stone Christ leaned against, & here is the English Hotel." Yonder is the arch where Christ was shown to the people, & just by that open window is sold the best coffee in Jerusalem. &c &c &c.

[Had Jerusalem no peculiar historic associations, still would it, by its extraordinary physical aspect, evoke peculiar emotion in the traveller. [As the sight of haunted Haddon Hall suggested to Mrs Radcliffe her curdling romances, so I have little doubt, the diabolical landscapes great part of Judea must have suggested to the Jewish prophets, their terrific theology.

[Wearily climbing the Via Dolorosa one noon I heard the muezzin calling to prayer from the minaret of Omer. He does the same from that of Mt Olivet.

[The olive tree much resembles in its grotesque contortions the apple tree — only it is much more gnarled & less lively in its green. It is generally planted in orchards, which helps the resemblance. It is a haunted melancholy looking tree (sober & penitent), quite in keeping with Jerusalem & its associations. There are many olives on the plain north of the walls. The Cave of Jeremiah is in this part. In its lamentable recesses he composed his lamentable Lamentations

[Inside the walls are many vacant spaces, overgrown with the horrible cactus.

[The color of the whole city is grey & looks at you like a cold grey eye in a cold old man, — its strange aspect in the pale olive light of the morning.

[There are *strata* of cities buried under the present surface of Jerusalem. Forty feet deep lie fragments of columns &c.

[Stones of Judea. We read a good deal about stones in Scriptures. Monuments & stumps of the memorials are set up of stones; men are stoned to death; the figurative seed falls in stony places; and no wonder that stones should so largely figure in the Bible. Judea is one accumulation of stones — Stony mountains & stony plains; stony torrents & stony roads; stony walls & stony feilds, stony houses & stony tombs; stony eyes & stony hearts. Before you, & behind you are stones. Stones to right & stones to left. In many places laborious attempt has been made, to clear the surface of these stones. You see heaps of stones here & there; and stone walls of immense thickness are thrown together, less for boundaries than to get them out of the way. But in vain; the removal of one stone only serves to reveal three stones still larger, below it. It is like mending an old barn; the more you uncover, the more it grows. — The toes of every one's shoes are all stubbed to peices with the stones. They are seldom a round or even stone; but sharp, flinty & scratchy. But in the roads, such as that to Jaffa, they have been worn smooth by continuous travel. — To account for this abundance of stones, many theories have been stated: *My* theory is that long ago, some whimsical King of the country took it into his head to pave all Judea, and entered into contracts to that effect; but the contractor becoming bankrupt mid-way in his business, the stones were only dumped on the ground, & there they lie to this day.

[There is some prophecy about the highways being prepared for the coming of the Jews, and when the "Deputation from the Scotch Church" were in Judea, they suggested to Sir Moses Montifiore the expediency of employing the poorer sort of Jews in this work — at the same time facilitating prophecy and clearing the *stones* out of the way.

The hills. Are stones in the concrete. Regular layers of rock; some ampitheaters disposed in seats, & terraces. The stone walls (loose) seem not the erections of art, but mere natural variations of the stony landscape. In some of the feilds, lie large grotesque rocks — all perforated & honey combed — like rotting bones of mastadons. — Everything looks old. Compared with these rocks, those in Europe or America look juvenile.

Caves. Judea honey combed with them. No wonder that the gloomy became retreat of tens of thousands of gloomy anchorites.

[There is at all times a smell of burning rubbish in the air of Jerusalem.

[The so-called Pool of Bethesda full of rubbish — sooty look & smell.

[Three Sundays a week in Jerusalem — Jew, Christian, Turk. And now come the missionaries of the 7th Day Baptists, & add a fourth. (Saturday — the Jews) How it must puzzle the converts!

[The road from Jaffa to Jerusalem in parts very wide & full of separate divergent foot-paths, worn by the multitude of pilgrims of divergent faiths.

[Arabs ploughing in their shirt-tails. Some of them old men. Old age is venerable, — but hardly in the shirt tail.

[Part of Jerusalem built on quarries — entrance from North wall.

[No country will more quickly dissipate romantic expectations than Palestine — particularly Jerusalem. To some the disappointment is heart sickening. &c.

[Is the desolation of the land the result of the fatal embrace of the Deity? Hapless are the favorites of heaven.

[In the emptiness of the lifeless antiquity of Jerusalem the emigrant Jews are like flies that have taken up their abode in a skull.

Christian Missions &c in Palestine & Syria

———— " ————

A great deal of money has been spent by the *English Mission in Jerusalem.* Church on Mt Zion estimated to have cost $75,000. It is a fine edifice. The present Bishop (Gobat, a Swiss by birth) seems a very sincere man, and doubtless does his best. (Long ago he was 3 years in Abyssinia. His Journal is published. Written in a strikingly unaffected style — apostolically concise & simple.) But the work over which he presides in Jerusalem is a failure — palpably. One of the missionaries under Gobat confessed to Mrs. Saunders that out of all the Jew converts, but one he beleived to be a true Christian, — with much more. All kinds of variance of opinion & jealousies prevail. The same man mentioned above also said to Mrs S. many things tending to the impression that the Mission was as full of intrigues as a ward-meeting or caucus at home.

I often passed the Protestant School &c on Mt Zion, but nothing seemed going on. The only place of interest there was the Grave Yard. I attended a Missionary meeting in Jerusalem (to raise money for some other far-away place) but was not specially edified. In a year's time they had raised for "foreign missions" about £3.10, or something of that sort.

At Smyrna the American Mission is discontinued. The sorriest accounts were given me there. No one converted but with a carnal end in view on part of convert.

At Joppa, M^r^ & Mrs Saunders from Rhode-Island. Mr Saunders a broken-down machinist & returned Californian out at elbows. Mrs. S a superior woman in many respects. They were sent out to found an Agricultural School for the Jews. They tried it but miserably failed. The Jews would come, pretend to be touched & all that, get clothing & then — vanish. Mrs S. said they were very "deceitful". Mr S. now does nothing — health gone by climate. Mrs S. learning Arabic from a Sheik, & turned doctress to the poor. She is waiting the Lord's time, she says. For this she is well qualified, being of great patience. Their little girl looks sickly & pines for home — but the Lord's work must be done.

Mrs Minot of Philadelphia — came out some 3 or four ago to start a kind of Agricultural Academy for Jews. She seems to have been the first person actively to engage in this business, and by her pen incited others. A woman of fanatic energy & spirit. After a short stay at Joppa, she returned to America for contributions; succeeded in the attempt & returned with implements, money &c. Bought a tract about mile & half from Joppa. Two young ladies came out with her from America. They had troubles. Not a single Jew was converted either to Christianity or Agriculture. The young ladies sickened &

went home. A month afterwards, Mrs Minot died, — I passed her place.

Deacon Dickson of Groton, Mass. This man caught the contagion from Mrs Minot's published letters. Sold his farm at home & came out with wife, son & three daughters, about two years ago. — Be it said, that all these movements combining Agriculture & Religion in reference to Palestine, are based upon the impression (Mrs Minott's & others') that the time for the prophetic return of the Jews to Judea is at hand, and therefore the way must be prepared for them by Christians, both in setting them right in their faith & their farming — in other words, preparing the soil literally & figuratively. = With Mr Saunders I walked out to see Mr Dickson's place. About an hour from Joppa Gate. The house & enclosure were like the ordinary ones of the better class of Arabs. Some twelve acres were under cultivation. Mulberry trees, oranges, pomegranates, —— wheat, barley, tomatoes &c. On the Plain of Sharon, in view of mountains of Ephraim. — Mr Dickson a thorough Yankee, about 60, with long oriental beard, blue Yankee coat, & Shaker waistcoat. — At the house we were ushered into a comfortless, barn-yard sort of apartment & introduced to Mrs D. a respectable looking elderly woman. We took chairs. After some introductory remarks the following talk ensued —

H.M. "Have you settled here permanently, Mr Dickson?"

Mr D. "Permanently settled on the soil of Zion, Sir." with a kind of dogged emphasis.

Mrs. D (as if she dreaded her husband's getting on his hobby, & was pained by it) — "The walking is a little muddy, aint it?" — (This to Mr S.)

H.M. to Mr D. "Have you any Jews working with you?"

Mr D. No. Can't afford to hire them. Do my own work, with my son. Besides, the Jews are lazy & dont like work.

H.M. "And do you not think that a hindrance to making farmers of them?"

Mr D. "That's it. The Gentile Christians must teach them better. The fact is the fullness of Time has come. The Gentile Christians must prepare the way.

Mrs D. (to me) "Sir, is there in America a good deal of talk about Mr D's efforts here?

Mr D. Yes, do they beleive basicly in the restoration of the Jews?

H.M. I can't really answer that.
Mrs D. I suppose most people beleive the prophecys to that effect in a figurative sense — dont they?
HM. Not unlikely. &c &c &c.
They have two daughters married here to Germans, & living near, fated to beget a progeny of hybrid vagabonds. — Old Dickson seems a man of Puritanic energy, and being inoculated with this preposterous Jew mania, is resolved to carry his Quixotism through to the end. Mrs D. dont seem to like it, but submits. — The whole thing is half melancholy, half farcical — like all the rest of the world.
Dr Kayok(?) English Consul. This gentleman, born in the Levant, was some years in England. He awaked great interest there in behalf of the Jews, and came to Joppa at last to start some missionary project, and was not unprovided with funds contributed by the pious in England. — Long since he gave up the whole project, engaged in trade, is now a flourishing man, & English Consul. At any hints in reference to Missions, he betrays aversion to converse. It is whispered that he was someway trickish with the funds.
Sir Joseph Montifiore. This Croesus visited Palestine last year, bought a large tract on the hill of Gihon & walled it in for hospital grounds. A huge man of 75, he was carried to Jerusalem from Joppa, on a litter borne by mules. They fleeced him sadly, charging enormous prices for everything he bought. Sir J. seems to have the welfare of his poor countrymen near his heart, and it is said, purposes returning here for life. —

The idea of making farmers of the Jews is vain. In the first place, Judea is a desert with few exceptions. In the second place, the Jews hate farming. All who cultivate the soil in Palestine are Arabs. The Jews dare not live outside walled towns or villages for fear of the malicious persecution of the Arabs & Turks. — Besides, the number of Jews in Palestine is comparatively small. And how are the hosts of them scattered in other lands to be brought here? Only by a miracle.

Strange revelation made to me by Mr Wood (of Concord N.H) American Consul at Beyrout, concerning hidden life of Mrs Minot. Considered by him & L. Napier as crazy woman. Also about Miss Williams — Campbellite &c. Mr Wood saw Mr Dickson going about Jerusalem with open Bible, looking for the opening asunder of Mount Olivet and the preparing of the highway for the Jews. &c

Jan 27th Got on board the Austrian steamer "Acquila Imperiale" at 1. P.M. yesterday, but did not sail till late in the evening. Much wind & sea all night. In morning coast in view, — Leabonon mountains — snow-topped — Mt Hermon not in sight — inland. — At 2. P.M came to anchor at Beyrout. — Hotel Bel View — dragoman to Warburton — Sirocco blowing. Town occupies tongue of land projecting from base of Leabonon. Lofty mountains all round. Walled town. Old ruins of castles of crusaders. Town between desert & sea — both eating at it — buried trees & houses — Rich gardens. — Pier washed by surf — like walking on reef. — Lovely situation of hotel.

Jan (26)th Monday. Fine day — warm. Strolled about. Lazy heave of sea on rocks. Beautiful walk to town. Consuls books. Interesting man. Luckless discussion at dinner. Young Prussian.

Jan 27, 28, 29, 30, 31 — At the hotel. Mt Leabonon — snow — sun — tropic & Pole brought into one horizon. *The gate.* Tarter couriers rushing in with tidings of war. — Quiet days — stroll out on sea shore — dash of billows — what is all this fuss about? &c. — Orientalls have no hearth — no bed. — Never blush. — The Pasha's ball — The Bashi Bazouk's interpretation &c — Mt Sun-Nin — River Adonis — Tranquil despondency — Burial of Janizary — Koran in palm — Party of the Pasha — interpretation of Bashi Bazouk. The Twelve Judges. — Mr Wood of Concord — the Consul.

Sunday February 1st 1857. Fine day — sea & wind abated. Paid passage (cheated) in Austrian Loyds steamer "Smirne" to Smyrna. Went on board at 3. P.M. Did not have chance to bid Mr Wood good bye. Sailed at sunset. One week at Beyrout. — Very slow boat — foul bottom. poor accomodations. — Unmannerly captain — scene at dinner table. — Captain been in America.

Feb 2d Monday. At 10. AM sighted Cypruss. on starboard bow. Coming near long reach of whitish & yellowish coast with lofty mountains inland. From these waters rose Venus from the foam. Found it as hard to realize such a thing as to realize on Mt Olivet that from there Christ rose. — About 5. P.M. came to anchor off Larnaca the port of Cypruss. Could not well go ashore. But saw pretty much all worth seeing from deck. A level country about the town. Turkish look. Palms & minarets — houses along the shore. Export wine here. Quite a scene among the boatmen alongside. Rivalry of five boatmen for one passenger. Sunset.

Feb 3^d^ Tuesday. Fair wind last night. At 11. A.M. came round ahead with a very violent squall. Continued blowing for rest of day, ship horribly pitching & rolling. Seas coming from all directions. Poor devels of pilgrims seasick.

Feb 4th Wednesday. Sudden change to very fine weather. The coast of Caramania in sight all day. Lofty mountains — 7000 feet according to chart. Yesterday, during squall, amusing conduct of *Panurge* a Greek — thought his hour was come. Also, amusing Scene in cabin at dinner. Democracy of Captain & officers. Engineer came in — sat down — drank to "the Queen!" — All Lloyds & M. I. built in England. Great source of wealth. — Beautiful evening — moonlight. Came up with Rhodes, but did not touch (though we had some Turk passengers for it) owing to the Captain's wanting to use the moonlight for getting through intricate part of the Sporades. Rhodes looked a large & high island with some few lofty mountains inland. Recent explosion of gunpowder magazine has destroyed good part of "Street of the Chevaliers." — One finds that, after all, the most noted localities are made up of common elements of earth, air, & water. — English (Cornish) engineer invited me down to his department, and afterwards to supper in his mess. He was somewhat under stimulants. Said (pointing to his engines) "A fine pair of tools, Sir." Quite in love with his engine. — Beautiful moonlight detained me on deck late, as well as dread of my birth. Retired about 11. but at 2 A.M. was fairly goaded on deck by intolerable persecutions of bugs. Have suffered beyond telling from this cause. Not a wink of sleep now for four nights, & expect none till I get to Smyrna. This affliction of bugs & fleas & moschitos fully counterbalances to me all the satisfactions of Eastern travel. —

Thursday Feb 5th. In among the Sporades all night. Standing on t'gallant forecastle by the bright moon, Captain & officers steered us through the entanglements of channels. At dawn were completely landlocked by islands & islets. Cos, a large island, one of them. Sailed close to several. Almost jump ashore. Deep water. So thick, hard to say how you got in, or how you are to get out. All isles rocky, naked & barren. Patches of verdure on some. Fire kindled on one. — Would think this were navigation for a skiff. Passed two or three small quaint Greek vessels. — A fine sail upon the whole. But the scenery is all outline. No filling up. Seem to be sailing upon gigantic outline engravings. Shadows however help the scene. Distinct black of near isle relieved against haze of one behind. Or, terraces of bright distinctness — dusky grey — deep purple — according to successive distances. — Serene morning. Pale blue sky. — Steered out from intricasies & saw Samos ahead, and Patmos — quite lonely looking. Patmos stands in fact quite isolated — the more so, apparently, from so suddenly coming upon it after the apple-like clusterings of the other isles. Patmos is pretty high, & peculiarly barren looking. No inhabitants. — Was here again afflicted with the great curse of modern travel — skepticism. Could no more realize that St: John had ever had revelations here, than when off Juan Fernandez, could beleive in Robinson Crusoe according to De Foe. When my eye rested on arid heigth, spirit partook of the barreness. — Heartily wish Niebuhr & Strauss to the dogs. — The deuce take their penetration & acumen. They have robbed us of the bloom. If they have undeceived any one — no thanks to them. — Pity that ecclesiastical countries so little attractive by nature. ——— Captain's story of Greek pilgrims — great part of profit of A. Lloyds from this source — Thick as cattle in pen sometimes. Save up their money for years. Like Mussulmen to Mecca. — Priest at Jerusalem sell them ticket for heaven Printed paper with Dove in middle & Father & Son each side. Divided into seats like plan of theatre on benefit night. Cant let you have *this* place — taken up. Nor *this,* but if *this* here in the corner will do — very good — may have it at 500 piastres &c. —— Engineer told me about his acquaintance with Mike Walsh on board this boat last year. Went to Crimea. At Trieste made speech in beer-shop to English engineers. Provoked suspicion of Austrian spy &c. Cornishman enthusiastically in love with magnanimous nature of redoubtable Mike. — He was out at elbows & borrowing money. The "eminentest" man in E.'s opinion.

Friday Feb 6th. A cold rainy night, last night. Choice between shivering & scratching. Took both. Horrible night. — Slept awhile on settee, awoke chilled through. — Another time was all but frantic with the fleas. — The Scratching ship. Captain with back-scratcher — Two men leaning up & rubbing against each other &c. Main diversion. — In the rain entered Smyrna bay at day break. Nearly two months since here before. Hills below looked green, but mountains covered with snow. — Ashore to hotel & breakfast. Rascally waiter. — Walked in bazaar. Got bill cashed. — While at breakfast felt very bad neuralgic pain top of head — owing to utter sleeplessness of last five nights. — At 5. P.M sailed in Paddle steamer "Italia" of Lloyd's Austriaco for Pireus. — An Austrian man-of-war in harbor. Midshipmen in queer little canoes — standing up. One — alternate blades of oars. — Smoking. Honest bobtail — Stimulated. Enjoyment. Padleling in wake of steamer. — Good nights' rest. Italian merchant of Ancona. — Dried up but merry. Smoking. "Estates of the Church — Estates of de Debel!" — His ship at Constant^ple^ Custom House. — Venetian & wife & child. — Windy boat Temple of winds. — No comfort on deck. — Albanian taking his wine — Greek Priest. — (Little present)

*Saturday Feb 7th* Came to anchor at Syra — after stopping at Scio — this afternoon. Blowing hard & remained through the night. Third time at Syra. Very cold to what it was before. (Feb 8th Sunday) At dawn got under weigh. Head wind, head sea — cold, comfortless. Turned in to berth till four o'clock. Could not view the islands, though passing many. — Towards sunset approached Pireus. — Bare & bald aspect of the shores & isles — Came to anchor at 7. PM. Bright moonlight, with traces of the recent gales. — Man-of-war at anchor. Got into boat, & ashore, & into old hack, and through a settlement like one on tow path of canal, to a M^c^Adamed road, straight as die, — & into Athens. Passed horse & foot patrol. — Greeks in cafes smoking. Tomorrow prepare for the Acropolis. — I saw it by moonlight from road.

Trying to be serious about St. John when from where I stood figure of Santon a Arab holy man came between me & island — almost naked — ludicrous chaced away gravity — solemn idiocy — lunatic — opium-eater — dreamer — yet treated with profoundest respect & reverence — allowed to enter anywhere. — Wretched imbecile! bare & beggarly Santon, miserable stumbling-block in way of the prophecies, since saint though thou art thou art so far from inheriting the earth that thou dost not inherit a shirt to thy nakedness!

Feb 8th Sunday. After tempestuous, cold passage, came to anchor at Pireus and by moonlight to Athens. Hotel d Angleterre. Alexander,

guide — with Boyd who wrote Murray's G. B. — *Acropolis* — blocks of marble like blocks of Wenham ice — or like huge cakes of wax. — Parthenon elevated like cross of Constantine. Strange contrast of rugged rock with polished temple. At Stirling — art & nature correspond. Not so at Acropolis. Imperceptible seams — frozen together. — Break like cakes of snow. —
Jupiter Olympus. Like clearing in woods. clump of columns — Two isolated at further end. — Tuft of sculpture at top — Palm tree — drooping of acanthus like palm &c — Prostrate pillar in railing, like grave. Roulaeu of guineas — massy — base leaning — fallen pine — fell straight — still symmetric even in its fall. Stood more than 2000 years — down at last. Same night pillar of Erectheum fell.

Feb 9th Monday. Viewed the ruins with Alexander — looked at his shop (Hymettos honey, Parnasus canes, Marathon necklaces of shell, views of Athens — dress &c.) — Mr Marshall of Boston or N.Y. at hotel. Been all over Meditterranean on ice business. Cut ice at Black Sea. — I imagined his story of life) Called on Dr King Consul. Greek wife. Invited to tea. His daughter been in America. Pleasant evening. — Cold, with intervals of snow & sun through the day.

Feb 10th Among the ruins — revisited them all. *Temple of Theseus* well preserved. Yellowish look — saffron — burnt in slow fire of Time. *Temple of Victory* — ressurection — figure of Victory tying her sandal — grace & loveliness of the whole conception. — Genoese Tower incorporating columns of Perysplea. — Pavement of Parthenon — square — blocks of ice. (frozen together.) — No morter: — Delicacy of frost-work. ——
Spent evening conversing with young English officer from Zephalonia — Told story of Lindy Foote's son. &c. — Saw the sunset from *Lyccabacus.* Lovely climb.

Feb 11th Wednesday. Clear & beautiful day. Fine ride on box to Pireus. Acropolis in sight nearly whole way. Straight road. Fully releived against the sky — Between Hymmettus & Pentelicus. Pentelicus covered at top with snow — looking down on its child, the Parthenon. — Ruins of Parthenon like North River breaking up. &c — At 2 P.M embarked in French steamer "Cydnus" for Messina. Noble vessel &

French-built. Two or three Englishmen on board — young men. Talk with them. Misseri (Eothen's) on board, going to England. Talk with him. — Sailed along coast of Morea — mountainous. Good bed & slept well.

Feb 12th Thursday. Head wind & not fair overhead. but fast steamer. Quite a number in Second Cabin. No land in sight to day.

Feb 13th Friday. Coasts of Calabria & Sicily ahead at day break. Neared them at 10 o'clock. Both very high & broken — picturesque. Many houses. Snow on tops of highest mountains. Fine sail in the straits. At 1 P.M. anchored in harbor of Messina. Fine harbor. Like lagoon. Rainy day. Landed at Police. Searched for papers &c. Hotel in noble street. Large church. Coat cleaned.

Feb 14th Saturday. Last night went to cafe near opera-house to meet, if I might, Dr Lockwood of the frigate. But did not. This morning pleasant weather. Many American vessels in port for fruit. This the season. Went on board one. Went off to friggate. Called on Cap. Bell. Saw Dr Lockwood. Went with him on donkeys to a high hill four miles distant. The telegraph. Dined with him & officers in ward-room of friggate. Passed off pleasantly. Then walked through the town with the Dr, and in evening went to the opera of Macbeth with him. Retired at 11 P.M. — The officers of U.S.F. Constellation are

Captain		Bell	Lieut	Faunteleroy. (Virginian)
1st	Lieut.	Porter	Mid.	Buchanan.
2d	"	Bankhead	Cap.	Clerk. Bell.
—	"	Spicer		

The forts of Messina command the town, not the sea. Large tract of town demolished, so as to have rest at command from fort. Dial in church. Streams from mountains coming through the town.

Feb 15th Sunday. Dr Lockwood called at hotel, sat, and then proposed long walk. Walked out in long suburbs skirting the sea. Calabria's mountains in sight. Salvator Rosa look of them. Met masquers on the road. Carnival. Walked 7 or 8 miles. sat on stones, much talk. Fine day. Enjoyed it considerably. Back to dinner at hotel by 6 P.M. Streets very lively in evening. Walked about with Dr. till 10 o'clock. Cafe — habitue's.

Monday & Tuesday 16 & 17 Feb. Neapolitan steamer for Naples started at 1 P.M to day. Took 2^d^ cabin passage. Repented it sorely in the end. Crossed the Straits to Reggio (St. Paul) lay there till midnight. By day break stopped at another place, high on hill, (Murat shot) and at noon at a third place on coast. Fine weather. Calm & beautiful. Populous shores & very mountainous & high. Scenery very fine. Sailed close in shore. Suffered again horribly from sleeplessness. (Saw Etna from Reggio)

Wed. 18 Feb. Ere day break we passed between Capri & main & entered bay of Naples. I was on deck. Dim mass of Vesuvius soon in sight. Recognized it from pictures of outline. Soon, *smelt* the city. Brilliant lights. — Detained on board till 9 A.M. by Police being dilatory. Went to *Hotel de Geneve* with some others. Struck by first appearance of Naples. Great crowds, noble streets, lofty houses. — At breakfast Rhinelander & Friedman said they were going to Pompeii. Joined them. R.R. same thing over the world. Passed through Portici, Resino, Torre del Greco. —— Pompeii like any other town. Same old humanity. All the same whether one be dead or alive. Pompeii comfortable sermon. Like Pompeii better than Paris. —— Guards there. Silent as Dead Sea. —— To Vesuvius on horseback. Vineyards about the base. Ashy climb. Hanging on to guide. Haggling. Old crater of Pompeii. Modern crater like old abandoned quarry — burning slagmass — Red & yellow. Bellowing. Bellows. flare of flame. Went into crater. Frozen liquorice. —— Came down with a rush. Dusk. Ride in dark. At Nunnziata got veturino to Naples. Cold ride, no coat, — back to hotel by midnight. Silent country & streets. One suburb. Ate & to bed.

Thursday Feb 19th. Sallied out for walk by myself. Strada di Toledo. Noble street. Broadway. Vast crowds. Splendor of city. Palace — soldiers — music — clang of arms all over city. Burst of troops from archway. Cannon posted inwards. Royal carriages in palace — royal steamers. To Capo di Monte in cab. Supurb palace, roads, grounds, & view. St. Januarius of the Poor. Catacombs — old man with lanthorn. Great extent. Old bones. Grimy. Could'nt get away. Thought crazy. — Walked about again. Bought good coat for $9. — Quays show little commerce. Wonder how live here. Magnificence of the city. Vesuvius in sight from square. Smoking. — Walked to Villa

Real — hotels — at Brittanique happened to see Townsend's name. — Dined there. Releived by hearing (tho' but indirectly) from home. To San Carlo at 10 o'clock. Fine house. Met English banker. Sentinel on stage &c.

Friday Feb 20th. Walked to Post Office with letters. Then took voiture for eastern part of bay. Posilipo — beautiful promontory of villas — along the sea — new road — till came in sight of bay of Pozzuoli. Went through Grotto of Sejanus to remains of school of Virgil & other ruins of villas. Ruined stone balcony overhanging deep cave & cliff. Isle of Nisida. Saw Baia — the end of the bay. Went to the Solfatara — smoke — landscape not so very beautiful. — Sulphurous & aridity, the end of the walk. (At Posilipo found not the cessation which the name expresses.) Passed lake of Agano (salt at bottom) (Avernus did not visit — much the same, I suppose) Visited Grotto del Cane. Old man leading poor patient little dog. Unlocked gate. — Dog keeled over, gasped, insensible. Dragged out & came to — lay on grass, rolled & walked patiently off. — Poor victim. — Returned to Naples by Grotto of Pausilipo. Very high. Scene of thoroughfare in Grotto. Smacking of whips, goats, twilight. — Sun streams through at sunset. — Villa Real — splendid equipages. Visited Virgil's tomb — mere ruin — high up. great view of bay & Naples & Vomero Mount & Castle of Elmo. Drove up to Elmo Castle. Long street. From balcony over garden of Church of San Martino got glorious view of bay & town. Sunset. White friars. — Drove to Cafe de la Europe for cheap dinner. Row with cabman. Dined & walked for an hour in Strada di Toledo. Great crowds. Could hardly tell it from Broadway. Thought I was there. — Cafes well filled. — Many lottery shops, all with little shrine of Virgin & child, lit — cheap decoration. Curious reflections. Religious inducement to wickedness. — Home by 9 & to bed.

Saturday 21st Feb. Upon going from chamber in morning encountered by jabbering man with document. Commissionnaire. Into breakfast room — people at table — "Do any of you speak French?" Whereupon Mr Rowse(?) spoke. Passport. &c. — Went to Rothschilds' for £20. No scrutiny as at other places. Went to Museum. A collection of them. *Bronze utensils from Pompeii & Herculaneum.* — Helmet & skull. — Dentist tools — Surgical tools — furnaces —

Mosaic tables & pavements — fishooks — mirrors for toilette — cash cabinets.

Terra cotta collection — mythological delineations.
Hall of bronze statuary. Plato (hair & beard & imperial) Nero (villianous) Seneca (caricature.) Drunken faun on wine skin. Augustus. horse — colossal head of horse — &c &c.
Paintings Madonna by Raffael — a Domenichino. Two small Correggios — (Could not see anything so wonderful in these last) But face of Raffael's Madonna touchingly maternal. A vast collection of other pictures I but glanced at.
Frescoes — from Diomed's house — fruit pieces &c from dining room.
Marbles. Hercules Farnese — colossal. gravely benevolent face. The group of the bull; glorious. — Tomb stones &c with inscriptions, identical with ours. ——
— Had to quit Museum ere through with it.
Went in voiture to Cathedral of St. Januarius. Very fine. Thence a promiscuous drive through the older & less elegant part of town. Long narrow lanes. Arches, crowds. ——
Tumblers in narrow street. Blocked way. Balconies with women. Cloth on ground. They gave way, after natural reluctance. Merriment. Turned round & gave the most grateful & graceful bow I could. Handkerchiefs waved from balconies, goodhumored cries &c — Felt prouder than an Emperor. Shabby old hack, but good fellow, driver. ———
Wonderful number of shops &c. Crowds of idlers. Lazzaroni troublesome. Stopped in at curious little old chapel. Statue in net. — Dismissed hack at hotel. — Walked on mole. Military continually about streets. — Curious bells near my room. Every ten minutes strike. Repeat each other. Conversation of bells. Tete-a-tete. —— Dined at hotel de Geneve at 5 P.M. —— Uncertain about diligence or veturino to Rome. Paid a Napoleon for getting passport in order.

Sunday 22[d] Feb. Breakfasted early and at 9 o'clock took train for Castleamarre (In the corner) with M[r] Rows of Brunswick (N.J) and young Englishman. — Volcanic formation along road. Crowds of hackmen &c. Veturino bargaining. Three horses, with cock feathers, abreast, to Sorrento for about a dollar. — Grand drive. Road. Windings broad sweeps & curves — ravines — bridge — terrace — rocks — inclined plain — heigth — sea — Sorrento. Tasso's house, hotel. Beauty of site on cliff overhanging sea &c. — Disappointment about veturino. Some mystery of general procedure. — Got man to speak English & engaged 1st seat in coupe for 24th Feb. — Mr R. a little queer at dinner. His sister affable.

Monday 23d Feb. Went to Museum after breakfast. Shut. Took hack and went on Pausipilo road. Fine morning. Repassed the scenery of the other day as far as hill (semicircular turn-out) whence you get view of bay of Pozzuoli. Drove to village of that name. Thence to Lake Avernus. In a crater. Lonely look. flags on water side. Meloncolly old temple. Curious they should have fabled hell here. Cave of Sybil. Gate. (Narrow one to hell, here) Torches. Long grotto, many hundred feet, fast walk. Came to sudden dive down — very narrow — Descent to Infernal regions, guide said — Came to pool — took me on his shoulder across — bath & bed of Sybil — oracle-place — Landed me on ledge of rock. — Many other caves to right & left. Infernal enough. — What in God's name were such places made for, & why? Surely man is a strange animal. Diving into the bowels of the earth rather than building up towards the sky. How clear an indication that he sought darkness rather than light. — Before coming to Lucrino (near the sea, divided by causeway; very stagnant & bad smell — "hotel" overlooking it) you see the New Mountain. Curious to see this stranger (parvenue) from the abysses taking his rank among the elderly mountains. But not so *new,* either. Could tell queer stories. "But that the secrets of his prison-house &c"

[Comparison between Avernus & Hinnom) New Mountain cultivated towards summit. Buildings on it. — Pozzuoli a great bay in bay. Drive to Baie. Along the shore. Road cut through ruins of old villas of Romans. Singular melting together of art in ruins and Nature in vigor. Vines overrunning ruins. Ruins here take the place of rocks. Arches, substructures, buttresses &c &c &c.

Temple of Venus. Round. Summit wavy with verdure — corpses dressed for a ball. Temple of Mercury. Low dome. Part fallen & below. Vines drooping down. Echo. Where art thou, Mercury — Where? —

[On the western shore of Italy is a bay &c. — A burning mountain — enumerate the momentoes of the remorselessness of Nature — ravages of war &c — burned city. Solfatara &c. —— Now, one would think if any *modern* city were here built &c, they would be sober in view of these things. But no. Gayest city in the world. No equipages flash like these; no beauties so haughty. No cavaliers so proud, no palaces so sumptuous. &c &c. — Apt representation of that heedlessness, benignly ordained, of man which prevents him one generation from learning from a past. — "Let us eat, drink & be merry, for tomorrow we die." Such seems the lesson learned by the Neapolitans from their scenery. — The beauty of the place, in connection with its perilousness. — Skaters on ice. — [Full, too, of monuments of the variety of old religions (Sybils cave) and yet the Romish superstition.

═══ Arrived at hotel at 4 P.M. & prepared to pack valise to leave at Diligence office overnight, after writing this scrawl of memorandum — Next for

Rome.

P.S. Wonderful old ruinous palace at Pausolippo. Sea-palace. —— The road. Villas, grots, summer-houses — ravines — towers &c &c &c. Such a profusion & intricacy of grotto, grove, gorge villa hill, that it takes some time & patience to disentangle such snarls of beauty.

— Of the ride to Pausillippo. —

Scene at dinner table tonight. Comments &c. The young Parisian, the fair young lady, the French judge with black cap on.

Tuesday Feb 24th At 8.A.M. started in diligence from P.O in Naples for Rome. Only Frenchman & self in coupe. Like balcony overlooking horses. Snug. Far preferable to steamer &c. — Fine level country about Naples. Vines abundant. Smart postilion — one continual gallop & crack of the whip from post to post. Change horses 8 miles. At least 100 horses at the diligence. At Fondi passed our veturino friend. Saw various ruins from time to time. At night fall entered among mountains. The tower & sea at Terracina. Night.

Wednesday Feb 25th At daybreak were on the Alban mount. At 10 A.M were in Rome. First letter from home. Stopped at hotel de Minerva. In square is obelisk on elephant. Walked to Capitol. Took view from tower. Whether it is having come from the East, or chafed mood, or what, but Rome fell flat on me. Oppressively flat. — Did'nt sleep any last night, though. — Tiber a ditch, yellow as saffron. The whole landscape nothing independent of associations. St: Peters looks small from Tower of Capitol. — Walked to St. Peters. Front view disappointing. But grand approach. Interior comes up to expectations. But dome not so wonderful as St: Sophia's. — Exhausted at 3. PM. Dined at 6 & to bed.

Thursday Feb 26. To Torloni's, banker, to find out about S. Shaw or letters. Learnt nothing. To Capitol & Coliseum. — Coliseum like great hollow among hills. Hopper of Greylock. Slope of concentric ruins overgrown. mountainous. Museum of Capitol. Hall of Emperors. "That Tiberius? he dont look so bad at all" — It was he. A look of sickly evel, — intellect without manliness & sadness without goodness. Great brain overrefinements. Solitude. — Dying Gladiator. Shows that humanity existed amid the barberousness of the Roman time, as it now among Christian barberousness. Antinous, beautiful. —— Walked to the Pincian hill —— gardens & statuary — overlooking Piazza del Populo. — (Music on Pincian) Fashion & Rank — Preposterous posturing within stone's throw of Antinous. How little influence has truth on the world! — Fashion everywhere ridiculous, but most so in Rome. No place where lonely man will feel more lonely than in Rome. (or Jerusalem). Fine view of St Peters from Pincian. — In the evening walked to Cafe Greco in Via Condotti. "English sculptor" with dirty hands &c. Dense smoke. Rowdy looking chaps. &c — Home & to bed. (Stopped at evening in picture dealers; offered a Cenci for $4. Surprising cheap). Fine lounge in Piazza di Espagna among picture & curiosity dealers, & in Via Condotti, also.

Friday Feb 27th Tried to find A. Consul, Page, & Jarves. Failed in all. — Went to Baths of Caracalla. — Wonderful. Massive. Ruins form, as it were, natural bridges of thousands of arches. There are glades, & thickets among the ruins — high up. — Thought of Shelley. Truly, he got his inspiration here. Corresponds with his drama & mind. Still magestic, & desolate grandure. — After much trouble & sore travel without a guide managed to get to Protestant Burial Ground & pyramid of Cestius under walls. Read Keats' epitaph. Separated from the adjacent ground by trench. — Shelley in other ground. Plain stone. — (Went from Caracalla to Shelley's grave by natural process) Thence to Cenci Palace, by way of Suspension Bridge, Isle of Tiber, theater of Marcellus (blacksmiths shops &c in arches — black with centuries grime & soot — built upon above & inhabited) & Orsini Palace & Ghetto. Tragic looking place enough. The big sloping arch. — Part of it inhabited, part desolate. — Thence to Farnese palace — finest architecture of all the palaces (private). Farnese Hercules & Farnese Toro formerly here. Now in Museum Borbonico, Naples. Thence to St. Angelo Bridge & St. Peters. And to dinner & bed. — Remarked the banks of Tiber near St: Angelo — fresh, alluvial look near masonry — primeval as Ohio in the midst of all these monuments of the centuries.

Saturday Feb 28th Lost time going after Consul &c. At 12 M. was at Borghese villa. Extent of grounds — peculiar odors of Italian garden — Deep groves — cold splendor of villa — Venus & Cupid — mischevous look of C. —— Thence to Villa Albani — along the walls — Antinous — head like moss-rose with curls & buds — rest all simplicity — end of fillet on shoulder — drapery, shoulder in the mantle — hand full of flowers & eyeing them — the profile &c. The small bronze Apollo. surprising how such a metal could be melted into such flexible-looking forms. Picture of Italian lady. —
— Thence to the gate Pia to fountain of Moses. Not bad — Ox drinking — pitchers &c crowded round. — Thence to baths of Diocletian — church — monument of 8 columns. — S. Rosa's tomb. The four fountains — Monte Cavallo — colossal horses from ruins of baths — like finding the bones of the mastadon — gigantic figures emblematic of gigantic Rome. Hill of Monte Cavallo. View of dome of St. Peters. — Thence by Trajan's forum home at 6 P.M. dinner & to bed. — Extent of ground not built upon within walls of Rome. Silence & loneliness of long streets of blank garden walls.

Sunday March 1st 1857. To Monte Cavallo — colossal equestrian group, found in Baths, basin also, obelisk — most imposing group of antiques in Rome. — People those Caracalla baths anew with these colossal figures — Gigantic Rome. — St. Peters in its magnitude & colossal statuary seems an imitation of these fragments. — The grass growing in the Square. The 4 Fountains. 4 Vistas — terminating with obelisks &c. — The private old palaces — The ruinous fountain of rocks, the vines &c trailing into pool. The mossy pillars & green ooze of loneliness. — The poor old statues in their niches — the gardens. — San Maria Maggore. — (The picture at home) Gold from Perue. — Trophies of Marius & several other ruins. The Porta Maggore. Finest ancient gate in Rome. Baker's Tomb. Acqueducts — mass of brick. To the basilica of St: John Lateran. Loneliness of the spot by Giovanni Gate (Naples) heigth looking down from walls — Splendor of private tomb there. 12 Apostles gigantic — drapery. — Did not visit Stairs &c — Walk along the walls outside. — Solitude & silence — passing gates walled up — passing the gate Totilla entered — perfect hush of all things — The gardens outside — To the Gate of St: Sebastian — ancient. Arch of Drusus — Columbaria — Dove-cote — The little busts. Darby & Joan, hand in hand — domestic expression — man the same —. Scipio's tomb. Extent of it — inscriptions — candles. — Notification over gate — Penny-Fair. — Palace of the Cesars — Went in — Great arch over arch — stairs — birds — stables. — Arch of Janus. — Cloaca Maxima — gloomy hole — trailing vines into the sewer. — Lost my way getting back. Stopped in at church. Animated preacher. Home by 5 P.M. Dinner & to bed.

March 2^d^ 1857. Vatican Day (Monday) From 12 to 3 in Museum; previously visiting the Loggie of Raphael & Sistine Chapel. The Loggie — piazzas — sky seen between columns — Adam & Eve — The Eve — Faded bloom of the paintings. — Staid in Vatican till closed. Fagged out completely, & sat long time by the obelisk, recovering from the stunning effect of a first visit to the Vatican. — Went to Piazza di Espagna, & home. — Sat awhile in the Rouses' room ere retiring. —— Hall of Animals — Wolf & sheep.

March 3^d^, Tuesday. Started with M^r^ & Miss R. to ascend St. Peters. Too late for time. — Visited Mosaic Museum in Vatican. Heads of Popes for St. Pauls. Rode to Palazzo Barberini to see Cenci. — Expression of suffering about the mouth — (appealing look of innocence) not caught in any copy or engraving. — Lovely little painting of Galatea in car — two swimmers in dark blue shadowed water — gleam of limbs. — A Holbein (Christ disputing with doctors) To San Maria Maggoire. To St. John Lateran — Corsini chapel — gems in crown — statue below in vault — "The Pietà" — Scala Santa — (5 stairs) pilgrims going up — penitents. — Walked to Trevi Fountain. — Very fine. — A cold, raw, windy, dirty & horribly disagreeable day. Dinner & to bed. — The Peruvian & Pole. — The Irish priest.

March 4th Wednesday. Ascended St. Peters. feilds & paddocks on top — figures of saints. — Met Mr & Mrs C. & brother on the church. — To Corsini Palace — paintings — large gallery — & very many first rate works. Holbein's Luther & wife — Magdalen of Carlo Dolci. — Battle scene of Salvator Rosa & one Calabrian scene. To church of St. Pietro in Montorio — Flagellation of Piombo — View of Rome. To the Fountain Paolina — largest in city. Another noble view. — Crossed the Janiculum Bridge to Saint Andrea delle Valle — Frescoed cupola — — Early to bed.

March 5th Thursday. To Coliseum. To Villa built upon arches of palace of Cesars. To Capitol. Through gallery a second time. Bronze Wolf. To Borghese Gallery. Danae. C. Borgia. To Pincian Hill. Cold grey windy day. Eye so bad had to go to room & to bed at 5 P.M. minus dinner.

March 6th Friday. Eye prevented me from doing or seeing much to day. To St. Peters — Borghese Gallery — Pincian — Saw the Pope in carriage — Funeral of French officer — lane among high walls crowned with green foliage — Talk with Mr R. in his room.

March 7th Saturday. To Sciarra Gallery. Faded splendor — balcony over Corso — closeness of a closet — The Cheating Gamblers (Honesty & Knavery — the self-possession & confidence of knavery — the irresolution & perplexity of honesty) — The Gloaming (to apply a Scotch word) of a scene between dusk & dark of Claude. Other Claudes (His first manner) All their effect is of atmosphere. He paints the air. Curious Holy Family of Albert Durer (the old nurse) A Lady by Titian — The crimson & white sleeves — The golden haze of his pictures (Danae) The Sciarra has been in Chancery. — *To the Rospiglioso gallery* — The terraced garden — 200 years old — the garden stairway in hollow — mossy balustrades — The lemon walk tiled over — The fish pond & fountains & violets wet with spray — — The Casino — bas-reliefs — Aurora — Floats overhead like sun-dyed clouds — The Mirror — the lovers seated there.

Sampson pulling down the temple — gigantic — unfortunate hint at fall of Aurora — The shot. —— *To the Quirinale Palace of Pope.* Vast hall — cold splendor — Marbles, paintings, &c &c &c Gobelins — The Palm — Sevres china — Guido's Annunciation (Raphaels') Fresco of the Swiss Guards looking down — boxes with ribands — *The Gardens* — A Paridise without the joy — freaks & caprices of endless wealth — rhuematics in gardener — As stone is sculptured into forms of foliage, so here foliage trained into forms of sculpture — Walls, niches, arches, casements, columns, bases, chambers (quarried out of foliage) — The arcades — leafy cloisters — The water-organ — the Vulcan's shop — the fountains. — *To Church out of Bath* — Monumental columns — Greek Cross. — To little gem of church in street leading to Porta Pia — The gem — the cherubs looking down from cupola — the precious marbles. — Dined on 19 cents at Lepri's in Via Condotti & home & to bed. Eye very troublesome. Hope it wont stay so.

March 8th Sunday To Jesuits Church — To Gibbon's church nigh Capitol — various columns rifled from ancient edifices — Gibbon's meditations — Christianity. — To Baths of Titus — overgrown — dark & intricate — resort of banditti once. — To Mamertine Prison. To Tarpean — dirty yard at base — Dignified Roman guide — *"Miserable!"* — Pitiable object. — To St Peters — tour of interior — Stuarts' tomb. The Popes monuments. To Pincian — great Sunday resort. — Dined on 17 cents & to bed at 11 PM after a talk with Mr R. in his room.

March 9th Monday. Vatican day. — Deliberate walk through the galleries. — Hall of Animals — Wolf & lamb, paw uplifted, tongue — fleece. Dog on stag, eying him. Lion on horse. — But Playing goats — the goat & kid — show a Wordsworthian appreciation of the gentle in Nature. — Frescoed ceilings which, like starry skies, no man regards — so plentiful are the splendors. — Coronation of the Virgin — Raphael — the faces so like his masters Perugino's in the next room. — Review of troops in St Peters piazza. — With Mr & Miss Rouse to St. Onofrio, church & monastery, where Tasso expired. On the Janiculum, fine view of Rome. Sad corridors, cloisters & no grass. Doleful old chamber — Wax cast. — Little sad garden, mouldering gateways. — Quaint church — damp & doleful. — New monument in wretched taste. — Stopped in at some churches & to Lepri, to soup & meat.

March 10th Tuesday. I begin writing here after more than one week's abstinence, oweing to state of my eyes and general incapacity. On the day of this date I went to the Doria Pamfili palace in the morning. Most elegant one in Rome perhaps. Two portraits of Raphael. One of Titian's women — profuse brown hair on Magdalen — Thought I detected a resemblance between it & his portrait of his wife — only the Magdalen idealized. Machiavelli's portrait disappointed me. Ugly profile, &c. Did'nt like it. Two large landscapes of Claude did not touch me. The "Gloaming" is the best. Brueghel's pictures much pleased me. The Elements & animals. — Lucretia Borgia — no wicked look about her. good looking dame — rather fleshy. —— To the Borghese gallery for third time. — The supurb table there — the tunnel cut thro' to street, & fountain. Have remarked before on pictures here. — To the studios. The English sculptor, Gibson. His colored Venus. Talk with him. The 7 branched candlestick &c. Art perfect among Greeks. Limit to human power, — perfection. — To Bartholomew's. His Eve. Bust of young Augustus — (Edition). To Page's. Thin socks. Titian — kneading of flesh — Middle tint. Long lecture. — Home, dinner, bed.

March 11th Wednesday. Started for Appian Way. Narrow, — not like Milton's Way — not suitable to dignity &c. Old pavement. Tomb with olive trees on it. sown in corruption, raised in olives. Same day, Grotto of Egeria. Nothing very beautiful or at all striking about it. No foliage, but one clump. — To St. Pauls, outside walls. Magnificent. Malaria among the gilding. Building against Nature. Pet of Pio's. The Catacombs — laberyth of them. —— Home at 3, changed room, had fire, and prepared for being laid up. No dinner.

Thursday March 12th. Crept out at 12 M. to Coliseum. Repeopling it, &c. The arch. Dined on fig & bread.

Friday March 13th. Fine day. To grounds of Villa Borghese. Great beauty of them. Fine rich odours of bushes & trees. The laurel &c. The closed villa, statues seen thro' railing. Silence & enchantment. "Glitter wide the halls, high the laurel grows &c. — Taken from scenery of Italian Villa. — Called on Page. Long lecture. Swedenburgh. Spiritualist. Thin Socks. Dined on a plate at Lepri's.

Saturday March 14th. Walked about to Trinita di Monte. Second visit to Albani Villa. Father Murphy. Mrs. S. Caryatide. The long lines of foliage — architecture of villa, richness of landscape. Fine site. — To B. of Diocletian Church. Fall of Simon Magus. Meridian line, — Moslems in St. Sophia: transverse.

Sunday March 15th. Attacked by singular pain across chest & in back. In my room till 5½ P.M. Dined at table d'hote. This day saw nothing, learned nothing, enjoyed nothing, but suffered something.

Monday March 16th Vatican day. — Afterwards to Pincian. Could not engage seat in coupe of diligence. Have to go to Florence by Civita Vechia. haze Sixtine Chapel — blue clouds, limbs.

Tuesday March 17th. To Frascati by R.R. Crossing Campagna by R.R. — Villa Aldrobrandini. Charming day & grounds. Avenues of trees. Laurel, cypruss, pine, olive. Rich masses of foliage. Stone seats at angles. View of Tusculum (Cicero) from top of hill, at end of long avenue of olives. The cave — skull. The fountain, seen through hall of villa. Maps. Mellow aspect of all. Willows advanced as far as middle of May with us. Felt the bracing, renewing air of these hills very sensibly. Air of Rome hypochondriac. — Fine neglect of grounds of villa. Omnibus riding through Rome to & from R.R.

Wednesday March 18. Breakfasted on 16 pennies at Caffe Nuovo. To Torlonia Villa — small chambers — theaters — arbored dessert room — colonade & sea — rich decorations. — Grounds. The cave — the tournament — the artificial ruins — the circus &c &c. Grounds small. Fine views. — Crawfords studio — Colossal America & various statues. Extent of studio. Indian, Backwoodsman &c &c.

Thursday March 19th. Engaging vetturo for C. Vechia. Old stable &c. — To Villa Doria Pamfili. Great extent. — rich green — Paridise within Paridise. Yellow villa. — long vista of green & green water. The cedars & pines. Avenues of olives. View of St. Peters. The terrace gardens — the form of the parterres — flourishes of chromoplates. Finer than English Park — richer foliage & sweeter atmosphere. Brilliant coloring & soft. — The Ghetto. The market (butcher) in old temple alley leading through between columns. Filth & crowd. Old clothes — babies in basket & babies sewed up. Fountain of 7 branch candlestick. Way in which old temples are used — churches — shops — alleis — blacksmiths — markets &c &c &c. View from piazza of San Pietro in Montorio. Best in Rome. In the evening at Caffe Nuovo — old palace. Deep recess of windows. Crowd of orderly well-dressed people. Magical guitarr man. Hush & applause.

Friday March 20th. At 6.A.M started for Tivoli. Chilly grey ride across Campagna. Lake Tartarus. Travetine. — Villa of Hadrian — Solemn scene & solemn guide — Extent of ruin, — fine site. Guide philosophising. — Tivoli on heigth. Temple of the Nymph overhanging — paths — gallery in rock — Claude — Not to Paradise, but Tivoli. — shading — middle tint — Villa of Mecanas. — Chill ride home in the evening. —

Saturday March 21st. Rainy. Run about getting my *vises.* Sam left his card. Saw him. Had letter from home to 20th Feb. All well. Met to part. — At 4 P.M. started in veturino for Civitta Veccia in company with Mr & Miss R. of New Jersey and an Italian lady. Desolate ride across desolate country. (Last view of St. Peters. Went out by gate near it.) At midnight stopped for three hours at lonely inn. Heard Meditterrean near. Rode on.

Sunday March 22d Arrived at C. Vecchia at 6 A.M. Crowds in streets. Sheepskin leggins &c. At 3 P.M. went aboard French steamer "Aventime", small craft. Great crowd. Turkish flag hoisted in honor of Turk envoy to Sardinia. Talked with him. His views of Mahomattism &c. Upper classes of Turkey indulge philosophical opinions upon religion &c. Repeated story of Abbots fire at Salonica. Same as I heard from Abbot himself. — Slept on settee (no berth).

Monday March 23d At Leghorn by daylight. Pleasant morning, though damp. Passports. Nothing special about Leghorn. At 10½ took 2d class car for Pisa. Walked at once to the Duomo &c ═ One end of it looks like coral grottoes in sea, — pearl diver. pillars in tiers. — St Peter's uplifted arm handle of bronze door. — *Baptistery* like dome set on ground. Wonderful pulpit of marble. — Campanile like pine poised just ere snapping. You wait to hear crash. Like Wordsworth's moore cloud, it will move all together if it move at all, for Pillars all lean with it. About 150 of 'em. There are houses in wake of fall. — *Campo Santa*. Beauty of bowered walks of stone. Frescoes. Wags who painted them. Tartarus — tooth-pulling — serpent looking in eye. Impudent — mouth. Esop might have designed it. The three kings. — The four monuments stand in commons — grass. grow out of ground. Come upon them as upon bouquet of architecture.

[Interior of duomo magnificent. St. Agnes. &c.

[Sea-chapel on river side. Collonaded Street. Silence of the Common. & River-side. At 5½ P.M took cars for Florence. Level plain richly cultivated. Mountains. At 8 P.M arrived at Florence. Hotel du Nord. Caffe Doney near it. To bed early, no sleep for 2 nights past.

Tuesday March 24th. Cold & raining all day. To Pitti Palace —— "It's as bad as too much pain: it gets to be pain at last" Heard this broken latter part of sentence from wearied lady coming from Uffizi Palace. — She was talking no doubt about excess of pleasure in these galleries. — Florence is a lovely city even on a cold rainy day. Ufezzi Palace. The Perseus of Cellini. Wandered about after leaving gallery Pitti. To the Duomo & Campanile. Came upon them unexpectedly. Amazed at their magnificence. Could not enter. Bought fine mosaics for one Napoleon. — Breakfasted to day at Caffe Doney.

Wednesday March 25th. Festa, galleries closed. To Pitti gardens, rather Boboli. Noble views of Florence & country. Strolled about generally to churches, piazzas, &c. At Santa Croce saw tombs of Dante, M. Angelo, Alfieri, and Machiavelli. Preacher near M.'s tomb. M. said naught. Crucifix held out towards him. Campo Santa here. — At Annunziata saw fine frescoes of A. del Sarto. Gamblers struck by lightning. — Animated appearance of streets. Walked over to Romana Gate, outside to Bellesgardo. Striking view from this hill of city & Vale d'Arno. Roundabout walk to get to it. Abruptly came upon it, by a narrow lane between high walls of gardens. The tower on the Vecchio palace the grand feature. — Came on violent rain; & walked home in it.

Thursday March 26th. Sunned myself after breakfast in Grand Ducal square. To the Uffizi gallery. Idle to enumerate. Grand view of tower of Vechio palace from head of gallery. View of covered way that crosses the Vechio bridge. — Not pleased with the Venus de Medici, but very much astonished at the Wrestlers & charmed with Titian's Venus. The Portraits of painters interesting. —— To the Accademia di B. Arti. — Giotto's paintings. Rich effect of gilding & raised parts. Here are predecessors of the Peruginos & Raphaels. Saw a large painting, not referred to in my hand book, which contained many faces, attitudes, expressions & groupings I had noted at Rome in Raphael. Undoubtedly Raphael took from this, or some yet older painting. But still more, the *whole spirit* was the same. — Could not get access to all parts of the Accademia. — But saw the statues, — such as they are. Returning, passed Ricardi palace — Immense arched & lowering pile, with massive and impending cornice. — Raining pretty much all day, at times violently. — At dinner table accosted by singular young man who speaks 6 or 8 languages. He presented me with a flower, and talked like one to whom the world was delightful. May it prove so.

Friday March 27th. At Caffe after breakfast sat musing upon caffes in general, & the young men frequenting them. Something good might be written on the "Caffe Doney", including that "Henry" & the flower-girls. — To the Museum of Natural History. Immense collection. Lapis lazuli — chrystal vessels, dragons, perfumers &c &c. Wax plants, seeds & germinations. Anatomacal preparations. Terrible cases & wilderness of rooms of them. — The Sicilian's work. N° 1. Interior of case, broken arches, skeleton thrown under arch — head of statue — dead expression — crown & scepter among bones — medallion — Death & scythe — pointing — tossed skeletons & tools. horrible humiliation. Cleft shows more temples & pyramid. *N° 2*. Vault — heaps — all colors from deep green to buff — all ruins — detached bones — Mothers children old men, intricacy of heaps. Man with cloth over face bringing down another body whose buff contrasts with the putrid green. *N° 3*. In a cavernous ruin. Superb mausoleum like Pope's, lid removed shows skeleton & putridity. Roman sarcophagus — joyous triumphal procession — putrid corpse thrown over it. — grating — rats, vampires — insects. slime & ooze of corruption. — Moralist, this Sicilian. (H.). — The final collection. —

Revisited Pitti Gallery. The 3 Fates of M. Angelo. Admirable expression. The way the one Fate looks at other — Shall I? — The expectancy of the 3^{d}. (Transition from splendid humanity of gallery to the Sicilian). The inlaid tables & pictures. S. Rosa's portraits (one autograph) Battle Peice. —— To Powers' studio. His America. Il Penseroso, Fisher Boy. — Saw him. Apron, plain man. Fine specimen of an American. — To the Cascine. — Dined at the Luna with the young Polyglot. Walk along river & home.

Saturday 28th March. Before breakfast ascended Duomo. Entered Ball. Fine morning & noble view. Parapet round the building. Fresco of dome. Immense foot five feet long by measurement. — Magnitude of dome. — After breakfast at caffe Doney, did some business & then to Ufizzi gallery for last look. Afterwards to Fiesole. Boccaccio's villa — Medicis villa. Franscican convent. View from windows. Old maps, — behind the age. ——— Etruscan wall. — To the Cascine & home. After dinner packed carpet bag & wrote this.

Sunday 29th April. Porter forgot to wake us at 3.AM. Diligence started without us. Run round the Duomo to the Gate. All day among hills. Crossed the Appenines. Grand scenery. Long reaches of streams through solitary vallies. No woods. No heartiness of scenery as in New England. Drawn by oxen part of the way. 4000 feet above sea. Deep banks of snow in places. Lonely houses. Villages. Grave & decorous people: Breakfast in the hut. Nothing of talk in the coupè: But much smoking:

Monday March 30th. Stopping at the "Three Moors." Fine day. Saw the leaning tower — black & grimy — brick. Its companion is of prodigious heigth. To the Gallery. The Madonna of the Rosary. A Circe. St. Cecilia. David Victorious. &c. — To the Campo Santa — Vast extent of sepulchral arcades. Splendor of some of the monuments. Arcade winding up the hill to church — three miles. Saw the University. The Court all coats of arms of students. Statue of the learned lady. Walked under the arcades in the evening. First thing at Bologna, tried Bologna sausage, on the principle that at Rome you first go to St. Peters.

Tuesday March 31st. After breakfasting with the young C. Traveller at caffe, started alone in diligence for Padua. — Polite elderly gentleman in diligence. A dead level country in strong contrast to last Sunday's travel. Ponds for hemp. Vineyards. Stone farm-houses & stone barns without sides. — At one P.M. came to Ferrara, where diligence stopped till 3. Went to see cathedral. Interesting old pile. Portico sustained by pillars resting on old hunchbacks. — The Last Judgement sculptured overhead. The Father in the angle of pediment. Below to right & left the elect & reprobate. The four figures stepping out of their stone graves, as out of bed. The legs thrown out in various attitudes. Capital. Grotesque figures. — Fine bell-tower, but incomplete. — The old palace of the ancient lords of Ferrara is surrounded by broad moat. Drawbridge &c. Massy brick arches over moat. — Ferrara is on a dead plane, grass grows all about, seems a human common. — Tasso's prison. Mere cider-cellar. Grated window, but not strong. Byron's name &c. Other scribblers. — From Ferrara to Padua went by smaller post. Austrain. Old fashioned vehicle. Mysterious window & face. Secret recesses. Hide. Old fashioned feeling. Crossed the Po, quite a broad stream & very turbid & rapid. Yellow as Missippi. Alluvial look. Old ferry boat. Austrain frontier. At dusk came to Rovigo, a considerable town. Saw two more leaning towers there; dismantled & ruinous. At midnight came to Padua, & to the hotel "Star of the East."

Wednesday April 1st. Rainy day. To the famous caffe of Pedrocci. Worthy of its fame, being of great size and well furnished. Got a grave dark guide & started with great-coat & umbrella to see the sights. — To the town hall. Wonderful roof (India) To the private palace to see the "Satan & his host." Fine attitude of Satan. Intricate as heap of vermecilla. Church of St. Anthony & Shrine. Supurb. Crutches & pictures. Bronze bas-reliefs. Goliath & David, &c. Promenade — The Brenta flowing round it. Pleasant aspect of Brenta winding through town. To Giotto's chapel. — The Virtues & Vices. Capital. The Scriptural pictures. — The Arena. — Fine church in vicinity. Old palaces & old arcades & old streets. At 2. P.M took cars for Venice. Raining hard. Comfortable cars. — Level country. Approaching Venice like approaching Boston from the West. — Into gondola to Hotel Luna. Dined at table 'dhote, & sallied out to piazza of St. Marco, & about there till 8 P.M.

April 2^d^, Thursday. Breakfast at Florian's, on roll. Ducal Palace Went into St. Mark's. Oily looking interior, reeking look, disappointed. Repairing dome — scaffold. To Rialto. Up Bell Tower. In gondola to Grand Canal & round by Guidecca. Dinner. Walk in St. Mark's. To bed. — No place like the St. M.s Square for enjoyment. Public ball room — no hours. Lights. Ladies taking refreshments outside (In morning they breakfast on sunny side). Musicians. singers. soldiers &c &c &c. Perfect decorum. Fine architecture. — In the evening met in Ducal Palace (the court) affable young man (Antonio) engaged him to meet me for guide tomorrow.

April 3^d^ Friday. To Glass bead manufactury. Drawing the rods like twine-making. cutting, rounding, polishing, coloring a secret. To Gold chain manufactury. Old Venetian gold. Various qualities. To Church St. Guovani Paoli. Monuments. The chapel with the beautiful bas-relief. Christ expounding to the doctors. To the Aresenl. Great basins. Turks standard. Lanterns. On the canals. Othello's house & statue. Shylocks. L. Byron's. Foscari Palace. Fine view of G. Canal. — After dinner in Piazza.

April 4th. Saturday Breakfast at Mindel's. Took gondola at Piazzetta for Murano. Village in water. passed cemetery, — on isle. — Gliding in to water village. Old church. Back & to Jesuit church. Marble drapery of pulpit. Astonishing what can be done with marble. Into Grand Canal. House of Gold. Duke of Bordeaux's. Dutchess de Berri's &c &c. Hotel de Ville — old palace — superb court. & stair case. Frescos of courtiers looking down & over balustrade beyond stair case. — To the bankers & Sardinian Consul. To Gallery, Titian's Assumption. The great black heads & brown arms. St. Mark coming to rescue. Venetian noble. Old pictures of Venice. — Grand saloons. — Titians Virgin in the Temple. After dinner, took gondola till dark on Canals. Old Palace with grinning monsters &c. Bought coat. To bed at 9½.

April 5th. Sunday Breakfast on St. Marks. Austrain flags flying from three masts. Glorious aspect of the basilica in the sunshine. The charm of the square. The snug little breakfast there. Ladies. Flower girls — musicians. pedlers of Adriatic shells. Cigar stores &c &c. — Sat in a chair by the arcade at Mindel's some time in the sun looking at the flags, the sun, & the church. (The shadow of the bell-tower. The Pigeons. People coming to feed them. — Took gondola. To the garden laid out by Napoleon. At end of Venice. (Like Battery at N. York) Fine view of lagoon & isles on two sides of Venice. To the Lido, from whence fine view of Venice, particularly the Ducal palace &c. Walked across the sand to the Adriatic shore. Calm waters. Long wide beach. — Through the grassy lagoon to Armenian Convent. Admirable retirement from the world, asleep in the calm Lagoon, the Lido a breakwater against the tumultuous ocean of life. — Garden, convent, quadrangles, cloisters, — View from library window — isles — [The city in the distance. Portraits of noble bearded old Armenian priests. Old printing presses. Turkish medal. M.S. Bible. Chapel. 8 worshippers, & 8 priests. Supurb vestments, blended with supurb light streaming in from shining lagoon through windows draped with rosy silks. chaunting, swinging silver censers — puff of incense at each worshipper. Great gorgeousness of effect. — The approach, gliding in — between grass. —

[Smell of stale incense peculiar to these old Churches. Only found out this — the cause of it — to day. — Back to the city. Mirage-like effect of fine day — floating in air of ships in the Malamocco Passage, & the islands. To the church of Santa Maria Salute. Octagonal. To the church of S. Giorgio Maggiore. Series of carvings in wood. Landed at steps of Ducal palace under Bridge of Sighs. Prison black as by fire. Also palace in parts. *Was* a fire here. Walked in piazza of St. Mark. Crowds of people promenading. Pigeons. Walked to Rialto. Looked up and down G. Canal. Wandered further on. Numbers of beautiful women. The rich brown complexions of Titian's women drawn from nature, after all. (Titian was a Venetian) The clear, rich, golden brown. The clear cut features, like a cameo. — The vision from the window at end of long, narrow passage. — Walked by moonlight & gaslight in piazza of St. Mark. Numbers of singers, & musicians. — The tumblers & comic actors in the open space near Rialto. The expression of the women Tumblers. —— The Ducal palace's colonade like hedge of architecture. — On these still summer days the fair Venetians float about in full bloom like pond lillies. — G. Canal not straight & stiff, but irregular with projections for advantageous fronts. Winds like a Susquehanha. View from balcony of Foscari palace. Best site. Huge timbers. Occupied as barrack. Austrain cots &

burnishing armor. Cooking & scrubbing in great hall. — On the canals of Venice all vehicles are represented. Omnibus, private coach, light gig, or sulky, pedler's cart, hearse. — [You, at first, think it a freshet, it will subside, not permanent, — only a temporary condition of things. — St: Mark's at sunset, gilt mosaics, pinacles, looks like holyday affair. As if the Grand Turk had pitched his pavilion here for a summers day. 800 years! Inside the precious marbles, from extreme age, look like a mosaic of rare old soaps. — — have an unctuous look. Fairly steamed with old devotions as refectories with old dinners. — In Venice nothing to see for the Venetian. — Rather be in Venice on rainy day, than in other capital on fine one. —

— My Guide. How I met him, & where. Lost his money in 1848 Revolution & by travelling. — To day in one city, tomorrow in next. Fine thing to travel. When rich, plenty compliment. How you do, Antonio — hope you very well, Antonio — Now Antonio no money, Antonio no compliment. Get out of de way Antonio. Go to the devel, Antonio. Antonio you go shake yourself. You know dat Sir, 'dat to de rich man, de poor man habe always de bad smell? You know dat Sir?

Yes, Antonio, I am not unaware of that. Charitably disposed. Old blind man, give something & God will bless you [Will give, but doubt the blessing]. [Antonio good character for Con. Man] Did not want to die. Heaven. You believe dat? I go dere, see how I like it first. — His rich anecdote. Byron swimming over every morning to wake a lady in palace opposite. The Prussian countess, cavalier sends. Very wicked lady but very happy. — Floating about philosophizing with Antonio the Merry. Ah, it was Pausillippo. — Whether saw the brother of E. of Austria or not. — Leaning over parapet. Boys. silver lace. Anxious to settle it; & in my favor, for I consider that some of the feirce democracy would not look with disrespect upon the man who had &c &c &c

April 6th. Left Venice at 5½ AM for Milan. Through Padua & Vicenza to Verona, where bride & groom entered the cars. Between Verona & Brescia had noble views of Lago di Garda, with Mount Baldus in distance. Villages upon its shore & on an island. Long vista of the lake between great overlapping mountains whose snows insensibly melted into the purples. Passed on the north continually by the first tiers of the Alps. R.R. over dead level of Lombardy plain. Rich cultivation. Mulberry trees, vines. Farm houses so unlike ours. No signs of hard work as with us. This region the scene of Napoleon's campaigns. At Coccaglio took diligence for Treviglio (18 m. from Milan). Rode from 1 PM till 6. In coupe. Arrived at Milan at 7½ P.M. Omnibus to Hotel de le Ville. Row at station between cabman & Austrain gen d'arm. Walked out to see the cathedral by night. Tour of shops &c A Canal.

April 7th Tuesday. To the Gallery. Very extensive, and some noble paintings. St. Catherine's Martyrdom. St. Mark at Alexandria is admirable for accuracy of architecture costume & expressions. To the Camp d'Armo. Arch. To the picture of Leonardo da Vincis. In suburb of Milan. Curious old brick church. Very old. Some trouble finding the refectory. At last directed to an archway where stood trumpeters. *Not* for Leonardo, though. Led through passages occupied by military (cavalry) to large court (like that of inn). Refectory a long, high, blank room, two ends painted. Great stage for copyists. Catching last hues of sunset. Whole picture faded & half gone. (Photograph copy of it I saw) — Significance of the Last Supper. The joys of the banquet soon depart. One shall betray me, one of you — man so false — the glow of sociality is so evanescent, selfishness so lasting. —— Leonardo & his oil, case of a great man (Wordsworth) & his theory. To the cathedral. Glorious. More satisfactory to me than St. Peters. A wonderful grandure. Effect of burning window at end of aisle. Ascended, — From below people in the turrets of open tracery look like flies caught in cobweb. — The groups of angels on points of pinacles & everywhere. Not the conception but execution. View from summit. Might write book of travel upon top of Milan Cathedral. Dined at 5 P.M. at table d hote of the Hotel d la Ville. Curious old gentleman there. Prided himself upon filling his glass. Young man. Talk. About cathedral.

April 8th Wednesday. Up at 5. AM. At 6½ started for Lake Como. Ride of hour & half in cars over dead rich plain. Took steamer at Como. Like going to Lake George. — Wonderful populousness of shores of lake. Abrupt rise of mountains. roads cut through rocks, windrows, ledges. View at Belleaggio of the three arms of the lake. Mountains rolled together in watery blue. Snow upon summits. Picturesque boats boarding at every village. Villages upon all kinds of sites. Some midway upon steep slopes as if they had slipped there in a land-slide. Churches on isolated peaks. Groups of hamlets — pinfolds. Villages by scores, a hundred. Terraced vegetation. Lone houses way up, here & there. Cascades. (under house) No trees. Back to Milan at 7 P.M.

Thursday April 9th. Up at 5. Scribbled here, and down to breakfast at 6½. at hotel. Young Parisian and lady there. At 9. o'clock started in diligence for Novara. Smart postilions, bugles under arm, glazed hat, metal band, jack boots. Over dead flat Lombardy plain, Alps in sight to the north. Passed many populous villages & towns. High cultivation of a most fertile soil. Crossed noble granite bridge of the Ticino. Came to Novara at 1½. Lunched there. Remained, waiting for train, 4 hours. Walked in boulevard on old walls — ancient brick fortress with deep, broad moat — Old duomo. Thorwalsden's angels. Old court. Baptistery. Wax work. Nails & hammer, hair &c. At 5½ took train for Turin. Fell in with Greek from Zephalonia ("English subject") Arrived at Turin 9.P.M. Adventure with omnibus, porters, and Hotel d la Europe. — At Novara, saw church with wooden architecture before it. Within, altar made into stage, where were pasteboard figures of scriptural characters. Exactly as in theatre. And lighted.

Friday April 10th. Very rainy. Breakfasted at caffe (gilded octagonal saloon) in Via di Po. Walked under the great arcades. Took view across to Colina. Visited Gallery. Admirable painting of "A Confessional". Some heads of Titian. 4 fine allegorical paintings — Earth, Air, Fire, Water. Rubens' Magdalen — excellently true to nature, but very ugly. Groups of children by Van Dyke — six in a row, heads, — charming. Teniers tavern scenes. The remarkable Teniers effect is produced by first dwarfing, then deforming humanity. Breughel — always pleasing. ——
— Piazza Castello, where hotel is, is the centre of Turin. Interesting old pile, with various fronts, and grotesque assemblage of various architectures. Turin is more regular than Philadelphia. Houses all one cut, one color, one heigth. City seems all built by one contractor & paid for by one capitalist. — Singular effect of standing in arch of castle, & looking down vista of Via di Grossa to Mount Rosa & her snows. —— Caught it unobscured by clouds early on the morning I

left Turin. — Boulevards around the town. Many caffes & fine ones — Laboring people & poor women taking their frugal breakfast in fine caffes. Their decorum, so different from corresponding class at home. — In the evening it cleared off. Went down to the Po again. Stood on steps of church there. To bed early.

Saturday April 11th. Bright weather. Up early to see Mount Rosa from the street. Saw it. Breakfasted on chocolate (Turin famous for it) on bank of Po. At 10 A.M. took cars for Genoa, over 100 miles. Pleasant for some time & passed through pleasant country. Very populous & highly cultivated. Approaching Appennines, noble scenery. Road built with great skill & cost. Numerous tunnels through hills at base of Appennines, till at last comes the grand Tunnel — 2 miles long. — Arrived at Genoa in rain at 3 P.M. Carpet bag fell from shoulder of clumsy porter. Afraid to look at Kate's affairs. —
— Stopped at hotel Feder on water side. Walked through Strada Nuovo &c. Palaces inferior to those of Rome, Florence, & Venice. One peculiarity is the *paintings of architecture* instead of the reality. All kinds of elaborate architecture represented in fresco. — Machiavelli's saying that the appearances of a virtue may be advantageous, when the reality would be otherwise. — Streets like those of Edinburgh; only still more steep & crooked. Ascended one for view. — Dined at table 'dhote. Fine room. The hotel occupies old palace. In evening walked on pavilion nigh port. Lofty hotels. Tower of the Cross of Malta. View of hills in distance.

Sunday April 12th. Breakfasted at Caffe. Chocolate. To the Public promenade on ramparts. Look off. Troops. Unhandsome set of men. To the Cathedral. White & black marble in alternate courses. The steps. The *Gridiron* bas-releif. Fine interior. Tower. — The Ducal Palace. All the world out. Numbers of women. The Genoese head dress. Undines and Maids of the Mist. Simple & graceful. Receipt for making a plain woman look lovely. Took omnibus (2 sous) to end of harbor. Light house (300 feet high) Ascended. Superb view. Sea coast to south. Promontory. All Genoa & her forts before you. The heigth & distances of these forts, their outlying loneliness. The bleakness, the savageness of glens between, seem to make Genoa rather the capital and fortified camp of Satan: fortified against the Archangels. Clouds rolling round ramparts aerial. &c. Took the East side of harbor, and began circuit of the 3[d] line of defences. Ramparts overhang the open sea, arches thrown over ravines. Fine views of sections of town. Up & up. Galley-slave prison. Gratings commanding view of sea — infinite liberty. Followed round & round. Nonplussed. Got to Public Promenade. Struck up steep lane to little church (fine view of sea from porch) Thence higher, and came to ramparts. Magnificent views of deep valley other side — & of Genoa & sea. Up & up. Finer & finer, till I got to the apex fort. Saw the two encircling vallies, and the ridge in which their heads unite to form the site of the highest forts. Great populousness of these vallies. Loneliness of some of the higher forts. Grounds enclosed by 3[d] circuit. Deep, woodless glens. Solitary powder magazines. Lonesome as glen in Scotch highlands. — With great fatigue descended by irregular path, coming out by Doria palace. Dined at table d hote. Greek next me. Gigglers opposite. — Walked over the port. Stopped in with Greek at garden-caffee. Beautiful spot with fountains arcades &c &c &c. In bed at 8½. — Threatening rain all day, but none.

Monday April 14th Chocolate at caffe. Old Wall of the Custom House. Visited the palaces. Different style from those of Rome &c. Large halls, preceding courts. But see Guide Book. Was shown thro' some palaces in great haste. Rosso palace in particular. — Very windy. To hotel early, effects of yesterday's work. Met Purser of Constitution at dinner. In bed by eight.

Tuesday Ap 15th Took cars at six A.M for Arona on Lake Maggiore. Met Liutent Fauntleroy at station. Pleasant ride across new country. At 2 P.M sailed from Arona in (Passed thro' Allessandia & Novara) small steamer. Cold passage. Scenery fine. White-wash brush. Confusion of seasons. Pourings of cascades, numbers of hamlets. The terraced isle. Came to Magadino at 7 P.M. Diligence to Bellinzona. Entered defile at dusk, and kept in it. Shadowy & vague approach among the roots of Alps. At Bellinzona out jumped Dr Lockwood just from Simplon. *April 16* At 2.AM started in diligence for crossing the San Gothard. Bow window. Silence, mystery. Steady roll of wheel. Dawn, zig-zags, Gorge, precipice, Snow. At Airolo breakfasted. M[r] Abbot accosted me. Storming violently. Hand sleds. Parties waiting at Airolo for three days. Started. Long train. Zig-zag. Houses of refuge. Discussion of the gods &c. Verge & brink of paths.

Summit. Hospice. Old stone warehouse. Scene there. Men in comforters, frozen horses. sleding goods. — Started again. Stoppage by goods coming the other way. Turning out. Floundering of horses. Descent. Like coming from the clouds. Noses of crags thrusting out — 10000 feet. Dinner at Andermatt. Wet through. Diligence. Devil's Bridge. Scenery through gorge. Green & white of grass & snow. Lime torrent. Altorf. Fluellen at 7 P.M. — April 17 Before breakfast next morning went out for view of Lake Lucern — Bay of Uri. Chapel. (seats Methodists) At 9. A.M. started for Lucern in steamer. Entrance of Bay of Uri. Tell's Chapel. At 11 came to Lucern. — Thorswalden's lion — living rock. Ramble with Abbot & fine views. Old Bridges.

Friday April 18. At 8 AM started in diligence for Berne. Coupe, only Abbot & me. Charming day & charming country. Swiss cottages. Thrift neatness &c. Dinner at inn. At 7 arrived at Berne, putting up at "The Crown." Went to terrace of cathedral for view of Bernese Alps. There they were — seen over the green.

Saturday April 19th. Walk on terrace. Cathedral. Spent whole day almost with Mr Fay & Abbot & daughter. Ride. Noble views of Alps. Rail Road building.

Sunday April 20th. At 10. AM. started in diligence (interior) for Basle. Fine day. At Solieure dined. Encountered a Mr Smyth merchant of N.Y. Supurb views of the Bernese Alps & Jura ranges all morning. Beyond Solure drew near Jura, — palisades — About high as Saddle Back. 4000 feet. Old castles. Entered by a remarkable defile. View of white Alps through defile. Ride across. — Took R.R at L—— and at 8 P.M put up at "The Wild Man" in Basle. Walked out, crossed the Rhine by bridge of boats. Deep, broad, rapid.

Monday April 21. At 5 A.M. off by R.R. for Strasbourgh. 90 miles. To the Cathedral. Pointed — pinnacles — All sprouting together like bed of what you call it? asparagus Brown free stone. The Clock &c. Crowd waiting. Ascent. Not fine as Milan. Platform on top. The Spire, inscriptions (1500) At 2 P.M. crossed with Mr Smyth to Kiel. Passports. French & German. Baden. Took cars for Heidleburgh. Californians. Lovely afternoon. Level country bounded by hills.

Great fertility. Getting the crops in. At 8 PM arrived at Heidleburgh. Hotel Adler.

Tuesday April 22. Up at 5 and mounted to Castle. Blossoms, grass, all things fresh round the charming old ruin. The chimney. vault. View of Necker. The University. — The cloven ruin. trees sprouting. defile in ruins. — Flower bed in banquet hall. Knights in green niches. — Students. Daguerotypes. At 2 P.M. took cars for Frankfort on Maine. At station encountered Dr Abbot again — bound to Frankfort. Same level fertile country as all way from Basle. At 4 PM came to Frankfort, stopping at Hotel . After dinner Smythe invited us to ride about town. — Goethe's statue. Faust's. Cathedral. Luther's preaching place. River side. Park. Jews quarter. Rothschilds home. &c &c &c.

Wednesday Apl 23. — After breakfast went in to see Abbot — found him smoking in bed & better. Went to Rothschilds. — Eminent hardware merchant. Aspect of cash-room. kegs, barrels, rolls, presses, weights & scales, coopers, carmen & porters. Drove about the town. Faust's statue. The "Ariadne" of H——. Rose light. Beauty and Deformity contrasted. At half past eleven A.M. started in cars for Wiesbaden, but by mistake arrived at Mayence — at 2 P.M. Took boat for Cologne. Mayence on low land, but covering large space, fine cathedral & buildings. Passed through Hock-land. Plenty of vineyards (sticks) down Rhine. Got to Cologne at 10 P.M. Rainy & cold all day. My partial companion. (from Boston?) Stopped at Hotel de Cologne.

Thursday April 24th At 5 o'clock got up, breakfasted & went to R.R. station, across river for Amsterdam. Through Duselldorff & Utrecht. Rainy, cold, hail at times & sleet. Rich country, level. — Entering Holland, began to look like a great heath — passed much waste, brown, muddy looking land — immense pastures, light green. Adventure after hotel in Amsterdam, where we arrived at 3½ P.M. Put up at last at the "Old Bible", upon which something good might be written in the ironical way.

April 24th (Mistake of a day before). Very cold & snowy yesterday afternoon. At ordinary a number of sea captains. This morning got a queer little old Dutchman for guide & went to Picture Gallery. Wonderful picture of Paul Potter — The Bear. — Keel hauling of a Dutch Surgeon. — The Syndics of Rembrandt & The Night Watch (shadows) — Portrait of a painter & his wife — admirable (Old Pedlers) The abandonment of good humored content. — Dutch convivial scenes. Teniers & Breughel. — Streets of Amsterdam like long lines of old fashioned frontispieces in old folios & old quartoes. Canals & drawbridges. Greasy looking old fellows — Teniers. — To the "Garden" & "Plantation." The pink-mouthed dog. The "Sloth". — View of city from cupola of palace. Red tiles of houses. The Port. The drop of gin. — Shape of Amsterdam like ampitheater, water all round it. — Broeck, did not see. place of cheese, butter, & tidiness. — The old galliot. Neat, & chest of drawers. — At 4½ took train for Rotterdam. Smoking cars. One all to myself. Passed through Harlem — Neat, like "Colonie" in Albany. Leyden, big cathedral. The Hague. Arrived at Rotterdam at 7½. Got guide & went to Dance Houses. Into three of them. Striking & pathetic sight. The promenading girls — music — their expression & decorum. — Villiany of the guide. To bed by 9½.

April 25th. With guide went to cathedral of St. Lawrence. (Forgot to say that while in Amsterdam visited the church there. Carved pulpit, &c but nothing inside) Fine view of Rotterdam & environs. House of Erasmus. At 11 o clock went on board steamer for London. Fair wind, but chilly. Passed several of the embankments. — The fat steward. At 7 o clock, strong, fair wind.

April 26th Monday. Made the mouth of Thames early, & steamed up, passed many objects of interest. The mammoth ship "Great Eastern". At 7 AM were at St. Catherine Wharf. Cab, & to Tavistock Hotel. Dreary Sunday in London. Walked to Hyde Park & in Kensington Gardens. Got an idea of them.

April 27th. To the Longman's &c

April 28th. To Madam Tussaud's. No where else in particular.

April 29th 30th — May 1st — Thursday, Friday & Saturday. —
Lay a sort of waterlogged in London. — Reverie at the "Cock".

Chrystal Palace — digest of universe. Alhambra — House of Pansi — Temple of ——. &c &c &c. — Comparison with the pyramid. — Overdone. If smaller would look larger. The Great Eastern. Pyramid. — Vast toy. No substance. Such an appropriation of space as is made by a rail fence. Durable materials, but perishable structure. Cant exist 100 years hence. — Beautiful view from terraces of Chrystal Palace. — Thames Tunnel.

Rode out in omnibus to Richmond. Several evenings at Hyde Park to see the equestrians. Fine & bold riding of the ladies. Poor devel looking over the rail. — Visited the Vernon & Turner galleries. — Sunset scenes of Turner. "Burial of Wilkie." The Shipwreck. "The Fighting —— taken to her last birth."

Sunday May 2d Left London by RR for Oxford. Clear day. Rich country. Passed through Berkshire. Level & fertile. Windsor castle in distance. Saw Reading, shire town of Berkshire. At 11½ arrived at Oxford. — Most interesting spot I have seen in England. Made tour of all colleges. It was here I first confessed with gratitude my mother land, & hailed her with pride. Oxford to American as well worth visiting as Paris, tho' in a very different way. — Pulpit in corner of quadrangle. Deer. Garden girdled by river. — Meadows beyond. Oxen & sheep. Pastoral & collegiate life blended. — Christ Church Meadow. Avenue of trees. — Old reef washed by waves & showing detached parts — so Oxford. Ivy branch over portal of St. John intertwining with sculpture. Amity of art & nature. Accord. Grotesque figures. Catching rhuematism in Oxford cloisters different from catching it in Rome. Contagion in Pamfili Doria but wholesome beauty in Oxford. Learning lodged like a faun. Garden to every college. Lands for centuries never molested by labor. Sacred to beauty & tranquility. Fell's avenue. Has beheld unstirred all the violence of revolutions. &c. — Steep roof. Spanish chestnut. Dining halls.

[Dormer window derived from gable, as spire from elevating & sharpening roof in snowy climates — final result of gradual process. — Stair case of Christ Church. Single pillar as in Paris chapel. Each college has dining room & chapel — on a par — large windows. Soul & body equally cared for. — Grass smooth as green baize of billiard table. — The picturesque never goes beyond this. — I know nothing more fitted by mild & beautiful rebuke to chastise the ranting of

Yankees. — In such a retreat Old Burton sedately smiled at men. — Improvement upon the monkish. As knights templars were mixture of monk & soldier, so these of monk & gentleman.

[These colleges founded as men plant trees. — Belfry cant ring bells, &c. Music coming out of church as beads ooze out of earthen pitcher. — Stopped at the "Mitre" at Oxford. — High Street.

Monday May 3^d^. Left Oxford at 9 A.M for Stratford on Avon. Changed for horse rail road. Stopped at the "Red Horse." — Shakspere's home — little old groggery abandoned. — cheerless, melancholly. Scrawl of names. — The church. Tomb stones before Altar, wife, daughter son-in-law. — New Place. — Walk to Hathaway cottage at Shottery. Level country. ———
At 3½ went on stage to Warwick. Cold & windy. Wonderfully beautiful country. — (Edge Hill). — Aspect of Castle nigh Avon. Walked about Warwick. Entrance very fine. Old gate &c. At 6½ took R.R. for Birmingham. Arrived before dark. Mob of chimnies. Like Newcastle-upon-Tyne. Stopped at Queen's, by R.R. Drove round town. City Hall, fine building. Parthenon. To bed early.

Tuesday May 4th. At 6 A.M. took RR for Liverpool. Like riding through burnt district — standing columns of pines, smoking or with shoots of flame from top. — The Chimnies.
Arrived at Liverpool at 12. M. — Secured my berth on "City of Manchester" by paying balance. Got letters from Brown, Shipley & Co. Saw Hawthorne. Called on Mr Bright. Got presents. Trunk. Packed. *The "Grecian"*

Wednesday May 5th. Fine day. At 10 A.M. got on board tender for steamer. — At 11½ — off for home.

Journal 1860

Journal Kept on board Ship "Meteor" Thomas Melville, Commander: From Boston to San Francisco. Herman Melville, Passenger.

1860 Wednesday May 30th

At 10½ A.M. Tom, Fanny, George Griggs, and I went off to ship in the stream. Beautiful day, and pleasant sail down the harbor. Mr Peabody was on board, and lunched in the cabin. We bade Fanny good bye, and I assisted her into the tug-boat, preparatory to its going ahead to tow. At ¼ past one P.M. pilot and tug-boat left us. Waved our handkerchiefs to Fanny, and the voyage began. —— Quite sea-sick at night.

June 8th Friday

During the past days cloudy, foggy rainy weather, with good breeze generally, and sailing Eastward, or little south of East. — Gulf Stream disagreeable. But this there is a change. Clear & bright — light breeze. Wind still from the South. Sent up sky sail yard. Crew busy in rigging &c

June 11th Saturday Lat. 33." 21. Long. 41. 37. Ther. 76." 74.
The same bright, clear weather, growing warmer each day. Feel very sensibly improving in appetite &c, after seasick qualmishness. Have seen flying-fish, weed, Portuguese-men-of-war, and several sail lately. This afternoon had a collision with an English brig from Pernambuco bound for Liverpool. She blundered down across our bow, & was locked with us for a time; ripping & tearing her sails. We also were damaged in fore-yard & main. At the moment of collision the Steward of the brig being in jeopardy, leaped aboard of us, and, the vessels separating, remained aboard, till taken off by boat sent from the brig. He told me that the Captain was asleep in his berth when we came together, and added the Mate was half-blind &c. It was altogether an instance of the grossest heedlessness possible on the part of the brig — quite unaccountable. — When it was plain that she purposed crossing our bow, and that it was out of the question for her to do so, Tom at once put his helm up, and by so doing, we came off with less damage than could have been anticipated.

June 12th Sunday
Came out to day in light clothes.

June 20th Monday Lat. 18." 30
During the past week took the Trades — crossed the Northern Tropic — and last night saw the Southern Cross — the North Star sensibly sinking. Unvarying fine weather. Went out to flying-jib-boom end this morning. Glorious view of the ship. Spend the day dipping into the "Quarterlies", — find methodical reading out of the question. Not yet completely settled in my stomach. Head all right, tho'.

Wednesday June 27th 4" Lat. N.
For four days past been in the Doleful Doldrums, — the whole ship's crew given up to melancholly, and meditating darkly on the mysteries of Providence. But this morning, we have a wind, and feel better.

Friday. June 29th
Crossed the Line last evening. Saw bonetoes under the bow.

Sunday July 8th 18. 30 S. L. 33 30 W. L.
For the last five or six days — Calm — profound at times. Few or no fish seen. A comet made its appearance to the N. W the other night, & was still visable last night. At 4½ P.M. yesterday the Calcutta sow commenced delivering her pigs, and about 6½ P.M. concluded. Eleven were born, but two were dead: Thus, nine "souls" have been added to our company. Some ten days since the Carpenter made a set of chessmen; and Tom and I have played a game or two every evening. This morning sprang up a breeze — — I hope it will continue

Sunday July 21 S. Lat. 43° — W. Lon. 49°
Clear fine mild day. Speckled haglets & other birds about. Since writing last, have had two hard blows. Have a stove up in the cabin. Play chess every evening. Put up cabin-stove yesterday — started it this morning. Quite comfortable & domestic in the cabin now.

Monday Aug 8
Since last date have had several gales, with snow, rain, hail, sleet, mist, fog, squalls, head-winds, refractory stove, smoky cabin, drunken ship &c &c &c. — In one gale, several men washed off the t'gallant forecastle, and the boy Charlie was sent flying into the pig-pen, which was stove, & the sow & little pigs came, with the deluge, aft. One (pigling) drowned, poor fellow. — A man hurt by a sea; assisted his chum in getting him into his berth, the crew being engaged taking in sail. — One of the gales lasted three days. In one we split the mainsail all to pieces, & the mizzen topsail, and a staysail. — Days short — but not sweet. Winter.

Tuesday Aug 7th
At daylight made the land — Fair wind & pleasant. — Made Staten Land & N. W. Coast of Terra del Fuego. Two sail in sight. Entered the Straits of Le Maire, & through the short day had a fine view of the land on both sides — Horrible snowy mountains — black, thunder-cloud woods — gorges — hell-landscape. Signaled ship "Black Prince" from New York. — There are three on the Sick List. The man hurt by the sea — one with a fever — the third, a boy with general debility. —

Wednesday. Aug 8th
Moderate breeze & fair, but thick. Could not see the land, tho' to be wished. Just before sunset, in a squall, the mist lifted & showed, within 12 or fifteen miles the horrid sight of Cape Horn — (the Cape proper) — a black, bare steep cliff, the face of it facing the South Pole; — within some miles were other awful islands & rocks — an infernal group. Tried to weather Cape Horn, as sloops weather Castle Garden Point N.Y. — but were headed off. Tacked ship to the southward.

Thursday Aug 9th
A gale of wind, with snow & hail & sleet. —

Ray, a Nantucketer, about 25 years old, a good honest fellow (to judge from his face & demeanor during the passage) fell this morning about day-break from the main topsail yard to the deck, & striking head-foremost upon one of the spars was instantly killed. His chum, Macey (Fisher) of Nantucket, I found alone in the upper cabin sitting over the body — a harrowing spectacle. "I have lost my best friend", said he; and then "His mother will go crazy — she did not want to let him go, she feared something might happen." —— It was in vain to wash the blood from the head — the body bled incessantly & up to the moment of burying; which was about one o'clock, and from the poop, in the interval between blinding squalls of sharp sleet. Tom read some lines from the prayer-book — the plank was sloped, and —— God help his mother. — During the brief ceremony, made still the more trying from being under the lee of the reefed spanker where the wind eddies so — all stood covered with Sou-Westers or Russia caps & comforters, except Macey — who stood bareheaded. —— The Chief Mate imputes the fall to the excess of clothing worn, — excess, not as regards comfort — but activity aloft. — The ship's motion very violent to day.

Friday Aug 10th
—— Calm: blue sky, sun out, dry deck. Calm lasting all day —— almost pleasant enough to atone for the gales, but not for Ray's fate, which belongs to that order of human events, which staggers those whom the Primal Philosophy hath not confirmed. — But little sorrow to the crew — all goes on as usual — I, too, read & think, & walk & eat & talk, as if nothing had happened — as if I did not know that death is indeed the King of Terrors —— when thus happening; when

thus heart-breaking to a fond mother — the King of Terrors, not to the dying or the dead, but to the mourner — the mother. — Not so easily will his fate be washed out of her heart, as his blood from the deck.

Miscellaneous Entries in the Journal Notebooks

MELVILLE made these miscellaneous entries at various times, not all determinable. For clarity, these entries, unlike those in the main text of the journals, are presented here by their page or other location in the notebooks, with that location reported in the outside margin of the Northwestern-Newberry page. Melville wrote some of these entries in ink, some in pencil; and since no priority has been determined for them, all entries have been presented on the page, with textual notes at the foot of the page (or on the following page) reporting which ones he wrote in ink and which in pencil. (Unless reported otherwise, the ink is the usual brownish-black color.) Melville's exact placement of words on the page is not reproduced. Here, as in the journal texts proper, his indentations have been observed, but not his lineation, except in lists and changes in topic. Illustrations are reproduced at seventy-eight percent of the original size. The same principles of transcription have been followed as for the journals proper (see pp. 236–42). For description and dating of these miscellaneous entries in the first four notebooks, see pp. 213–30 in the NOTE ON THE TEXT and the discussions at 139.1–20, 147.1–9, 153.1–16, 154.1–6, and 157.8–10. For the abbreviations used in the footnotes, see p. 543.

[A, inside rear cover]

Oct. 15.	small bottle of stout (Dinner)
One bottle	"
two bottles	(one at night)
one bottle	(one at night)
" "	afternoon
" "	"

138.1–6 Oct. . . . "] *entry written in the upper left corner; the first line in ink, the remainder in pencil*

[B, front pastedown]

Allan	18		*Mama*	
$3.	Tickets	— 1.00	$1.	Mal
.75	Change	— .25	.50	Stan
.12½	Play			
1.	Supper	(Albany		

Friday
87½ Fare to Staten Island
87½ " back

Paid 50 cts For Mama

Saturday Greenwood

Ferry &c 14
Carriage 2.50
Ferry &c 12

Sunday, from Albany 37½

Albany — Augusta

Car fare $1.00

Ferry (1 & ½ Fares,) — 29
Mama to Lathers 60

139.1–20 Allan . . . 60] *entire page in pencil, written over earlier erased pencil notations*
139.1 18] *crossed through several times*
139.1 *Mama*] *lined through*
139.2 Mal] *written at far right margin*
139.3 .50 Stan] Stan *written at far right margin, then* .50 *and* Stan *lined through*
139.9 back] *connected by a curving line to* Paid *below*

[B1] Hair cut Saturday 9th June 18 St.
3. P.M.

Gabriel Miss
buss
Harlem & North

25
Washing Edinburgh

9 Shirts
1 Night Shirt
7 Hankerchiefs
2 Pair Stockings
Draws & undershirts

Red marked
laundry List

140.1–15 Hair . . . List] *with the exception of notations reported below, all in pencil, then erased; in pencil by ESM over erasures in upper part of page:* Herman Melville's Journal

140.6 25] *in ink*

140.7–13 Washing . . . undershirts] *laundry list written possibly in indelible pencil, possibly in ink, then incompletely erased*

140.9 9] *written over* 8 *or possibly vice versa*

140.14–15 Red . . . List] *boxed; below* List *in lower center of page are (1) impressions made by writing on a superimposed sheet, or sheets (the writing included a list with numbers in a column:* 1 / 1 / 2 / 1 / 1) *and (2) a formerly attached clipping:* "The Rev. Alex. J. D. D'Orsey, B.D., of Corpus Christi College, English Lecturer at Cambridge, and Lecturer in Public Reading at King's College, London,".

Captain R. J Fletcher. 1st Mate, Pendleton(?) — 2[d] Mate, Stokes. } Independence [B96]

——— " ——— " ———

Captain Griswold, 1st Mate Smith. 2[d] Mate } Southampton.

Conversations with the Colonel on fixed fate &c. during the passage.

The Perjurer — [B270]
"Hard is the choice when one is compelled either by silence to dye with grief or by speaking to live with shame."

141.1–9 Captain . . . passage.] *in ink*
141.1 R. J] *inserted above caret*
141.2 Independence] *inserted slantingly after brace*
141.6 Southampton.] *inserted slantingly after brace*
141.8–9 Conversations . . . passage.] *across center of page; the ink shows that this notation goes with succeeding pages B97–99, included in the 1856–57 journal, pp. 49–50*
141.10–12 The . . . shame."] *in pencil on top quarter of page, then erased*
141.11 compelled] *before canceled* by

[B271] Memoranda of things on the voyage
——— " ——— " ———

The pirate & the missionary. —— "All right" with a knowing look, wife on his arm. (Cap: Fletcher).

Smuggling grog — mustard bottle on his leg — skin in meat.
(Fletcher)

[B272] Fletcher's story about the catamount pursuing the runaway sailor thro' the horrible woods of Perue along the sea-coast. Leaping from bough to bough — He slept with his knife in his hand. —— (Recalled the "Opium Eater" & "crocodile")

Rousseau a schoolmaster. (2^d Vol, near beginning) "could have killed his scholars sometimes".
Dr Johnson an usher — "intolerable" (Vol. 1st) (Other allusions in 1st Vol Boswell)
3^d " P 220 — Do

"A finer man never broke the world's bread" — "If you have friends on the look-out I have a friend at the helm." — "Did that hamper of wine & those two hams send that man to jail?"

Allusion to *Cannibals* 17th page of Sir Thomas Browne. "Vulgar Errors" (Also page 57 of B. Jonson.

Indian (Gay-Head) Sweetheart flogged.

Ordering Sir Richard &C

[B273] A Dandy is a good fellow to scent a room with.

A comical duel Ben Jonson — page 51 ("Out of his humor") Fly — wounding our clothes.

Talk as much folly as you please — so long as you do it without blushing, you may do it with impunity —
— (B.J. p 54)

142.1–8 Memoranda . . . (Fletcher)] *page in ink*
142.1 the] e *rewritten*
142.10–31 Fletcher's . . . &C] *with the exception of notations reported below, all in ink*
142.17–19 (Other . . . Do] *inserted in pencil after* (Vol. 1st)
142.22 friends] *inserted with caret above canceled* men
142.26 *Cannibals*] ni *written over* a
142.27 (Also . . . Jonson.] *inserted in pencil in right margin*
142.29–31 Indian . . . &C] *these lines and rules in pencil*
142.31 Ordering] *written over* Ording
142.33 A . . . with] *in ink;* A . . . good *rewritten over original pencil; remainder of page in pencil*

[B276] Books obtained in London 1849
" "

Books	Source	£. S. D
Ben Jonson. folio 1692		.13.
Davenant. " 1673		.10.
Beaumont & Fletcher folio		.14.
Hudibras 18 mo. (old)		2.
Boswell's Johnson (10 vol. 18 mo.)		21.
Sir Thomas Browne folio. 1686		
3 copies of Mardi, from Bentley		
2 copies of "Redburn" from Bentley		
Guide Book for France	From Mr Murray.	
" " " Germany		
Knight's London (3 vol oct:)		1 .10. 0
Lavater		10.
Rosseau Confessions (		11.
Castle of Otranto		1.
2 plays of Shakspeare		. 2
Charles Lamb's works (octavo)	From Mr Moxon.	
Final Memorials of Lamb		
Guzman 3 Vol.		3.
Chatterton 2 "		
Old Map of London (1766.)		3. 6
Anastasius (2 vol)	Bentley	
Calleb Williams (1 vol)	Do	
Vathek (1 vol)	Do	
Corinne "	Do	
Frankenstein "	Do	
Aristocracy of England	Bow Street	5.
Marlowe's Plays	Do	
Autobiography of Goethe	(Bohn)	3.
Letters from Italy (Goethe	Do.	3.
Confessions of an Opium Eater.		1 6.

144.1–32 Books . . . 6.] *with the exception of notations reported below, all in ink*

144.1 1849] *inserted in pencil after* London

144.3–32 Ben . . . Eater.] *check marks before items 1, 3, 5, 6, 13, 16-19, 21, 22, 24, 25*

144.3 folio] *followed by an earlier pound sign between the two columns, imperfectly rubbed out*

144.3 1692] *inserted in pencil above* Ben Jonson

144.4 1673] *inserted in pencil above* Davenant

144.8 1686] *inserted in pencil after* folio.

144.15 Confessions (] *single open parenthesis followed by incomplete letter*

[B276]

[B277]

Books obtained in Paris
—— " —— " ——

Telemachus — About 2 francs.
Anastasius (2 Vol) " 4 "
Views of Paris. (R.R. Station.)

Books obtained in Germany
—— " —— " ——

"Lays & Legends of the Rhine"	.	Coblentz.
"Up the Rhine"	.	Cologne
Panorama of the Rhine	.	"

Paris "Curios"
— " —

Medal of Napoleon & Josephene	.	5 francs
" (Battle)		1 "

Porcelain stoppers — Cologne.
2½ Groschen (6 pence)

[B278]

Copy of

146.1–16 Books . . . pence)] *in ink*
146.11 *Paris*] *written along left margin; placed here editorially*
146.17 Copy of] *in ink, centered at top of page*

Dr O. S. Root. [B281]
Rev. George R. Entler
Harford, Cortland Co. NY
Dr Robert Campbell.
George S. Willis
James Colt Jr.
Rockwell & Colt
Julius S. Rockwell.
Philip Marett Esq. New Haven
Conn.
Metropolitan N.Y.

Monday 19 Nov: [B282]
6½ P.M. Haymarket with Mr Langford.
Tuesday 20th
Mrs Lawrence, Clarendon, 8. P.M. (call)
Wednesday 21
9½ P.M. Langford 3 Furnival Inn
Supper.

Thursday 22

Friday 23
Murray's ¼ before 7 — dine, Lockhart.

Cannibals [B283]
Execution
Terrapin

147.1–11 *Dr* . . . N.Y.] *in ink; italicized names incompletely underlined*
147.7 Rockwell & Colt] *after canceled* Lawyer
147.11 Metropolitan N.Y.] *below this line, lower third of page torn off*
147.12–21 Monday . . . Lockhart.] *in blue ink*
147.12 Monday 19 Nov:] *originally* Tuesday 20th Nov. *centered at top of page, then canceled, and corrected date inserted above at left*
147.14 Tuesday 20th] *interlined*
147.22–24 Cannibals . . . Terrapin] *in pencil, centered at top of page*

[B284] *M. F. Tupper* — Albany, Guildford — By London Bridge — about 20 miles (Hatchards')

Lord John Manners — town address N° 3 Albany. — Belvoir Castle, Leicester.

Longmans 37 Paternoster Row.

Mr Langford Furnival's Inn. (3)

Mulligan (Wm) 45 Walker St — N.Y.

Lady Elizabeth Drummond 2 Bryanston Square. & Cadland, Southhampton.

U.S. Legation 1 Upper Belgrave Street.

J. Bates 46 Portland Place. Near Park Crescent. } New Road omnibus

Russell Sturgis 27 Upper Harley Street

Edward Moxon 44 Dover Street, Piccadilly. Nearly opposite St. James' Street — back of Murray's.

G J Adler No 3 Rue de la Convention, Paris.

Albert Smith 14 Percy Street, Bedford Square.

J Bates (country address) East Sheen, Surry.

Duke of Rutland's is in Leicester.

R. M. Milnes Fryston, Ferrybridge, Yorkshire.

Richard Bentley 29 Broad Street, Brighton.

Robert Francis Cooke. 4 Elm Court, Temple.

Alfred Henry Forrester (Crowquill) 3 Portland Place, North Clapham Road.

John Miller, Tavistock Street, Covent Garden.

Mr Cleaves — 9 King's Bench Walk, Temple. (11 O'Clock, Friday)

John Foster 58 Lincoln's Inn Fields

George C. Rankin Esq. 25th Reg. Nat. Inft. Hadgeepore, Punjab.

148.1–29 *M.* . . . Punjab.] *in ink, except for notations reported below*
148.1 *F.*] *crossed a second time with blue ink*
148.1 Guildford] o *inserted above in blue ink*
148.6 *Langford*] ford *inserted with caret above canceled* don *(underlined)*
148.8 Bryanston] *original final* e *canceled in blue ink*
148.10 Belgrave] *after canceled* Berkely
148.11–16 Near . . . Square.] *in blue ink except underlining under* Albert Smith *where usual brownish-black ink appears*
148.11–12 New Road omnibus] *inserted slantingly after brace*
148.15 *J*] *converted from another letter*
148.26 (11 O'Clock, Friday)] *on rear pastedown just across from* Temple.
148.28–29 George . . . Punjab.] *added in pencil during 1856–57 voyage*

[B284]

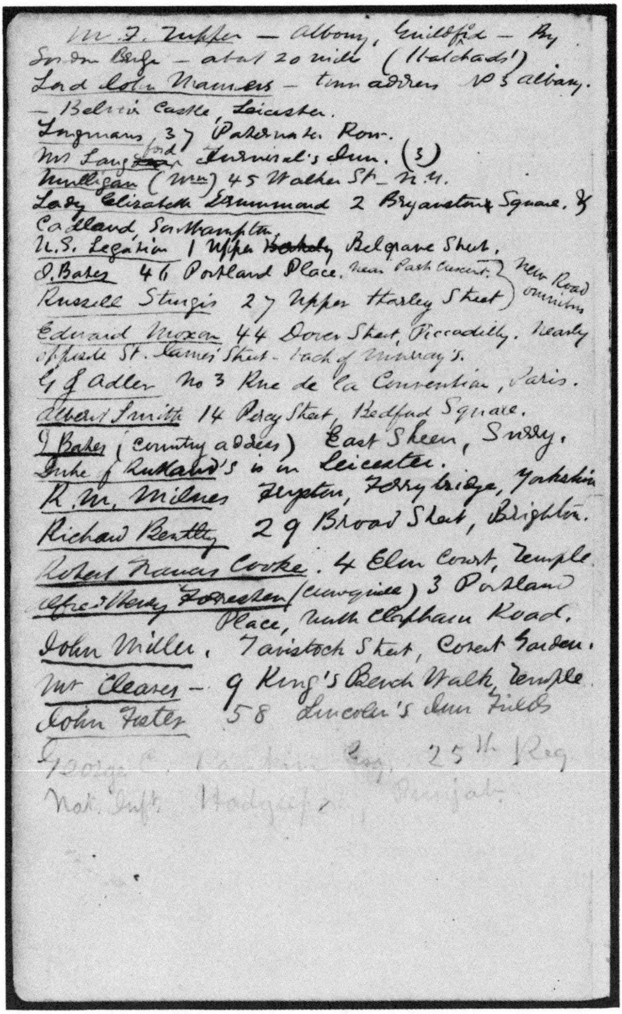

[B, rear pastedown] 14 S. for spoon.

L. J. Manners
Belvoir Castle
Leicester

Sampson Low 169 Fleet St:
Harpers Agent.

[C, inside front cover] Sn

Straps for gaiters

[C43] "Bobby Jock." — Dispute whether any men are content. Foolish fellow found. Said he was content — perfectly. — Sure? — Yes. — Never annoyed by anything? No. — Think. — No — But think — Yes, there is one thing, when I go into the streets all the boys cry out There goes Silly Bobby.

Captains wives at sea. Ship cast away while Captain holding his wife's head — sea-sick.

≡ The Juggler's Exposure in Edinburgh &C.
(Story of the Pantaloons in the Indes)
(Taylor's offer to be cicerone.)

150.1 14 . . . spoon.] *in ink*
150.1–3 L. . . . Leicester] *in pencil*
150.4–5 Sampson . . . Agent.] *in ink*
150.6 Sn] *in ink, in top left corner; in pencil below, notation by ESM, written large:* Herman Melville's Journal
150.7 Straps for gaiters] *in pencil*
150.8–18 "Bobby . . . cicerone.)] *in ink*
150.11 Yes] *after rubbed-out* Oh
150.13 Silly] *written over rubbed-out* Foolish

"Bobby Lock." — Dispute whether any men are content. Foolish fellow found. Said he was content — perfectly. Sure? — Yes. — Never annoyed by anything? No. — Think. — No — But think — Yes, there is one thing, when I go into the street all the boys cry out There goes Silly Bobby.

Captain's nerves at sea. Ship astray while Captain holding his nose. Cause — sea-sick.

: The Juggler's Escapism in Edinburgh &c.
(Story of the Pantaloons in the Indies)
(Taylor's offer to be cicerone.)

[C43]

[C44]

Cemeteries

Memoranda

Dardeneles

On the Bridge.

[D, front pastedown] Sanders

American Gentleman at Jaffa

[D, front free endpaper, recto] Bought this book at Bazaar in Constantinople

152.1–4 Cemeteries . . . Bridge.] *in pencil, centered, and written large on top half of page*

152.5–6 Sanders . . . Jaffa] *in pencil, at top of page*

152.7 Bought . . . Constantinople] *in ink, centered, in two lines, in upper quarter of page, with large notation by ESM in pencil centered below:* Herman Melville's Journal

[A pocket-compass were very useful in Constantinople. [D, front free end-paper, verso]

For the Story { [Pera, the headquarters of embassadors, and where also an unreformed diplomacy is carried on by swindlers, gamblers, cheats. No place in the world fuller of knaves.

[Contrast of Dardeneles with Sts: of Gibralter.

[Salonica is, next to Constantinople, the cheif place of commerce in European Turkey.

[Entering Europe by back door

[Man is a noble animal, splendid in epitaphs &c — (Inscription of the onion in Cheops)

[Lore of the "Bible" — Amsterdam — like the "Press"]

The Burnt Districts.

153.1–2 A . . . Constantinople.] *in pencil, with ink bracket added before* A

153.3–5 For the Story] *these words and brace in pencil*

153.3–15 [Pera . . . Districts.] *in ink*

153.13 [Lore] *before opening bracket, in left margin, two short horizontal lines with wavy scrawl between*

[D145] Frescoes of Travel

by

Three Brothers

Rosseau	}	Venice
Cicero		Olympus
Byron		Parthenon
Haydon		Leonardo.

Poet, Painter, and Idler.

J. C. should have appeared in Taheiti.
— Land of palms. —
Palm Sunday — Beautiful Gate.
—— " ——

Jerusalem seen from Bethalem Road.

Spinoza, Rothschild &c. &.

Goods laid up in mosque — Maccabees —
Same in Temple — ("M. 2B. 3C.) (Note)

Noah after the Flood.

Eclipse.
Cap. Pollard.
of *Nant.*

154.1–5 Frescoes . . . Idler.] *title, columns of names, and brace in ink*
154.5 Idler.] *after canceled* Scholar
154.6–8 J. C. . . . Gate.] *these lines and division mark in pencil, then lined through in pencil*
154.10 Jerusalem . . . Road.] *in red pencil, then lined through in black pencil*
154.11 Spinoza . . . &.] *in red pencil*
154.12–13 Goods . . . (Note)] *these lines and brace in pencil*
154.14–16 *Noah . . . Nant.*] *in ink*

Subjects for Roman Frescoes [D146]

{*A group of cyprusses* in Villa D'Este.
Whispering apart like Angelo's "Fates"

{From *Tartarus to Tivoli*
is but a step or two

{The Cenci portrait

{Sixtus V[th] — His obelisks &c
Sprung from the people — What it was to be Pope in those days. No democracies — Only way of rising to preeminence — & such preeminence. — What he did in order to be this.

155.1 *Subjects . . . Frescoes*] *in pencil, in two lines, written large*
155.2–6 *A group* . . . portrait] *in pencil, except for ink brace before* The Cenci
155.2 *cyprusses*] es *added (not underlined)*
155.7–11 Sixtus . . . this.] *these words and brace in ink*

[D147] Oxford

— " —

(Transferred from small pocket book)

It was in Oxford that I confessed for the first, & with glad gratitude, my mother land. — Oxford to an American of taste as well worth seeing as Paris. — — Pulpet in corner of quadrangle. — Deer — green gardens — water courses — sheep — meadow beyond. — rafters of roof of cloister of Spanish cedar. —

Spire offspring of peaked roof. Final result of elevating & sharpening a roof in snowy countries.

Dormer window of gable.

Meadows of Christ Church.

Old reef washed by waves — standing fast — so Oxford. — Ivy branch interleaving with twigs of sculpture over Gothic door. — Union of Art & Nature.

Contagion in Pamfili Doria, but *wholesome* beauty in Oxford.

[D148] Learning in Oxford lodged like a baron Garden to every college. Lands for centuries never violated by sordid labor — profane hand of enterprise — sacred to beauty & tranquillity.

Fell's avenue of elms.

Every college has dining halls & chapel — soul & body equally provided for.

The picturesque in sculpture goes not beyond Oxford.

Grass smooth as green baize of billiard table.

I know nothing more fitted by a mild & beautiful rebuke to chastise the sophomorean pride of America as a new & prosperous country.

In such a retreat old Burton composed his book, sedately smiling at men

[D149] They have beheld all revolutions unchanged. Improvement upon the monkish cloister As Knights-templers were half soldier half monk — so these half monk half gentleman.

These colleges founded as men plant trees — for posterity

156.1–18 Oxford . . . Oxford.] *in ink*
156.10–11 Final . . . countries.] *inserted in ink, in right margin, marked for transposition by paired X's with dots in the interstices*
156.19–32 Learning . . . men] *in ink*
156.20 sordid] *after canceled* labor
156.24 Every college has] *inserted in left margin before* Dining *(vestigial capital)*
156.33–38 They . . . posterity] *in ink*
156.35 soldier half] half *miswritten* have
156.37 founded] *inserted above caret*

[D147]

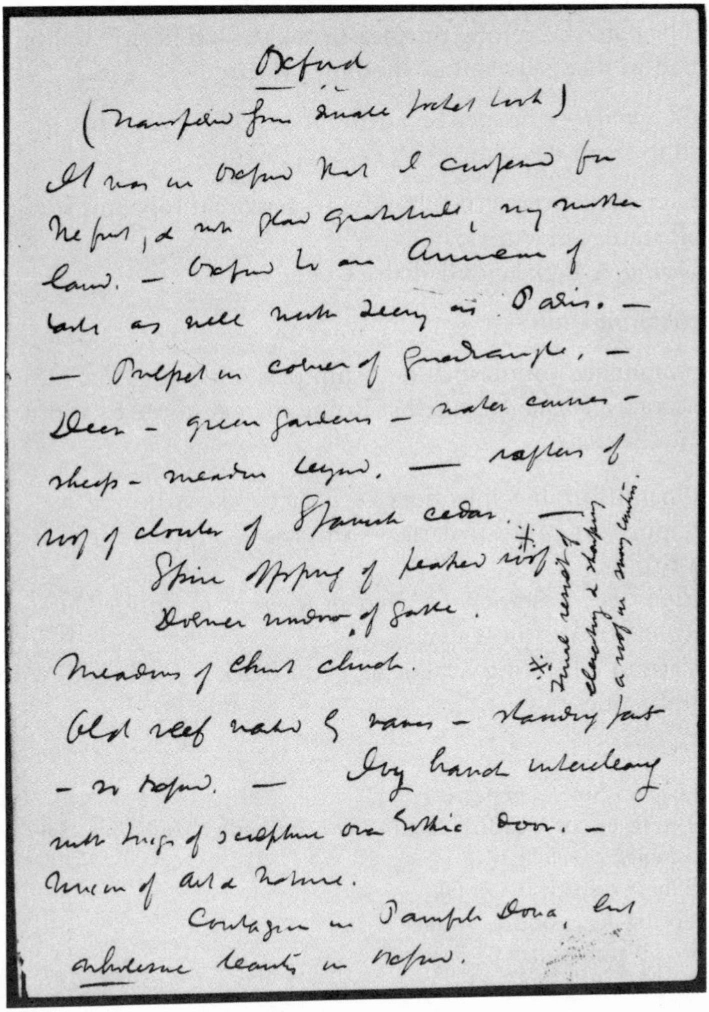

[D230] The Vatican (A volume)
Busts of Titus & Tiberius (side by side)
Rome.

Bitterness — Dead Sea. (Bitterness of Death)

[The cyprus in the Villa D'Este
Whispering like Michael Angelo's "Fates"
"Dolce Niente" (Sung softly)

[D232] [Seeing is beleiving.
The pains lie among the pleasures like sand in rice, not only bad in themselves, but spoiling the good.

St Sophia — Suspended from above like fully blossomed tulip from its stem. —

Colisseum. great green hollow — restore it repeople it with all statues in Vatican
Dying & Fighting Gladiators.

Restoring ruins —

7 branched candlestick — Sculptor's criticism.
More imagination wanted *at* Rome than at home to appreciate the place

Uncomfortable splendors — palaces like dripping ice. — Supurb St Paul's malaria — Smyrna robe splendor in richest folds.
Ruins look as much out of place in Rome as *in British Museum.*
Rivers of Virgin water.
Vatican like long walks in great Park — arbored with arabesques.

158.1–5 The . . . Sea.] *in pencil*
158.5 (Bitterness of Death)] *inserted in pencil with a wavy line above and another below*
158.6–8 [The . . . softly)] *in ink*
158.9–11 [Seeing . . . good.] *in ink*
158.12–28 *St* . . . arabesques.] *in pencil*
158.13 from] *after canceled* by
158.25 *much*] inserted above

[D233]

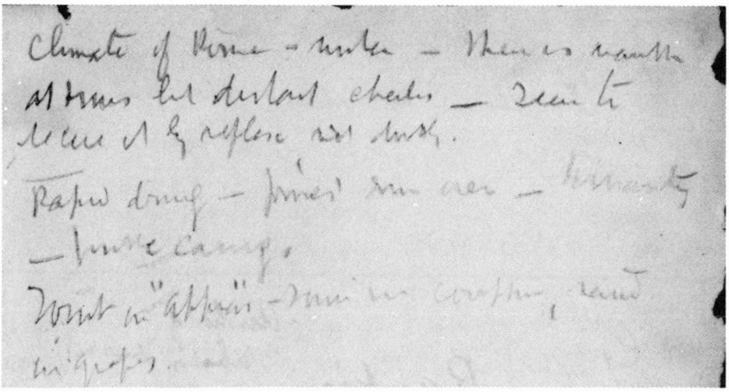

Climate of Rome — winter — there is warmth at times but distant cheerless — seem to receive it by reflex not directly. [D233]

Rapid driving — priest run over — humanity — public carriage.
Tomb on "Appian" — sown in corruption, raised in grapes.

De Leon Consul at Alexandria. [D234]
George Wood (Concord N.H.) " " Beyrout
Daniel McCartan. Poughkeepsie.

G. C. Rankin Author of *"What is Truth?"*
E.I.U.S. Club
14 St James Square.

159.1–8 Climate . . . grapes.] *in pencil*
159.9 De Leon . . . Alexandria.] *in ink*
159.10 George] *inserted in pencil before* ink Wood
159.10 (Concord N.H.)] *inserted in pencil before rest of line in ink*
159.11 Daniel . . . Poughkeepsie.] *in pencil*
159.12 G. C. Rankin] *in ink, written large*
159.12 Author . . . *Truth?"*] *inserted just above in ink*
159.13–14 E. . . . Square.] *in ink, written large*

Editorial Appendix

HISTORICAL NOTE
By Howard C. Horsford

TEXTUAL RECORD
By Howard C. Horsford
with Lynn Horth

RELATED DOCUMENTS
By Harrison Hayford

THE FIRST *of the three parts of this* APPENDIX *is a Historical Note on the background and composition of the journals, contributed by the primary volume editor, Howard C. Horsford. The second part, the Textual Record, consists of a note on the text and editorial principles of this edition; discussions of Melville's numerous references and of certain problematical readings; textual notes on features of the manuscripts; and a report of line-end hyphenation. The third part presents related documents: two sets of Melville's memoranda in books, and further records of his trips abroad.*

To insure uniform textual policy in all volumes of the Northwestern-Newberry Edition, the same three editors, Harrison Hayford, Hershel Parker, and G. Thomas Tanselle, participate in the planning and establishment of textual policy for all volumes, except as otherwise noted; even when other editors are named (as in the case here of writings edited from manuscript), the final decisions still rest with one or more of these editors, as noted in individual volumes. Final responsibility for all aspects of every volume is exercised by the general editor, Harrison Hayford.

Editorial work on the Northwestern-Newberry Journals *volume was begun in 1965 under an initial grant from the U.S. Office of Education. Howard C. Horsford undertook in 1965 to revise the earlier editions from the manuscripts on the principles of the Edition, and to supply annotations and materials for the textual notes (see p. 212). Subsequent changes in the principles of the Edition with respect to manuscripts not intended for publication required his later reworking the texts he contributed in 1969. From 1986 to publication of the volume in 1989, he was in constant consultation with Lynn Horth in her editorial work on it as stated below; he reviewed all changes by the series editors and read all the successive proofs. While the Historical Note and the Discussions are substantially those he originally supplied, they have been so revised and supplemented that not all textual readings, facts, opinions, or turns of phrase are now his, and consequently not all can be attributed to him. His few disagreements with readings adopted in the text by the series editors are all reported in the Discussions with his preferred readings marked (H). Likewise, some textual decisions and emphases of opinion may not be those preferred by one or another of the editors involved.*

Lynn Horth, as executive editor of the Edition, under grants from the National Endowment for the Humanities, assumed full-time responsibility for verifying Horsford's texts from the manuscripts, for checking and augmenting the Discussions, and for developing the Textual Notes and the Note on the Text. She operated the word processor to produce the crucial disks from which the text was typeset, proofread the whole repeatedly, and supervised the other proofreadings. She also selected the illustrations and directed preparation of the maps.

G. Thomas Tanselle, as bibliographical editor of the whole Edition, wrote the sections on textual policy and textual apparatus for the final form of the Note on the Text, adapting materials supplied by Horsford and following, where applicable, the basic pattern and wording set by the series editors in other volumes. In addition, he approved all information presented in the Textual Record.

Harrison Hayford took primary responsibility for shaping the materials supplied by Horsford to conform with the patterns established for the whole Edition in the intervening years. He prepared the Related Documents and worked closely with Lynn Horth in verifying the texts from manuscripts and photocopies and in proofreading at all stages.

Alma A. MacDougall, as editorial coordinator of the Edition since 1981, contributed to every aspect of the volume. She supervised its production, provided copyediting and proofreading, assisted in verifying the texts, and prepared the index.

The editors were given frequent aid and counsel by the bibliographical associate, Richard Colles Johnson. In the initial stages Joel Myerson, as contributing scholar, supervised assembly of materials. In later stages Robert C. Ryan, the manuscript associate, reexamined numerous difficult textual readings in the manuscripts. R. D. Madison, editorial associate, consulted on nautical matters. Staff members of the Newberry Library deserve thanks for indispensable assistance: Kenneth Cain for photographing illustrations, Thomas Willcockson for making or adapting the maps, John Aubrey and Jerrylyn Marshall for finding books. Further assistance was given by Paula Backscheider, Theresa Biancheri, Ann Larson, Lee C. Mitchell, Carla Reiter, Catherine Strassner, Cynthia Warner, Mary Valentine, and the late Sheila Robertson. The assistance of others is acknowledged at appropriate points in the EDITORIAL APPENDIX.

Authorization to edit manuscripts and permission to publish material from their collections has been granted by (1) the Houghton Library, Harvard University; (2) the Newberry Library, Chicago (Melville Collection); (3) the New York Public Library, Astor, Lenox and Tilden Foundations (Duyckinck Collection and Melville Family Papers, Gansevoort-Lansing Collection, Rare Books and Manuscripts Division); and (4) the British Museum. The editors have also made use of materials in the collections of the New York Public Library, Northwestern University Library, the Library of Congress, the Berkshire Athenæum, the Boston Athenoeum, the Widener Library of Harvard University, the University of Rochester Library, the Herrick Memorial Library of Alfred University, the Walter C. Hinkle Memorial Library of the State University of New York, Agricultural and Technical College at Alfred, the Philadelphia Free Library, and the U.S. Naval Academy Museum. They are indebted for information and assistance to Nicolas Barker, Ruth T. Degenhardt, Dr. Estelle Foote, Alan Frost, Norma Higgins, Jean Lang, Daniel Owen, Kathleen Reilly, and Karen Tschang.

Renewed acknowledgment is made here to those whose assistance was recorded by Eleanor Melville Metcalf in her edition of the 1849–50 journal and by Howard C. Horsford in his Princeton (1955) edition of the 1856–57 journal. With the permission of Princeton University Press, the present edition draws freely on the annotations and index and adapts the maps in that edition. Use of annotative material from the Metcalf edition is acknowledged by the initials EMM.

Melville in his late twenties, before his first European tour. An oil portrait (ca. 1845–47) by Asa Weston Twitchell (see p. 254 below). Courtesy of the Berkshire Athenaeum, Pittsfield, Massachusetts.

Historical Note

IN EACH of the three journals presented in this volume Herman Melville recorded his actions and observations on a single trip from home. The first journal covers his business trip to London and side-excursion to the Continent in 1849–50; the second, his health-excursion to England, the Near East, and Europe in 1856–57; and the third, his voyage for the same purpose around Cape Horn to San Francisco in 1860. The three journals thus record the only extended trips he took during his career as a professional writer, after his first merchant-sailor voyage to Liverpool in 1839 and his whaling and naval cruises in the Pacific in 1841–44. Those earlier voyages yielded materials for the six books of his early literary career: *Typee* (1846), *Omoo* (1847), *Mardi* (1849), *Redburn* (1849), *White-Jacket* (1850), and *Moby-Dick* (1851). In the preface to *Omoo* he declared that "No journal was kept by the author during his wanderings in the South Seas," and nothing in the form or content of any of these six books suggests that he worked from a journal in writing it.[1]

1. See the Northwestern-Newberry edition of *Omoo* (1971), p. xiv; see also the Hendricks House edition (1969), p. 343, note 2.20. In the section on "Sources" at the end of this NOTE its documentation is explained and its short citations are given in

The three journals presented here are Melville's only known writings in this form, and there is no evidence that he wrote any others. Unlike his great contemporaries Emerson, Thoreau, and Hawthorne, he kept no habitual journal of his days and thoughts; and if he ever, like Whitman or Henry James, kept any sporadic ones or any notebooks of memoranda or notes for literary use, none are known to survive.[2] The first two of the present journals, one written near the peak and the other near the end of his years as a professional writer, both show clear signs that he kept them at least in part to supply matter for future literary use; and indeed he drew upon both for subsequent fictional or poetic pieces. The ensuing NOTE places each journal in the context of Melville's literary career, discusses its general character, and points out such later literary uses.

II

The main reason Melville went to London in 1849 was to conduct negotiations for the publication in England of his fifth book, *White-Jacket*. Its American edition, to be published by Harper & Brothers, was already in proofs, of which he took a set with him as the basis of his negotiations and as printer's copy for the English edition.[3] Another,

---

full. Parenthetical references to the texts of the journals are by page and line of the present edition.

2. Such memoranda do survive in at least three of his books: on the endpapers of Volume VII of Shakespeare's *Dramatic Works* (Boston: Hilliard, Gray, 1837; Sealts 460), as well as of Hawthorne's *Mosses from an Old Manse* (New York: Wiley & Putnam, 1846; Sealts 248), and on paper bound into Owen Chase's *Narrative of . . . the Whale-Ship Essex* (New York: Gilley, 1821; Sealts 133). All three sets of notes are reproduced and transcribed in the Northwestern-Newberry Edition: the first and third in Volume VI, *Moby-Dick* (1988), pp. 955–95; the second in the present volume, pp. 599–607. The notebook in which Melville and his wife recorded his 1857–60 lecture engagements and fees has no literary memoranda; see Volume IX, *THE PIAZZA TALES and Other Prose Pieces, 1839–1860* (1987), pp. 799–807. His nearest surviving approach to another journal—apart from letters covering several days—was written on the blank front leaves of *A History of the County of Berkshire, Massachusetts* (Pittsfield, 1829; Sealts 216) as a memorandum (not daily entries) of an agricultural inspection tour of the county, July 18–20, 1850; this memorandum (with other notes) is reproduced and transcribed in the present volume, pp. 589–98 (see also Volume VIII, *Israel Potter* [1982], p. 186, n. 12).

3. For publication details cited here and below, see the HISTORICAL NOTE in the Northwestern-Newberry edition of each book.

more loosely defined reason was to travel for a few months in Europe, perhaps as far as Rome. His 1849–50 journal is his day-by-day record of that trip.

Financial as well as personal and literary motives impelled Melville's decision to make the trip. The unusually long time he had devoted to *Mardi* had financially dangerous consequences. True enough, *Typee* and *Omoo* had brought him considerable international acclaim, but *Mardi*, for which he had high ambitions, puzzled even well-disposed reviewers and was savaged by others. His marriage in August of 1847, to Elizabeth, daughter of Chief Justice Lemuel Shaw of Massachusetts, was auspicious; but for economy he and his next younger brother Allan, also newly wedded, had set up joint housekeeping in New York, where they could make a home for their brides, widowed mother, and unmarried sisters. Within two days of each other, in February of 1849, two infants had been added to the crowded household: Malcolm, the son of Herman and Elizabeth, and Maria, the daughter of Allan and his wife.

In the early months of 1849 Melville managed to conclude the bargaining for the English edition of *Mardi*. Next he wrote another fictional narrative, *Redburn*, based on his own early voyage to Liverpool, and arranged its American and English publication. Then at once he dashed off during the hot, cholera-ridden summer months a fourth such narrative, *White-Jacket*, derived from his own service aboard the frigate *United States*. These two books were written in such haste and under such pressures that ever afterward he professed to scorn them, particularly *Redburn*. In this 1849–50 journal, for instance, twice he slightingly calls *Redburn* a "thing" (31.21–22, 47.15).

By summer's end Melville was in debt to Harper & Brothers, his American publishers, by just over $1,300, including an advance of $300 for *Redburn* and another of $500 for *White-Jacket*. The problem confronting him was to secure the best possible terms for English publication of the latter. John Murray III, whose firm was then perhaps the most distinguished in England, had brought out *Typee* and *Omoo*, but in the relatively inexpensive Colonial and Home (later Home and Colonial) Library series. That series was aimed principally at the colonial market, notably Canada, which had been forbidden cheap non-British editions by the copyright legislation of 1842. But the series, really neither cheap nor "light" enough for colonial tastes, had not been very successful. Moreover, there had been some objection to the inclusion in a "Home" series of Melville's two South Seas narratives because they were "licentious" and "lascivious." In any event, Murray canceled the series in 1849 and in late February refused *Mardi*, giving as his reason (according to John R. Brodhead, who acted as Melville's agent in London) that it was "fiction" and didn't "suit him."[4] However, when Brodhead at once took it to Richard Bentley, who liked to publish American writing and had a long fiction list, Bentley quickly accepted *Mardi*, gave a 200-guinea advance, and published it in mid-March. But when he was offered *Redburn* in June in a letter from Melville, he naturally hesitated in view of both the severity of important reviews *Mardi* was receiving and its lagging sales. Even more troublesome was the judicial decision just handed down (described below) that appeared to devastate British copyright protection for foreign works. Nevertheless, on June 20 he wrote accepting *Redburn*, and though he offered an advance of only £100 instead of the £150 Melville had asked, Melville accepted the offer a month later.

Such was the problematic situation Melville faced in August with the English placing of *White-Jacket*, which was written as hastily and under the same pressures as *Redburn*, and with even more distractions. Surely he was weary from his summer's unremitting labor, was manifestly irritated with the necessity he had been under of writing to suit popular taste, and possibly felt short of experiences to make into further books. At any rate, along with a tourist's pleasurable anticipations (and perhaps an inadmissible wish for a recess from a demanding household), he thought it worthwhile to deal with British publishers face to face. For the four earlier books he had had to depend upon intermediaries, but now he hoped that in spite of the aggravated uncertainties of copyright, he could strike a better bargain in person.[5] By the end of August he had resolved upon a trip to London and the Continent which would replenish his pockets, spirits, and literary materials.

4. Barnes (1974), pp. 143–46; Paston (1932), p. 53; see also the discussion at 18.3 in the DISCUSSIONS section below.

5. Although N. P. Willis in January of 1850 wrote that before sailing Melville did not know about the newest adverse ruling, his foregoing correspondence with Bentley and Brodhead shows that he did. See the Northwestern-Newberry edition of *Redburn* (1969), p. 320, and Melville's letter to Bentley, July 20, 1849.

III

For the crossing, Melville engaged passage on the big new packet *Southampton*, a sailing ship (slower but less expensive than a steamer) on which he enjoyed the unshared luxury of a first-class cabin. Departure from the ship's usual East River pier had been scheduled for October 8 (a Monday, and one of the four-times-monthly regular dates), then postponed to the tenth, then to the eleventh, because of violent autumnal storms. The *New York Journal of Commerce* for the tenth reported that the weekend storm was the worst of the season, with unusually high tides, flooded wharves, and great damage to shipping. Its next issue, for Saturday the thirteenth, added that "another rain storm commenced early last Wednesday evening, and continued most of the time until we went to press." Melville went aboard on that Wednesday, the tenth, but with some embarrassment returned home again for the night; the ship cleared at last on the eleventh, ahead of a strong northwest wind. Although he expected that, as was often done, friends would accompany him to the Narrows, then return on the tug with the pilot, no one went because the day was so rainy. But by early the next week the ship was beginning to get Gulf Stream weather.

On the North Atlantic route, dominated by American ships, though the great days of the fast-sailing packets were ending, the *Southampton* had just been launched; advertisements by the owners promised, "These ships are all of the first class, and are commanded by able and experienced navigators. Great care will be taken that the beds, wines, stores, &c., are of the best description. The price of cabin passage is now fixed at $75 outward [recently reduced because of competition with steamships], for each adult, without wines and liquors."[6] Packet ships out of New York were, in fact, known for good tables, with fresh meats, milk, and eggs, from a virtual farmyard on the upper deck. Commonly breakfast was served at eight, lunch at noon, dinner at four, and tea at eight in the evening, even if dinner might already have lasted as long as two hours. For the rest, as Melville's journal notes, the hours were often occupied with impromptu entertainments devised by the passengers. Eastbound, at least, the packets were nearly as fast as the early steamers, and their

6. *New York Journal of Commerce,* e.g., Saturday, October 6, 1849.

superior accommodations helped keep them in competition. Westbound, however, especially in winter, without favoring winds and a course north of the now adverse current of the Gulf Stream, the passage could be very much rougher and very much slower, longer by five hundred or even seven hundred miles in January gales, with a consequent additional fare of one guinea for the extra meals. To meet North Atlantic winds and seas, these square-rigged, three-masted ships were constructed to be the strongest afloat; late ones might, like the *Southampton*, have three decks. But no matter how violent the passage, owners expected the captains to carry all possible sail; the hard-driven crew did not like the service and was usually a rough, tough lot. Besides the captain, packets carried a first and second mate, a third on larger ships, commonly a steward or two, and on the London route a stewardess. While ordinary seamen disliked the service, to be captain was a high ambition, and because of his relative intimacy with passengers a successful captain had also to be a sociable, intelligent host. He was paid a substantial portion of the passengers' fares, and popular ones like Captain Griswold might also expect gifts from them. Melville found Griswold congenial and in London collected money among the passengers to present him a book. In other ways, too, Melville much enjoyed the trip, showing off in the rigging, visiting the seasick, and engaging in long philosophical, theological, and political discussions, particularly with George J. Adler, a scholar of German literature and philosophy. As momentous as anything on Melville's whole trip, in its aftereffects upon his thought and writings, was his congenial companionship with Adler on the ship, in London, and in Paris.[7] With Adler and Dr. Franklin Taylor (Bayard Taylor's cousin) Melville enthusiastically projected an excursion across Europe, into Greece, and on to Constantinople, Jerusalem, and Egypt—perhaps, somehow, even to Spain. Less intoxicatedly he still hoped to see Rome.

With considerable self-consciousness and a wry flourish, Melville concluded his journal's shipboard entries in early November as the ship approached the English coast: "This time tomorrow I shall be on land, & press English earth after the lapse of ten years — *then* a sailor,

7. The importance of the relationship with Adler, in the foreground of *Moby-Dick*, is discussed by Lee (1974), Heffernan (1986), and Marovitz (1986). For Adler, see the discussion at 4.13.

now H.M. author of 'Peedee' 'Hullabaloo' & 'Pog-Dog' " (12.6–9). Before, in June of 1839, he had been only an impoverished greenhorn, not quite twenty years old when he left his home in upstate New York to ship on his first voyage, as a "boy"—the lowest class of common sailor— aboard the *St. Lawrence*, a Liverpool trader. Now, just past thirty, a husband, a recent father, and a popular author, he was ready to enter London with letters of introduction from and to important people, and entrée to negotiate with the most distinguished publishers in England.

Once ashore on November 5, Melville kept up his journal faithfully. As for his way of making its entries, he did not usually write down a day's events at that day's end, though in contrast to his practice in the two later journals he was conscientious in keeping it, usually writing up a day first thing the next morning, at other times "bringing up" several past days at a time. As a journal, its appeal is only secondarily literary, yet it has the interest of showing a young writer, of remarkably lively and independent mind, still in the first flush of his success, somewhat anxious about money and the unsettled state of copyright, but fundamentally confident in his new powers, glad for the sea-change and to be footloose for a while and traveling, but also in the end eager to get home to his wife and child.

Neither in this journal nor in the two later ones are current affairs recorded beyond passing allusions. That Melville was nevertheless much interested in them had been attested a few months earlier by the sections of political allegory he added to *Mardi*, and it was to be shown in after years by his response in poetry to the actualities of the Civil War. But in the 1849 journal, among many things not mentioned, or only obliquely alluded to, is, for example, the sordid death of Poe—while Melville was waiting to board, the *New-York Tribune* of October 9 carried the news and Rufus Griswold's pseudonymous hostile account of Poe's life. Or the Gold Rush—the *Tribune* of October 10 devoted its feature article and half its back page to the arrival of the ship *Empire City* with a million dollars in gold and the latest California news. The devastating cholera epidemics in both New York and London—like that dramatized in *Redburn*—are only indirectly mentioned in the journal, and no mention is made of the Irish famine, or the revolutionary uprisings of 1848 and their aftermaths, or the emergence of Louis Napoleon; only very indirectly do we hear of the tense state of Paris—though all of these had been treated in

Mardi. Walking in London through the appalling slums around Seven Dials and St. Giles, as he did repeatedly, Melville must have been as acutely aware of misery as his Redburn had been in Liverpool. But this awareness is not reflected in the journal. (Curiously enough, however, three years later in a list he made for his uncle Peter Gansevoort, who was on his way to London, he recommended the gin shops of this area as one of the sights to see.)[8]

Possibly all along and clearly at times, Melville had in mind that he might make literary uses of what he was seeing. Most notably, his entry for December 18 records that he looked over "a lot of ancient maps of London" and bought one, explaining, "I want to use it in case I serve up the Revolutionary narrative of the beggar" (43.15–17). The beggar was Israel Potter, whose *Life and Remarkable Adventures* (Providence, 1824), so this entry reveals, he already thought he might "serve up." This possible future use doubtless accounts for many other entries about London atmosphere and places. For other uses, one entry (November 10), for example, comments on a possible sketch about the lord mayor's banquet ("A good thing might be made of this," 15.25–26), and another (December 16) on what he was missing by declining an invitation to the duke of Rutland's great country place: "If I do not go, I am confident that hereafter I shall upbraid myself for neglecting such an opportunity of procuring *'material'* " (42.1–3). And in fact Melville did use some of his London and Continental experiences, not only in brief passages of *Moby-Dick* and *Pierre* but also at length in both *Israel Potter* (1855) and some of the magazine pieces he wrote in the dogged years after the failure of *Pierre:* in the second parts of the unpublished "Two Temples" and of "Poor Man's Pudding and Rich Man's Crumbs," and in the first part of "The Paradise of Bachelors and the Tartarus of Maids."[9]

In very little is Melville's 1849–50 journal like those, say, of Hawthorne, Emerson, Thoreau, or Dana. Nor do we find in it what Clarel found in the dead Celio's "journaled thoughts"—a "second self" (*Clarel* [1876], 1.19.25–26). Primarily it is not meditative or

8. This list is reprinted below, pp. 620–23.

9. For specific uses in *Moby-Dick*, see, e.g., the discussions below at 13.6, 33.19, 33.34, 35.26–27, 35.33, 37.9–10, 42.27–28, and 42.37; for *Pierre*, 33.34 and 37.9–10; for *Israel Potter*, 14.28, 18.26, 21.6, 29.12, 32.19, 35.33, and 43.15–16; for "The Two Temples," 12.13, 14.7, and 16.2; for "Poor Man's Pudding and Rich Man's Crumbs," 15.19; and for "The Paradise of Bachelors and the Tartarus of Maids," 16.6, 24.9–10, 25.32, 44.23, 45.23, and 46.23.

even pointedly observant, so far as one can tell from its mere words. It is largely a nominal (though characteristically alert) record of events, of people met—reminders, perhaps, of some things to retell at home in the family, of the bargaining with publishers, of a number of disappointments, and rather oddly—considering Melville's exuberance on shipboard—of inferable loneliness or diffidence. At least, so one might interpret the degree to which he at first keeps up shipboard acquaintances, then seeks out friendly Americans in London, and delays presenting his letters of introduction, or the eagerness with which in Paris, speaking no French, he seeks out the more cosmopolitan George Adler.

By contrast, when he returned to London more than seven years later, he was, to judge from his 1856–57 journal, weary if nothing more and perhaps dispirited from the winter's traveling around the Mediterranean, and he seems then to have engaged in virtually no activity; but in this earlier journal he seems indefatigable. He records walking all day and many evenings; seeking out well-known pubs to have at least one quaff (though for economy's sake usually eating at cheap and obscure places); inveterately going to theaters at all levels; developing his interest in old books as he browsed in bookstores of all kinds; following the advice of guidebooks about sights to see and things to do (and going far beyond them in frequently seeking the disreputable districts and the unspeakable horrors of the mid-century slums). He is also a frequent churchgoer, but perhaps in large part because there was almost nothing else to do on a Sunday in Victorian London. A proposal in 1856 to open even such decorous and educational establishments as the British Museum and the National Gallery, for example, was shouted down from the pulpits.

For his sightseeing, Melville had the use of several guidebooks. A later letter (February 2, 1850) refers to at least five that he took with him, borrowed from George Duyckinck, who had been in Europe the year before, and whose older brother Evert had been Melville's chief New York literary adviser and book-lender since he supervised the publication of *Typee* in 1846. The borrowed two his letter refers to "for Northern & Central Italy" he could not in the end use, but he doubtless profited from the borrowed copy of *Cruchley's Picture of London* that had (he apologized) suffered an unaccountable "accident in the back."[10] The two for Italy were surely handbooks published by

10. For George and Evert Duyckinck, see the discussion at 3.14. Fourteen

John Murray (on October 20, for instance, Melville records reading about Venice in "Murray"), and so also probably were the other borrowed two not named. The Murray *Handbook* series, first compiled and organized by John Murray III, whom he met in London, and the now even more famous Baedekers, originated at nearly the same time in the 1830's. Karl Baedeker freely acknowledged taking over innovations from Murray, but his guides were less "literary," more flatly factual, though perhaps more reliable in detail than Murray's, and in any case none of them was translated into English until 1861. Until well down toward the end of the century, then, guidebook references in the accounts of writers like Hawthorne or Henry Adams or Henry James are usually to Murray. Whatever the other two guidebooks Melville borrowed from George Duyckinck may have been, Murray himself gave Melville copies of his *France* and his *Continent*. The latter guide Murray had personally put together as a young man; it covered the Low Countries, north Germany, and the Rhine, and was the first in a long and profitable line. Perhaps Melville also used Murray's new *Handbook for London* (1849), compiled in encyclopedia form by Peter Cunningham; he mentions it without comment in a journal reference to meeting Cunningham at a dinner (44.24–25). And in this encyclopedic genre, late in his stay he bought Charles Knight's *London* (not at all useful as a guide, however), probably in anticipation of future literary use, in working up Israel Potter's *Narrative*, for example. Murray's *France* would not have helped him in Paris, which that guide omitted because of the excellence of the local Galignani *Paris Guide*. Perhaps Melville found adequate the book his New York friend Dr. Augustus Gardner had given him, *Old Wine in New Bottles* (1848), an account of his life as a medical student in Paris in the earlier 1840's; while not a "guide," this was quite detailed and extensive in its coverage of Parisian scenes.

Many of the journal's entries concern Melville's meetings, dinners, and conversations with men of some social and literary prominence. He even exchanged bows with Queen Victoria (November 22). Nevertheless, we may regret that most of the literary figures seem now but minor ones. What major ones might not Melville have met through the widely acquainted Monckton Milnes, to

---

editions of *Cruchley's Picture* were published between 1831 and 1849; Sealts (166) reports the one Melville borrowed as the eleventh edition (1847) since that is the one preserved in the Duyckinck Collection in the New York Public Library.

whom he had two gilt-edged letters of introduction that he did not manage to present? He narrowly missed meeting John Forster, Dickens's close friend and later biographer. Both *David Copperfield* and *Pendennis* were being serialized at just this time, and several other men Melville did meet could have introduced him to their authors. (Dickens, like Melville, was in the crowd that witnessed the hanging of the Mannings.) Apparently nothing had come of Melville's request through his father-in-law for a letter from Emerson to Carlyle. The painter Charles R. Leslie, whom he also met but with whom he narrowly missed spending Christmas, could have introduced him to the great old painter J. M. W. Turner. So could the aged poet Samuel Rogers, who near the end of Melville's visit invited him for not one but two of his famous "breakfasts" (December 20 and 23), presumably finding something congenial in the young American author introduced by a letter from Edward Everett, president of Harvard and a former American minister to England. All this is not to underrate the personal interest and contemporary importance of individuals he met, like the great bookman Henry Stevens, the publisher Charles Knight (whose *Penny Cyclopædia* Melville had plundered and was to plunder further), the London *Handbook* writer Peter Cunningham, or even the lionized J. G. Lockhart (Scott's son-in-law), the artist John Tenniel, and the author of *Eöthen*, Alexander Kinglake. But by now none of these figures, set beside Melville himself, looms large. At Rogers's, or Murray's (November 23), or Bentley's (December 18), the guest list is pleasant but distinctly safe, as some of Melville's amused and acerbic comments suggest. He was keenly aware of differences in manners and personalities among the literary set, and between those he encountered at Murray's table and those at the table of the wealthy American banker Joshua Bates (November 24).[11]

One topic reported frequently in the journal, Melville's visits to the Inns of Court and the courts themselves, may have had a special impetus directly related to his troublesome copyright problem. The courts just at this moment were exacerbating the vexed question of copyright protection. Without international agreement, and notwithstanding Dickens's singling out American "pirates" for heated

11. For varying interpretive commentaries on Melville's London visit, see Mumford's paraphrase of the journal (1929), Horsford (1984), Wallace (1985), Bezanson (1986), Heffernan (1986), and Hershel Parker in the Northwestern-Newberry edition of *Moby-Dick* (1988), pp. 602–6.

accusations, many English publishers also profited from the confusion. Because of the ambiguities of British law, publishers who believed their rights were violated had to take individual cases to one or another court to secure either injunctions or damages, but in the tangle of overlapping jurisdictions among the several English courts, such individual decisions provided only uncertain precedent for other courts. After 1839, there had been, it is true, a brief period when the balance of these decisions began to favor the rights of foreign authors if their publication in England preceded or was simultaneous with publication elsewhere. In that period Murray and Bentley, as reputable publishers, had been willing to recompense Melville. But that favorable state of affairs was now seriously jeopardized. The copyright legislation enacted in 1842 had become a source of new litigation, and in three major cases, the two most recent in 1849, the rights of foreign authors were once again highly impaired. The two cases immediately affecting Melville's interests in London both involved the music publisher Boosey's trying to protect his rights to the score of Bellini's opera *La Sonnambula*. As recently as June in the case of *Boosey v. Purday*, the Court of Exchequer had decided against Boosey, while in the late fall, just as Melville was making his discouraging rounds, the similar case of *Boosey v. Jefferys* was moving in the same court to a similar rejection of claims for damage.[12]

The situation in the late 1840's, then, bore hard on the principal publishers of American writing, Blackwood, Murray, and especially Bentley. Given these circumstances, it is easy to see why Bentley, the first one to whom Melville took *White-Jacket*, though willing to accept it and pay £200 for the first thousand copies, initially felt he could offer no advance (no money on the spot or negotiable note)—a condition essential to Melville's projected Continental and Near Eastern (or Roman) trip. It is even easier to see why Murray, to whom he took it next, rejected *White-Jacket* as "not in his line" (though as far as Murray's criterion of factuality mattered, the career of its narrator was not observably less factual than that of the narrator of *Typee* and *Omoo*). So also, of course, for the other publishers to whom Melville successively offered his new book—Colburn, Longman, Moxon possibly, Bogue, Chapman & Hall, and Bohn. Melville knew their unanimous rejection made the jaunt to Rome, much less to the Near East, impossible, but, pending further negotiations with Bentley, he

12. See Barnes (1974), chap. 8, esp. pp. 153, 158, 162, 166–67, and 172.

took a two-week flying trip to Paris (including Versailles), Belgium, and the Rhine. It is perhaps not easy to see why Bentley in the end, already edging into financial troubles on other counts, with the unsuccess of *Mardi* large on his ledgers and the future of *Redburn* not yet established, agreed to an "arrangement" (Melville's word) to take on *White-Jacket.* By the terms of the contract they signed on December 17 he purchased outright for £200 the copyright to an initial edition of one thousand copies (exactly his original offer), and instead of an advance "guarantee" against half-profits (as for *Mardi, Redburn,* and later *The Whale*) he paid Melville in full that day with his note for £200 at six months. The crucial clause in the contract—what now made him willing to give this note at once—would seem to be that Melville, in turn, guaranteed, as for none of his other books, that should Bentley incur a loss through inability to establish copyright (i.e., through piracy) he the author would within a year "make good such deficit in whatever manner" Bentley might then require. (Most obviously, Bentley might require Melville to pay back his loss. He never did so despite a substantial one, since it was not due to piracy.) A week later Melville managed with the help of a new London friend, David Davidson, to get the note discounted for £180, thereby sacrificing £20 to secure ready money.[13] (He had already in London received and with Davidson's help negotiated Bentley's six-month £100 note in advance for half-profits from *Redburn.*)

The next month, January of 1850, Bentley was able to write the London *Times* a justifiably self-righteous reply to "An Importer of Foreign Books." "Importer" had deplored the unsettled state of copyrights, using for an example what he claimed was the failure of Melville, who had "wearily hawked" *White-Jacket* "from Piccadilly to White Chapel," to find any publisher willing to risk taking it.

13. See footnote 14. Bentley's copies of his contracts with Melville are in the British Library, Melville's in the Houghton Library of Harvard University. Later, when Bentley accepted *The Whale* (the title of *Moby-Dick* in England) in July of 1851, the copyright situation was temporarily better: in May, on appeal, the Court of Error had reversed the judgment in the case of *Boosey v. Jefferys.* (This alone may have made Bentley willing for this next book to revert to a half-profits contract, into which was written a clause exempting Melville from refunding Bentley any part of the £150 advance; see Hayford, 1971.) On further appeal, however, when Jefferys carried the case to the court of last resort, the House of Lords, the Law Lords rendered the unanimous opinion (August 1, 1854) that no foreigner was entitled to British copyright protection unless he was present in Britain when the work was published there.

Bentley thus could rightly say that "Importer" was misinformed inasmuch as he himself had just dealt with Melville generously despite the risk of pirating.[14]

Melville's main business in London was thus concluded with fair success, though on terms that meant he could not for the present afford the jaunt to Rome or beyond. He took ship for home on the *Independence* on Christmas Day, facing a little unhappily the rough, slow, mid-winter passage of the North Atlantic by sail, but at least with a "Hurrah & three cheers" (40.34) and a letter of credit for £180, the discounted proceeds from Bentley's note. Remarking in his journal at sea on December 29 that "No events happen" and that for that reason he would keep "no further diary" for the return passage, he made only one more dated entry, on January 30, 1850, when he noted sighting the pilot boat off New York. Meanwhile during the voyage, evidently, he jotted a few notes from conversations and reading, and also made lists of the books he had obtained in London, Paris, and Germany—some three dozen. A good number of them, along with his English and Continental experiences of the past ten weeks, would strongly affect his own writings in the new decade, first among them *Moby-Dick*.

IV

Melville's second journal was the record of his next trip abroad in 1856–57, at the end of seven years of intense literary labor and increasing financial pressures that had placed him in sore need of both physical and mental restoration.[15] He had arrived home from England on February 1, 1850, reinvigorated in body and mind as well as in literary inspiration. In a continuing surge of energy he launched

14. See *Log*, I, 361–62; Leyda queries there whether "Importer" may have been David Davidson or Thomas Delf; Melville's journal shows that he kept Davidson informed and did not meet Delf. As to "generosity," no writer now commanded the sums paid to Scott and Byron earlier in the century; to cite payments one American writer received earlier and later, Cooper found his value declining from a high of £1300 to £100. As it turned out, Bentley in March of 1852 had a deficit still of £173/9/6 on *White-Jacket* to report to Melville. See Gettmann (1960), pp. 4–5, 7, 83, and the Northwestern-Newberry edition of *White-Jacket* (1970), p. 407.

15. See the HISTORICAL NOTE to the Northwestern-Newberry edition of *The Confidence-Man* (1984), pp. 257–76, for a survey of these years.

into writing the book that would become *Moby-Dick* a year and a half later; took his family out of the heat of New York City to Pittsfield for the summer; engaged in the now-famous August Berkshire festivities with other literary figures including Hawthorne; wrote about Hawthorne's *Mosses from an Old Manse* and entered into an intense, if curtailed, friendship with him; bought the farm he named Arrowhead; and in late September moved his family out of the city into this rural quiet. In the sweep of an extraordinary flood of creativity that continued into the next spring and summer, he wrote Evert Duyckinck on December 13 of 1850 that he could use fifty fast-writing youths to execute all the "future works" he had teeming in his mind.[16] The ensuing long winter, while an intensely creative one, entailed also the relative isolation but enforced intimacy of extended family in a farmhouse; and in the spring the necessities of farm labor, not much more congenial to Melville than those of Brook Farm had been to Hawthorne, began to fret him. In his letters he complains repeatedly about the state of his eyes. An irritable or a gloomy note begins to edge into his letters to Duyckinck and Hawthorne, culminating in the remarkable one to Hawthorne in early June of 1851 that voices anger at the necessity of writing for dollars, irritation with the necessity of bringing his *Whale* to some sort of hurried conclusion, and grim presentiment of ultimate failure.[17]

Despite the relative American success of *White-Jacket*, meanwhile, Melville was still in debt to the Harpers, who refused his request for an advance on the new book; in debt also to his father-in-law and to an old friend, T. D. Stewart, for money used to purchase and refurbish Arrowhead; and now with a second child on the way. Yet for the moment he had the release of the novel's completion and its publication in November of 1851, and the overwhelming gratification of Hawthorne's understanding it. But its mixed reception was disappointing, perhaps infuriating, to Melville. Failure to reach an agreement with Bentley for the English publication of *Pierre*, the "romance" he had begun about the time *Moby-Dick* was published, was another disappointment; its disastrous reception and sales failure a

16. Thoughts impelling some of these may have gone into *Moby-Dick*; unfortunately, the only thoughts preserved in journal or notebook fashion are the memoranda cited in footnote 2 above.

17. See also Elizabeth Shaw Melville's later recollection of his writing *Moby-Dick* under "unfavorable circumstances" (Sealts, 1974, p. 169).

year later must have been extraordinarily painful to him, all disclaimers notwithstanding. A still further blow was the great fire at Harper & Brothers in December of 1853, which burnt the stock of his books in print, except for a few copies of *Mardi* and *Moby-Dick* and 110 copies of *Pierre*. Though the stereotype plates themselves were undamaged in underground vaults, there was little enough reason for Harpers to reprint such slow-selling books (they did so, however, in 1855).[18]

Nevertheless, Melville's taxes had to be paid and his children—now including a second son, after a while a daughter, and then another—had to be provided for, as well as his wife and at times his widowed mother and spinster sisters. While the family busied itself again with attempts to obtain him a consular post, Melville moved off on a new literary tack. He began writing magazine pieces, for which *Harper's New Monthly Magazine* and *Putnam's Monthly Magazine* were willing to pay him well. A conspicuous aspect of this considerable body of work is its recurrent theme of defeat, injury, or loss met with pride and endurance. This theme undoubtedly accords with Melville's own state of mind and health, though to just what degree is uncertain. Elizabeth Shaw Melville's letters, various family ones, and her brief memorandum in after years express anxiety regarding his overwork and mental strain. Perhaps family concern was exaggerated in 1853, but real enough were debilitating attacks of rheumatism in 1855 that put the part-time farmer helplessly on his back just when crops needed attention. Such physical limitation was a severe reversal for the nimble sailor who just a few years before had delighted in cavorting in the rigging, showing off before the passengers bound for London.[19]

For all this, by mid-decade Melville's narrative about the old Revolutionary War "beggar" Israel Potter, a project he had kept in

18. A curious sidelight on the Harper firm's having accepted not only *Moby-Dick* but *Pierre* is offered by an early memorandum for its editorial readers of novel manuscripts: "Stupidity and vulgarity . . . they will quickly recognize—and I hope they will keep their eyes open to detect the atheistic or agnostic element which nowadays pervades so many stories. We should be wicked if we knowingly disseminated such books . . ." (quoted by Harper, 1912, p. 548).

19. Sealts (1974), p. 169; see also Metcalf (1953), chap. 10, or *Log*, I, 468–69, and II, 502, 507, 519, and 521. Leon Howard (1951) believed Elizabeth usually exaggerated Melville's condition, but his mother's letters corroborate her view of it.

mind at least since London, was well enough along to begin magazine serialization in July of 1854. There were enough pieces from *Putnam's* to publish with a newly written opening sketch as *The Piazza Tales* in May of 1856; and by the beginning of October *The Confidence-Man* was in the form of printer's copy. On October 10, the day before he sailed once more for Europe, Melville discussed its publication arrangements with Dix & Edwards, his new American publishers.[20]

Meanwhile, the state of Melville's finances had become all but disastrous. Despite his unremitting desk labor, he simply could not, unaided, support his household. The necessary aid, a bitter gall to his pride, repeatedly came from his father-in-law. Melville had been in debt to Chief Justice Shaw ever since the 1847 purchase of the New York City house and that of the farm in 1850; but as Shaw tactfully wrote later, he had always considered these moneys he lent to Melville as, in a way, advances on his daughter's ultimate inheritance.[21] Furthermore, Melville remained in debt to his several American and English publishers for advances.[22]

On top of all this, as Shaw's 1860 letter recalls, in 1856 he advanced another "fourteen or fifteen hundred dollars" to cover Melville's "outfit and . . . expenses" for the 1856–57 trip. As Shaw wrote at the time to his son Sam, already in Europe, Elizabeth was again deeply anxious about her husband's health, attributing "severe nervous affections" to intense overwork. The family therefore considered it urgent that Melville should break off his writing and take a European tour for four or five months. Elizabeth and the two little

20. It now seems clear that arranging an English edition was not a primary motive for the trip and that his wife's later report that he "took manuscript books with him for publication" is mistaken. See the Northwestern-Newberry edition (1984), pp. 311–13.

21. Shaw's letter to Melville, May 15, 1860, outlining the history of their financial dealings, is printed in full in Metcalf (1953), pp. 180–82. Two earlier letters of Melville to Shaw, in May of 1856, indicate other vexing mortgage complications, caused by the debt of some $2,000, plus accumulated interest, owed to T. D. Stewart, who was pressing for payment. See Barber (1977), pp. 418–21.

22. Howard (1951, pp. 208, 233–34) mistakenly took at face value the annual published Pittsfield property declarations to mean that Melville kept and jealously guarded a slowly growing, rather substantial cash "nest-egg" in reserve through all these years. But the declarations were actually *pro forma*, and family letters (such as those listed in footnote 21 above) published after Howard's biography contradict them.

girls would stay at her father's home in Boston and the two boys, both older, with other relatives.[23] Whatever his own view of the state of his health and finances, this excursion seemed necessary, and Melville accepted it.

V

The journal Melville kept on his 1856–57 trip (October 11 to May 8) is often painful to read, not merely for its editors because of its passages of cramped handwriting and its compressed, sometimes erratic, spelling, but more essentially to any reader because of the grimly skeptical and even morbid states of mind it now and again reveals. Of course, it is also true enough that Melville wrote much of the journal under the most adverse conditions, tormented by fatigue and sore eyes, by fleas and sleeplessness, by the innumerable discomforts and ills of mid-century, midwinter travel in the Levant and the Mediterranean. (Guidebooks like the one for Egypt published by his old acquaintance John Murray strongly recommended not starting until late winter, beginning with Egypt and only then working slowly north through Palestine and Syria with the spring. If Melville was aware of this ideal calendar, he could not afford to wait several months to meet it.) But even such an explanation does not account for the long passages written during the enforced layovers in his Alexandria and Jaffa hotels, where the pressured, near illegibility of his hand is a kind of barograph for the weather of his mind.

Surely the underlying causes of this journal's special quality reach much deeper, and its value is correspondingly more profound. His 1849–50 journal is interesting as the record of a popular, healthy, largely confident young author going out to meet the publishing and literary world of London. He expected to encounter interesting people, his prospects were reasonably good, he was going to be footloose for a time, and, with whatever emotional contradictions, free of a crowded and distracting household of obligations. But that journal remains almost entirely an account of surfaces.

When Melville took the steamer *Glasgow* on October 11, 1856, for Glasgow—with unformed plans for London, Europe, and Italy—seven years to the day after his 1849 embarkation, all those factors,

23. Metcalf (1953), p. 159, or *Log,* II, 521 (Sept. 1).

saving only the obligations, had radically altered. His friend Evert Duyckinck reported him "right hearty" on the eve of his departure from New York. But on the other side in Liverpool the more penetrating Hawthorne, who soon found himself and Melville "on pretty much our former terms of sociability and confidence," remarked that Melville looked "a little paler, and perhaps a little sadder, . . . with his characteristic gravity and reserve of manner." Melville told him he felt better than when he left America but also said that "he did not anticipate much pleasure in his rambles, for that the spirit of adventure is gone out of him." Much "overshadowed" as he seemed, Hawthorne hoped he would "brighten as he goes onward."[24]

In considerable part this brightening did come, but slowly. Unlike the 1849 journal, in which excited entries began almost before the ship left harbor, this 1856 journal has no entries at all for the two-week Atlantic passage (October 11–26). Only a later memo shows that once again Melville had found a congenial fellow-passenger and had "Conversations with the Colonel on fixed fate &c. during the passage" (141.6–7). There is only a later three-page summary of the first three days ashore in Scotland (October 26–28), then a ten-day gap, part of it spent in travel with "an American theological student, very uninteresting, but better than nobody," and then a similar "Memorandum of stay in Liverpool" (November 8–18) that records even his meetings with Hawthorne only elliptically and omits all mention of a whole day's excursion to Chester with him. The memorandum was made just before (or perhaps after) embarking from Liverpool for the Mediterranean—as he had only in the past week resolved to do, bypassing London and the Continent, largely for reasons of economy—on the steamer *Egyptian* on November 18. Only then do more-or-less daily entries begin.[25]

24. *The English Notebooks* (1941), pp. 432–37. Hawthorne's full entry is reprinted below, pp. 628–33.

25. For discussion of when he made the memorandum for Scotland, see p. 221 below. Fortunately he wrote a fuller account in a letter to his brother Allan from Liverpool, including more about the colonel, George Rankin, with whom he conversed philosophically on the *Glasgow* (see also the discussion at 141.6), and the comment on the uncongenial Presbyterian theological student; the entire letter is reprinted below, pp. 624–27. That the Liverpool memorandum was jotted in retrospect no doubt explains the omission of the excursion with Hawthorne. In any case, the 1856 journal is quite like the 1849 one in its virtually complete lack of references to current affairs—for example, to the aftermath of the Crimean War, or the news of

But as the Mediterranean sun warmed away the November chill, Melville's spirits and health clearly improve, and the entries become more full and lively. Though the impatient wait (January 1–4) in Alexandria and the dreary, unpleasant delay (January 19–25) in Jaffa overshadow the accounts of Egypt and Palestine, Melville appears to have enjoyed thoroughly the crowds and exotic color of Constantinople (December 12–18) and Cairo (December 30). One or two lapses in health curbed his otherwise indefatigable sightseeing, but in the brief Rome meeting (March 21) with his young brother-in-law Sam Shaw, he reported himself much improved, and Sam found him now sunburnt and stout.[26] In the Near East he had interested himself in people and sites; here in Italy, with an energy and catholicity of taste to be found nowhere in Hawthorne's notebooks, he persistently widened and deepened his understanding of art, even when, as a tyro, he was still echoing contemporary conventional judgments.

At first conscious of expense (as the letter to his brother Allan cited in footnote 25 emphasizes), Melville endured the discomforts of obscure inns and second- or third-class ship passage; as he found his money holding out, however, he began engaging the better seats on the European diligences to view the passing landscape, or visiting famous cafés and places of entertainment. But the astonishing pace Melville had kept up inevitably began to slacken. The languor of Venice becomes appealing, the entries once more perfunctory. And by London, which he had so vigorously enjoyed seven years before, he is hardly interested enough to stir from his lodgings. This in spite of the fact that the London "Season" of this spring promised to be particularly brilliant, prompted by the engagement of the Princess Royal to Prince Frederick William of Prussia; especially notable were Charles Kean's elaborately magnificent productions of Shakespeare and the opening of the great new Reading Room of the British Museum, on May 2.

For all the energy, the interest in experience, and gregarious encounters this journal displays from time to time, there is no overlooking the pervasive skepticism, the bleak irony, and the recurrent wea-

---

Sir Richard Burton's setting out the first week of October to seek the source of the Nile, or the election campaign of Buchanan and the first Republican candidate, John C. Frémont, let alone the increasingly divisive issue of slavery and imminence of civil war.

26. See the discussion at 113.17.

riness. Occasionally it leads to rhetorical overkill, as in the overwrought passage on the bitterness of the Dead Sea (83.19–22), or to mere intellectual petulance, as in the deprecation of Niebuhr and Strauss for destroying the romance of myth (97.18–20). Nevertheless, places of death, of darkness, confinement, or constraint both fascinate and provoke a nervous timorousness in the once fearless sailor; almost compulsively he seeks to climb out or up. In Constantinople he is haunted by Near Eastern wailing for the dead (62.30–35), in Cairo appalled by disease and blindness (74.11–14), no doubt an especially threatening subject for him, in Florence gruesomely fascinated by the grisly wax representations of plague deaths (115.26–38). Metaphysical speculation had greatly excited him in 1849 on the way to London; now it is a kind of grinding obsession, or so it seemed to Hawthorne in his notebook passage about their conversation on the Southport sands. However much Melville enjoyed large parts of this trip—and one ought not minimize that—an observation he added later may be even more to the point: "The pains lie among the pleasures like sand in rice, not only bad in themselves, but spoiling the good" (158.10–11).

Though Melville may at first have been unenthusiastic, as he told Hawthorne in Liverpool, such a trip to Italy and the Levant was one he had anticipated for a long time. Perhaps it had its first major impetus when he was on his third and last whaler, the *Charles and Henry*, in late 1842 and early 1843. He could have read in that ship's little library *A Visit to Constantinople and Athens* (1836) by the Reverend Walter Colton, chaplain to the U.S. frigate *Constellation*, a ship which, by a nice coincidence, Melville encountered pleasantly on this trip.[27] Or perhaps it had begun, if a passage in Chapter 1 of *Redburn* is autobiographical, with a youthful awe of the famous Near Eastern traveler John L. Stephens and his *Incidents of Travel in Egypt, Arabia Petræa, and the Holy Land* (1837). As a young author in New York Melville had met Bayard Taylor in the first flush of success with *Views A-Foot* (1846), his account of vagabonding in Europe; shortly after, on the ship to London, he encountered Taylor's cousin and fellow wanderer, Dr. Franklin Taylor. Recurrently in his 1849 journal, Melville recorded enthusiastic conversations with Dr. Taylor, laying out plans

27. Heflin (1974), pp. 6–27.

for inexpensive travel in Italy and the Levant, a "glorious Eastern jaunt."[28]

But certainly public interest in traveling to Europe, and even to so seemingly remote, dangerous regions as the Near East and Africa, was very extensive. Mediterranean piracy had been largely suppressed, and with the Crimean War the Turkish government had come to look more tolerantly on "infidels." J. Ross Browne, whose *Etchings of a Whaling Cruise* (1847) Melville had reviewed and had drawn upon for *Moby-Dick*, wrote up his comic version of Syrian travels in *Yusef* (1853), and Melville's acquaintance and friendly reviewer N. P. Willis had recently (1856) reissued *A Summer Cruise in the Mediterranean* (1853), his account of cruising as a guest on the *Constellation*; Bayard Taylor's even more recent *Central Africa* (1854) and *Lands of the Saracen* (1855) were but two of the better among many similar accounts (several of which are mentioned in the discussions of passages in the present edition).

In much of what Melville saw and noted, his experience did not differ remarkably from that of many other travelers, lay and clerical. For every country he visited, excepting only Palestine, Murray had long since provided a handbook; it is indicative of the popularity of even that ill-governed territory, ill-prepared with tourist accommodations, that Murray issued his *Handbook for Travellers in Syria and Palestine*, in two parts, the very next year, 1858. And within ten years, Mark Twain would write from the much publicized first conducted tour to the Holy Land the travel letters that went into *Innocents Abroad* (1869). Murray not only provided the handbooks, his writers of them provided the attitudes and even a good deal of the language for many of the early accounts; and in this respect, too, Melville, in much of this journal, does not appear particularly original. Mark Twain in his preface offered to see with his own eyes, but Melville often sees with eyes quite like those of his contemporaries and recent predecessors. Yet he does not always do so. Any comparison of Melville's memoranda on Egypt, say, with the conventional meditations of popular writers like A. W. Kinglake or the pious Prime brothers, S. I. and W. C., on time, history, and immortality, points a notable difference.[29]

28. See entries for October 15, 18, 26, and November 17.

29. See Henry Nash Smith (1962) on Mark Twain's echoes of Kinglake and

Along with its unconventional entries, this 1856–57 journal has many that differ significantly from any in his own 1849 journal, not only in their pervasive dispirit but in several other important ways also. For one thing, with the example before him of some of the writers just mentioned, he may have had the idea of writing a travel book. Certainly his uncle Peter Gansevoort thought he ought to.[30] His two books of most nearly pure invention, *Mardi* and *Pierre*, had been signal failures, while the last of his store of travel experiences had been pretty well exhausted by the Mississippi riverboat milieu of *The Confidence-Man*. As Emerson had already noted wryly in "The American Scholar" (1838), "Authors we have, in numbers, who have written out their vein, and who, moved by a commendable prudence, sail for Greece or Palestine." Melville's 1856–57 journal, in any case, beginning only when England has been left behind, tends even in its most prosaic passages to be somewhat more detailed, partly because where so much of the 1849 journal was occupied with individual people, especially publishers, this account is chiefly of sights, sounds, exotic color, of immersion in the crowds in Constantinople and Cairo, of the quality of the Palestinian landscape, and of the social scene in Naples, Rome, and Venice. It is in conjunction with passages like these that there occasionally appear comments like "Something comical could be made out of all this" (82.21–22) and cryptic little reminders (sometimes contemporaneous, sometimes added later): "enumerate," "For Note," "For Con. Man," "For the Story," and similar phrases, as well as the constant "&c. &c. &c.," all of which imply possible future uses.

Another way this journal differs, particularly in its long retrospective entries on his observations in Egypt and in Palestine but also more briefly elsewhere, is that Melville meditates or comments on the implications and significance of what he has seen far more often than in the earlier journal.[31] One brief example is the passage suggested by his visit to the volcanic region west of Naples with its

even of W. C. Prime, whose sentimental rhetoric he professed to scorn (pp. 28–29). Franklin Walker (1974) gives an engaging account of the writings of three "irreverent pilgrims"—Melville, Browne, and Mark Twain.

30. See *Log*, II, 587 (Dec. 17).

31. Some of these comments might have disturbed Chief Justice Shaw, who was severe in his judicial treatment of irreverence and blasphemy. See Levy (1957), pp. 48–58, and all of chap. 4 for Abner Kneeland's trials in the 1830's for blasphemy.

fabled grottoes and sulfurous vapors: "What in God's name were such places made for, & why? Surely man is a strange animal. Diving into the bowels of the earth rather than building up towards the sky. How clear an indication that he sought darkness rather than light" (104.18–22).

A still further difference this journal offers is that in its entries we have a chance, however limited, to see something of the process of Melville's thinking and writing, both at the time of composition and on later perusals. In the 1849 journal, except for an occasional false start canceled and some harsh personal descriptions later inked out, the manuscript shows scarcely any alteration. In this 1856–57 journal, however, and particularly in the passages written at Alexandria and Jaffa, where enforced waiting left him time for deliberate composition, a number of pages are difficult to transcribe intelligibly in their entirety, so as to show the order of the cancellations, insertions, and restorations, as idea crowds on idea, phrase replaces phrase. Many of these changes, in the same ink, were made during the compositional process or soon after; others were penciled in at some later time or times.

Let a single not too complicated example suggest the revision process (the passage is reproduced below). In Alexandria, thinking about the impression the Pyramids had made on him, Melville first wrote, "And one seems to see that as out of the crude forms of the natural earth they [*i.e., Egyptian priests or wise men*] could evoke by art the wonderful [wonderful *canceled and* transcendent *inserted*] mass & symmetry & unity [& unity *canceled, then restored by dashed underlining*]

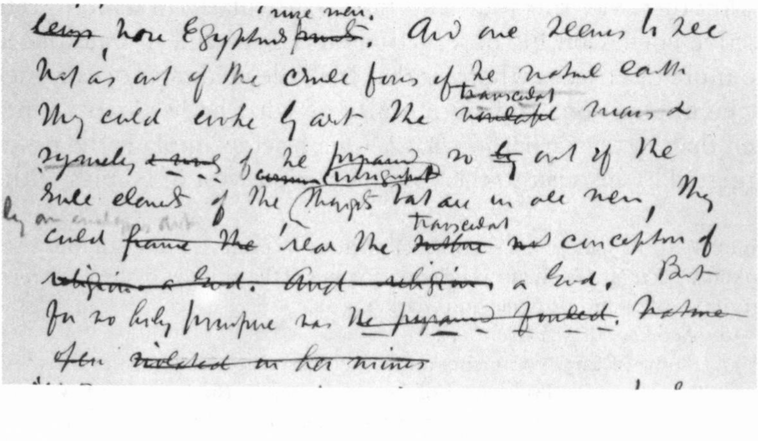

of the pyramid so by [by *canceled*] out of the rude elements of the thoughts that are in all men, they could frame the [frame the *canceled*] rear the sublime [sublime *canceled*; transcendent *inserted above*] not [not *canceled*] conception of religion. [religion. *canceled*] a God. And religion [a . . . religion *canceled*] a God. But for no holy purpose was the pyramid founded. [*last three words canceled, then restored*] Nature often violated in her mines. [*sentence canceled*]." Then, or shortly after, Melville inserted "common" above "the thoughts", canceled "common" and inserted "insignificant", circling it and connecting it to a caret between "the" and "thoughts". (The inferred time-sequence may not be altogether accurate.) At some later time, when Melville reworked the whole page with a pencil, in the above passage the first inserted "transcendent" was canceled, then marked for restoration. Next, the partial phrase "mass & symmetry" was canceled. Finally, in the last clause of that sentence a new phrase, "by an analogous art", was inserted to give the reading: "they could by an analogous art rear the transcendent conception of a God."[32]

Besides the kind of compositional and revisory processes suggested by the above example, the journal's pages show many markings which Melville made in it later for various literary purposes. The later times, whatever their exact dates, at which Melville did so were, as now seems likely, some while after he had completed his return trip, through Italy, Switzerland, Germany, Holland, and England, and his homeward Atlantic crossing from Liverpool to New York (May 6–19), on the steamer *City of Manchester*. He made no dated journal entries during the crossing.

Whatever intentions Melville may have had in keeping the journal, he told his wife's older half-brother, Lemuel Shaw, Jr., soon after his return that he intended to write no more "at present."[33] Yet over the succeeding years he wrote a good deal, and in the course of doing so he consulted this journal. His markings in it show he used it for at least two of the three seasons of lectures he gave, 1857–60, almost certainly for the poetry he began writing about then, and most nota-

32. The passage occurs on manuscript page D23, 78.33–38 in the present text. Horsford's 1955 edition of this journal, pp. 273–86, offers type-facsimile representations of the most difficult manuscript pages, D22–23, D38, and D40–47; also photofacsimiles of D23, 38, 43, and 145. For explanation of manuscript pagination see pp. 213–32 in the NOTE ON THE TEXT.

33. See *Log*, II, 580 (before June 2), or Metcalf (1953), pp. 165–66.

bly for *Clarel*, the major work he concentrated on from probably the later 1860's to its publication in 1876. For these purposes his markings and additions to the original entries are variably related and of various kinds: words, phrases, observations, and tentative titles, marginal scorings, underlining, and other attention-arresting devices, sometimes in ink, sometimes in ordinary pencil, sometimes with a kind of red crayon or pencil.

Some of the memoranda added on the pages immediately following the last dated entry (Wednesday, May 5, 1857, recording his boarding ship at Liverpool for New York) were tentative titles: "Frescoes of Travel" or *"Roman Frescoes"* (154.1, 155.1). Perhaps they were for the travel work or works (of whatever sort) that he did not write, or perhaps for his first lecture. The title most commonly given that lecture in newspaper reports was, however, "Statues in Rome."[34]

At the Boston dinner Lemuel Shaw, Jr., gave to welcome Melville home in May, Oliver Wendell Holmes called a lecturer a "literary strumpet," but of course Dr. Holmes himself was lecturing on the burgeoning lyceum circuit, as were many other prominent literary men, including Bayard Taylor, George William Curtis (who seems to have helped Melville get started), and Thomas Starr King, whom Melville was to meet in San Francisco in 1860.[35] The first of the three lectures, "Statues in Rome," delivered in the 1857–58 season, depended heavily on Melville's recent observations, recorded in this journal; the third lecture, "Traveling," in the 1859–60 season, drew on it only occasionally and more generally. As it happens, the journal entries for late February into April of 1857 in Rome and Italy are marked scarcely at all, perhaps because his memory was still so fresh when he composed the lecture in the fall of that year. Some of the memoranda he recorded after the last travel entry can, however, be related to material in the lecture. Often enough, too, the lecture appears to have lifted, bodily, ideas and even whole passages from the journal, not only about Rome but about things Melville had observed

34. The three lectures for Melville's three lecture seasons have been reconstructed from newspaper reports by Merton M. Sealts, Jr., first in *Melville as Lecturer* (1957) and later, with revisions, in the Northwestern-Newberry edition of *THE PIAZZA TALES and Other Prose Pieces, 1839–1860* (1987).

35. See *Letters*, pp. 188–89 (Sept. 15), and pp. 201–2 below.

elsewhere in Italy, principally Naples and Florence, even in England, and from recollections of Paris in 1849.

Two instances of Melville's drawing upon the 1856–57 journal may be cited here for their exemplary qualities. The first is the prominent use in the lecture of his own observation of the bust of Tiberius, and of another tourist's remark about it (106.13–15). The second shows how an idea grew and changed as he reflected on it. Initially he records his idea of repeopling Caracalla's Baths with gigantic figures like the Horse-Tamer group before the Quirinal Palace (107.34–35); nine journal pages later, this has become repeopling the Coliseum (111.30–31). Finally, among the memoranda at the journal's end the image later used in the lecture has emerged as: "*Colisseum*. great green hollow — restore it repeople it with all statues in Vatican Dying & Fighting Gladiators" (158.14–16).[36]

Melville delivered the lecture on "Traveling" only three times, in the winter of 1859–60; no manuscript is preserved, and its contents are known from a single incomplete newspaper account. This account indicates in a general way that it included some references to his 1856–57 travels—the discomforts of the Levant, including fleas, the irritations of tedious passport regulations and attendant bribery, the beauty of Naples, the sobriety of Turks, the honesty of infidels, and the trickery of Christians. But these remarks as reported are so general that nothing more than casual recourse to the journal for them can be usefully surmised.

Melville began writing poetry seriously in these years, seriously enough and extensively enough that he had a book of poems ready in 1860 for publication, though it found no publisher; and he continued writing poems for the rest of his life. Most of them are difficult or impossible to date very precisely.[37] But whenever written, many of them make direct and repeated levy on the experiences recorded in the journal. Still, as with the lectures, there is very little in the way of supplementary marking of the journal related to them. Quite possibly in reading it over for other purposes Melville was prompted, incidentally as it were, to render his imaginative impressions in poetic

36. Northwestern-Newberry *Piazza Tales* volume (1987), pp. 404–5. See also the discussions at 102.35, 106.12, 108.21, 111.30, 114.16, 115.4, and 117.28.

37. See Shurr (1972), pp. 6–7; and the HISTORICAL NOTE to the Northwestern-Newberry *Published Poems* volume (forthcoming).

Melville in 1861. Photograph, courtesy
of the Berkshire Athenaeum.

form. But even the passages on the Egyptian desert and the heavily reworked ones on the Pyramids (75.3–17, 78.7–38) only indirectly foreshadow his two published poems on these subjects, "In the Desert" and "The Great Pyramid." Both were among eighteen poems in a section titled "Fruit of Travel Long Ago" in *Timoleon (*1891), all of which directly relate to experiences recorded in the journal in passages without later markings suggesting such use; their dates of composition are conjectural.

For *Clarel*, published in 1876, Melville from the 1860's into the early 1870's much more evidently read and reread his journal, especially of course the Palestinian section.[38] First of all, it may be that the speculative title "Frescoes of Travel by Three Brothers Poet, Painter, and Idler" (154.1–5), whether or not related to early ideas for a travel book or his first lecture, was a contributing idea to the structure of *Clarel*, the idea of observation and meditation from multiple perspectives.[39] It is certainly true that multitudes of descriptive details as well as the linear narrative movement of *Clarel* depend closely and extensively on matters recorded in the journal: descriptions of places and sights, prototypes of characters, reflections made at the time, and so on. However, the first two parts of *Clarel*, "Jerusalem" and "The Wilderness," show the closest correlation with the journal; the last two parts, as Walter E. Bezanson demonstrates (see footnote 38), begin to show Melville's characteristic habit of greater reliance on secondary works, such as Arthur P. Stanley's *Sinai and Palestine* (1863), which he bought in 1870 (Sealts 488).

All the same, even in these two later parts (whenever they were written), Melville demonstrably returned to his journal, as evidenced by his additions and special markings in it. The comparison of the monks at Mar Saba to Shakespeare's samphire gatherers (*Clarel*, 3.9.41), for example, derives not from an observation in Jaffa he wrote at the time, but from an addition he made later in pencil on the same page (see the textual note at 83.38). In a different way, the unexpected view of distant Jerusalem from the Bethlehem plain (*Clarel*, 4.1.176–87) stems from two passages in the journal: the origi-

38. See Walter E. Bezanson on the probable history of composition in the HISTORICAL NOTE to the Northwestern-Newberry edition (1990) of *Clarel* (as in the Hendricks House edition [1960], p. xxxiii). See also Howard (1951), pp. 297–98.

39. Mumford (1929), p. 308.

nal observation (84.26–28), which was later boxed in heavy red lines, and repeated, again in the same red crayon or pencil, in the notes that follow the last journal entry (154.10).

These and certain other instances of borrowings in *Clarel*, such as details about the Timoneer, or the wistful association of Jesus with Tahiti, or the complex association of goods deposited for safekeeping in the Temple with the apocryphal Book of Maccabees, point to Melville's reading and rereading, using and marking his 1856–57 journal as he worked upon the poem, at least into the early 1870's.[40]

VI

Melville's third journal, the last and briefest, was kept during his voyage from Boston around Cape Horn to San Francisco from June to October of 1860, on his brother Captain Thomas Melville's ship *Meteor*—once again for his health. This journal occupies only six sides on four leaves and has but fourteen sporadic dated entries for the voyage of 134 days. For his 8 days ashore in San Francisco there is no journal at all, and none for his 24-day return trip by ship to Panama, by rail across the isthmus, and again by ship to New York.

The three years between Melville's return from Europe in May of 1857 and his sailing on this voyage at the end of May of 1860 were troubled and indecisive, but not empty of consequence. The Melvilles, Shaws, and Gansevoorts continued to worry about his health and state of mind, neither of which kept him from traveling the lecture circuit by train, stage, and boat in those three winters.[41] Sooner or later, as indicated by the summary above, Melville was engaged in other kinds of writing than for lectures. The notations he made in the 1856–57 journal imply that he was thinking of various other projects. Perhaps one project was travel pieces or a book like those of the popular Bayard Taylor. A sequel to *The Confidence-Man* may have been another, but if so that must have died when its pub-

40. See the discussions at 84.28 and 154.6. For some of Melville's other uses of this journal in *Clarel*, see the discussions at 55.30, 55.37, 58.22, 64.11, 79.17, 79.21, 80.19, 81.29, 82.34–35, 83.18, 83.22–23, 84.10, 84.18, 84.19, 84.28, 84.37, 85.14–15, 85.21, 85.22, 90.8, 108.31, and 154.1–16. From Bezanson's unpublished dissertation, "Herman Melville's *Clarel*" (Yale, 1943), the Northwestern-Newberry edition includes a tabulation of passages in the 1856–57 journal that were drawn upon in *Clarel*.

41. See footnote 34.

lishers, Dix, Edwards & Company, dissolved in late April in the 1857 financial panic and the successor company (in which George William Curtis was a partner) soon failed and sold the stereotype plates of their books at auction in September (though those of *The Confidence-Man* and *The Piazza Tales* were withheld).[42]

When he was invited in August of 1857 by the newly established *Atlantic Monthly* to contribute, Melville replied he would be glad to do so though he could not say when. By the next year George Duyckinck reported him "busy on a new book," and by May of 1859 he had "two Pieces" to submit to some magazine, perhaps *Harper's* or the *Atlantic*. Quite possibly these "Pieces" were poems and the "new book" was poetry. In any event just before his 1860 trip Melville had a collection of poems ready for publication. He was characteristically self-mocking in his letter asking Evert Duyckinck to help Elizabeth and Allan find a publisher for the manuscript he left with them, but his memorandum to Allan detailing his wishes was serious. Besides, his purchases and markings of poetry volumes during the past three years show he had undertaken a serious study of the craft of poetry.[43] Whatever merits these poems may have had, no publisher was found for them then. Some were possibly among early poems he seems to have burned, but versions of others were doubtless in his privately printed *Timoleon* (1891), and still others were left unpublished. On his 1860 voyage, meanwhile, he had some of them in hand or head, or possibly was writing new ones, for in a later letter (May 25, 1862) he reminded Thomas of a moonlight night at sea when he "repeated" to him "three cables' length" of verses.[44]

Nevertheless, while all of this suggests an active life as lecturer and writer, Melville's once robust health was periodically impaired. After his return from the 1856–57 trip, he had said that though better he was not perfectly well, and his wife's late memorandum notes that after serious back trouble in March of 1858—when not yet thirty-nine—"he never regained his former vigor & strength." (A serious

42. As to a sequel, see Horsford (1952), pp. 85–89; also the Northwestern-Newberry edition of *The Confidence-Man* (1984), pp. 312, 315–16, its *Piazza Tales* volume (1987), pp. 499–500, and p. 187 above.

43. See *Letters*, p. 200, *Log*, II, 615–16, and Metcalf (1953), pp. 182, 183–84; for his purchases see, *passim, Log*, II, and Sealts, *Melville's Reading*.

44. See below, p. 645; also *Letters*, pp. 213–15; Howard (1951), pp. 263–65, discusses poems of this apprenticeship. See also Shurr (1972), pp. 4, 168–80.

Melville (seated) and his youngest brother, Thomas, captain of the *Meteor*, a few days before their 1860 voyage to San Francisco. From an ambrotype in the collection of Harrison Hayford.

road accident in November of 1862 further debilitated him.) From time to time in family letters there are rejoicing remarks on his good health, but these imply an underlying concern. Certainly Melville was ready to give up the farm after his return from Europe in May of 1857. He tried to sell the rest of his land and almost bought a house in Brooklyn, and once again the family bestirred themselves to obtain him a government appointment, this time in the New York Customs House, but with no results.[45]

After these three dispiriting years, Melville was invited in early May of 1860, by his brother Tom, captain of the California-China clipper *Meteor*, to sail with him to the Pacific and prospectively around the world. He soon determined to do so. The ever-kindly Chief Justice Shaw wrote him on May 15 commending the idea as a "permanent benefit" to his health, and outlining plans to relieve Melville of all debt to him by taking over title to the farm and giving it to Elizabeth in anticipation of her inheritance.[46] A few days before sailing, the brothers had their picture taken together, an ambrotype (reproduced opposite) which shows them both heavily bearded, looking very much alike despite Herman's more than ten years' seniority. Tom's ship had arrived in Boston on April 28, from Manila and Calcutta. This course was a frequent extension for clippers beyond the California run, especially as competition for fewer cargoes intensified, with steamships taking more of the intra-American trade. Depending on cargo availability, then, the ship's route beyond San Francisco on this voyage was uncertain, but at the outset Melville expected to sail around the world. So he wrote Evert Duyckinck on May 28 from the *Meteor*, in Boston Harbor two days before sailing:

> I anticipate as much pleasure as, at the age of fourty, one temperately can, in the voyage I am going. I go under very happy auspices so far as ship & Captain is concerned. A noble ship and a nobler Captain—& he my brother. We have the breadth of both tropics before us, to sail over twice; & shall round the world. Our first port is San Francisco, which we shall probably make in 110 days from Boston. Thence we go to Manilla—& thence, I hardly know where.[47]

45. Sealts (1974), p. 169; Hayford and Davis (1949), pp. 168–83, 377–88.

46. Metcalf (1953), pp. 180–82.

47. See pp. 634–35 below; also *Moby-Dick*, chap. 52: "Round the world! There is much in that sound to inspire proud feelings; but whereto does all that circumnavigation conduct? Only through numberless perils to the very point whence we started, where those that we left behind secure, were all the time before us" (p. 237).

At the height of excited commercial competition for the premium California trade, the *Meteor* had been launched in South Boston in 1852 and bought by the firm of Curtis & Peabody. She was a medium clipper and like most of them was built more for speed than tonnage. (For comparison, her size, 1068 tons, was less than half that of Donald McKay's great *Sovereign of the Seas,* 2421 tons, launched the same year; her dimensions were 195 feet long, 36 wide, 24 deep.) She was described as "a splendid ship, with a sharp bow ornamented with the representation of Atalanta picking up the golden apples."[48] When Melville's youngest and perhaps favorite brother took over as her second captain, having been first mate, he was not yet twenty-nine years old. On his first voyage from New York to San Francisco in 1859, the *Meteor* matched the record of fifteen and a half days from fifty degrees South Pacific to the equator. Since the peak year of 1854, however, the profitability of clippers in the California run had been in a decline that was accelerated by the panic of 1857, and with the Civil War their marvelous era ended.[49] In 1860, nevertheless, the *Meteor*'s owners must have had a cargo waiting for her in Boston. On May 30, scarcely a month after docking, she sailed again, with Herman Melville aboard. She arrived in San Francisco 135 days later, on October 12. Her run this summer was close to the average time of 133 days for ships following Lieutenant Matthew Maury's *Sailing Directions,* though ordinarily the best sailing season east to west was late fall, when one had reasonable expectations of good winds in the North Atlantic and relatively easy passage by Cape Horn.[50]

The Atlantic route recommended by Lieutenant Maury to get the greatest advantage of winds and currents bore nearly east to the sixty-fifth meridian, then by stages past the Brazilian shoulder of South America, standing some distance off the coast to avoid adverse land winds, thence to the Straits of Le Maire between Staten Island and the

48. Howe and Matthews (1926–27), II, 394.

49. Many were seized and destroyed by Confederate cruisers, and to avoid similar fates others were sold abroad, to British firms especially. Subsequently, the *Meteor* was engaged under another captain in local trading between Hong Kong, Singapore, and Bangkok and was sold to a British firm in 1862.

50. Rydell (1952), in chap. 8, "The Clipper Ship Era," gives a detailed account of this decade; see also Cutler (1930). The record time from New York to San Francisco was just over 89 days. For Maury, see *Explanations and Sailing Directions,* 8th enl. ed. (Washington, D.C., 1858–59).

extreme southeast point of Argentina. Sailing ships ordinarily avoided the Straits of Magellan because of dangerously narrow channels and unpredictable currents, tides, and winds. To go farther south, however, around the barren island of Horn with its forbidding cape, meant facing its very strong, east-bearing current, with great rolling swells, icebergs, and gale-force winds three-fourths of the time. The thousand miles between the two Atlantic and Pacific points on latitude 50 degrees south have the fiercest gales, and the time through that leg of the voyage was regularly specified in ships' records. Once a ship was in the Pacific, Lieutenant Maury recommended first working west and north to the equator between 105 and 125 degrees west and then heading directly for the central California coast.

Except that Captain Thomas Melville initially sailed much farther east than usual, the *Meteor's* published record indicates that he probably followed this general course. The ship took the thirty days of June from Boston to the equator and was in the Straits of Le Maire on August 7. She had crossed 50 degrees south in the Atlantic on August 1, Melville's birthday (not celebrated by any journal entry for this day), and because of the gales his journal describes she spent fifteen days reaching 50 degrees on the other side on August 16. Northbound in the Pacific, the *Meteor* crossed the equator again on September 13, but thereafter encountered light winds and calms, including four days only 160 miles off Point Reyes, California. During the calm, one afternoon Melville drew a picture of Arrowhead, with himself approaching in the carriage pulled by "Charlie," and family figures out to meet him (see p. 642 below). The delay made for the ship's relatively slow thirty-day passage to harbor on October 12.

When Melville was not seasick (unaccustomedly so) or knocked about by the ship's pitching, he engaged in the pastimes meagerly described in the few entries of the 1860 journal. He had a gam with a whaler in the Pacific.[51] He wrote a few family letters to be mailed

51. See Heflin (1975) for a reminiscence of the Pacific gam, thirty-odd years later by the whaleship's captain. Signing himself "A Member of the Clan," this captain, in the Nantucket *Inquirer and Mirror* (Dec. 31, 1892), after praising highly the cetological accuracy of *Moby-Dick*, said, "I had the honor of entertaining Mr. Melville for a day on board of my ship in mid-ocean, and found him a gentleman in every sense of the word. He was on his way to California, in ship Meteor, of Boston, commanded by his brother." This gam is mentioned as lasting an hour in Melville's letter to his son Malcolm reprinted below, pp. 635–37.

from San Francisco. He read a fair amount. In the farewell letter of May 28 he had told Duyckinck, "I have a good lot of books with me—such as they are;—plenty of old periodicals—lazy reading for lazy latitudes." His journal calls these "the 'Quarterlies'," best fit for the tropics which would make "methodical reading out of the question" (132.25–26). Eleven surviving "books" (including works of more than a single volume) contain jotted notations that attest where or when (or both) he had them in hand on the voyage. First in this respect was Alexander Campbell's *Sketches of Life and Character*, given him by Allan in 1849, which he soon passed on to Tom: "At sea. June, 1860." In the South Atlantic he recorded the ship's latitude in Hawthorne's *The Marble Faun*. In five of the works he wrote "Cape Horn" (followed in three of these by a "2") but no month. These works were the first volume of Milton's *Poetical Works*, Chapman's *Iliads of Homer*, Homer's *Batrachomyomachia*, Bulwer-Lytton's translation of Schiller's *Poems and Ballads*, and a volume with the New Testament and Psalms. Having made the rough passage of the Horn and sailing north, he placed "Pacific Ocean" and successive dates in five volumes: September 4 in Béranger's *Songs*, September 14 ("Gulf of Mexico") in Wordsworth's *Complete Poetical Works*, September 21 in the second volume of the Milton set, September 22 ("Sunday afternoon") in Cary's Dante, and October 3 ("700 miles from San Francisco") in Chapman's *Odysseys of Homer*.[52]

The 1860 journal ends abruptly after two extended entries for August 9 and 10, occupying nearly a third of the whole, about the shocking death of a young sailor named Ray who fell from a yardarm, off the pitch of the Cape. After that, for the whole Pacific passage to San Francisco, from mid-August to mid-October, Melville kept no further account, at least none that is now known. Preserved are only two letters. One of these is a three-page letter he wrote on September 2 to his seven-year-old daughter Bessie that told her simply about the sea-birds. The other is a detailed eight-page letter he wrote on September 1 and 16 to his eleven-year-old son Malcolm in which he spent two of its pages telling of the young sailor's fall and death. Letters to his wife (September 22, October 19) and to her

52. For the complete dating and placing Melville put in each work, see (in order) Sealts 117, 247, 358b, 277, 276, 439, 65, 58, 563a, 358b, 174, 278.

father (October 16?) are not extant, though some of their content is mentioned in letters among the family at home. A surviving note from Melville to his wife's half-brother Sam gives no details about either the voyage or San Francisco, where he wrote it on October 16, four days after his arrival on October 12.[53]

About Melville's week in San Francisco, October 12 to 20, very little is known. Apart from his note to Samuel Shaw, we now have nothing from his own pen. Local newspapers announced the *Meteor*'s arrival—two of them giving "Kay" rather than "Ray" as the dead sailor's name. They welcomed Melville's coming, evidently had been told he would be there for some time, and expressed hope that local literary societies would prevail on him to speak. Predictably, Melville seems to have visited at least one book store, for it appears that on his third day ashore, pursuing his study of poetry, he bought Charles Mackay's edition of *Songs of England*, which he misleadingly inscribed "H Melville N.Y. Oct 15th 1860," when in fact he was in San Francisco (Sealts 342).

On October 18 the *Daily Alta* announced his imminent departure. One bright episode, on October 19, the last day of his stay, has only recently come to the notice of his biographers. It was reported on the same day with tantalizing brevity by Thomas Starr King in two letters to friends in New York. To "Dear Randolph" (identified as Randolph Ryer, a very old friend newly rich in business) he wrote: "I have just returned from Mrs. Fremont's where I have made a visit with Herman Melville, who is visiting San Francisco. He brought a letter of introduction from Dr. Dewey. We had a fine time with Mrs. F. The Col. was at home." To Henry W. Bellows (later to be the Melvilles' pastor in New York), King's letter reported the visit in a sentence word for word the same as the first one just quoted. This episode involved Melville with four nationally famous figures of the era. Orville Dewey, who supplied him the letter of introduction, most likely at the request of Chief Justice Shaw, was a native of Berkshire County, loyal to it throughout his distinguished career as a Unitarian minister in various cities including New York and at this time Boston. Thomas Starr King, to whom Melville presented Dew-

53. For the possibility that Melville made further journal entries that have not been preserved, see p. 232. His letters to Bessie and Malcolm are reprinted below, pp. 635–41.

ey's letter (probably overcoming inhibitions as in London) was an equally distinguished Unitarian minister, for the past ten years in Boston, and also a successful lyceum lecturer as Melville was not; earlier this same year he had moved to San Francisco and was becoming one of the state's leading men. Jessie Benton Frémont was the daughter of the redoubtable thirty-year senator from Missouri, Thomas Hart Benton, over whose strong opposition she had in 1841 married John C. Frémont, the dashing explorer of the West. Colonel Frémont had meanwhile won both notoriety and popularity, especially for his part in the "conquest" of California in the late 1840's, and had become very rich since 1849 from California gold and real estate. In 1856 he was the first Republican candidate for president, losing to James Buchanan. In their fine new home at Black Point overlooking the Golden Gate, Jessie Frémont, herself highly literate, held her salon, receiving the city's intellectual elite and literary visitors. During the "fine time" King and Melville had with her on their visit, the one topic of conversation mentioned in King's letter to Ryer was her willful marriage—which she brought up, evidently in the presence of her husband the colonel, who was "at home": "It is the 19th anniversary of her wedding,—when all Washington was horror struck, as she said, because she had made '*such* a foolish match.' " King's letter goes on, "Now that Fremont's mills turn out $16,000 a week in solid gold I suppose Washington would pass a different judgment. She *is* a superb woman."[54]

The next morning, October 20, Melville sailed on the *Cortes* (or *Cortez*) for Panama City. At some point, presumably during his week in San Franciso, though it is not clear just when or why, he had given up any notion of traveling on with Tom. Perhaps there was not the ready cargo for the Far East that they had originally counted on;

54. The *New Melville Log* documents the newspaper reports and the letters cited in this paragraph. Alan Trachtenberg called Jay Leyda's attention to King's letter to Bellows (at present unlocated), as cited by Peter E. Palmquist in *Carleton E. Watkins: Photographer of the American West* (published for the Amon Carter Museum by the University of New Mexico Press, Albuquerque, 1983), pp. 12–13. Hershel Parker located King's other letter about the episode, in the Thomas Starr King Papers in the Bancroft Library, University of California, Berkeley; the quotations are given here by permission. A play about Melville's visit to San Francisco is now being written by Tony Gilgallen, making use of his discoveries about various local happenings at the time of Melville's visit.

perhaps the owners changed intentions because of a better cargo,[55] perhaps, as Melville wrote his wife (according to his mother's letter cited below), the voyage was not improving his health; or perhaps, as his biographer Leon Howard implies, he just wanted to get back to his family again.[56] In any event, Melville chose not to wait and sail with Tom.[57]

About Melville's three-week return trip to New York via Panama, again we have nothing he may have put on paper en route or later. Of the surviving books he marked on the outward voyage, only one (the Wordsworth) carries his notations of date and place during the homeward trip to show he had it in hand then. Perhaps once again he was traveling light and had left most of his "good lot"

55. According to Pony Express news from California, by October 31 the *Meteor* had begun loading one hundred tons of wheat for England (*New-York Times*, November 12, 1860). She sailed in mid-November for Falmouth, England, where she arrived in late February of 1861.

56. See Howard (1951), pp. 266–69.

57. The posting of the letters Melville had written on shipboard and the dating of those he wrote or probably wrote in San Francisco are uncertain evidence regarding the time of his changing plans. The September 16 part of the shipboard letter to his son Malcolm describes the way it will be carried from San Francisco by way of Panama to New York. Any announcement of his intended return home, written to his wife in the implied enclosing letter to her on the twenty-second, would not reach there before he himself did. But though he did not in fact mail Malcolm's letter the way he had planned, the route it apparently came by would have taken just about as long. The envelope, besides carrying the notation of its posting in San Francisco, October 19, is also marked "Overland"; this indicates that it was carried by the government-contracted Overland Mail Company, in which case it would ordinarily reach St. Louis in about three weeks, by way of Los Angeles, Texas, and Arkansas. If so, and forwarded as it was from Pittsfield to Boston, once again it would hardly have reached his wife before Melville himself arrived, still less at any time before November 5. For on that date, his mother wrote her brother that she and her resident daughter had heard from Elizabeth, reporting a Pony Express letter speaking of his unimproved health. (The dramatic, newly inaugurated but short-lived Pony Express, without government contract, promised ten days from Sacramento to St. Joseph, Missouri, but it was expensive, five dollars an ounce.) And in a curiously phrased addition, the senior Mrs. Melville remarked, "He had written us to come by Steamer — Lizzie writes" (Metcalf, 1953, p. 189). Does this mean he was coming by steamer, or the letter was? And was the letter the one to Elizabeth, or another to his mother? Melville's one extant communication from San Francisco, a note to Elizabeth's half-brother Sam Shaw, dated October 16 and, so it says, to be enclosed in a longer letter to Chief Justice Shaw, apologizes for its brevity by announcing ambiguously, "In a few days I shall be at sea again."

of books and his other gear aboard the *Meteor* with Tom, as he had left his trunk and excess baggage behind in Liverpool with Hawthorne in 1856. If so, before the books reached his hands again they had completed the long cruise with Tom from which he had removed himself. In 1866 Mark Twain was to take the same trip—San Francisco to New York—and later to make good literary use of it, but if Melville had ever entertained such a motive nothing came of it.

At least his means of transport and accommodations, afloat and ashore, can be described. Steamship connections between New York and San Francisco including the land transit of the Panama isthmus had been dramatically energized by the Gold Rush. By 1855, the Panama Railroad had been completed, initially supervised by Melville's admired travel writer, John L. Stephens, and the independent Atlantic and Pacific steamship lines had agreed on mutual schedules for through passage.[58] Somewhat surprisingly, most years of the decade it appears that at least three-quarters as many passengers wished to travel east as west.

Cornelius Vanderbilt had characteristically muscled into control of the Atlantic line, and had as well obtained a sizable holding in the Pacific Mail Steamship Company. But the latter was still managed in excellent fashion unlike its Atlantic counterpart; it was well-staffed, officered, and provisioned, with three departures a month from San Francisco, scheduled on the first, eleventh, and twentieth. Wooden side-wheel steamers were becoming a little dated and more expensive to operate, but passengers liked them because they were wide and steady, without the vibrations and rolling of the narrower screw-steamers. Especially on the less stormy and warm Pacific leg, the upper-deck cabins and promenades were spaciously comfortable. Entertainment included dancing, amateur theatricals—and gambling.

On the Pacific side, ships stopped at Manzanillo or Acapulco for coal and fresh provisions; in the Caribbean, ordinarily either Havana or Kingston, Jamaica, depending on which end of Cuba the ship

58. For Stephens see p. 185 above. Melville had shown an earlier interest in Central America. He had bought from Harper & Brothers in 1855 Robert Tomes's *Panama in 1855. An Account of the Panama Rail-Road, of the Cities of Panama and Aspinwall* (Sealts 528) and Ephraim G. Squier's *Waikna* (Sealts 485), an account of exploring the Mosquito Coast, i.e., coastal Honduras. Melville had met Tomes through Evert Duyckinck in 1848 and given him a copy of *Moby-Dick* in 1852, and Tomes was one of the party at Daniel Shepherd's on the eve of Melville's departure for Scotland in 1856.

rounded. The western leg of the trip took thirteen or fourteen days to Panama City; the railroad scheduled two trains a day each way (forty-seven miles, four hours, $25 plus ten cents a pound for baggage), so that passengers could move from one ship to the other with minimum delay. From Aspinwall (now Colón) on the north side, where the railroad had been built out to an island with deep-water docking, the usual time to New York was another nine to eleven days. In early 1860 fares rose again so that by first-class cabin a through ticket (including rail fare) cost $225 eastbound, $25 higher than westbound.

The *Cortes*, on which Melville left San Francisco, Captain Richard H. Pearson commanding, carried 250 passengers and more than a million dollars in specie. Stopping at both Manzanillo on October 27 and Acapulco on the twenty-eighth, they arrived at Panama City in the early afternoon of November 4.[59] Presumably, Melville with other passengers took the quite decent train the same afternoon and either boarded ship overnight, or stayed at one of the hotels that had sprung up in busy, Yankee-ized Aspinwall.[60]

Melville's remaining passage on Vanderbilt's *North Star*, however, under Captain A. G. Jones, was doubtless a different story so far as comfort was concerned. It, too, was a wooden side-wheeler of nearly 1900 tons, built on Long Island in 1853 and used by Vanderbilt that summer as a private yacht, carrying his family and a large party to Europe and the Mediterranean.[61] But any ship, whatever its previ-

59. The *Cortes* had been launched in New York in 1852, for local Atlantic coast service, but was immediately transferred to the Pacific where she served uneventfully until the early 1860's. She was a characteristic wooden side-wheeler of something over 1100 tons, with three decks; there is a picture of her in Kemble (1943), facing p. 52. Transferred to China service, she burned at Shanghai in 1865.

60. There are 1861 pictures of these trains in Kemble (1943), facing p. 117. As early as 1853, there were five hotels; the City Hotel, for example, was two hundred by sixty feet with surrounding galleries on both floors, could seat two hundred people in the dining room and bar, and could accommodate five hundred comfortably if cots were placed on the screened galleries (Kemble, p. 187). Richard Henry Dana, Jr., had found Aspinwall in the summer of 1859 a "Dismal place. Swamp, torrid marsh, hot, damp, a mist of vapors, like smoke, at sun-rise, all full of miasma. . . . Aspinwall not intended to be lived in by whites. Worst place I ever saw" (*Journal* [1968], III, 842).

61. An amusingly, grossly sycophantic account of the commodore, the guests, and the trip was given by the quasi-"chaplain," the Reverend Dr. John Overton Choules, in *The Cruise of the Steam Yacht North Star* (1854); a sketch of the two-masted, two-stack ship adorns the title page and is embossed on the cover. Thereafter the ship

ous service, controlled by and contributing to the greed of the old commodore, was notorious for insolent and infrequent service, inadequate staffing and provisioning, and filthy conditions. One outraged account of a Vanderbilt ship, just over a month before Melville's passage, declares:

> We are assured that a more filthy, nasty, pigstie could not be found any where. . . . The dirty, greasy table cloths were rendered still more disgusting by being used at night as pillows by the niggirs. . . . The food is represented as abomnible; the staterooms uncleaned; in fact everything a perfect disgrace to both captain and owners.

The *North Star* seems no exception; on an 1863 trip, a *New York Herald* reporter claimed it was overloaded by nearly three hundred passengers, with only two out of seven lifeboats ready for launching, and only four toilet facilities for some three hundred passengers in the first and second cabins.[62] Nevertheless, the *North Star* evidently made a fast trip, for Melville landed in New York on November 12. He could have read in the *Times* of that day the latest Pony Express news mentioning the *Meteor*. He went on to Boston where his family was with the Shaws, and in early December he returned to Pittsfield to ready the cold house for their homecoming. By this time Tom and the *Meteor* were on their way to England, and perhaps it was at this Christmas season that he composed the poem "To Tom" (see p. 647 below).

Inevitably, Melville was again at restless loose ends. His volume of poems—which, though he could hardly have expected much financial return, had nevertheless been prepared with anxious care—remained unaccepted. In the following years, whatever the disappointment of this first attempt at publishing poetry, he continued his study of other poets and his writing of poetry. Poems stirred by the Civil War appeared in *Harper's Monthly*, and the collection *Battle-Pieces* in 1866, the first full year of peace. At the end of 1866, the acquaintance he had made in Switzerland in 1857 with the New York

---

served on the New York–Aspinwall run until 1865, with occasional charter service (at a price) for the government during the war; it was broken up in 1866.

62. These accounts are in Kemble (1943), pp. 162, 155–56; see also pp. 96, 160. A passenger list for Melville's trip appeared in the *New-York Times* for November 14. Dana, too, on the first leg of his trip around the world, found his ship "*filthy*. No care of water-rooms. . . . In 1st cabin, no change of bed linen for whole passage—11 days—no cleaning out. Bad smell of dining-room, scarcely tolerable" (*Journal*, III, 841).

banker Henry Smythe[63] resulted at last in his government appointment as Inspector of Customs in New York City, a post he held for nineteen years, the rest of his working life. The rest of his writing life was devoted mainly to his poetry. Whether coincidental in timing or not, *Clarel*, the major work of this period, was published in the centennial year 1876. Two privately printed collections followed: *John Marr and Other Sailors* (1888) and, in the last year of his life, *Timoleon* (1891). In his desk at the end, besides unprinted verse and accompanying prose, much of which he was shaping for further publications, there was the ballad that had grown into the unfinished manuscript of *Billy Budd, Sailor*. In all of these published and projected volumes were materials reminiscent of experiences recorded in one or another of the three journals presented in this volume of his *Writings*.

SOURCES

REFERENCES TO DATES, events, and documents that are not otherwise documented in this NOTE are based upon the following printed sources: *The Letters of Herman Melville*, ed. Merrell R. Davis and William H. Gilman (New Haven: Yale University Press, 1960), of which a revised edition will appear as Volume XIV of the Northwestern-Newberry Edition of *The Writings of Herman Melville;* Jay Leyda, *The Melville Log* (New York: Harcourt Brace, 1951; enl. ed., New York: Gordian Press, 1969), a revised edition of which, titled *The New Melville Log*, edited by Jay Leyda and Hershel Parker, is forthcoming from Gordian Press; Merton M. Sealts, Jr., *Melville's Reading: A Check-List of Books Owned and Borrowed* (Madison: University of Wisconsin Press, 1966; rev. and enl. ed., Columbia: University of South Carolina Press, 1988)—cited as "Sealts" and followed by an entry number; and previously published volumes of the Northwestern-Newberry Edition. All documents are quoted *literatim;* any variation between a document as transcribed in these sources and as printed in this NOTE is based on an examination of the original. Quotations and citations from Melville's works (and page references cited) follow the already published or forthcoming Northwestern-Newberry texts.

63. See the discussion at 125.22.

The following works are cited in the footnotes to this NOTE only by author and date: Patricia Barber, "Two New Melville Letters," *American Literature*, XLIX (November, 1977), 418–21; James J. Barnes, *Authors, Publishers and Politicians: The Quest for an Anglo-American Copyright Agreement, 1815–1854* (Columbus: Ohio State University Press, 1974); Walter E. Bezanson, "*Moby-Dick*: Document, Drama, Dream," in *A Companion to Melville Studies*, ed. John Bryant (Westport, Conn.: Greenwood Press, 1986); Carl C. Cutler, *Greyhounds of the Sea* (New York: Putnam's, 1930); Richard Henry Dana, Jr., *The Journal of Richard Henry Dana, Jr.*, ed. Robert F. Lucid (Cambridge: Harvard University Press, 1968); Royal A. Gettmann, *A Victorian Publisher* (Cambridge: Cambridge University Press, 1960); J. Henry Harper, *The House of Harper* (New York: Harper & Brothers, 1912); Nathaniel Hawthorne, *The English Notebooks*, ed. Randall Stewart (New York: Modern Language Association of America, 1941); Harrison Hayford, "Contract: *Moby-Dick*, by Herman Melville," *Proof*, I (1971), 1–7; Harrison Hayford and Merrell R. Davis, "Herman Melville as Office-Seeker," *Modern Language Quarterly*, X (June–September, 1949), 168–83, 377–88; Thomas F. Heffernan, "Melville the Traveler," in *A Companion to Melville Studies*, ed. John Bryant (Westport, Conn.: Greenwood Press, 1986); Wilson L. Heflin, "New Light on Herman Melville's Cruise in the *Charles and Henry*," *Historic Nantucket*, XXII (October, 1974), 6–27; Heflin, "Death of the Arctic Fleet," *Melville Society Extracts*, No. 21 (February, 1975), 10; Howard C. Horsford, "Evidence of Melville's Plans for a Sequel to *The Confidence-Man*," *American Literature*, XXIV (March, 1952), 85–89; Horsford, "Melville in the London Literary World," *Essays in Arts and Sciences*, XIII (September, 1984), 23–42; Leon Howard, *Herman Melville* (Berkeley and Los Angeles: University of California Press, 1951); Octavius T. Howe and Frederick C. Matthews, *American Clipper Ships, 1835–1858* (Salem: Marine Research Society, 1926–27); John H. Kemble, *The Panama Route, 1848–1869* (Berkeley and Los Angeles: University of California Press, 1943); Dwight A. Lee, "Melville and George J. Adler," *American Notes and Queries*, XII (May/June, 1974), 138–41; Leonard W. Levy, *The Law of the Commonwealth and Chief Justice Shaw* (Cambridge: Harvard University Press, 1957); Sanford E. Marovitz, "More Chartless Voyaging: Melville and Adler at Sea," *Studies in the American Renaissance*, 1986, 373–84; Herman Melville, *Clarel*, ed. Walter E. Bezanson (New York:

Hendricks House, 1960); Melville, *Journal of a Visit to Europe and the Levant, October 11, 1856–May 6, 1857*, ed. Howard C. Horsford (Princeton: Princeton University Press, 1955); Melville, *Omoo*, ed. Walter Blair and Harrison Hayford (New York: Hendricks House, 1969); Eleanor Melville Metcalf, *Herman Melville: Cycle and Epicycle* (Cambridge: Harvard University Press, 1953); Lewis Mumford, *Herman Melville* (New York: Harcourt, Brace, 1929); "George Paston" [Emily M. Symonds], *At John Murray's* (London: Murray, 1932); Raymond A. Rydell, *Cape Horn to the Pacific: The Rise and Decline of an Ocean Highway* (Berkeley: University of California Press, 1952); Merton M. Sealts, Jr., *The Early Lives of Melville* (Madison: University of Wisconsin Press, 1974); Sealts, *Melville as Lecturer* (Cambridge: Harvard University Press, 1957); William H. Shurr, *The Mystery of Iniquity: Melville as Poet, 1857–1891* (Lexington: University Press of Kentucky, 1972); Henry Nash Smith, *Mark Twain: The Development of a Writer* (Cambridge: Harvard University Press, 1962); Franklin Walker, *Irreverent Pilgrims: Melville, Browne, and Mark Twain in the Holy Land* (Seattle: University of Washington Press, 1974); Robert K. Wallace, "The 'Sultry Creator of Captain Ahab': Herman Melville and J. M. W. Turner," *Turner Studies*, V (Winter, 1985), 2–20.

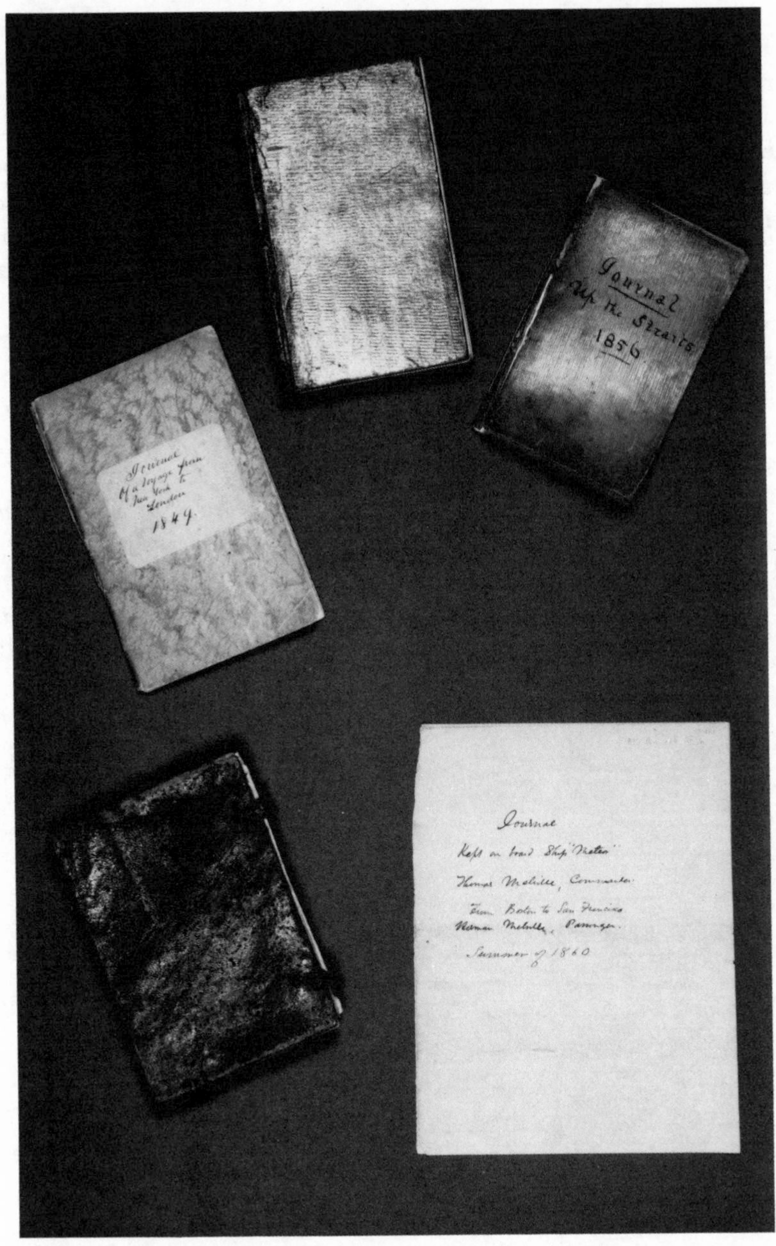

The five manuscript notebooks Melville used for his journals (top: A, B, C; bottom: D, E). By permission of the Houghton Library, Harvard University.

Note on the Text

OF THE THREE journals in this volume, the first two are written in four blankbooks of varying sorts, the third on four loose leaves apparently from another blankbook. For convenience all five of these are called "notebooks" here and are designated as A, B, C, D, and E. The journal of 1849–50 was written in A and B; the journal of 1856–57, barely begun in B, was written in C and D; and the journal of 1860 was written on leaves of E. All five were donated to the Harvard College Library (and are now in the Houghton Library of Harvard University) in 1937 by Melville's granddaughter, Eleanor Melville Thomas Metcalf, to whom they had descended through her grandmother (Elizabeth Shaw Melville, Melville's wife) and her mother (Frances Melville Thomas).

The manuscript notebooks are the only authoritative source for the texts of the journals, none of which was written for publication or was published during Melville's lifetime. Each of the three, however, has been separately edited and published in the twentieth century: the 1849–50 journal, edited by Eleanor Melville Metcalf (1948); the 1856–57 journal, edited first by Raymond Weaver (1935) on the basis of the transcription in a Columbia University M.A. essay by Gerald M.

Crona (1933), then by Howard C. Horsford (1955) on the basis of his Princeton Ph.D. dissertation (1951); and the 1860 journal, anonymously edited (1929). (For full citations see pp. 232–36.)

For the Northwestern-Newberry texts of the 1849–50 and 1856–57 journals, Horsford, the primary editor (who had already in 1951 verified his dissertation text from the manuscripts), initially (1966) made one collation of the manuscript journals in photocopy against the printed texts of the earlier editions (Metcalf, 1948; Horsford, 1955) and later (1967) verified the resulting texts by a complete collation with the manuscripts. For the text of the 1860 journal he made a transcription (1967) from photostats, which he verified from the manuscript; it was verified again by an independent transcription (1986) from the manuscript by Harrison Hayford. Together Lynn Horth and Harrison Hayford made one complete collation (1986) of Horsford's resulting texts with the manuscripts. In the course of Horth's keyprocessing of the texts (1986–89) Hayford, Horth, and Horsford read her numerous successive printouts against photocopies of the manuscripts, thus progressively verifying the texts.[1] All along, undeciphered words and words whose readings were at issue among these editors were reexamined in the manuscripts by one or more of them, as well as by Robert C. Ryan, the Manuscript Associate. In most instances the majority decision resolved such issues satisfactorily. Every word in the final text still not thus deciphered satisfactorily is reported in the DISCUSSIONS (with photofacsimiles): (1) as "conjectural" if the editors can find no satisfactory reading; (2) as having "possible" alternative readings; (3) as preferred by the majority, though not by Horsford, the primary editor, whose preferred reading is listed as "possible" and labeled (H).[2]

Since no new complete independent transcriptions of the 1849–50 and 1856–57 journals were made from their manuscripts for the Northwestern-Newberry edition, it is proper to refer to these newly edited texts as "revised." Acknowledgment is thereby made that they are based, though they do not rely, upon the earlier editions of Metcalf and Horsford, which were transcribed from the manuscripts and which incorporate the contributions of those editors in deciphering

1. The final text was transmitted to the printer in the form of computer disks, and the resulting proofs were read three times against photocopies of the manuscripts.

2. Readings which fall into these three categories occur at some sixty points.

Melville's frequently difficult and sometimes baffling handwriting.[3] Nevertheless, the Northwestern-Newberry text of the 1849–50 journal differs from the Metcalf edition at numerous points in spelling, punctuation, and capitalization on almost every page (mainly because of different editorial policies) and in wording at some dozen points; and the Northwestern-Newberry text of the 1856–57 journal differs repeatedly from the Horsford Princeton edition in spelling, punctuation, and capitalization on almost every page (mainly for the same reason) and differs in wording at some ninety points.

The following pages describe the five manuscript notebooks, report earlier editions of the journals, set forth the textual policy of the present edition, and describe the textual apparatus.

THE MANUSCRIPT NOTEBOOKS

NOTEBOOK A: BEGINNING OF THE 1849–50 JOURNAL. The notebook given the Houghton Library number Ms Am 188 (371), which is designated A in this edition, was made for a pocket account book. It measures 18.4 by 12 cm. Eleven sheets of lined white paper were folded once to make twenty-two leaves. The resulting forty-four unnumbered pages are lined horizontally in light blue and vertically with one red margin line 2 cm from the left edge and by a double red line 3.2 and a single red line 1.2 cm from the right edge. The cover, a single piece of light cardboard pasted over with orange marble-patterned paper, now faded, was wrapped around the folded leaves and center-stitched with them by two loops of thread. The spine is now worn through, so that the front and back segments of the cover are separated, as are also those of the sheets forming the first six and the last six leaves. On the front of the cover is a plain white label (6.1 cm high by 8.3 cm wide) on which Melville wrote in ink the notation: "Journal / Of a Voyage from / New York to / London / 1849."

Melville's manuscript journal, written in brownish-black ink, occupies only the first twenty-four pages, here designated A1–24; the

3. The text of the Weaver (and Crona) edition of the 1856–57 journal does not underlie any of Horsford's successive transcriptions, although he and the Northwestern-Newberry editors consulted its readings in verifying their own. No use was made of Metcalf's more literal transcription for her edition of the 1849–50 journal (in the Melville Collection of the Houghton Library, Ms Am 188 (371.2)).

Herman Melville's

Journal
Of a Voyage from
New York to London
1849

Thursday Oct 11th After a detention of three or four days, owing to wind & weather, with the rest of the passengers I went on board the tug-boat Goliath about 12½ P.M. during a cold violent storm from the West. The "Southampton" (a regular London liner) lay in the North river. We transferred ourselves aboard with some confusion, bore up our anchor, & were off. Our pilot, a large, beefy looking fellow resembled an oysterman more than a sailor. We got outside the "Narrows" about 2 O'clock; shortly after, the "tug" left us & the Pilot. At half past 5. P.M. saw the last of the land, with our yards square, & in half a gale.

Notebook A, page 1 (script about original size); NN3.2–3.11.

Cathedral. Mysterious hint dropped me
about my green coat. Talked with the
Pilot about the perils of the Channel. He
told a story of running down a brig in a
steamer &c. — It is now eight o-
clock in the evening. I am alone in
my state-room — lamp in tumbler.
Spite of past disappointments I feel that this
is my last night aboard the Southampton.
This time tomorrow I shall be on land,
& press English earth after the lapse of
ten years — then a sailor, now H. M.
author of "Peedee" "Hullabaloo" & "Pog-Dog".
— For the last time I lay aside my
"log," to add a line or two to Lizzie's
letter — the last I shall write aboard.
— ("Where dat old man?" — "Where books?)"
First words of baby Malcolm's)

Notebook A, page 24 (script about original size); NN12.1–12.12.

remainder are blank.[4] Melville left the inside front cover blank, but on the inside back cover he listed mostly in pencil the bottles of stout he ordered aboard ship in October of 1849. At the top of A1 Melville wrote the same notation as on the front label. On this first page he also wrote the date to the left of the vertical margin line and the entry proper on the lines to its right (see the photofacsimile on p. 214). On all succeeding pages, however, though he continued to write the dates in this left margin, often fencing them with one or two horizontal and vertical lines, he wrote the text completely across the page, enclosing the dates with script.

On certain pages Elizabeth Shaw Melville later penciled identifying additions. These occur on A1, where she wrote across the top margin, above Melville's own notation, "Herman Melville's"—and on pp. A13, 14, 18, 19, and 24, where she wrote identifications of pet names, in Melville's entries, for herself and their son Malcolm and of phrases from Malcolm's baby talk (see the photofacsimile of A24, on p. 215).

NOTEBOOK B: CONCLUSION OF THE 1849–50 JOURNAL. When Melville arrived in London, he stopped using his partly filled notebook A in which he had written aboard ship; instead he began his London entries in a second one, which the Houghton Library numbers as Ms Am 188 (372) and the present edition designates as notebook B. Melville made no notation on its cover.

Composed of twelve sewn gatherings, this notebook has covers with a thin, reddish-brown leather (now rebacked with similar leather) over heavier cardboard, trimmed flush with the paper, making a volume 17.8 by 11.5 cm, and 2 cm thick. The paper is pale blue, glazed, and unlined; it is watermarked "TOWGOOD / 1849". The gatherings comprise 144 leaves, of which the first and last were pasted down to the front and back covers, leaving 142 free leaves. The resulting 284 pages are unnumbered; they are here assigned the numbers B1–284. At both the front and the back, a separate strip of a

4. Locations in the present edition of manuscript notebook pages described here may be found by consulting the TEXTUAL NOTES, where the first word on each notebook page (e.g., A6) is keyed to the Northwestern-Newberry (NN) page and line in which it occurs (parenthetical reference numbers below for individual words likewise indicate NN page and line). Melville's miscellaneous entries at the front and back of the manuscript notebooks are printed separately on pp. 137–59, where manuscript locations appear in the outside margins.

For the Journal of voyage out, see the small paper book

I commence this Journal at 25 Craven Street, Strand, at 6 1/2 P.M. on Wednesday Nov 7th 1849—having just arrived from dinner at a Chop House, and feeling like it.

Mon: Nov: 6th 1849. Having at the invitation of McCurdy cracked some Champagne with him, I retired about midnight to my state-room; and at 5 in the morning was wakened by the Captain in person, saying we were off Dover. Dressed in a hurry, ran on deck, & saw the lights ashore. A cutter was alongside, and after some confusion in the dark, we got off in her for the shore. A comical scene ensued. The boatmen saying we could not land at Dover, but only at Deal. So to Deal we went, & were beached there just at break of day. Some centuries ago a person called Julius Caesar jumped ashore about in this place, & took possession. It was Guy Fawke's Day also. Having left our baggage (that is Taylor, Adler & self) to go round by ship to London, we were nobly unincumbered; & I proposed walking to Canterbury—distant 18 miles, for an appetite to breakfast. So, we strode thro' this quaint old town of Deal

Notebook B, page 3 (script about original size); NN12.13–12.29.

proved agreeable in the end. She had resided some time in China — I talked with her some time. Besides these, there was a duodecimo footman, or boy in a light jacket with bell-buttons. — [illegible] [illegible] [illegible] [illegible] [illegible] Conversed with Dr Holland, a very eminent physician, it seems — & a very affable intelligent man, who has travelled immensely. After the ladies withdrew, the three decanters — Port, Sherry & Claret — were kept going the round with great regularity. I sat next to Lockhart, and seeing that he was a customer who was full of himself & expected great homage; & knowing him to be a thorough going Tory & fish-blooded Churchman & conservative, & withall, Editor of the Quarterly — I refrained from playing the snob to him, like the rest — & the consequence was he grinned at me his ghastly smiles. — After retiring to the drawing room, coffee & tea were served, & I soon after came away. [illegible] — Oh Conventionalism, what a ninny, thou art, to be sure. And

Notebook B, page 30 (script about original size); NN25.36–26.16.

slightly brighter green-blue paper has been added to reinforce the hinge between the last free leaf and the cover.

Melville used the notebook for certain miscellaneous entries apart from his dated journal entries. The front pastedown and the first page, B1, he used for memoranda, mostly penciled, of various items at different times unrelated to this trip; all of these were later erased, presumably by Melville himself but possibly by his wife, who wrote on B1 "Herman Melville's / Journal" in pencil. Melville's journal entries begin about a quarter of the way down B3 (see the photofacsimile on p. 217). In the space above, Mrs. Melville wrote a notation in pencil across the top, "For the Journal of voyage / out, see the small paper book"—that is, notebook A. For his 1849 entries in this notebook, Melville left no margins; he commonly underlined the initial date and made the entry proper continuous with it. At first Melville's script is rather smaller and more deliberate than that of his shipboard writing in notebook A; it is in brownish-black ink throughout, except for one long passage in blue ink from the bottom of B13 to the middle of B20, two words on B23, a mixture of both inks on B28, all blue ink on B282, and four addresses in blue ink on B284. On B87 Mrs. Melville added, in pencil, an identification of the pet name of their eight-month-old child. In this notebook, a few derogatory passages were deleted by lining and cross-marking, but not so heavily that they cannot be accurately deciphered for inclusion in the text. These deletions were evidently made by Melville himself within a few days, upon reconsideration, since the ink used for both the entries and the deletions appears to be the same and since no evidence of such treatment by other hands occurs in the journal notebooks or the other manuscripts he left unpublished. These passages occur on B24, 30 (reproduced opposite), 33, 34, 38, and 84 (one word).

Melville's day-to-day entries for the 1849–50 trip to London and the Continent end on B95. (His brief renewed use in 1856–57 of this notebook, pages B96–99 and B284 [for one address], as well as his later use of its front pastedown is discussed below.) However, he used the top of B96 to list the officers of his ships out and back. After B99 the pages are blank until B270, at the top of which Melville entered in pencil the words "The Perjurer" followed by a brief quotation from Ben Jonson—all subsequently erased. Pages B271, 272, and 273 contain a variety of memoranda, some in ink and some in pencil, regarding anecdotes he heard or passages he read while homeward

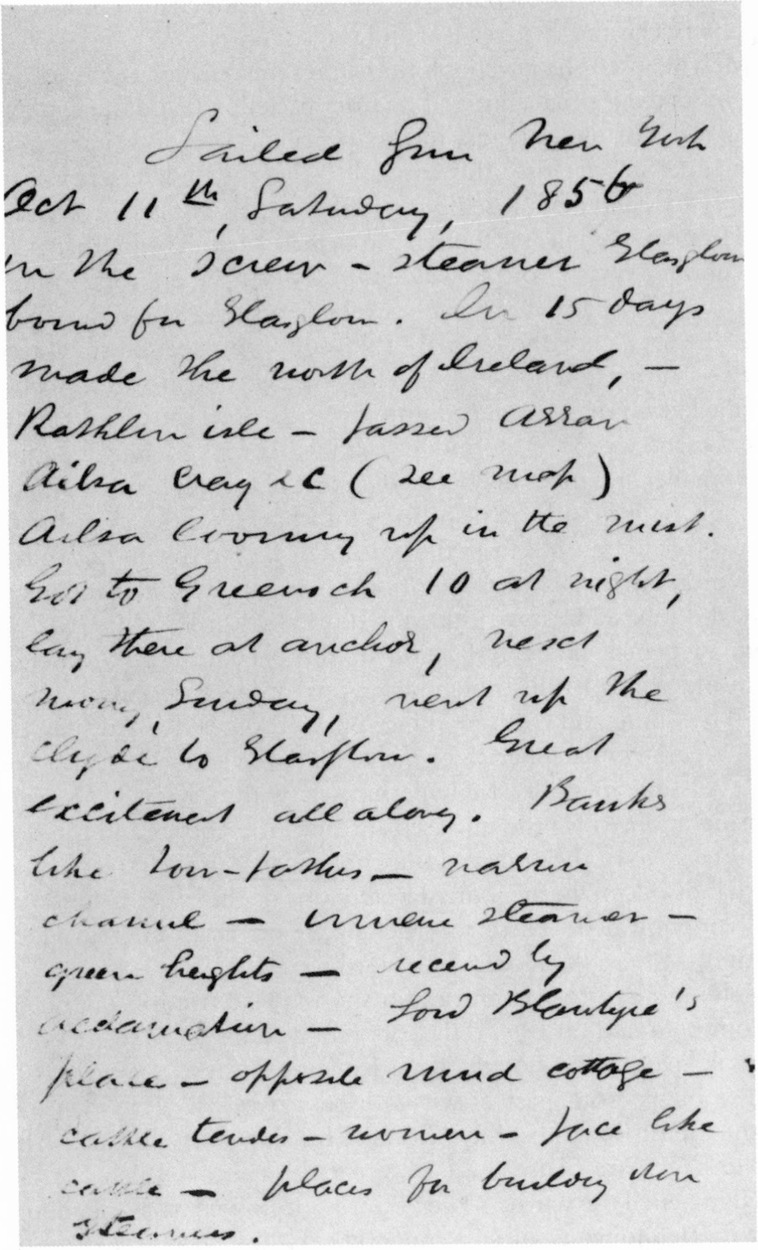

Sailed from New York
Oct 11th, Saturday, 1856
in the screw-steamer Glasgow
bound for Glasgow. In 15 days
made the north of Ireland, —
Rathlin isle — passed Arran
Ailsa Crag &c (see map)
Ailsa looming up in the mist.
Got to Greenock 10 at night,
lay there at anchor, next
morn, Sunday, went up the
Clyde to Glasgow. Great
excitement all along. Banks
like tow-pathes — narrow
channel — immense steamer —
green heights — second by
acclamation — Lord Blantyre's
place — opposite mud cottage —
cattle tender — women — face like
cattle — places for building iron
steamers.

· Notebook B, page 97 (script about original size); NN49.2–49.10.

bound after Christmas of 1849. Pages B274 and 275 are blank; B276 and 277 contain lists Melville made then of books (and "Curios") he had obtained in London, Paris, and Germany. Page B278 is blank except for the incomplete notation "Copy of", and B279 and 280 are also blank. The lower third of B281–82 is torn out; but the upper part of B281 carries names and some later American addresses, and that of B282 lists in blue ink times and places of his various engagements in London. On B283, in pencil, are the three words "Cannibals / Execution / Terrapin" (perhaps referring to his notation on B272 concerning Sir Thomas Browne's allusion to cannibals). Finally, B284 and the inside of the back cover (rear pastedown) carry an extensive list of addresses, primarily English, made during his 1849–50 London trip (he added the final address on B284 during his 1856–57 trip).

NOTEBOOK B: BEGINNING OF THE 1856–57 JOURNAL. Melville made memoranda and journal entries relating to his 1856–57 trip in three separate notebooks, B, C, and D. When he set off in 1856, he took notebook B with him, apparently intending to make renewed use of it since the bulk of its pages remained blank from the 1849–50 trip.[5] For whatever reasons, however, he put no shipboard entries in it on the passage from New York to Glasgow. Only after making his way to Edinburgh did he make use of it, and that simply for a laundry list he jotted on B1. And only later, perhaps in Liverpool, did he enter in it, on pages B97–99, a brief retrospective summary of his crossing to Glasgow (adding on B96 a memorandum of shipboard conversations with "the Colonel"), and of two days sightseeing thereabouts. This writing is all in similar handwriting and pale gray-brown ink. One problematic matter is that he initially dated (on B97, reproduced opposite) the retrospective summary 1857; this year was later corrected in the margin in pencil to 1856 (and was still later erased). The initial dating 1857 (otherwise hard to explain) could well mean that he in fact did not record the summary until sometime in 1857—or even later. In any case, a likely supposition is that when he determined to travel light on his Mediterranean trip he packed away this modestly bulky volume among other excess baggage in the trunk he left behind

5. In Horsford's 1955 edition of the 1856–57 journal, this notebook, since it was the first of the three that Melville used for that journal, was designated as A; its redesignation here as B (to mark it as the second of the five notebooks he used in all for journals) should be noted by readers consulting both editions, as should the redesignation here of Horsford's 1955 B as C and of his C as D.

Memorandum of stay in Liverpool

Begun and continued at sea, which accounts for the part of the writing.

Saturday, Nov 8th. 1856. Arrived from York, through Lancaster, at 1. P.M., having passed through an interesting country of manufactures. A rainy day. Put up at "White Lion Hotel" Dale St. Dined there at ordinary. Before sitting down, asked bar-maid, "How much?" Curious to observe the shrinking expression, as if shocked at the idea of anything mercenary having part in the pure hospitality of an ordinary. Host a bowler at table. Comical affectation of a private dinner party. All thought of the public house banished. Entertaining his friends. "Will you have some ale?"— But charged in the bill.— Affectation of the institution

Notebook C, page 1 (script about original size); NN50.10–50.21.

in Liverpool with Hawthorne at the American consulate. With him instead he carried the much smaller pocket memorandum book, presumably bought in Liverpool, that is here designated notebook C.

NOTEBOOK C: CONTINUATION OF THE 1856–57 JOURNAL. At the end of Melville's brief retrospective account on B97–99 Elizabeth Shaw Melville later penciled the notation: "Continued in small mem. book / — marked 'Journal up the Straits' — / Sailed from Liverpool to Con- / stantinople Nov. 18 — 1856". The "small mem. book" to which her notation refers is the one numbered by the Houghton Library as Ms Am 188 (373) and here designated as notebook C.

Notebook C was made by folding twelve sheets of off-white paper once to make twenty-four leaves, of which the first and last were pasted down, front and back, to the thin, tan-leather cover wrapped around the leaves, with the leaves and cover center-stitched. The remaining twenty-two leaves, or forty-four pages, show faint horizontal lines and are unnumbered; they are here numbered C1–44. Such evidence as the vestigial stitch holes in the spine of the cover and sheets indicates that the present stitching was not the original one; and the evidence of pinholes and creasings in the leaves shows that for a time they were in an unstitched state and suggests that Melville was then using some of his entries on certain of them, probably for other writings. The notebook measures 16.5 by 10.5 cm. On its front cover Melville printed in dark ink with a blunt pen in large letters the notation: "*Journal* / Up the Straits / *1856.*"

Inside, on the upper left corner of its front pastedown, is Melville's ink word-start "Sn", and across the upper center, his penciled memo "Straps for gaiters". Just below, Elizabeth Shaw Melville later wrote in pencil the notation "Herman Melville's / Journal". (These inscriptions are now barely visible because the paper has browned severely from its pasting to the leather.) Also, on C42 Mrs. Melville penciled her notation of the journal's sequence: "Continued in leather / covered book 'bought in / Constantinople' — Dec 16 — / 1856 — ". Melville's day-to-day entries occupy C1–42; C43 has his miscellaneous memoranda in ink, C44 four items in pencil. In the journal the date of each entry is commonly followed by the first words of the entry proper, the writing occupying the whole page— with no significant margins—and generally following the faint (perhaps because faded) lines on the paper (see the photofacsimile of C1, opposite).

minaret. The light loft nest of pigeons.
From the gallery, without, all round, another
glorious view. (Three great views of Constantinople)
All important to one desirous to learn
something of the topography of Pera &c.
After much study succeeded in understanding
the way to the two great bridges. Came
down, & crossed the first bridge. There
took a boy-guide to the bazar. (All
the way from the G. Tower down steep
hill to bridge, a steady stream of people)
Immense crowds on the Constantinople side.
× Way led up steps, into × large court
mosque bazaar
surrounding mosque. There clothes bazar,
most busy scene; all the way to the
Bazar by this route — crowd, crowd, crowd
full of dense
— from the Fez caps, the way seemed
paved with tiles. — The Bazar is formed
× of hundreds narrow aisles, overarched;
and along the sides looks like lines
of show-cases, a sort of sofa-counter before
them (where lads, customers recline) and
a man in each. Persian bazaar, superb.
Pawnbrokers here. Money changers, bullion

Notebook C, page 35 (script about original size); NN63.24–64.1.

Melville's handwriting at places in notebook C becomes quite difficult to read, sometimes because of haste, and evidently it later perhaps gave trouble even to Melville himself, for in the upper right corner of C1 he added in pencil the elliptical and apparently garbled notation: "Began and continued at sea, which accounts for the part of the writing." When he actually began using notebook C is uncertain. The retrospective quality and brevity of its early entries, together with significant omissions (even of a day with Hawthorne in Chester), indicate that, as in his previous abbreviated account of his arrival and stay in Glasgow, he delayed a while in Liverpool before writing in his journal. But the entry for his next-to-last day in Liverpool (Monday, November 17) refers to "today"—an indication that his later pencil notation is not accurate in saying he "began" the use of this notebook at sea.

Melville's repeated later re-perusals of notebook C are evidenced by a number of his later additions: of words, phrases, and attention-arresting devices, some in black pencil and some in red pencil, and perhaps a few inserted words or phrases in an ink that appears distinctly fresher and darker, but possibly only because the pen that made each of them was newly dipped. These additions were chiefly made on the later pages, where his arriving at and exploring Constantinople are recorded (see, for example, the photofacsimile of C35, opposite). Some of them may be associated with his writing poems after he returned home; in at least three cases, on C19, 26, 36, his additions cannot be earlier than the later entries in D (the third of the notebooks for this trip) to which they allude. Among his later changes and additions, besides the penciled note on C1, are those which occur on C18, 19, 23, 24, 26–32, 34–37, 39–41, 44, and perhaps 15; this last, however, may have been made by a still later reader, perhaps the journal's first editor, Raymond Weaver, who did make various pencil notations on Melville's manuscripts.

NOTEBOOK D: COMPLETION OF THE 1856–57 JOURNAL. When Melville had filled notebook C, he began to use a new one; on the recto of the front free endpaper (actually its original second leaf) he wrote: "Bought this book at / Bazaar in Constantinople". This notebook is numbered by the Houghton Library, in sequence with the three earlier ones, as Ms Am 188 (374); it is designated here as notebook D.

The notebook has ten center-sewn gatherings, each of twelve leaves, of which the first and last are pasted down to the front and

Constantinople

Tuesday, Dec 16 [Continued from Small Notebook]

1856

Wandered about in vicinity of Hippodrome till nearly dusk; lost myself, & finally came out at a gate on the Sea of Marmora. Returned to Tophanna by kayack. Interesting appearance of the walls here. Owing to the height of the shore above the sea, the fortifications here present a wall on the water side, but only a parapet on the land. Hence, from the sea, the towers look immensely lofty; & they are of all shapes; in some parts their windows are formed by the open spaces of the battlements. In some parts, there are balconies. Several gates & archways are to be seen walled up. Collonades are disclosed, closed up. Pilasters. The fall, or rather crumbling away of the wall at one angle discloses a solitary column of white marble, looking strange as the remainder of a body masoned up in a tomb. Reminded me of the Abbotsford walls — only on a grand scale. When large masses of the masonry have fallen, they lie like rocks, in confused heaps, the mortar as hard as the bricks & stone. — At dinner to day the French attache estimated

Notebook D, page 1 (script about original size); NN66.20–66.36.

back covers (and now separated at the hinge), leaving 118 leaves. The 236 unnumbered pages are here numbered D1–234, beginning with the recto of the third original leaf, since Melville treated the second leaf as a free endpaper. The unlined paper, of poor quality, has browned and begun to disintegrate as well as to separate at the folds and to pull away from the threads that sew the gathered sheets and from the four cords that attach them to the boards at the spine. The cover is of roughly grained leather (with a tuft of animal hair still remaining) mounted over the front and back boards and wrapped around the spine; it has two leather loops on the front cover, intended to be fastened over the fore-edge to two corresponding leather thongs (now broken off) inserted in the back cover. The notebook measures 17.0 by 12.5 cm and is 2.3 cm thick.

Melville made no notation of its contents on notebook D. In the top left corner of the front pastedown, he penciled a brief notation: "Sanders / American gentleman at Jaffa". On the recto of the free endpaper is Melville's penned notation about its purchase. Immediately below, Elizabeth Shaw Melville noted in pencil: "Herman Melville's / Journal". The verso of the free endpaper carries a variety of Melville's jottings in ink (with two later ones in pencil)—not necessarily all made at the same time, and probably mostly or wholly dating after Melville's return home. Though most of them deal with the Near East, at least one refers to Amsterdam, which he saw near the end of his trip.

The journal proper begins on the recto of the next leaf (the second after the one pasted down) where the present numbering starts as D1 (reproduced opposite). Each entry usually begins immediately following its date, and thereafter runs edge to edge of the paper. In certain places, however, where Melville is writing a retrospective and continuous travel account that goes on through the night, he gives the date of the new day in the running account, not on a new line. Also, on some pages jotted notations in the same ink (evidently contemporaneous) are squeezed into the narrow margins (see, for example, the photofacsimile of D7, on p. 228).

In two major instances, the entries do not run consecutively with events: in both Alexandria and Jaffa, while waiting for ships, Melville writes long retrospective accounts of his impressions and activities in Egypt and in Palestine; in Jaffa he evidently carries on a double set of entries—day-to-day events there, and the intensively worked-over

Spent an hour conversing with him & his brother. Got a guide (a grave serious man with a figured coat carrying a silver mounted mace in a velvet scabbard in one hand, and a heavy silver mounted cowhide in the other) and went to Bazaar, to see the slaves. Failed. Went up Mt Pagus. A large circuit. The interior strewn over with fragments of stones, looking like a broken moor. Commands a superb view of bay & town of Smyrna. An old ruinous mosque within. A Boston name written there. Descended, & went to the Caravan Bridge, a great resort on holydays, and country gate of the town. There passed a constant succession of trains of camels, horses, mules, & donkeys. Sometimes a horse leading a camel-train, sometimes a donkey, sometimes a donkey also following. Horsemen with arms. Buffalo.— The camel a most ungainly creature from his long curved & crane-like neck, (which he carries stiffly like a clergyman in a stiff cravat) his flattery-looking forelegs, & his long lank hind ones, he seems a cross between an ostrich & a gigantic grasshopper. His hoof is spongy, & covered with hair to the ground, so that walking upon these muddy lanes, he seems stalking along on four mops.— The cemeteries very,

Carries his neck out like a turtle. Has a way of turning his head so as to bring his face & tail face eye together. Tail like an eel. Some hold it & steer him.

Camel seems built by nature with special precautions against man's use. The hump in way of saddle, but rather ornament than otherwise here.

[A sort of seam— tuck.— Many of the sides— length. Ornamentation is seen as in most of the [illegible]

Notebook D, page 7 (script about original size); NN69.18–70.6.

account of Palestine. Consequently this account is separated from preceding and following daily entries by unused pages, and a blank page intervenes before the account of missionary activities.

Thus, writing of one sort or another occupies both sides of the free endpaper, then D1–30, then D32–50, then D52–59, and then D61–144 (with the intervening pages blank). On D144 the entries proper conclude with Melville's departure from Liverpool for home. (His subsequent notes and jottings are taken up below.)

With one major exception Melville made these original entries in ink—on D62 in Beirut either his pen or his ink supply failed temporarily and he finished several lines of the entry in pencil. In two notable places, as well, he revised the writing heavily and extensively—in the considered accounts of Egypt and of Palestine (see the description and photofacsimile of a passage from D23 on pp. 188–89 above). His revisions, however, consist of at least two stages. First, there are his immediate revisions as he searches for more vivid or more precise phrasing; these are incorporated in the text of the present transcription. Next, evidently much later, Melville made further changes, including additions and devices for emphasis in both black and red pencil and perhaps some in ink. Very likely there were substages within these two main stages. None of these secondary revisions, since they were all made later, are included in the present text; they are described in the TEXTUAL NOTES and are discussed more extensively in the section of the HISTORICAL NOTE about Melville's later use of this material for his lectures and poetry (pp. 189–94 above).

Following the last of the entries proper, there begins on D145, the next recto, a series of jottings and memoranda, many of which are related both in their purport and in their media—various combinations of black and red pencil and apparently different pen and ink—to Melville's revisions and later perusals noted above. These run from D145 to D149, after which are eighty blank pages. Similar jottings and notations begin again on the fifth page from the end (where the present text's numbering resumes with D230) and conclude on D234 with a brief list of names and addresses, three of which (but not a fourth) are certainly connected with this 1856–57 trip. Finally, the rear pastedown bears a label with the Houghton Library number; it also carries slight fragments, on six glue-spots, of a newspaper or magazine clipping subsequently removed.

Of the five journal notebooks, D presents the most frequent difficulties for reading Melville's handwriting. This fact may account for some further minor later penciled markings, which evidently are not Melville's own. These markings all consist of faint marginal X's or underlinings (or both) associated with especially difficult scrawls, but they do not include the few instances where presumably Melville himself corrected his own difficult words by partly rewriting them in pencil. The following are examples from the notebook's first few pages: on D1 there is such a marginal penciled X beside the line containing a quite obscure "immensely", and one also on D2, where the difficult word is "swarms". Again on D16, "brooches" is singled out by an X and underlining, and on D18 "friable" by underlining. Melville's own later pencilings are not as faint or reticent as these, which must have been made by some later perplexed reader, perhaps Raymond Weaver. Consequently, these marks have not been reported in the textual notes.

NOTEBOOK E: THE 1860 JOURNAL. Melville made only a few intermittent journal entries during his voyage to San Francisco in 1860. He made them on four leaves of machine-made blue paper with chain lines, lightly lined in darker blue, each leaf watermarked "JOYNSON / 1855" and measuring 24.8 by 19.4 cm. These leaves are now separate and may have been so when Melville inscribed them; however, since the left edge of each is torn (all with the same matching tear) while the other three edges are all machine cut, it seems likely that at the time Melville inscribed them the leaves were still in a notebook (or quired block) and were only subsequently torn from it at one pull. At some time—whether during their inscription or later—the leaves were folded backward into a packet, probably first with two horizontal folds making thirds, then later with three horizontal folds making fourths (the front of the first sheet, with the notation, is most soiled at its middle and bottom quarter creases). The four leaves now have the Houghton Library number Ms Am 188 (375); in this edition they are designated as notebook E and their eight pages as E1–8. (The pages were numbered 1–6 in pencil—perhaps by Mrs. Melville—beginning with the verso of the first leaf, where Melville's entries begin, and leaving the verso of the last unnumbered.) Melville wrote in ink on E1, the recto of the first leaf, the notation: "Journal / Kept on board Ship 'Meteor' / Thomas Melville, Commander: / From Boston to San Francisco." Later, he added on the

1860 1

Wednesday May 30th At 10½ A.M. Tom, Fanny, George Griggs, and I went off to ship in the stream. Beautiful day, and pleasant sail down the harbor. Mr Peabody was on board, and lunched in the cabin. We bade Fanny good bye, and I assisted her into the tug-boat, preparatory to its going ahead to tow. At ¼ past one P.M. pilot and tug-boat left us. Waved our handkerchiefs to Fanny, and the voyage began. —— Quite sea-sick at night.

June 8th Friday During the past days, cloudy, foggy rainy weather, with good breeze generally, and sailing Eastward, a little south of East. — Gulf Stream disagreeable. But this Noon is a change. Clear & bright — light breeze. Wind still from the South. Sent up sky sail yard. Crew busy in rigging &c

June 11th Saturday The same bright, clear weather, growing warmer each day. Feel very sensibly improving in appetite &c, after seasick qualmishness. Have seen flying-fish, weed,
Lat. Portuguese-man-of-war, and several sail lately.
33." 21. This afternoon had a collision with an English brig
Long. from Pernambuco bound for Liverpool. She blundered
41. 37. down across our bow, & was locked with us for
Ther. 76." 74. a time; ripping & tearing her sails. We also

Notebook E, page 2 (reduced to 65% of original size); NN131.5–132.8.

next line: "Herman Melville, Passenger." Below this, still later, Elizabeth Shaw Melville added, also in ink, "Summer of 1860". At some point the third leaf, E5–6, evidently was separated from the others, for she penciled across the top of E5 the identification: "From a journal on the 'Meteor' commanded by Capt. Thomas Melville, bound for San / Francisco"; and in the left margin just above the date "Monday / Aug 8" she penciled the year "1860".

Melville's journal entries begin on E2, the verso of the first leaf (reproduced on p. 231), and continue successively, recto and verso, through E7. His writing is all in dark ink, in unusually clear handwriting. Since the entries break off abruptly, in mid-voyage, it is at least possible that Melville kept further entries that are not preserved, but there is no evidence that he did so, and the fact that he left the last four lines of E7 and all of E8 blank casts doubt upon the possibility. On E2 and E3 a faint pencil line down the left side, about 2.7 cm from the left edge, makes a ruled margin. In these two margins, and in equivalent but unruled margins on the other pages, Melville wrote all the days, dates, latitudes, and longitudes, to the left of the entries themselves.

EARLIER EDITIONS

FROM THE 1849–50 journal, Raymond M. Weaver, in his biography *Herman Melville, Mariner and Mystic* (New York: George H. Doran, 1921), quoted and paraphrased extensively from notebook A and notebook B. The first complete journal transcription from both notebooks was made by Eleanor Melville Metcalf for the edition that she titled *Journal of a Visit to London and the Continent, 1849–1850* (Cambridge: Harvard University Press, 1948); her text and annotations, under the same title, were published in a separate English edition (London: Cohen & West, 1949). In the American edition her text occupies pages 3–88, her substantial annotations, pages 91–175; the first manuscript page (A1) is shown in photofacsimile facing page 4, a deleted passage (B24) facing page 40, and the list of "Books obtained in London" (B276) facing page 86. Mrs. Metcalf's editorial policy differed somewhat from that of the present edition, but apart from her misreadings of some words, her changes in spelling and punctuation, and her inconsistency in the treatment of ampersands, dashes, and the like, her transcription is substantially accurate, as determined by the numerous manuscript (and photocopy of manuscript) collations performed for the Northwestern-Newberry edition. A considerable part of Melville's journal account in notebook A of the voyage to England (but not his subsequent account in notebook B of his movements in England and Europe) was included by Jay Leyda in *The Portable Melville* (New York: Viking Press, 1952), pp. 386–93. Leyda included many more excerpts, from both notebooks—with individual passages rearranged in order to date them as entries—in *The Melville Log* (New York: Harcourt, Brace & Company, 1951), I, 318–25.

From the 1856–57 journal, Weaver first published in his biography, pp. 354–57, a frequently inaccurate extract from the account of Saturday, December 13, Melville's first day in Constantinople (C23–29). Subsequently Weaver edited a complete, but still fairly inaccurate, transcription of the 1856–57 journal, including the four pages from B, all of C, and all of D. Earlier than his own final text, Weaver states in his introductory note, was one prepared by his Columbia University M.A. student, Gerald M. Crona; Weaver acknowledges that "his text is the basis of mine."[6] As his title for this first published

6. Crona's M.A. essay (Columbia, 1933) is titled: "A Transcription from a Photostatic Copy of Herman Melville's *Journal of His Voyage to Constantinople and the Holy Land, 1856–1857.*" Crona's title made clear that he worked not from manuscript but from photostats. His four-page introduction acknowledged the kindness of Mrs. Metcalf in placing them at his disposal, and of Weaver in helping him secure them; but he mentioned no further assistance Weaver may have given him, either by furnishing him any already transcribed passages or by criticizing this pioneer transcription. Unlike Weaver's text, Crona's does not include the portion of the journal in notebook C; it is even more sparingly annotated and shows lack of acquaintance with many proper names Crona misreads. Wrong readings occur on almost every page, not all of which Weaver later corrected in his own text. Weaver's two hyperbolical and imprecise accounts of his prolonged struggle with the 1856–57 journal, in a note in the publisher's prospectus (1935) for the edition and in a textual note in his undated introduction to it, leave uncertain just how much he worked from the manuscript notebooks and how much from photocopies, how much he himself had already transcribed before Crona began, and how much, if anything, he supplied initially for Crona's text or later to correct it. While he leaves the whole chronology of his dealing with this journal likewise unclear, this much emerges: around 1920 Eleanor Melville Metcalf gave him access to it; in the early 1920's he "withheld" it (and the 1849–50 and 1860 journals) from the Constable Edition's added Volume XIII, *Billy Budd and Other Prose Pieces* (1924) as too difficult to decipher ("Already," he writes, "I had slaved over this *Journal* for two years," and "for the first half of it I had a text that at best was very tentative; for the second half I had a text as hopeless and as fragmentary as a papyrus frayed down the center and with every other word obliter-

edition of the complete journal, Weaver adapted (supplying the dates of the whole trip) Melville's notation on the notebook C portion only: *Journal up the Straits: October 11, 1856 – May 5, 1857* (New York: The Colophon, 1935). According to its colophon, the book, "made by the Pynson Printers from plans by Bruce Rogers, was undertaken in the winter of 1932. After having encountered more than the usual vicissitudes of editing and publishing it is now completed in May 1935." Its frontispiece, a "photogravure portrait of Herman Melville is now first reproduced from a photograph in the possession of Mrs. Henry K. [Eleanor Melville] Metcalf. The photograph was made in Pittsfield, Massachusetts in the early sixties, and the author's signature is reproduced from an autograph in the collection of Mr. Weaver." (See p. 192 in the present edition.) (In the prospectus cited in footnote 5, the less positive statement is that the photograph was "taken, it is thought, in the early '60s at Pittsfield, Mass.") A photofacsimile of one leaf from notebook D, manuscript pages 43 and 44, in true size, is bound in between pages xvi and xxvii. There was a detailed review of Weaver's edition by Robert S. Forsythe in *American Literature*, VIII (March, 1936), 85–96.

Jay Leyda supplied a number of significantly better readings (with assistance from Howard C. Horsford) in the lengthy extracts from the 1856–57 journal that he included in *The Melville Log*, II, 525–77. The passages of this journal in Leyda's *The Portable Melville*, pp. 564–

---

ated"); for the rest of the 1920's no work is specified; in the winter of 1932 publication of the edition was undertaken; sometime around 1930 (apparently) Weaver set Crona to work on a transcription, and Crona completed his M.A. essay in 1933; in the spring of 1935, after delays that distressed the publisher, the prospectus appeared, and in May the edition itself. The prospectus, a center-stapled pamphlet of sixteen pages, is titled: *Prospectus of a Hitherto Unpublished Work by Herman Melville JOURNAL UP THE STRAITS Now to Be Published by The Colophon*. It was "Distributed to a few Bookmen in the Spring of 1935 by The Editors of The Colophon, from their offices, 229 West 43rd Street, New York." The prospectus reproduces in photofacsimile part of a sentence from page D71 with the phrase "Rouleau of guineas" [NN99.10, "Roulaeu"], to exemplify Weaver's tormenting difficulties in deciphering Melville's hand and the help he got from friends. But no mention is made of Crona. A concluding "Note to Melville Collectors" apprises them that the prospectus "contains information not in the book itself"; but much of the information, whether conveyed in Weaver's own note or in the publisher's words (evidently inspired by what he told them), is imprecise, as indicated above, or unreliable. For some background relating to the Constable texts, see Philip Durham, "Prelude to the Constable Edition of Melville," *Huntington Library Quarterly*, XXI (1957–58), 285–89.

75, were all from D, the fourth of the five notebooks (with acknowledgment of Horsford's assistance—by error naming the 1849–50 journal).

Howard C. Horsford edited from photocopies and the manuscript notebooks a new and largely accurate transcription of the whole journal, with an introduction and extensive annotations, as his Princeton Ph.D. dissertation (1951), titled the same as the version he later published, *Journal of a Visit to Europe and the Levant, October 11, 1856–May 6, 1857* (Princeton: Princeton University Press, 1955). In this edition photofacsimiles of four manuscript pages are included: D23, 38, 43, and 146 (facing, respectively, pages 274, 275, 242, and 243). Horsford's textual policy—far more rigorously applied—differed from that of Crona and Weaver in presenting, notebook page by page, a somewhat more literal transcription of Melville's erratic handwriting and spelling. His introduction included a valuable three-page description of these and of the problems they offer, which began with the remark, "The difficulties of Melville's handwriting and the vagaries of his spelling enjoy a not undeserved notoriety . . . . But it is only just to Melville to remark that although his hand virtually comprises a private system of penmanship, once one has become familiar with it, it presents real difficulties only at intervals. At such times, however, only inspired guess-work is of any avail" (p. 43). Horsford's description concluded with a statement that rendered his policy of transcription close to that of the present edition: "In view of these and similar problems, then, absolute fidelity in the transcription of the text has had to be tempered with a reasonable expediency, if only for the sake of typography. As a general editorial principle, I have attempted to give Melville the benefit of every possible doubt. Where a word is clearly misspelled, it is left unchanged . . . . Otherwise, where in my judgment only simple or careless elision is involved, I have silently restored the word to its full form" (p. 46). Horsford's 1955 edition included within the text bracketed editorial information, footnote numbers, and other symbols, unlike the Northwestern-Newberry edition, which presents Melville's final wording in clear text on the page, without editorial matter. Corrections, alternative readings, and textual policy in this 1955 edition were discussed by William H. Gilman and by Horsford in a review and replies in *American Literature*, XXVIII (March, 1956 and January, 1957), 82–93, 520–24.

The 1860 journal was not quoted in either Raymond Weaver's biography of Melville (1921) or Lewis Mumford's *Herman Melville*

(New York: Harcourt, Brace, 1929). Its complete text first appeared, edited anonymously, in the *New England Quarterly*, II (January, 1929), 120–25, in a mostly accurate transcription. Jay Leyda printed much of the journal, with some corrections and certain rearrangements of the order of passages for purposes of dating, as entries in *The Melville Log*, II, 618–23, and also in *The Portable Melville*, pp. 587–92.

TEXTUAL POLICY

THE TEXTS presented in this volume, as in other volumes of the Northwestern-Newberry Edition, are critical and unmodernized. They are *critical* in that they do not aim to correspond exactly to the documentary form of the texts but instead incorporate some editorial alterations designed to bring the texts nearer to Melville's intention. They are *unmodernized* in that they do not aim to bring spellings and punctuation into conformity with any presumed modern usage or with the modern idea that consistency in such matters is desirable. Because the single source for the texts of each of the journals is Melville's handwritten original and because the journals are private writings, not intended for publication, the implications of these two words, however, are somewhat different here from what they are for the texts of works published during Melville's lifetime or works of the kinds normally intended for publication.

In the case of such works, critical editors whose goal is a text reflecting the author's intention at a particular time must use their judgment to decide which features of the documentary text (or texts) were supplied by someone other than the author and without the author's full concurrence and, in addition, which were slips made by the author. When, as here, it is clear that no one but the author was responsible for the extant documentary texts, only the latter of these categories is relevant, and the central editorial problem becomes how to define the "slips" that will be corrected. Of course, one could argue that none of them should be corrected and that the text should be presented *literatim*, without critical editing (except for the compromises that are inevitable whenever handwriting is transferred to print). Every text can usefully be presented either way—either as a literal transcription (or reprinting) of an existing text (thus emphasizing the text of a *document*) or as a critically edited text (and therefore emphasizing the intended text of the *work*, which is but imperfectly represented by the documentary text or texts). For private writings as well as those intended for publication, every feature of a document prepared by the author may be significant as psychological evidence; the difference between the two situations is that private writings are not subject to the same conventions of spelling, punctuation, and usage as are published writings, and all idiosyncrasies in them can be thought of as integral elements of the style, and therefore as features not merely of the document but of the work as well. This line of reasoning leads toward the production of noncritical texts. On the other hand, a distinction can be made between idiosyncrasies not intended by the author (such as the transposition of two letters) and those that can be regarded as private usages (such as spellings that would have been considered incorrect according to the conventions of the time and therefore would probably not have been tolerated by a publisher). This line of reasoning leads to the production of critical texts. The Northwestern-Newberry editors, cognizant of the merits of both these approaches, have decided to follow the latter as more compatible with the goal of the Edition as a whole to provide reading texts reflecting Melville's intentions.

The critical texts in this volume therefore attempt to present Melville's intentions in the act of writing: they aim to eliminate his slips of the pen but to retain other odd spellings that appear to have been what he intended at the time. In determining what falls into each category, the editors have had to expand the concept of an unmodernized text to include any spelling that seems intended. Unmodernized critical texts of works intended for publication normally alter spellings that do not conform to what was considered standard at the time (recognizing that some variations in the spelling of particular words were conventional in certain periods). But for private writings the standard of what was expected in print does not apply; the author was not writing for others' eyes and was under no constraint to conform to any convention whatever. That the author may simply not have known the standard spellings for certain words is similarly irrelevant; the author may have wished to be "correct," but, if it is clear that an unconventional spelling was intended at the moment of writing, that spelling would be retained under the policy followed here. Implementing this policy requires two kinds of editorial decisions: (1) determining what spelling to adopt when the handwriting is either unclear or elided; (2) determining, when the handwriting is clear, which unconventional spellings are slips and which are intended.

UNCLEAR HANDWRITING AND ELIDED HANDWRITING. In thinking about this problem, one must begin with the recognition that even the production of a noncritical transcription necessitates critical judgment in transferring a handwritten document into print. Although one's goal would be the exact transcription of the documentary text, subjective judgments are involved in deciding what in fact that text consists of, for the individual standard letterforms of a type design cannot reproduce all the ways in which words may be represented in handwriting—such as with half-formed letters, extraneous strokes, or even indeterminate scrawls—and in any case the point of a transcription is to provide a specialist's interpretation of what is ambiguous in the document. How to transcribe unclear handwriting and elided handwriting must therefore be faced whether one's goal is a noncritical or a critical text. *Unclear handwriting*—here defined to mean the writing in those words where the author was attempting to form all the actual letters (as opposed to eliding some) but did not form them all completely or added extraneous strokes—would probably be handled the same way in both kinds of editions: the context would suggest what letters were intended, and those letters would be placed in the text. Thus a letter that could be read as either *i* or *e* would be reported as one or the other depending on what seemed required by the context; and a superfluous stroke falling between *a* and *d*, but in the context not representing an additional letter, would be ignored. *Elided handwriting*—here defined to mean the writing in those words where the author, instead of forming or half-forming all the actual letters, used one or more strokes or a wavy line to stand for some of them—might be handled differently in the two kinds of editions: a noncritical text might attempt to suggest the nature of the elision, whereas a critical text would report the intended letters. Thus the former might print *ig* and the latter *ing* where a wavy line vaguely resembling *ig* was obviously intended to mean *ing*. A good case could be made, however, for adopting *ing* under these circumstances even in a noncritical text, arguing that the goal of the edition is not the imitation of the strokes of the handwriting but the reporting of the letters they are meant to stand for. Certainly a critical text, like the one offered here, should take this approach.

Elisions are in fact one of the prominent characteristics of Melville's handwriting, often occurring in such combinations as *ance*, *ence*, *ment*, *ing*, *ion*, or *ious*, whether used medially or terminally. They must be distinguished from two other kinds of shortening also common to his hand—abbreviated words and fused letters. Abbreviated words by definition involve the intentional omission of one or more letters (the letters that are present may or may not be clearly formed), whereas elisions by definition are ambiguous strokes that presumably represent the unformed letter or letters in the word. In some instances it is not easy to distinguish an abbreviation from an elision, but the critical editor must make the attempt, because the distinction is important. An abbreviation, as an intended form of a word, has an existence independent of the fully spelled words it is linked with, and an author's choice of one or the other at a given point in a private piece of writing is a stylistic feature that should be respected by a critical editor. An elision, in contrast, does not signal an intended shortening of a word but is simply the paleographical evidence of a hurried attempt to represent the full word, and the critical editor should spell an elided word out in its conventional form (unless the author, when forming all the letters of the word, habitually used another spelling). Melville's habitual use of fused letters must also be distinguished from his elisions: fusions are places where a single stroke does double duty as the ending stroke of one letter and the beginning stroke of the next. Although fusions often pose problems in reading Melville's hand, they do not—once they are identified—pose problems for transcription, because both letters in each instance are actually present (if sometimes only in part) and both would therefore be included in either a critical or a noncritical text.[7]

UNCONVENTIONAL SPELLINGS. Even when the handwriting is clear, critical editors still have a decision to make: whether the spelling that is clearly present is the one the writer intended. Melville's manuscripts are filled with peculiar spellings, and a noncritical text would incorporate all of them. But when the aim is to reflect his intention at the moment of writing, there is obviously a distinction to be made between, on the one hand, spellings like "Publlic" (118.6), "dentention" (3.3; for "detention"), or "twon" (52.24; for "town")

7. The fullest description of the characteristics of Melville's handwriting is the one provided by Merrell R. Davis and William H. Gilman in their edition of *The Letters of Herman Melville* (New Haven: Yale University Press, 1960), pp. xxi–xxv (to be reprinted in the Northwestern-Newberry revised edition of the *Letters*). Further discussion of elision, fusion, and expansion (their term for the addition of superfluous strokes) can be found in their account.

and, on the other, those like "greivously" (11.6), "supurb" (15.31), or "invisable" (57.37). The former are examples of what are often called "slips of the pen," in which the writer, preoccupied by the idea being expressed, reverses two letters or mechanically repeats or anticipates one or more letters. The latter are examples of conceivable spellings: that is, whether or not they are justified by etymology, they are conceivable in that they reflect pronunciation. The former could not have been intended by Melville; it is more accurate to call them "miswritten" than "misspelled," and a critical editor should correct them. The latter may well (and in many instances one can say that they certainly do) represent Melville's intention at the time of writing, whether or not he spelled the same words in other ways at other times, and a critical editor should allow these spellings to stand.

This policy has been applied conservatively in the present volume: the spellings that seem clearly to be instances of miswriting (there are 107 of them) are altered to standard spellings, but all the other spellings are retained as they occur in the manuscripts. The basic guideline for making these decisions is to treat as miswritten any spelling that seems inconceivable as Melville's intended spelling, either because its pronunciation would not resemble that of the intended word or because its sequence of letters is alien to the way letters are combined in English. Although such decisions inevitably rest on editorial judgment, that judgment has operated within a framework established by a strict definition of the characteristics of miswriting. To be eligible for consideration as miswriting, a word must exhibit at least one of the following five features:

(1) *repetition*—The addition of one or more extraneous letters often takes the form of a mechanical repetition, as in "guidedd" (15.7), "Iiago" (22.14), "Cafffe" (112.23), "Publlic" (118.6), and "affablle" (118.9); sometimes the repetition is not consecutive, as in "rifleld" (110.18), and sometimes even a whole word is repeated, as in "to to" (28.1), or an ending is repeated from the previous word, as when "though though" (98.35) is written for "though thou".

(2) *anticipation*—Another kind of addition results from the anticipation of letters that are to follow, either in the same word—as in "dentention" (3.3), "adjoinging" (20.26), "artistocracy" (41.37), "Asaia" (68.35), "Backswoodsman" (112.28), and "breksfast" (118.34)—or in a succeeding word—as when "lasted" (5.31) is written for "last" in anticipation of "drifted" two words later, or "and" (45.33) for "an" in anticipation of the next word "old", or "schoof"

(102.8) for "school" (the next word is "of"), "no" (104.25) for "not" (the next word is "so"), and "blacks" (119.23) for "black" (the next word is "as").

(3) *metathesis*—Transpositions of one or more letters, creating words that cannot possibly have been intended, occur in Melville's (as in nearly everyone's) handwriting: examples are "Sclliy" (10.17), "forigen" (15.27), "Pariasin" (34.6), "twon" (52.24), both "corss" (75.15) and "acorss" (125.26), "tonuge" (95.6 and 110.27), "Itialn" (107.15), and "realtiy" (123.17,20).

(4) *omissions*—Some clearcut omissions (that is, not instances of elision) create groups of letters that Melville cannot have intended as words, such as "shool" for "school" (32.15) or "Ise" (75.6) for "Isle". Uncompleted words such as "disappoint" for "disappointment" (88.18) also fall into this category.

(5) *misplaced familiar combinations of letters*—Several insertions, omissions, and substitutions seem to have resulted from a tendency to form familiar combinations of letters. For example, in writing the name "Sam" Melville added an *e*, unconsciously creating the common word "Same" (29.6); he also added an *e* to "Both" (39.33), presumably because his hand automatically formed the common sequence of letters constituting "the". The same kind of automatic reaction may explain the *l* in "imbible" (37.28) as well as the substitution of "than" for "that" (90.26) and "that" for "than" (132.17).

It is obvious that these five categories must be interpreted in the light of the general guideline stated earlier, for not every word that falls into these categories is an example of miswriting. For instance, the repeated *d* in "guidedd" (15.7) and *l* in "affablle" (118.9) make those words miswritten, whereas the repeated *r* in "Canterburry" (12.28) and *l* in "collonade" (74.38) do not, because the latter are (and the former are not) conceivable English combinations of letters; and the metatheses in "forigen" (15.27) and "corss" (75.15) produce miswritten words, whereas those in "beleives" (5.1) and "heigth" (60.6) do not, because the latter are (and the former are not) pronounceable as the intended words—"heigth" of course representing a common, if nonstandard, pronunciation. (It may be noted that "beleives" and "heigth" were common lifelong spellings of Melville.) The characteristics placing words in one of the five categories enumerated here, therefore, are a necessary but not a sufficient condition for considering those words miswritten.

There is one further way in which the present text departs from

Melville's inscription in his notebooks: it incorporates only his final wording at points where he made revisions at the time of his original inscription.[8] The presence of canceled wording is one of the common characteristics of private documents, and a literal transcription would have to include this wording.[9] It is not part of what Melville intended, however, and is therefore not incorporated in the Northwestern-Newberry text (though it is reported in notes).[10] Reported separately (pp. 137–59) are the miscellaneous notations that Melville made at the front and back of notebooks A, B, C, and D.

TEXTUAL APPARATUS

THE TEXTUAL apparatus in this edition enables readers to reconstruct certain features of the manuscripts and provides them with an explanation of the reasoning that underlies the transcription at individual difficult points.

DISCUSSIONS. These discussions identify conjectural readings and supply photoreproductions of them, in context, at approximately original size. (In the reproductions some features of the originals may not show, while some apparent features may be due to marks showing through from the other side.) They also point out Melville's errors in dating, call attention to other errors (such as omitted words or mistaken identifications), provide relevant contexts for Melville's allusions, and indicate the standard spellings for persons and places mentioned by Melville. A chronology and a map of the entire trip are

8. For treatment of Melville's later revisions that are not incorporated in the text, see p. 229 above.

9. Parts of words and punctuation marks that Melville did not actually strike through in his cancellation of the passages in which they stand are considered canceled in accordance with Melville's evident intention and are not included in the text or distinguished from other canceled matter in the textual notes. Similarly, several vestigial words, capital letters, and plurals, which Melville let stand through incomplete revision, are altered in the text to fit the revised context; these vestigial manuscript readings, however, are reported in the TEXTUAL NOTES. Omitted words, however, are not supplied, nor are Melville's factual errors, such as incorrect dates or days, corrected; these are identified in the DISCUSSIONS.

10. A minor additional departure from Melville's inscription is the omission (in six instances in his 1849 journal) of his repetition of the date of an entry after beginning a new manuscript page; these redundant date lines are reported in the TEXTUAL NOTES.

supplied for the first two journals; maps of London, Paris, Constantinople, Jerusalem, Naples, and Rome are also provided.

TEXTUAL NOTES. These notes, which also cite readings in the text by page and line numbers, record (1) the words with which individual manuscript pages in the five journal notebooks begin; (2) the readings of the manuscripts at those points where the present editors have made alterations to correct miswritten words; (3) letters, words, or phrases Melville (by lining out, erasing, or rubbing out the ink) canceled at the time of original inscription; (4) the locations of words that Melville added at that time on the same line or inserted above lines, below lines, or in margins, along with a description of his means (if any) of showing where the words were intended to be read; (5) his marks of emphasis (such as circling, boxing, oversize lettering, and multiple underlining); (6) his occasional repeated date lines in the 1849 journal, which are omitted from the text (see footnote 10 above); (7) Melville's cancellations and additions made at a subsequent sitting, whether soon or in later years (in pencil unless otherwise noted); and (8) extra-textual markings and notations by Melville himself and his wife. Unless otherwise reported in these notes, the writing is in the ink described above for each notebook. After the closing bracket, all words in italics are editorial, and all in roman are authorial. These notes do not attempt to describe the handwriting at points that can be considered unclear or elided; but the problems posed by some of these instances, as well as some of the possible solutions, are taken up in the DISCUSSIONS.[11] Textual notes for the miscellaneous entries are presented at the foot of the page or on the following page (see p. 137); these notes specify the medium of all markings on the page.

REPORT OF LINE-END HYPHENATION. Since some compound words are hyphenated at the ends of lines in the manuscripts, the

11. The textual notes also do not report changes from the manuscripts that are purely a matter of design. The following are regarded as such and therefore nontextual: the lineation and placement of titles; the spacing between journal entries; the placement, spacing, lineation, and various scorings of date lines (here uniformly printed in italics); the use of lines under superscript letters; the length of hyphens, dashes, and lines (here standardized to four lengths: the ordinary hyphen, an em dash, a two-em dash, and a three-em dash to mark places where Melville used one to fill out a short line of writing); and the placement of punctuation in relation to quotation marks when that placement is indeterminate in the manuscript (in such cases the punctuation has been uniformly placed outside the quotation marks in conformity with what appears to have been Melville's dominant practice).

intended forms of these words become a matter for editorial decision. When such a word appears elsewhere in the manuscripts in only one form, that form is followed; when its treatment is not consistent, the form which occurs more times in analogous situations is followed. If a word does not occur elsewhere in the manuscripts, the form is determined by a survey of similar words, by the usage in mid-nineteenth-century dictionaries, such as Worcester's *A Universal and Critical Dictionary of the English Language* (Boston, 1847) or Webster's *American Dictionary of the English Language* (Springfield, Mass., 1848), and by any relevant evidence in other Melville manuscripts. The first list in the REPORT OF LINE-END HYPHENATION records these decisions, by listing the adopted Northwestern-Newberry forms of compounds that are hyphenated at the ends of lines in the manuscripts. The second list is a guide to the manuscript forms of compounds that happen to be hyphenated at the ends of lines in the Northwestern-Newberry edition. No editorial decisions are involved in this second list, which is needed for making exact quotations, in respect to these words, from the present edition.

To sum up, then, the text of this edition can be described as one that attempts to reflect Melville's intention by expanding elisions, correcting slips of the pen, and omitting canceled material. The guiding rule, as for the treatment of manuscript material in other volumes of the Northwestern-Newberry Edition, is that unclear, conjectural, and elided words are transcribed in standard spelling (unless Melville habitually spelled them differently), but words that are clearly spelled unconventionally (except for those classified as miswritten) are retained as Melville wrote them. Although the apparatus provides readers with evidence regarding miswritten words and cancellations, it cannot—short of offering a complete manuscript facsimile—make available the evidence for the editors' decisions about how to read all that is unclear and elided in the original manuscripts. Even a photofacsimile is not an adequate substitute for the original, and certainly no transcription can be. But transcriptions have contributions of their own to make, and the present critical transcription is offered as an attempt to establish the text Melville intended as he wrote his journals, along with information to help readers understand the nature of the documents and the private writings they contain.

Discussions

THESE discussions of adopted readings and of Melville's references are keyed to page and line of the journal texts and (unlike the texts) supply now-standard spellings for proper names. The discussions correct Melville's frequently wrong dates and misspelled proper names; for commentary on textual decisions, see p. 212 above. Discussions for the first two journals are preceded by a chronology and a map of the entire trip (see pp. 248–49 [1849–50] and pp. 380–83 [1856–57]); maps are also supplied for London (pp. 272–73), Paris (p. 334), Constantinople (p. 399), Jerusalem (p. 435), Naples (p. 457), and Rome (p. 463). See below for a list of abbreviations and of short titles for frequently cited works; citations for other works are given in full at the first occurrence and by author or short title thereafter (to locate the full citations readers may consult the index). Unless otherwise specified, all quotations from Melville's writings (and page references cited) follow the Northwestern-Newberry (NN) Edition (poems cited as unpublished by Melville will be found in the forthcoming NN volume *BILLY BUDD, SAILOR and Other Late Manuscripts*). All quotations are presented *literatim* (except for the silent correction of several typographical errors in secondary sources); any variation between a document as transcribed in the works listed below and as printed in these discussions is based on an examination of the original. Likewise, any discrepancy in identifications or other factual matters between the works listed below and these discussions is based on further investigation.

ABBREVIATIONS AND SHORT TITLES

A, B, C, D, E	the five manuscript notebooks
Bercaw (followed by entry number)	Mary K. Bercaw, *Melville's Sources* (Evanston, Ill.: Northwestern University Press, 1987)
Central Italy	*A Handbook for Travellers in Central Italy. Part I. Southern Tuscany and Papal States*, 4th ed. (London: Murray, 1857)
Continent	*Hand-book for Travellers on the Continent*, 6th ed. (London: Murray, 1849; 11th ed., 1856)
DAB	*Dictionary of American Biography*
DNB	*Dictionary of National Biography*
Egypt	*Hand-book for Travellers in Egypt* (London: Murray, 1847, 1858)
EMM	Eleanor Melville Metcalf, ed., *Journal of a Visit to London and the Continent by Herman Melville, 1849–1850* (Cambridge: Harvard University Press, 1948)
ENB	Nathaniel Hawthorne, *The English Notebooks*, ed. Randall Stewart (New York: Modern Language Association of America, 1941)
ESM	Elizabeth Shaw Melville, wife of Herman Melville
FINB	Nathaniel Hawthorne, *The French and Italian Notebooks*, ed. Thomas Woodson (Columbus: Ohio State University Press, 1980)
France	*Hand-book for Travellers in France*, 3d ed. (London: Murray, 1847; rev. 1848)

Galignani	*Galignani's New Paris Guide* (Paris: Galignani, 1848; 1851; 1864)
Greece	*Handbook for Travellers in Greece* (London: Murray, 1854)
(H)	a reading preferred by Howard C. Horsford
HCL-M	Melville Collection (Harvard College Library) of the Houghton Library of Harvard University
Letters	*The Letters of Herman Melville*, ed. Merrell R. Davis and William H. Gilman (New Haven: Yale University Press, 1960) [Revised and enlarged edition forthcoming as NN vol. XIV]
Log	Jay Leyda, *The Melville Log*, 2 vols. (New York: Harcourt, Brace, 1951; New York: Gordian Press, 1969) [Forthcoming: *The New Melville Log*, ed. Jay Leyda and Hershel Parker (New York: Gordian Press)]
M	Herman Melville
Northern Italy	*Handbook for Travellers in Northern Italy* (London: Murray, 1842; 6th ed. 1856)
NYPL-D	Duyckinck Collection, Rare Books and Manuscripts Division, the New York Public Library
Rome	*A Handbook for Travellers in Central Italy. Part II. Rome and Its Environs*, 4th ed. (London: Murray, 1856)
Sealts (followed by entry number)	Merton M. Sealts, Jr., *Melville's Reading: A Check-List of Books Owned and Borrowed*, rev. and enl. ed. (Columbia: University of South Carolina Press, 1988)
Southern Italy	*A Handbook for Travellers in Southern Italy*, 2d ed. (London: Murray, 1855)
Turkey	*A Handbook for Travellers in Turkey*, 3d ed., rev. (London: Murray, 1854)

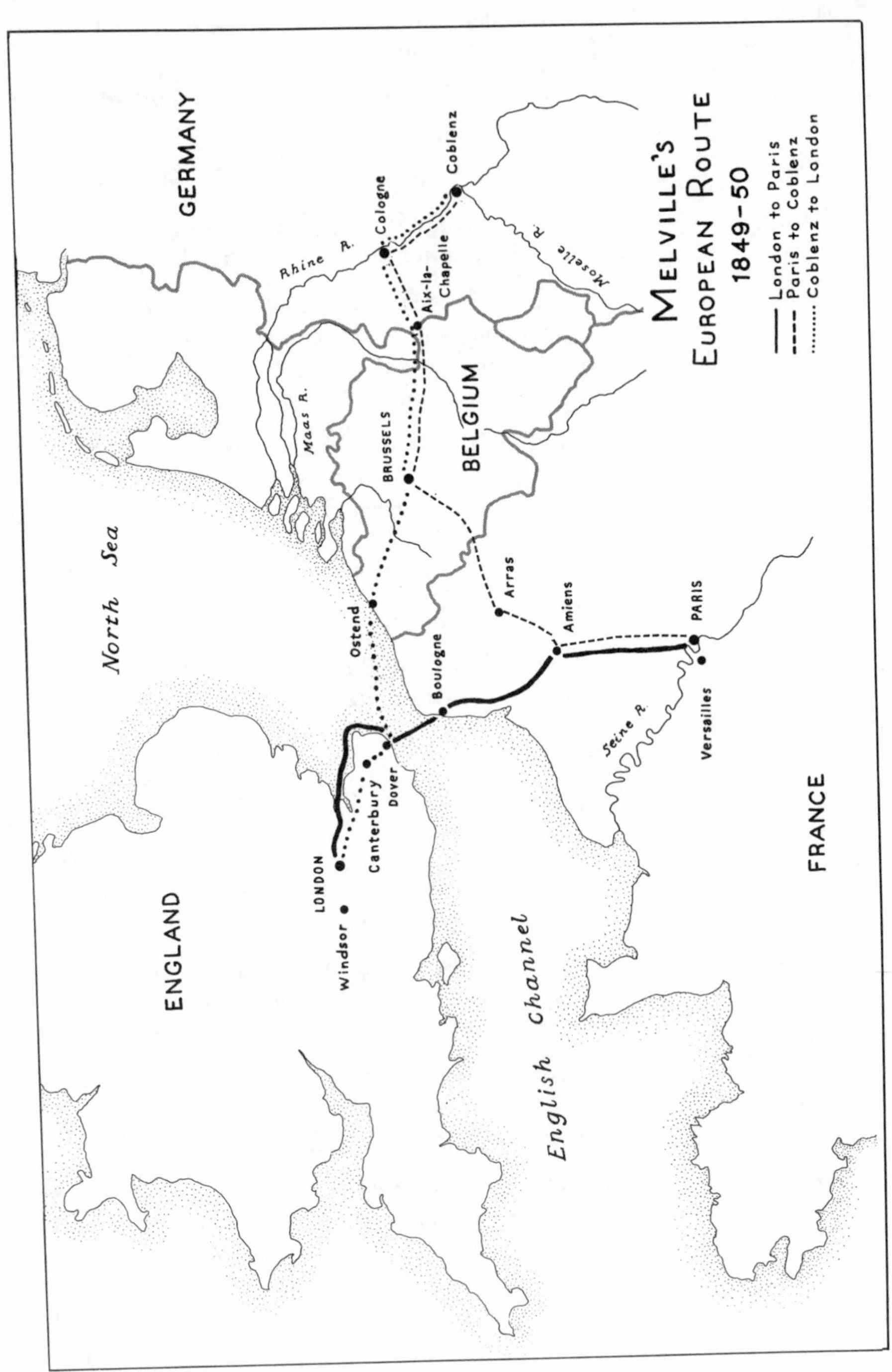
MELVILLE'S
EUROPEAN ROUTE
1849–50
London to Paris
Paris to Coblenz
Coblenz to London
GERMANY
Coblenz
Cologne
Rhine R.
Aix-la-Chapelle
Moselle R.
BELGIUM
Maas R.
BRUSSELS
North Sea
Ostend
Arras
Amiens
PARIS
Versailles
Seine R.
Boulogne
Dover
Canterbury
LONDON
Windsor
ENGLAND
English Channel
FRANCE

CHRONOLOGY OF THE 1849–50 TRIP

[NN numbers in the first column indicate the beginning of a dated entry; events of that day are sometimes covered in the next day's entry or in external sources cited in the discussions. Bracketed dates correct those in the journal; see the appropriate discussions.]

3.3	Oct. 11, 1849	Sailed from New York
10.29	Nov. 1	Landfall, Start Point, England
12.16	[5]	Debarked at Deal; to Canterbury
13.16	6	To London
14.19	9	Lord mayor's investiture
16.5	11	Excursion to Hampton Court
16.27	12	First meeting with Richard Bentley
17.16	13	Hanging of Manning couple
17.29	14	First meeting with John Murray
19.5	16	Murray declines *White-Jacket*
19.35	17	Excursion to Dulwich
23.26	21	Excursion to Greenwich
24.20	22	Excursion to Windsor
25.1,20	23	Dinner at Murray's
26.21,35	24	Dinner at Joshua Bates's
28.12, 29.23	25	Dinner with Henry Stevens
29.3, 30.11	27	Channel steamer to France
30.23	28	To Paris
29.10, 30.35	29	Lodging on Left Bank
33.32	Dec. 6	Excursion to Versailles
34.8	7	To Brussels
34.34	8	To Cologne
35.25, 36.33	9–10	To Coblenz
38.4	11	Return to Cologne
38.23	12	To Brussels and Ostend
39.7	13	Arrived at Dover and in London
40.18	15	Agreement with Bentley for *White-Jacket*
43.12	18	Dinner at Bentley's
43.36	19	Visit to Gansevoort Melville's lodging and death site; dinner with the Cookes
44.22	20	Breakfast with Samuel Rogers; dinner at Erechtheum Club
46.6	22	Second dinner at Erechtheum Club
46.20	23	Second breakfast with Rogers
47.5	24	To Portsmouth
47.25	[25]	Embarked for New York
	Jan. 31, 1850	Arrived in New York

JOURNAL 1849–50

3.4 weather] See an account of the violent autumnal storms and of packet ship travel, p. 169.

3.6 "Southampton"] Newest (launched and entered service 1849) and largest (1,300 tons, with three decks, 181 ft. long) of the "Black X" line to Portsmouth and London; it was kept in packet service until 1865, then disappeared into transient freight-carrying (R. G. Albion, *Square-Riggers on Schedule* [Princeton: Princeton University Press, 1938], pp. 282, 299).

3.14 Allan] M's next younger brother (1823–72); see p. 167. George was the younger brother (1823–63) of Evert Duyckinck (1816–78) and his associate in editing the New York *Literary World.* M knew Evert rather better but was also on good terms with George. It was George, back only a year from Europe, who loaned M several guidebooks for this trip, who seems to have put M in touch with London book dealers, and for whom M brought back an antique bronze medal from the Latin Quarter of Paris (see the discussion at 146.13 and *Letters*, p. 103 [No. 71]).

3.15 a rich merchant] Robert H. McCurdy (1800–1880), "one of the famous New York merchants of fifty years and more ago" (Lyman H. Weeks, ed., *Prominent Families of New York* [New York: The Historical Co., 1897]); originally partner in a commission dry goods firm, McCurdy, Aldrich & Spencer, 30 Broad St., he also became director or incorporator of banks and insurance companies. M's fellow passenger was his older son, Theodore Frelinghuysen McCurdy; apparently he settled later in Norwich, Connecticut, and was still alive in 1884 (E. E. Salisbury, "The Griswold Family of Connecticut," *Magazine of American History*, XI [1884], 333). This trip was a McCurdy family affair: John Griswold, operator and part owner of the shipping line, was an uncle; R. H. Griswold, the captain for this trip, was a cousin once removed; see the discussion at 10.33.

3.20 state-room] See p. 169; customarily, fare (seventy-five dollars at this time) was for double occupancy, with fifty percent added for single occupancy (Albion, *Square-Riggers*, p. 235).

4.12 passengers] *Log*, I, 318 (Oct. 11), reprints one list from an unidentified newspaper clipping; several New York papers printed such lists, often differing in details of initials and spelling. One of the fuller ones, in the *New York Journal of Commerce* (October 13, 1849), has here been slightly amplified from others: "In the ship Southampton for London—Herman Melville, Theodore F McCurdy, Miss Wilbur, Miss Gelston, Wm Mulligan, Ferdinand Rusch, Mr Brown, Theodore Timpson, and Miss LeCain

[L Cain?], New York; Mrs Keese, James D Keese, and Hobart Keese, New Haven; Wm Hart and lady, Troy; Miss Ada Kingsford, Va; Mr Jell, Canada; Robert T [J?] Taithorn C[anada] W[est]; G J Adler and Balthazar Frewlin [Prewlin?], Switzerland; Mrs J H Stokes and 3 children, Mrs Moore, Mrs N W Gould and James Wells and lady, London; L [C?] A Morin, Paris; Frank Taylor, M D, ship's surgeon, of Pa." M's name leads all these lists, whether because he was first to engage passage or was considered most noteworthy. (Only Mulligan's home address, 45 Walker St., New York, appears in M's address list at the end of this journal [148.7]; see also the discussion at 14.20.)

4.13 M[r] Adler] George J. Adler (1821–68), born in Leipzig but brought to the U.S. in 1833; within two years of graduation from New York University as valedictorian (1844), he was appointed Professor of German (an unremunerated position because German was not a part of the regular curriculum). His enormous labors on his *Dictionary of the German and English Languages* (1849), published just before this trip, had shattered his health, as he told M. Their conversations on the voyage over and in London and Paris contributed vital intellectual impulse and substance to *Moby-Dick*, as Dwight A. Lee ("Melville and George J. Adler," *American Notes and Queries*, XII [May/June, 1974], 138–41) and Sanford E. Marovitz ("More Chartless Voyaging: Melville and Adler at Sea," *Studies in the American Renaissance*, 1986, 373–84) argue. Some of M's London book purchases, notably of works by Goethe, may reflect his influence (see p. 144 and Adler's letter, p. 618). His continued "many regards" for M were shown a year later by the just-published, inscribed copy of his translation of Goethe's *Iphigenia in Tauris* (New York, 1850), which he sent to M, who noted in it: "Received Jan. 8th, 1851. Pittsfield." (Sealts 229; Bercaw 300). He returned to New York in 1852, but a recurrence of hallucinations and paranoia led to his permanent commitment to the Bloomingdale Asylum in October of 1853. He was able to write or translate several more works on German grammar, Provençal poetry, and other literary subjects, to lecture on such varied ones as Arabian poetry, Goethe's *Faust*, and Roman literature, and to support himself by giving private lessons in Latin and German. His apologia, *Letters of a Lunatic; or, A Brief Exposition of My University Life, during the Years 1853–54*, was privately printed in 1854. At his death the *New-York Times* (August 25, 1868) carried an editorial; M and Evert Duyckinck attended his funeral (*Log*, II, 697 [Aug. 25, 1868]).

4.18 Taylor] The ship's passenger list names Dr. Frank[lin] Taylor as ship's surgeon, but the brief allusions to him in biographies of his cousin differ as to his profession. Somewhat older than Bayard, Frank too was born in rural southeastern Pennsylvania and earned his own education. Frank encouraged Bayard in his career, inviting Bayard to accompany him to Europe (1844), where Frank studied at Heidelberg and (according to Bayard's widow) received a Ph.D. (*Life and Letters of Bayard Taylor*, ed. Marie Hansen-Taylor and Horace E. Scudder, 2 vols. [Boston: Houghton, Mifflin, 1884], I, 37, 50; Marie Hansen Taylor, *On Two Continents* [New York: Doubleday, Page, 1905], p. 92). One biography of Bayard refers to Frank as an M.D., another as a schoolteacher (Rev. Russell Conwell, *Life, Travels, and Literary Career of Bayard Taylor* [Boston: Russell, 1879], p. 306; Albert H. Smyth, *Bayard Taylor* [Boston: Houghton, Mifflin, 1896], p. 37). The travel book that established Bayard's fame, *Views A-Foot* (New York: Wiley & Putnam, 1846), was dedicated: "To Frank Taylor, these records of the pilgrimage, whose toils and enjoyments we have shared together, are affectionately inscribed by his relative and friend. . . ." M had purchased the book in December of 1846 (Sealts 495; Bercaw 688). M later notes (18.14–15) that Frank Taylor was going to accompany McCurdy to Jerusalem and the Levant.

Bayard Taylor (1825–78) briefly adopted the first name "James" early in his career. With little formal education, he became a prolific and popular travel writer, poet, novelist, and man of letters; his major work, a translation of Goethe's *Faust* (1870–71), was admired both at home and in Germany. He served in 1862 as secretary of legation at St. Petersburg and in 1878 as minister to Germany, where he died. After his first popular book, he moved to New York late in 1847 and wrote briefly for the Duyckincks' *Literary World*, then for Horace Greeley's *Tribune*. He was handsome, had unusual personal charm, and according to Smyth, his biographer, was literally "mesmeric." By February of 1848 he had met M, to whom he was "obliged to write" and read a Valentine verse at a literary party given by Anne Lynch (*Log*, I, 272 [Feb. 13–14]). On the eve of M's 1856–57 trip, with Taylor now a celebrated traveler and M in eclipse, Evert Duyckinck recorded in his diary that M "said of Bayard Taylor that as some augur predicted the misfortunes of Charles I from the infelicity of his countenance so Taylor's prosperity 'borne up by the Gods' was written in his face" (*Log*, II, 523 [Oct. 1]). One trait M may have responded to in Taylor was his "robust use and praise of alcohol" *(DAB)*. One of his later books was reputedly the first American novel of idealized open love between men, *Joseph and His Friend* (New York: Putnam & Sons, 1870), first serialized in the *Atlantic Monthly*, 1870.

4.23 Scotch artist] William M. Hart (1823–94), born in Scotland but currently a resident of Troy, New York (see the passenger list in the discussion at 4.12), where his patron was Dr. J. H. Armsby of Albany (see the discussion at 7.3).

4.26–27 several Frenchmen & Englishmen] Among cabin passengers only one, L. A.—or C. A.—Morin, whose name M elsewhere misspells "Moran" (10.11), is listed as from Paris; similarly (apart from two Canadians) only four English matrons and the husband (James Wells) of one are listed as, nominally, from "London."

4.34–35 *Colredegian*] Samuel Taylor Coleridge (1772–1834), though beginning as a more or less radical "Unitarian" occasional preacher, reverted like his friend Wordsworth to a more orthodox though liberal Christian faith. M had borrowed *Biographia Literaria* (New York: Wiley & Putnam, 1847) from Evert Duyckinck in February of 1848, and had alluded to it as a book read by the frigate's "transcendental" chaplain in *White-Jacket*—and also to Coleridge's brief enlistment as a trooper (chaps. 38, 13, pp. 155, 51; Sealts 154; Bercaw 147). M was also evidently acquainted with *Notes and Lectures upon Shakespeare and Some of the Old Poets and Dramatists* (London: Pickering, 1849; Sealts 155; Bercaw 149). Here M presumably refers to Coleridge's later works that were important in renewing a philosophical basis for Christianity in the light of German historical criticism. M's own unorthodox religious and philosophical attitudes were already evident in his recent *Mardi* (1849), but perhaps his serious religious questioning as well as his spoofing of biblical literalism in *Moby-Dick* owed much to these prolonged shipboard conversations with Adler, as perhaps also did his apparent reading in German higher criticism (see, e.g., 97.18–20). The familiar quotation about the disputations of the fallen angels is from *Paradise Lost*, II, 557–61.

6.10–11 Corposant balls] The bluish electrical glow of corona discharge at the ends of masts and yards; they appear in the "Candles" chapter (119) of *Moby-Dick* and in *Clarel*, 3.12.93.

6.15–16 I alone . . . tale] An allusion to the iterated words of the messengers of disaster in the Book of Job; used as the epigraph to the Epilogue of *Moby-Dick* (p. 573).

6.17 European tour] *Holidays Abroad; or, Europe from the West* (2 vols., New York: Baker & Scribner, 1849), by Caroline Stansbury Kirkland (1801–64); she is now considered more interesting for *A New Home* (1839), her earlier work about life in frontier Michigan; her later writing consisted of travel letters and other collections. M presumably met her and Bayard Taylor at Anne Lynch's 1848 Valentine party (*Log*, I, 272 [Feb. 13–14]). Her book on Europe had just been published; it reports her travels in 1848, from Liverpool through England, France, Savoy, and Italy, and back to England by way of Switzerland and the Rhine, territory M himself substantially traversed seven years later.

6.37 "Omoo"] M's second book, *Omoo*, published in the spring of 1847 and generally favorably reviewed. The lady was Janet Wallace Hart, the wife of William Hart (see the discussion at 4.23).

7.3 Armsby] James H. Armsby, M.D. (1809–75), professor of anatomy and physiology at the Medical College in Albany, of which he was a cofounder. The oil portrait of M by Asa Weston Twitchell (1820–60) of Albany and Troy was painted between 1845 and 1847, while M was still living with his mother (EMM). First reproduced in EMM, it is now in the Berkshire Athenaeum, Pittsfield, Massachusetts (see p. 164).

7.18 cheap European travel] M originally hoped to make a trip more extended than merely to London. Here, direct and extended acquaintance with Taylor, who knew a good deal first hand about cheap traveling, reinforced the desire. Bayard Taylor's account of traveling afoot with this cousin had aroused so much wistful inquiry from readers that he added a chapter to the eighth edition (1848), giving a detailed accounting of expenses. For most of two years, he reported basic expenses of $472, including ship passage; in southern Germany, he claimed, one could travel "comfortably on twenty-five cents a day." Perhaps Frank Taylor's account of the Rhine and Heidelberg motivated M's quick Rhine excursion this midwinter (December 8–11, a rather oddly bleak time for sightseeing) and even his return there in 1857.

7.25 "Powell"] Thomas Powell (1809–87); see also 39.35 and accompanying discussion and 42.23–25. He was an English poet, dramatist, and journalist who had emigrated to New York early in 1849, having fled prosecution in England for forgery and theft. As a bluff, hearty representative of the British literary scene, Powell was immediately welcomed into the Duyckinck circle and became a valued contributor to the *Literary World*. By June Melville knew him well enough to give him a copy of *Mardi*. By the time he gave Melville good advice about asking the price before drinking alcoholic beverages, Powell had been arrested in New York for forging letters of credit and had lied his way out of the situation. His *Living Authors of England*, announced before Melville's departure, was published by Appleton in November of 1849—a slapdash assemblage of scurrilous gossip, intimate anecdotes, extended quotations (for padding), and some offhand but frequently pointed literary commentary, full of morsels to feed the avid American appetite for news from the great literary capital, London. The *Literary World* and many papers welcomed Powell's gossip, but others were offended by it, and some reviewers were outraged at his gratuitous slurs against the greatest American author, Washington Irving. Powell's *Living Authors of America* (published by Stringer & Townsend) appeared in 1850 (meant to be only an initial selection of American writers, not including M or Hawthorne, but no other volumes followed), a compilation even more padded and digressive than his first one. See the HISTORICAL NOTE to the NN *Moby-Dick*, pp. 607–9, and Hershel Parker's forthcoming *Herman Melville and the Powell Papers*.

7.31 Barney . . . Orianna] Identified in penciled additions by ESM as family pet names for their first son, Malcolm (also "Macky"), eight months old on this day, and herself ("Lizzie"). "Oriana," the heroine's name in the medieval romance *Amadis of Gaul*, was frequently applied by Renaissance poets to Queen Elizabeth. EMM adds that "Barney" was the nickname of a boatsteerer, William Barnard, on M's first whaler, the *Acushnet*; M listed his name among those of other shipmates when one of them, Henry Hubbard, visited him in 1853 (see G. Thomas Tanselle, "Two Melville Association Copies: The Hubbard *Whale* and the Jones *Moby-Dick*," *Book Collector*, XXXI [1982], 170–86, 309–30; reprinted with slight changes in the NN *Moby-Dick*, pp. 997–1004).

7.35 An Irish lady] Identified by M three days later (Saturday) as Mrs. Gould, who appeared on the passenger lists nominally as from London and on all of them with the initials N. W. EMM seems mistaken in identifying her as the opera and light-opera singer Julia Gould: Julia was born in London, not Ireland, and in none of her several marriages was "Mrs. N. W. Gould." A more likely identification appears in T. Allston Brown, *History of the American Stage* (New York: Dick & Fitzgerald, 1870): "Gould, Mrs. — Born in Killarney, Ireland. Made her American *debut* at Niblo's Garden, New York" (p. 147). Possibly, then, she was the wife of the long-time concert and stage guitarist Napoleon W. Gould, a mainstay of the various Christy's Minstrels troupes from at least the late 1840's on (see George C. D. Odell, *Annals of the New York Stage*, vols. V–IX [1843–75] [New York: Columbia University Press, 1931–37]).

8.10 in Murray] I.e., in one of the guidebooks issued by M's first English publisher, John Murray, and loaned to M by George Duyckinck (see pp. 173–74)—one of the editions of *Hand-Book for Travellers in Northern Italy* [by Sir Francis Palgrave], 1842; the most recent was the third, updated in 1847.

8.20 Pickwick] Dickens's *Posthumous Papers of the Pickwick Club* was published in parts in both London and Philadelphia in 1836–37, with many subsequent editions.

8.31–32 La Place] Pierre Simon, marquis de Laplace (1749–1827), the noted mathematician and astronomer, famous for his work in celestial mechanics and probability theory. Where Newton, with an as-yet-unperfected mathematics, thought it might be necessary from time to time for a divine hand to correct the observable anomalies in the workings of the solar system, the refinements and corrections of errors by Laplace and Lagrange seemed to explain phenomena so satisfactorily that Laplace could assert the system was in fact entirely self-maintaining. Hence, his famous reply (quoted here by Adler) when Napoleon remarked to him that he had left God out of his theories in his *Traité de mécanique célèste* (1799–1825): "Sire, je n'avais besoin de cet hypothèse" ("Sire, I had no need of that hypothesis").

9.23–24 "Bradshaw's . . . Guide"] In the 1840's and after, Bradshaw's, a Manchester firm, issued a variety of regularly updated guides under slightly different titles according to areas and extensiveness of coverage; the one M saw here was probably *Bradshaw's Continental Railway, Steam Navigation, and Conveyance Guide*, an extremely useful compendium of detailed timetables; M bought one of these at Galignani's in Paris, see pp. 616–19 below.

9.33 Lamertine] Alphonse de Lamartine (1790–1869), a principal figure in early French sentimental romanticism, greatly admired as poet, novelist, and for a period as political leader. At first a moderate royalist, he moved toward democratic circles, and after the upheaval of 1848 he was briefly one of the five members of the Executive Committee of the provisional government. But inexperience and the intolerable pressures of the unsettled situation, which, it was said, he more than any other single man had helped bring about by his inflammatory speeches and historical writing, led to his early political demise. His *History of the Girondists* was published in translation by Harper & Brothers, M's American publisher, in 1847. *Clarel*, 2.16.50–56, alludes to "poor Lamartine—a latter palmer" (in 1832–33), and to his "fine social dream" defeated by "that realist how grim," Fate.

9.34 Corinne] *Corinne* (1807), by Mme. de Staël (née Anne Louise Necker, 1766–1817), a travel novel of sensibility, extravagantly admired in the early half of the century. Being the wife of the Swedish diplomat Baron de Staël-Holstein gave the author relative security during the revolutionary turmoil, but her opposition to Napoleon provoked him into exiling her and suppressing her work. Whether the "curious discussion" here of "Lamertine & Corinne" was about the quality of their relative "sensibilities" or about their political relations to the two revolutionary governments and the two Napoleons is not evident—perhaps the latter, in view of the debate two days later about monarchy versus republics. M obtained from Bentley a copy of Isabel Hill's translation of the novel, which Bentley had published in 1833 (see M's book list, 144.26; Sealts 486; Bercaw 666).

10.3 "Where dat old man"?] Identified in a penciled note by ESM as "Macky's baby words," which if true would make Malcolm indeed a precocious infant at something less than eight months. M quotes the words again in the entries for October 30 and November 4, and ESM glosses them the same way (see the reproduction on p. 215 above). He also included the question, referring to Ahab, in the final chapter of *Moby-Dick* (p. 567).

10.7–8 a criminal charge] This kind of amusement on a long sailing voyage was not invented by M; Fanny Kemble records a similar entertainment (cited by Albion, *Square-Riggers*, p. 242). In either case the practice may have been modeled on the parody "Judge and Jury," which M later saw in London, perhaps at the suggestion of George Duyckinck (see 17.13 and accompanying discussion).

10.17 Scilly Island] Twenty-eight miles southwest of Land's End, Cornwall, the Scilly Islands were the customary landfall for packets bound for Portsmouth and London (M noted them again on the voyage home, 47.36).

10.25 Lizzard Light] On the Lizard headland, the southernmost point of England and the Cornish peninsula; Start Point (mentioned in the next entry) is the southeast point of Devon, ten miles below Dartmouth.

10.33 Captain Griswold] Robert Harper Griswold (1806–82) was born in Lyme, Connecticut, the ninth child of Governor Roger Griswold, and the grandson of Governor Matthew Griswold. By 1829 he was second mate to his brother, and by 1833 a captain (Albion, *Square-Riggers*, p. 336). The success of most packet captains required a capacity to deal with the cabin passengers on three- to five- or six-week passages. The family memorial states: "He was a favorite commander of packet-ships of the John Griswold Line [named for an older cousin], sailing between New York and London, a man of much reading, and, in his prime, of elegant manners and great personal beauty. He died in Lyme in 1882, after years of lingering infirmity and pain" (Salisbury, "The Griswold Family," p. 329). In 1849 he was listed as regular captain of the *Northumberland*, so this was perhaps a special trip on the brand new *Southampton* of the "Black X" line (see the discussion at 3.6). See also p. 169 and the discussion on Robert McCurdy at 3.15. Timpson was a fellow passenger (see the discussion at 4.12).

11.8–9 Bill of Portland] The southern extremity of the high, semi-detached limestone peninsula on the coast of Dorset, below Weymouth and some forty to fifty miles west of the Isle of Wight. Its highest point is 458 feet. Portland stone is a very fine grade of limestone. "The Needles" mentioned in the next entry are three isolated and pointed masses of chalk, one hundred feet high, at the western extremity of the island.

11.11 metaphysics] Following preposition lacking (presumably "with"); the error occurred as M turned over his page (see also the discussion at 38.26).

11.35 Beachy Head light] Dungeness is a low, shingled point on the southwest Kentish coast, twenty miles from Dover. But M is confused here: Beachy Head, which he names next in sequence, is in fact near Eastbourne on the Sussex coast, thirty-five or so miles *west* of Dungeness. It is a precipitous chalk headland, 575 feet high, once surmounted by the Belle Tout Lighthouse.

12.2 green coat] A source of increasing unease (cf. 13.26–27) until he bought a new coat in London on December 14 (39.37–40.1). No doubt British notions of propriety in dress were involved; in 1856, for instance, a professor from West Point was denied admission to a royal levee because he was dressed in a frock coat, black neckcloth, and yellow waistcoat (James Pope-Hennessy, *Monckton Milnes*, 2 vols. [London: Constable, 1949–51], II, 36). M took the green coat back to New York (see *Letters*, pp. 105–6 [No. 74]). See also the discussion at 15.1 in the NN *Moby-Dick*.

12.5 lamp in tumbler] Probably a lamp suspended in gimbals to remain upright irrespective of the ship's motion; there is such a lamp in Father Mapple's sermon on Jonah in Chapter 9 of *Moby-Dick* (pp. 44–45).

12.8 ten years] Since July and early August of 1839, in Liverpool, while M was a novice seaman on the *St. Lawrence*. (The two quoted phrases at the end of this entry were identified in pencil by ESM as "First words of baby Malcolm's"; see the reproduction of this manuscript page on p. 215, also the discussion at 10.3.)

12.11 Lizzie's letter] Not preserved, but see *Log*, I, 326 (Nov. 4, 1849), for Allan's reference to it. (No. 310 on the "Check List of Unlocated Letters," *Letters*, p. 311.)

12.13 Craven Street] An ancient street running between the Strand, just east of Trafalgar Square, and the river at Hungerford Stairs, scene of Dickens's youthful humiliation in the blacking warehouse; it was just east of Hungerford Market (see the illustration on p. 287; the market was demolished in 1860 for Charing Cross Station and Hotel). By the nineteenth century, the street was mostly occupied by either lodging houses or the offices of architects and solicitors; in his entry for December 23, M calls his address at No. 25 a "house" (47.2). In "The Two Temples" (unpublished by M) the impoverished narrator in the second part speaks of his "cold and lonely bed far up in an attic of Craven Street, looking down upon the muddy Phlegethon of the Thames" (NN *Piazza Tales* volume, p. 311), but the houses at the river end of Craven Street were 30 and 31, not 25. Most accounts of Benjamin Franklin's eighteen years as American agent in London assert he lived at No. 7, which is what M would have thought, but more recently it has been determined that his lodging for most of the time was No. 36, then later at No. 1—*Survey of London: The Strand* (vol. 18 of series), ed. Sir George Gates and Walter H. Godfrey (London: London County Council, 1937); plates 16–23 are photos of the street, individual houses, and selected interiors; note especially plate 20.

12.16 *Nov: 6th*] Error for November 5. M realized his one-day error when he made the entry for the next day, which he initially dated as the seventh and then corrected to the sixth without correcting this error.

12.24 Caesar] His landings, in 55 and 54 B.C., are believed to have taken place here or nearby, toward Sandwich; the treacherous shoals offshore at the entrance to the Thames estuary made for much rescue and salvage work for the Deal boatmen and pilots, "beyond all others . . . famed for skill and daring. . . . A fine, stalwart, broad-shouldered set, . . . not over-refined in manners, nor choice in language" (Charles Knight, *Knight's Excursion Companion* [London: Knight, 1851], Excursion IV, p. 2). Possibly M remembered that in Captain Frederick Marryat's *Poor Jack* (London: Longman, Orme, Brown, Green, & Longmans, 1840) much of the action takes place in and around Deal. The book was among the few aboard his third whaler, the *Charles and Henry* (see the discussion at 15.38; the book list is in Sealts, *Melville's Reading*, pp. 247–50).

12.29 Cinque Ports] Deal, like other small Channel ports, was added later as a "Member" to the original Cinque Ports, and attached to Sandwich, one of the five responsible for furnishing ships to the royal fleets. In *Bleak House* (London: Bradbury & Evans, 1852–53), Dickens describes Deal in (ostensibly) the 1830's: "At last we came into the narrow streets of Deal: and very gloomy they were, upon a raw misty morning. The long flat beach, with its little irregular houses, wooden and brick, and its litter of capstans, and great boats, and sheds, and bare upright poles with tackle and blocks, and loose gravelly waste places overgrown with grass and weeds, wore as dull an appearance as any place I ever saw" (chap. 45, p. 436). As one of the Cinque Ports, Sandwich anciently had been prosperous, but it was now inland some two miles, a somnolent, shabby village though with architectural remnants of its former eminence.

12.33 "Richboro' Castle"] Richborough, like Sandwich a mile distant, had long since been silted off from shipping lanes. The fortification guarded Rutupiae, chief Roman port on the east coast after A.D. 43. In the nineteenth century, much of the northeast wall remained standing, several hundred feet long, some twelve feet thick at the base, and from twenty to thirty feet high. Elsewhere the walls were broken down, though the interior five acres, overlaying a sizable masonry platform, still stood above the surrounding fields

(*Knight's Excursion Companion*, IV, 7–8). The antiquary William H. Rolphe of Sandwich in 1849 was excavating an amphitheater on the south side, a walled ellipse of 200 by 116 feet (EMM, pp. 98–100, citing Charles Roach Smith, *The Antiquities of Richborough, Reculver, and Lyme, in Kent* [London: Smith, 1850]). In *Clarel*, 2.20.35–37, shards may be of tile-like brick "Such as in Kent still serve that end / In Richborough castle by the sea— / A Roman hold."

13.6 Cathedral] In naming Henry II, who was buried at Fontevrault, France, M has a memory lapse or is confused by the association with Becket. The tomb here is that of Henry IV (d. 1413) and his second wife; it is on the north side of Trinity Chapel, the site of Becket's magnificent shrine until it was destroyed under Henry VIII, leaving only the deeply worn pavement. The tomb of Edward the Black Prince (d. 1376), son of Edward III, is across the chapel on the south side. Becket's assassination, prompted by the hasty words of Henry II, took place (December 29, 1170) in the northwest transept; a small slab marks the reputed spot where Thomas fell, replacing according to tradition the blood-stained fragment of pavement sent to Rome. The description of the *Pequod* includes this image: "Her ancient decks were worn and wrinkled, like the pilgrim-worshipped flag-stone in Canterbury Cathedral where Becket bled" (*Moby-Dick*, chap. 16, p. 69; see also the discussions at 35.26–27 and 42.27–28 in the present volume).

13.10 Dane John] The park and promenade, in the southwest angle of the old City wall, surrounded a tumulus eighty feet high of unknown origin; M's later London acquaintance Charles Knight (see the discussion at 46.21) speculated that the name might be a corruption of "donjon." By M's time the lime trees of the park, laid out in 1790, made a long archway, and the walk on the ramparts, fifteen feet wide, passed several of the old watch-towers. The West Gate on the road to London is the only survivor of the original six gates, "a striking and picturesque object, standing between two lofty and spacious round towers, and being embattled, portcullised, and machicolated" (*Excursion Companion*, III, 5).

13.13 theater] The play, a simple-minded farce, was Douglas Jerrold's *The Housekeeper* (1833), identified by M when he saw it a second time in London on December 14 (40.14): in the time of George I, the Lady Felicia takes the guise of a housekeeper to win the love of her cousin and foils a plot to restore the Stuart Pretender. Perhaps M had a warm feeling about Jerrold because of the highly enthusiastic and sympathetic review of *Typee* in *Douglas Jerrold's Shilling Magazine*, III (April, 1846), 380–83; reprinted in Watson G. Branch, *Melville: The Critical Heritage* (London: Routledge & Kegan Paul, 1974), pp. 70–73; see also Hugh W. Hetherington, *Melville's Reviewers* (Chapel Hill: University of North Carolina Press, 1961), p. 26.

13.20 Tunbridge] Tonbridge, forty-one miles from London, has the ruins of a Norman castle built by a kinsman of William the Conqueror. Penshurst Place, thirty-seven miles from London, came to the Sidney family in 1552; Sir Philip was born there in 1554.

13.20–21 Arrived . . . dinner] The shortest route to London was the direct route through Rochester; the railroad came by a roundabout inland route to join the line from Dover, entering London from the south and terminating at a big new Italian-palazzo station at London Bridge, just upstream from the Tower. The new bridge, opened only eighteen years before, was an oft-recommended vantage to get a sense of the crowded river and the turmoil of the metropolis (see the entry for November 9, 14.23-24). Poultry, only a long block (by way of the new King William Street) from the bridge, is the short section of the main thoroughfare across London, between Cheapside on the west and Cornhill to the east; it was just then on the point of being widened and rebuilt.

13.26 Queen's Hotel] At St. Martin's le Grand, a long walk back to the vicinity of St. Paul's, not far from where they had just eaten.

13.28 Concerts] To reach the Drury Lane Theatre, on Catherine Street just east of Covent Garden, meant another two-mile walk back toward M's lodging. The original theater, burnt, altered, or rebuilt a number of times, had been replaced in 1812. Louis Antoine Julien had been an immensely successful dance band composer and conductor in Paris until driven out by debts. Though a highly mannered showman (e.g., conducting Beethoven with a jeweled baton and new white gloves presented to him on silver salvers), he nevertheless satisfied vast audiences with popular music while educating them to the best. The new season had just opened and this evening's program included the *Roman Carnival* overture of Berlioz, a selection from Donizetti's *Lucrezia*, several selections from Meyerbeer's new *Le prophète*, several German lieder, "Home, Sweet Home," instrumental solos and duets including "Rule, Britannia!," and the first performance for these concerts of Mendelssohn's Grand Symphony in A Minor. All this between eight and eleven in the evening (advertisement, London *Times*, November 6). The theater had recently been refurbished: "A great improvement has been made. . . . The reading-room is more than ever an object of attraction, the tables being covered with daily and weekly newspapers, monthly and quarterly magazines, miscellanies, and periodicals of every description, in almost every known language of civilized Europe" (*Times*, November 3).

13.30 Redburn] When John Murray declined *Mardi* (see above, p. 168), Richard Bentley quickly took it up, then more hesitantly *Redburn*, which he published (September 29) in two volumes. Early English reviews were generally favorable; the judicious praise in the November number that M saw of *Bentley's Miscellany* was therefore not merely the kind of house "puffing" for which Bentley, like his initial partner Henry Colburn, was scorned by more gentlemanly publishers. See Hetherington, *Melville's Reviewers*, pp. 135–40; Royal A. Gettmann, *A Victorian Publisher* (Cambridge: Cambridge University Press, 1960); also the NN *Redburn*, pp. 332–41.

13.30–31 the Row] Paternoster Row, principal center for book dealers, just north of St. Paul's; it was described about this time by the Boston publisher James Brown of Little, Brown: "Paternoster Row I was greatly disappointed in. Instead of a street full of splendid booksellers' shops, it is a narrow lane barely admitting a carriage: dirty, dark, gloomy and disgusting. . . . In this mean street, however, are sold more fine books than in any other market in the world" (quoted in Henry W. Boynton, *Annals of American Bookselling, 1638–1850* [New York: Wiley & Sons, 1932], p. 170). See also 21.21–22,26.

13.32 Blackwood's] M seems to have thought the fourteen-page, unsigned review in the November number of *Blackwood's Edinburgh Magazine* was by its violently polemical editor "Christopher North" (John Wilson)—"the old Tory"—but more likely it was by Frederick Hardman. It was the longest and one of the three most adverse British notices. While praising some elements of style and characterization, it bore down on the weaknesses: inconsistencies in Redburn's characterization, the figure of Harry Bolton, the London excursion; it showed at best a patronizing condescension to Americans (Hetherington, *Melville's Reviewers*, pp. 140–41; Hershel Parker, "A Reexamination of *Melville's Reviewers*," *American Literature*, XLII [May, 1970], 226–32—see p. 228). Granting M's self-protective irony here, the passage fits in with his persistent denigration of *Redburn* as a mere hurried potboiler (see also 14.11–12, 31.21–22. 47.15, and the discussions at 14.11 and 47.15).

13.37–38 American Bowling Saloon] See the discussion at 24.4.

14.2–3 Blackwall R.R. Station] The London and Blackwall Railway, north of the river, ran on elevated arches through a region of crowded poverty for the short three miles between Fenchurch Street Station, near the Tower, and the great dock area at Blackwall; that evening, so M could have read next day in the *Times*, the inept engineer of a baggage train rammed the rear coaches of a passenger train in Stepney Station, seriously injuring eight.

14.3 Docks] London was later than Liverpool in constructing gigantic and enclosed wet docks to alleviate the crowding of river shipping, obviate the problems of tidal change, and forestall wholesale thievery. The East India Docks were the third to be opened, in 1806, and deep enough to handle the largest ships. The Custom House, just west of the Tower, had hours ten to four indoors, or nine to four at the waterside office, in winter. Passenger luggage was inspected in the Steam Packet Baggage Warehouse, where duty was assessed on articles like books, millinery, eau de cologne, prints, and shoes. *Knight's Cyclopædia* (London: Knight, 1851) quotes an 1850 complaint, in a journal of the "highest authority," which asks rhetorically of recent travelers "whether they ever experienced, in any country, a similar amount of annoyance? It is in vain that everything dutyable is at once produced by the sufferer; the most literal search is insisted on; packages are wrenched asunder. . . . The chances are many against the preservation of any of the more fragile objects" (p. 124).

LYCEUM THEATRE

14.7 Theater] The Royal Lyceum was near the east end of the Strand, redecorated in 1847 by its manager, Mme. Vestris. The illustration above is from *Tallis's Illustrated London* by William Gaspey (London: Tallis, 1851), I, facing p. 226. Peter Cunningham, writer of Murray's *Modern London* (1851), called it "very beautiful" and listed its specialties as extravaganzas, vaudeville, and farce. As advertised in the *Times*, November 7: "This Evening will be presented *Not a Bad Judge*. After which, *Beauty and the Beast*. Characters by Messrs. Rafter, F. Matthews, and Harley; Mrs. C. Horn, Miss Matindale, Miss Kenworthy, and Mde. Vestris. To conclude with *A Practical Man*." Charles Mathews (1803–78), whom M saw in *A Practical Man*, was the husband of "Mme. Vestris," Lucia Elizabeth Mathews (1797–1856). She began in Italian opera, then moved to English drama, remaining popular with a large audience for a certain archness and easy, roguish manner. He had no range beyond comedy, but was equally popular for a light touch and excellent mimicry. George Henry Lewes, in his retrospective assessment of

Mathews's career, acknowledged his limitations but admired his sophistication and finesse (*On Actors and the Art of Acting* [London: Smith, Elder, 1875], pp. 59–72).

The nature of the program M saw this night is suggested by excerpts from earlier *Times* accounts: "Mr. Planché's excellent burlesque of *Beauty and the Beast* was revived . . . with great splendour, the scenery being radiant with all the etherial hues of Mr. Beverley." And, "Mr. Boyle Bernard . . . has provided the Lyceum with a most genial farce, entitled *A Practical Man*. . . . The plot of this piece is literally nothing. Its object is to develope the peculiarities of a restless individual, acted by Mr. Charles Mathews, whose brain is swelling with the biggest schemes, but is totally destitute of the decision requisite to carry them into execution. . . . Scattered papers, upset washhand-stands, and smashed images mark the progress of the 'practical man.' " (Thursday, November 1, and Monday, October 22).

M's experience here and similar ones with the gallery are combined in the second part of his "The Two Temples," where this night's hawker of porter becomes a boy-agent of sentimentally renewed goodwill. The audience and the height of the gallery are described: "Quiet, well-pleased working men, and their glad wives and sisters, with here and there an aproned urchin, with all-absorbed, bright face, vermillioned by the excitement. . . . The height of the gallery was in truth appalling. The rail was low. . . . And like beds of glittering coral, through the deep sea of azure smoke, there, far down, I saw the jewelled necks and white sparkling arms of crowds of ladies in the semicirque" (NN *Piazza Tales* volume, p. 313).

14.11 Bentley's] At 8 New Burlington St., a short street connecting Regent Street and Savile Row; for Bentley, see the discussion at 16.27. M's general disparagement of *Redburn* explains his finding the serious English critical notices of it "laughable." Hetherington (pp. 135–42) describes and excerpts a number, of which by this date only two, *Britannia* and *Blackwood's*, were adverse. (See Parker's criticism of Hetherington cited in the discussion at 13.32; also the NN edition of the novel, pp. 332–41.)

14.13 Murray's] At 50 Albemarle St., a few blocks southwest of New Burlington Street, running into Piccadilly; for Murray, see the discussion at 18.3. Hawthorne described the street as "one of hotels, principally, with only a few tradesmen's shops, and . . . a quiet, aristocratic aspect," where Murray's door, showing only a brass plate with the engraved name, was so inconspicuous he missed it at first (*ENB*, p. 224). The illustration opposite appears on p. 515 of "The House of Murray" by F. Espinasse, in *Harper's New Monthly Magazine* (September, 1885), 501–22.

14.13–14 National Gallery] The gallery proper was then housed in the western half of the building recently erected on the north side of uncompleted Trafalgar Square. Only a scant 220 pictures occupied one small room and three moderate-sized, ill-lighted ones (*Knight's London*, 6 vols. [London: Knight, 1841–44], VI, 241–42; see also 42.37–38, where M names a few paintings). The public was admitted free on Monday through Thursday from ten to five.

14.15 Chancery Lane] Running north to Holborn from Temple Bar, this street links the old Inns of Court; the old Lincoln's Inn gateway opened off the lane to the west, with the "fields" beyond. Once an open waste, site of executions and haunt of rabble, it had been slowly reduced to a twelve-acre square with walks and enclosing rails, second oldest and one of the finest and largest of London's public gardens. Dickens's *Bleak House* (1852–53) opens on such a dark November late afternoon:

> Implacable November weather. As much mud in the streets, as if the waters had but newly retired from the face of the earth. . . . Smoke lowering down from chimney-pots, making a soft black drizzle, with flakes of soot in it as big as full-grown snow-flakes—gone into mourning, one might imagine, for the

Murray's, 50 Albemarle St.

death of the sun. Dogs, undistinguishable in mire. Horses, scarcely better. . . . Foot passengers, jostling one another's umbrellas, in a general infection of ill-temper, and losing their foot-hold at street-corners, where tens of thousands of other foot passengers have been slipping and sliding since the day broke. . . .

. . . Gas looming through the fog in divers places in the streets. . . . Most of the shops lighted two hours before their time—as the gas seems to know, for it has a haggard and unwilling look.

The raw afternoon is rawest, and the dense fog is densest, and the muddy streets are muddiest, near that leaden-headed old obstruction . . . Temple Bar.

14.16 Princess's Theatere] Originally built in 1830 as a bazaar with a large concert room, it had been remodeled in 1841 for theater purposes. *Cruchley's Picture of London* (a copy of which M had borrowed from George Duyckinck) described it as "capable of containing upwards of 2000 persons. . . . The pit has backs and covered seats; . . . for taste, decoration, brilliancy and beauty, [it] is allowed to be the most elegant and commodious theatre in Europe" (quoted from the thirteenth edition, London, 1848, pp. 154–55). Under the management of Charles Kean (see the discussion at 40.13–14) it was notable for its staging and performances of Shakespeare; the advertisement in the *Times* for November 8, however, lists: "Mr. J. M. Maddox, Sole Lessee and Manager, Duchess-street. This Evening will be presented *Don Pasquale*. Don Pasquale, Mr. H. Corri; Dr. Malatesta, Mr. Richard Latter; Ernesto, Mr. Allen; Norina, Mdlle. Nau. After which, *The First Night*. To conclude with the new ballet, *Les Patineurs*." The *Times* (October 2) described a performance: "An English abridgement of the French piece, *Le Père d'une Débutante*, under the title of *The First Night*, followed the opera, and chiefly through the spirited and characteristic acting of Mr. Wigan, who acted the part of Achille Talma Dufard, the father, . . . was received with shouts of laughter throughout." At the "half price," M and his friends presumably missed Donizetti's opera buffa. The ballet was from Giacomo Meyerbeer's new opera *Le prophète*, just produced in London in July; it was inserted to capitalize on the new rage for roller-skating. See the discussion at 14.31.

14.20 Mulligan] William Mulligan on the ship's passenger lists, whose address is listed among others at the end of the journal notebook (148.7). (EMM identifies him therefore as one of the masters of the school, Mulligan and Roberts, at that address.)

14.21–22 "Lord Mayor's Show"] M's vantage on Cheapside, presumably for the return of the procession, was but a few steps from the hotel and post office. After election in September, the lord mayor of the City is regularly invested in office this day, November 9. Since 1215, by agreement with King John, the new head of the City Corporation has journeyed to Westminster for royal approval, accompanied by elaborate pageantry using both river barge and coach. This year the Honorable Thomas Farncomb, wharfmaster, ship owner, merchant, and banker, in his scarlet or purple robes, richly furred, wearing gold chain and collar, had departed the Guildhall, just north of Cheapside and Poultry, at eleven; preceded by innumerable constables, banners, dignitaries of the Worshipful Company of Tallow-chandlers, a fully rigged ship drawn on wheels, the lord mayor's bargemaster and bargemen, City Corporation functionaries, heralds and armored knights, trumpeters and kettle-drummers, the two City sheriffs in their chariots with retainers, the retiring lord mayor (newly titled Sir James Duke), the new lady mayoress, liveried servants, marshalls, swordbearers, criers, bailiffs, mounted honor guards, and others, he would have moved—by the time M saw him—by a circuitous route to London Bridge, thence by water to Westminster, returning by way of Blackfriars Bridge, St. Paul's Churchyard, Cheapside, and King Street (*Times*, November 10).

14.25 Edgeware Road] The route of M's walk is a little obscure: he must first have walked over to the south side of the river perhaps by London Bridge near the Tower. How he then recrossed is uncertain; Westminster Bridge had settled badly, and was said to be closed entirely after 1846, and if so he could have taken the Hungerford foot bridge to Westminster. His subsequent ramble was on the north side of the river—through the parks to the Edgware Road (as it is now spelled) near the Marble Arch.

14.28 (Dante's)] M's later dinner-acquaintance Peter Cunningham wrote in Murray's *Modern London* that London Bridge is

> the one the Foreigner naturally sees first, and it is the spot above all others calculated to impress him most with the power and ceaseless activity of this great capital. The bridge itself, crowded with an ever-moving line of people and vehicles, and lined at the same time with the heads of curious spectators . . . all gazing upon the busy waters below, is a curious picture. . . . On the other hand, the water below is equally instinct with life; above bridge we see the stairs of the penny iron steam-boats, landing and taking in West End or Greenwich passengers, amid a perfect din of bell-ringing and cloud of steam-blowing. Below bridge we see the 'Pool,' with its fleets of colliers moored in the stream. (p. xvi)

M in 1853 recommended sauntering on the London bridges to his uncle Peter Gansevoort (see pp. 620–23).

In the *Inferno*, Dante uses Dis, the name of the Roman god of the underworld, as an alternate name for Satan, and thus "city of Dis" means lower Hell, the inner fortified city that the poet and Virgil approach in Canto VIII and enter in Canto IX, moving on down from the fifth to succeeding circles of Hell.

> But on mine ear
> Sudden a sound of lamentation smote,
> . . . .

> "Now, my son,
> Draws near the city, that of Dis is named,
> With its grave denizens, a mighty throng."
> . . . .
> We came within the fosses deep, that moat
> This region comfortless. The walls appear'd
> As they were framed of iron.
> . . . .
> . . . his eye
> Not far could lead him through the sable air,
> And the thick-gathering cloud.

(VIII, 62–63, 66–67, 74–76, and IX, 5–7, in the H. F. Cary translation, 1845, which M had bought in 1848 [Sealts 174; Bercaw 190].)

Though the earlier London (1776–1823) of Israel Potter would have been rather different, M was sufficiently struck by this present observation to entitle Chapter 24 of *Israel Potter* "In the City of Dis," which begins by describing Israel's entrance over London Bridge to his long impoverished exile: "It was late on a Monday morning, in November—a Blue Monday—a Fifth of November—Guy Fawkes' Day!—very blue, foggy, doleful and gunpowdery, indeed, as shortly will be seen,—that Israel found himself wedged in among the greatest every-day crowd which grimy London presents to the curious stranger. That hereditary crowd—gulf stream of humanity—which, for continuous centuries, has never ceased pouring, like an endless shoal of herring, over London Bridge" (p. 158). (On Guy Fawkes Day, November 5, M had landed in England.) See also *Clarel*, where Jerusalem, from Mt. Olivet, suggests "the city Dis aloof" (1.36.29)—this view is illustrated below on p. 427.

14.29–30 cast iron Duke] Undoubtedly M refers to the memorial to Arthur Wellesley, the first duke of Wellington, the victor of Waterloo and late prime minister (still alive in 1849), standing opposite his residence—threatening it according to hostile critics—at Apsley House, Hyde Park Corner. Subscribed by the "ladies of England" in 1822, it was cast from cannon captured in Wellington's victories over Napoleon, more or less modeled on one of the two colossal Dioscuri (or Horse-Tamers) before the Quirinal Palace in Rome (see the 1856–57 journal, 107.26–27), and miscalled "Achilles." The phrase "Iron Duke" was given currency by *Punch* in 1845, but similar phrases, "man of iron" and the like, had long been used. (See Elizabeth Longford, *Wellington, Pillar of State* [New York: Harper & Row, 1972], pp. 415–17.)

14.31 Adelphi Theater] The Adelphi area was a group of buildings, streets, and extensive terraces built by the Adam brothers in the late eighteenth century on vaultings over the low riverbank, just east of M's lodging. *Cruchley's Picture of London* (p. 156) noted the theater for "the performance of burlettas, ballets, and pantomimes . . . [w]ell supported by a judicious choice of comic votaries. . . . The interior is handsomely decorated. It opens at half-past six, and commences at seven o'clock. . . . Gallery, one shilling." The *Times* advertisement for November 9: "*The Sons of Mars*. Characters by Messrs. Cullenford, Boyce, Hughes, P. Bedford; Mesdames Celeste [the manager], Woolgar, F. Matthews, E. Chaplin, and Turner. After which, *Domestic Economy*. To be followed by *A Bird of Passage*. To conclude with *Mrs. Bunbury's Spoons*." If M's "good piece" refers to the principal one, it was an adapted French play about a lieutenant, his friend—a younger heedless soldier—and the friend's sister, who unbeknownst to her brother loves and is loved by the lieutenant though promised to an unlikable captain. "This story is devoid neither of interest nor of ingenuity, but it is not expansive enough . . . to fill up satisfactorily . . . two hours. . . . The acting deserves just praise. Madame Celeste, as the soldier boy, . . . adequately represented his heedless gaiety" (*Times*, October 23). If M stayed for any of the one-act farces, he saw in Mark Lemon's *Domestic Economy* a cross-grained rustic who insists on exchanging roles with his wife: "The distress which John Grumly has to endure from his domestic employments . . . is most ludicrously portrayed. . . . The offspring of the couple, an unlucky urchin, ever tumbling into washing-tubs or upsetting flour-boxes, is cleverly acted" (*Times*, November 9). In Sterling Coyne's new extravaganza, the courtship of Mrs. Bunbury, a pastry cook, by several practical-jokester rivals is "only the preliminary to a grand skating scene . . . on the frozen lake. . . . The dances, executed with skates running on little wheels, are exceedingly well managed" (*Times*, October 16).

14.36 Wrote him] This letter, and the one to which Bentley was replying, are Nos. 311 and 312 on the "Check List of Unlocated Letters," *Letters*, p. 311.

15.3 lounged . . . day] Cunningham advised visitors that this day, Saturday, was the "aristocratic" day for sightseeing and that Monday was generally a workman's holiday (*Modern London*, p. xxvi). M's "sauntering" has begun with visits to the great lawyer and lawyer-training centers, taken in order from his lodging. He will spend more time on later visits to them (see the entries for November 11, 16.6–8, December 20, 44.22–29, and December 21, 45.46–34), but evidently on this Saturday he saw principally exteriors, courtyards, and gardens. Hawthorne on a first visit to the Temple precincts in 1855 found the large garden bordering the river pleasant but rather unimpressive, though he was struck by the quietness and the "many large, solemn, and serious edifices of dark brick"; when he walked through again in November of 1857, almost exactly eight years after M, he found the trees leafless but the grass still green and huge quantities of golden chrysanthemums blooming about the borders (*ENB*, pp. 217–18, 596). New Hall, at Lincoln's Inn, was the new (1846) great hall and library whose interior M viewed later (December 21); there is a contemporary sketch in *Knight's Cyclopædia*, p. 450.

15.5 Cock Lane] A small street north of St. Paul's. In early 1762 William Parsons drew crowds to his house here by claiming it was haunted by the ghost of a (he said) murdered wife. The "Cock-Lane ghost" is well known from Boswell's *Life of Johnson* (Saturday, June 25, 1763) but often with the wrong idea that Johnson believed in, rather than helped expose, the imposture. Chapter 69 of *Moby-Dick* ends thus: "Are you a believer in ghosts, my friend? There are other ghosts than the Cock-Lane one, and far deeper men than Doctor Johnson who believe in them" (p. 308). Chapter 17 of *The Confidence-Man* alludes to "some cavernous old gorge in a city, like haunted Cock Lane in London" (p. 85). Something of the lane's dinginess in the shabby neighborhood of Newgate and Old Bailey, near Smithfield, remained in M's mind in 1857 when he described Cairo streets (see the entry for January 3, 73.20–21, 74.4–5,7–8). Smithfield was still the great cattle and farm market, with adjoining slaughterhouses (shown below, from *Tallis's Illustrated London*, I, facing p. 224); its noisome filth less than half a mile north of St. Paul's (memorialized in Dickens's *Oliver Twist* and *Great Expectations*) led to its closing in 1855. On Saturdays, however, the principal market was hay and straw; big days

Smithfield Market

for cattle were Mondays and Fridays. M refers to the cattle in *Moby-Dick* (chap. 105, p. 460) and in *Israel Potter* (chap. 25, pp. 164–65). Smithfield was the site of Bartholomew Fair from 1133 to 1855.

15.6 Charter House] Sir Thomas Sutton founded Charterhouse in 1611 as a "hospital" for aged pensioners and as a boys' school. The Carthusian monastery, dissolved by Henry VIII, had passed through a number of hands before Sutton's purchase and bequest of £200,000. Its magnificence had consternated contemporaries like Bacon: "For to design the Charter House, a building fit to be a Prince's habitation, for a hospital is as if one should give in alms a rich embroidered cloak to a beggar" (quoted in *London Past and Present* [London: Murray, 1891], I, 364, Henry B. Wheatley's three-volume updating of Cunningham's encylopedic *Handbook for London, Past and Present* [London: Murray, 1849]). The eighty pensioners were chosen from penniless gentlemen, soldiers, and merchants impoverished by piracy or shipwreck, and servants of the royal household. *Knight's London* (II, 113–32) gives a mid-nineteenth-century description of the precincts, including the kitchen with two enormous chimneys, part of the original monastic edifice. Sutton was buried in the chapel under what Wheatley describes as a "sumptuous monument" (*London Past and Present*, I, 363). Edward Law (1750–1818) had been a vigorous, hasty-tempered, and highly prejudiced lord chief justice (appointed 1802 and created Baron Ellenborough). He had entered the school in 1761, and at his desire was buried in the chapel, "in grateful remembrance of his education there." Thomas Howard, duke of Norfolk, had been one of the earlier buyers of the property (1565). In the summer of 1570, while he was being held in the Tower, Elizabeth ordered him removed to his own house for fear of the plague, but suspicions of his continuing negotiations for marriage with Mary Queen of Scots led to his reconfinement in the Tower, trial, and execution in 1572.

15.11 Goswell . . . Barbican] Goswell Road, northward beyond Charterhouse, as M may have recalled from his shipboard reading, was the residence of Pickwick. The Barbican, south and east of Charterhouse, and so named from a watchtower or "barbican" of the old City wall, was a street Milton once lived on; Dryden's *MacFlecknoe* had enthroned Shadwell there in a neighborhood of brothels; and it figures in Chapter 25 of *Israel Potter* (pp. 164–65).

15.12 St Swithin's] A church designed by Christopher Wren on Cannon Street, near the approach to London Bridge; its only notable feature was the London Stone, a much-worn block from the street now in the wall, believed to be the "milestone" for England. (After the church was destroyed by bombing in World War II, the stone was relocated in the wall of a nearby bank.)

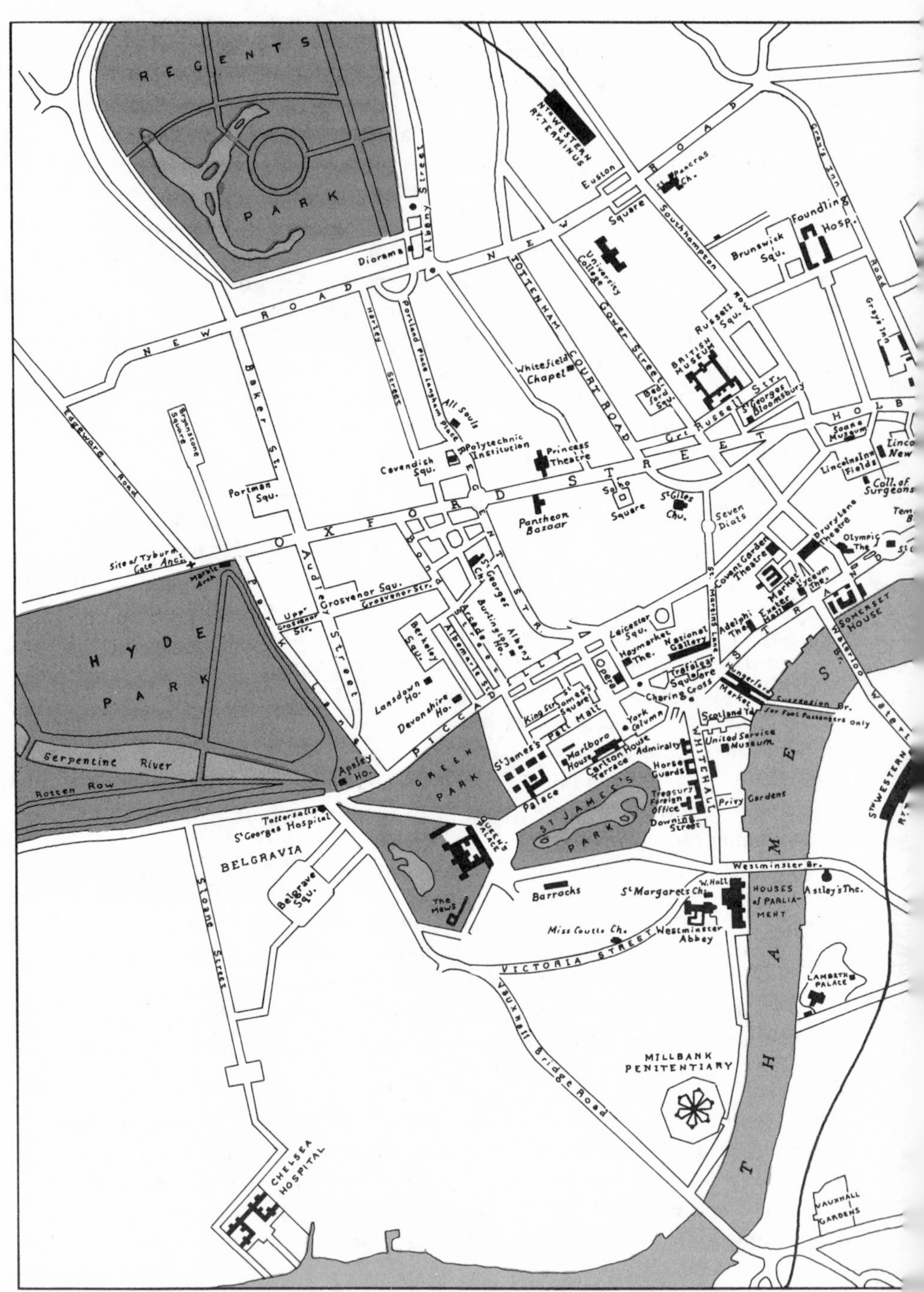

London, circa 1850. Based on the fold-out map

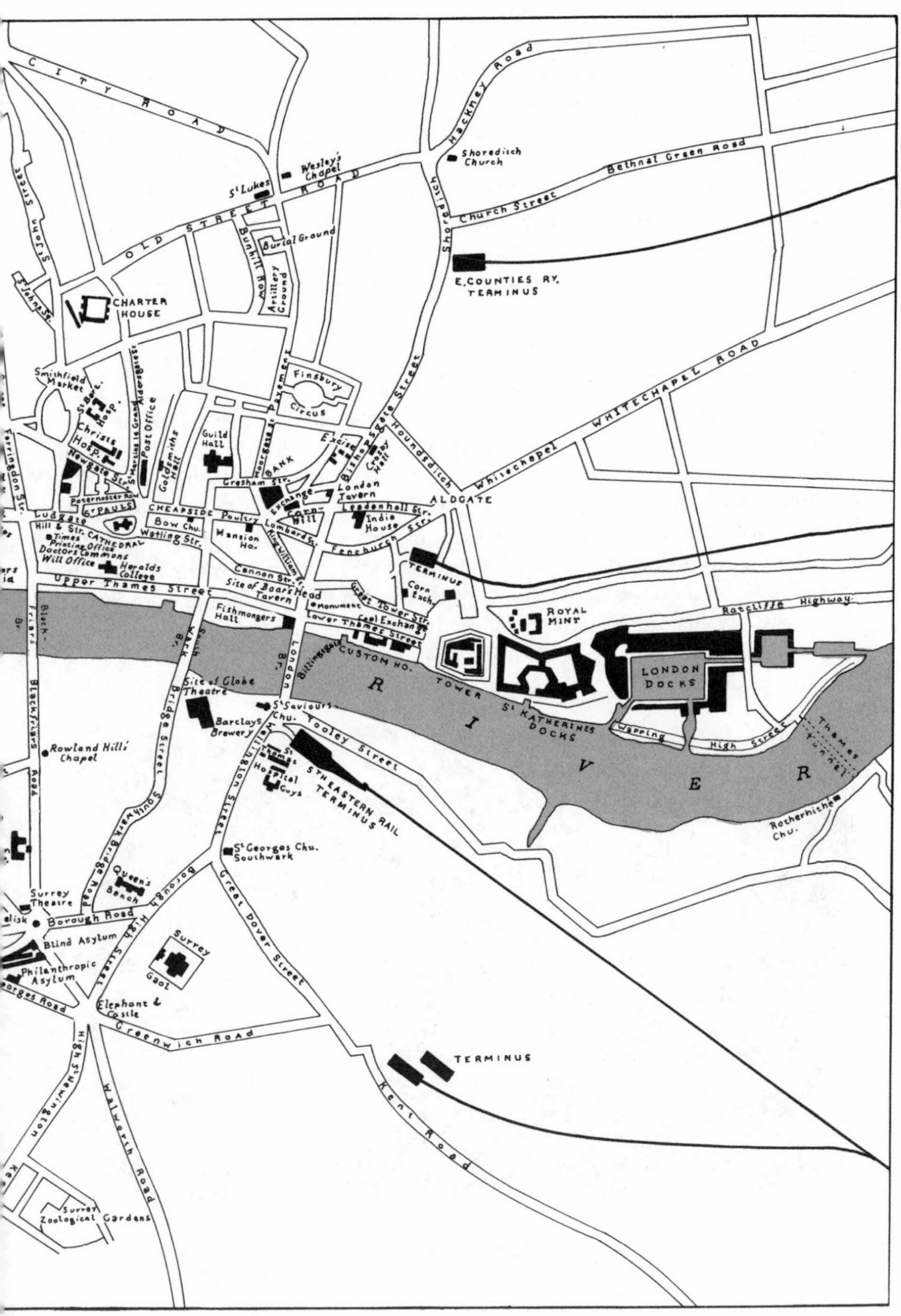

included in Cunningham's *Modern London* (Murray, 1851).

15.15 Whittington] Richard Whittington (d. 1423), immensely wealthy merchant and thrice lord mayor, was not a communicant of St. Swithin's parish but of the next west, St. Michael Paternoster Royal. His actual birthplace was in Gloucestershire, and even in the famous legend he was returning there in discouragement. What M was shown was probably a place off Moor Lane, just north of the Guildhall. A rambling, half-timbered building illustrated in Sir Walter Besant's *Mediæval London* (2 vols. [London: Black, 1906], I, 250) is called Whittington's house and located in "Swithin's Passage, Moor-Lane." But records of the college he founded located his house one tenement away from his parish church where he is buried (Besant, II, 379).

15.19 Guildhall] Originally a twelfth-century building, as the center of City government the Guildhall had been constantly embellished by later wealthy merchants; though substantially burned in the Great Fire, it was rebuilt in the existing walls (the illustration below is from *Tallis's Illustrated London*, I, [249]). The great hall, where state occasions like the lord mayor's banquet were held, was 152 feet long, 49 wide, and 89 feet to the roof ridge (Hawthorne gives an extensive description in 1856, *ENB*, pp. 379–80). M may have read the lengthy *Times* account on Saturday, November 10, which described the elaborate decorations for this occasion, with mirrors, trellises, conservatory plants, aviaries, a fountain, and sculptures of classical divinities. The assembly of nine hundred began before six, and at seven the lord mayor accompanied by state dignitaries and ambassadors proceeded to the

The Guildhall

high table (Mrs. Farncomb, the lady mayoress, was conducted by Lord John Russell). Besides listing the eminent guests, the *Times* gives the separate bills of fare for the high table and the lower hall; the following is a sampling of the high table menu: ten tureens of turtle, thirty entrées, one boiled turkey, two roast pullets, two dishes of fowls, two dishes of capons, two hams ornamented, one stewed rump of beef, sirloin of beef, three roast turkeys, three pheasants, two geese, two dishes of partridges, one dish of wild fowl, two peafowls, and so on and so on, concluding with, in part, pineapples, grapes, ice creams, apples, cakes, nuts, conserves, and brandy cherries. The quantities for the lower hall were proportionate. What M later "made of this" was the second part of "Poor Man's Pudding and Rich Man's Crumbs," published in *Harper's New Monthly Magazine*, June, 1854 (NN *Piazza Tales* volume, pp. 297–302). Its setting is the great 1814 banquet for the victors in the Napoleonic Wars, but the helpful officer, the back-alley entrance, and the litter within come from this day's experience.

15.28–29 Bank & New Exchange] The Bank of England, next east from the Guildhall, was essentially the financial center of the nineteenth-century world; its neoclassic facade had been altered in 1848 to make it more "impressive" and changes were still going on. The "New" Exchange was the recently erected building of the Royal Exchange (dedicated by the queen in 1844); M had only to cross Threadneedle Street to reach the "chief commercial building of the greatest commercial city of the world" (*Knight's Cyclopædia*, p. 603). The following Wednesday (November 14) M attempted to see the quarters of Lloyd's (see 18.7 and accompanying discussion).

15.29–30 Fish Street Hill . . . Tower Hill] Fish Street Hill, formerly the main approach to old London Bridge, is distinguished by two of Wren's greatest works, the church of St. Magnus Martyr and the imposing monument commemorating the Great Fire: M mentions neither here, but he had mentioned the latter in a letter to John Murray in September of 1846 (*Letters*, p. 46), in *Omoo* (chap. 53, p. 204), *Redburn* (chap. 30, p. 142), and was to mention it in *Israel Potter* (chap. 25, p. 161) and in his 1856–57 journal (59.23) for a comparison in Constantinople. At the Tower, according to *Knight's Cyclopædia* (p. 192), "though far too little of the Tower is open to the public, for the parts that are shown, the Regalia and the Armoury, the charge is . . . only sixpence to each, and they are open every day except Sundays and church holidays. The number of persons who visited the Tower in 1849 was 45,474." Open from ten to four, with warders conducting tours every half hour. At the time of M's visit, the collection of armor was exhibited in the Horse Armoury, a one-story building erected in 1825 alongside the central keep, the White Tower. "On the north side, in a recess, is an equestrian figure, in an Asiatic suit of great antiquity. . . . It consists of what might be termed the ordinary dress of a knight of that period, namely, minute iron rings joined together into a network enveloping the entire body" (p. 191). *Cruchley's Picture of London* (p. 199) adds that it was supposed to have belonged to Bayezid I. The brass cannon of the Knights of Malta (now in the Small Arms Room, White Tower) was one of the few items to be saved from a disastrous fire in 1841; of "exquisite workmanship" and "finely ornamented," the barrel was covered with figures in alto relievo and with laurel branches and medallions, on a carriage carved to represent two Furies. The French had taken it at Malta in 1798, and a British frigate took it from the French transport. Accompanying it was the banner of the last Grand Master of the Knights.

15.32–33 headsman's block] Both block and ax were exhibited on the ground floor of the White Tower, in the crypt of the chapel. The fourth earl of Kilmarnock, William Boyd (1704–46), was a late convert to the Stuart cause, so he confessed, because of his impoverishment by a careless and dissolute life. When Charles the Young Pretender was defeated at Culloden, Kilmarnock was taken. According to *Knight's London* (II, 248), he, Lord Balmerino, and "the treacherous and profligate" Simon Lord Lovat were all beheaded for their part in the Scottish rebellion of 1745. (Lovat's execution in 1747 was the last beheading in England.) Hawthorne described the block in 1855 as "of oak about two feet high, with a large knot in it, so that it would not easily be split, . . . with a hollow, to accommodate the head and shoulders. . . . There were two or three very strong marks of the axe, in the part over which the neck lay" (*ENB*, p. 215).

15.35–36 London Docks] These two great docks (shown opposite, from *Tallis's Illustrated London*, II, facing p. 164), next in sequence immediately east of the Tower, were guarded but open to visitors. M was now entering, of course, a major lower working-class and sailor district. Ratcliffe (or "Ratcliff") Highway (later St. George Street and still later The Highway) was a busy thoroughfare toward Limehouse, while Wapping High Street along the river was where Nelson outfitted himself and where pirates like Kidd were hanged. To Hawthorne in 1855, Wapping was a "dingy, shabby, and uninteresting region. . . . Many ale and spirit-shops, apple-stands, fish and butcher's stalls, all on the poorest scale. . . . On the whole, the place is dreary" (*ENB*, pp. 233–34). As late as 1890, Wheatley in revising Cunningham would describe Ratcliffe Highway: "From end to end the street has a maritime savour. . . . The very churches and institutions—Seamen's Mission Hall, Seamen's Chapel, Seamen's Free Reading-Room, Bethel Station; and, unfortunately, flaring drinking, dancing, and music rooms, and haunts of a far worse order. Here, among other 'dens,' are the Chinese opium-smokers' sties" (*London Past and Present*, III, 150). The area also received extensive notice in Bracebridge Hemyng's section on London prostitution, added to Henry Mayhew's *London Labour and the London Poor* (4 vols. [London: Woodfall, 1851–62], IV, 210–72).

LONDON DOCKS

15.37 Tunnel] The Thames Tunnel, originally a foot passageway opened six years earlier; its two parallel passages, separated by a thick open-arched brick wall, ran for thirteen hundred feet under the riverbed from Wapping to Swan Lane, Rotherhithe. For a penny, M would have descended a sixty-five-foot vertical shaft by means of a spiral staircase to the gas-lighted passage. "The arches are to some extent occupied as a bazaar, and the walls of the shafts are decorated with paintings, each panel containing a subject selected from English or Colonial scenery . . . executed with great boldness of style and much brilliancy of colour" (*Knight's Cyclopædia*, p. 552). Hawthorne and his son Julian (*ENB*, pp. 232–33) found it a gloomy, dungeon-like place, and the shops under the arches, kept by women, full of cheap jewelry and trumpery; at one of them M bought two medals for Evert Duyckinck's little sons (see *Letters*, p. 103 [No. 71]), though he seems not to have crossed under. The place made some impression on him: two comparisons in *Moby-Dick* (the chest of Ahab's imagined ideal man—in chap. 108, p. 470—and legendary accounts of whale length—in chap. 105, p. 460) use the tunnel for analogy, and it was one of the very few things M visited on his brief return to London in May of 1857 (128.7). The illustration below is from the 1851 edition of *Knight's London,* III, 49.

15.38 "Poor Jack"] Across from the docks, the south bank parish had been largely occupied by families connected with ships, but of late its riverfront had become drab with an unbroken chain of warehouses, the river itself dense with shipping, especially the dingy coal carriers. The epithet "Poor Jack" had more than one association for M. Among the "patriotic verses, full of sea-chivalry and romance" by Charles Dibdin (1745–1814), upon which M comments in Chapter 90 of *White-Jacket* (pp. 382–84), the one titled "Poor Jack" celebrates the views of a hardy British naval seaman. But the name was also a generic term for boat tenders, odd-job men around the wharves, stray waifs and beggars. As such, it provided the title for Captain Marryat's novel (1840), which was included in the small library of M's third whaler, the *Charles and Henry* (see the discussion at 12.24). Nine-year-old Tom (often called Jack), son of a long-absent sailor, leaves his termagant mother to pick up a precarious living by his wits. "Indeed I was now what is termed a regular *Mud-larker*, picking up halfpence by running into the water, offering my ragged arm to people getting out of the wherries, always saluting them with, 'You havn't got never a halfpenny for poor Jack, your honour?'"; and shortly, by resourcefulness and fighting ability, he beats the other boys for the "office" or "avocation" of "Poor Jack" of the Greenwich waterside (pp. 46, 49, 50, 56). (See also the discussion at 23.32, for the novel's association with old pensioners at Greenwich.) M may have had in mind the particular "Poor Jack" he saw here this day when some months later he wrote the first paragraph of Chapter 57 of *Moby-Dick*: "On Tower-hill, as you go down to the London docks, you may have seen a crippled beggar (or *kedger*, as the sailors say)" (p. 269); but unlike the one in *Moby-Dick* this Poor Jack was probably not displaying a painted whaling scene in which he lost a leg.

15.38 Took a steamer] *Knight's London* (I, 15–16) eulogizes a similar twilight trip with a certain equivocality edging its mid-Victorian, bourgeois complacency:

> A bell is ringing; we pass through a toll-gate, paying four-pence, and in a few seconds are on board one of the little steam-boats, bearing the poetical name of some flower, or planet, or precious gem. . . . Threading its way through a dozen other steam-winged vessels, the boat darts towards the Surrey shore; and her prow is breasting the ebbing tide. What a gorgeous scene is now before us! The evening sun is painting the waters with glancing flames; the cross upon the summit of that mighty dome of St. Paul's shines like another sun; churches, warehouses, steam-chimneys, shot-towers, wharfs, bridges—the noblest and the humblest things—all are picturesque. . . . In truth, this juxtaposition of the magnificent and the common fills the mind with as much food for thought as if from London Bridge to Westminster there was one splendid quay, curtaining the sheds, and coal-barges, and time-worn landings which meet us at every glance. . . . Whilst we rush under the mighty arches of the iron bridge, and behold another, and another, and another spanning the river, looking as vast and solid as if they defied time and the elements; and also see the wharfs on the one bank, although the light be waning, still populous and busy,—and the foundries, and glass-houses, and printing-offices, on the other bank, still sending out their dense smoke,—we know that without this never-tiring energy, disagreeable as are some of its outward forms, the splendour which is around us could not have been. . . . The dirty Whitefriars is the neighbour of the trim Temple. Praised be the venerable Law which has left us one green spot, where

trees still grow by our river-side, and which still preserves some relics of the days that are gone!

M particularly recommended such an excursion to his uncle Peter Gansevoort (see pp. 620–23). The view shown below of the gardens from the river is from *Tallis's Illustrated London*, I, 45.

TEMPLE GARDENS.

16.2 Saturday night] The impoverished narrator in the second part of M's "The Two Temples" takes a similar Saturday night walk: "A stranger in London on Saturday night. . . . What shall I do with myself this weary night? . . . So on I drifted amid those indescribable crowds which every seventh night pour and roar through each main artery and block the bye-veins of great London, the Leviathan. Saturday Night it was; and the markets and the shops, and every stall and counter were crushed with the one unceasing tide. . . . The unscrupulous human whirlpools eddied me aside at corners, as any straw is eddied in the Norway Maelstrom. . . . I staggered on through three millions of my own human kind. The fiendish gas-lights shooting their Tartarean rays across the muddy sticky streets, lit up the pitiless and pitiable scene" (NN *Piazza Tales* volume, pp. 309–10). However, the theater in which he finds refuge, the "Temple Second," was not the "penny theater" below but clearly Covent Garden. By the 1851 census, the population of the city was 2,362,236 (Francis Sheppard, *London, 1808–1870* [Berkeley and Los Angeles: University of California Press, 1971], p. 138).

16.3–4 Penny Theater] These theaters, called "gaffs" by their street-folk patrons, flourished by the hundreds in all the poor districts of London; jerry-built out of old warehouses, stables, or stores, using the flimsiest props and sleaziest costumes, they were crowded up to six or nine times a night by a couple of hundred youngsters, with perhaps a few adults. By Victorian standards, the audiences were unspeakably rowdy, boisterous, and addicted to the most degraded language and delight. Programs, not more than an hour long at most, often included a bawdy song-and-dance interlude, two plays—say *Hamlet* or *Lear* cobbled up in twenty minutes, or the most fantastic melodrama or outrageous farce, often as many as ten or twelve new ones a week. A vivid earlier description with extracts of audience conversation and actors' dialogue is James Grant, *Penny Theatres, from* SKETCHES IN LONDON, *1838* (reprinted by The Society for Theatre Research, London, 1952); Henry Mayhew's section on the "Penny Gaff" in his *London Labour and the London Poor* (I, 40–42) describes a particular visit contemporary with M's. (EMM, pp. 106–7, quotes from a number of pamphlets in the Harvard Theater Collection.)

16.6 Temple Church] The church of the Knights Templars, in the Temple precincts, is in two parts, the older Round Church (1185) and the Choir (before 1240). A great crust of later ornamentation and alteration had recently been removed (1839–42), restoring the original Crusader-Norman style under the influence of Saracenic magnificence. Hawthorne found it wonderfully beautiful, and its windows especially splendid (*ENB*, p. 598). Full choral service was performed by the Temple choir, six men, eight boys, with one of the best organs in England. The recumbent effigies (nine, not ten) in the Round Church had been much battered and covered with paint and whitewash, but the recent restoration, so *Knight's Cyclopædia* claimed, resulted in "the very beautiful and noble effigies which once more grace the floor of the Temple Church in their pristine state" (p. 440). Hawthorne, at least, found them the best preserved he had seen. As M notes, those with

[Effigies of Knight Templars.]

legs crossed, it was thought, had been on a Crusade or at least vowed to do so. These effigies (pictured on p. 281 above, from the 1851 edition of *Knight's London*, III, 314) are described in Part I of M's "The Paradise of Bachelors and the Tartarus of Maids": "Go view the wondrous tombs in the Temple Church; see there the rigidly-haughty forms stretched out, with crossed arms upon their stilly hearts, in everlasting and undreaming rest" (*Harper's New Monthly Magazine*, April, 1855; NN *Piazza Tales* volume, p. 317). Again, in *Clarel*, 4.2.110–15, he recalls

> . . . those monk-soldiers helmet-crowned,
> Whose effigies in armed sleep, lie—
> Stone, in the stony Temple round
> In London; and (to verify
> Them more) with carved greaves crossed, for sign
> Of duty done in Palestine.

What M in his journal calls the heads of the "damned" were thought to be, rather, representations of Purgatory, constituting half the circle of sixty-four heads decorating the arcade in the aisle: "The half-circle that was most carefully restored—the left or northern—presents but comparatively few exceptions to the painful character expressed by all the heads on that side, and which has been marked throughout by the nicest discrimination of the different kinds of manifestation of pain applicable to so many different classes of individuals. . . . There is one head, combining a mingled sensation of physical and mental horror which surpasses description—it is ghastly—fearful!—it is as if all the worst passions of man's nature had been gathered together in one point and then smitten with some intolerable agony" (*Knight's Cyclopædia*, p. 439). M particularly commended a visit to the church to his uncle Peter (see pp. 620–23 below).

16.9 took a buss] According to contemporary estimates, some seven hundred omnibuses in London, with two hundred more in the environs, ran every few minutes; as a rule they carried thirteen inside, several more outside, for a usual fare of sixpence the first four or five miles. (See Sheppard, *London*, pp. 120–22, for a modern estimate of these numbers.) By the route M took, mostly north of the river, the distance would be about fifteen miles, though he must have crossed the river before Kew, which is on the south bank, as is Richmond. The famous gardens at Kew were a favorite residence of George III, who enormously enriched the gardens, begun by his father, with worldwide specimens. (Both the actual and M's fictional Israel Potter, working as gardeners, encounter the king here—see chap. 5 of *Israel Potter* and the discussion at 43.15–16 below.) The gardens had been made national and public in 1840; M apparently did not enter, but passed along the southeast boundary. Sir William Chambers (1726-96), successful architect and principal instigator of the eighteenth-century Chinese craze, was first employed by the mother of George III. From a youthful trip to China, he brought back sketches that informed the oriental embellishments at Kew, most importantly the great pagoda of 1761 near M's route. Called the most ambitious of chinoiserie garden structures in Europe, its ten stories, 160 feet high, were once ornamented with glazed tiles and eighty garish iron dragons.

16.12 Richmond Hill] Richmond Park was enclosed as a great chase by Charles I; it was usual to approach it from the north, as M did, which afforded the view from the terrace of Richmond Hill. *Knight's Cyclopædia* (pp. 17–18) rhapsodizes about the prospect that M admired:

> Richmond . . . is recognized as the most beautiful of English villages. . . . Suddenly the long anticipated prospect bursts upon the view. . . . It is a purely *beautiful* landscape that is spread before us. . . . Wood and water, softly-swelling hills and hazy distance, with village spires and lordly halls, are blended in beautiful harmony. . . . A vast expanse of country stretches far away till the distance is closed by the hills of Buckinghamshire on the north-west, and the Surrey downs on the south-east; and all this intermediate space is one wide valley of the most luxuriant fertility, but appearing to the eye a succession of densely-wooded tracts, broken and diversified by a few undulations of barer uplands. . . . In the midst the broad placid river, studded with islets, and its surface alive with flocks of swans . . . majesty is added to the exceeding loveliness by Windsor's royal towers. . . . Nothing, however, but poetry can properly describe the surpassing beauty of the prospect, and the poetry that does well describe it—that of Thomson—will at once recur to every one.

16.16 Thompson] The poet James Thomson (1700–1748), with the success of "The Seasons" (1726–30), began in 1736 his lifelong residence at Richmond, where he wrote "The Castle of Indolence" (1748); only Tennyson was more popular after 1850. Alexander Pope (1688–1744) began his residence in his famous villa and gardens a mile and half west across the river in 1719.

16.17–18 Hampton Court] This palace was open, free of charge, from ten to four every day but Friday in winter; for a small fee a gardener would show special outside features. Cardinal Wolsey's great palace and gardens with subsequent additions, residence of twelve successive sovereigns, had been neglected after George II; only since 1838 had the gardens and palace been open to the public, under repair and restoration. Entrance was recommended from the west for the effect of Wolsey's Tudor Gothic, but M must have crossed the river from the northeast and entered by way of Wren's massive brick emulation of Versailles for William III. Much of Charles I's remarkable collection of paintings had been sold off by the Commonwealth, but others had been brought from other palaces, many only copies, or misattributed, as may be the case with the Titian and the Guido Reni M mentions; most of the original great Van Dycks were gone, but among those remaining was one of Charles I's mistress, Margaret Lemon. Of the two "Court Beauties" series, M doubtless refers to those from the court of Charles II, painted by Sir Peter Lely; those commissioned in rivalry by Queen Mary of Orange from Sir Godfrey Kneller "look as uniformly dull as those of Charles are uniformly impudent" (*Knight's Cyclopædia*, p. 64). The Rembrandt M mentions is the head of a rabbi. The glory of Charles's collection, however, was the series of Raphael cartoons (now in the Victoria and Albert Museum); M's reference to the poor lighting is probably to this series, not the almost equally famous Mantegna cartoons, *The Triumph of Caesar*. The original ten Raphael cartoons represented the Acts of the Apostles, painted on paper and cut in strips to guide the tapestry weavers of Brussels, commissioned to make the hangings for the Sistine Chapel. After much damage, the seven remaining were bought by the then Prince Charles in Genoa; reserved from the sales after his execution, they were continually mishandled but finally reassembled, probably under William III, and pasted on linen. Wren constructed a special gallery for them, but they were hung too high, almost above the twelve north-facing windows opposite—thus the common complaint about the lighting. Perhaps this partly explains Hawthorne's dismissal of them (even though predictable) as dull and uninteresting; *ENB*, p. 286. An account of their history and recent condition is given by John K. G. Shearman, *Raphael's Cartoons* (London: Phaidon, 1972).

Among the ornate State Beds were William III's, hung with crimson velvet; Queen Anne's in crimson, yellow, and white cut velvet; George II's queen's in crimson damask; and George III's queen's in elaborately embroidered lilac satin. East of Wren's facade the great formal French garden stretched to the river; the south gardens were from Tudor and Stuart times. Nearby on the north were the "Wilderness" with its famous maze, followed by the eleven hundred acres of Bushy Park with its fountain, basin, and a magnificent avenue of chestnuts and limes. (M's return by rail meant recrossing the river to take the short branch line to ugly new Waterloo Station on the south bank, opposite his lodging.)

16.27 Bentley] Richard Bentley (1794–1871), from a family of printers and publishers, entered briefly and unhappily into partnership with the notoriously cheapjack Henry Colburn in 1829. However scorned by other publishers, he early recognized the importance of fiction and the uses of advertising. He began his successful "Standard Novels" series with Cooper's *The Pilot* (1831) and remained loyal to the end of Cooper's career, as he did to such other Americans as William Prescott, Francis Parkman, and George Bancroft. His *Miscellany* was initially successful, with Dickens as editor and *Oliver Twist* as a serial, but by the time of M's visit it had declined drastically, contributing to the financial bind Bentley was in from the mid-1840's through the mid-1850's. He published *Mardi, Redburn, White-Jacket,* and *The Whale*; and despite continuing losses he would also have published *Pierre* had M allowed the "alterations" he diplomatically called for in a letter of May of 1852. He began "with real admiration of your genius," but went on to state that changes were necessary to make M's work "properly appreciated here." (See Bernard R. Jerman, "'With Real Admiration': More Correspondence between Melville and Bentley," *American Literature*, XXV [November, 1953], 307–13; the NN revised *Letters* volume; the NN *Pierre*, pp. 378–79; and Gettmann, *A Victorian Publisher*. See also 13.29 and p. 179 above.) The portrait below is reproduced from *Extracts from* LE LIVRE (Edinburgh: Clark, 1886), facing p. 1.

17.3 St James] St. James's Street, lined with the splendid clubhouses of nineteenth-century London, continues Albemarle Street south of Piccadilly to St. James's Palace, beyond which is St. James's Park. In 1845–46 M's brother Gansevoort, while secretary of legation, had lodged nearby at 1 St. James's Place; see 44.20 and accompanying discussion.

17.4 Cigar Divan] The Divan, at 101 Strand, consisted of "a long room . . . fitted up in a style of oriental taste, which, when lighted, is very brilliant; large looking glasses decorate each end of the room; the walls present tasteful scenes and landscapes; the furniture, consisting of ottomans and couches, covered with leather. On the tables are scattered the leading journals of Europe, with chess, draughts, &c. Entrance, one shilling, which entitles the party to a cup of coffee and a cigar" (*Cruchley's Picture of London*, p. 245). EMM (p. 113) notes the allusion in Part I of "The Paradise of Bachelors and the Tartarus of Maids" where the narrator ironically tries to imagine ancient Knights Templars "in their red-cross mantles smoking cigars at the Divan!" (NN *Piazza Tales* volume, p. 317).

17.7–8 London Coffee House] On Ludgate Hill, not far from the Old Bailey; after it opened in 1771, it became the center of a club devoted to scientific and philosophical discussion, including Joseph Priestley and Benjamin Franklin as members. In the nineteenth century, it continued to be frequented by Americans, who knew it for good wine and quiet dinners (Robert E. Spiller, *The American in England* [New York: Holt, 1926], p. 271).

17.9 Joseph Harper] Joseph Wesley Harper, Jr. (1830–96), son of the third of the four Harper brothers (Eugene Exman, *The Brothers Harper* [New York: Harper & Row, 1965], p. 292). First of the family to go to college, he had just graduated from Columbia, valedictorian of the class of 1848, and like all the Harper sons and grandsons immediately entered apprenticeship to the firm's business. M's impression of the prosperous younger man may have been a little jaundiced: he wrote (and later canceled) the remark "A regular Yankee." Though a good-natured jokester, young Harper was genial and especially charming, both a business genius and ethically upright; devoted to literature, he shared his gentle father's tact in literary correspondence and ultimately became in effect editor-in-chief. Unlike his uncles, he later took an active part in the struggle for international copyright. (A late picture of him appears with the memorial notices in *Publishers' Weekly*, July 25, 1896, pp. 156–57, 159; see also Exman, *The House of Harper* [New York: Harper & Row, 1967], pp. 143–44, 154; his cousin, J. Henry Harper, *The House of Harper* [New York: Harper & Brothers, 1912], pp. 45, 316, 433, 640–41; John Tebbel, *A History of Book Publishing in the United States*, 3 vols. [New York: R. R. Bowker, 1972–78], II, 191, 193; and Donald Sheehan,

This Was Publishing [Bloomington: University of Indiana Press, 1952], p. 11.) The Harpers had first declined *Typee*, but accepted *Omoo*, took over *Typee*, and published all of M's books through *Pierre*; then their *New Monthly Magazine* published seven pieces and two of the poems later collected in *Battle-Pieces* (1866), which was also published by them.

17.13 "Judge & Jury"] Renton Nicholson (1809–61), with a partner, established the Garrick's Head and Town Hotel at 27 Bow St. (facing the Covent Garden theater) near the famous central Bow Street Police Office—with a certain appropriateness, as he himself was often in jail for insolvency; there he presided as "The Lord Chief Baron" over the Judge and Jury Society. The humorous mock trials attracted even M.P.'s and peers, with occasions of "real eloquence, brilliant repartee, fluent satire, and not unfrequently . . . indecent witticism" (*DNB*). Later Nicholson added what may have been risqué "poses plastiques" and "tableaux vivants." M later recommended this sight to his uncle Peter, though with a wrong address (see pp. 620–23). ("Stetson" is unidentified.)

HUNGERFORD MARKET.

17.17–18 Hungerford Bridge] This brief-lived suspension bridge for pedestrians, almost next door to M's lodging, led from Hungerford Market to Southwark, from which it was about a mile's walk to the Surrey County Gaol, a large, plain, three-story quadrangle fronting on an open space used for public executions. The illustration above is from *Tallis's Illustrated London*, I, facing p. 88.

17.18–19 the Mannings] George and Marie de Roux Manning, she a lady's maid, he a publican, were found jointly guilty (October 26) of murdering a friend of hers in August, burying his body beneath the kitchen flagstones, and robbing his lodgings; in the weeks since, the *Times* (for example) had carried numerous accounts of them and their mutually recriminatory statements, each for the "good" of the other's soul piously calling on the other to acknowledge sole guilt—accounts or similar ones that M probably saw in his reading of the daily papers (as he says he did about another current event at 15.26). The most famous account of the execution is in the first of two outraged letters written by Dickens to the *Times* (November 14) after accompanying John Forster (see the discussion at 40.4) at midnight to witness the gathering crowd:

> I believe that a sight so inconceivably awful as the wickedness and levity of the immense crowd collected at that execution this morning could be imagined by no man, and could be presented in no heathen land under the sun. . . . As the night went on, screeching, and laughing, and yelling in strong chorus of parodies on Negro melodies with substitutions of "Mrs. Manning" for "Susannah," and the like were added. When the day dawned, thieves, low prostitutes, ruffians and vagabonds of every kind, flocked on to the ground, with every variety of offensive and foul behaviour. Fightings, faintings, whistlings, imitations of Punch, brutal jokes, tumultuous demonstrations of indecent delight gave a new zest to the general entertainment. When the sun rose . . . it gilded thousands upon thousands of upturned faces, so inexpressibly odious in their brutal mirth. . . . When the two miserable creatures . . . were turned quivering into the air, there was no more emotion, no more pity, no more thought that two immortal souls had gone to judgment, no more restraint in any of the previous obscenities, than if the name of Christ had never been heard.

The adjoining news account in the *Times* reported that the prisoners shook hands as they were being hooded, she veiled and blindfolded, then again just before the drop. The hanging took place on the roof of the jail at 9 A.M. before thirty thousand spectators, and, according to the news account, "on the outskirts of this great mass of human beings were, grouped in smaller numbers, a very different class . . . who had paid their two or three guineas to gratify a morbid curiosity, and who . . . from their luxurious homes, came to fill the windows, the gardens, and the housetops of a few miserable little houses. . . . The best view . . . is to be obtained from the tenements at the west end of Winter-terrace." M bought a broadside of the execution and sent it to Lemuel Shaw; it is reproduced in *Log*, I, 331 (Nov. 13, 1849). Albert Borowitz, in *The Woman Who Murdered Black Satin* (Columbus: Ohio State University Press, 1981), gives an exhaustive account.

17.25 Regent's Park] The park and the area leading to it along Regent Street were developed early in the century by the Prince Regent and John Nash, his favorite architect, as a fashionable and profitable real estate venture, an "aristocratic 'garden city'" (Sheppard, *London*, p. 113). The zoo (fee one shilling, open from nine to sunset) in the northeast quarter of the park prompted Knight's frequent superlatives: "If one were desired to name the most delightful lounge in the metropolis . . . the Zoological Gardens . . . must, we think, be the chosen place" (*Knight's London*, V, 257); by his enumeration, this traditional cage, pit, and pond type of zoo seems to have had a large variety of specimens. Through a tunnel, one passed under the park road to the northwest extremity where "a remarkably lofty building appears before us, with an enclosed yard . . . the giraffe-house and park. . . . It is difficult to resist the impression, that these most beautiful and delicate, but, to the very eyes that behold them, almost incredibly tall creatures cannot belong to any part of our planet. . . . There are now four here; two adult males and one female, and one young one born in the Gardens, and enjoying, we are happy to say, excellent health" (V, 270). (As to the "Dreary & rainy day" when M was there—evidently the weather had changed from the bright sunny morning described in Dickens's letter, quoted in the preceding discussion.)

17.28 letter home] No. 313 on the "Check List of Unlocated Letters," *Letters*, p. 311.

17.30–32 Taylor . . . designs] For Taylor see the discussion at 4.18; his "designs" may have been to borrow money from the two ladies or to be employed by them as a private doctor or as a "cicerone" on a European tour, but he ended up by accompanying the wealthy young McCurdy, as this day's entry notes further along. As to Taylor as a possible "cicerone" see the discussion at 150.18, and as a private doctor see the headnote to "The Two Temples" in the NN *Piazza Tales* volume, pp. 702–3 (which errs in reporting that McCurdy's "rich merchant" father also accompanied them).

17.33–34 the Abbey & Westminster Hall] In the abbey, the Chapel of St. John the Baptist is next but one to the ornate Chapel of Henry VII; in its center is the tomb of Thomas Cecil (d. 1622), eldest son of Elizabeth's Lord Burleigh. His first wife, Dorothy Nevill, lies to his right with her effigy above. His surviving second wife, Frances Bridges, indignantly refused the left side and was buried at Winchester. (Nave and choir were open to the public; the chapels required a fee.) When the old Palace of Westminster, housing Parliament, across the street from the abbey, burned in 1834, the great hall survived; in 1849 it was still surrounded by the various attached law courts, other shabby buildings scheduled for demolition, and beyond by the rising pile of the new Houses of Parliament. The south end of the hall had been opened for the construction of the great staircase that was to rise to the central hall of the new building.

18.1 Vauxhall] The gardens, about a mile upriver on the south bank, had been a famous resort since the Restoration; but its graveled walks, colonnades and pavilions, bowers, music, dancing, fireworks, cafés, and other entertainments closed within ten years of M's visit.

18.3 Murray] John Murray (1808–92), third of the line, rather more cautious than his father, who had published such notables as Byron, Scott, and Austen, followed his father's loss of interest in imaginative literature and nearly always declined to accept poetry or fiction. The firm was perhaps the most influential of English publishers, with a long list of important books in history, travel, and discovery. A staunch conservative churchman, all the same he published the two great scientific works of his time, Charles Lyell's

JOHN MURRAY III.

Geology (1830–33) and Charles Darwin's *Origin of Species* (1859), but he sternly reprobated anything tinged with freethinking. It was a distinct advantage to M that Murray published first *Typee*, then *Omoo*, even though in the cheap "Colonial and Home Library" series. With *Typee*, Murray had been troubled by its possible fictitiousness; in his refusing *Mardi* (an avowed "romance") and later books, one consideration was objections like those in a reader's letter to him about the inclusion of *Typee* and *Omoo* in a series listed as containing *"nothing offensive to morals or good taste"*: "Their tone is, I think, reprehensible throughout. They are not works that any mother would like to see in the hands of her daughters. . . . I think it important to elicit . . . some assurance that there shall not appear in his series another volume similar in character" (quoted by "George Paston" [Emily M. Symonds], *At John Murray's* [London: Murray, 1932], pp. 53–54). Murray himself had traveled widely in his youth; vexed by the lack of reliable, systematic sources of information, he personally devised the first of the spectacularly successful Murray *Handbooks* (so named by his father). Winters he held office hours from ten to five at 50 Albemarle St., where he lived above the office with his wife (m. 1847) and daughter (b. 1849), and where twice a week he carried on the long tradition of hosting literary dinners. J. Henry Harper called him the "finest specimen of an English gentleman I ever met. Tall, willowy, and of fine presence, he entertained with the courtesy of a Chesterfield" (*The House of Harper*, p. 394). The portrait here is reproduced from p. 520 of "The House of Murray" by F. Espinasse, in *Harper's* (September, 1885), 501–22.

18.7 "Loyd's"] Lloyd's was in the new Royal Exchange, which M had noted before (see 15.28–29 and accompanying discussion); the truncated triangle of the building enclosed a large inner court, surrounded by an arcade with shops below and more shops and offices above. The famous association of underwriters and center of marine and mercantile intelligence occupied quarters on the main floor, approached by a wide flight of stairs and an imposing vestibule. For the general public there was an "Enquiry Room" on the ground floor, giving out freely the latest information on any ship; on the main floor, three large rooms accommodated respectively the Underwriters, the Merchants' Room, with an unparalleled file of provincial and foreign newspapers, and the Captains' Room, where refreshments as well as ships and ships' stores were sold.

18.11 Stibbs] Edward C. Stibbs, 331 Strand (EMM). In the list of books he bought in London, M records the price of the Beaumont and Fletcher folio as fourteen shillings, the Jonson as thirteen shillings (144.5,3). The first was *Fifty Comedies and Tragedies* . . . (London, 1679; HCL-M; Sealts 53; Bercaw 53); it is rather extensively marked by M, who used it in one of the epigraphs to "The Encantadas" (*Putnam's Monthly Magazine*, March–May, 1854; see the NN *Piazza Tales* volume, p. 605) and somewhat confusingly inscribed it: "Herman Melville London, December, 1849. (New Year's Day, at sea)" and "1850." The other was *The Works of Ben Jonson* . . . (London, 1692; now in the New-York Historical Society; Sealts 302; Bercaw 405); it too is annotated by M and similarly inscribed. M's entries at the end of this journal notebook cite Jonson four times (141.10–12, 142.27,35–36,38–40; see the discussion at 142.35). Some years later (1858), George Duyckinck gave M the Chapman translation of the Homeric works that he took with him on his 1860 trip around Cape Horn (see p. 200).

18.15 New Strand Theater] A small place near Somerset House and Stibbs's bookshop, it was also known off and on as Punch's Play House, a name suggesting its principal fare—dance, burlesque, and farce. *The Clandestine Marriage*, however, was the well-known comedy (1766) by David Garrick and the elder George Colman, suggested by Hogarth's *Marriage-à-la-Mode*. The younger daughter of a socially ambitious merchant has secretly married his clerk, but Sir John Melvil, though betrothed to the elder daughter, declares his passionate attachment to the younger and persuades the father to the change. This affronts the father's wealthy sister Mrs. Heidelberg, while the already married younger daughter confusedly implores aid from Melvil's uncle, Lord Ogleby, himself an amorous old beau too ready to enter these lists on his own. The contretemps is resolved when the lover found in the daughter's bedroom proves to be her husband. For Mrs. Julia Glover (1779–1850), who had been on the stage some sixty years, "Mrs. Heidelberg" was one of her best-known parts, suited to her "admirable vein of comedy and her joyous laugh" (*DNB*), and perhaps to her growing corpulence. She had recently joined William Farren at the Strand, where they repeated their best parts, opening with this play just two nights before M attended. The *Times* of November 13 reported that "the combination of these veteran artistes . . . drew a crowded audience; and so great was the manifestation of feeling . . . that it elicited a special acknowledgment." William Farren (1786–1861) followed his father into acting, beginning in the provinces early in the century. He had played many of the classic comic roles as well as secondary roles like Polonius, Kent, and Casca, but he was preeminent in the portrayal of old men. Lord Ogleby was a principal one of these, and George Henry Lewes devotes a chapter to analyzing Farren's skill (*On Actors*, pp. 51–58). Sometime after 1862 in his copy of William Hazlitt's *Lectures on the English Comic Writers* (Sealts 263b, p. 189), M annotated a passage that praises Farren: "F. in Lord O. I saw in London in 1849. An old man then; but his acting —— I have never seen anything like it" (quoted by permission of Frank H. Waring). Henry Leigh Murray (1820–70) had begun only ten years before, mostly in Scotland, but had returned to London in 1844 and frequently played secondary Shakespearean roles. He had just joined Farren at the Strand, where he was also stage manager. His reputation was due more to an easy naturalness than to vigorous style or remarkable talent.

18.21 Special Thanksgiving day] Proclaimed in gratitude for the cessation of the cholera that had broken out in June, the most devastating epidemic yet: though reports vary, September deaths reached more than sixty-six hundred, and the summer's total in London, fourteen to sixteen thousand; for England and Wales, more than fifty-three thousand (Sheppard, *London*, pp. 267, 269, 273; Altick, *Victorian People and Ideas* [New York: Norton, 1973], p. 45).

18.26 Primrose Hill] Rising just north of Regent's Park to the gentle height of 200 or so feet, with Hampstead Heath beyond reaching to some 440 feet; for the "curious view," see the discussion on Sadler's Wells at 19.24–25. In Chapter 24 of *The Confidence-Man* the philanthropic Cosmopolitan proposes to the misanthropic Missouri bachelor that they "embark for London—I staying with my friends nigh Primrose-hill, and you putting up at the Piazza, Covent Garden" (p. 137); the ironic point raised apparently being whether a misanthrope would be wiser to live merrily right in town, "in the flower market," like Diogenes, or "skulking" outside it, "in the pine-barrens," like Timon. See also the NN *Israel Potter*, pp. 175–76, for Melville's use in that book of this Primrose Hill view and his other London observations (chaps. 24–25). In this, as in such passages as the last paragraph of "I and My Chimney" (*Putnam's Monthly Magazine*, March, 1856; NN *Piazza Tales* volume, p. 377), M is no doubt alluding to his own shunning of New York City to live in rural Pittsfield, Massachusetts (1850–63).

18.30 Mt Washington] M and his bride had visited Mt. Washington in New Hampshire on their wedding trip from Boston to Montreal and Quebec in August of 1847.

18.30–32 Crossed . . . Bank] M and Adler went through what were then the northern environs of the metropolis by a route that circled down into the City proper from the north. The name King's Cross referred to a hideous statue of George IV (which did not long survive) placed where Gray's Inn Road starts south. The general area around it was one of the worst of the city slums; Sir Walter Besant (*London in the Nineteenth Century* [London: Black, 1909], pp. 272–73) quotes a description published in 1854 of the appalling stenches, piggeries, stables, garbage heaps, cesspools, and lack of water or any sanitary facilities whatsoever, together with the subhuman life monstrously overcrowded in these "rookeries." Construction of new rail lines and stations, like the one then being built at King's Cross, had devastated whole districts and forced the displaced poor to crowd in the remaining tenements. Dickens's *Dombey and Son* (London: Bradbury & Evans, 1848) describes the slightly earlier destruction (where M had passed just to the west) by the London and North-Western line's entry to Euston:

> Traces of its course were visible on every side. Houses were knocked down; streets broken through and stopped; deep pits and trenches dug in the ground; enormous heaps of earth and clay thrown up. . . . Here, a chaos of carts, overthrown and jumbled together, lay topsy-turvy at the bottom of a steep unnatural hill; there, confused treasures of iron soaked and rusted . . . Babel towers of chimneys, wanting half their height; temporary wooden houses and enclosures, . . . carcases of ragged tenements, and fragments of unfinished walls and arches, and piles of scaffolding, and wildernesses of bricks, and giant forms of cranes, and tripods straddling above nothing. (chap. 6, p. 46)

18.31–32 Angel Inn] Chiefly famous earlier as the last stop for travelers before entering the city from the north, en route to the Smithfield markets, via St. John Street; they gathered there for mutual protection against highwaymen infesting the intervening open fields. The seventeenth-century structure had been rebuilt and then modernized since Hogarth's engraving *The Stage Coach* depicted the courtyard.

18.34 Elephant & Castle] A well-known tavern (built ca. 1674, rebuilt 1824) about a mile beyond London Bridge at the Southwark intersection of most of the important roads and omnibus lines south and east. (The district and tavern were destroyed in World War II, but the name remains for today's even busier junction.) One explanation derives the tavern's name from a sign that pictured an elephant with a castle-like howdah; a more popular one traces it to a corruption from the time of Charles I's brief engagement (when prince) to L'Enfanta de Castille. (For two early views of it, one by Rowlandson, see H. D. Eberlein and A. E. Richardson, *The English Inn, Past and Present* [Philadelphia: Lippincott, 1926], pp. 46, 140.)

18.38 "Edingburgh Castle"] Neither Cunningham nor Cruchley mentions this "noted place," but a slightly later London directory gives its address, 332 Strand, next door to the bookseller Stibbs (see 18.11, 20.26–28, and accompanying discussions) and thus close to M's lodging. M commended it to his uncle Peter Gansevoort (see pp. 620–23).

19.6 British Museum] Open Mondays, Wednesdays, and Fridays, ten to four in the winter, admission free. M would have entered under the imposing new portico in Great Russell Street, through litter and scaffolding for the new building whose construction had been going on in stages since 1823. Hawthorne, too, mentions "a hand and arm up to the shoulder, fifteen feet in length, . . . of some stone that seemed harder and heavier than granite"; he gives its size once as fifteen feet, later as six, still later as ten feet (*ENB*, pp. 243, 591, 612). Others identified it as possibly part of the statue of Thotmes III, whose head Giovanni Belzoni had found at Karnak in 1818. The black basalt Rosetta Stone, taken from the French in 1802, was also displayed in the Egyptian Gallery, ground floor, west wing. Most of the great Assyrian sculptures Austen Henry Layard was sending back from Nineveh were still temporarily stored, but some of the larger ones were displayed in the entrance hall. M's "&c." of course embraces a multitude of treasures, including the famous Elgin Marbles.

19.8 Murray was not in] This is the probable time M wrote the note described in a Sotheby sales catalogue (London, 1975):

> to the publisher John Murray: written in Murray's office in Albemarle Street during the publisher's absence, proposing to call back at 4 p.m. in the hope of seeing his correspondent and discussing with him "some final arrangement concerning the book I left," 19th-century note (?by the recipient) at foot of page identifying Melville as "author of Typee" integral address leaf with autograph address ("John Murray Esq. / Present") and remains of wafer seal: in fine condition.

The note was purchased by H. Holdsworth Rawnsley for £750 ("Melville for Sale," *Melville Society Extracts*, No. 26 [June, 1976], 18–19).

19.8 by the "Canada"] Mail to the U.S. left Liverpool by the new Cunard steamers, usually on Saturdays, occasionally Wednesdays. M's letter to Allan is No. 314 on the "Check List of Unlocated Letters," *Letters*, p. 311.

19.9 Seven Dials] About a half mile north of M's lodging, an intersection of seven streets named for a column with sundials that once stood in the center. A dark, noisome place in the nineteenth century, a notorious thieves' quarter, with narrow streets, gin shops, and idlers, it was also a center for ballad printers and mongers. The area through which M walks, and returns to the next day, stretched from west of Lincoln's Inn nearly to Regent Street, north past Soho and St. Giles nearly to Bloomsbury and the British Museum, and contained some of the most terrible rookeries. In Dickens's *Bleak House*, Tom-all-alone's is there, with its denizen the pitiful crossing-sweeper Jo, and the pestilential graveyard where Captain Nemo lies and Lady Dedlock dies. Dickens's descriptions of it are powerful (e.g., chaps. 16 and 22); Lord Shaftesbury's in 1847 was quasi-official:

> . . . tight avenues of glittering fish & rotten vegetables, with doorways or alleys gaping on either side—which, if they be not choked with squalid garments or sickly children, lead the eye through an almost interminable vista of filth and distress. . . . The pavement, where there is any, rugged and broken, is bespattered with dirt of every hue, ancient enough to rank with the fossils, but offensive as the most recent deposits. The houses, small, low, and mournful, present no one part, in windows, door-posts, or brickwork, that seems fitted to stand for another week—rags and hurdles stuff up the panes, and defend the

passages blackened with use and by the damps arising from the undrained and ill-ventilated recesses. (Cited in Sheppard, *London*, p. 4–5.)

Crowding this area were swarms of recent famine-stricken Irish immigrants, as well as Londoners displaced by such new thoroughfares as New Oxford Street being driven through the St. Giles neighborhood just at this time (see Sheppard, pp. 6 and 14). The regular summer epidemic of cholera struck most viciously in these places. For whatever reasons, M made a point of suggesting a visit there to his uncle Peter (see pp. 620–23 below).

19.11 "Hand Books"] On Murray's famous *Handbooks*, see pp. 173–74; also the discussion at 18.3. These were his pride, and he himself had compiled the first ones for northern Europe and later those for as far south as Switzerland and upper Italy. The probable editions of the two given to M were his *Hand-Book for Travellers on the Continent . . . Holland . . . Northern Germany, and along the Rhine . . .*, sixth ed. (1849), and *Hand-Book for Travellers in France . . .*, third ed. (1847; or revised? 1848).

19.13–14 "Mitre Tavern"] Just off the west end of Fleet Street and adjacent to the Inner Temple, this claimed to be the favorite resort of Johnson, Boswell, Goldsmith, and their friends, and displayed a cast from Joseph Nollekens's bust of Johnson; however, though M here appears to be following the Murray *Handbook for London* by Cunningham, it seems now generally held that this tavern, originally Joe's Coffee House, took the new name only after the original Mitre at 39 Fleet St. was razed, four years after Johnson's death. Hawthorne and his son Julian found it behind a front of modern shops, through an archway, with a low, somber coffee room, "a good, plain, respectable eating-house" (*ENB*, p. 252). Like the Cock and the Rainbow, where M also tries the ale or stout (but not the food, possibly because of cost), these three taverns on or near Fleet Street were recommended for their steaks, chops, joints, and kidneys; customary dining hours in the West End were three to seven. The Dr. Johnson Tavern (mentioned later in this entry) was named for association with the several lodgings Johnson occupied in this general neighborhood—the last, where he died, at 8 Bolt Court, off Fleet Street.

19.23 Cap: Griswold] Passengers frequently gave gifts to popular captains; see Albion, *Square-Riggers*, p. 154. The initial "P." following perhaps refers to Adler's fellow Swiss: in one passenger list (New York *Evening Post*, October 12), his name is spelled Balthazar Prewlin rather than Frewlin as in other papers.

19.24–25 Sadler's Wells Theater] Like many other pleasure resorts in the higher country north of the City, especially patronized in the summer, the theater had developed out of a music house at a "holy well" rediscovered in the seventeenth century, and still retained pleasant aspects of its semirural site. An "Old Playgoer," however (writing in *Gavarni in London*, ed. Albert Smith [London: Bogue, 1849]), writes: "Sadler's Wells, too, was quite a provincial theatre. You got such a view from the heights of Islington over London that the afternoon walk was equal in itself to the performance. Few can understand now how this could have been, as they look down upon the hazy glare that seems to choke and burn up the outskirts of Clerkenwell at their feet" (p. 46). In a working-class suburb, it had a reputation for low amusements and rowdy audiences. But with the repeal of restrictive licenses for the two West End "legitimate" theaters, the distinguished actor Samuel Phelps ventured to take over its management in 1844 and began transforming it—and its audience—with notable productions of Shakespeare and other reputable drama. It was not small (seating twenty-six hundred) but, in contrast to the fashionable West End playhouses, was unusual in having few boxes; its very large pit, whose benches had been made reasonably comfortable with backs, afforded inexpensive entertainment to large crowds. Books like those of Knight or Cruchley, however, still spoke condescendingly of its "variety of minor entertainments. . . . Comic pantomimes are a species of entertainment for which this house has always been celebrated. It is open at half-past five, and commences at half-past six, . . . pit, one shilling" (*Cruchley's Picture of London*, p. 158).

19.25 One of Colley Cibber's comedies] For this night, the advertised program read: "This evening will be presented *She Would and She Would Not*. Don Philip, Mr. H. Marston; Trappanti, Mr. Hoskins; Don Manuel, Mr. A. Younge; Octavio, Mr. G. K. Dickinson; Hypolita, Miss Fitzpatrick; Rosara, Miss T. Bassano. After which, *The First of May*. To conclude with *The Tobit Dog*." In the initial production (1702) Cibber himself played the part of Don Manuel; this is accounted one of his best comedies. Don Manuel, a testy, tyrannical father, breaks the betrothal of his daughter to Octavio for a better match to Don Philip, son of a friend, but not known by sight. Philip, scorned by Octavio's sister, has agreed, but the sister realizes her mistake and follows in disguise, pretending to be Don Philip; she "marries" the daughter, to prevent Philip's doing so, to help her brother, and to fool Don Manuel. All is discovered and the proper lovers united. The actor M saw, Anthony Younge, had been recruited from minor theaters by Samuel Phelps and trained in Phelps's style, subordinating actor entirely to the role. In repertory, Younge became First Old Man, known for playing the comic roles traditionally assigned to that position, such as Dogberry or Sir Andrew Aguecheek, without clowning; so an 1850 spectator wrote: "A. Younge in Autolycus display'd a versatility and loss of self quite refreshing in a Comic Actor," and compared him favorably to better known personalities (cited in Shirley S. Allen, *Samuel Phelps and Sadler's Wells Theatre* [Middletown,

Conn.: Wesleyan University Press, 1971], p. 205; Younge is mentioned also in Dennis Arundell, *The Story of Sadler's Wells, 1683–1964* [London: Hamilton, 1965]).

19.31 Temple Bar] Removed in 1870; the structure M saw, designed by Wren to replace the one destroyed by the Great Fire, marked the boundary of the City proper, where the sovereign ritually asks permission of the lord mayor for entry, and where Fleet Street and the Strand change names.

19.31 "Cock Tavern"] Of several by that name, this one (now torn down) was at 201 Fleet St., opposite the Middle Temple; famous enough in the Restoration, it was later restricted to men and became known for its Jacobean carved oak chimney piece and long low room subdivided by settees. M's parenthesized "(Tennyson's)" refers to the poet, with whom it was a favorite haunt. Tennyson's "Will Waterproof's Lyrical Monologue, Made at the Cock" (1842) had rendered the tavern an attraction to Americans moved by the poem's discreetly bibulous and sentimental melancholy; M's sister Augusta had received the 1842 *Poems* as a gift in 1844 (Sealts 507b). Cunningham's *Modern London*, the 1851 updating of Murray's handbook for Crystal Palace visitors, listed the Cock (p. xxxv) among the chief "after-theatre" houses, along with the Rainbow (see 21.10 and accompanying discussion) and others; M visited the Cock again on December 16 (41.18–19), and it was one of the few places he made a point of revisiting in 1857 (127.34). M alludes to it in *Clarel*, 4.19.33–34.

19.35 Dulwich gallery] The localities and villages M mentions were already disappearing in the urban sprawl south of the river; however, this gallery, whose building and virtually all its paintings had been bequeathed in 1811 to the college that housed it, lay at "the end of a pleasant, quiet, and rather countrified village, . . . among fine old elms, and at the back of the old-fashioned, comfortable-looking 'God's Gift College at Dulwich,' which Edward Alleyn, the actor, founded in 1613" (*Knight's Cyclopædia*, p. 735). In November admission was by a free ticket secured in the city, from eleven to three every weekday but Friday. Whatever M's enthusiasm, its few Italian paintings were considered mostly inferior and misattributed; more exceptional was its extensive selection of Dutch and Flemish genre paintings, a continuing interest of M's. Bartolomé Murillo's peasant pictures (a Spanish flower girl, two Spanish boys, and two Spanish boys together with a Negro boy) were called outstanding. A "Europa" was attributed to Titian; of a number of Claudes, Ruskin thought the *Landscape with Jacob and Laban* to be "one of the most genuine" known to him; a Salvator Rosa *Soldiers Gambling* was usually mentioned; and the "Venus" may be one that shows her gathering Hesperidean apples, attributed merely to the "Italian School." Knight rather depreciated the many paintings by Philips Wouwerman, but one of a farrier may have attracted M's notice because of the mottled horse. Guido Reni's *St. John in the Wilderness* seems to be the one M mentions, and so also Nicolas Poussin's *Assumption of the Virgin*. Such a collection of genre paintings had many old men, but possibly M refers to Adriaen van Ostade's *Man Smoking*. Sir Joshua Reynolds's *Mrs. Siddons* was only partly by him and merely a repetition of his famous original; his *Death of Cardinal Beaufort* was a sketch.

20.16 Colbourn] Henry Colburn (d. 1855) was one of the most enterprising of the newer publishers; his popular titles and aggressive huckstering, advertising, and promotion of them were scorned by more sedate publishers and editors. Having broken the agreement dissolving his brief partnership with Richard Bentley, not to publish in London, he resumed on his own at the Great Marlborough Street address (close to Bentley's establishment) and amassed a considerable fortune with such writers and books as Captain Marryat, G. P. R. James, Edward George Bulwer-Lytton, and Burke's *Peerage*. He has been described as "a small bustling bundle of energy with no scruples whatever, . . . wholly indifferent to book-design and workmanship," completely lacking in literary taste, open-handed and obsequious to promising authors or social superiors but imperious and unsympathetic to the rank and file (Michael Sadleir, cited by Gettmann, *A Victorian Publisher*, p. 16). Although Colburn refused *White-Jacket* on M's terms promptly enough, in general he "seemed incapable of decision . . . from the choice of a proffered book to the quantity of sugar he should put in his teacup. There was lamentable hesitation in all he did or said, seldom uttering more than half a sentence, and leaving it uncertain what he thought" (Samuel Hall, cited by Gettmann, p. 17). In light of the above characterizations, no reason for Murray's "instigation" of M to offer *White-Jacket* to Colburn is immediately apparent, and he may seem condescending; but he knew why he had refused it, and perhaps the reason for Bentley's hesitancy—M's hitherto regular publishers—and must have had well-informed reason to think its best chance, on Melville's desired terms, might lie with Colburn. As it turned out, Bentley alone of the publishers to whom M offered it esteemed him and his "genius" highly enough to risk taking it, even though he did so only on an "arrangement" that modified M's terms. (See the discussion at 16.27 and pp. 176–77.)

20.28 Davenant . . . Hudibras] According to his later list (144.4,6), Melville paid ten shillings for the first of these and two shillings for the second. Sealts identifies the first as "D'Avenant, Sir William. The Works . . . London, Herringman, 1673," inscribed "Herman Melville London, December, 1849. (New Year's Day, At sea)" and annotated; the second as

"Butler, Samuel. Hudibras. The First [-Third and Last] Part . . . London, Baker, 1710. 3 pts. in 1 v. Rebound" (Sealts 176 and 104; Bercaw 192). Sealts adds that M gave the Butler to Evert Duyckinck, quoting from M's letter to him of February 2, 1850. The inscriptions are: "L. Duval" / "R. Miles / 1765" / and "Evert A Duyckinck / from H. M. / Feb 2d 1850. / 85 years after that Mr. Miles the old Englishman, in silk small clothes, bought the work at some stall—*you* own it now—who will own it next?" (NYPL-D; see also *Letters*, pp. 102–3). In the letter to Duyckinck, M wrote that he bought the book at "Stribbs's in the Strand"—i.e., Stibbs's bookstore, which as M notes was next to the Edinburgh Castle. The "very civil, intelligent young man" may have been a clerk, not Stibbs the bookseller himself, with whom he had already established a more personal acquaintance (see the discussions at 18.11 and 18.38).

20.29 St: Giles] Again, as on the day before, M's circular itinerary is taking him through the dreadful rookeries lying north of his lodging and Trafalgar Square, those near the eighteenth-century church of St. Giles in the Fields being among the most crowded due to the building of New Oxford Street. The recent novel *Ranthorpe* (London: Chapman & Hall, 1847) by George Henry Lewes opened with a description of the area around Holborn, also on a cold November night:

> Holborn was noisy, murky, and sloppy. A drizzling rain descended through the haze: the chilling haze of a London winter night. Streams of brilliant gas, reflected from gilded lamps and pillars in those splendid mockeries named gin-palaces, flashed at intervals through the darkness, calling attention to the orgies there perpetrated: where brutal violence, sodden depravity, low cunning, vice in all its hideousness, and poverty in its desperate wretchedness, had assembled. . . . There were the brawls of miserable women reeling from public houses; and the scuffles with pickpockets emerging from Saffron Hill. . . .
>
> Amidst this noisy, cheerless scene, standing at one of the numerous bookstalls, was a youth . . . . (pp. 2, 4)

What M saw as he went down Nash's fashionable Regent Street was of course a different matter, though Nash's colonnade sheltering the walk at the Quadrant had just been pulled down (1848).

20.36–21.2 St: Dunstans . . . Bow Church] Recently rebuilt (1831–33), the first church sat back from Fleet Street at Chancery Lane. The second, St. Mary le Bow, is east of St. Paul's. This church, and especially its elaborate 235-foot tower and steeple, was considered one of Wren's masterpieces; the interior was 65 feet long, nearly as wide, and reached 38 feet to a coved and paneled roof. (By well-known tradition, those born within sound of Bow church's famous peal of ten bells are authentic Cockneys.)

21.4 Doctors Commons] Just south of St. Paul's, Doctors' Commons was—until torn down a few years after M's visit—a "College," that is, a place of study and practice for doctors of law; certain courts also sat here. Richard H. Dana, Jr., in his 1856 journal, fretted over the multiple fees paid to successive clerks for the privilege of seeing Shakespeare's will (*The Journal of Richard Henry Dana, Jr.*, ed. Robert F. Lucid, 3 vols. [Cambridge: Harvard University Press, 1968], II, 759), but whether or not M knew about the will, he could not have seen it on a Sunday.

21.6 Printing House Square] The area, famous to students of Shakespeare as the site of the Blackfriars Theatre, is just up from Blackfriars Bridge; the hall was the post-fire seventeenth-century headquarters and dispensary of the Apothecaries' Company, while the nearby square took its name from the publication center of the London *Times*. M tramped on two successive Sundays, November 18 and 25, through the back streets of London, perhaps in part because there was almost nothing a visitor could do of a drizzly Sunday in Victorian London except go to church or walk the streets. But his repeated walks through such areas (see also the discussion at 20.29) imply a deep interest on his part, probably both from his social sensitivity and his wish to absorb background for his story of Israel Potter (see 43.15–17 and accompanying discussion)—in which he eventually described this milieu, though less extensively than he expected to at first (chaps. 24 and 25 of *Israel Potter*). In his last days before leaving England in 1857, Hawthorne, too,

> walked the streets a great deal, in the dull November days. . . . There is a dull and sombre enjoyment always to be had in Holborn, Fleet-street, Cheapside, and the other thronged parts of London. It is human life. . . . I have never had the same sense of being surrounded by materialisms, and hemmed in with the grossness of this earthly life, anywhere else . . . ; but . . . it is really an ungladdened life, to wander through these huge, thronged ways, over a pavement foul with mud, ground into it by a million of footsteps; jostling against people who do not seem to be individuals, but all one mass . . . ; everywhere, the dingy brick edifices heaving themselves up, and shutting out all but a strip of sullen cloud that serves London for a sky;—in short, a general impression of grime and sordidness, and, at this season, always a fog. (*ENB*, p. 607)

21.9 wrote Lizzie] No. 314 on the "Check List of Unlocated Letters" (*Letters*, p. 311); this is apparently the one M sent "by the Herman" the next day (see 22.8–9).

21.10 Rainbow tavern] At 15 Fleet St., by the Inner Temple Gate, "a well-conducted and well-frequented tavern, (famous for its stout)" (Cunningham, *Handbook for London* [1849], II, 689). The reference to Tennyson parallels the previous allusion at the Cock Tavern (see 19.31–32 and accompanying discussion); there seems no special association of Tennyson here except as he liked to frequent with friends these taverns along the Strand and Fleet Street when he came to town (*Alfred Lord Tennyson; A Memoir, by His Son* [Hallam Tennyson], 2 vols. [London: Macmillan, 1897], I, 183–84).

21.13–14 St: Bride's Church] Founded by Saint Bridget in the sixth century, near the east end of Fleet Street, and accounted one of Wren's "glories." Until a few years before, however, it was so surrounded by houses as to be invisible from the street, but after a neighborhood fire the adjacent ground was left open. Presumably even so neither its exterior nor its principal interior ornament, the elaborate stained-glass window after Rubens's *Descent from the Cross*, was very visible at a November eventide.

21.19 Thomas Delf] Export Bookseller, 16 Little Britain (EMM), i.e., just east of the Smithfield markets. It was Evert Duyckinck who supplied the letter of introduction about which M later wrote him from Paris (December 2, 1849): "Mr Delf I was not so happy as to see when I called there" (*Letters*, p. 95). Delf was at times a trans-Atlantic negotiator for authors and publishers; just at this time, as agent for the Boston firm of Ticknor & Fields, he was assembling De Quincey's writings for a collected edition, while young James T. Fields was enlisting Evert Duyckinck's aid in New York (W. S. Tryon, *Parnassus Corner: A Life of James T. Fields* [Boston: Houghton Mifflin, 1963], p. 131). As well as suggesting a reason (besides book buying) for Duyckinck's letter, the connection may have contributed to M's purchase and enthusiastic reading of the *Opium-Eater* during his last days in London (see the entries for December 22 and 23).

21.20 David Davidson] London agent of the New York dealers and publishers Wiley & Putnam until the dissolution of the partnership in 1848. It was Davidson who in a spirited 1847 competition bid the then unheard-of price of five hundred pounds for a Gutenberg Bible for James Lenox, the first copy to cross the Atlantic, now a treasure of the New York Public Library (Wyman W. Parker, *Henry Stevens of Vermont* [Amsterdam: Israel, 1963], pp. 174–75). Stevens (whom M subsequently met on November 24), Lenox's usual agent, wholly approved Davidson's discretion, but evidently thought that Davidson felt some animus toward him (Henry Stevens, *Recollections of James Lenox*, ed. Victor H. Paltsits [New York: New York Public Library, 1951]; in a note, p. 26, Paltsits miscalls him "Daniel"). Davidson was a friend of both Evert and George Duyckinck ("Young D's" was doubtless an introductory letter from George, the younger brother); after Davidson's return to New York, M had further contact with him as indicated by two letters from M to George (December 13 and 20, 1858) about Davidson's possibly arranging a lecture engagement for M in Jersey City, of which nothing came (*Letters*, pp. 192–93; Merton M. Sealts, Jr., *Melville as Lecturer* [Cambridge: Harvard University Press, 1957], p. 78). See also the discussions at 30.7 and 46.6–7 for letters from Davidson to George Duyckinck concerning M. Davidson's address was The Aldine Chambers, 13 Paternoster Row.

21.21 J. M. Langford] Joseph Munt Langford (1809–84), drama critic for the London *Observer* and head of the London branch of the publishers William Blackwood & Sons, at 37 Paternoster Row. He also dabbled in playwriting. Besides introducing M to other critics (see the entry for November 19, 22.9–12), he gave a supper for him (November 21, 24.7–15). In April of 1856, when M's younger brother-in-law, Samuel Shaw, went to Europe, M wrote a letter of introduction for him to Langford (*Letters*, p. 180). The letter M carries here must be from Mrs. Charles D. Welford, whom he probably knew through her husband's partnership in Bartlett & Welford, booksellers at 7 Astor House, New York, a popular meeting place for collectors and literary men in the 1840's (Helmut Lehmann-Haupt, *The Book in America* [New York: Bowker, 1939], p. 194). Both Welfords were English, she the daughter of the Mrs. Daniel on whom M calls on December 14 and 16 (see the discussion at 40.5). In New York Welford had perhaps contributed to M's growing interest in old books. He was a good friend of the English publisher Edward Moxon (see 23.3–9 and accompanying discussion), and after Bartlett withdrew from their partnership in 1849, he joined with Charles Scribner and later returned to England as his agent. Welford was described as brilliant, extraordinarily able, and "a veritable storehouse of bibliographical lore"—see Tebbel, *History of Book Publishing*, I, 317, and Roger Burlingame, *Of Making Many Books* (New York: Scribner's Sons, 1946), pp. 78, 162–64.

21.23 McCready . . . Smith] For Macready and Smith, see 22.12–14, 24.9–12, 14–15, and accompanying discussions.

21.26 Longmans] The Longman firm, in Paternoster Row, prided itself on being the second oldest publishing house in London. M's giving "37" for the address (148.5) may be an error for No. 39, the firm's regular address, unless it also occupied space at No. 37, which was Blackwood's address after 1845. The Longman firm had been associated with such great ventures as Chambers's *Cyclopædia*, Johnson's *Dictionary*, and the phenomenally successful *Edinburgh Review*; they had published many of the Romantic poets and in 1849 had just issued the widely acclaimed first two volumes of Macaulay's *History of England*. Through some now-unknown arrangements, directly involving Hawthorne but apparently not M himself, in 1857 they took on the English edition of *The Confidence-Man* (see the discussion at 127.31). For a picture of the Row and the Longman establishment before its burning in 1861 see *The House of Longman, . . . 1724–1924*, by Harold Cox and John E. Chandler (London: Longmans, Green, 1925), at p. 81. Thomas (1804–79), fourth of the name, and his brother William (1813–77), were now the principal partners among several associates; William, whom M probably saw, generally supervised the literary department. He was a vigorous outdoorsman and was "noted for his courtesy to men of letters" (*DNB*).

Lord John Manners

21.30–31 Lord John Manners] Lord John James Robert Manners (1818–1906), younger son of the duke of Rutland (see 22.31 and accompanying discussion), was associated fervently with Disraeli in the Young England opposition to Sir Robert Peel, and had accompanied him on the tour of the industrial districts that supplied the depiction of misery and squalor in Disraeli's *Sybil* (1845). Manners disclaimed connection with Bentley's newspaper *Young England*, which promoted the views of Disraeli, Manners, and others, but apparently knew Bentley well enough to leave his letter there, probably at the instance of N. P. Willis, whom M mentions just below (for a discussion of Bentley and Manners see Gettmann, *A Victorian Publisher*, p. 144). Manners's oldest sister, Lady Elizabeth Frederica (mentioned later in this entry), had married Andrew Robert Drummond from a banking family, and the next oldest (also mentioned later), Lady Emmeline Charlotte Elizabeth, had married the Honorable Charles James Stuart-Wortley-Mackenzie. The portrait of Manners is reproduced here by courtesy of the Trustees of the British Museum.

21.33 Monckton Miles] Richard Monckton Milnes, later Baron Houghton (1809–85), still single in 1849, had rooms at 26 Pall Mall, where as both an active member of Parliament and a literary figure (minor poet and first biographer of Keats) he held notable breakfasts rivaling those of Samuel Rogers (see 44.29–32 and accompanying discussion) for the variety, liveliness, and wit of those invited. M's brother Gansevoort not long before his death had breakfasted there with, among others, Thomas Macaulay and Richard Cobden ("Gansevoort Melville's 1846 London Journal," ed. Hershel Parker, *Bulletin of the New York Public Library*, LXIX–LXX [December, 1965–February, 1966]; see entry for March 11, 1846, LXX, p. 120). Besides this new letter to Milnes from Manners, M already carried one from Edward Everett, solicited by M's father-in-law; for Everett's letters, see 22.26–27, the discussion at 22.28, and pp. 610–14. M recorded the address of Milnes's country place (148.19), and though he might not have had an experience like Henry Adams's encounter with the flamboyant young Swinburne there in 1862, M's not meeting Milnes was a regrettable missed opportunity (see *The Education of Henry Adams* [1907; Boston: Houghton Mifflin, 1918], pp. 139–41).

21.38 portraits] Cunningham, in Murray's *Handbook for London* (1849, I, 7), lists also portraits of Scott, Southey, Crabbe, Hallam, Lockhart, and Irving. Of special interest to M may have been the portraits of celebrated voyagers hung in the dining room; travel books were prominent in Murray's list.

22.2 Willis] Nathaniel Parker Willis (1806–67) was a journalist, poet, editor, dramatist (*DAB*); he was probably the best-paid American "magazinist" in the early 1840's (Henry A. Beers, *Nathaniel Parker Willis* [Boston: Houghton Mifflin, 1885], p. 262). His use of Washington Irving's *Sketch Book*, by "Geoffrey Crayon," as a model for travel descriptions and mildly fictional sketches is proclaimed in the title of his *Pencillings by the Way* (London: Macrone, 1835), and his ingenuous ego in the title of *People I Have Met; or, Pictures of Society and People of Mark* (New York: Baker & Scribner, 1850). By his extraordinary ability to make friends, in the 1830's and early 1840's he quickly won his way into upper-class English circles. At the time of M's trip Willis was in New York editing the *Home Journal*, whose frequent notices of M were friendly and generous. He was profuse in both the use and the offer of letters of introduction, and although the acerbic Harriet Martineau was scornful of his ostentatious generosity, he was no doubt motivated by genuine good feeling. Besides these two letters M had just received, he probably carried others by Willis from New York. At any rate, in the *Home Journal* of November it was probably Willis who wrote of M: "With his genius, the popularity of his books in England, and the extraordinary charm of his narrative powers in conversation, we predict for him an 'open sesame' through the most difficult portals of English society" (*Log*, I, 328 [Nov. 8, 1849]). Willis set off unintended consequences when he printed in the January 12, 1850, *Home Journal* a quotation from a letter M wrote him while in London (see the discussion at 40.9–11, pp. 618–20 below, and the NN *Moby-Dick*, p. 608; also p. 609 in that volume for the open sniping between Willis and the Duyckinck camp soon after M's return to New York City). Later Willis's involvement in the sordid Forrest divorce case may have had some effect on Melville's elaborations of *Pierre* (see the NN *Moby-Dick*, p. 697). (See also 73.5–6 and accompanying discussion for M's encounter with the frigate *Constellation*, on which Willis had spent a number of months in 1833; Willis had also known the frigate *United States*, on which M's service in 1842–44 supplied the experiences underlying the *White-Jacket* he was now trying to sell.)

22.2 Tupper] Martin Farquhar Tupper (1810–89) published between 1838 and 1842 his extraordinarily popular *Proverbial Philosophy*, which sold 1.5 million copies in America, he claimed, as well as being extensively extracted in Willis's *Home Journal*. His autobiography, *My Life as an Author* (London: Low, Marston, Searle & Rivington, 1886), displays an immense naive vanity, and his *Philosophy* was but a collection of truisms and commonplaces. (M noted his country address on the last page of this journal notebook, 148.1–2.)

22.5 the Albany] A fashionable address on the north side of Piccadilly, with suites of rooms or dwelling houses for single "gentlemen"; Manners occupied No. 3 (so M noted it, 148.3). Belvoir Castle is the country seat of the dukes of Rutland (see 22.31–32, 39.22, and accompanying discussions).

22.8 Wrote him] No. 316 on the "Check List of Unlocated Letters," *Letters*, p. 311.

22.12 Mcready] The *Times* review of the Macready performance in *Othello* M saw here may have been by John Oxenford, a playwright and self-taught translator (see the discussion at 47.18, on M's purchase of Goethe's autobiography), who began writing the drama criticisms for the *Times* about this period; its tone fits his reputation for uncritical amiability. From the issue of Tuesday, November 20:

> Though Mr. Macready's impersonation of Othello is less identified with himself than that of Macbeth or King Lear (the greatest of all), the character of the Moor is always one . . . [that] has always proved attractive.
>
> A leading peculiarity in his delineation . . . is the subduing . . . those passionate outbreaks which, with many actors, constitute almost the substance of the character. . . . He gives the most intellectual rendering of the great scenes with Iago; he elaborates the progress of jealousy . . . with the utmost minuteness. . . . But all the emotion is subdued . . . till the decisive moment, when the actor at last works on the masses by a burst of agony. . . . An apt key-note [is] that tenderness of nature which Mr. Macready makes especially prominent in the Moor's character. . . .
>
> . . . Mr. Wallack, ever a popular favourite, plays Iago with much spirit, and Miss Reynolds gives a picturesque version of Desdemona.
>
> The house was well filled, and all the principal artists were loudly called.

William Charles Macready (1793–1873), despite his contentious temper and chronic discontent with matters theatrical, including fellow actors, became quickly preeminent, especially in Shakespearean roles, for which he insisted on returning to the original texts. In the fall of 1849 he was doing *Hamlet, Macbeth, Lear,* and *Othello*, alternating the role of Iago with James Wallack (see the following discussion). George Henry Lewes said his voice was "extensive in compass," containing tones "that thrill, and tones that weep" but otherwise mannered; Lewes admired his lesser roles but added, "he fails in the characters which demand impassioned grandeur. . . . His Macbeth and Othello have fine touches, but they are essentially unheroic—their passion is fretful and irritable" (Lewes and John Forster, *Dramatic Essays* [London: Scott, 1896], p. 132).

On his final American tour (1848–49) Macready had been the occasion of the notorious Astor Place riots in New York; partly because of the American actor Edwin Forrest's misplaced hostility, aggressive partisans tried to disrupt Macready's performances, and in the culminating violence (May 10, 1849) twenty-two people were killed. M, along with Duyckinck, Irving, and others, had signed a published petition urging Macready to continue (May 8; *Log*, I, 302).

22.14–15 Wallack . . . Miss Reynolds . . . Roderigo] James W. Wallack (1791?-1864) was better known for his career in America, notably as manager of Wallack's Theater, Broadway and 13th Street, New York. His portraits show a dark, handsome man; his deportment was described as dignified, his acting as lacking in fervor—better in melodrama and light comedy.

Jane Louisa Reynolds (1824–1907) both acted and sang; Macready's own comments on her were often impatiently critical— for example, her performance of Desdemona in 1850: "the awfully bad acting of Miss Reynolds" (*The Diaries of William Charles Macready, 1833–1851*, ed. William Toynbee, 2 vols. [London: Chapman & Hall, 1912], II, 476).

The "Roderigo" was Charles Selby (1802?-63), who also wrote farces and adaptations from the French. His acting career was mostly in character parts, his reputation that of a useful and responsible actor, with a "good stage presence."

22.16 Buckstone] John Buckstone (1802–79), like many actors, also wrote plays; he quickly developed a reputation, especially for "low" comedy. Primarily, his style was to play himself, not a character, but though his manner was criticized as too broad, his infectious self-complacency and overflowing good humor gained him enthusiastic audiences. "Added to a countenance peculiarly fitted to express humour in all its varieties and transitions, he had an evident enjoyment of the droll conceptions he was embodying" (*DNB*). His plays (between one and two hundred) were successful for the same qualities; *Alarming Sacrifices* was evidently a late substitution for the advertised *Guardian Angel*.

22.19 Lockhart] See 25.27–31 and accompanying discussion.

22.28 Rogers] For Samuel Rogers, see 44.29–32 and accompanying discussion. The letter was from Edward Everett, who had written it and the one to Monckton Milnes at the request of M's father-in-law, Chief Justice Shaw. Everett was currently president of Harvard and recently American minister to the Court of St. James's (1841–45). This letter and his covering letter to Shaw are reprinted below, pp. 611–14.

22.28 St James' Place] An L-shaped enclave off St. James's Street, just north of the palace; M's brother Gansevoort had lived at No. 1 during his brief tenure as secretary of the American legation (1845–46); see 44.20 and accompanying discussion.

22.30 the American minister] Abbott Lawrence (1792–1855), appointed minister to the Court of St. James's by the new president, Zachary Taylor, had arrived in September. Beginning as a farm boy with little education, he came to Boston in 1808 to join his brother Amos in founding the great textile mills at Lowell and Lawrence. As the leading merchant of Boston, he was "prompt, energetic, with an intuitive insight into the characters of men, with sound judgment, and an openness of character. . . . He took a deep interest in all matters of public concern, in politics, political economy, finance. . . . He won the favor of all parties, by his general intelligence, and by his genial and affable manners" (Freeman Hunt, ed., *Lives of American Merchants*, 2 vols. [New York: Derby & Jackson, 1858], II, 334–35; the portrait reproduced here faces p. 331). M noted the address of the legation as 1 Upper Belgrave St. (just west of the gardens of Buckingham Palace); see 148.10. It has been suggested that Abbott Lawrence was M's model for the "gentleman with gold sleeve-buttons" in Chapter 7 of *The Confidence-Man* (see William Norris, "Abbott Lawrence in *The Confidence-Man*," *American Studies*, XVII [Spring, 1976], 25–38; Helen P. Trimpi, *Melville's Confidence*

Abbott Lawrence

Man and American Politics in the 1850s [Hamden, Conn.: Archon Books, 1987], pp. 103–5; and the NN edition, pp. 35–42, 291–92).

22.30 Davis] John Chandler Bancroft Davis (1822–1907), nephew of the historian George Bancroft, had succeeded John R. Brodhead as secretary of legation on August 31, acting as chargé d'affaires until the arrival of Lawrence. After trying law briefly, he resumed diplomatic service as assistant secretary of state in 1869, and played a prominent part in the *Alabama* claims settlement. M had been in correspondence with Davis (or Brodhead—not knowing just when the secretaryship was changing hands) during August, about the delivery of proofs of *Redburn* to Bentley (*Letters*, pp. 89–90). This was a function Brodhead, a friend of Gansevoort's, had taken on when Gansevoort died and he succeeded him as secretary (see *Letters*, pp. 48–49 [No. 29, Dec. 30, 1846]).

22.31–32 Duke of Rutland] John Henry Manners (1778–1857), fifth of the title, for seventy years; father of Lord John Manners (see the discussion at 21.30–31), who became seventh duke, upon the death of his older brother, in 1888.

22.34 Clarendon Hotel] At the south end of New Bond Street, and listed as one of the two best in Murray's *Handbook for London*.

22.37 Bryanston Square] Some blocks north of Oxford Street above Park Lane. In his address list (148.8) M specifies Lady Elizabeth Drummond's as No. 2.

23.1 Russell Sturgis] Sturgis (1805–87) was one of the transplanted New Englanders who became powers in British banking. After a Boston career in law, then the China and Philippine trade, he had just come to London with his family in the spring to join Baring Brothers; he soon became a full partner (1851) and eventually succeeded Joshua Bates (see 23.2 and accompanying discussion) as senior partner (he was a cousin of Mrs. Bates). (Ralph W. Hidy, *The House of Baring* [Cambridge: Harvard University Press, 1949], pp. 395, 579–80, n. 11.) Henry Adams, writing in his *Education* (chap. 8) of the dark days when his father was American minister in London in the winter of 1861–62, has very kind words for these banking Americans, and especially for Mrs. Sturgis (see 27.32 and accompanying discussion); M meets them all later (November 24) at the country house of Bates. A portrait of Sturgis is reproduced in Hidy, facing p. 410, and in *Some Merchants and Sea Captains of Old Boston*, issued by the State Street Trust Co. (Boston, 1918), facing p. 1. It shows a wide-eyed, rather narrow-jawed face, with a high, balding forehead. According to M's address list (148.12), Sturgis lived at 27 Upper Harley St., the short northern extension of Harley Street, leading up to Regent's Park, some three-quarters of a mile from Bryanston Square.

23.2 Portman Square] M errs here, but noted the address correctly—46 Portland Place (a block or two east of Harley Street)—at the end of the journal notebook (148.11). In 1861 Minister Charles Francis Adams took up residence nearby, and his son Henry sometimes uses Portland Place in his *Education* as a kind of generic center of gloom and anxiety for the little colony of Americans in the winter of 1861–62. An exceptionally wide street, it continued to be highly fashionable; Henry James, for example, makes this the address of the big town house of Maggie and Prince Amerigo in *The Golden Bowl* (1904).

23.2 Joshua Bates] Bates (1788–1864), also from Massachusetts, had an early failure because of the War of 1812, but another merchant whom he had impressed sent him to England as his agent. He soon became a partner of one of the young Barings (also half-American on the mother's side), then was taken into the big banking house as one of three managing partners. (For much of the nineteenth century, Baring Brothers was the most important merchant banking partnership with American connections; it became both the official fiscal agent in England of the U.S. government and the major channel for British investment in America.) In addition to being the firm's expert on American affairs, Bates was the genius of the internal organization and administration of its worldwide interests. A description of him in the 1840's speaks of his patience, equanimity, and good temper, his nerve, self-possession, and self-confidence. By the 1850's he was probably the most influential foreigner in private life in England, trusted absolutely for his judgment, fairness, and integrity. (It was not irrelevant that his daughter was married to the Belgian ambassador, who as representative of King Leopold, uncle of Prince Albert and Queen Victoria, was especially intimate with the royal family; see the discussion at 27.12.) He tended to prefer English to American life, but his benefactions to the Boston Public Library are recorded in the Proceedings of the Trustees as *A Memorial of Joshua Bates* (Boston, 1865). Among his friends and visitors were both Coleridge and the future Napoleon III. (See also Hidy, *House of Baring*, pp. 82–85 and *passim*; also *DAB*.) A portrait bust is pictured in the *Memorial*, and a three-quarter-length painted portrait in Hidy, at p. 71, depicting a face rather round, serious but open and friendly. When M met him, he had just been in America, including Boston, in the spring, where he very likely knew Chief Justice Lemuel Shaw.

23.3 Moxon] Edward Moxon (1801–58), unlike Murray, resisted the swing away from poetry (being a poet himself); when Wordsworth died in 1850, Moxon had published extensively not only the late laureate but all six major candidates for the new appointment. He first became friends with Lamb in 1824, and through him with Samuel Rogers (who helped finance his publishing venture). Moxon's marriage in 1833 to the orphan who lived with the Lambs increased the intimacy; ultimately Lamb's library came to him, and he sold some sixty items to his close friend Charles Welford, the New York bookseller discussed at 21.21 above. (Lamb was a favorite of the Duyckinck circle; the *Literary World*, February 5, 1848, listed these items; it also gave a florid account of a re-auction of certain ones, November 4, 1848; see the Dibdin Club's reprint of the original catalogue, *A Descriptive Catalogue of the Library of Charles Lamb* [New York, 1897].)

Moxon planned to publish Lamb's complete works and did manage to get out much of it that year. *The Works . . . A New Edition,* 1848 (Sealts 316) is presumably a reprint of the 1840 octavo edition in five parts; the present location of M's set is unknown. M received this gift the next day, along with Thomas Noon Talfourd's *Final Memorials of Charles Lamb*, in two volumes, published by Moxon in 1848 and inscribed, "To Herman Melville, Esq. with the Publisher's Regards" (Sealts 317). (M lists both sets among his London acquisitions, 144.18–19; the latter, annotated, is now in the Princeton University Library.) Earlier in 1849 M had already bought Lamb's *Specimens of English Dramatic Poets* (Sealts 318), possibly because of the interest of either or both Welford and Duyckinck; and on shipboard, so he wrote Richard Henry Dana, Jr., after his return, he had "found a copy of Lamb . . . not having previously read him much, I dived into him, & was delighted. . . . So I was very sincere with Moxon, being fresh from Lamb" (May 1, 1850; *Letters*, p. 108). Moxon had published Dana's *Two Years before the Mast* in 1840; at Chief Justice Lemuel Shaw's request Dana had written a letter to Moxon for M (reprinted pp. 614–15). M had thanked Dana before sailing (October 6, 1849; *Letters*, pp. 92–93), and in the May 1 letter to him after his return he described this meeting:

> I was ushered into one of those jealous, guarded sanctums, in which these London publishers retreat from the vulgar gaze. It was a small, dim, religious looking room—a very chapel to enter. Upon the coldest day you would have taken off your hat in that room, tho' there were no fire, no occupant, & you a Quaker.—You have heard, I dare say, of that Greenland whaler discovered near the Pole, adrift & silent in a calm, with the frozen form of a man seated at a desk in the cabin before an ink-stand of icy ink. Just so sat Mr Moxon in that tranced cabin of his. I bowed to the spectre, & received such a galvanic return, that I thought something of running out for some officer of the Humane Society, & getting a supply of hot water & blankets to resuscitate this melancholy corpse. But knowing the nature of these foggy English, & that they are

> not altogether impenetrable, I began a sociable talk, and happening to make mention of Charles Lamb, and alluding to the warmth of feeling with which that charming punster is regarded in America, Mr Moxon brightened up—grew cordial—hearty;—& going into the heart of the matter—told me that he (Lamb) was the best fellow in the world to "get drunk with" (I use his own words) & that he had many a time put him to bed. (*Letters*, pp. 107–8)

Though by 1849 Moxon was declining into the illness of his last years, by other accounts he was commonly much more genial than at first with M. He meant his "establishment," as he called it, to rival such literary gathering places as Murray's in the next street. His original interest in poetry and drama was supplemented by a growing interest in travel narratives, but like Murray's not in fiction. M lists his address, at 44 Dover St., "Nearly opposite St. James' Street — back of Murray's" (148.13-14).

23.11–12 Mr & Mrs Lawrence] Abbott Lawrence (see the discussion at 22.30) had married Katherine Bigelow, of a distinguished legal and political family of Medford, Massachusetts, in 1819. M's wife, as a nineteen-year-old in 1842, had attended her sewing circle (see *Log*, I, 125 [Jan. 10]). This hostile description of her (as far as "reptiles & crawling things") M soon heavily crossed and lined out. (Eleanor Melville Metcalf, with photographic help at the Morgan Library, first read the deleted words [see photofacsimile in EMM, facing p. 40]; with minor exceptions, the present reading accords with hers.) M a week later changed his opinion, in his entry on November 27 (probably it was at this time that he censored his initial remarks about her); but Henry Bright, Hawthorne's friend and M's 1856 Liverpool acquaintance, more nearly agreed with M's first impression:

> Even in England they [American women] forget that they have superiors, and Mrs. Abbott Lawrence scarcely exaggerated the complacent self-reverence of her countrywomen when she said, "I entertain for the Queen a feeling, not exactly of friendship, for I am not intimate enough for that, nor of loyalty, for I am not a British subject, but rather a sentiment of attachment and sympathy which one lady in an exalted position always entertains for another." Or to take another instance when she wrote to the Queen begging to present Mrs. Peabody to her,—"I may assure your Majesty in requesting this favour that I am doing what is with me an unusual thing, for at Boston the Lawrences are more in the habit of conferring than of requiring a favour." (*Happy Country This America*, ed. Anne H. Ehrenpreis [Columbus: Ohio State University Press, 1978], p. 375)

Hawthorne called a version of the second anecdote one of the "queer stories" the English tell (*ENB*, p. 281).

23.19 Lady Bulwer] Presumably the Honorable Georgiana Wellesley, niece of the Duke of Wellington, who had recently married Sir Henry Bulwer, the even more recently named British ambassador to Washington (April 27, 1849).

23.24 Haymarket] Cunningham's *Modern London* (pp. xliii–xliv) innocently advised the visitor that the Haymarket was a place one must see on an opera or theater night, with a crush of carriages and cabs—and throngs of orderly and disorderly people moving among the brilliantly lighted taverns and shellfish shops. But Cruchley strenuously cautioned the stranger to beware the sharpers, swindlers, confidence men, pickpockets, and prostitutes thronging the place at all hours. M's "singular interview" may have been with any one of these, but most likely with a prostitute. Hemyng, in the section on prostitution added to Mayhew's *London Labour*, declares that the Haymarket was frequented by a high class of "ladies of the evening," and estimated their number here and in Regent Street at more than eight thousand (IV, 217, 213). The French writer Hippolyte Taine, after a walk along the Strand and Haymarket in the 1860's, observed: "Every hundred steps one jostles twenty harlots; some of them ask for a glass of gin; others say, 'Sir, it is to pay my lodging.' . . . The deplorable procession in the shade of the monumental streets is sickening; it seems to me a march of the dead. That is a plague-spot—the real plague-spot of English society" (quoted in Sheppard, *London*, p. 367). In a medical-legal assessment of the question written eight years after M's visit, William Acton argued that an adjoining street, the one "connecting Leicester Square with the bottom of Regent Street . . . , a thoroughfare infested with loitering prostitutes," ought to be cleared. The Haymarket had acquired such "an evil notoriety" that its frequenting should no longer be tolerated (*Prostitution* [London: Churchill, 1857, 1870], pp. 232–33). Hawthorne, walking about here in 1855, also noted, "At every street corner, too, under archways, and at other places of vantage, or loitering along, with some indescribable peculiarity that distinguished her, and perhaps turning to re-tread her footsteps, was a woman. . . . One feels a curious and reprehensible sympathy for these poor nymphs; it seems such a pity that they should not . . . find what they seek!—that any of them should tramp the pavement the whole night through, or should go hungry and forlorn to their beds" (*ENB*, p. 232).

23.28 Greenwich Hospital] After 1873 the Royal Naval College; the original palace of Henry VIII and Elizabeth was replaced by Charles II, given to the Royal Navy by William and Mary, and rebuilt by Wren and Sir John Vanbrugh for its pensioners (the picture here is from *Tallis's Illustrated London*, II, facing p. 91). The painted hall (where Nelson lay in state) and the chapel, surmounted by their great domes, are in the structures farther from the river; still farther is the great wooded park, rising 180 feet to the observatory and the terrace. Of the view from the terrace the commonly ecstatic Charles Knight wrote: "The great city looms out of its canopy of smoke—

dim and shadowy—venerable in its associations with the past—sublime in its present aggregation of riches and poverty, of hope and fear. But the park is full of light and cheerfulness;—green lawns and leafy avenues" (*Cyclopædia*, p. 23). In the chapel, large enough to hold thirteen hundred pensioners, together with officers and families in the gallery, Benjamin West's picture of Saint Paul's shipwreck hung over the altar; M may have had it in mind in Chapter 2 of *Moby-Dick*: "that tempestuous wind . . . kept up a worse howling than ever it did about poor Paul's tossed craft" (p. 10). The principal showplace, however, was the painted hall (in the winter open from ten to three except Mondays and Fridays; fee, three pence), originally the dining room until the pensioners became too numerous. In 1823 it was made into the Naval Picture Gallery; *Knight's Cyclopædia* numbered 139 paintings of admirals and seamen, from Ralegh and Drake to the heroes of the Napoleonic Wars. That part particularly designated the Nelson Room contained, as Hawthorne wrote in 1855, "two coats of Nelson, under separate glass-cases. One was the coat which he wore at the battle of the Nile, and is now much eaten by moths. . . . The other was the coat in which he received his death-wound, the bullet-hole being visible in the shoulder. . . . On the breast of the coat are sewn three or four orders of knighthood, the glitter of which is supposed to have drawn the enemy's aim. . . . Over the coat is laid a white waistcoat, with a large bloodstain upon it, out of which all the redness has been discharged" (*ENB*, p. 217). Even his pigtail was preserved. The painted ceiling M notes represented William III and Mary with many allegorical symbols.

Greenwich Hospital

23.31–32 Pensioners at dinner] At this time the hospital could accommodate at most 2,710 men; dressed in blue coats, some in cocked hats, others in caps, and carrying whatever eating utensils they wished, they now gathered in basement dining halls in groups of four to apportion out the meal's allowance, either to carry back to their separate "cabins" or to eat at parallel rows of benches. M recommended this time for visiting to his uncle Peter (see pp. 620–23): "Go to Greenwich hospital in the *morning* so as to see the pensioners at dinner. (An American negro is among them)".

23.32 The negro] The immediate context of this cryptic item places the Negro at the mess with no hint that M talked with him or why he noted him; so—except that he was American—does M's advice to his uncle three years later, as quoted in the preceding discussion. But in *Billy Budd, Sailor* (written ca. 1885–91) occurs a passage that blends this entry's Negro with its "old pensioner" with whom M had a "talk" outside on a hill some while after dinner; the passage is about certain "sanctioned irregularities" in the British navy of Nelson's time: "the same thing was personally communicated to me now more than forty years ago by an old pensioner in a cocked hat with whom I had a most interesting talk on the terrace at Greenwich, a Baltimore Negro, a Trafalgar man." There is no way of knowing whether this blending of (American) Negro at dinner and old pensioner on the terrace was a confusion of M's memory or a deliberate imaginative fusion of the two for his fictional purposes. See the note on the passage (leaf 97, p. 156) in Harrison Hayford and Merton M. Sealts's edition (Chicago: University of Chicago Press, 1962), which also discusses other sources than the old pensioner for M's information about the "sanctioned irregularities." As to sources, it may be added, much of Marryat's *Poor Jack* (see 15.38 and accompanying discussion) is closely associated with Greenwich and its pensioners, among whom is a comic American Negro singer, wounded at the Battle of the Nile and "still alive" in the 1840 of the novel's ending.

23.34 Story of Charles II] No remarkable story about him and Greenwich has surfaced. Eleanor Melville Metcalf quotes a suggestive communication to her from Vice Admiral Sir E. J. Patrick Brind, of the Royal Naval College, Greenwich: "There is no reliable personal story about King Charles II at Greenwich and there is nothing in the archives to that effect. There is however a tale, which is not believed by the historians, that Nell Gwynne used a certain room in the College" (EMM, p. 129).

24.2–3 Fleet Market] Formerly it occupied the center of what is now Farringdon Street, built over Fleet Ditch between Fleet Street and Holborn; officially it had been closed in 1829 but either there or in the relocated Farringdon Market (at right angles and supposedly devoted to fruits and vegetables), some of the old butcher shops must have persisted.

24.4 American Bowling Saloon] M had already stopped here on November 6 (13.37–38). About his beating Davidson on this visit, Leon Howard in his biography (Berkeley and Los Angeles: University of California Press, 1951) remarks, "Melville's Honolulu experience stood him in good stead" (p. 144)—in reference to a report that one way M supported himself during his summer there (1843) was by "setting up pins in a ball alley" (*Log*, I, 166 [May?, 1843]).

24.6 Lavater's Phisiognomy] The treatise on physiognomy is listed by M among the books he acquired in London (144.14). Sealts (122) does not identify the edition. Johann Kaspar Lavater (1741–1801), a Swiss poet, theologian, and mystic, as well as a student of faces, brought out the original four-volume edition of his famous work in 1775–78. The British Museum catalogue lists various English translations and abridged editions. Several allusions to Lavater and the pseudoscience of physiognomy, both earlier and later than this purchase, and usually facetious, occur in M's writings, including *Mardi* and *Moby-Dick*.

24.7 lodgings] M lists them as "Furnival's Inn. (3)" (148.6). The inn, on Holborn, once an Inn of Chancery attached to Lincoln's Inn, had in the nineteenth century ceased to have any connection with the law and had been rebuilt for "chambers."

24.9 Albert Smith] Hardly the Cockney M calls him, Smith (1816–60) was trained in medicine and surgery, but by 1841 he had turned to his real interest in comic or satiric essays, novels, theatrical burlesques and extravaganzas, still later becoming a comic lecturer and stage entertainer himself. When M met him, he was recently back from Constantinople and the East, a trip that resulted in *A Month at Constantinople* (London: Bogue, 1850). M noted his address at 14 Percy St., Bedford Square (148.16). Years later M gave his wife Smith's *Natural History of the Ballet-Girl*, 1847 (inscribed to her, June 13, 1886), with which she associated also Smith's *Natural History of the Gent*, 1847 (Sealts 474, 475). However much a humorist, something of Smith's bourgeois complacency is suggested by a passage on the first page of his frontispiece for the French caricaturist's *Gavarni in London* (London: Bogue, 1849). Describing the swarming slums that so interested M and so appalled Gavarni in his visit this year, Smith spoke of the street life, especially of the children, and added: "Their parents live huddled up in dirty single rooms, repelling all attempts to improve their condition—for, 'The People,' we regret to say, are naturally fond of dirt." In 1856 Hawthorne found Smith "a little flashy and rowdyish, but a good-hearted man, and an agreeable companion" (*ENB*, p. 326).

24.9–10 Tom Taylor] Taylor (1817–80), educated at Glasgow and Cambridge, had briefly been professor of English literature at the University of London, then a lawyer. But upon settling in London he became a journalist, especially with *Punch*, of which he eventually became editor. Even more he made a mark as a playwright, sometimes in collaboration with Smith, and chiefly in domestic comedies: one of his best known was *Our American Cousin* (1858), with Edward Askew Sothern creating the role of Lord Dundreary in New York. In 1849 his new play *Diogenes and His Lantern* opened just after M's departure. He was also something of an art critic, and M later bought the 1853 edition of his *Life of Benjamin Robert Haydon* (Sealts 262). In 1856, Hawthorne first saw Taylor at a distance—"a tall, slender, dark young man"—and a few days later met him at a dinner given by Henry Stevens; not completely impressed, he summed up Taylor as a "sensible, active-minded, clearly perceptive man, with a humorous way . . . but without originality, or much imagination." Still later that year, though liking him better, Hawthorne was still equivocal, finding him "a gentleman of very questionable aspect—un-English . . . with a great beard of soft black" (*ENB*, pp. 311, 327, 378).

Such convivial suppers, especially an even more joyous one in Robert Cooke's chambers in the Temple (see the entry for December 20), provided M the experiences behind Part I of his "The Paradise of Bachelors and the Tartarus of Maids" (NN *Piazza Tales* volume, pp. 316–35).

24.19 Accepted] M's note accepting the invitation from Joshua Bates is No. 317 on the "Check List of Unlocated Letters," *Letters*, p. 312.

24.21 for Windsor] The London and Great Western Railway left from Paddington, reaching Windsor twenty-one miles away by a branch line. According to Knight's *Excursion Companion* (VII, 2), the State Apartments were open Mondays, Tuesdays, Thursdays, and Fridays from eleven to three in winter, but visitors had to obtain tickets in advance from certain shops in London or Windsor. An attendant accompanied them through the few open sections in the northeast part. A set of Gobelin tapestries depicting the biblical Queen Esther hung in the Queen's Audience and Presence Chambers; others hung in the Ballroom. In the Guard Chamber, last of the open rooms, was the shield (once attributed to Cellini) that Francis I presented to Henry VIII; damascened with gold and silver, its figures represented scenes from Caesar's life. Here also a bust of Nelson surmounted a pedestal cut from the mainmast of the *Victory*. Knight added to his account of the State Apartments: "Most visitors acknowledge to feeling disappointment. . . . In truth, too little is shown of them to admit of their being fairly estimated. The carpets are taken up, the whole of the furniture is jealously concealed under brown-holland coverings" (No. VII, p. 10).

From the tower, eighty feet above a forty-two-foot mound, one could look north out over the steep chalk cliff to the Thames Valley and Eton; to the south, over the Great Park and Windsor Forest; reputedly, on a good day one could see parts of twelve counties. The Long Walk was then a broad avenue of lofty elms, leading three miles south to a large equestrian statue of George III. The six hundred feet of Royal Stables were new, housing the royal stud, including the Arabians presented by the pasha of Egypt, the children's ponies, and Albert's personal horse, together with many carriages. The picture of the castle below is from *Tallis's Illustrated London*, II, facing p. 108.

Windsor Castle

24.27 Queen Dowager] From the Court Circular for November 22 in the *Times* of the next day: "The Queen and his Royal Highness Prince Albert went this morning to visit her Majesty the Queen Dowager at the Priory, Stanmore"; Adelaide, widow of Victoria's uncle, William IV, had long been a semi-invalid, and died ten days after this, December 2.

24.30 Kalydore] A contemporary advertisement for Rowlands' Kalydor, A. Rowland & Sons, London, reads: "An Oriental Botanical Preparation, for Improving and Beautifying the Complexion and Skin. It eradicates Freckles, Tan, Pimples, Spots, Discolorations, and Other Cutaneous Visitations." Victoria, less than five feet tall, was, as discreet contemporaries preferred to phrase it, not notable for her beauty. Only a few months older than M, she was by now the mother of six children, four months pregnant with the seventh, and just over the chicken pox. Caroline Kirkland wrote in the travel book M had liked on shipboard, "She seemed to us much plainer in every respect than any picture of her we had seen. Her complexion is far from clear. . . . The Prince looks like a substantial German baron, not ill-favored, but quite behind the notion one gets of him from his portraits" (*Holidays Abroad*, I, 91).

24.38 my reply] No. 318 on the "Check List of Unlocated Letters," *Letters*, p. 312.

25.10 Bogue's] David Bogue (d. 1856 at age forty-four) began as an assistant to an Edinburgh bookseller; by 1836 he was in London, by 1840, in business for himself. After 1843 his bookselling and publishing were conducted at 86 Fleet St., not the Strand (Frederic Boase, *Modern English Biography* [Truro: Netherton & Worth, 1892]). He sold prints and among various sorts of books published the two by Albert Smith that M later gave to ESM (see the discussion at 24.9). He originated (1846) a project that Henry George Bohn (see the discussion at 26.32) soon merged into the long-lived Bohn Standard Library series.

25.17 figs] His granddaughter notes: "Melville must have been fond of figs all his life. One of my own earliest remembrances of his room in Twenty-Sixth Street, New York, was the bag of figs on his paper-piled table" (EMM, p. 131). She cited from Raymond Weaver's biography (New York: Doran, 1921) her earlier record of this: "Yet lo, the paper-piled table also held a little bag of figs, and one of the pieces of sweet stickiness was for me" (p. 379); reprinted in Merton M. Sealts, Jr., *The Early Lives of Melville* (Madison: University of Wisconsin Press, 1974), pp. 177–79.

25.18 Wrote Lizzie & Allan] Nos. 319 and 320 on the "Check List of Unlocated Letters," *Letters*, p. 312.

25.21 Murray's . . . invitation] Murray and his wife commonly hosted two dinners a week in season; Thackeray wrote of such occasions: "Everybody had the same dinner in London—the soup, fish, saddle of mutton, boiled fowls, three or four entrées, confectioner's sweets, cheap champagne and hired waiters" (paraphrased in Paston, *At John Murray's*, p. 67). The "footman" whose legs M disparages was doubtless the butler, James Mills, a devoted and lifelong retainer who was more widely read than many of the guests (Paston, p. 307). Some of his comments about this "stiff" dinner M soon crossed out; see the reproduction on p. 218 above and the textual notes at 26.1–4 and 26.14–15.

25.27 Lockhart] John Gibson Lockhart (1794–1854) was best known for his biography of his father-in-law, Sir Walter Scott, but also for his youthful savaging of Keats and the "Cockney School" of poets. He came to London in 1825 to edit Murray's *Quarterly Review*, the Tory, High Church counter to the Whig *Edinburgh Review*. His intimates regularly drew the contrast between the public man, chill, formal, aloof (because shy), and the husband, father, and friend of deep feeling and warm affections. John Wilson, his one-time associate at *Blackwood's*, described him as having "an e'e like an eagle's, and a sort of lauch about the screwed-up mouth o' him that fules ca'd nae canny, for they couldna tholl the meaning o't" (quoted in Henry Curwen, *A History of Booksellers* [London: Chatto & Windus, [1873]], p. 214). His nineteenth-century biographer cites a more flattering inventory: "I used to think him the most wonderfully handsome man I ever saw. . . . His finely cut classical features, his marvellously clear complexion, white even to pallor . . . and the jet black hair grouped in the clustering curls . . . made a lasting impression on me" (Andrew Lang, *The Life and Letters of John Gibson Lockhart*, 2 vols. [London: Nimmo, 1897], II, 329). By 1849, however, family deaths, fragile health, and his younger son's scandalous and defiant behavior were prematurely aging him. For much of these last years he was living on only bread and butter, becoming thin to emaciation.

25.32 Cook] Robert Francis Cooke (1816–91) was Murray's cousin and partner; after being a Longman apprentice, he joined Murray's in 1837. He sometimes accompanied his good friend George Borrow in wandering among the gypsies. In Part I of "The Paradise of Bachelors and the Tartarus of Maids" he is described fictionally as "that fine Barrister, Bachelor, and Bencher, R. F. C. . . . At the core he was a right bluff, care-free, right comfortable, and most companionable Englishman. If on a first acquaintance he seemed reserved, quite icy in his air—patience; this Champagne will thaw" (NN *Piazza Tales* volume, p. 319). See the discussion at 44.22.

26.4 Dr Holland] Henry Holland (1788–1873)—later Sir Henry (1853)—was physician for queens including Victoria, the ladies of London, prime ministers, ambassadors, even the future emperor Louis Napoleon. Yet he resolved to limit his professional income to five thousand pounds in order to devote his leisure to study and travel. His then wife was the witty daughter of the famous wit Sydney Smith. Dr. Holland's early book of travel in the eastern Mediterranean, *Travels in the Ionian Isles* (London: Longman, Hurst, Rees, Orme, & Brown, 1815), would have interested M.

26.28 Chapman & Hall's] Then at 186 Strand; notable as publishers (with one long intermission) of Dickens, beginning with *Pickwick*, which they had commissioned (1836–37). The partners now were the cousins Edward (1804–80) and Frederic (1823–95) Chapman, William Hall having died in 1847. If M saw Frederic, he met a bluff, cheery businessman (Edgar Johnson, *Charles Dickens* [New York: Simon & Schuster, 1952], II, 943) and keen sportsman. The quiet, retiring Edward was usually the judge of literature—he was the one who insisted that Pickwick be illustrated as fat.

Portraits of both and a drawing of the shop are in the company history, *A Hundred Years of Publishing*, by Arthur Waugh (London: Chapman & Hall, 1930).

26.32 H. G. Bohn's] Henry George Bohn (1796–1884) at first collected and sold valuable old books at 4 York St., Covent Garden, then sold "remaindered" books, then in 1846 began to reissue cheap editions of a "solid and instructive kind" in various Bohn series that made a major contribution to the current book-trade revolution and also made him wealthy. With wide cultural interests, energetic and shrewd, he superintended every detail of his business and did much of the editing and of the translating of Continental works.

27.3 Stevens] Henry Stevens (1819–86), bookman. One of M's most interesting new acquaintances and probably a major contributor to his involvement with old books (reflected in the bibliographical taxonomy of whales in chap. 32 of *Moby-Dick*). See the discussion at 29.37–30.1. A Vermont Yankee, Stevens graduated from Yale, then studied law one year (1844) at Harvard (where he met his friend J. C. B. Davis), but in 1845 his

Henry Stevens

lifelong bibliomania led him to London, where he very soon became a major dealer in important manuscripts, books, and collections, "the most colorful book agent of the nineteenth century" (Parker, *Henry Stevens*, p. 120; the frontispiece is reproduced opposite). For England, he was a major supplier of the American collection (more than one hundred thousand volumes by 1865) that Antonio Panizzi was assembling at the British Museum; for America, he was a principal buyer for the great collections of John Carter Brown in Providence and James Lenox in New York, and for the Smithsonian Institution and the Library of Congress. At this time a bachelor, he and Davis both lived at Morley's Hotel and often entertained visiting Americans. In 1850 he described himself as a "hearty, fat, plump, jolly red-faced bachelor," while Francis Parkman called him "the only man I know in London who can do anything except invite you to a stiff-necked, white cravated dinner party" (Parker, *Henry Stevens*, pp. 134, 147). Sometimes Yankee-sharp in his dealings, to his many friends he seemed at once sanguine and candid yet crafty and finally enigmatic. He had known M's brother Gansevoort in London, had breakfasted with him in April of 1846, only a month before he died (May 12, 1846), and had been one of the twelve persons at his funeral in Westminster Abbey (Hershel Parker, "Gansevoort Melville's 1846 London Journal," *Bulletin of the New York Public Library*, LXX, 129; Wyman W. Parker, *Henry Stevens*, p. 83; 1969 supplement to *Log*, II, 915 [May 18]). Stevens had recently spent many months in Boston and New York (1847–48), making his headquarters at Bartlett and Welford's bookstore, at No. 7, The Astor House (Stevens, *Recollections of James Lenox*, ed. Victor Paltsits, pp. 102–3; see also the discussions on Davidson and Langford, at 21.20 and 21.21). In the spring of 1856 Hawthorne and Davis were dinner guests at the now-married Stevens's house and saw his extensive personal collection of books and manuscripts (*ENB*, pp. 326–27).

27.7 Dolly] M's granddaughter's note, presumably based on family tradition, assures us this was "a nickname for his wife. Also the name of the ship which takes the narrator of *Typee* to the Marquesas" (EMM, p. 132).

27.12 Bates'] The banker's "country address" was in the village of East Sheen, near Richmond Park, just east of Richmond; it is noted in M's list (148.17). The nephew (of the new second Baron Ashburton, William Bingham Baring) was perhaps Henry Bingham Mildmay (1828–1905); Alexander Baring, first Baron Ashburton and senior partner in Baring Brothers when Bates became one, had just died (1848); his son-in-law Humphrey Mildmay had also been made a partner with Bates, and young Henry Mildmay (named like his uncle for his grandmother's Philadelphia family) was just now being groomed by Bates to take a place in the firm (Hidy, *House of Baring*, pp. 43, 44, 395, and 421). The "Baroness" M could not identify was possibly Bates's daughter Elizabeth, who in 1838 had married the brilliant young Baron Jean-Sylvain van de Weyer (1802–74), long-time Belgian minister to the Court of St. James's; he kept the legation in Bates's big town house in Portland Place where, because he spoke English so well, he was sometimes mistaken for the American minister. As a young man in 1830 he was central in installing Victoria's beloved uncle Leopold as king in the newly established state of Belgium, and as a result he and his wife were on intimate terms with Victoria and Albert. In 1861 Mrs. Bates and her daughter were important to the Charles Francis Adams family in the first difficult London months of his term as U.S. minister.

27.19 Peabody] George Peabody (1795–1869), another naturalized Massachusetts Yankee at the center of British banking, began as a prosperous merchant in Baltimore and New York, despite an impoverished boyhood and rudimentary education. He had come to England in 1827 and settled permanently in London ten years later. He and his later partner Junius Morgan became friendly rivals of the Barings and Rothschilds. His enormous benefactions on both sides of the Atlantic were memorialized in Peabody institutes or museums in Baltimore, at Harvard and Yale, and in his native town of South Danvers, now renamed Peabody; also in housing for the London poor, to which he ultimately gave $2.5 million; and in the $3.5 million Peabody Southern Educational Fund for the American South, especially for Negroes. He used his home and wealth to further Anglo-American understanding. A lifelong bachelor, he was especially kind to younger men and women, who found him acute, strong, and yet benevolent—as M at once saw him, "a very fine old fellow." (For his connection with M's brother Gansevoort, see 28.3–6.)

27.22 Captain Chamier] Frederick Chamier (1796–1870), retired naval officer and imitator of Marryat's sea novels (see also the discussion at 47.28). His valuable later work was the publication of his revised and extended edition (London: Bentley, 1847) of William James's *Naval History of Great Britain* (London, 1822–24), which is cited in *Billy Budd, Sailor*. Possibly the daughter told M about Chamier's recent experiences in revolutionary Paris.

27.32 Mrs Sturgiss] Russell Sturgis's second wife was Julia A. Boit (for her husband see the discussion at 23.1). Henry Adams much later wrote about his memories of her in 1861: "Mrs. Russell Sturgis was one of the women to whom an intelligent boy attaches himself as closely as he can. . . . The kind of education he [Adams] most required was that of a charming woman, and Mrs. Russell Sturgis, a dozen years older than himself, could have good-naturedly trained a school of such, without an effort. . . . During two years of miserable solitude, she was in this social polar winter, the single source of warmth and light" (*Education*, chap. 8, p. 122). In an 1864 letter he wrote, "all the harm that I know of her is that she likes the flavor of a dinner and a good glass of wine" (*The Letters of Henry Adams, 1858–1868*, ed. J. C. Levenson, Ernest Samuels, Charles Vandersee, and Viola Hopkins Winner [Cambridge: Harvard University Press, 1982], p. 464).

28.4 Gansevoort] M's older brother (1815–46) had been a rabble-rousing Democratic orator in Polk's 1844 presidential campaign; in reward, after office-seeking disappointments, he was appointed secretary of legation in London (July, 1845), where his rhetorical extravagance and Anglophobic reputation caused Minister Louis McLane some embarrassment. He arranged John Murray's acceptance of *Typee* (published in 1846 as *Narrative of a Four Months' Residence among the Natives of a Valley of the Marquesas Islands*), the manuscript of which he had brought to London, and also its acceptance there by George Palmer Putnam for Wiley & Putnam in New York. At McLane's, Gansevoort had dined with Peabody, N. P. Willis, and Washington Irving on January 18, 1846. His having "shunned society," so he wrote his brother Allan, was to economize so he could later dress appropriately for fashionable society (Parker, "Gansevoort Melville's 1846 London Journal," *Bulletin of the New York Public Library*, LXIX, 652). His journal in early 1846 repeatedly refers to depression and indifferent health; by early April he was seriously ill. On April 3 he wrote M, "I sometimes fear that I am gradually breaking up. . . . It is becoming a toil to me to make the exertion necessary to dress to go out. . . . I think I am growing phlegmatic & cold. . . . My circulation is languid. My brain is dull. . . . A degree of insensibility has been stealing over me, & now seems permanently established, which, to my understanding is more akin to death than life" (Eleanor Melville Metcalf, *Herman Melville* [Cambridge: Harvard University Press, 1953], p. 35). On May 12, he died, with symptoms of cerebral anemia (Howard, *Herman Melville*, pp. 96–97).

28.9–11 silence . . . mysteries] See *Pierre*, the first paragraph of Book 14: "All profound things, and emotions of things are preceded and attended by Silence. . . . Silence is the general consecration of the universe. . . . Silence is at once the most harmless and the most awful thing in all nature. It speaks of the Reserved Forces of Fate. Silence is the only Voice of our God" (p. 204).

28.24 Leicester Square] Only a few blocks northwest of M's lodging, the square had long been a center for artists (e.g., Hogarth and Reynolds), the quasi-raffish, and successive waves of foreign exiles following Continental revolutions—most recently that of 1848. Of the several French establishments in the vicinity, perhaps the best known was the Sablonière hotel, where M does breakfast later (December 16). There was also a Hôtel de

Provence and, in an adjoining street, a Hôtel de Versailles. The French cuisine was reputedly excellent. M recommended the square, with its emigrants and good breakfasts, to his uncle Peter (see pp. 620–23).

28.34 Aldgate Pump] M is wandering in the working-class east district of the City, beyond the Bank of England and north of the Tower; the pump, at the junction of Leadenhall and Fenchurch streets, was locally famous for its water until closed for impurity in 1876. Whitechapel Road is the continuation of Aldgate High Street northeast beyond the former City wall. Though a wide thoroughfare, with the kingdom's largest haymarket, it was bordered by "one of the very worst localities in London; a region of narrow and filthy streets, yards and alleys, many of them wholly occupied by thieves' dens, the receptacles of stolen property, gin-spinning dog-holes, low brothels, and putrescent lodging-houses,—a district unwholesome to approach and unsafe for a decent person to traverse even in the daytime" (Wheatley, *London Past and Present*, III, 500). Bayard Taylor, in *Views A-Foot* (1846), writes of entering the City by way of Whitechapel and mentions his "humble lodgings at the Aldgate Coffee House, where I slept off fatigue for a shilling a night, and walked up Cheapside or down Whitechapel . . . hunting out my way to churches, halls and theatres" (p. 44).

Jews had long inhabited the area—the Jewish Burial Ground (where the first Rothschild was buried) was just north of Whitechapel. According to Eleanor Melville Metcalf, "Moses & Son" was probably "Elias Moses and Son, wholesale and retail clothiers, tailors, hatters, 83–86 Aldgate Street.—*Post Office London Directory*, 1847" (EMM, p. 134).

29.2 "Oh . . . charms"] From the well-known opening lines of William Cowper's "Verses, Supposed to Be Written by Alexander Selkirk" (1782) (the castaway original of Robinson Crusoe):

> I am monarch of all I survey,
> My right there is none to dispute,
> From the center all round to the sea,
> I am lord of the fowl and the brute.
> O solitude! where are the charms
> That sages have seen in thy face?
> Better dwell in the midst of alarms,
> Than reign in this horrible place.

29.3 Morley's] A fashionable hotel at 4 Trafalgar Square, just up the street from M's lodging, where both Stevens and Davis lived and where Gansevoort had become a friend of the Morleys. In 1855 Hawthorne found it very spacious and more like an American hotel than any other he had seen in England (*ENB*, p. 211). The Reverend J. W. Newton, born in Connecticut, received a commission from Pennsylvania in 1844; he had last been at sea in March of 1848.

29.7–8 bound for Boulogne] *Cruchley's Picture of London* lists the principal steamship firm as the General Steam Navigation Co., with offices in Lombard and Leadenhall streets and in Regent Circus, Piccadilly, "whose splendid, conveniently arranged, and powerful steam ships leave London" for Boulogne, etc. (p. 274). Via the Thames, the trip was 110 miles, took twelve hours, and cost fifteen shillings. The Nore anchorage over a sandbank at the mouth of the Thames is especially famous for the 1797 mutiny in the Royal Navy, the historical background for *Billy Budd, Sailor*.

29.12 Bussy] Now more accurately Buci, a short, curving street not far from the ancient church of St. Germain-des-Prés on the Left Bank, terminating near the Pont Neuf. (Michelin still stars the area for its ancient, "picturesque" buildings and narrow, twisting streets.) The area was one of the two principal centers of unrest on the Left Bank in the uprising the previous year, 1848. The address seems to have been recommended by M's recent friend Dr. Augustus Kinsley Gardner, who had been a young medical student in Left Bank Paris a few years earlier. M had met Gardner in the Duyckinck circle in 1847, and he had inscribed to M his recent book, *Old Wine in New Bottles; or, Spare Hours of a Student in Paris* (New York: Francis, 1848; HCL-M; Sealts 222). Gardner himself may have lodged here, or certainly nearby, as indicated by his references to the Luxembourg Palace, the School of Medicine, the morgue at the Pont St. Michel, and so on. In M's *Israel Potter* (chaps. 8 and 9) the description of Franklin's once aristocratic neighborhood in the Latin Quarter, where Israel stays briefly, is drawn from this experience of M's. From Chapter 8: "The Latin Quarter still retains many old buildings whose imposing architecture singularly contrasts with the unassuming habits of their present occupants. In some parts its general air is dreary and dim; monastic and theurgic. In those lonely narrow ways—long-drawn prospectives of desertion—lined with huge piles of silent, vaulted, old iron-gated buildings of dark grey stone, one almost expects to encounter Paracelsus or Friar Bacon" (p. 47). The business of the bottle of brandy is elaborated in Chapter 9, and more details are supplied: a dark tessellated floor, two mahogany chairs and a bed, a cracked marble washstand, a water vessel without handle, a great square mirror, artificial flowers, and so on.

29.26 Mrs Lawrence] The last sentence about her is repeatedly lined through, as were the "bitter things" M wrote on first meeting her (23.14–24; see the discussion at 23.11–12). "Earl Cadogan's house" is presumably at the address listed in Cunningham's *Modern London* (1851) for the residence of the American minister, 138 Piccadilly. For the office of the legation see 22.29 and 148.10.

29.35 Livingston & Wells] Their New York office (at 10 Wall St., also the address of Allan's law office and Gansevoort's before him) advertised the firm as an "Express agency / Goods bought to order and shipped / Letters & newspapers forwarded / Semi-agency for travellers, assist in business / forwarding luggage, transmit funds / Drafts and remittances". (The "cheque" Davidson gave M was for the discounted proceeds of Bentley's hundred-pound advance on *Redburn*; see p. 177.)

29.36–37 shoveled the sovereigns] Richard Henry Dana, Jr., in 1856 also went to a London bank on "Lombard street, so famous in history, where so much of the money of the world is gathered, a narrow, winding, dingy street. . . . There were clerks, some weighing gold in scales, some shoveling it out upon the counter, with little brass shovels, like those used in sugar barrels" (*Journal*, II, 718).

29.37–30.1 Stevens . . . Museum] Any bibliophile might dream of such a private showing as M was given, by such a guide (see the discussion on Stevens at 27.3). The library had been settled a few years before in the ground floor of the north wing and part of the east wing of the new building; it was not freely open to the general public, but Stevens had early secured access to its treasures through his relationship as agent for Americana with the Keeper of Printed Books, the future famous Principal Librarian, Antonio Panizzi. Though young, the library was well on its way to eminence, with 435,000 books by the end of 1849. Charlemagne's Bible (in the Vulgate) was said to have been revised by Alcuin for the emperor. Shakespeare's signature in Florio's 1603 translation of Montaigne's *Essayes* (no longer considered authentic) was a happy combination for M since both were favorite writers; he had bought books by each at the same time in January of 1848 (Sealts 366, 460a) and had acquired and delighted in a set of Shakespeare's works (Sealts 460) in February of 1849; allusions to both writers crop up in *White-Jacket*, and both influenced *Moby-Dick* and *Pierre* (Bercaw 634, 502). The Codex Alexandrinus, one of the three oldest Greek manuscripts of the Bible, is in four volumes, in uncial letters on thin vellum of the fifth century. Among the Saxon and medieval manuscripts were the famous Cottonian and Harleian collections, including the unique *Beowulf*. The "comical librarian" could be a nobody or possibly either the excitable Italian emigré Panizzi—just then deeply involved with a royal commission investigating the conduct of the library—or the Keeper of Manuscripts, Sir Frederic Madden, jealous of Panizzi and frequently described as "fiery" (see Edward Miller's biography of Panizzi, *Prince of Librarians* [London: Deutsch, 1967]).

30.7 "Blue Posts"] At 13 Cork St. (north of Piccadilly and beyond the Burlington Arcade); "a good, homely well-cooked English dinner may be had at a reasonable rate at the Blue Posts Tavern. . . . The landlord is famous for his baked punch" (Cunningham, *Handbook for London* [1849], I, 233). N. P. Willis described it: "This is a snug little tavern, with the rear of its two stories cut into a single dining-room, where chops, steaks, ale, and punch, may be had in unusual perfection. It is frequented ordinarily by a class of men peculiar, I should think, to England—taciturn, methodical in their habits, and highly respectable in their appearance—men who seem to have no amusements and no circle of friends, but who come in at six and sit over their punch and the newspapers till bed-time, without speaking a syllable" (*People I Have Met*, p. 37). M mentioned this occasion in a letter to the Duyckincks (from Paris, December 2; *Letters*, p. 95). After M again invited him out to dine (December 21; see 46.6–7), Davidson wrote (December 24) to George Duyckinck: "I am very much obliged to you for an introduction to Hermann Melville Esq—we passed two evenings together which considering the dinner and breakfast he had to do here was fortunate—I suppose I was not exactly the kind of man to bring him out—still we had a pleasant brace of evenings. One at the Mitre Tavern Fleet St where we sat right opposite to D^r^. Johnsons corner in which these was a manner eating stewed mutton for dinner with his pint of 'af n'af at six o'clock in the evening—doing our well done 'steaks we adjourned (by omnibus) to the 'Blue Posts' Cork Street, Burlington Arcade and had a pint of real punch at the very table you, and Boot*lare* (Butler) and I blue posted a dinner once upon a time" (NYPL-D; see the discussion at 46.6–7 for the continuation of this letter).

30.8 Wrote Allan] No. 321 on the "Check List of Unlocated Letters," *Letters*, p. 312.

30.14 Tilbury Fort] The principal defense above the mouth of the Thames, on the north bank opposite Gravesend.

30.21 Passport] Murray's *Continent* (1849) advised that passports were usually obtained from the minister of the country of debarkation and visaed by those of other countries; passports for France were issued, for five shillings, at the General Consulate, 47 King William St., London Bridge. Entry permits (seven shillings) issued by the Prussian consul (106 Fenchurch St.) would serve for Belgium and the Rhine. Murray's *France* (1848) adds,

> The passport which a traveller brings with him into France is not valid for travelling through the country, nor for quitting it, until it has received the signature of the Minister of the Interior. It is therefore taken away from the traveller at the sea-port where he lands . . . and is forwarded by the police to

> Paris, while a temporary passport, *Passe Provisoire*, is given him to carry him on to Paris, and 2 francs must be paid for it. . . .
>
> The first care of the traveller after landing . . . should be to obtain his passe provisoire, which is often a tedious business, owing to the number of applicants all eager to secure their papers in time to start. . . .
>
> On reaching Paris, the "Passe Provisoire" must be taken or sent to the Préfecture of police, where the original will be given in exchange for it. It is better to send a valet de place or commissionnaire for it than to go for it: the commissionnaire being known to the officials is more likely to be attended to than a stranger, speaking French perhaps scarcely intelligible. (p. xvii)

(This account, doubtless written before the 1848 upheaval, still applied according to the 1853 *France*; and M did have some problems—see the entries for December 3 and 4.)

Nearly a quarter of Boulogne's twenty-nine thousand inhabitants were English, but Murray's 1848 *France* lists no Hotel Bedford. M's habit of traveling light, here with one "little portmanteau," saved him money; the clearing and porterage of luggage was charged by number of pieces.

30.23 train for Paris] Trains reportedly covered the 156 miles in ten hours, by way of Abbeville, Amiens, Pontoise, and St. Denis, and were recommended as the most economical, least fatiguing means of travel. Dr. Gardner (*Old Wine*, p. 12) described first- and second- (but not third-) class accommodations, observing that unsnobbish, wise travelers would choose the comfortable second class.

30.28 Rue de la Convention] The former rue du Dauphin, renamed after the 1848 upheaval (today rue St. Roch)—a short street connecting the rue de Rivoli, near the northeast corner of the Jardin des Tuileries, and the rue St. Honoré.

30.29 "Meurice's"] Murray's *France* described the hotel as "a comfortable and well-managed house, much frequented by Americans: bed 3 fr. per day . . . dinner at table-d'hôte, without wine, 4½ fr." *Galignani's New Paris Guide* for 1848 added, "To an English traveller few hotels in Paris offer so many advantages as Meurice's, 42, rue de Rivoli. It is situated in a fine and agreeable spot, facing the Tuileries" (p. 14). Thackeray (*Paris Sketch Book* [London: Macrone, 1840]) observed wryly: "If you cannot speak a syllable of French, and love English comfort, clean rooms, breakfasts, and waiters; if you would have plentiful dinners, and are not particular . . . concerning wine; if, in this foreign country, you *will* have your English companions, your porter, your friend, and your brandy-and-water . . . with your best English accent, shout out boldly, MEURICE!" (I, 22). Eight months before M, another Englishman found the three hundred rooms were small but with good beds, chests of drawers, and stoves (J[ohn] B[ill], *The English Party's*

Excursion to Paris [London: Longman, 1850], p. 26). The illustration below of the rue de Rivoli is from *Paris and Its Environs*, ed. Thomas Forester (London: Bohn, 1859), facing p. 46.

RUE DE RIVOLI.

30.32 Galignani's] Galignani's Reading Room was through a gateway and courtyard at 18, rue Vivienne—a few blocks northeast of M's hotel; it was "a great resource to the Englishman in Paris: here he will find all the best newspapers of all the world; here he will meet with his friends, a list of his countrymen visiting or residing in Paris being kept here, and may supply himself with books, or subscribe to the circulating library" (Murray's *France*). The traveler could subscribe to the Reading Room's services for ten sous a day, three francs a week (*Galignani's New Paris Guide*; Bill, *English Party's Excursion*, p. 55). The Galignani firm published many English books, usually pirated, and in 1850, a few months after M's visits to the Reading Room, included *Redburn* (without authorization) in the "British Library" series published jointly with Jules Baudry.

30.33 Palais Royal] As M observes below, renamed the National after Louis Philippe was deposed in 1848. Facing the Louvre a short distance east of M's hotel, it was built for Cardinal Richelieu, but before 1789 buildings and galleries for shops were added around the gardens. After many changes and rebuildings, the quadrangle complex now contained the Théâtre Français, the Théâtre Montansier (or du Palais Royal) and many of the most elegant and expensive shops, cafés, and restaurants of the city. Galignani recommended: "The best time for seeing this brilliant bazaar is in the evening, when the garden and arcades are brilliantly illuminated and full of people; the shops of the watchmakers and jewellers will then particularly strike the visitor's eye. The Palais Royal has been called, not without reason, the Capital of Paris" (p. 176). The interior of the palace proper, however, had been vandalized in the recent uprising, and repair was slow. The illustration below is from Bohn's *Paris and Its Environs*, p. 74.

PALAIS ROYAL.

30.36 Concorde] The modern Place de la Concorde was just being completed; the 1848 revolution had started with disturbances here, and here the new constitution had been proclaimed a year before (November, 1848), but its gory history reached back to the executions of Louis XVI and Marie Antoinette, with the subsequent guillotining of some twenty-eight hundred persons, including a figure fascinating to M, Anarcharsis Cloots (to whom he refers in *Moby-Dick*, chap. 27; *The Confidence-Man*, chap. 21; and *Billy Budd, Sailor,* chap 1). The Place de la Concorde and the adjoining Champs Élysées, as Dr. Gardner described them, presented, especially on holidays, "many objects of interest and amusement. Independently of its agreeable walks, the gorgeous Place Concorde, glittering with gilded gas-posts and fountains—the magnificent Obelisk of Luxor . . . ; numberless vehicles of the wealthy, flashing with gold and silver, and bearing, beside the driver, one or two pampered lackeys, who, from their stand upon the rack behind, look down with scorn and pity upon all they pass; the numerous booths of mountebanks with the never-to-be-forgotten Punch and Judy, and other similar shows; and, in addition to the whole, the crowds of people of all classes and ages, who throng the *trottoirs*, present altogether a rare combination of novelty, fun, and splendor" (*Old Wine*, pp. 64–65).

30.38–39 garrisoned town] Elected president by the provisional government (December, 1848), Louis Napoleon acted to acquire absolute authority; he sent French troops to Rome in the spring to destroy the Roman Republic and restore Pope Pius IX; at home he cultivated the conservative, Catholic, and monarchical elements, repressed the radicals, muzzled the press, and used his cudgel-bearers, the "Ratapoils," to terrorize socialist opposition. In June of 1849 he had put down an armed revolt. As late as 1851 a British visitor claimed there were still sixty thousand troops, besides the Garde Nationale, stationed in Paris (Sir Francis Head, *A Faggot of French Sticks; or, Paris in 1851* [New York: Putnam, 1852], p. 169).

30.39 Wrote . . . Adler] Nos. 322 and 323 on the "Check List of Unlocated Letters," *Letters*, p. 312.

31.2 Bourse] On the rue Vivienne; within the Salle, a large ground floor hall, was the "corbeille," a circular enclosed space toward one end, around which the authorized brokers shouted their offers.

31.4 Bordeaux] Galignani advised that one could find plentiful dinners for two francs; in the vicinity of the Palais National, twenty-two to thirty sous would buy soup, two dishes at choice, bread, dessert, and a "modicum of wine."

31.11–12 "Cafe Francais"] Galignani did not list such a café in this general area.

31.13 Notre Dame] The cathedral had suffered much damage in the Revolution and for some years after 1793 had been converted into a "Temple of Reason." Napoleon returned it to the Church in 1802, but restoration did not commence until 1845.

31.15 Place de la Bastile] About a mile's walk from the Île de la Cité; the huge plaza, built by Napoleon in 1803, occupies ground somewhat east of the site of the infamous Bastille prison. It had been the place of the 1848 insurgents' strongest barricade and therefore much damaged. The 170-foot column in its center, with interior stairs and a statue of Liberté on the sum-

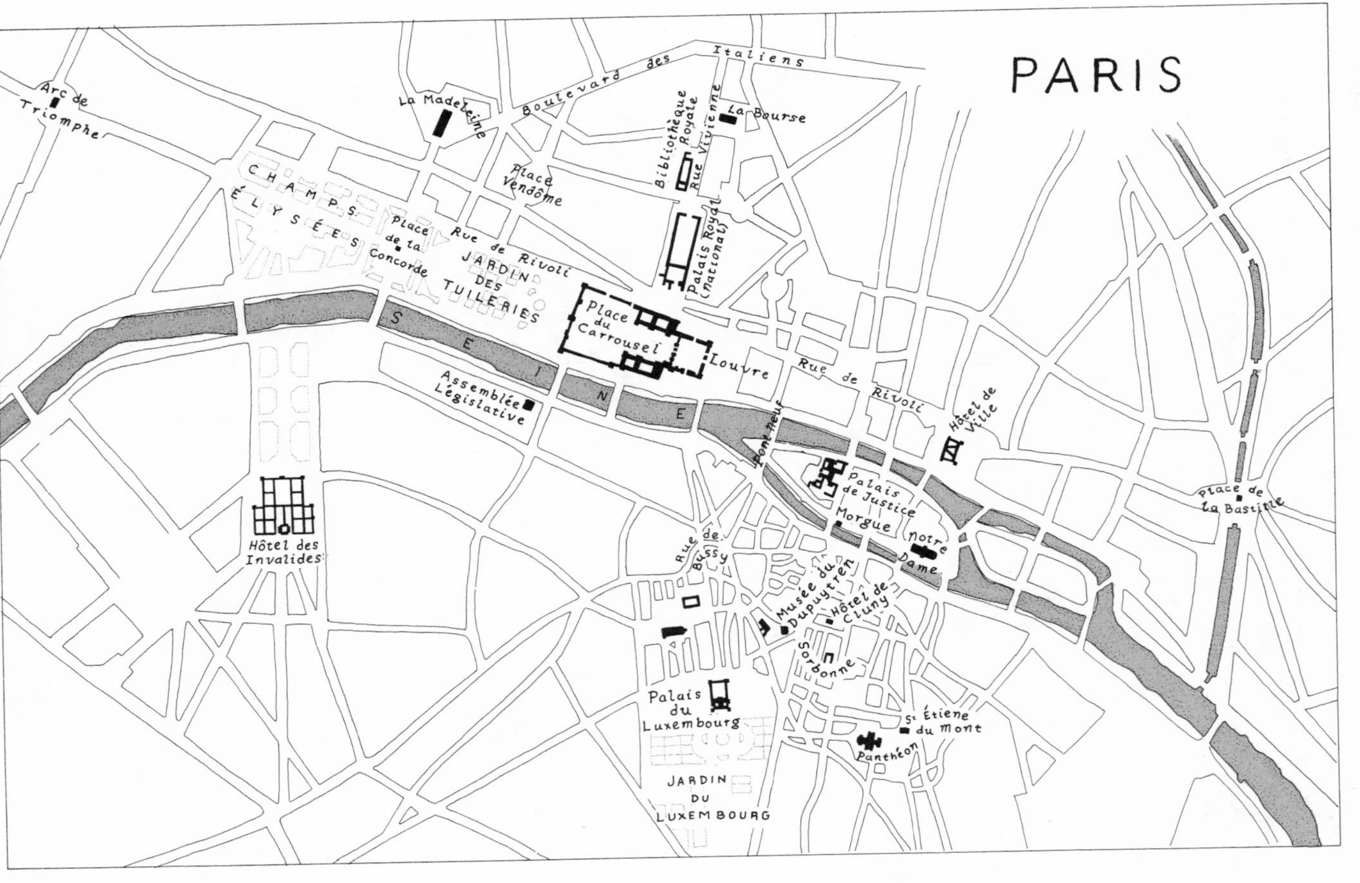

Paris, circa 1853. Based on the separately issued map *Nouveau Plan Itinéraire de Paris* by Charpentier (Paris: Danlos, 1853).

mit, originally memorialized the Parisians killed in the 1830 uprising, but later also those of 1848, who were buried there. An English gentleman's contempt is expressed in this contemporary description:

> I found myself in a large, long, irregular, uncomfortable-looking open space. . . . I saw before me a lofty bronze column, surmounted by a perfectly naked, lengthy, thin, herring-stomached, long-backed, flying-Mercury-looking mountebank, with a pair of wings on his shoulders, the whole newly gilt all over, as if it had just flown . . . from California.
>
> On the outside of the column, from the bottom to the top, in three strata, each representing the result of one day's revolutionary havoc, were inscribed . . . a variety of names. . . .
>
> The monument was surrounded on all four sides by massive iron railings, within which, at the foot of the column all the way round, I observed a confused pile of faded wreaths. (Sir Francis Head, *A Faggot of French Sticks*, pp. 49–51)

31.17 Louvre] According to Galignani, open daily except Monday; foreigners needed a passport, except on Sunday, a public day (M must have used his "passe provisoire"—see the discussion at 30.21). Most of Napoleon's spoils from Egypt and Italy had been returned, but there were still some remarkable items in the Musée des Antiquités—the Musée Grec et Romain was "exceedingly choice," especially in its Greek collection, the famous *Venus de Milo*, for example, which had been found in 1820 and bought by the French government. When M saw the building, with its west-reaching wings leading to the still-extant Palais des Tuileries, it had been saved from decrepitude by Napoleon I and partly restored, but complete restoration and the added wings were yet to be finished by Napoleon III. The great Galerie d'Apollon, for example, was not finished until 1851.

31.21 California] The steamer *Empire City* had arrived in New York on Sunday, November 11; on Monday and Tuesday, Horace Greeley's *Tribune*, for example, exulted over the news that the California Constitutional Convention had unanimously adopted an anti-slavery provision; it reported that the ship carried a million dollars in gold, printed a letter from Bayard Taylor traveling cross-country from San Francisco to the Sierra mines, and gave glowing accounts of further gold discoveries, the most "magnificent" a great vein on Colonel Frémont's ranch. But M may have seen the *Tribune*'s summary edition "for European Circulation" of November 14, carried on the *Hibernia* sailing the same day. *Redburn* had been published in New York by Harper & Brothers on November 14; the Duyckincks' *Literary World* (November 10) had printed two advance chapters (*Log*, I, 329).

31.33 Sorbonne] A half-mile's walk from M's lodging, just across a street running south of the Hôtel de Cluny (see the discussion at 33.19) and just off the rue de la Harpe (now the boulevard St. Michel). Notices of lectures open to the public were posted at the porter's lodge, entrance to the inner quadrangular court. The work of Victor Cousin (1792–1867), a famed eclectic philosopher, was no doubt known to M's companion Adler if not to M. An enormously popular lecturer at the university, he remained its virtual head while minister of public instruction under Louis Philippe.

31.35 Pere le Chaise] Père-Lachaise, the famous cemetery on high ground to the northeast, overlooking the city and the Seine Valley. Though approached through a poor district, it seems to have attracted most visitors, even those who scorned the ostentatious bourgeois monuments rapidly filling the permanent grave precincts—for example, the supercilious Sir Francis Head, who wrote: "My eyes and mind were completely bewildered by the sudden appearance of a forest of monuments, which looked as if the tenants of the innumerable graves before me had, one and all . . . arisen to declare that even in the republic below ground there exists the same desire for distinction which the soi-disant republicans of Paris . . . are everywhere displaying" (*Faggot of French Sticks*, p. 451). The "tomb" of Abelard and Héloïse—"the most picturesque and interesting monument in the cemetery" (Galignani, p. 280)—is not far inside the main entrance; it is a small chapel (fourteen by eleven feet, twenty-four feet high) in thirteenth-century style, built out of the ruins of Abelard's Abbey of the Paraclete, near Troyes. Inside, Abelard's recumbent effigy, originally in the Priory of St. Marcel, near Chalon-sur-Saône, where he died, is watched over by a statue of Héloïse. (In *White-Jacket*, chap. 44, M speaks of the emasculation of more than one hated master-at-arms by a frigate's crew as his being "served . . . as his enemies served Abelard"; p. 190.) In *Old Wine* (p. 234) M's friend Dr. Gardner severely disparaged the cemetery; M wrote its name and a page reference (along with three other items) on the verso of the rear free endpaper of his presentation copy from Gardner (Sealts 222).

31.36 Abattoir of Popincourt] This great slaughterhouse (listed by Galignani as a "must" visit) was the largest of the five erected outside the city by Napoleon's order, to remove the activity from the central areas. Sir Francis Head, who visited two others, describes them as extraordinarily well managed, humane, clean, and free of offensive odor. This one was a short half mile west of the cemetery.

31.37–38 Boulevards] The "Grands" Boulevards (still three-starred by Michelin) follow the late medieval ramparts of the city on the north running in an arc from the Madeleine past the Opéra and ending at the Bastille; they are variously named, de la Madeleine, des Capucines, des Italiens, and so on. According to Galignani, "The Boulevard des Italiens in particular . . .

[presents] on a fine autumnal evening a scene of the utmost gaiety; the effect is indescribable; a confusion of colours and images bursts upon the eye, and the whiteness of the houses, broken at intervals by dark masses of verdure, form a beautiful contrast to the blaze of light issuing from the splendid 'cafés' and club-houses, while the glaring gas-lights without illuminate the groups seated round the little marble tables; rattling equipages rush by, and all the world seem entranced at this hour in the pleasure of perfect idleness" (p. 476).

32.3 Rachel] Élisa Félix (1820–58), unhappy child of poor Jewish parents, was—and still is—considered among the greatest of actresses. Because of her, the tragedies of Corneille and Racine were revived, Racine's Phèdre being her greatest role. Dr. Gardner wrote: "The great tragic actress was . . . when I saw her, the only performer of any eminence on the French stage. . . . With difficulty I obtained a ticket, four days previous to her appearance. . . . The fame, which she enjoys, I am convinced . . . is richly deserved" (*Old Wine*, p. 252). Galignani described the lining up for tickets: "The Theatres of Paris are well regulated. . . . The visitors who await the opening of the doors are arranged in files of two or three abreast; and although the crowd probably consists of several hundreds, but little pressure or inconvenience is felt. . . . Such, indeed, is the ardour for theatrical amusements exhibited by the population of Paris, that a crowd, or *queue* as it is commonly called, may always be found at the door . . . for several hours before the time of admission" (p. 456). M's letter to Evert Duyckinck the next day (December 2) also jokes about his disappointing experience: "The other evening I went to see Rachel—& having taken my place in the *'que'* (how the devel do you spell it?) or tail—& having waited there for a full hour—upon at last arriving at the ticket-box—the woman there closed her little wicket in my face—& so the 'tail' was cut off" (*Letters*, p. 94; see p. 616 below).

32.9 St Roche] On the rue St. Honoré, a little west of where M had breakfast; its north-south axis and unusual length (due to successive additions after its founding by Louis XIV) gave St. Roch its principal distinction. The elliptical Chapel of the Virgin is under the cupola; the side chapels had been newly decorated with paintings earlier in the century. Galignani twice singled out the church, not for these features but for its music and the spectacle of High Mass on Sunday morning at ten: "St. Roch, though not remarkable for any architectural beauty, is the richest church in Paris, . . . and on high festivals mass is celebrated with great pomp and solemnity. On these occasions, the music and singing are so remarkable that the influx of strangers . . . often excludes all possibility of entrance" (p. 233).

32.10 Madeline] Begun by Napoleon as a Greek-style "Temple of Glory," the Madeleine in the form M saw it had been finished only since

1842. Hawthorne, too, in January of 1858 was rhapsodic about the "glorious and gorgeous" church, and describes at length an elaborate funeral much like the one M had seen at St. Roch (*FINB*, pp. 18–21). It also was famous for its sacred music.

32.12 Invalids] If M viewed the locales in the order he names them here before reaching the Hôtel des Invalides, he engaged in some circuitous backtracking. Built by order of Louis XIV to house as many as seven thousand disabled war veterans, the hotel and its esplanade are still called by Michelin the finest architectural composition in Paris. (Its population by the mid-nineteenth century was some three thousand; Jérôme Bonaparte had recently been appointed governor.) As one entered the Court of Honor from the north or riverfront, the dining rooms were on the ground floor to the right (now part of the Musée de l'Armée). The veterans sat twelve to a round table; the officers in their hall also sat in twelves, but on chairs, not stools, and with plate given by Napoleon's Austrian empress. The Church of St. Louis was the original chapel in the center of the complex; here still hung 250 captured battle standards, though most of the original thousands had been burnt before the entrance of the Allies in 1814. The Algerian trophies were from the conquest completed in 1847. The adjacent Church of the Dôme was closed to visitors for the ongoing construction of Napoleon's tomb; meanwhile, his body since its return from St. Helena in 1840 was lying in one of the side chapels. In the Council Chamber area, a gallery had been set up with many portraits of military commanders.

32.14–15 Thence . . . Luxemburgh] M's walk of something over a mile was taking him in part through one of the most elegant and palatial residential districts of Paris, that of the old nobility in the Faubourg St. Germain. Marie de Médicis's Luxembourg palace, only a few hundred yards from M's lodging, had been the seat of the Directory during the Revolution, then of the Consuls, then of Napoleon's Senate, and after 1814 of the Peers. After the Revolutions of 1848 it was briefly abandoned until Napoleon III

PALACE OF THE LUXEMBOURG.

restored the Senate. It was open all days but Mondays, from ten to four, to visitors with a passport. The gallery in the east wing, which had once housed Rubens's twenty-four paintings from the life of Marie de Médicis, was now devoted to the works of living French artists. The assembly room, the first-floor Salle des Séances, a semicircular chamber with hemispherical vault, had been specially constructed in 1844—Dr. Gardner called it "extremely beautiful" (*Old Wine*, p. 127). Marie's formal gardens south of the palace had been partly laid waste in 1792 to build popular cafés, ballrooms, and fairgrounds but were now being restored and replanted. The illustration here is from *Galignani's New Paris Guide* (1864), facing p. 374.

32.18 Richelieu] The cardinal (1585–1642) built the Sorbonne in 1624–42 for the theological faculty; the church (the only remaining original part) has in its south transept his white marble tomb, on which his reclining effigy is represented as upheld by Religion while at his feet sits the weeping figure of Science (portraits of his nieces).

32.18–19 Panthenon] The Panthéon, an imposing edifice on the highest ground of the Left Bank, was begun as a church in the eighteenth century at the tomb site of Ste. Geneviève, patron saint of the city, and was converted in the Revolution to a temple to the illustrious dead of France. The remains of Mirabeau and later those of Voltaire and Rousseau were brought here. Dr. Gardner devoted several pages to it, including this passage:

> Under the temple are the tombs of those, whom France has pronounced worthy of a place of such distinction. The guide proceeds with a lantern through its chilly passages, and, as he comes to each monument, arranges his company, so that they can have an advantageous view, taps it with his cane, and after a suitable preparatory hawking and hemming, commences his history. . . . [The memories of these famous men], like wild beasts in a menagerie, are "stirred up" by a chattering guide, and their merits canvassed by the stupid Englishman, who says "well that's did,"—and the curious Yankee, who asks "have you ever saw?"—neither of whom have ever read a syllable of their writings.
>
> . . . The ashes of about thirty eminent persons now find a resting place in these caverns, enclosed in marble cenotaphs or urns. (*Old Wine*, p. 301)

M's comment "still building" refers to repairs from bad damage in 1848; this high ground had been the insurgents' most formidable Left Bank redoubt, with the Panthéon the headquarters from which they repelled troops for two days until artillery dislodged them.

32.19 old church] The nearest one is that of St. Étienne-du-Mont, diagonally across the street; its unusual sixteenth-century Gothic construction is unlike anything else in Paris. M's return to the river took him through the pre-Haussmann medieval Latin Quarter (which he would describe in Chapter 8 of *Israel Potter*) probably to the Pont des Arts or the Pont des Sts. Pères, now Pont du Carrousel, which in turn led him across to the Place du Carrousel—the open space between the wings of the Louvre and the then-still-standing Palais des Tuileries (pictured below, from *Galignani's New Paris Guide* [1864], facing p. 145).

PALACE OF THE TUILERIES (VIEW FROM THE PLACE DU CARROUSEL).

32.25–27 sallied . . . apartment] M was taking a rather roundabout way to his lodging; the nineteenth-century city morgue, of which Gardner and others made much (see the discussion at 32.34), was on the south bank of the Île de la Cité, east of the Pont St. Michel.

32.29–30 Continental Guide] A fragment of a map from *Bradshaw's Continental . . . Guide* survives with M's signature and his note, "Bought at Galignani's, Paris, Dec: 3d 1849." (see the discussion at 9.23–24). The fragment is reproduced and identified below, pp. 616–19.

32.30–31 Rue de la Fontane Moleire] Now simply the rue Molière, just west of the Palais National (Royal).

32.31 Thence walked] Galignani described the mile and a quarter walk from the Place de la Concorde down the Champs Élysées to the Arc de Triomphe as "a charming place for pedestrian exercise not only during the fine weather but also in winter" (p. 191). Some years later, however, Hawthorne, though impressed by the architecture of Paris emerging under Napoleon III, found the Champs Élysées in midwinter a grassless, dusty waste of barren white soil, the merry-go-rounds, booths, tables, and restaurants almost empty (*FINB*, pp. 14, 21). The arch was started by Napoleon in 1806 to commemorate Austerlitz and finished in 1836 under Louis Philippe. Its summit at 164 feet could be reached by a spiral staircase of 273 steps.

32.32 Bought little medal] Among the list of purchases at the end of this journal notebook M included two items under "*Paris* 'Curios' ": "Medal of Napoleon & Josephene" and another of "(Battle)"; the second seems the likely candidate from this occasion. See 146.13 and accompanying discussion.

32.34 Police] The prefecture was adjacent to the Palais de Justice on the Île de la Cité. (M apparently evaded the passport problems mentioned by Murray [see the discussion at 30.21] but had some "Develish nuisance" the next day about his passport visa to leave France—see 33.7–8 and accompanying discussion.)

32.34 Morgue] Pictured above, from Dr. Gardner's *The French Metropolis. Paris; As Seen during the Spare Hours of a Medical Student*, 2d ed., rev. (New York: Francis, 1850), facing p. 320. See also the discussion at 32.25–27. This was, as Gardner says, a grisly popular visiting place for tourists:

> Near the Pont St. Michel is situated a structure, which attracts the notice of every stranger visiting the city, in consequence of the publications of travelers; and yet it is a building possessing no interest in itself. Composed of stone, without pretension; plain, and even insignificant; without a sign or flag, or anything else to distinguish it, every body would be in danger of overlooking one of the most extraordinary places in Paris, were it not for the number of people seen constantly entering, and soon returning. . . . [One enters] a small room, divided into two parts by a glass partition. . . . The crowd of dirty blouses, charcoal-men, washer-women, and hucksters of all sorts, is so great, that we are kept for some time at a little distance. A quantity of clothes is hanging on nails around the apartment. . . . Iron frames supporting inclined boards to the number of eight or ten were arranged round the room . . . . On these, directly underneath the collections of clothes, were outstretched the

> bodies of their wearers, stripped naked, with the exception of a slight covering of small size about the loins. . . . [On each] a constant shower of water was projected . . . from a cock, which was fixed above. (*Old Wine*, pp. 320–22)

32.34 "Rosbeuf"] I.e., "Rosbif"; twice above (31.19, 32.1) M misspelled this French word as "Rosbeef"; here his variant misspelling perhaps reflects the French word "boeuf" ("beef"). For a probable identification of the café, see p. 618 below.

32.36 "Opera Comique"] The original Théâtre des Italiens gave the name to the most fashionable of the great boulevards. According to Galignani, "The light, agreeable character of the music, which formerly distinguished the Opéra Comique, has given place of late years to a more elaborate style, more scientific perhaps, but less popular. Auber and Halévy, however, preserve the ancient character of this school" (p. 460).

33.1 Cafe de Foy] At the Palais National, listed by Galignani among the most splendid: such cafés "rank among the most remarkable features which distinguish Paris to the eye of a stranger. . . . When lighted up at night, the effect, either seen from the exterior or within, is perfectly dazzling. . . . In the interior . . . you see yourself reflected by mirrors, remarkable for their size and number; you find yourself bewildered with the blaze of light, amidst the confused glitter of gilding, painting, and glass; . . . and the effect is heightened by the degree of taste and luxury displayed. . . . Here it is, in these spacious rooms, resplendent with decoration and brilliant with light, that the character of the French people may be seen . . . . At almost all these places coffee, chocolate, tea, ices, liqueurs, etc. are to be obtained" as well as light suppers (p. 17).

33.3 "Bibliotheque Royale"] On the rue Vivienne in a huge mansion that once belonged to Cardinal Mazarin, where the royal library had been transferred in the eighteenth century; no longer "Royale" but "Nationale." In the first-floor public areas were five sections devoted respectively to printed works, manuscripts, engravings, antique marbles, and a collection of medals, coins, and other objects. In one gallery was the bronze sculpture called the "French Parnassus," slopes covered with figures in classical attire, representing individuals of French genius located with a degree of elevation according to imputed merit. The section of manuscripts open to the public included fifth- and sixth-century missals, writings in Coptic, Persian, Indian, Arabic, Ethiopian, Chinese, Japanese, Armenian, and other languages, as well as autograph letters by Franklin, Henry IV, Louis XIV, Voltaire, Racine, Molière, Corneille, and Rousseau, which were, according to Galignani, "arranged under glass frames for the inspection of visitors" (p. 228). The galleries of engravings held 1,300,000 plates, though the principal ones (including fourteen from the sixteenth century, among them several by Dürer) were shown in the first few rooms; the Holbeins and other Dürers were kept with the German school, to be viewed only upon special request.

33.7 passport] The entry for December 5 (33.25–27) shows the difficulty of getting visas from the Belgian and Prussian ministers. M had already made a trip (Monday, December 3, 32.33-34) to the prefecture to pick up his passport. Now something else had come up evidently requiring a return trip—perhaps a missing stamp or signature. Furthermore, the Prussian legation required the passport overnight. William C. Rives was serving his second appointment as American minister in Paris (1849–53); the ministry was at 11, rue de Penthièvre, a mile or so west of the Bibliothèque Nationale.

33.8 nuisance] Possibly "nonsence".

Minister about passport. Thence to the Prefecture of Police &c. Devilish nuisance, the whole of it.

33.10 Telemachus] *Les aventures de Télémaque* (1699) by Bishop François Fénelon (1651–1715), presumably in an English translation (edition unidentified; Sealts 212). The imaginary adventures of the son of Odysseus, it was written for the bishop's pupil, the son of the dauphin, but it brought the author into disgrace because it was seen as a satire on Louis XIV and his policies. M listed the book, among others purchased in Paris, as costing "About 2 francs" (146.3).

33.12 Cafe Anglais] In 1848 Galignani did not list it among the "most splendid and attractive" cafés in Paris, but added it to the list in the 1851 edition. Both editions recommended the Café Cardinal, on the rue Richelieu a few steps away (1848, pp. 17–18). In a less than usually jaundiced tone, Sir Francis Head described such a café on the fashionable boulevard des Italiens:

> I found myself comfortably seated in a small octagonal room, chastely painted, brilliantly illuminated by gaslights, reflected in and multiplied by plate glass. . . . In this little chamber . . . were negligently scattered a quantity of small tables . . . ; there advanced towards me, whisking the tail of a white napkin as if to intimidate me, a very respectable man . . . dressed in a white neck-cloth, a very well-made dark cloth jacket . . . [and a floor-length] white apron. . . . In

> the fore and back ground of the picture there continually crossed and recrossed . . . a number of respectable, attentive, well-behaved waiters . . . with hair plastered by oil. (*Faggot of French Sticks*, pp. 45–47)

33.17 the stalls] The thousands of old books and prints for sale, just as today, would have attracted M, while his lack of proficiency in French, and of money, would have inhibited book purchases.

33.18 Museum] At 15, rue de l'École de Médecine, virtually next door to M's lodging. Dr. Gardner described it:

> [Near the School of Anatomy] is the celebrated Museum of Dupuytren, so called in honor of the distinguished surgeon, who left seventy thousand dollars for the establishment of a professorship of pathological anatomy. . . . The collection is . . . not very large. It, however, contains many objects of interest, which are arranged along the walls in glass cases. It embraces all the varieties of disease, but is particularly rich in those of osseous structure, and wax casts, and representations of syphilitic diseases. This is open to the public every Thursday. . . . For myself, accustomed to see suffering and death, and *never* affected at any period of my life, . . . let me acknowledge, that the contemplation of these horrors, arranged together, and displaying such a loathsome catalogue of deformities . . . for the *first* time sickened and unmanned me. (*Old Wine*, pp. 69–70)

(On the verso of the rear free endpaper of the copy Gardner gave him, M wrote four Paris items, the first is: "Museum of Duypuytren 69". See p. 174 and the discussion at 29.12.)

33.19 Hotel de Cluny] Near the museum and across a street from the Sorbonne (see the discussion at 31.33), the princely fifteenth-century city residence of the abbots of Cluny was built in flamboyant Gothic style over vast Gallo-Roman ruins. It suffered much neglect after it became state property in the Revolution, was purchased by a private citizen to house his fourteen hundred works of medieval art, then at his death bought back by the state, combined with the city-owned ruins of the Roman Palais des Thermes, and opened as a museum in 1844. It was open to foreigners, noon to four, Wednesdays, Fridays, and Sundays. Though most of its art works were religious, many early Renaissance ones used classical mythology, but none showing Leda and the Swan was mentioned in guidebooks. The most famous tapestries were two series, of David and Bathsheba, and of the Lady and the Unicorn. Galignani called the chapel "a most extraordinary monument" and noted its central pillar supporting the ribbed fan vaulting, and its elaborate tracery decoration (see the discussion at 128.33). From the chapel, a winding staircase led down to the vestibule of the Roman palace, thought to have been Julian the Apostate's residence when he was proclaimed emperor. Its only "perfect part" was the great hall, thought to be the frigidarium of the baths. With a guide one could venture beyond into the "cellars," supposedly the tepidarium. Melville later used the Hôtel de Cluny, the winding stair, and the ruined Roman baths in the crucial metaphor for Ahab's deep inner mysteries in Chapter 41 of *Moby-Dick* (pp. 185–86), where, as here, he evidently misapplies the French word "Thermes" (baths) as the name of a person. The illustration below is from *Picturesque Views of the City of Paris and Its Environs,* drawings by Frederick Nash, text by John Scott and M. P. B. de la Boissière (London; Longmans, Hurst, Rees, Orme, & Brown, 1823), II, n.p.

Hôtel de Cluny, Courtyard

33.24 Palace of the Deputies] The former Palais Bourbon, on the left bank, became the National Assembly after 1848. In an inner court, the Provisional Government had erected for the new Assemblée Législative what Galignani called an "uncouth temporary building" (p. 341) that first established the now classic distribution of seats by political ideology, right and left. Galignani went on to advise that while ordinarily one could enter the palace by asking at the door, for any important debate it was advisable to secure a ticket from a Representative or from the minister of one's own country.

33.34 Versailles] Trains left the St. Lazare depot, locals every half hour, express every hour, for the fourteen-mile trip. Galignani advised leaving Paris by nine in the morning to give time for looking around the exterior before the doors opened at eleven. The palace had been devastated during the Revolution and everything movable dispersed. Napoleon and after him the restored Bourbon kings began making repairs and moving in art works to establish a museum. Dr. Gardner, who devoted three long chapters to a description of it in the mid-1840's, wrote: "The American, who has never been accustomed to see more than four or five hundred pictures at a time, is bewildered with the immense multitude all around him. For hours and hours he walks through continuous galleries and smaller rooms. . . . The very immensity of the collection to be seen, prevents his properly observing any" (*Old Wine*, p. 179). Battle pictures in the Historical Section were from all periods, including the Revolution and the Napoleonic Wars. M alludes to them in Chapter 56 of *Moby-Dick*: "Go and gaze upon all the paintings of Europe, and where will you find such a gallery of living and breathing commotion on canvas, as in that triumphal hall at Versailles; where the beholder fights his way, pell-mell, through the consecutive great battles of France; where every sword seems a flash of Northern Lights, and the successive armed kings and Emperors dash by, like a charge of crowned centaurs?" (p. 267). According to Galignani, the royal suites had been restored with great care, especially the bedroom of Louis XIV, the "gem" of the palace; the exception to historical accuracy in this room, however, was what Galignani called the well-known "Titans" by Paul [Paolo] Veronese, which was brought from Italy by Napoleon and used to ornament the ceiling (p. 527). A portrayal of Jupiter hurling thunderbolts, it was retitled *Jupiter Punishing [or Fulminating] the Vices* when moved to the Louvre shortly after M's visit. The Bassin d'Apollon (sculpted by Jean-Baptiste Tuby, 1635–1700), is the principal feature of the great Allée to the west: the god issues from the water in a chariot drawn by four horses, surrounded by dolphins and sea monsters. However, the eloquent literary use M later made of a Versailles fountain figure was not of the Apollo he notes here but of the Enceladus (from the Bassin d'Encelade, sculpted by Gaspard Marsy) he does not mention; he wrote (1852) of Pierre's vision of a fallen, half-buried mountain rock as the cast-down Titan Enceladus: "Not unworthy to be compared with that leaden Titan, wherewith the art of Marsy and the broad-flung pride of Bourbon enriched the enchanted gardens of Versailles;—and from whose still twisted mouth for sixty feet the waters yet upgush . . . ; piled with costly rocks, and with one bent wrenching knee protruding from the broken bronze;—not unworthy to be compared with that bold trophy of high art, this American Enceladus, wrought by the vigorous hand of Nature's self, it did go further than compare;—it did far surpass that fine figure molded by the inferior skill of man. Marsy gave arms to the eternally defenseless; but Nature, more truthful, performed an amputation, and left the impotent Titan without one serviceable ball-and-socket above the thigh" (*Pierre*, bk. 25, chap. 4; pp. 345–46).

34.12 2^d class cars] Two trains daily covered the 228 miles from Paris to Brussels in twelve and a quarter hours, though there were several changes to make between lines. (M's "Doual" is Douai.) Murray's *Continent* (1849) called railway travel very cheap for passengers, but the charges for baggage by weight very high. In general Belgium had not been bothersome about passports, though officials were stricter after the uprisings of 1848; however, functionaries were considered frequently insolent and dilatory. Travelers were warned, on the other hand, that French officials very strictly examined passports of those departing through Valenciennes; Quièvrain is the first village on the Belgian side. M's history, like his geography, is a little askew: the kingdom of the Netherlands, arbitrarily established by the post-Napoleonic Treaty of Vienna (1815), broke apart in 1830, and the modern Belgian kingdom was then established (Joshua Bates's son-in-law Baron van de Weyer being an important member of the revolutionary group; see 27.21 and the discussion at 27.12).

34.20 Hotel de France] From the Gare du Midi in the Senne Valley the old Brussels streets climbed to the plateau on the east, past the modern Mont des Arts and Parc de Bruxelles to the rue Royale, where the hotel was "highly recommended; comfortable and moderate" (about twelve francs a day including Bordeaux wine—Murray's *Continent*, p. 162).

34.26–28 "There . . . chivalry"] M quotes accurately this famous passage of Byron's *Childe Harold's Pilgrimage*, Canto III, stanza xxi (though without indicating the line break after "then"); Harold, contemplating the field of Waterloo, evokes the duchess of Richmond's equally famous ball in Brussels the night before the battle. A reputed site of the ball was on the rue Royale of M's hotel. M was well versed in Byron but Sealts reports no *Childe Harold* he owned at this time. An excursion to Waterloo, some twelve miles by carriage, would have taken eight hours (including three on the site) and cost twenty francs.

35.2 Boulevards] In the newer, upper town a large square had been laid out with avenues of trees and statues. Murray (*Continent*, p. 162) considered the adjoining Royal Palace unremarkable. The new Botanic Gardens, near the old city gate north of the park, were open only after ten o'clock, Tuesdays, Thursdays, and Saturdays. Murray described Brussels as a small Paris and spoke of its "miniature" boulevards, along which M walked to the northern station for the train to Cologne.

35.3 seat for Cologne] Distances and times: to Liège, some seventy-one miles, four hours; Aix (Aachen), another thirty-four miles, two and a half hours, plus another hour at Belgian customs; to Cologne, over forty-three more miles, two and a half hours. At the Prussian border a passport admitted one quickly; baggage was examined at Aix or Cologne. Liége was called the Birmingham of the Low Countries, including the smoke and dirt: "The staple manufacture is that of firearms; Liége is, in fact, one great armoury" (Murray, *Continent*, p. 180). Beyond Liège the railroad crossed the northern remnants of the ancient mountain chain underlying the Ardennes—the country's poorest, least populous, and least advanced part. This section of the railroad had been completed only in 1844, because of great construction difficulties, nineteen tunnels in Belgium alone. On the Prussian side great viaducts and long tunnels descended to the Rhine Valley and the station outside the north city wall of Cologne.

35.18 a Hotel] Murray's *Continent* (p. 251) recommended the Hôtel de Cologne, on the Rhine quay close to the steamer landing, because it was "moderate and quiet"; the Rheinischer Hof, which M reached by mistake, also on the quay, was "good, clean, and well conducted, though dear."

35.26–27 cathedral . . . tower] Work on this "St. Peter's of Gothic art" began in 1248 but halted in 1509, with the taller of its two towers only a third of their planned five-hundred-foot height, and the crane on its top that M saw still there in 1849 (see "Der Dom" in the illustration on p. 350). Restoration was now proceeding, and the nave, aisles, and transepts had been reopened with a temporary wooden roof. In a small chapel behind the unfinished choir in the shrine of the Three Kings (the reputed bones of the Magi brought from Milan by Barbarossa), one saw three skulls with the names Gaspar, Melchior, and Balthazar spelled out on the reliquary in precious stones. M bought a memento here, which he later gave to his wife's younger half-brother, writing in February, 1850: "I send Lemuel a little medal (not silver) which I bought in the famous cathedral of Cologne" (*Letters*, p. 104 [No. 72]). An image from M's enforced day in Cologne emerged a year or more later in Chapter 32 of *Moby-Dick*: "But I now leave my cetological System standing thus unfinished, even as the great Cathedral of Cologne was left, with the crane still standing upon the top of the uncompleted tower. For small erections may be finished by their first architects; grand ones, true ones, ever leave the copestone to posterity. God keep me from ever completing anything" (p. 145). A second image passed into his description of the *Pequod*: "her masts stood stiffly up like the spines of the three old kings of Cologne" (chap. 16, p. 69)—probably in allusion to their upright figures in relief on the reliquary. See also the discussions at 13.6 and 42.27–28.

35.28–29 *"valet de place"*] Murray (*Continent*, p. 207) recommended using such a guide as indispensable, but one attached to a hotel, since with freelancing youths the traveler risked "falling into bad hands," or "finding himself in situations in which it will be neither agreeable nor creditable to be placed."

35.33 old town] For all its medieval associations nineteenth-century Cologne had its filth and stenches. So Samuel Prime: "This city of 60,000 . . . is celebrated for its fine cathedral, its abominable smells, and its . . . [Cologne water]. As the city is planted on a hill-side having a steep descent to the river, it is strange indeed that its reputation for filthiness should be so well deserved. Coleridge says that he counted seventy-two distinct smells" (*Travels in Europe and the East*, 2 vols. [New York: Harper & Brothers, 1855], I, 288). Though in this entry M does not mention Cologne perfume, in Chapter 91 of *Moby-Dick* he jokingly makes a neophyte French whaleship captain who was "a Cologne manufacturer before" insist on taking the oil from a fetid dead whale (p. 405), and in Chapter 9 of *Israel Potter* jokes again by making Yankee-bumpkin Israel—in Franklin's Latin Quarter room drawn from M's Paris one—sniff soap and artificial flowers and puzzle about a bottle of eau de cologne he thinks looks like Franklin's white wine (pp. 49–51). Originally a Roman colony (hence its name), Cologne became an archbishop's seat under Charlemagne and reached its walled extent between the twelfth and the fifteenth centuries. Peter Paul Rubens (1577–1640) was born not in Cologne (as Murray says) but in Siegen, a village to which his father and family had been confined until 1578. M's error again indicates his reliance on Murray's guidebook. Marie de Médicis (1573–1642), widow of Henry IV, after exile and escape from the France of Cardinal Richelieu and her son Louis XIII, died in Cologne—reputedly in the misnamed birthplace of Rubens, 10 Sternen Gasse; her heart was buried under the floor of the cathedral between the High Altar and the shrine of the Magi.

36.9 Jesuits' Church] The church was said by Murray to be a "gorgeous combination of Gothic and Italian architecture" but "overloaded with gorgeous decorations" (*Continent*, pp. 253, 257). The museum M visited, which became the Wallraff Richartz, had mostly early specimens of local painters, unnamed and uncatalogued. "Schefferen" is unidentified.

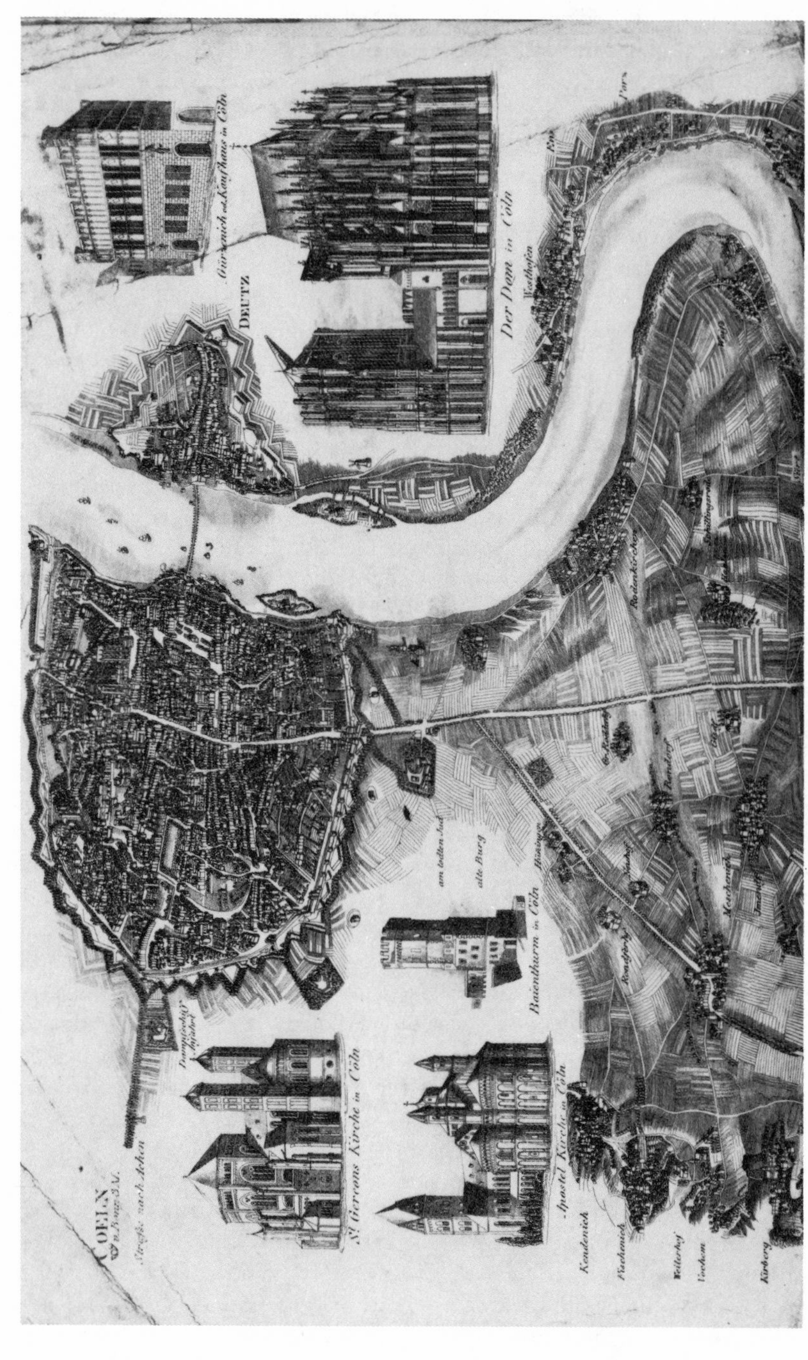

Panorama of the Rhine: Cologne

36.13 Rubens] Rubens was baptized in St. Peter's, and he presented to it the painting M saw, one of his best known from his last years. The painting actually portrays the martyrdom of Peter—not the removal of Christ from the cross that is traditionally meant by "Descent from the Cross"; a copy was exhibited free, while to see the original required a fee, fifteen groschen, to the sacristan.

36.15 purchased some books] On M's book list are two items obtained in Cologne: "Up the Rhine" and "Panorama of the Rhine" (146.9–10). Sealts identifies the first (280) as some edition (London or Frankfort? 1840?) of Thomas Hood's *Up the Rhine*; he leaves the second (396a) unidentified; a computer search done through the Online Computer Library Center (OCLC) indicates that there were several nineteenth-century works with the title *Panorama of the Rhine*, including a pictorial one done by Friedrich Wilhelm Delkeskamp (Frankfurt-am-Main: Borniger & Collin, [1837]), the illustration opposite is from a copy in The Newberry Library.

36.17 German dinner] Murray advised that in northern Germany the best dinner was table d'hôte; it was customarily served at one or two o'clock. The noted sociological journalist Henry Mayhew described one satirically: the room "spacious as a music-hall"; fountains, mirrors, diorama paintings of Rhine scenery; a musicians' gallery; "tables, which strike one as being as long as a railway platform, [that] reach two and three times up and down the room, . . . generally lined all the way with fresh faces every day"; a babel of French, English, and Germans who assembled at the loud sound of a bell. The menu was lengthy: a thick soup; a roast or *bouilli* served sliced with gravy or sauce, pickle, and potato; then one of a variety of specialty meats, like raw salmon, or sausage, with vegetables like red cabbage or sauerkraut; an entrée, as of fish or calf's head; a pudding or other sweet; then a substantial baked meat, veal or mutton, with stewed or preserved fruit; salad and fowl or field birds; and finally a dessert of fruit, cakes, and nuts. Mayhew commends the multilingual young waiters' great skill but was astonished at the price: "English readers . . . will marvel when they hear that a dinner, consisting of eight courses, is put upon the table at a charge which varies between eighteen pence and two shillings per head" (*The Rhine and Its Picturesque Scenery* [London: Bogue, 1856], pp. 235–40).

36.25 bridge of boats] Until the next decade, a long, floating causeway resting on a string of barges crossed the Rhine from Cologne to the fortified suburb of Deutz (see the illustration opposite). From it one got the best view of the city. Mayhew's *Rhine* has a picture of the waterfront from it, and a lengthy description of the bridge and view at dusk (pp. 46–50).

36.28–29 for Coblentz] Boats from Cologne were better than those from Düsseldorf with no sleeping accommodations or restrictions on overcrowding. First- and second-class cabins differed little. The time to Coblenz was about eight hours upstream (five hours return). Whatever "grand sight" M saw at night, the major Rhine scenery commenced only after about twenty miles, near Bonn.

37.1 *Rudenshimer*(?)] M's question mark indicates his uncertainty about the spelling of "Rüdesheimer."

37.8 *"Giant Hoff"*] The Geant Hof, nearest to the boat landing, was described by Murray as "very good and moderate"; beds were fifteen to twenty-one silver groschen; breakfast, twelve; table d'hôte with wine, twenty-four.

37.9–10 Bridge of Boats] The ancient city of Coblenz stands in the southwest angle of the confluence of the Rhine and Moselle rivers; as at Cologne, a bridge laid over linked barges crossed the Rhine. Murray remarked, "No town on the Rhine surpasses Coblenz in the beauty of its situation," and "the views from the centre of the bridge of boats" and other sites "are all fine" (*Continent*, p. 279).

Ehrenbreitstein

37.10 fortress] By the Treaty of Vienna, Coblenz had been awarded to Prussia, becoming the capital of its Rhenish provinces, not least because it was the great fortified center toward the French border. The greatest fortification was Ehrenbreitstein, atop a four-hundred-foot, precipitous ridge opposite the junction of the rivers. Reduced to ruin by the French, it was being enormously rebuilt by the Prussians. Murray called it the most interesting object in the vicinity for both its majestic towering appearance from below and the magnificent vistas it gave from above. Mayhew pictured it (reproduced opposite) and devoted a four-page description to " 'the Gibraltar of the Rhine' " and its site (*Rhine*, pp. 226–30). Entry, by way of a long, fortified roadway slanting up the face of the rock, required a permit from the commandant, but with a passport this was easily secured by a valet de place. M's association here in 1849 of the Quebec citadel (visited on his 1847 honeymoon) and this fortress is repeated in his description (written in 1850–51) of Father Mapple's lofty pulpit as "his little Quebec" and, with its Bible, as "a self-containing stronghold—a lofty Ehrenbreitstein, with a perennial well of water within the walls" (*Moby-Dick*, chap. 8, p. 39). In 1852 he developed in *Pierre* the "curious" paradox he noted here, juxtaposing wine and guns: "As the vine flourishes, and the grape empurples close up to the very walls and muzzles of cannoned Ehrenbreitstein; so do the sweetest joys of life grow in the very jaws of its perils" (bk. 4, chap. 2; p. 69). In *Clarel*, 4.18.1–7, he called three mountain-top convents massed about the Church of the Nativity in Bethlehem "an Ehrenbreitstein."

37.14 half Italian] Coblenz, like Cologne, had been a principal city on the old trade route to Italy; two interesting old churches were St. Castor, founded by Charlemagne's son Louis, at the confluence of the rivers, whose oldest parts showed the first signs of Lombard style in the Rhineland, and the Liebfrauenkirche, its oldest parts dating from 1259 and displaying Romanesque towers. Mayhew writes of the "old and new towns pinnacled with their many quaint steeples—the rude, bell-shaped spires of St. Florin—the bulbous mosque-like tops of those of the *Liebfrauen-Kirche* . . . seeming almost like a bit of turner's work—and the slated domes of the squat, round towers of the Priests'-house, looking in the distance like helmeted giants in their suits of mail—and the square turrets of *St. Castor*, with their low steeples, like crayon points, standing between the streams" (*Rhine*, pp. 220–21).

37.15 bridge . . . Metternich] The fourteen high arches of the bridge across the Moselle dated from the fourteenth century: "It is in this quarter of the town, too, that the most antiquated and interesting buildings of Coblenz are to be found: the 'Metternicher-hof,' or 'Stammhaus' (family-house) of the late Austrian prime-minister, is close at hand, though the house itself has little remarkable about it, for it is merely a large, plain, pea-green-coloured building, with the words 'METTERNICHER-HOF' worked in the iron ties outside the front walls" (Mayhew, *Rhine*, p. 223). Prince Metternich (1773–1859), wily diplomat, Austrian chancellor, and master of the reactionary Congress of Vienna, had fled Vienna for England in the Revolutions of 1848, and had just returned to Brussels in October of 1849.

37.20 German officers] "Nor are the *tables d'hôte* themselves without their sprinkling of officers; the hat-stand in the corner of the room is covered with their helmets, and their swords occupy the place usually devoted to the umbrellas. You will generally find one entire wing of the dinner-table particoloured with the Prussian uniforms, for the officers dine all together, and, according to the popular report, make sad havoc with the fare" (Mayhew, *Rhine*, p. 233; he goes on to describe their eating habits, their manners, and in a page-long, small-print footnote, their smart appearance contrived with very low pay, and their ubiquity—"the country is overrun with troops like rats in a barn").

37.24 "Governor of Coney Island"] Humorous sobriquet of Guilbert Davis, a wine merchant, as identified in EMM, which quotes two books by acquaintances of M. The *Reminiscences of Richard Lathers* (New York: Grafton Press, 1907) lists him as "the popular Guilbert Davis, called by his sporting friends 'Governor of Coney Island' " (pp. 38–39). Lathers and M's brother Allan were married to Thurston sisters, whose family were intimate neighbors of Davis on socially select Bond Street in New York City. (For Lathers see also the discussion at 139.1–20.) Lathers refers to Davis's knowing M in Evert Duyckinck's congenial basement literary gatherings (1847–50), and to his own visits, as a Pittsfield neighbor, with M at Arrowhead in the 1860's (*Reminiscences*, pp. 61, 328–29, 407). Dr. Gardner tells of encountering Davis in the Jardin des Plantes in Paris among the exotic mounted birds, "looking equally sharp, a representative of the American Eagle—the 'Governor of Coney Island,' who says 'I am the Governor of Coney Island—probably as well known, as any man in New-York. I've been to Europe fifteen times, Spain five, Russia six, England nine times, and traveled more in France, than any man, that ever lived. Poh! these things are nothing; in Rome they are twice as fine; I have just come from there; I am a wine merchant, that's why I travel so much. . . . ' and thus he went on without interruption, occasionally deigning to look over his spectacles" (*Old Wine*, p. 257).

38.12–13 Drachenfells . . . Nuns] M omits most scenic Rhine sites between Coblenz and Bonn but names these imposing downriver ones. Rising precipitously from the east bank, the several volcanic peaks, cones, and ridges collectively known as the Siebengebirge (though more than seven) include Drachenfels nearest the river, the lair of the dragon slain by Siegfried in the epic *Nibelungenlied*. Slightly upriver on the west bank, the rocky eminence of Rolandseck opposed to Drachenfels makes the "portal" to the upper Rhine; the castle ruins and desolate arch atop the ridge make a striking scene from the river. In eponymous legend Charlemagne's nephew Roland stood vigil here for his lost betrothed, who believing him dead had taken the veil in the nunnery of Nonnenwerth on the island. Mayhew (*Rhine*, p. 160) mentions but disparages the opinion of Americans who liken Hudson to Rhine river scenery, whereas M here prefers the Hudson.

38.16 Steinberger] From the celebrated twelfth-century vineyards of the (suppressed) Cistercian Abbey of Eberbach in the Rhinegau; like the Rüdesheimer M had sampled earlier, it was one of the premier wines of the region.

38.20 presents] M listed as "Curios" purchased in Cologne (see 146.15) porcelain stoppers for which he paid two and a half groschen (sixpence). One of these he gave to Evert Duyckinck: "Do not despise it—there is a sermon in it. Shut yourself up in a closet, insert the stopper into a bottle of Sour Claret, & then study that face" (*Letters*, p. 103 [Feb. 2, 1850]).

38.26 whole] No noun follows (apparently omitted in starting a new notebook page; cf. the discussion at 11.11).

38.31 antique gate-way] The Eigelstein Thor in the remains of the twelfth-century north wall, outside of which was the station.

38.33 Aix la Chapelle] After Napoleon's defeat Charlemagne's northern capital had been awarded to the Prussians, as Aachen, and was being extensively rebuilt. The "town-house" or city hall (Rathaus or Hôtel de Ville) in the center was a fourteenth-century structure. The nearby cathedral embodied both a lofty fourteenth-century choir and much of the ninth-century octagonal "chapel" built by Charlemagne for his tomb. The tomb had been twice opened: his throne there was now in the gallery, his skull and a legbone were shown among the relics in the sacristy, and his other bones had just been rediscovered (1847) in a chest.

39.2–8 ride to Ostend . . . arrived at Dover] The train trip from Brussels to Ostend took about six hours. The Channel crossing from Ostend was recommended as shortest, sixty-three miles, with steamers daily in four to five hours; passage in the forecabin, ten shillings.

39.9 "The Gun"] The Gun Hotel, Shorn Street, listed as cheap and tolerably good (*A Handbook for Travellers in Kent and Sussex* [London: Murray, 1858]), advertised itself as next door to the Custom House, near the landing for the Ostend Mail Packets, and only a minute's walk from the railroad station.

39.11 "Anastasius"] A monotonously long but popular picaresque novel (1819) by Thomas Hope (1770?–1831) about a ruthless Greek adventurer in the Levant. The two-volume edition M had bought in Paris for "about" four francs (Sealts 281, probably the Baudry edition; see 146.4) was confiscated by customs because of the 1842 restrictions on foreign editions of English books. Later, in London, Bentley gave M John Murray's two-volume 1836 edition—doubtless after M told him this tale of woe—perhaps when they dined on December 18, or perhaps on the twentieth when M saw him again and noted getting "some books out of him"; but the date M put in both volumes with his signature was December 19, when they did not meet (HCL-M; Sealts 282; Bercaw 372). EMM (p. 143) points out passages interesting for their "suggestiveness in relation to the writing of *Moby Dick*," about ceremonies consecrating brotherhood and about the Ramadan and its fasting.

39.12–13 train for London] A distance of eighty-eight miles; at Ashford (twenty-one miles) the line became the one M had previously traversed from Canterbury.

39.18 Rogers] See the entry for December 20 (44.29–32, and accompanying discussion), when M has the first of two breakfasts with the old poet.

39.22 Belvoir Castle] The castle (pronounced "Beever") was close to the border (on the Leicestershire side) between Lincolnshire and Leicestershire, a hundred miles north of London, and had been rebuilt after a fire in 1816. M would have seen one of the finest private picture galleries in England. (See the discussions at 21.30–31 and 22.5.) M's writing first "M^{r}" then "The Duke of" before "Rutland" was perhaps a deliberate assertion of the democratic principles that all along flavor this journal, as in his account of Murray's dinner party on November 23. His tone and implications in the journal are best caught in Lewis Mumford's paraphrase, recounting the London visit (*Herman Melville* [New York: Harcourt, Brace, 1929], pp. 119–31).

39.30 wrote . . . Allan] See the discussion at 40.9–11.

39.35 "Powell Papers"] For Powell, see the discussion at 7.25. Under the heading "A Scoundrel Branded" the *New-York Tribune* for November 20 carried a long quotation from a letter by Charles Dickens to Lewis Gaylord Clark, the editor of the *Knickerbocker Magazine* and longtime opponent of M's friends Evert Duyckinck and Cornelius Mathews. Too impatient to wait for the December issue of his magazine, Clark was rushing into print Dickens's exposure of Powell as a forger and a thief who had fled England to avoid prosecution. The publication of this sensational article in the *Tribune* led to a flurry of attacks on Powell and on Mathews (who was implicated by Powell's praise of him in his chapter on Dickens in *Living Authors of*

America), and led to legal retaliation by Powell (he charged several newspaper editors with libel and had one or two of them arrested) and eventually to his use of the scurrilous *New York Herald* as a forum for his self-vindication and for an attack on Irving and Melville. See the NN *Moby-Dick*, pp. 606–10. Allan probably accompanied the November 20 article from the *Tribune* with some early responses to it, and may have included some attacks on Powell's book which antedated the publication of Dickens's exposé.

40.4 Foster] Though M misspells the name, this is John Forster (1812–76), since 1833 the chief literature and drama critic for the *Examiner*, who lived in "well-known chambers at 58 Lincoln's Inn Fields" (*DNB*). (Forster complained that his lifelong effort to get his name spelled with the medial *r* imperfectly succeeded—footnote to Chapter 5 of his Dickens biography, *The Life of Charles Dickens*, 3 vols. [London: Chapman & Hall, 1872–74].) A lawyer, scholar, biographer, intimate with distinguished literary and intellectual men, now best known as Dickens's intimate friend and biographer. Had M accepted Forster's breakfast invitation, for Sunday, December 23 (see December 21, 46.3–5), he would have encountered his loud voice and authoritarian manner, but might have divined his underlying honesty, tenderness, tolerance, and generosity. We are not told who wrote M's letter of introduction to him; surely not Powell, and not Willis, whom Forster scorned almost as much as Lockhart did. (M listed Forster's address, 148.27).

40.5 Mrs: Daniel] The mother-in-law of the New York bookseller Charles Welford (see the discussion at 21.21). She lived at an address in Lincoln's Inn Fields (see the entry for December 16), near, it seems, to the Royal College of Surgeons, No. 40, which housed an extensive museum of anatomical preparations, human, animal, and paleontological, and which M's elliptical sentence may mean he also visited. Possibly her husband was George Daniel (1789–1864), miscellaneous writer, devoted book collector, and close friend of Charles Lamb, whose books Welford purchased from Moxon (see the discussion at 23.3). In the letter M sent this same day to Evert Duyckinck (December 14; see 40.9–11 and accompanying discussion), M wrote: "I this morning did myself the pleasure of calling on Mrs: Daniel for the first. I saw her, & also two very attractive young ladies. Had you seen those young ladies, you would have never told Mrs: Duycknk of it. You must on no account tell Mrs Welford of this; for those nymphs were her sisters" (*Letters*, p. 96). For M's subsequent visit the following evening (December 15), see the December 16 entry, 41.13–18.

40.8–9 "Independence"] See 42.27–28 and accompanying discussion.

40.9–11 Thence . . . Judge] Of these five letters, according to *Letters* only the one to Duyckinck (No. 69) is known to survive; an excerpted paragraph of the one to Willis (No. 70) was printed in his *Home Journal*, January 12, 1850 (see the discussion on Willis at 22.2 and pp. 618–20); of the ones to ESM, Allan, and Lemuel Shaw there is no trace (Nos. 324, 325, and 326 on the "Check List of Unlocated Letters," *Letters*, p. 312).

40.13–14 Kean . . . Jerrold] Charles John Kean (1811?-68), son of the famous Edmund Kean, began his career as a child. By 1847 he had been in America three times. His spectacular productions were more notable than his acting, which was marred by many mannerisms, a harsh voice, and an inflexible presence. Both Forster and Lewes found things to praise in his performance but on the whole were severe (see *Dramatic Essays*, pp. 41–48, 107–12, and *passim; On Actors*, pp. 12–22). His wife, Ellen Tree (1805–80, m. 1842), acted in many companies, worked with Fanny Kemble, and was reputed competent. The Keans commonly played Mondays, Wednesdays, and Fridays; this Friday evening Kean played Sidney Maynard, Buckstone acted Simon Box, and Mrs. Kean the part of Felicia. Jerrold's play was followed by *The Wonder, Box and Cox*, and *Who's My Husband*. (Theaters had just reopened after the funeral of the Dowager Queen Adelaide the previous day.) For M's earlier viewing of the Jerrold play on November 5, see 13.12–15 and accompanying discussion; for his earlier evening at the Haymarket when Macready, Buckstone, and Wallack also acted, see the entry for November 19, 22.12–17, and accompanying discussions.

40.19 Holywell Street] A narrow lane now demolished but then opening off the east end of the Strand, at the church of St. Clement Dane's. Sir Walter Besant (*London North of the Thames* [London: Black, 1911], p. 329) has a drawing of it and regrets the disappearance of this "survival of old London" and its "picturesquely old" houses "with pointed gables." In 1855 Hawthorne described it as "a narrow lane, filled up with little bookshops and bookstalls, at some of which I saw sermons and other works of divinity, old editions of the classics, and all such serious matters; while, at stalls and windows close beside them (and, possibly, at the same stalls) there were books with title pages displayed, indicating them to be of the most abominable kind" (*ENB*, p. 248). It was notorious for the sale of pornography and other "low publications" (Wheatley, *London Past and Present*, II, 228; Mayhew, *London Labour*, IV, 210). It was one of the addresses of the prolific concocter, publisher, and purveyor of pornography William Dugdale (Steven Marcus, *The Other Victorians* [New York: Basic Books, 1966], p. 74), along with others who put out the "latest hair-raising episodes concocted by Holywell Street hacks" (Richard D. Altick, *The English Common Reader* [Chicago: University of Chicago Press, 1957], p. 5). (See also Marcus, p. 98, for a quotation from the anonymous Victorian memoirs *My Secret Life*, describing this street and its use by doxies "to relieve their bladders.")

40.20 Rosseau's Confessions] *Confessions* (1781, 1788), by Jean Jacques Rousseau (1712–78). M includes this book on his acquisitions list (144.15), an English translation, as shown by a quotation from its second volume among his "Memoranda of things on the voyage" (142.15–16). The edition is not identified by Sealts (429); see Bercaw 590.

40.21 "Knight's London"] This work, titled simply *London*, was both edited and published (1841–44) by Charles Knight (1791-1873), whom M will meet on December 23 (see the discussion at 46.21). It is a collection of discursive essays by various writers on subjects ranging from aspects of historical London to contemporary shops and advertising, illustrated by 650 wood engravings, and issued first in 150 parts then in six volumes, octavo. In his book list (144.13) M notes the set he bought as in three volumes, octavo, costing him one pound and ten shillings. Sealts (312) locates no three-volume edition before 1851 (Bohn); but the six-volume set issued (not rebound or reprinted) in three volumes was offered for sale at the price M paid as early as 1847 in Bohn's ("remainder") catalogue, which does not state whether with Knight's imprint or Bohn's (as later, e.g., 1851, reprinted). (See Bercaw 422.) For visitors to the 1851 exposition Knight revised and condensed the work into the one-volume *Cyclopædia of London*, frequently cited in these discussions.

40.26 Arcade] "Burlington Arcade, Piccadilly, is a covered avenue, upwards of 200 yards in length, with elegant shops on each side, fitted up with great taste. . . . It is lighted by gas; and in an evening presents a brilliant appearance" (*Cruchley's Picture of London*, p. 188). It was also, like Regent

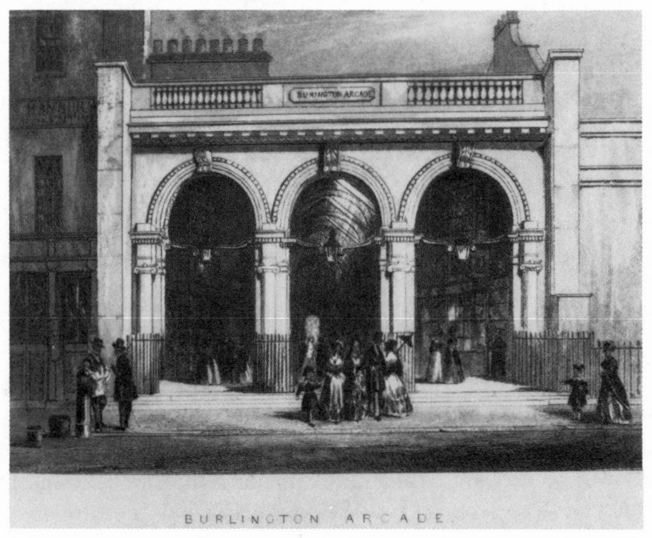

BURLINGTON ARCADE.

Street, the haunt of the better class of prostitutes, especially in the afternoon (Mayhew, *London Labour*, IV, 217, 251; see the discussion at 23.24). The reproduction above is from *Tallis's Illustrated London*, I, facing p. 154.

40.28 "The University bread trencher"] On M's last day in London (December 24, 47.19) he bought another for his wife's stepmother, Hope Savage Shaw, which he sent her from New York via her son in February of 1850 with a note: "I am sure you will not refuse to gratify me, by accepting a little present which Sammie brings with him. . . . It is called a 'University Bread Trencher' and has recently been generally introduced among English families. Some three or four centuries ago this article was used in the University Dining Halls. So that the present fashion is only the revival of a very ancient one. . . . Samuel will instruct you more particularly touching the mode of using it" (*Letters*, p. 104).

40.35–41.1 arrangement . . . March] For the contract arrangement see pp. 176–77. Apparently Bentley published *White-Jacket* on February 1, 1850, seven weeks in advance of its New York publication; beginning the next day, reviews in London were mostly favorable (see the NN edition, pp. 429ff.).

41.4 Wise's book] Henry A. Wise (1819–69) was an American naval lieutenant, the first of whose several books had just been published by Baker & Scribner (1849) in New York under the pseudonym Harry Gringo: *Los Gringos; or, An Inside View of Mexico and California, with Wanderings in Peru, Chili, and Polynesia.* It is not clear why Melville spoke (or what he said) about the book to Bentley, who by mid-January of 1850 published it although another (apparently authorized) English edition had already appeared (*Log*, I, 362 [Jan. 19]). Sealts (559a) locates no copy belonging to M. The book was Wise's own disgusted account of Polynesian life, with his view that it had benefited from missionaries, "progress," and justifiable French occupation, a view antithetical to M's. Despite this, Wise paid "the faint tribute of my own individual admiration to Mr. Melville," adding: "Apart from the innate beauty and charming tone of his narratives [i.e., *Typee* and *Omoo*], the delineations of Island life and scenery, from my own personal observation, are most correctly and faithfully drawn" (p. 398). Wise then gave a report (pp. 398–99) of his inquiries around Tahiti about M and real-life people in his books, including Fayaway and a baby of hers—too young to be M's. Many years later (1886 or 1887), M himself told a fanciful barbershop tale about recognizing a year-and-a-half-old "son" at Nuku Hiva—by the actual dates, only fifteen months after his one-month stay there in the summer of 1842 (see Merton M. Sealts, Jr., "Additions to *The Early Lives of Melville*," *Melville Society Extracts*, No. 28 [November, 1976], 12). Possibly M had met Wise through Willis or Duyckinck, both of whose journals reviewed Wise's book, but the connection remains unclear.

41.20 Tristam Shandy] M omits here the second *r* from "Tristram" in the title of the great novel (1760–67) by Laurence Sterne (1713–68), and the name was printed that way both in *Israel Potter*, in a passage (chap. 13, p. 82) remarking that a "good-natured English clergyman" wrote this book, and in "Cock-A-Doodle-Doo!" (*Harper's New Monthly Magazine*, December, 1853; see below). While M's book list does not include any copy he bought in London (see p. 144), and Sealts (490) records only this unidentified copy among M's owned or borrowed books, M must have read deeper into the work in coming months, for its influence on *Moby-Dick* has often been noted (see Bercaw 670) and is unmistakable in the last paragraph of Chapter 26, upon which Luther S. Mansfield and Howard Vincent comment: "Much of the latter half of this paragraph would seem to be Melville's transmutation for his serious purpose of the comic invocation in . . . Book 9, chap. 25" (Hendricks House edition [New York, 1952], p. 665). In "Cock-A-Doodle-Doo!" the same passage seems to be involved when the narrator tries to read his impatient creditor "a fine joke about my Uncle Toby and the Widow Wadman," one that must be about her concern over the sexual mutilation he—like Ahab—has possibly suffered (see the NN *Piazza Tales* volume, pp. 272–73, and the discussion on p. 695 in that volume).

41.21 Hotel de Sabloneire] See the discussion at 28.24.

41.24 my famed namesake] Henry Melvill (1798–1871), "the most popular preacher in London" (*DNB*), at this time principal of the East India College, and later chaplain to the queen and canon of St. Paul's. Some three years later he was described as tall, slightly bent, quite gray-haired, "his face strongly marked by benevolence and thought," with "high cheekbones and a large mouth" (Prime, *Travels*, I, 112). His leanings were evangelical, his style rapid, earnest, emphatic, but ornate. Commonly he spoke for three quarters of an hour. (EMM, p. 148, notes that the London *Times* just the day before, December 15, had carried a long account of the East India College and its preparation of young men going into missionary service to deal with "all the phases of Oriental vices and deceit, dissimulation and treachery.") The church, on Goswell Road (Pickwick's street), seems to have been of no particular distinction.

41.37 aristocracy] EMM notes (pp. 148–49): "Melville was enough interested to buy a book on the *Aristocracy of England*, of which he made use two years later in the opening book of *Pierre*, 'Pierre Just Emerging From His Teens.' He seems to have had an inherited interest in his own aristocratic strain, and a natural philosopher's curiosity about the 'preservation and beautifying influences of unfluctuating rank, health, and wealth.' Note that he wants to know what an aristocratic heritage does to human beings to affect the quality of their feeling and thinking—'what it really and practically is.' " Melville included a book of that title on his list of books acquired in London (144.28; see Sealts 288).

42.15 An article] In an extended note EMM (p. 149) identifies this as a letter "on Sunday-School Education" signed "Publicola," addressed to the editor of the *Weekly Dispatch* (December 16, 1849), and located by F. C. Francis of the British Museum. The writer of the letter uses the term "Sunday-School Education" only ironically, to describe the qualities of sectarian bigotry in much of what passed for national public education.

42.17 Steamer] Westbound, the usual route lay north of the eastbound one (avoiding the Gulf Stream), and against midwinter Atlantic gales the distance might be seven hundred miles more for a sailing ship (average time was thirty-five days; see p. 170). By regular Cunard steamer service between Liverpool and New York (from 1848 on), however, one could cross in less than half the time of a sailing packet (Albion, *Square-Riggers*, p. 258).

42.27 "Independence"] This sailing ship had been launched in New York in 1834 for service on the Liverpool route but transferred to the London-Portsmouth, Red Swallowtail line in 1847. It measured 732 tons, was 140 feet long, with a 32-foot beam, and undoubtedly had two decks. In the demise of sailing packets, it was retired in 1852. The regular departure dates were advertised as from London on the sixth, thirteenth, twenty-first, and twenty-eighth, and from Portsmouth on the first, eighth, sixteenth, and twenty-fourth of every month (see, e.g., *New York Journal of Commerce*, October 6, 1849). Captain Artemas T. Fletcher (M's "R. J" at 141.1 is mistaken), born in Charlestown, Massachusetts, about 1814, generally commanded another ship, but he had begun as first mate of the *Independence* in 1840 (Albion, *Square-Riggers*, pp. 278–79, 282–83, 298, and 335). Because of the rigors of the westbound winter passage, more travelers were taking the steamers, and a packet might be nearly empty of cabin passengers—the packets therefore began carrying more and more emigrants steerage. Westbound, the shortest time of the *Independence* was twenty-six days, its longest, forty-nine, and its average, thirty-four. This crossing was to take thirty-six days.

42.27–28 old ship . . . small . . . ancient] The same adjectives occur in the description of the *Pequod*: "She was a ship of the old school, rather small if anything. . . . Her ancient decks were worn and wrinkled" (*Moby-Dick*, chap. 16, p. 69). See also the discussions at 13.6 and 35.26–27.

42.37 National Gallery] On his two prior visits (November 8, 14.13–14—see the accompanying discussion—and November 12, 16.29), M singled out nothing for mention. Though the gallery had a few fine paintings, critical observers considered it shamefully deficient as a national collection: "The building in Trafalgar Square, in the western wing of which the national collection of pictures is deposited . . . is universally condemned as inelegant in itself, and unworthy of its purpose. The rooms, too, are small and ill-lighted, and hardly sufficient for even the present scanty collection; altogether, indeed, the National Gallery is a discredit to the nation" (*Knight's Cyclopædia*, p. 724). The writer conceded, however, that Rembrandt was "nobly represented" by not less than six paintings, some among his best. Two of the portraits were once thought to be of Jews: that of the rabbi, so-called, is now labeled *Man in a Cap*, though possibly the model was Jewish; the other (part of the Beaumont collection) variously known as "Portrait of a Jew" or of a "Jew Merchant," is now only doubtfully attributed to Rembrandt and labeled *A Seated Man*. EMM (p. 151) quotes the 1847 catalogue: "A very powerful representation of an unpolished wealthy individual. The rough features, the grizzly beard and warm fur cap [make for] a sort of savage dignity." EMM also quotes its descriptions of the Gaddi paintings (but in later catalogues the attribution was merely to the school of Taddeo Gaddi, himself the Florentine pupil of Giotto: two apparently companion paintings of various saints may have been the wings of an altarpiece; the modern catalogue no longer lists them). Not mentioned by M was a painting by Guido Reni (now considered a copy) that he mock seriously criticized in *Moby-Dick*: "Guido's picture of Perseus rescuing Andromeda from the sea-monster or whale" (chap. 55, p. 261). The painter of "Murder of the Innocents" was not Reni but Raphael; this work (apparently a fragment of a cartoon for a tapestry) was at this time generally believed to be by Raphael and to be part of the *Acts of the Apostles* (so *Knight's London*, VI, 246, and Richard Cattermole, *The Book of Raphael's Cartoons* [London: Bohn, 1845], pp. 12, 19, 20), which M had seen at Hampton Court (see the discussion at 16.17–18). According to the director of the Berlin Royal Gallery at the time, the series from the life of Christ was apparently started by Raphael but the three-part *Murder of the Innocents* was executed by Giulio Romano (Dr. [Gustav F.] Waagen, *Treasures of Art in Great Britain*, trans. Lady Eastlake, 3 vols. [London: Murray, 1854], II, 406–7). But for a long time no such work has been listed in the gallery's catalogues under Raphael, Reni, or Romano.

43.1 Vernon Gallery] Formed in 1847 by the gift of Robert Vernon (1774–1849), who had made a fortune in the Napoleonic Wars, the collection included more than 150 British works by, among others, Hogarth, Gainsborough, Reynolds, Lawrence, Landseer, and Constable; it was to become a substantial basis for the National Gallery (where M visited it in 1857—see 128.10 and accompanying discussion) but was still in Vernon's Pall Mall residence at this time.

43.6 pocket Shakspeare] Edition and titles unidentified by Sealts (463). M's book list includes "2 plays of Shakspeare" costing him two pence (144.17). M's spelling of the name varies in his letters and other manuscripts; here it agrees with that adopted in the title and introduction of his surviving set of *The Dramatic Works* (Sealts 490); see the NN *Moby-Dick*, pp. 955–57. Cf. the discussion at 129.8–9.

43.9–10 letter for a Duke] No. 327 on the "Check List of Unlocated Letters," *Letters*, p. 312.

43.15–16 maps of London] The one M bought is unidentified by Sealts (330a); it is listed as "Old Map of London (1766.) 3.6" among M's London acquisitions (144.22). This entry is the unique evidence that M had already found and considered making literary use of the little book *Life and Remarkable Adventures of Israel R. Potter* (Providence, 1824), which was the basis for his *Israel Potter*, first serialized in *Putnam's Monthly Magazine* (July, 1854–March, 1855) then published by Putnam (1855). The copy of the *Life* now in HCL-M, as noted by Sealts (407), is not M's original copy (see the NN *Israel Potter*, pp. 277–85, and its reproduction of the *Life*, pp. 286–394).

43.18–19 Chatterton . . . Guzman] This set of *The Poetical Works of Thomas Chatterton*, in two volumes (Cambridge: Grant, 1842), is now in the Berg Collection of the New York Public Library (Sealts 137); M marked both volumes (EMM quotes examples) and wrote in the first (after his name with "London Dec 19. 1849"): "Bought at a dirty stall there, and got it bound near by." Sealts (9) does not identify the edition of Mateo Aleman's *Guzman de Alfarache*—a Spanish picaresque romance first translated into English as *The Rogue* (1622). Both works are on M's book list (144.20–21), where the cost given for *Guzman* is not two but three shillings. (See Bercaw 6 and 132.)

43.21 "Redburn"] The review (presumably by Evert Duyckinck) appeared in the November 17 number, with wholly approving comments and extensive quotation from the book. Reprinted in Branch, *Melville: The Critical Heritage*, pp. 201–2. Hetherington, *Melville's Reviewers*, pp. 143–44, and EMM, pp. 153–54, quote much of it.

43.28 my reply] No. 328 on the "Check List of Unlocated Letters," *Letters*, p. 312.

43.33 "White Jacket"] By October 6 M had a "printed copy of the book" (possibly meaning proofs) in the American edition and its "plate-proofs, all ready to go into my trunk" (*Letters*, pp. 91–92); in this journal (18.5) he refers to these as "proof sheets." His late revisions on them and other differences between the American and English editions are discussed in the NN edition, pp. 408, 446–47.

44.3 Bell] Robert Bell (1800–1867), an Irishman active in London since 1828, an editor, biographer, novelist, and playwright. Bentley had just published his *Wayside Pictures through France, Belgium, and Holland* (1849). Later, he brought out annotated editions of the English poets, some of which (including his eight-volume Chaucer, 1854–56) M owned (see *Letters*, p. 252 [No. 208]; Sealts 56, 138, 139).

44.6 the comic man] Alfred H. Forrester (1804–72) shared the pseudonym "A. Crowquill" in illustrating his brother's—Charles Robert Forrester's—contributions to *Bentley's Miscellany*, 1840-41, and he also used it for his own popular children's books, burlesques, and sketches, many in early volumes of *Punch* and later in the *Illustrated London News*. For his design skills, he was long associated with staged pantomimes. In 1849 he had just written and illustrated *A Goodnatured Hint about California* (London: Bogue, 1849).

44.8 daughter . . . sons] Of the four Bentley sons, the third, George (1828–95), joined and succeeded his father in the business; in 1849 he had just returned from Rome, where he had witnessed the occupation by French troops. M's letter of June 27, 1850, to Bentley proposing the book that became *Moby-Dick* recalls this occasion (but not that the daughter was married): "I have not forgotten the very agreeable evening I spent in New-Burlington Street last winter. Pray, remember me to M[r] Bell & Alfred Crowquill when you see them. With compliments to Mrs Bentley and Miss Bentley" (*Letters*, p. 110).

44.13 Browne] Sir Thomas Browne (1605–82). M's reading of his works, borrowed in March of 1848 from Evert Duyckinck (to whom he spoke of Browne in *Religio Medici* as a kind of "crack'd Archangel," *Log*, I, 273 [March 18]), had conspicuously affected the style of *Mardi*, as it would that of *Moby-Dick*. Among M's memoranda on the homeward voyage is one recording an allusion to cannibals in Browne's "Vulgar Errors," which he was reading in his newly acquired volume (see 142.26–27 and accompanying discussion). In his book list M recorded this copy as "folio. 1686" (144.8); Sealts (90) identified it as *The Works* (4 pts. in 1 vol., London, 1686)—the first collected edition—the present location of M's copy is unknown. (See Bercaw 83.)

44.14 Boswell's Johnson] Sealts (84) lists this ten-volume set as possibly either the Murray printing of 1839 or the Bohn printing of 1848; both of these printings were from the plates of the original Murray 1835 eight-volume *Life* (edited by John Wilson Croker) and of his added two volumes of Johnsoniana (later in 1835, when Murray supplied new title pages for all ten volumes). It appears that by 1848 Bohn had taken over Murray's stock and plates; he subsequently issued some sets with mixed Murray/Bohn imprints. Whatever the imprints of M's ten-volume set, its contents were those of Murray's original 1835 edition and of all Murray and Bohn printings with later dates. (Bohn also issued in 1849 the eight-volume *Life,* from the same plates, in his Shilling Series.) M listed the set among books bought (144.7) and noted among his memoranda three passages that struck him as he browsed in the *Life* on the voyage home (see 142.17–19 and accompanying discussion). Several passages in *Moby-Dick* reflect his further reading in it. See annotations in the Mansfield-Vincent Hendricks House edition and Bercaw 72.

44.17 Atkinson] Doubtless the George Atkinson who in turn called at M's lodging on Sunday, December 23; he was presumably the barrister who, in an 1849 directory, had two addresses: 37 Gordon Square and 1 Inner Temple Lane at 16 Fleet St. This George Atkinson (1809–91) became a barrister of the Inner Temple in 1840 and was the author of legal treatises and most recently (1849–50) of *The Worthies of Westmoreland* (Boase, *Modern English Biography: Supplement* [Truro: Netherton & Worth, 1908]). M's connection with him is unknown but possibly came through Henry Stevens: in the late 1870's Stevens prepared a catalogue of the "Percival Library," property of a Mrs. George Atkinson, deceased (Parker, *Henry Stevens*, pp. 328–29).

44.19 Moore the apothecary] Partner in Moore & Illingworth, surgeons, 1 Arlington St. (EMM). Arlington Street runs south from Piccadilly, north of St. James's Place (see the following discussion and the discussion at 22.28). Moore seems to be the Edward D. Moore who attended the dying Gansevoort (*Log*, I, 213–14 [after May 6, 1846]; *Letters*, p. 30n.).

44.20 N° 1] No. 1, St. James's Place was Gansevoort's residence in London; he dates his diary from there a number of times as well as four of his letters to Murray, printed in Merrell R. Davis, *Melville's MARDI* (New Haven: Yale University Press, 1952), pp. 219–21. EMM identifies the address only as the Railway Coffee House, from an 1847 London directory.

44.22 Elm Court, Temple] Robert Francis Cooke's address (at No. 4) is on M's list (148.21). Strictly speaking, it was the address listed in an 1849 directory as that of William Henry Cooke, his brother; but Robert seems not to have been a barrister as suggested by M's portrayal of him in Part I of "The Paradise of Bachelors and the Tartarus of Maids" (see the next discussion and the discussion at 25.32). Charles Lamb's essay "The Old Benchers of the Inner Temple" describes his own childhood recollections of the Temple precincts (where he was born) and characterizes with whimsical affection a few of the old barristers who frequented the terrace then. "Benchers" were members of the governing bodies of the Inns of Court.

44.23 A set of fine fellows] Peter Cunningham (1816–69) had just compiled for Murray the two-volume *Handbook for London, Past and Present* (1849), a monumental collection of antiquarian lore, arranged in encyclopedia form. (The introduction by Michael Robbins to the reprint of the 1850 edition [East Ardsley: EP Publishing, 1978], pp. i–xiii, gives an account of Cunningham and the book.) All subsequent works on the city have been indebted to him (*DNB*). Chief clerk in the government audit office, he also edited many literary works and was involved in the controversy about the authenticity of Shakespeare's signature in the volume of Montaigne M saw in the British Museum on November 25 (30.3–4; see also the discussion at 29.37–30.1).

The grandfather of the Woodfall whom M met was Henry Sampson Woodfall (1739–1805), publisher of the *Public Advertiser*, in which the "Junius" letters (1769–72) scathingly attacked various public figures from a Whig point of view; "Woodfall's Junius," its author's identity a mystery, was long popular. Perhaps the grandson whom M met was Henry Dick Woodfall, also an eminent printer. "Comical" Mr. Rainbow (the adjective was subsequently heavily lined out) is not listed in contemporary city directories, but Boase's *Modern English Biography* lists J. M. Rainbow (1800–1853), an actuary for an insurance company. "Stone" was the brother-in-law of the painter Charles R. Leslie whom M met three days later, as M subsequently recalls (45.10–11; see also the accompanying discussion and the discussion at 46.24); he was probably Mrs. Leslie's brother Samuel, mentioned in Leslie's *Autobiographical Recollections* (ed. Tom Taylor [Boston: Ticknor & Fields, 1860], pp. 327, 336).

This occasion, fictionalized as to season (May), the bachelorhood of all nine partakers, and the profession of Robert Cooke, as well as amplified from other genial London dinners, became the basis of the first part of M's "The Paradise of Bachelors and the Tartarus of Maids." Though Robert Cooke's brother is not mentioned here (see the discussion at 44.22; also 44.35–36 and accompanying discussion), the pair are apostrophized in that piece: "if the having warm hearts and warmer welcomes, full minds and fuller cellars, and giving good advice and glorious dinners, spiced with rare divertisements of fun and fancy, merit immortal mention, set down, ye muses, the names of R. F. C. and his imperial brother" (NN *Piazza Tales* volume, p. 318). Presumably the actual menu was more or less the one recounted in the piece: from ox-tail soup through turbot, roast beef, mutton, turkey, chicken pie, and game fowl, to tarts and puddings, cheese and crackers, with claret, sherry, ale, port, and unnamed wines.

44.29 Rogers] Samuel Rogers (1763–1855), poet, banker, bachelor, wit, dilettante, and friend of leading figures, built and decorated his house with "exquisite taste" at 22 St. James's Place, looking out on Green Park.

His poems (written many years earlier) were elegantly conventional, but he was offered the laureateship (declined) on Wordsworth's death (he had written *Italy: A Poem*, from which are taken the illustrations on pp. 501 and 511 below). Privately, he was generous and kind: he had helped Moxon (his publisher) set up in business; but in public he could be quite formidable, as Sir Henry Holland, whom M had met at Murray's, described:

> Wealthy, unmarried, highly cultivated in all matters of literature and art, his conversation seasoned with anecdote and personal sarcasms uttered in a curious sepulchral voice, he gained and kept a higher place than his poetry alone would have procured for him. . . . In society his most severe sarcasms were often hidden under honeyed phrases. . . . He . . . [was] intolerant to all that presented itself in social rivalry to himself. The usurpation by others of talk at a dinner table, or an interruption to one of his own anecdotes, was sure to provoke some access of bitterness bitterly expressed. These feelings increased with increasing age. They were somewhat curiously modified in the distrust with which he latterly regarded his own memory—rarely venturing upon an anecdote without a *caveat* as to his having told it before. (*Recollections of Past Life* [New York: Appleton, 1872], pp. 208–9)

Sometime after 1862 in his copy of Hazlitt's *Lectures on the English Poets* (bound with Sealts 263b, p. 177), M annotated a derogatory comment on Rogers: "This is pretty much all spleen. Rogers, tho' no genius, was a painstaking man of talent who has written some good things. 'Italy' is an interesting book to every person of taste. In Hazlitt you have at times to allow for indigestion" (quoted by permission of Frank H. Waring). Caroline Kirkland, into whose recent book M had looked on shipboard, described her experience: "The amenities of his house are so charming, that nobody has been able to be silent about them. A breakfast with him is among the much-coveted and long-remembered pleasures of the traveller. . . . We found Mr. Rogers in a quiet parlor, rich in gems of art from cornice to floor, and looking upon a garden. . . . Elegance has devised nothing beyond what we find at a London breakfast like this. The service, partly of gold, was altogether precious. . . . The refreshments, mingled with flowers, were delicate enough for Ganymede to have served" (*Holidays Abroad*, I, 75–77). Rogers's private collection of art was one of the finest in Europe. Murray's *Handbook for London* listed more than thirty of its paintings individually. His Turners may have especially interested M and in combination with others seem clearly to have influenced descriptive passages in *Moby-Dick* (see Robert K. Wallace, "The 'Sultry Creator of Captain Ahab': Herman Melville and J. M. W. Turner," *Turner Studies*, V [Winter, 1985], 2–20; for examples of Turner's work, see the illustrations on pp. 450, 468, 501, 511, and 519 below.). Among the "superb paintings" M saw were ones attributed to

Samuel Rogers's breakfast room

Claude, Giorgione, Reni, Veronese, Raphael, Rubens, Reynolds, and Gainsborough. When the collection was sold after Rogers's death in 1855, it brought fifty thousand pounds. This breakfast room, its walls crowded with paintings, is pictured above, from the *Illustrated London News*, January 5, 1856, p. 5.

44.33 got some books] Listed by M as so obtained are three copies of *Mardi* and two of *Redburn* (144.9–10), Hope's *Anastasius* in two volumes, William Godwin's *Caleb Williams*, William Beckford's *Vathek*, Mme. de Staël's *Corinne*, and Mary Shelley's *Frankenstein* (144.23–27). All except *Anastasius* were Bentley's own publications, as reported by Sealts (see 282, 225, 54, 486, and 467).

44.34–35 Erechtheum Club House] The house was "formerly the town depôt of Wedgewood's famous ware," in St. James's Square, at the corner of York Street; the club was notable for its scientific and literary membership and its good dinners (John Timbs, *Clubs and Club Life in London* [London: Chatto & Windus, [1872]], p. 260).

44.35–36 Cooke's brother] William Henry Cooke (1811–94) had been made a barrister in the Inner Temple in 1837 and took his Oxford M.A. in 1847. He later (1863) became a Bencher and Queen's Counsel. His writings were principally on legal and Temple history and antiquarian subjects (Boase, *Modern English Biography: Supplement).* See the discussions at 25.32 and 44.22.

44.37 Reform Club House] Organized in the 1830's by liberal members of Parliament at the time of the debate over the Reform Bills, the club's imposing new house on Pall Mall—in Italianate style by Sir Charles Barry, architect of the new Houses of Parliament—was considered the most palatial in London. When M gained admission on December 24 (see 47.15–18) with an order from Cooke (see 46.18–19), he noted the great two-story central hall with surrounding colonnades of twenty columns at each of the two levels. Cunningham advised the visitor to procure admission to some of these clubs, including the Reform, "famous for its central hall, and its kitchen planned by M. Soyer" (*Modern London*, p. xix).

44.37–38 Privy Gardens] These were the remaining three acres or so of the private grounds of old Whitehall Palace, between Whitehall and the Thames. Fronting the river was a row of houses, the middle one (No. 4) occupied by Sir Robert Peel (1788-1850) until his accidental death six months after M's visit. Americans at this time would know his effort to remove the grain duty to relieve the Irish famine, and M would know about his settling the Oregon question (in June of 1846, just before he resigned as Prime Minister), which had so agitated M's fiery nationalist brother Gansevoort before and during his brief London service.

44.38 New Houses of Parliament] After the 1834 fire gutted the old buildings, the new structure designed by Barry was begun in 1840; by 1849 the nine-hundred-foot river front had been completed, with most of the clock-tower and central tower but not the west side and the royal tower. "A strange medley this line of exterior here presents—bald looking Tudor architecture . . . —old decayed brick-work—wooden erections towering up, and running about in various directions—and over all the gorgeous architecture of the new pile gradually stretching forth its bulk" (*Knight's Cyclopædia*, p. 75). Since 1847 the House of Lords had been open to visitors on Wednesdays and Fridays, but trying to get in on a Thursday caused M's trouble and delay.

45.2 Tenniel] John Tenniel (1820–1914), later a *Punch* cartoonist and famous as the illustrator of Lewis Carroll's *Alice* books, was commissioned to do one of the frescoes in an upper waiting hall of scenes from British poets; M mentions three of the four then complete: Tenniel's *St. Cecilia*, J. R. Herbert's (1810–90) *Lear Disinheriting Cordelia*, and Charles Cope's (1811–90) *Griselda* from Chaucer.

45.7 Surrey Theater] At the south end of Blackfriars Road, beyond Blackfriars Bridge. It had a tradition, as an outlying theater, of circus-ring spectacles, melodrama, and pantomimes. What M's unwilling loss of time at the Houses of Parliament made him too late to see were the Christmas pantomimes, the most elaborate ones, with remarkable transformations, spectacular scenes, and marvelous stage effects. Forrester ("Crowquill"—see 44.6 and accompanying discussion), who was a principal designer and deviser of scenery and effects, no doubt meant to give M a behind-the-scenes view of the machinery. (EMM identifies the new pantomime in rehearsal as *The Moon Queen and King Night; or, Harlequin Twilight.*)

45.11 Leslie] M met the expatriate American painter two days later on December 22 (see 46.24 and accompanying discussion). As by not meeting Milnes and Forster, by not meeting Leslie earlier in his visit M missed his chance of introduction to a wide circle of interesting people. See Wallace, "Sultry Creator."

45.17 Miller] John Miller, listed in a directory of 1849 as an American bookseller and the "diplomatic despatch agent, American Legation, 26 Henrietta St., Covent Garden"; at the end of this journal M listed his address as Tavistock Street, Covent Garden (148.24), possibly his residence. M knew Miller's name earlier from dependence on the legation staff for assistance in the English publication of his books, after Gansevoort's death (see *Letters*, p. 58 [March 31, 1847]). In 1855 Miller served Hawthorne in an official capacity from Henrietta Street: "The business of forwarding despatches to America, and distributing them to the various legations and consulates . . . must be a pretty extensive one; for Mr. Miller has a large office, and two clerks in attendance" (*ENB*, p. 207).

45.18 White Jacket] The book was actually published on February 1; see the discussion at 40.35–41.1.

45.23 Cleaves] Though M misspells his name with a final *s*, this is surely J. J. Cleave, a barrister at 9 King's Bench Walk, Inner Temple, according to a directory of 1852; this address and the hour of M's appointment with him the next morning (eleven o'clock, Friday) are among the addresses at the end of the journal (148.25–26). He may have been at the previous night's dinner in the Temple: among the nine guests in the first part of "The Paradise of Bachelors and the Tartarus of Maids" was one "from 'No. ——, King's Bench Walk, Temple' " (NN *Piazza Tales* volume, p. 319). Or else M conflated these two dinners in that piece. In it he also incorporated the "mull of snuff" going "the rounds" (p. 323).

45.27 Library] Since Cleave's address was in the Inner Temple, the reference to manuscripts suggests that he took M to the Inner Temple library, much the better of the two Temple collections; it had an array of valuable manuscripts, "consisting of original letters from kings and queens of this country, diplomatists, foreign agents, and other distinguished personages" (H. H. L. Bellot, *The Inner and Middle Temple* [London: Methuen, 1902], p. 49). Conversely, the hall of the Middle Temple was more famous and interesting than that of the Inner Temple, which was small and poor imitation Gothic. The former hall, one of the best extant specimens of Elizabethan construction with its great hammer-beam ceiling, Knight called the most sumptuous as well as largest hall in the several Inns of Court. Hawthorne, in his account eight years later in 1857, was eloquent: "Truly, it is the most magnificent apartment that ever I stood within; very lofty, so lofty indeed that the antique oaken roof was quite hidden, as regarded all its details, in the sombre gloom that brooded under its rafters." After a lengthy description then of the paneling, the great painted windows, the screen and other furniture, he concludes: "I do hate to leave this hall without expressing how grave, how grand, how sombre, and how magnificent, I felt it to be" (*ENB*, p. 597). Eminent members of the Middle Temple had included Ralegh, John Ford, Clarendon, Evelyn, Burke, Sheridan, Blackstone, and Thomas Moore. Cunningham noted in his *Handbook for London* (1849) that many portraits of the Benchers were, however, "chiefly copies, and not very good" (p. 140). The tables were contemporaneous with the hall, those below the dais made from the timbers of Drake's *Golden Hind*.

45.30 New Hall] Hawthorne, also in a gloomy December (1857), wrote: "We gained admission into the noble Hall, which is modern (finished only some ten or twelve years ago) but built in antique style, and as stately and beautiful an interior as ever I beheld; the most so, indeed, it seems to me, . . . with its lofty oaken roof, its panelled walls, with the windows high above, and the great arched window at one end, full of painted coats of arms, which the light glorifies in passing through" (*ENB*, p. 607). The library, built at the same time and in the same Tudor Gothic style, was only a little smaller; the huge kitchen beneath the hall (forty-five ft. square and twenty ft. high) was vaulted and pillared like a crypt.

45.32 the courts] Out of term time, the old hall was used for sittings of the lord chancellor—and Dickens's infamous Court of Chancery in *Bleak House*; the two vice chancellors' courts occupied a square of buildings adjoining the Chancery Lane gatehouse. The "old fellow nearly asleep" was Charles Pepys (1781–1851), earl of Cottenham, who had been elevated to the peerage on assuming the chancellorship. He had resigned the office after failing to reform the harshest features of the old system, and after his reappointment in 1846 was in failing health and frequently absent; he again resigned in 1850, just before major reforms began in 1852. The famous opening installment of *Bleak House* was to appear in March of 1852.

45.34 Rolls' Court] The Master of the Rolls sat in the buildings across Chancery Lane when not in term at Westminster. (The site is now occupied by the Public Record Office.) His jurisdiction was much the same as the lord chancellor's. At this time the master was Henry Bickersteth (1783–1851), Baron Langdale, who was admitted to the bar from the Inner Temple in 1811. He succeeded Cottenham as Master of the Rolls when the latter first became lord chancellor; he too was much interested in law reform, and had the highest reputation for patience, painstaking care, impartiality, and sound reasoning. What the "strange story" Cleave (apparently) told M may have been is problematic, since he was known for a most admirable public and private character.

46.4 declined] No. 329 on the "Check List of Unlocated Letters," *Letters*, p. 312.

46.6–7 Blue Posts] Davidson wrote two days later (December 24) to George Duyckinck an account of both his earlier (see the discussion at 30.7) and recent evenings with M: "The second evening was at the Blue Posts for the entire thing commencing on beefsteaks and ending on empty pitchers, or in other words from six till half past eleven—damages—paid by Melville 14/2 sterling. We asked each other in the small smoking room—which we had to ourselves with a fine fire—Where,—said he—Where—said I—where said we bothe to gether—where in America can you find such a place to dine and punch as this?" (NYPL-D).

46.11 my money] See p. 177.

46.12 "The Opium Eater"] Listed by M as "Confessions of an Opium Eater" (144.32). The edition of Thomas De Quincey's *Confessions of an English Opium-Eater* (1822) is not identified by Sealts (180). In all, four "editions" (i.e., printings) of the same text and pagination (206 pp.) had been issued in London (1822, two in 1823, 1826), plus a different cheap fifth edition (1845, 49 pp.) in Smith's Standard Library; M's copy was most likely from one of the first (textually identical) four. In any event, this first version was relatively short, originally two magazine articles; the more familiar 1856 edition was considerably expanded and revised. M alludes once to the book in his shipboard "Memoranda" (142.13). Influences upon several passages in *Moby-Dick* and *Pierre* have been suggested (e.g., in notes to the Hendricks House editions of *Moby-Dick* [New York, 1952] and *Pierre* [New York, 1949]; see Bercaw 203). See 142.13, "crocodile", and the accompanying discussion.

46.14 Baring Brothers] The firm's address was at 8 Bishopsgate. Hawthorne described the edifice as an unmarked house, standing back from the street behind an iron fence (*ENB*, p. 256). Dana, entering, found himself in a "small room, plain and unpretending, where some dosen or more clerks were writing at enormous folio ledgers. This is the counting-room of the Barings. In the back-room . . . in a plain box, sat Mr. Russell Sturgis, to whom I presented my letter of credit. . . . Mr. Bates . . . came in from a small parlor. . . . In these plain rooms is done a money business unparalleled in America, and rarely equalled in Europe" (*Journal*, II, 717–18). Melville had dined with both these important bankers on November 24 (see 27.12–17 and the discussions at 27.12 and 23.1).

46.21 Charles Knight] Knight (1791–1873) throughout his career was an actively idealistic proponent of making good literature available inexpensively to the laboring classes. He was manager of what M means by "popular publications" for the Society for the Diffusion of Useful Knowledge (though by no means so utilitarian or self-deluded as many of its members) and brought out the Libraries of Useful Knowledge and of Entertaining Knowledge; he published the *Penny Magazine* and the *Penny Cyclopædia*. His considerable (and willing) losses on these ventures were partly offset by sales of works aimed at intelligent but not affluent readers (Altick, *English Common Reader*, pp. 282–83 and *passim*). M had just bought an edition of his *London* (see the discussion at 40.21) and unquestionably owned a set of the *Penny Cyclopædia*, as proved by his heavy use of its articles in his books from *Mardi* through *Moby-Dick* and in *Israel Potter* (see Bercaw 544). In Altick's judgment: "*His Passages of a Working Life* [3 vols., 1864–65] is one of the most readable and continuously interesting of Victorian autobiographies. It reveals him—and all contemporary evidence substantiates this impression—as an attractive person, energetic, idealistic (though without the stridency of the typical Victorian zealot), resilient (as he certainly had to be), and thoroughly in love with life" (*English Common Reader*, p. 281). He also shared the nineteenth-century enthusiasm for progress, industrial development, and the visible evidences of a materialistic ethos—an outlook increasingly uncongenial to M.

46.23 Ford] Richard Ford (1796–1858) was a scholar, amateur artist, and connoisseur whose famous Murray *Handbook for Spain* (1846) was so outspoken about religion and politics that its first edition had to be withdrawn. The *Times* obituary article said, "So great a literary achievement had never before been performed under so humble a title" (*DNB*). Ford may have been a guest at Cooke's dinner in the Temple, or, as suggested in the discussion at 44.23, M may have taken details from several dinners he attended: one of the nine guests in Part I of "The Paradise of Bachelors and the

Tartarus of Maids" "had lately returned from a trip to Old Granada, and, of course, was full of Saracenic scenery" (NN *Piazza Tales* volume, p. 321).

46.24 Leslie] See the discussion at 45.11. Charles Robert Leslie (1794–1859) was born in London of American parents, grew up in Philadelphia, returned to London in 1811 to study painting, and except for an unhappy winter as instructor at West Point, remained there the rest of his life. His paintings often depicted scenes from standard fiction, frequently humorous, at which he excelled. Tom Taylor (see the discussion at 24.9–10) edited Leslie's *Autobiographical Recollections* (1860), in which he described Leslie as "equable, affectionate, self-respecting to the point of reserve and reticence; valuing good taste and moderation as much in art as in manners; averse to exclusive theories or loud-sounding self-assertion in all forms" (p. xiv).

46.28 Rogers] For Rogers, see the discussion at 44.29, with illustration of the breakfast room on p. 369. Such literary breakfasts usually began at half past nine or at ten, and lasted for up to two hours, with enough guests for variety but not too many for general conversation (Harold G. Merriam, *Edward Moxon* [New York: Columbia University Press, 1939], p. 55). If the reason Rogers entertained M alone the first time (after their back-and-forth efforts at meeting) poses a question, why he invited M with the Procters and Kinglake this time does not. Likely he associated M as sea writer with "Barry Cornwall," Procter's pseudonym as author of his most popular poem "The Sea"—little knowing that in anonymously reviewing a realistic whaling-voyage narrative a couple of years earlier M had quoted that poem for ridicule (but also Byron's "Roll on, thou dark and deep blue ocean, roll!"): "Give ear, now, all ye shore-disdaining, ocean-enamored youths, who labor under the lamentable delusion, that the sea—the 'glorious sea' is always and in reality 'the blue, the fresh, the ever free!' Give ear to Mr J. Ross Browne, and hearken unto what that experienced young gentleman has to say about the manner in which Barry Cornwall has been humbugging the rising generation on this subject" (review of Browne's *Etchings of a Whaling Cruise*, in the *Literary World*, March 6, 1847; NN *Piazza Tales* volume, p. 208).

Bryan Waller Procter (1787–1874), barrister, commissioner of lunacy, and popular poet, especially admired for his lyrics as in *English Songs* (1832), was a schoolmate of both Byron and Sir Robert Peel and a friend of Leigh Hunt, Lamb (whose biography he wrote, 1866), and Dickens. The pseudonym "Barry Cornwall" was a rough anagram of his name. Hawthorne wrote of him in 1854: "A plain, middle-sized, rather smallish, English-looking gentleman, elderly, . . . with short white hair. Particularly quiet in his manners; he talks in a somewhat feeble tone and emphasis, not at all energetic. . . . I liked him very well; he talked unaffectedly. . . . Nothing remains on my mind of what he said, except that, in his younger days, he was a scientific pugilist. . . . On the whole, he made a pleasant and kindly, but not a powerful impression" (*ENB*, p. 62). In inviting the Procters, Rogers perhaps also had in mind his idea of having M "meet some ladies" (44.31–32). Mrs. Procter had great gifts socially and intellectually; after her husband's death she remained the center of admirers of her shrewdness and wit, and the *Dictionary of National Biography* quotes one writer as saying, "Her spirits often had to do for both." Procter is still in the *Oxford Dictionary of Quotations* (1979), as well as Bartlett's (1980) and Stevenson (1967), for the lines M ridiculed.

Rogers probably invited Kinglake as another writer of exotic travels. Alexander William Kinglake (1809–91) explained the title of his travel book as meaning, in Greek, "from the early dawn"—"from the east" (p. vii): *Eöthen; or, Traces of Travel Brought Home from the East* (London: Ollivier, 1844). It is an impressionistic account of the young man's travels in the Levant around 1835. Along with Eliot Warburton—another youthful Levantine traveler—Kinglake had studied law in Procter's office. Warburton's book, *The Crescent and the Cross* (in two parts) had also come out in London in 1844 and been published by Wiley & Putnam in 1845; his and Kinglake's books are early Victorian classics of eastern travel. By coincidences, M encountered their respective dragomen in 1857 on his own Levantine travels—see 95.5–6, 100.2–3, and accompanying discussions. M's interest in the Near East suggests a topic of some of the conversation at Rogers's breakfast table.

47.5 *Quebec Hotel*] On the west side of Bath Square (EMM), near the tip of Portsmouth Point, overlooking the narrow channel leading into the inner harbor from the outer roadstead of Spithead (see also the discussion at 47.28). The point "may be considered as an integral part of the town. It consists of one large, and well-built street, called *Broad-Street*; in which, and in *Bath-Square*, are the offices and stores of the principal Ship-Agents . . . and many excellent Inns and Taverns, of which may be particularly noticed . . . the *Quebec Tavern*, in the Square, which is the chief rendezvous for the . . . Havre Packets" (Henry Slight, *A Metrical History of Portsmouth* [Portsmouth: Hollingsworth & Price, 1820], p. 68). Of some hundred public houses in the town, at least half were on the point, "a picturesque, heterogeneous assemblage of taverns, liquor-shops, eating-houses, cook-shops, tailors, drapers, pawnbrokers, watch-jobbers, and trinket-merchants, backed by a warren of mean streets and alleys. It was a place throbbing with life and excitement" (Geoffrey J. Marcus, *Heart of Oak* [London and New York: Oxford University Press, 1975], p. 144). Here were taverns known to Nelson and his captains—and frequented by Marryat's young midshipmen; just below M's hotel was the Sally Port, to and from which swirled the negotiators for the great mutiny of 1797, and where Nelson embarked for the last time to join the *Victory* in the Spithead anchorage.

47.10 Somerby] The *New York Herald* of February 1, 1850, lists the (cabin) passengers just arrived on the *Independence* as: "H Melville of New York; H G Somerby, of Newburyport; J W Jones, of England; Rebecca Jones, do; J Scott, lady and two children; Mrs Thor and son, France; Mr Alexander, of Jersey; Mr Erricson, of Sweden" (*Log*, I, 364); Parker is unidentified.

47.15 thing] M's slighting reference (as at 31.21–22) is to *Redburn*, published by Bentley in two volumes.

47.18 bought some books] Among these books were two that M bought at H. G. Bohn's establishment, York Street, Covent Garden (see the discussion at 26.32); these were books in the Bohn Standard Library series (Nos. 31, 43). The first contained *The Autobiography of Goethe* (Oxenford translation), which ran over into the second, where *Letters from Italy* took pp. 237–450; they were not issued as a two-volume set, so M on his list (144.30–31) entered them (as he bought them) separately, with the price for each, three shillings. M's copy of the first is now unlocated; in the second (HCL-M; Sealts 228) he wrote: "Herman Melville Bought at Bohn's Dec 25. 1849." The date is a slip for December 24 (see his error the next day—47.25–26—in dating Christmas as the twenty-sixth) or is perhaps the date of inscription, not purchase. For discussion of M's copies of these books see Harrison Hayford, "Melville's German Streak," in *A Conversation in the Life of Leland R. Phelps* (Durham, N.C.: Duke University Center for International Studies, 1987); see also Bercaw 296.

47.19 bread trencher] See the discussion at 40.28.

47.21 Bazaar] The Lowther Arcade or Bazaar at the west end of the Strand (just up from M's lodging) was an "elegant avenue" surmounted by glass domes, "replete with taste. . . . The first-floor consists of rooms, capable of being applied to those neat trades which are devoted to the supply of the female toilette" (*Cruchley's Picture of London*, p. 190).

47.22 Waterloo Station] To Portsmouth by the London and South-Western Railway from this station (nearest M's lodging across the river), through Winchester, the distance was ninety-four miles; it involved either a final ferry trip across the harbor mouth from Gosport on the west to Portsmouth on the east, or one on a short branch line around the upper margin of the harbor and entry by way of the eastern suburbs outside the fortifications.

47.25 *Dec 26.*] Error for December 25.

47.28 the town] Old Portsmouth, small and crowded within its extensive fortifications in the nineteenth century, occupied the southwest angle of Portsea Island, where the inner harbor emptied into the great roadstead of

Spithead, between the east end of the Isle of Wight and the Hampshire coast. Forming the near side of the narrow channel is Portsmouth Point (the site of M's hotel), a short, blunt, semidetached peninsula pointing northwest into the inner harbor. Immediately adjacent north and east of here along the inner line of the harbor was the much larger suburb of Portsea, with the gun wharves, arsenals, building slips, and drydocks of the naval yards. Thus the otherwise enthusiast for Victorian industry Charles Knight: "Be it however understood . . . Portsmouth and Portsea are anything but beautiful towns. . . . Everything looks, and breathes, and smells of soldiers, and sailors, and docksmen" (*Excursion Companion*, IX, 5). A slightly earlier description of the groggeries and brothels along the landing in Portsea beach is more censorious:

> This is called the Commons hard; and both it and the row opposite are much devoted to the sale of frippery, so that this is neither the most cleanly nor the most moral spot in England. It is the great landing-place from the ships in the harbour—at least for the common sailors and those who keep up intercourse with them. . . . This Common hard displays no very pleasant scene [even] in times of peace, . . . but as such scenes are inseparable from places where sailors resort in great numbers, it is probably better to have it thus concentrated. (Robert Mudie, *Hampshire*, 3 vols. [Winchester: Robbins, [1838]], II, 210–11; there are a number of engravings of Portsmouth town and harbor scenes in this section, probably not much changed ten years later.)

When Dana stopped overnight in 1856, the place was unusually busy because of the recent end of the Crimean War, but otherwise his evening tour of the town included much of what M would have seen in the early morning:

> No town in England is so completely naval and military as Portsmouth; and now the return of the Crimean regiments makes the town fuller than usual. . . .
>
> How redolent is everything of the gigantic naval force of England. Sailors swarming about the countless grog shops and unconcealed brothels, singing, loud talking, lounging . . . , women swarming like fire flies in a field. How narrow and crooked are the bye streets and lanes, and how old, and low roofed, and redolent of tobacco smoke and grog are the rooms. (*Journal*, II, 803)

47.28 "North Corner"] This in particular was a resort of petty officers: so writes Frederick Chamier (see the discussion at 27.22) in *The Life of a Sailor* (London: Bentley, 1832), when the gunner and the boatswain (Mr. Pipes) quarrel about being a "gentleman": "Mr. Pipes had, it is true, been all his life before the mast, and had associated with the very best society at either North Corner or the Point; but he was an officer by virtue of his warrant, and that warrant made him likewise a gentleman" (quoted in C.

Northcote Parkinson, *Portsmouth Point* [London: University Press of Liverpool, 1948], pp. 124–25). The northwest corner of the Royal Dockyard (farther north of the point along the inner harbor) was and is called the "North Corner," with a North Corner Jetty, and it would be the resort of chiefs and petty officers (letter to Howard C. Horsford from G. P. B. Naish, the Honorary Secretary of the Society for Nautical Research, National Maritime Museum, Greenwich).

M's "short stroll" before breakfast must have been limited to the point and immediately adjacent Portsea (entry to the dockyards was restricted), but he would have had a clear view of the *Victory*, Nelson's flagship at Trafalgar, which until the twentieth century was kept at anchor out in the harbor. Though it was then treated as a "ship in ordinary," with its masts, rigging, sails, and guns in storage, its floating hull was never allowed to deteriorate, and everything aboard was kept shipshape. One could visit the ship by hiring a boatman along the public docks, but M did not have the time. His remembered beachside view of it and his feeling for Nelson prompted a passage in *Billy Budd, Sailor*: "Nevertheless, to anybody who can hold the Present at its worth without being inappreciative of the Past, it may be forgiven, if to such an one the solitary old hulk at Portsmouth, Nelson's *Victory*, seems to float there, not alone as the decaying monument of a fame incorruptible, but also as a poetic reproach" (chap. 4; Hayford-Sealts edition, p. 57).

47.33 Jones] See the passenger list quoted in the discussion at 47.10.

48.7 *Jan: 30th*] Possibly M has the date wrong, or else after he wrote this the entry of the packet into the harbor was delayed: New York papers of February 1 and 2 list the arrival of the *Independence* on January 31.

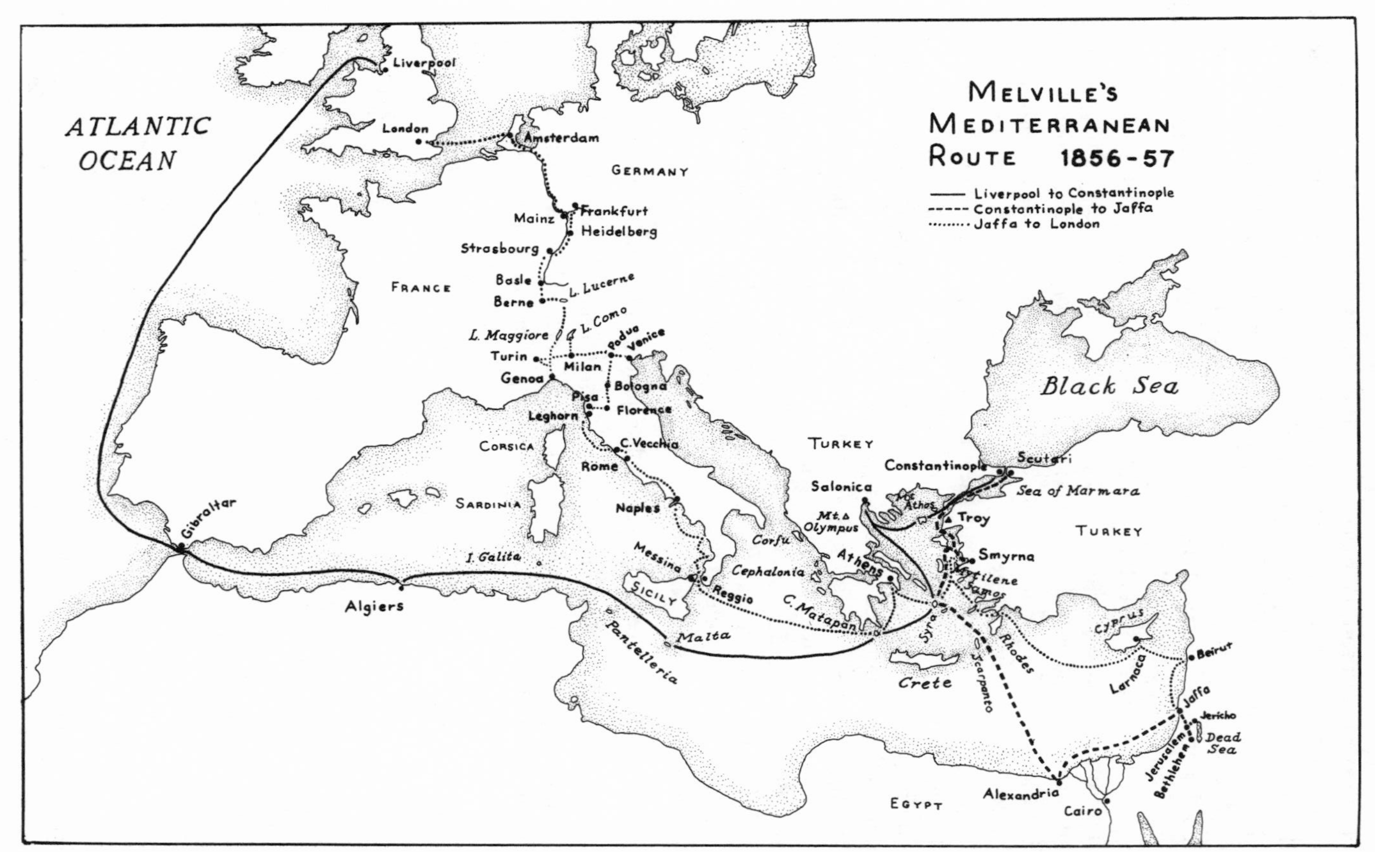
MELVILLE'S MEDITERRANEAN ROUTE 1856-57
Liverpool to Constantinople
Constantinople to Jaffa
Jaffa to London
ATLANTIC OCEAN
Liverpool
London
Amsterdam
GERMANY
Mainz
Frankfurt
Heidelberg
Strasbourg
FRANCE
Basle
Berne
L. Lucerne
L. Maggiore
L. Como
Turin
Milan
Padua
Venice
Genoa
Bologna
Pisa
Florence
Leghorn
C. Vecchia
CORSICA
Rome
SARDINIA
Naples
Gibraltar
I. Galita
Messina
SICILY
Reggio
Algiers
Malta
Pantelleria
Corfu
Cephalonia
C. Matapan
Athens
Mt. Olympus
Salonica
TURKEY
Athos
Constantinople
Scutari
Sea of Marmara
Black Sea
Troy
TURKEY
Smyrna
Mytilene
Samos
Syra
Rhodes
Scarpanto
Crete
Cyprus
Larnaca
Beirut
Jaffa
Jericho
Jerusalem
Bethlehem
Dead Sea
EGYPT
Alexandria
Cairo

CHRONOLOGY OF THE 1856–57 TRIP

[NN page and line numbers in the first column indicate the beginning of a dated entry; events of that day are sometimes covered in the next day's entry or in external sources cited in the discussions. Bracketed dates correct those in the journal; see the appropriate discussions.]

49.2	Oct. 11, 1856	Sailed from New York
49.6	26	Arrived in Glasgow
50.1	28	Excursion to Dumbarton and Loch Lomond
50.12	29–Nov. 8	Glasgow, Stirling Castle, Edinburgh, North Berwick, Abbotsford, Melrose, Newcastle-upon-Tyne, York, Lancaster, to Liverpool
51.1	Nov. 11	To Southport with Hawthorne
51.10	13	Returned to Liverpool
51.17	15	Excursion to Chester with Hawthorne
51.23	18	Sailed from Liverpool
52.6	24	Gibraltar
52.20	26	Algiers
52.33	29	Malta
53.13	Dec. 2	Arrived in Syra
54.25	5	Departed Syra
54.32	6	Arrived in Thessalonica
56.33	9	Departed Thessalonica
57.8	10	Sea of Marmara
58.5	12	Arrived in Constantinople
64.23	16	Excursion up Bosporus
68.3	18	Excursion to Scutari; departed Constantinople
69.9	20	Arrived in Smyrna
70.36	23	Departed Smyrna
71.21	24	Arrived in Syra
71.22	25	Departed Syra
72.34	28	Arrived in Alexandria
73.7	30	Arrived in Cairo
73.12	Jan. 1, 1857	Returned to Alexandria
79.1	4	Departed Alexandria
79.4	6	Arrived in Jaffa; departed for Jerusalem

79.29	Jan. 7	Arrived in Jerusalem
80.1	10–16?	Three of these days were spent in the excursion to the Jordan and the Dead Sea (Jericho and Bethlehem)
80.4	[18]	Departed Jerusalem; arrived in Ramleh
80.9	[19]	Departed Ramleh; arrived in Jaffa via Lydda
82.4	[24]	Departed Jaffa
95.1	[25]	Arrived in Beirut
95.14	27–31	Party of the Pasha
95.23	Feb. 1	Departed Beirut
95.29	2	Larnaca, Cyprus
97.35	6	Smyrna
98.16	7	Arrived in Syra
98.37	8	Departed Syra; arrived in Pireus and Athens
99.30	11	Departed Athens and Pireus
100.7	13	Arrived in Messina
101.1	16	Departed Messina
101.9	18	Arrived in Naples; excursion to Pompeii and Vesuvius
102.5	20	Excursion to Posilipo
103.33	22	Excursion to Castellammare and Sorrento
104.7	23	Excursion to Pozzuoli and Baia
105.25	24	Departed Naples
105.33	25	Arrived in Rome
111.22	March 11	Excursion along Appian Way
112.14	17	Excursion to Frascati
113.10	20	Excursion to Tivoli
113.17	21	Departed Rome
113.24	22	Arrived in and departed Cività Vecchia
113.31	23	Arrived in Leghorn; departed for Pisa and Florence
116.9	28	Excursion to Fiesole
116.17	29	Departed Florence; arrived in Bologna
117.1	31	Departed Bologna for Ferrara and Padua
117.24	April 1	Departed Padua; arrived in Venice

120.32	April 6	Departed Venice for Milan
121.31	8	Excursion to Lake Como
122.6	9	Departed Milan for Turin via Novara
123.6	11	Departed Turin for Genoa
124.24	[14]	Departed Genoa for Switzerland via Lake Maggiore
124.32	[15]	San Gotthard Pass
125.7	[16]	Arrived in Lucerne
125.13	[17]	Departed Lucerne for Berne
125.21	[19]	Departed Berne for Basle
125.29	[20]	Departed Basle for Strasbourg and Heidelberg
126.3	[21]	Departed Heidelberg for Frankfurt
126.14	[22]	Departed Frankfurt for Mainz and Cologne
126.26	[23]	Departed Cologne for Amsterdam
126.34	24	Departed Amsterdam for Rotterdam
127.20	25	Departed Rotterdam
127.26	26	Arrived in London
128.13	May [3]	Departed London for Oxford
129.7	[4]	Departed Oxford for Stratford-on-Avon, Warwick, and Birmingham
129.19	[5]	Departed Birmingham for Liverpool
129.26	[6]	Departed Liverpool
	19	Arrived in New York

JOURNAL 1856–57

49.2 Sailed] The *Glasgow*, operated by the Glasgow and New-York Steamship Co., measured 1,962 tons; it had been built in 1851 and was captained by John Duncan. First-class fare was seventy-five dollars. Departure lists in New York papers totaled eighty passengers; M's account of his fellows, in his letter to his brother Allan from Liverpool, is unenthusiastic (see p. 624 below).

49.4 Rathlin . . . Crag] All craggy, mountainous islands: Rathlin, a small one just north of County Antrim, Ireland; Arran, the large island well up in the Firth of Clyde; Ailsa, a small, bare granite peak rising abruptly to 1,114 feet at the mouth of the firth. Conceivably, M as a youthful sailor to Liverpool in 1839 could have seen Ailsa in passing. A two-paragraph description of it (with details from the *Penny Cyclopædia*) is given in *Israel Potter* as John Paul Jones maneuvers his ship in the vicinity (chap. 15, p. 97).

49.5 Greenoch] At this thriving little port on the south bank, twenty-five miles downstream from the city, as M was helping a sailor lower a boat, he was struck across the nose by a coil of stiff rope. When he wrote Allan two weeks later he said he was by then pretty well healed but had looked as if he "had been in a bar-room fight" (see p. 625).

49.8–9 Lord Blantyre's place] The picturesque ruins of the priory of Blantyre on the south bank, just downriver from Glasgow; Charles Walter Stewart (1818–1900) was twelfth and last lord. Wordsworth quotes his sister Dorothy's description, from 1831, in his note to the sonnet "Bothwell Castle": "On the opposite bank, which is finely wooded with elms and other trees, are the remains of a priory built upon a rock; and rock and ruin are so blended, that it is impossible to separate the one from the other. Nothing can be more beautiful than the little remnant of this holy place; elm-trees . . . grow out of the walls, and overshadow a small, but very elegant window. . . . The river Clyde flows on smooth and unruffled below" (*Yarrow Revisited, and Other Poems* [London: Longman, Rees, Orme, Brown, Green, & Longman, 1835], p. 42). M may have recalled from newspaper accounts that Mrs. Manning, whom he saw hanged in London (see the entry for November 13, 1849, and the discussion at 17.18–19), had once been Lady Blantyre's maid.

49.10 pace] Possibly "face" (H).

cattle tenders — women — face like cattle — places for building iron steamers.

49.11 old cathedral] Behind the twelfth-century Cathedral of St. Mungo, the Necropolis rose on the terraces of a three-hundred-foot hill; atop, the statue of John Knox on a Doric column had been erected in 1824. Hawthorne in 1856 and 1857 found the cathedral good but somewhat small, in excellent repair, its monuments few, and its crypts impressive (*ENB*, pp. 330, 511).

49.18 poverty] The squalor of the poor districts, especially the "Gorbals," has been notorious down to the present. Hawthorne thought that "the poorer classes of Glasgow excel even those of Liverpool in the bad eminence of filth, uncombed and unwashed children, drunkeness, disorderly deportment, evil smell, and all that makes city-poverty disgusting"; he remarked how the principal streets, like the High, in this district near the cathedral and university swarmed with "the lower orders . . . so that it is difficult to make one's way among the sallow and unclean crowd, and not at all pleasant to breathe in the noisomeness of the atmosphere." But he inclined to consider the newer parts, the west end, "the stateliest city I ever beheld" (*ENB*, pp. 329, 512).

49.19–21 University . . . Street] The university, founded in the mid-fifteenth century, was on High Street, the old thoroughfare from cathedral to river. Hawthorne twice described its generally Tudor architecture, in the prevailing dark gray granite, as cold and hard (*ENB*, pp. 329, 512–13). The forty acres of Kelvingrove or West End Park, high and terraced, were a popular promenade that could be entered from Sauchiehall Street, an avenue of fashionable shops.

50.1 Loch Lomond] The lake, northwest of Glasgow, was a common way to enter the romanticized Highlands. Hawthorne twice began the usual tour this way: a river steamer to the town of Dumbarton, a short railroad trip to Balloch on the lake, and then a steamer the length of the lake (*ENB*, pp. 330, 514, 517).

Dumbarton Castle, anciently one of the strongest fortresses in Scotland, occupies a basaltic height "bulging up out of the Clyde, with abrupt decision, to the height of five hundred [actually 240] feet. Its summit is cloven in twain, the cleft reaching nearly to the bottom on the side towards the river" (*ENB*, p. 514). Hawthorne describes the flights of ascending stairs, the views from the summits, the armament, the sheep, the remnants of ancient weaponry in the armory, and especially "the sword of William Wallace. It is a formidable-looking weapon, made for being swayed with both hands, and, with its hilt on the floor, reached about to my chin" (*ENB*, pp. 514–16). Wallace (?1272–1305), Scottish hero of the war against Edward I, and legendarily gigantic, was imprisoned here, then removed to London and executed. (The village furnaces were from old glassworks, once its principal industry.)

50.5 Levern] I.e., Leven, the river connecting the Clyde with Loch Lomond.

50.12 Arrived from York] M's itinerary after Glasgow is detailed in his long letter to his brother Allan begun in Liverpool on Monday, November 10 (see p. 625): Glasgow for "three or four days," then to Edinburgh for "five days, I think," and then Scott's Abbotsford and Melrose, and also Perth and Stirling. That recollected order may be inaccurate: Perth and Stirling might have been better accommodated between Glasgow and Edinburgh. Visiting Perth seems to imply M was following his father's footsteps into the ancestral Melville country in Fifeshire (William H. Gilman, *Melville's Early Life and* REDBURN [New York: New York University Press, 1951], p. 13), though he did not call on anyone because of the ugly injury to his face. Thereafter he entered England by way of Berwick and Newcastle, stayed a day in York, then went on to Liverpool. Excepting Perth, Hawthorne had made a similar excursion—by way of the Highlands—the preceding May and substantially repeated it with his wife in June of 1857.

50.14 Dale St:] Together with its Water Street extension, this street in the city's commercial center runs at right angles to the river and central docks; Hawthorne's consulate was just one block over and nearer the river on parallel Brunswick Street. The hotel, originally an eighteenth-century inn, seems to have been too small to have been listed in guidebooks, but according to Mr. J. F. Smith, Liverpool City Librarian, an 1855 city directory locates it at No. 69; William Rowell, proprietor. In mid-century Liverpool an ordinary bedroom would cost about $1.50, food of the plainest kind without wine, $3.00 a day. M's letter to Allan, however, says he spent only $35.00 altogether in his two weeks of traveling.

50.22 Exchange] Some blocks nearer the river than M's hotel, the Town Hall marks where Dale becomes Water Street. The Exchange buildings front on the open quadrangle behind the hall, in the center of which is the Nelson monument. However fictionalized, Chapter 31 of *Redburn* probably reflects M's feelings in 1839 as he wandered the streets:

> The ornament in question is a group of statuary in bronze, elevated upon a marble pedestal and basement, representing Lord Nelson expiring in the arms of Victory. . . . Victory is dropping a wreath on the dying admiral's brow; while Death, . . . a hideous skeleton, is insinuating his bony hand under the hero's robe. . . . I never could look at Death without a shudder. . . . How this group of statuary affected me, may be inferred from the fact, that I never went through Chapel-street without going through the little arch to look at it again. (pp. 155–56)

50.29 Rock Ferry] A small suburban town across the River Mersey where the Hawthornes took temporary residence in 1853 before settling in adjoining Rock Park; they had left those quarters, however, when his ailing wife, Sophia, and their two daughters went to Lisbon for the winter of 1855–56.

50.32 docks] Perhaps Liverpool's most interesting feature, constructed to provide berths at a constant level independent of the twenty-foot river tides. Since M had first explored them in 1839 (see *Redburn*, chap. 32), eight or more big new docks and several landing stages had been added, the Huskisson in 1852 (named for William Huskisson, 1770–1830, mercantile statesman and first casualty of the new railroad age, killed by an engine at the opening of the line to Manchester). The second paragraph of *Billy Budd, Sailor* recalls Prince's Dock, nearest the end of Dale/Water Street.

50.34 Consulate] Hawthorne had been appointed to the lucrative post in 1853 by his old friend President Franklin Pierce; in the first pages of his English notebooks he described the "rascally set of sailors," dirty and desperate, thronging the entry, the two rooms overlooking the noisy, busy dock area, the grim decorations of his twelve-by-fifteen-foot private office, and his prospective daily routine (*ENB*, pp. 3–4). (The building is pictured in Raymona E. Hull, *Nathaniel Hawthorne: The English Experience* [Pittsburgh: University of Pittsburgh Press, 1980], p. 19.) Ordinarily, Hawthorne did not make a record daily; in this case he waited a week and a half to write up M's visit and their excursion to the medieval city of Chester, which he had already visited often and described (see pp. 628–33 below).

50.35 "Anderson's"] On Exchange Street, just off Dale Street and near the Exchange; its midday crowds of businessmen were considered a characteristic sight.

51.2 Southport] A middle-class resort north of Liverpool on the Irish Sea. After his wife and daughters returned from Lisbon in June, 1856, Hawthorne moved the family to Southport on September 16 in the hope that the sea air would be beneficial to her health. He described the railroad trip along the coast as dreary, through the "dismal outskirts" of the city, then along a "wide monotony" of plain shut off from sight of the water by low dunes (*ENB*, p. 397). The town itself was primarily a summer resort, out of season very windy and rather desolate. After a winter there, he called it "as stupid a place as ever I lived in" (p. 461). Their lodging, in a tall stone house called Brunswick Terrace, fronted the beach; they had three rooms (with another for the governess) and a "parlor," the initial furnishings of which he described as shabby, with an old carpet, a square table in the center, some chairs, a long sofa, and other odds and ends. They prepared their own meals, but he did not say with what cooking facilities (pp. 425–26). M barely mentions this visit in his letter to Allan (p. 626). (The house is pictured in Hull, *Nathaniel Hawthorne*, p. 101.)

51.6 walk by the sea] Fronting the town was an elevated embankment and promenade along the shore, but as Hawthorne repeatedly noted, at low tide the beach stretched seaward an "interminable breadth of sands, stretching out to the horizon" (*ENB*, p. 425). See pp. 628–29 below for Hawthorne's account of this walk.

51.7 & Fox & Geese] This may mean they played "Fox and Geese," a game using a board with pegs or draughtsmen, or, as suggested by A. H. Lewis of Southport, England, in a letter to Howard C. Horsford, that they visited and drank stout at the public house called "The Fox and Goose," which still exists in Cable Street, Southport, only a short distance from the site of Hawthorne's home.

51.7–8 Julian . . . Una] M had known the Hawthorne children during Hawthorne's Berkshire year (1850–51): Una (b. 1844), Julian (b. 1846), and Rose (b. 1851).

51.12 writing letters] One of these was part of the letter to Allan begun November 10 (printed below, pp. 624–27; No. 130 in *Letters*, pp. 182–86). Cited in that letter are also letters to M's mother, to ESM, to John Murray, and to Richard Bentley (Nos. 345–48 on the "Check List of Unlocated Letters," *Letters*, p. 313).

51.13 "Old Swan"] A hamlet, three miles out on the main road leading east; nearby were small sandstone quarries. Perhaps this was M's nostalgic renewal of a summer walk he took along this road in 1839, if the one taken by the narrator in *Redburn* (chap. 43) was autobiographical.

51.14 Bright] Henry A. Bright (1830–84), of a wealthy nonconformist family, a minor poet and a scholar whom Hawthorne claimed he liked better than anyone else he met in England. (See Hull, *Nathaniel Hawthorne*, p. 24, for a youthful portrait.) A few years earlier, Bright had made a tourist circuit in America; Longfellow's letter from Cambridge introduced him to Hawthorne in Concord (September 25, 1852), who passed him on to Catherine Maria Sedgwick at Lenox, but not to M, though Bright stayed overnight in Pittsfield. His journal of this trip has been edited by Anne H. Ehrenpreis as *Happy Country This America* (cited in the discussion at 23.11–12). Bright's church was the Renshaw Street Unitarian Chapel, described by Hawthorne as neat but plain and not very large, though the "Unitarian sect in Liverpool have . . . great wealth and respectability." In the small adjacent graveyard were tombs of several men whom Hawthorne admired, including the troubled and sometimes skeptical theologian Joseph Blanco White (1775–1841). M wrote Bright a note just before leaving Liverpool (November 18), thanking him for his "kind perseverance concerning 'Blanco White' " (*ENB*, p. 50; *Letters*, pp. 186–87). In his copy of Hawthorne's *Our Old Home* (Boston: Ticknor & Fields, 1863), p. 7, M underlined the word "Bright" in Hawthorne's punning reference to him—"Bright was the illumination of my dusky little apartment, as often as he made his appearance there"—and wrote at the bottom of the page, "His name. A son of one of the great Liverpool merchants" (Sealts 249).

This visit to the consulate, incidentally, was for Hawthorne to visa M's passport; he signed and endorsed it: "Exhibited at the Consulate of the United States of America at Liverpool this 14th November 1856 Good for Constantinople (via Malta & Gibraltar) Egypt & a tour about the Continent." At the Ottoman consulate he also got his Turkish visa. (Passport in the Berkshire Athenaeum; see *Log*, II, 524 [Oct. 7].)

51.15–16 Free Library & Cemetery] The Free Public Library, then on Duke Street, was one of the first such municipal institutions to be opened in Great Britain. (Sailor Redburn was booted from the lyceum reading room, chap. 42.) Not far from either chapel or library is St. James's Cemetery, one of the new Victorian parklike ones. It had been created out of a quarry, and Hawthorne considered it a pretty place, with paths and luxuriant shrubbery, many monuments on the floor of the deep valley, and other tombs hewn in the walls (*ENB*, p. 26). In America, Bright (see the preceding discussion) had toured cemeteries, which he called "the usual *park* of an American town" (*Happy Country*, p. 162), notably with Longfellow through Mt. Auburn Cemetery in Cambridge (p. 384).

51.17–18 Toxhete . . . Hall] Toxteth Park was a favorite residential district on high ground to the southeast; its promenade gave extensive views of the city, harbor, and Welsh hills beyond. St. George's Hall, a little east of M's hotel, had just been completed (1854)—a much-praised public auditorium and municipal court building in Greco-Roman temple style. Its huge organ boasted the innovation of steam-powered bellows. (Perhaps M in this entry retrospectively conflated this Saturday with the Friday preceding or the Sunday following: the long Saturday excursion he and Hawthorne took to Chester surely allowed no daylight time for these other activities, so late in an English autumn. In any case, M mentions neither the Chester trip this Saturday nor his meeting with Hawthorne on Monday; see pp. 628–33.)

51.19 trunk] Without explaining what change made the trunk now superfluous, M wrote Allan that he expected to leave it in Liverpool "as I told you" (see p. 626), and Hawthorne notes that M left it at the consulate, "taking only a carpet-bag to hold all his travelling-gear" (see p. 633).

51.21 "Egyptian"] M had found the ship the previous Thursday, at the Wellington Dock, and wrote Allan that night about the expected Monday departure (see p. 627 below). The ship belonged to the Levant Screw Steam Shipping Co., and plied between Liverpool and Black Sea ports, chiefly with textiles for freight. M regularly misspelled the captain's name, Robert Taitt, as "Tate." (Ships were often delayed in Liverpool by the strong prevailing westerlies blowing up the River Mersey; steam power was doubtless less affected than sail, but high winds and tide might make it difficult to leave the protecting dock.)

52.4 ships] The treaty ending the Crimean War (1853–56) had been signed the previous March. Initially (February, 1854), transports carried British troops only to Malta as a kind of demonstration; by September, however, the total fleet, warships and transports, arriving at the Crimea numbered 150.

52.8–9 "Apes . . . Hercules"] Jebel Musa (ca. 2,300 ft.) in Morocco, across from Gibraltar, is infested with monkeys of the same variety as Gibraltar. At Ceuta, Mt. Hacho (636 ft.) directly opposite Gibraltar makes the traditional other Pillar of Hercules. (Like Ailsa Craig, Bass Rock—mentioned later in this entry —is a high, isolated crag, in this case in the mouth of the Firth of Forth, presumably seen by M on his way south from Edinburgh.)

52.24 Morisco] Usually a Moor of Spanish birth. In Cervantes's novel (M had bought the Charles Jarvis translation in 1855—HCL-M; Sealts 125; Bercaw 122), the story told by the Morisco maiden involves no description of Algiers, but in Chapters 37–41 a once-captive Spanish captain does describe the city and his escape with the beautiful daughter of his captor. (Evidently M's ship did not dock at Algiers; unless for pressing reasons of cargo, difficulties with quarantine in later ports generally precluded any debarkation or even any stay in the Algerian harbor.)

52.34 Pantalaria] Pantelleria: some sixty or seventy miles southwest of Sicily, a place of exile or a penal colony since Roman times and doubtless well supplied with the political prisoners of the tyrannous Bourbon, King Ferdinand ("Bomba") of the Two Sicilies; see the discussion at 101.29.

53.3 Malta harbor] American men-of-war in the Mediterranean Squadron often spent time here; some years before, Lieutenant Francis Schroeder, secretary to the commodore, wrote this impressionistic passage:

> Our little voyages [around the peninsula-divided harbor] were delightful under the steepling battlements and cliffs, the deep coves, and among the warlike scenery of Malta. The superb and lofty ramparts and towers surmounting the precipices over the sea, and environing the curious harbours; the massive city, perhaps the best built in the world, and seeming rather to have been excavated and carved on the rocks; the climbing "streets of stairs," the arched piazzas on the cliffs, and mighty parapets bristling with cannon, tier over tier; and then the constant associations with the glorious past, with which the mind is filled on every side by some monument or grand work of its old masters [the Knights of Malta]. (*Shores of the Mediterranean*, 2 vols. [New York: Harper & Brothers, 1846], II, 76–77)

53.12 Morea] The medieval name for the classical Peloponnesus, south and west of the Corinthian isthmus; Cape Matapan is its southern extremity.

53.14 Syra] With the advent of steamships, this island port in the Cyclades became for a while the principal transshipping point for Levantine commerce, the most populous and important in the new Greek nation. During the Middle Ages pirates had driven the inhabitants to a "new town" on the mountain above; after independence, refugees from other islands resettled the port, and the "new town" became Old Town. The Psariote refugees were believed to have the least intermixture of foreign blood, and were described as handsome in the manner of classical sculpture, agile, but loquacious, disputatious, and lively. (M's recollections of Syra and other islands inform the poems "Syra" and "The Archipelago," both included in *Timoleon*, 1891; NN *Published Poems* volume, pp. 307–11.)

53.25 bemired] A conjectural reading, as is "lemons" (H).

picking of rags, carry water casks, lemons &c.
&c — still gave some notion of Greek
aspect. Picturesqueness of the whole.

53.30 sugarloaf] In speaking of the conical hill behind the harbor M appears to echo Murray's *Greece* (1854), which likened it to a "huge sugarloaf covered with houses" (p. 307). The church of St. George at the top was built by the Capuchins as headquarters for their eastern missions. Among the many visible islands unnamed by M are Delos, Tenos, Myconos, Naxos, and Paros.

54.24 Loyd's] Presumably the agent for Austrian-Lloyd's Mail Steam Packet Co., a thriving Mediterranean carrier on several of whose ships M later took passage. The transaction is obscure: perhaps M had intended to transfer to a ship for Alexandria (or Palestine) but changed his mind to remain with the Black Sea–bound *Egyptian*. (Successive editions of Murray's *Greece* reiterated the general advisability for autumn and winter travelers to start with Malta and Egypt, then move on to Palestine and Greece with early spring.)

55.2 Salonica] Thessalonica had been fortified by the Venetians (not the Genoese) during their struggle with the Turks. From the harbor, these white walls rising on the amphitheater of surrounding hills had a strikingly beautiful appearance, belying the squalor and filth within.

55.7 ship's agents] The Abbots (sometimes spelled with two *t*s) were an Anglo-Greek family whose grandfather had brought the British Levant Co. to Thessalonica in the late eighteenth century. One grandson, Henry, owned extensive tracts of timber on Mt. Olympus, where the Englishman M met may have been bird-shooting (see the discussions at 55.28 and 55.30). It was the once extremely wealthy and extravagant "Djékis" (i.e., John), however, who had created the luxurious country estate out of rocky ground some seven kilometers northwest of town, and who is at least partly the prototype of the self-satisfied wealthy merchant in *Clarel*. By one later account, he employed six hundred laborers to clear the land, construct a high wall and a tower-like house from the rocks, move soil, plant rare trees and ornamentals, and build a bath house. A seated portrait of the plump Djékis is reproduced in Ekaterina Georgoudakis's article, "Djékis Abbot of Thessaloniki and the Greek Merchant in Herman Melville's *Clarel*," *Melville Society Extracts*, No. 64 (November, 1985), 1–6.

55.9 mosques] Except Constantinople, no Byzantine city had more interesting churches; the crypt of St. Demetrius reputedly held the remains of the city's patron saint. Nineteen years later, Charles Dudley Warner called the basilica the most perfectly preserved of the city's thirty-seven former churches, with five aisles, and some "fine mosaics of marble, beautiful in design and color" (*In the Levant* [Boston: Osgood, 1877], p. 331). The circular church of St. George was built on the model of the Roman Pantheon, its walls eighteen feet thick and its inside diameter, eighty. The ceiling mosaics, largest extant of that art, represented fourteen saints in the act of adoration; "enough remains of the architectural designs, the brilliant peacocks and bright blue birds, to show what the ancient beauty was, but the walls of the mosque are white and barn-like" (Warner, p. 330).

55.14 triumphal arch] Of the city's three, the one M notes was doubtless that of Constantine, near the east end of the main thoroughfare; on the arch, otherwise in ruinous state, the double range of bas-reliefs around the piers had been preserved, though defaced. In the Jewish quarter, near the church of St. George, was the propylaeum of the ancient Hippodrome, a fine colonnade of five Corinthian pillars, with entablature and attic; from its location, this is surely what M saw, though he wrote "3".

55.22–23 Five Points] The most notorious slum district in mid-century New York, just off Broadway at the intersection of Cross, Anthony, Orange, Mulberry, and Little-Water streets.

55.24 great fire] Later (March 22, 113.29), M describes this as on Abbot property. London papers varied slightly in details; the *Times* of August 4, 1856, reported "a most fearful and destructive explosion occurred . . . on

Friday, the 11th of July. A fire broke out in the quarters of the European warehouses, and caused the ignition and explosion of 240 barrels of gunpowder in the store of a French merchant." On August 6 a "telegraphic despatch" in the *Times* added that a Greek merchant who caused the fire had been arrested and that at least seven hundred were killed or wounded.

55.28 Duckworth] Unidentified. No man of that name was found in a thorough examination of the history of the Duckworth family and of the voluminous printed and manuscript resources of the British Library and the Public Record Office covering the personal and official correspondence of the Foreign Office with the Embassy at Constantinople and with the Consulate at Thessalonica. It seems probable that M mistook the name.

55.30 *shooting . . . Tempe*] From Murray's *Greece*: "So many Englishmen now visit Greece . . . every winter for the purpose of shooting, that it is necessary to point out some of the best stations, where they may combine good sport with safe harbours for their yachts" (p. 18). In *Clarel*, Glaucon, the lightsome young man from Smyrna, claims: "Fine shot was mine by Nazareth; / But birding's best in Tempe's Vale: / From Thessalonica, you know / 'Tis thither that we fowlers stray" (2.5.45–48).

55.34 tomb stones] Older tombs of Turkish males were commonly adorned by sculptured turbans; stones for women were marked by a conventionally carved leaf or shell.

55.37 Abbots place] In *Clarel*, the English-Greek merchant from Thessalonica has "High walled, / An Eden . . . nigh his town, / Which locked in leafy emerald / A frescoed lodge. There Nubians armed, / Tall eunuchs virtuous in zeal, / . . . / Patrolled about his daughter" (2.1.138–44).

56.9–10 arms . . . compass] M used this anecdote in three different poems: (1) "The Admiral of the White," left in manuscript with an ESM annotation indicating "Herman gave this to Tom"; (2) *Clarel*, 3.12.56–128 (the story told by the Timoneer); (3) "The Haglets," a poem earlier published as "The Admiral of the White," on May 17, 1885, in the Boston *Herald* and (with eleven stanzas omitted) in the *New-York Tribune*, before it appeared, mostly unchanged from the *Herald* version, under its later title, in *John Marr and Other Sailors* (1888; *Published Poems*, pp. 218–25). (See also the discussion at 133.11.) In each case a store of arms deflects the ship's compass and causes her destruction.

56.30 assassinated] The French police reported sporadic plots on the life of Napoleon III, but there seem to have been no actual attempts at this time; in Naples, however, in the fall of 1856 a soldier rushed upon the king with a bayonet, and possibly some confused version of this had reached Thessalonica.

56.31 mosque] Charles Dudley Warner recalled seeing the mosque in 1875:

> On our way to the Mosque of St. Sophia, we passed through the quarter of the Jews. . . . These are the descendants of Spanish Jews, who were expelled by Isabella. . . .
>
> The Mosque of St. Sophia . . . copied in its proportions and style from its namesake in Constantinople, is retired, in a delightful court, shaded by gigantic trees. . . . Birds sang in the trees without disturbing the calm. . . . We were shown also a magnificent pulpit of the latter beautiful stone [verd antique] cut from a solid block, in which it is said St. Paul preached. As the Apostle, according to his custom, reasoned with the people . . . in a synagogue, and this church was not built for centuries after his visit, the statement needs confirmation. (*In the Levant*, pp. 329–30)

56.35 "beys effendi"] Bey was a hereditary rank originally for holders of imperial fiefs, later extended to certain military officers; "effendi" was a general title of courtesy for gentlemen.

57.5–6 Sinope] In a disastrous battle, a Russian naval force destroyed a Turkish squadron and this Black Sea port on November 30, 1853, precipitating French and English entry into the Crimean War.

57.6 "Ashmacks"] Also "yashmack," a heavy veil, usually of white muslin, covering all but the eyes of Turkish women.

57.8–9 Lemnos . . . Imbros] Both islands are at the north end of the Sporades, straddling the entrance to the Hellespont. M echoes Milton's description of Mulciber's fall (*Paradise Lost*, I, 745–46), "from the Zenith like a falling star, / On Lemnos th' Ægaean Isle."

57.11 new castles] In 1659 Mehmed IV erected "new" fortifications on either side of the entrance to the Hellespont against the Venetian threat; those farther up, erected by Mehmed II near the modern town of Dardanelles, had proved insufficient. (Mistakenly, M just below calls these latter also "New.") M's description here of the appearance of Asia is amplified in his entry for December 19, written about the outward-bound trip, and at some later time he penciled in here a forward-looking reminder: "For Asia here see 2d book (Lion)"—a reference to his description (at 68.35–36) of its color as like the Asiatic lions in menageries.

57.17 Abydos] Commonly identified with the modern Point Nagara, at the narrowest part of the straits, near the town of Dardanelles. Here the distance to the opposite Cape Sestos is scarcely a mile, and, in emulation of

Ovid's Leander, Byron swam the channel in seventy minutes, May 3, 1810. This was also the traditional site of the bridge (which M mentions below) built to carry the Persian troops into Europe; the mouth of the Granicus River, site of a major victory for Alexander, is on the Asiatic side, just down from the Sea of Marmara.

58.7 Prince Islands] Nine small islands, ten or eleven miles south of the city, valued as a resort for their mild climate.

58.8 Invisable confounds] Both words conjectural. Possibly "Invisable companions" or "Innumerable companions".

58.14 "Anastasius"] The picaresque novel (1819) by Thomas Hope, a pirated copy of which M had bought in Paris in 1849 then lost to English customs, but later replaced by a copy from his English publisher, Bentley (see 39.10–12 and accompanying discussion, also 144.23 and 146.4). Hope's description of the approach to the city (chap. 3) was much quoted by other travelers, and M could have been reminded of it by (for example) Murray's *Turkey* (third ed., 1854, pp. 54–55).

58.22 Golden Horn] Turkish Stamboul (now the older part of modern Istanbul), occupies a triangular promontory based on Europe, bounded by the Sea of Marmara on the south and the long, deep estuary of the Golden Horn to the northeast. At the apex, jutting into the Bosporus, is the State Palace—the Porte of the former sultans—and the Seraglio, mostly unused by this time in the nineteenth century. Stamboul was primarily Turkish in population, as was Scutari, the populous suburb across the Bosporus in Asia Minor, where Florence Nightingale had ministered to the English military hospitals. Most foreigners lived in the suburbs north of the Golden Horn, Galata on the inner shore, Top-Khaneh along the Bosporus, and Pera on the hill above; here were most of the diplomatic corps, wealthy merchants, and European hotels. M's hotel was not identified in Murray—perhaps Captain Taitt recommended it. In *Clarel*, Mortmain calls the "wive's–wine" of treacherous women "Tofana-brew" (2.36.90–91), and Rolfe recalls:

In Pera late an Asian man,
With stately cap of Astracan,
I knew in arbored coffee-house

On bluff above the Bosphorus.
Strange lore was his, and Saadi's wit:
Over pipe and Mocha long we'd sit
Discussing themes which thrive in shade.
(4.16.190–96)

58.23 caique] Eliot Warburton, like many others, describes them: "These graceful boats are the principal means of transit along the Bosphorus . . . ; their bows are very sharp, and rise so far out of the water, that only one half of the caïque rests upon the water. Their sides are formed of a single plank of very thin beech, and are quaintly adorned with gilding and oak-carving; you recline on silk cushions that supersede all seats, and are thus shot along with incredible rapidity" (*The Crescent and the Cross*, II, 187). See the illustration on p. 403 below.

58.29 assassins] Several letters of Emilia Hornby, the wife of Edmund (later Sir Edmund) Hornby, English diplomat in Constantinople from 1855 to 1865, mention the increased danger caused by the war and the mutual antagonisms of Turk, Greek, English, and French: "Pera is in a dreadful state of confusion. Ruffians and outcasts of all kinds have increased a hundred-fold. . . . There are no police or guards of any kind, and murders and all sorts of outrages are perpetrated in the crowded streets even by day, and still more in the utter darkness and confusion of the nights" (*In and around Stamboul* [Philadelphia: Challen & Son, [1858]], p. 128).

58.30 *Burnt Districts*] As most travel writers duly noted, devastating fires were all too common because of flimsy wooden construction, narrow, crowded streets, and inadequate, old firefighting equipment. Just a month before M's arrival the London *Times* correspondent in Turkey reported a fire in a Pera back-street that consumed several hundred houses (November 25, 26). M may have known Bayard Taylor's account:

> Constantinople has been terribly ravaged by fires, no less than fifteen having occurred during the past two weeks. Almost every night the sky has been reddened by burning houses. . . . The [recent] fire on the hill of Galata threatened to destroy a great part of the suburb of Pera. It came, sweeping over the brow of the hill, towards my hotel, turning the tall cypresses in the burial ground into shafts of angry flame, and eating away the crackling dwellings of hordes of hapless Turks. . . .
>
> To those initiated into the mysteries of Turkish politics, these fires are more than accidental; they have a most weighty significance. They indicate either a general discontent with the existing state of affairs, or else a powerful plot against the Sultan and his Ministry. (*The Lands of the Saracen* [New York: Putnam, 1855], pp. 351–52)

58.31 cemeteries] Since the custom was to plant a cypress at each grave, all Moslem cemeteries could seem like "forests"; none were treated with special piety but served rather as public resorts. Of the three principal ones in Pera, the smaller Turkish one was probably on M's route this morning.

59.4 gardens] As noted, the grounds and buildings had not been regularly occupied for some time because recent sultans preferred new palaces north along the Bosporus except for rare state occasions. Because of British and French help (and pressure) during the war, heavy restrictions on foreigners visiting this and other places had been much reduced. The walls enclosed a hill in three terraces, with cypress, plane, and other trees, garden houses, and kiosks; on the upper level were the palace proper and government offices. (Taylor describes fully the gardens, buildings, and following sights M mentions; *Lands of the Saracen*, pp. 346ff.)

59.5 St Sophia] M saw this most famous monument of Byzantine architecture, just southwest of the Seraglio Gate, under the best conditions for the time, though new plaster covered its Christian mosaics; it had been repaired and renovated in 1849 by order of the sultan. With relaxed restrictions on infidels, admission to this and other mosques cost only about two shillings.

59.12 Hippodrome] Begun by Severus and completed by Constantine on the model of the Roman Circus Maximus; its present shape was obscured by encroaching buildings in this area near St. Sophia. Along the original Spina only parts of three of the many ancient monuments remained: a sixty-foot Egyptian obelisk (with the inscription of Theodosius that M misremembers below); the eighteen-foot base, cast from Persian booty to hold the golden tripod of Apollo brought here by Constantine from Delphi; and the base of a masonry column once ninety-four feet high, covered with bronze plates. The bases of all three had just been excavated in 1856 by the noted archaeologist C. T. Newton, as described in his *Travels and Discoveries in the Levant* (2 vols. [London: Day & Son, 1865], II, 25–38). Reputedly, the heads of the three serpents who constitute the Delphian tripod were struck off at one sword blow by the conqueror Mehmed II; a part of one was in the Imperial Museum.

59.12–13 six towered mosque] On the southeast edge of the Hippodrome area; Sultan Ahmed I is said to have worked on it once a week with his own hands in the seventeenth century; zealots forced him to add a seventh minaret to the great mosque in Mecca lest his six here seem presumptuous. Effectively this was the state mosque, where all the chief festivals of the Prophet were celebrated. (Taylor describes it, *Lands of the Saracen*, pp. 349–50.)

59.19 to of] Intervening word lacking (presumably "be").

59.21 "Burnt Column"] The Column of Constantine (also known as the Porphyry or the Hooped Column) reached 120 feet high, made up of eight superimposed drums of porphyry; it was later strengthened by hoops of bronze, and once surmounted by a statue of Apollo; it marked the site of Constantine's Forum on the next hill west of St. Sophia. For the London Fire Monument, see the discussion at 15.29–30.

59.24 Cistern] This was Philoxenus, west of the Hippodrome, one of nineteen known cisterns of Greek construction. It was described by the Reverend Walter Colton (see the discussion at 73.6): "One of these [cisterns] is now dry, and partially filled with earth; but it still presents the spreading arch of its dome, sustained by six hundred marble columns, each column consisting of three, rising one above the other. It has the appearance of a superb subterranean temple, and there is now little to oppose this idea but an assembly of silk-twisters who flit among the columns, plying their task in the spectral twilight" (*Visit to Constantinople and Athens* [New York: Leavitt, Lord, 1836], pp. 65–66; revised and edited as *Land and Lee* by Rev. Henry T. Cheever [New York: Barnes, 1851]).

59.36 quincus] I.e., "quincunx".

59.37 Bazarr] Every traveler visited the great bazaar west of St. Sophia, the largest in the city and perhaps in the East; its miles of streets were covered with stone vaulting and lighted by small domes, its various shops grouped according to kind.

> The scene of the bazars is very curious; the luxurious shopman reclining on his ottoman, with his long chibouque and loose costume, the customer taking his seat opposite, and examining and chaffering about the article wanted. Turkish ladies peering through the closely latticed litter. . . . Far in the long vista of bazar are various animated groups, like some great fancy fair; there dashes along a group of glittering lancers under the sounding archways; here a staid dignitary pauses at a divan . . . , and a camel kneels to add fresh stores to the motley collection of goods. (Schroeder, *Shores of the Mediterranean*, I, 130–31)

60.5 Watch Tower] Built of white marble in the early nineteenth century, just west of the bazaar, the Serasker Tower commanded a view (by contemporary accounts) worth every fatiguing step of the ascent. The surrounding military center had been converted from an old imperial seraglio.

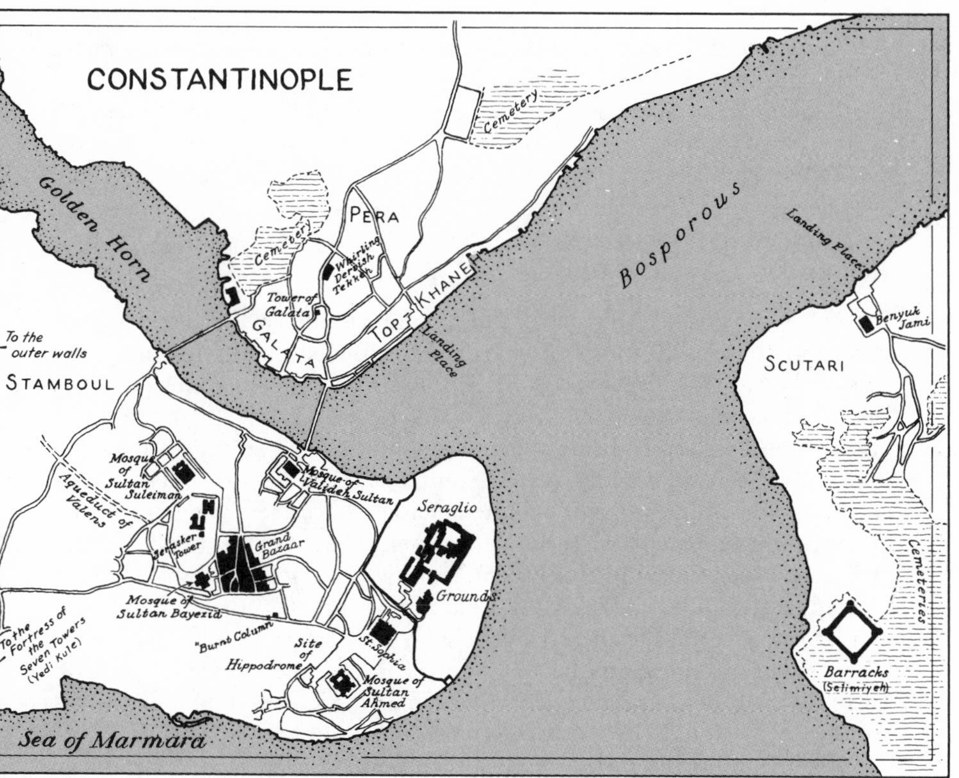

60.10 Pigeon Mosque] The Mosque of Bayezid II, built 1497–1505 by the son of Mehmed II the Conqueror. The myriads of sacred pigeons were said to be descendants of a pair bought from a poor woman by Bayezid and presented to the mosque.

60.15–16 Mosque of Sultan Sulyman] Built (1550–57) by Suleiman "the Magnificent" and considered the most beautiful example of Osmanli architecture. Barely smaller than St. Sophia and the Mosque of Ahmed, it was decorated with all the splendor the sultan could command at the height of the Turkish empire. What M calls "a kind of altar" is the "mihrab" that in every mosque marks the direction of Mecca; this one was pure white marble, bordered by choice Persian tiles and flanked by great gilt candelabra.

60.25–26 chests & bags] In the mosques of both Suleiman and Ahmed, a gallery area was set off and guarded, where travelers could deposit goods for safekeeping (see 153.12–13). M had used the allusion to Matthew 6:19 in *Moby-Dick*, chap. 16, where Peleg and Bildad arrange Ishmael's pay (p. 76).

60.39 Great crowds] Galata, along the north shore of the Golden Horn, was settled by Genoese allies of the Byzantines against the Venetians. Although it was the center of foreign mercantile activity, it was crowded with innumerable alleys and lanes of unsurpassed filth and wretchedness. It was infested, too, by the dangerous riff-raff of Europe, especially since the war. The population of Istanbul, so Lord Carlisle was told, was about 750,000—roughly 240,000 Turks, 300,000 Greeks, 200,000 Armenians, and 10,000 Jews and other Europeans (*Diary in Turkish and Greek Waters* [Boston: Hickling, Swan, & Brown, 1855], p. 32).

61.15 crowns . . . Sultans] M means plumed and jeweled state turbans, probably those in the tombs of Suleiman (mentioned later in this entry) and his celebrated favorite Roxalana in the gardens adjoining the mosque. Here also lay Suleiman II, Ahmed II, and others. It was described by Colton: "In the rear of the mosque, beneath the shade of the evergreen, stands the mausoleum of the royal founder. It is a beautiful pavilion, constructed of marble and adorned with a maze of delicate columns. In the centre repose the remains of the monarch in a marble coffin, beneath a covering of embroidered velvet, on which the town of Mecca, from which it was brought, is represented with singular vividness. At the head rolls the rich turban, ornamented with a tuft of heron's feathers, studded with the most precious gems. Several large tapers are constantly burning around it, and one individual, at least, may always be seen kneeling near, and reading the Koran, or praying for the repose of the soul" (*Visit to Constantinople*, pp. 54–55). Similarly, Bayard Taylor mentions the turban, sword, and jeweled harness at the tomb of Ahmed, whose mosque M visited also on this day (*Lands of the Saracen*, p. 350).

61.16 many] Possibly "wavy".

the crowns of the late Sultans. Then took
through great gateway, & behind many curtains
of [illegible], at the [illegible], [illegible]. Near the

61.24 Walls] After St. Sophia, visitors considered the great ancient walls the city's most impressive sight. Those across the promontory's landward base, the most massive and complex, withstood assaults for a thousand years. The city's fall to Mehmed the Conqueror (1453) was due less to the breach in them made by the first major use of cannon than to the confusion caused by the loss of defending leaders. The complete circuit, twelve miles, took five hours—M probably went horseback as indicated by his use of the verb "ride" and the aftereffects next day. Murray suggested hiring a horse from "Wepler, a German, who keeps a livery stable near the Hanseatic legation. . . . 40 piastres [about nine shillings] per diem" (*Turkey*, 1854, p. 66).

61.26 Sweet Waters] The Sweet Waters of Europe, a pretty, parklike, semirural retreat on the lower two and a half miles of two of the streams that flow into the Golden Horn. Its bridges, meadows, and groves made it a favorite resort of the wealthy, especially women; Mrs. Hornby describes her encounter there with the principal sultana and others from the royal harem (*In and around Stamboul*, pp. 371–81).

61.27 land wall] Constantine XI Palaeologus was killed on May 29, 1453, not here but defending the fourth gate, after the city was already effectively lost; on June 1, the victorious Mehmed entered through it.

61.38 garden spots] Vegetable gardens were planted in the old moat, partly filled with rich soil. Here, as later in Italy (111.24), M's allusion is to I Corinthians 15:42 ("So also is the resurrection of the dead. It [the body] is sown in corruption; it is raised in incorruption"). His parodic tone is symptomatic of his having made up his mind, as he told Hawthorne (see p. 628), "to be annihilated."

62.5 Greek Church] St. Mary ad Fontem, beyond the second gate. (It is not certain which guidebook—Murray's or some other—M is referring to here.) The chapel over a nearby spring dated only from 1833, but the site was holy for many centuries. A few fish curiously marked with light and dark coloring were explained by legend: when told the Turks had captured the city, an incredulous monk frying fish near the spring declared he would believe this news when his fish would jump from the pan into the water, only to see the fish do so. Colton adds that the original "Balukla, or Church of Fishes," was destroyed by Turks during the Greek War of Independence (*Visit to Constantinople*, pp. 91–92).

62.12–13 Seven Towers] Yedi Kule, the great fortress at the southwest corner of the city's land and sea walls, was reconstructed by Mehmed II in 1457 as the first imperial residence; it later served as state prison for ambassadors of nations warring with the sultan and sometimes for sultans recalcitrant to Janissary rule.

62.18 Válens(?)] M's questioned identification was correct; the aqueduct ascribed to Valens, Roman emperor of the East from 364 to 378, was built between the third and fourth hills in the city to carry water to the imperial palace. Of the original length of thirty-two hundred feet, about twenty-six hundred remain in two tiers, eighty-two feet above the valley.

62.21 Dervishes] As distinct from "howling" dervishes, the whirling ones worked themselves into ecstatic religious trance by increasingly rapid revolutions; many nineteenth-century travelers described them. Public performances were on Tuesdays and Fridays in the large Pera monastery or "Tekkeh," along M's probable return route. (The Christian "Shakers" of New England and New York who interested both Hawthorne and M manifested their religious ecstasy by shaking in a way that gave them their popular name.)

62.22–23 cemeteries of Pera] The great Moslem and Armenian cemeteries on the heights above the Bosporus; see 58.31–32 and accompanying discussion. Eliot Warburton called the view "one of the finest in the world: here all the gay people of the Frank [European] city assemble in the evening, and wander among the tombs with merry chat and laughter; or sit beneath the cypress-trees, eating ice and smoking their chibouques" (*The Crescent and the Cross*, II, 189). Mrs. Hornby's description reads:

> What a vast place it is, and how truly magnificent are its funereal trees! . . . Fancy the effect of a forest of such as these, with innumerable turbaned stones—some slanting forward, some upright, some fallen. . . . The eye follows with awe many a winding, rugged pathway through this silent forest of the dead. . . . The Pera side of this cypress-wood is much frequented, and is untidy, dirty, and noisy; but on this side, all is silent. . . . Many of the stones seem to be of great antiquity, . . . rapidly crumbling away. . . . But every now and then you come upon a fresh and splendid group. . . . I saw several painted a brilliant blue, and richly gilt. (*In and around Stamboul*, pp. 214–15)

62.25 Armenian funerals] Mrs. Hornby describes Greek and Armenian burial grounds and their use as resorts, also Greek and Armenian funeral processions, remarking "the women usually take a last adieu within the walls of the house, tearing their hair and garments with loud lamentations, after the fashion of the East" (*In and around Stamboul*, pp. 242–44).

62.36 *Street sights*] See the entry for November 9 (14.23–24) in the 1849 journal for another example of M's recurrent attraction to crowd scenes. (J. Ross Browne devotes a comic chapter—15—to the difficulties of the crowded streets, bridges, bazaars, and boats of Stamboul, in *Yusef; or, The Journey of the Frangi* [New York: Harper & Brothers, 1853].)

63.1 filthy streets] A staple comment by travelers; see also p. 186.

63.8 Consto[ple] bridges] The illustration opposite shows the arched bridges and the caiques and other watercraft described in this passage, as well as the "fine effect" of the mosques built "judiciously on the domed hills

of the city" (from *Beauties of Bosphorus* by Miss Pardoe, with drawings by William H. Bartlett [London: Virtue, 1839], n.p.).

63.14–15 Never wearied . . . them.] M's meaning is made unclear by his omission of the grammatical subject of "wearied" and uncertain reference of "them". The most likely meaning is that the "loquacious" Greek guide boys unweariedly leaned over the bridge rail and talked to sailors on the boats below. By his own account, M himself had not since his arrival in Constantinople two days earlier talked with the boys often or long enough to account for the expression "Never wearied"; since both he and they were on the bridge, he would not have leaned "over" the bridge rail to talk; and he can scarcely have shared with them enough of any language in which to converse very much; at 61.6–7 he had complained of "not being able to talk to a fellow being." Conceivably, there is a misreading of one or more of the three cited words.

Guide boys on the bridge. Greeks. Handsome faces. Lively, loquacious. Never wearied leaning over the balustrade & talking with them ✗ View from bridge, the quay

The Tower of Galata

63.21 Genoese Tower] Also variously known as the Tower of Galata, of Christ, or of the Cross, illustrated here from *Picturesque Europe*, ed. Bayard Taylor (New York: Appleton, 1879), p. 316. About 150 feet high and part way up the hill between the docks and the Pera heights, it was rebuilt in 1348 by Genoese subjects and allies of the Byzantine emperor who were settled at Galata.

63.32–33 clothes bazar] In the square enclosure of the Mosque of the Valideh Sultan, near the shore of the Golden Horn and the south end of the Galata bridge.

64.7 Schiller's Ghost-seer] In *Der Geisterseher* (1787–89), an unfinished Enlightenment novel by Johann Schiller (1759–1805), a mysterious "Armenian"—in fact a disguised priestly agent of the Inquisition—pursues a prince in Venice with apparently supernatural but actually merely magical events ("juggling" tricks) to effect his conversion to Catholicism. A translation titled *The Ghost-Seer!* was issued by Colburn and Bentley (1831), divided between Nos. 9 and 10 of their Standard Novels series; in No. 9 a first part of it was bound after Mary Shelley's revised *Frankenstein*; in No. 10 a second part after Charles Brockden Brown's *Edgar Huntly* (the "Armenian" appears in the first part). The copy of *Frankenstein* with the first part (No. 9, probably in a Bentley reprinting, e.g., 1849) that was given to M by Bentley in London in 1849 (see 144.27) is now unlocated (Sealts 438a/467).

64.9–10 Tower of Fire Watchman] The Serasker Tower, previously visited (see 60.5–10 and accompanying discussion).

64.11 Disciplining the barbarians] This pithy ironic phrase is developed in a debate in *Clarel* (4.12.77–81) about the ethics of "Christian" Western civilizations:

> . . . But preach and work:
> You'll civilize the barbarous Turk—
> Nay, all the East may reconcile:
> That done, let Mammon take the wings of even,
> And mount and civilize the saints in heaven.

64.14–15 Croton water pipes] Water from Croton Lake some forty miles north of New York reached the city via large pipes laid across High Bridge in 1842 and was distributed about the city by lines of iron pipe. Possibly M saw some of them being installed when he was in New York in the early 1840's, or at some time walked on the promenade built atop the aqueduct at High Bridge.

64.19 Buyakderre] Buyukdereh, a pretty village on the European shore of the Bosporus, twelve miles (an hour and a half by steamer) north of Constantinople. Warburton describes it as "a very picturesque village, with green verandahs, and red-tiled roofs, and a pretty little quay, and other seaport appendages in miniature. Men-of-war, with flags of the different nations which the ambassadors resident here represent, are moored a short distance from the shore. . . . The view . . . reaches through a vista of high cliffs and fortresses to the Black Sea . . . ; the vine-clad hills and grassy cliffs are mottled with the bright garments of the Greek inhabitants, and the whole scene is full of interest and animation" (*The Crescent and the Cross*, II, 186–87).

64.32 Ontario] Possibly M saw this lake (and Niagara Falls) on his trip west to Illinois in the summer of 1840 (Howard, *Herman Melville*, p. 33); the spontaneous comparison here suggests a personal recollection, whereas the reference in Chapter 61 of *Moby-Dick* could stem from a Cooper novel: "seated like Ontario Indians on the gunwales of the boats" (p. 283).

65.5 "Royal Albert"] Flagship of Admiral Lord Lyons, commander of the British Mediterranean Fleet.

65.14 from they spring] A word (presumably "which") is lacking after "from" (the error occurred as M inserted these three words—see the textual note at this point).

65.25 Banvard] John Banvard (1815–91), an American painter of vast scenic panoramas on immense lengths of canvas that were unrolled past the audience. M may have seen the Mississippi Valley one, which was advertised as three miles long; and as a source for "The River," a discarded chapter of *The Confidence-Man*, he may have used an edition of Banvard's book, *Description of Banvard's Panorama of the Mississippi River* (Boston, 1847, etc.); see the NN edition, pp. 511–15. (Banvard exhibited a panorama of the Ohio Valley in London in the winter of 1849–50 while M was there.)

65.31 "Arabas."] Mrs. Hornby: "A huge kind of wagon, made of dark oak, rudely carved and ornamented, and drawn by two white oxen, caparisoned in the most fantastic manner. . . . A handsome canopy of scarlet cloth, (sometimes even of velvet), embroidered with gold and trimmed with gold fringe, protects the vailed ladies, children, and black slaves inside from the sun" (*In and around Stamboul*, pp. 69–70).

66.33 Abbotsford] Sir Walter Scott's famous residence; M's visit to it during his stay in Edinburgh is reported in his letter to his brother Allan from Liverpool but not in his journal memorandum (see p. 625).

67.1–2 fortress . . . name] The fortress of Rumeli Hisar, built by Mehmed the Conqueror in 1452 on the European shore of the Bosporus halfway to the Black Sea, in preparation for his final assault on the city. Its three great towers represented the three occurrences of the letter *mim* (M) in his name as spelled in Arabic.

67.17–18 silent . . . streets] Mrs. Hornby commented: "Turn right or left out of this busy path, and you find yourself as it were in a city of the dead—closed lattices, and not a sound to disturb the profound silence of the steep and narrow streets, across which sometimes trails a neglected trellised vine" (*In and around Stamboul*, p. 94).

67.25 *The dogs*] Samuel I. Prime (brother of W. C. Prime, target of Mark Twain's satire in the Holy Land) described them: "As the dogs—a 'peculiar institution' of the city—act as scavengers, all the refuse from the houses is thrown into the street for their consumption. The dogs belong to no one in particular, but to every body in general. I counted five dying or dead, whom I had to step over or around" (*Travels*, II, 244–45).

67.26 prarie] This acceptable variant spelling occurs once in *Moby-Dick* and also in M's manuscript of his 1849 review of Francis Parkman's *The California and Oregon Trail*. See in the NN *Moby-Dick* the discussion at xi.29 (p. 813), and in the NN *Piazza Tales* volume the discussion at 232.20 (p. 641).

67.38–68.1 No drunkards] Many travelers noted both the admirable dignity and sobriety of ordinary Turks and the intemperance, promiscuity, and corruption of the upper and official classes.

68.2 fountain] The Fountain of Ahmed III (1728), considered the city's most beautiful; a square marble building, it combined wall and basin jets, ornamented with finely carved arabesques and inscriptions in gold on blue and green backgrounds.

68.4 Scutari] The most Asiatic suburb, on terraces up the Asian shore; this was where Florence Nightingale was active in the great military hospital and suffered her own illness.

68.7 Palaces] The European shore north of Constantinople was lined with extravagant palaces of successive sultans, their sisters, mothers, and court officials; the newest (1853) at Dolmabahçe was white marble in a showy, neo-Italian Renaissance style, of deplorable taste.

68.9–10 barracks . . . Cemeteries] The barracks M notes were the Selimiyeh (1807), near the shore in a former summer palace, rebuilt after burning in a Janissary revolt. The cemetery, Benyuk Mezaristan, was the largest and most beautiful of oriental burial grounds. M's later marginal note "Turks want to be buried in Asia" alludes to a wish stemming from their common belief that the Empire would ultimately be expelled from Europe. In a note to his Civil War poem "On a natural Monument," in *Battle-Pieces* (1866), M speaks of "the old turbaned head-stones and cypresses in the interminable Black Forest of Scutari" (*Published Poems*, p. 134); and in "The Continents" (unpublished by M) he refers to that Turkish burial preference:

From bright Stamboul Death crosses o'er;
Beneath the cypress evermore
His camp he pitches by the shore
Of Asia old.

. . . .

Even so the cleaving Bosphorous parts
Life and Death.

68.12 Water mosque] Perhaps the Benyuk Jami, built by a daughter of Suleiman the Magnificent, near the Scutari boat landing.

68.14 Tenedos Wine] The light wine from the small island of Tenedos at the mouth of the Hellespont (behind which Homer's Greeks withdrew to deceive the Trojans) was much esteemed in Constantinople.

68.18 Acadia] Possibly the old wooden paddle-wheel steamer of this name operated by Cunard on the Atlantic until 1850 had been transferred to the new Mediterranean line established in 1852.

68.24 Plain of Troy] These plains adjoining the mouth of the Hellespont had always been held the site of the epic battleground. The archaeologist Heinrich Schliemann (who began his excavations in 1870) later described the so-called "Tumulus of Achilles" as a large conical hill on a projecting headland about 250 yards from the Hellespont, and visible from the sea at a great distance; he found nothing but pottery in it and another nearby mound (Leo Deuel, *Memoirs of Heinrich Schliemann* [New York: Harper & Row, 1977], pp. 299–300).

69.15 Mount Pagus] The five-hundred-foot hill directly behind the south edge of Smyrna is crowned by ruins of the Acropolis that M visits later. The view here of the harbor of Smyrna is reproduced by permission of the U.S. Naval Academy Museum.

69.18 Consul, a Greek] Edward S. Offley, an American though born in the Levant, was the third of his family to hold the post; they were part of the American mercantile establishment in Smyrna, a principal entrepôt for American-Levantine trade. (In 1811, David Offley, a Philadelphia Quaker, had founded the first American commercial house there—see James A. Field, Jr., *America and the Mediterranean World, 1776–1882* [Princeton: Princeton University Press, 1969], pp. 117, 235, or David H. Finnie, *Pioneers East* [Cambridge: Harvard University Press, 1967], pp. 14, 26, 34.) Among others, Colton and M's friend Willis speak warmly of Smyrna's charms, the extensive American presence, and the Offleys' hospitality. (Field, p. 198, summarizes many such accounts.)

69.25 mosque] The martyred Polycarp (A.D. 69?–155?) preached from the original church, within the walls of the Acropolis.

69.26 Caravan Bridge] Many travelers described the city's color, variety, and vivacity and the great camel caravans bringing in trade goods—especially the figs and other fruits for which Smyrna was famous. The bridge across the Meles River was the main approach from the surrounding country, its immediate vicinity thronged with cafés, inns, and polyglot loungers. An especially colorful description is Thackeray's in Chapter 6 of *Notes of a Journey from Cornhill to Grand Cairo* (London: Chapman & Hall, 1846).

69.36 stalking] Possibly "stilting".

ostrich or a gigantic grasshopper. His hoof is spongy, & covered with hair to the ground, so that walking thro' these muddy lanes, he seems sitting along on four mops. —The cemeteries very

70.13 American Mission] From the time of *Typee* and *Omoo* M was critical as to the effect of missionary efforts; his account here is a little misleading and shows this bias (as later in Palestine and Beirut). Western missions, both British and American, were heavily directed to the conversion of the Jews, especially because of the millennial expectations tied to that event but partly also because it was a capital offense for a Moslem to convert, and partly because Greek, Armenian, and Roman hierarchies alike violently opposed Protestant proselytizing. Thus, though the American Board of Commissioners for Foreign Missions chose Smyrna as an initial base because of its prosperous American mercantile colony and relatively benign Turkish administration, the field of major missionary concern was always Syria and Palestine. The Americans therefore relinquished Smyrna to the English Missionary Society and the Church of Scotland and concentrated their resources in Beirut. (Another reason the mission appeared "hopeless" was that disease and death took a constant toll of all missionaries and wives.) See also the entry for January 23 (81.5–15) and the passage on "Christian Missions" (91.29–94.38); also Finnie, *Pioneers East*; Field, *America and the Mediterranean World*; A. L. Tibawi, *American Interests in Syria* (Oxford: Clarendon Press, 1966); and Robert L. Daniel, *American Philanthropy in the Near East* (Athens: Ohio University Press, 1970).

70.15–16 the chaplain] The Reverend William B. Lewis was appointed chaplain in 1840; just why M found him a "curiosity" is not made clear by other accounts, which occasionally praise him.

71.23 old style of almanack] By mid-nineteenth century the calendar of the Greek Orthodox Church was twelve days behind that of the West.

72.14–15 Contrast . . . archipelago] M's poem "The Archipelago" in *Timoleon* (1891) recalls this contrast and uses his recurrent example of barren Delos (*Published Poems*, pp. 307–8).

72.18–19 Delos . . . sea] A small island in the Cyclades and according to myth the only place to accept Leto when she was ready to give birth to the twins Artemis and Apollo. Delos was said to have been a floating island, hovering just beneath the sea's surface until commanded by Poseidon to emerge and stand firm to receive Leto.

72.30–31 "Sailing Directions"] Probably a version of *Sailing Directions for the Eastern Portion of the Mediterranean Sea . . .* , one of a series of such navigational aids published by John Imray & Son, London. (Despite the presence of U.S. naval vessels in the Mediterranean since the Barbary wars, the internationally famous American "Sailing Directions" compiled by Lieutenant Matthew Maury covered only Atlantic, Pacific, and Indian Ocean routes.)

72.35 Pompey's Pillar] Common misnomer for a column honoring Diocletian—along with Cleopatra's Needles the only important monuments of antiquity remaining in Alexandria. Like many travelers, Samuel Prime described it:

> There, on this height commanding the city and a view far out to sea, stands, "solitary and alone," the column of Diocletian, or popularly known as Pompey's Pillar. One must see it to appreciate the striking beauty of a single pillar of polished red Syenite, rising ninety-eight feet and eight inches from the ground to the top of the capital. The column, without the pedestal and capital, is an unbroken block of granite, nine feet in diameter. . . . The face of the monument has been injured by the itching for notoriety, which has induced European travellers to inscribe their names on it with paint. (*Travels*, II, 403)

M had referred to it (without having seen it) in *Mardi* (chap. 75, p. 229) as a symbol of antiquity, in *Redburn* (chap. 41, p. 206) as like the smokestacks at the Liverpool railway tunnel, and in *Moby-Dick* (chap. 103, p. 454) as like a whale's spine.

73.2 Cleopatra's Needles] The two obelisks called by her name had no real connection with Cleopatra (69–30 B.C.), but were erected at Heliopolis (ca. 1500 B.C.) by Thotmes III, and were brought here by the Romans. "One of them is lying on and under the sand, where it fell from its pedestal. The other is standing one hundred and fifty feet from it—a single shaft of red Syenite, about seven and a half feet through at the base. . . . The one that is lying prostrate . . . has been given away by the government to England and France; but neither is disposed to carry it off" (Prime, *Travels*, II, 402). The second (some 60 feet high and 180 tons) was moved to London in 1878, the first (somewhat larger) to New York's Central Park in 1880.

73.3 Canal] Silting had long isolated the declining port of Alexandria from the Nile, but the imperious Mehemet Ali, nominal viceroy of Egypt, decreed construction of the canal in 1819. Eliot Warburton devoted several paragraphs to its brutal history: "In the greatness and the cruelty of its accomplishment, this canal may vie with the gigantic labors of the Pharaohs. 250,000 people . . . were swept from the villages of the Delta, and heaped like a ridge along the destined banks of that fatal canal. They had only provisions for one month. . . . They tore up that great grave——25,000 people perished, but the grim contract was completed, and in six weeks the waters of the Nile were led to Alexandria" (*The Crescent and the Cross*, I, 35). The pasha's garden, near the shore, was reported to be hardly worth the easily obtained permission to enter.

73.4 De Leon] Edwin De Leon (1818–91), a lawyer, editor, and fiery southern articulator of the Young America political fervor, had been appointed consul general in Egypt (1854–61) by President Pierce, despite the

Young Americans' preference for Stephen Douglas (Field, *America and the Mediterranean World*, pp. 239–41); Gansevoort Melville vociferated similar expansionist enthusiasm as a campaign orator for Polk in 1844. Later De Leon was a Confederate diplomatic agent in Europe; he wrote a novel, works on Egypt and Turkey, and two volumes of reminiscences, *Thirty Years of My Life on Three Continents* (London: Ward & Downey, 1890).

73.6 Constellation] The original *Constellation* was familiar to M from his Pacific years; he had seen it and the *United States* in Honolulu in 1843 during the uproar over the temporary British annexation, and again in the harbor of Callao, Peru, in January of 1844. (Still earlier, as M probably knew, survivors of the famous sinking of the *Essex* by an enraged whale in 1820 were signally aided by the *Constellation* and its commander. See Thomas F. Heffernan, *Stove by a Whale* [Middletown, Conn.: Wesleyan University Press, 1981], pp. 99ff., with a picture of the ship drawn in 1831, on p. 98.) N. P. Willis had spent time on the *Constellation* in the Mediterranean, and its former chaplain, Walter Colton, had written his *Visit to Constantinople and Athens* (1836) on one of its cruises (a book in the library of M's last whaler, the *Charles and Henry*). It was one of the six original frigates—including the *Constitution* and the *United States*—authorized in the unsettled late eighteenth century. Completed at Baltimore in 1797, she played a distinguished part both in the undeclared naval conflict with revolutionary France and against the Barbary pirates. In 1853–54, however, she was nominally "rebuilt" as a twenty-two-gun sloop-of-war and thereafter served as a training ship; one of her functions, like that of the *United States*, was to "show the flag" on foreign stations, and as such she served repeatedly in the Mediterranean Squadron (the only ship on station during the Civil War). In 1856 the ship had just been in Constantinople in mid-November. (For M's friendship with Willis, see the 1849–50 journal, 22.1–2 and accompanying discussion; Willis's *Summer Cruise in the Mediterranean*, 1853, was a recent reprint of that part of his earlier *Pencillings by the Way*, 1835.) But whether the ship M saw here (and again in Messina where her officers are named—see the entry for February 14 and the discussion at 100.16–17) was merely a modification of the original he once knew, or in all essentials a new ship under the old name, is hotly argued by Howard I. Chapelle and Leon D. Pollard in *The Constellation Question* (Washington, D.C.: Smithsonian Institution Press, 1970). The ship has been "restored" as a historic shrine; for a 1968 picture, see *The Constellation Question*, p. 123. See also the discussion at 124.23.

73.7 To Cairo] By the newly opened railroad, 130 miles, either four or six hours, express or regular. On this route M placed the scene of the poem "A Rail Road Cutting Near Alexandria in 1855" (unpublished by M). Shepherd's Hotel was accounted one of the best in the Near East (though not by Mark Twain in *Innocents Abroad* [Hartford, Conn.: American Publishing

Co., 1869], pp. 615ff.), with charges of about sixteen shillings a day. De Leon described it in the 1850's as very oriental, with stone walls four feet thick, much used by British travelers to and from India (*Thirty Years*, I, 158).

73.8 Lockwood] John Alexander Lockwood (1811–1900) of Kent County, Delaware, entered the navy as an assistant surgeon, was promoted, and served at the Naval Academy as surgeon and professor of chemistry until 1849. (His brother Henry was the professor of mathematics on the *United States* and later at the academy—who may have suggested M's friendly caricature of the "Professor" in Chapter 83 of *White-Jacket*, pp. 415, 345ff.) Lockwood was new (1856) on the *Constellation* but in Honolulu in 1842 M may have heard of the sensation he and others, including the later Admiral Andrew Foote (see the discussion at 99.28), had created in 1839 by sponsoring a pamphlet (Samuel N. Castle, *An Account of the Visit of the French Frigate L'Artemise to the Sandwich Islands; July, 1839* [Honolulu, 1839]) that defended Protestant missionaries menaced by the efforts of a French frigate to force the Hawaiian king to accept Catholic missionaries. In a later pamphlet, *Flogging in the Navy* (1849), Lockwood attacked that abuse at the same time as M did in *White-Jacket*.

73.9–10 Citadel] Built by Saladin (1166) on an eminence southeast of Cairo as a defense against Crusaders. Visitors extolled the grandeur of the view west across the teeming city and its four hundred mosques to the Pyramids and along the fertile valley, far into the delta on the north (see also 74.28–75.2 and the discussion at 74.34). The illustration below is from *The Nile Boat; or, Glimpses of the Land of Egypt* by William H. Bartlett (London: Hall, Virtue, 1859), facing p. 60.

Cairo, from the Citadel

73.12–13 Victoria Hotel] Not mentioned in Murray's 1847 or 1858 *Egypt*, but William Prime described it as comfortably kept by an Englishman though not on the fashionable Grand Square (*Boat Life in Egypt and Nubia* [New York: Harper & Brothers, 1857], p. 496).

74.4–5 Cock Lanes] See 15.5 and accompanying discussion.

74.13 Children opthalmick] Thackeray was appalled by the "children sitting in the doorways, their eyes completely closed up with the green sickening sore, and the flies feeding on them" (*From Cornhill to Grand Cairo*, chap. 14, p. 241). The theme of "too much light" is developed in M's poem "In the Desert" in *Timoleon* (*Published Poems*, p. 314).

74.25 Black crape] Travelers often commented on the veiled women's bulky overgarments, kohl-darkened eyelids, and henna-stained fingernails. Thus Warburton: "A procession of women waddles along, wrapped in large shroud-like veils from head to foot, with a long black bag, like an elephant's trunk, suspended from their noses" (*The Crescent and the Cross*, I, 25, see also p. 69).

74.27 silks . . . donkeys] A Flaubert letter from Cairo in 1850 is graphic:

> It is like being hurled while still asleep into the midst of a Beethoven symphony, with the brasses at their most ear-splitting, the basses rumbling, and the flutes sighing away; each detail reaches out to grip you; it pinches you; and the more you concentrate on it the less you grasp the whole. Then gradually all this becomes harmonious and the pieces fall into place. . . . But the first days, by God, it is such a bewildering chaos of colours that your poor imagination is dazzled as though by continuous fireworks as you go about staring at minarets thick with white storks, at tired slaves stretched out in the sun, . . . at the patterns of sycamore branches against walls, with camel bells ringing in your ears and great herds of black goats bleating in the streets amid the horses and the donkeys and the pedlars. As soon as night falls, everyone goes about with his cloth lantern, and the pashas' grooms run through the city brandishing great lighted torches. . . .
>
> In Europe we picture the Arab as very serious. Here he is very merry, very artistic in gesticulation and ornamentation. . . . You hear the loud *zagárit* of the Arab women in the streets: swathed in veils and holding their elbows well out as they ride on their donkeys, they resemble nothing so much as black full-moons coming toward you on four-legged somethings. (*Flaubert in Egypt*, trans. and ed. Francis Steegmuller [London: Bodley Head, [1972]], pp. 79–80)

74.34 Mosque] Within the Citadel walls, the imperious viceroy Mehemet Ali had begun in 1824 the as-yet-incomplete new mosque to house his tomb, elaborate in rose marble and alabaster. In 1811, to break the power of the Mameluke mercenaries in Egypt, Ali entertained several hundred in the Citadel, closed the gates, and ordered the massacre, from which, reputedly, only Emim Bey escaped, by leaping his horse over a gap in the ancient walls (see *Clarel*, 1.21.30–39). The fourteenth-century Mosque of Hassan below the Citadel near Emim Bey's landing-spot on the southwest side was called the most beautiful example of Arabic architecture anywhere; in Cairo legend the sultan ordered the architect's hand cut off lest he build a rival.

75.3 *Pyramids*] The customary several-mile donkey ride to the Pyramids was the background for the poem "The Dust-Layers" (unpublished by M). Just over a decade before, Lieutenant Schroeder wrote of a similar excursion: out of the city and through the garden groves upriver four miles or so to the river crossing at Isle Roda, each donkey accompanied by an indefatigable runner with a sharp prod. "The scene was truly lovely; the battlements of the citadel and palace just tinted with the sunlight, minarets capped with gold, and the dark walls of the city yet in shadow. . . . We rode through pretty avenues, along little artificial water-courses overhung with fruit-trees, dripping with dews and freshness." On the island was the Nilometer, whose daily readings of the river level during the annual inundations were proclaimed by street criers throughout the city. By Arab tradition this island was where the infant Moses was found. Ibrahim, son and successor of Mehemet Ali, had extensive gardens laid out on it by an English horticulturist. The Pyramids (shown below, from *A Practical System of Modern Geography* by J. Olney [New York: Robinson, Pratt, 1836], p. 230; Sealts 390) were seven miles distant where watered fields and groves abruptly met the western desert. There swarming Bedouins helped visitors clamber up the two- to five-foot ledges—as Schroeder describes them, one at each elbow, another behind pushing, and a boy offering water at each pause. (In Mark Twain's *Innocents Abroad*, chap. 58, the scene was little changed.) On the north side of the Great Pyramid of Cheops, the entrance to its inner recesses was some sixty feet up, about three and a half feet square, descending one hundred feet in a smooth inclined plane before rising again to the innermost chamber (Schroeder, *Shores of the Mediterranean*, II, 35–49).

Pyramids and Sphynx.

75.23 fainted] Possibly "failed" (H).

75.30 Mammoth Cave] This notation may imply that M visited the famous Kentucky wonder on his return trip from Illinois in 1840.

75.34 Moses learned] Acts 7:22: "And Moses was learned in all the wisdom of the Egyptians." Warburton offers an observation parallel to M's in his speculative chapter on ancient magic and arcane wisdom: "Moses was well skilled in this [magic], as in all other 'learning of the Egyptians' " (*The Crescent and the Cross*, I, 99).

75.38–76.1 As long . . . pyramids] The following passage and M's extension of it at 78.7–38 contributed to his poem "The Great Pyramid" in *Timoleon* (*Published Poems*, pp. 315–16). In *Clarel* (1.17.56–62) he associated with pyramids the Illinois Indian mounds, which he possibly saw in 1840 (see the discussion at 75.30). Also in *Clarel* (2.11.55–61), the Pyramids and Cheops are types of "the imperishable Past."

76.6 Notch of White Mountains] M and his bride saw this part of New Hampshire on their wedding trip to Montreal and Quebec in August of 1847.

76.15–16 Theory . . . pyramids] M's fanciful theory of the Pyramids is one that De Leon attributed to the former Armenian official Hekkekyan Bey (*Thirty Years*, I, 177; *The Khedive's Egypt* [New York: Harper & Brothers, 1878], pp. 198–99).

76.26 *Shoobra*] In the village of Shubra, two and a half miles north of the city, Mehemet Ali had built a kiosk and extensive gardens (see Warburton's extravagant romantic description, *The Crescent and the Cross*, I, 50–52). The avenue leading there was a shady and fashionable promenade for the well-to-do native and foreign residents.

76.28 moscho] I.e., "mosquito". Many variant spellings for this word are reported by the *Oxford English Dictionary* and the *Dictionary of American English* but not the forms M wrote here and at 79.10 ("moschits"), both of which may be either colloquial or miswritten.

76.34 *great square*] Lieutenant Schroeder described in detail the Esbekyeh (or Usbekeeh), on or near which were the chief foreign hotels like Shepherd's, expensive shops, cafés, and the like:

> It is in the form of a circle, with a diameter of about a third of a mile, surrounded and traversed with avenues of sycamore and acacias, or carobs. Around the outer avenues is a canal of twenty-five feet width, which encompasses the whole park, and handsome bridges cross it at frequent intervals. On the outer side of the canal is the spacious, circular street, new built in modern design; and the whole thus composes one of the finest public places I know. (*Shores of the Mediterranean*, II, 31)

He further described the prancing horses, caparisoned dromedaries, ladies carried and guarded by ferocious slaves, Jews, Armenians, Turks, sherbet and tobacco dispensers, jugglers, and dancing girls.

ALEXANDRIAN DONKEY-BOYS.

77.5 *donkey boys*] Pictured above, from Samuel Prime's *Travels*, II, 398. Mark Twain's account of them in Alexandria is similar to M's but more comic:

> We found an army of Egyptian boys with donkeys no larger than themselves, waiting for passengers—for donkeys are the omnibuses of Egypt. . . . The boys crowded about us, clamored around us, and slewed their donkeys exactly across our path. . . . They were good-natured rascals, and so were the donkeys. We mounted, and the boys ran behind us and kept the donkeys in a furious gallop. . . . I believe I would rather ride a donkey than any beast in the world. He goes briskly, he puts on no airs, he is docile, though opinionated. Satan himself could not scare him, and he is convenient—very convenient. When you are tired riding you can rest your feet on the ground and let him gallop from under you. (*Innocents Abroad*, pp. 611–12; chap. 58 also describes the sturdy but motley donkeys of Cairo.)

77.12 bray] Possibly "boy"; the heading indicates that the passage is to be about both donkeys and donkey boys, and such a boy as M describes might seem more likely his idea of "the original Egyptian" than a donkey's bray.

Account of donkey & donkey boys. Wonderful endurance of both. Run, like deer (the boys). Stick in hand, barefooted & barelegged. Pursue the donkey, talk to him, remonstrate, admonish. Donkey trips nimbly. [Tell 'Constantinople'] Boy once pushed him. Donkey is one of the best fellows in the world. It is the patience & honesty of the donkey that makes him so abused & despised. He is so useful & indispensable, that he is contemned. He is so unresisting. Type of honesty, &c. As for his bray, that is the original Egyptian. Run donkeys like rats. Their saddles, very curious. High balled pommel. Then of donkeys. A great love for them. Necks.

77.17 Mohawk Flats] Along the Mohawk River near Schenectady, New York, these lands were very fertile and free of timber, a prize for early settlers. When M saw the Nile Delta, the annual autumn inundation had receded and a new planting was well along. Delta soil was reputed unlike any other, up to sixty-three percent sand and water and very friable—seed could be simply scattered on the surface, then trampled in. Where the land could be irrigated year round, two, sometimes three, crops would be grown, but scarcely four.

77.20 Pigeon houses] Lieutenant Schroeder also describes the pigeon-cotes: "Our village of this morning was distinguished by sixty or seventy enormous pigeon houses, built in conical domes of the mud of the Nile, . . . rising much higher than the walls. . . . These pigeon establishments are built in rows of tall cones, and myriads of pigeons are flying about their tops" (*Shores of the Mediterranean*, II, 27–28). The embankments M noticed were commonly causeways raised above the annual flooding.

77.28 Dipping & machines] In 1851 M's Berkshire neighbor and later his editor, George William Curtis, in a book that mentions M, described the two methods of raising water into the irrigation ditches: the primitive shadoof consists "simply of buckets swinging upon a pole, like a well bucket, and dipped into the river and emptied above by another into the channel. There are always two buckets, and the men stand opposite . . . plunging the bucket rapidly"; the more recent sakia "is the great instrument of irrigation. It is a rude contrivance of two perpendicular wheels, turned by a horizontal cog. The outer wheel is girdled with a string of earthen jars, which descend with every revolution into the pit open to the river, in which the wheel turns. As the jars ascend they empty themselves into a trough, thence conducted away. . . . The sakia is worked by a pair of oxen. Upon the tongue of the crank which they turn, sits a boy, drowsing and droning, and beating their tail-region all day long" (*Nile Notes of a Howadji* [New York: Harper & Brothers, 1851], pp. 140–41, 138–39).

77.37 Grand Square] The Place Mehemet Ali, center of European life, dominated by a great equestrian statue of the late viceroy.

78.38 founded] See the textual note at this point for M's subsequent penciled notation (reproduced below): "Explorers commencing out 30 miles in Desert" ("commencing" is a conjectural reading). Of the many expeditions exploring and excavating the antiquities of Egypt, possibly the one M had in mind was the greatest of mid-century explorations, the Prussian expedition led by Karl Richard Lepsius, 1842–45; one of the sites it explored was the depression of the Faiyum, some thirty miles west of the Nile. M could have seen descriptive articles in contemporary periodicals, or in Lepsius's *Letters from Egypt, Ethiopia, and the Peninsula of Sinai* (London: Bohn, 1853).

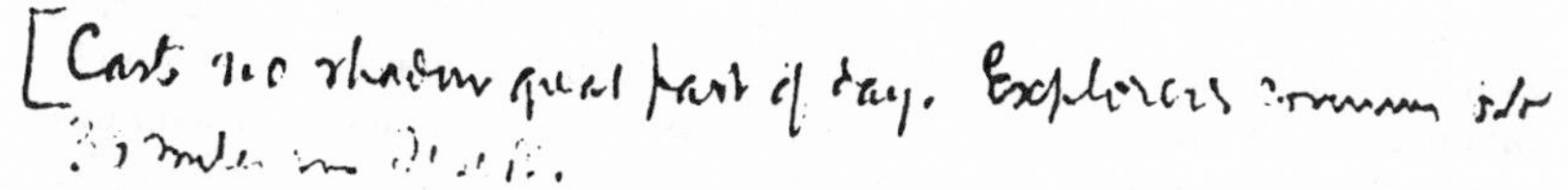

[Cast no shadow great part of day. Explorers commencing out 30 miles in Desert.

79.1 Jaffa] M's passage was probably on an Austrian-Lloyd steamer, which had a scheduled departure on Fridays, the day he expected to leave. The trip usually took most of three days and cost twenty-seven florins for second class, but well-advised westerners took first class if possible. Debarkation in the open roadstead about a mile off shore at Jaffa, however, was so treacherous and so confused by the clamor of local boatmen that many preferred to land at Beirut and travel to Palestine overland—as did both J. Ross Browne and Mark Twain with his fellow Innocents.

79.7 dragoman] The common Levantine term for guide and general factotum. J. Ross Browne, after a seriocomic description, lists the duties:

> He is interpreter of the party; he usually provides the provisions, horses, mules, tents, &c., and charges so much a day for the whole; he speaks various languages, seldom less than five or six; is expected to know all about the country, and something more. He is responsible for the name of every village and town, . . . for every moral and physical defect in the horses and mules; for every shower of rain, . . . for every headache and fit of indigestion, . . . for the amount of fleas, . . . for the sterile and unsatisfactory character of the scenery, . . . for the roughness of the roads . . . [and so on at length]. (*Yusef*, pp. 178–79)

Actually, for the trip to Jerusalem, about forty miles, twelve hours by horse, no guide was really needed, the road was so well traveled.

79.9 Ramla] M more often spells it "Ramlah" (80.5,8,9), but in *Clarel*, 1.1.41, the more common "Ramleh".

79.10 moschits] I.e., "mosquitos". See the discussion at 76.28.

79.16 ride . . . hills] The route, the climb through the mountains, and the first view of Jerusalem are described in innumerable travel accounts, of which the most immediately available to M was perhaps Bayard Taylor's *The Lands of the Saracen*. Later, the most ironic was Mark Twain's *Innocents Abroad*. It was customary to break at Ramleh (identified as the biblical Arimathea), about three hours from Jaffa, but well-advised travelers stayed at Latin, Russian, or Greek monastic hospices (as M did on his return, January 19), not in native hostelries, where, as Browne and M both discovered, the fleas were vicious:

> I have looked in vain for a scientific description. . . . The *Pulce granda*, or Syrian flea, is of a lively disposition and irregular in his habits, given to late hours and disturbances of the peace. . . . Human blood is his food; he prefers Christians to Arabs as an article of diet; has great vigor of muscle and capacity for digestion; carries in his mouth a long harpoon, which he throws with great skill; uses likewise a boarding-knife and patent forcing-pump. . . . Wounds produced by this ferocious animal are unpleasant, but not fatal. Constant depletion, however, may dest[r]oy life; hence, by repeated attacks, a man may be altogether dried up; in which case he becomes a dry subject. (*Yusef*, pp. 346–47)

Warburton describes the trip in detail in *The Crescent and the Cross*, Part II, Chapters 6 and 7. Melville used details from his trips both to and from Jerusalem in *Clarel*, 1.1.

79.17 Meditterranean Hotel] This had also been Bayard Taylor's hotel (*Lands of the Saracen*, p. 58); one of the three principal lodgings, it was sometimes considered the least bad, though damp (from the Pool of Hezekiah immediately at the rear), with high charges and bad food. Its location on Jerusalem's west side near the main or Jaffa Gate put it near the Church of the Holy Sepulchre, just to the north. M's room was evidently on

POOL OF HEZEKIAH.

the back side, and he puts Clarel into a room similarly located but with some interior details from the Jaffa hotel where M stayed on his return trip (see the entry for January 22). The illustration above is from *Walks about the City and Environs of Jerusalem* by William H. Bartlett (London: Virtue, 1844), facing p. 97.

79.21 view] This survey of landmarks is partially duplicated in *Clarel* (1.1.128–71), as is M's later wandering among the nearby hills (1.10, "Rambles"). David Street was the principal east-west thoroughfare, leading from the Jaffa Gate; the Street of the Patriarchs, or Christian Street, was a narrow lane descending toward the Church of the Holy Sepulchre.

79.25 damaged dome] Even though this dome dated from only 1810, when the church was rebuilt after a disastrous 1808 fire, its fall was constantly threatened until new iron-ribbed vaulting was supplied in 1868. The landlord's claim about the inception of the Crimean War was hyperbolic. The real cause, of course, the rivalry of Russian, English, and French interests in the Near East, was expressed in the czar's claim in the name of the Greek church to protection of the principal Christian sites; Louis Napoleon, seeking to bolster his new imperial title, was concerned to dispute that claim in his professed championing of the Latin church.

79.29 *Jan 7th*] Error for January 8; see the discussion at 80.1 below.

79.30 *Jan 8th*] Error for January 9; see the discussion at 80.1 below.

79.31 *Jan 9th*] Error for January 10; see the discussion at 80.1 below.

79.32 Frederick Cunningham] Son of Charles Cunningham (of A. & C. Cunningham, Boston merchants and shipowners in the Mediterranean, China, and West Indies food trade); when his father retired in 1849, Frederick (1826–64), with his cousin Charles W. Dabney, Jr., took over the West Indian business. His application for a passport, together with that for his wife (née Sarah M. Parker) and for a daughter, had been received by the State Department as recently as October 30, 1856.

80.1 *Jan 10th*] Error for January 11. At this point M recognized that he had made "some mistake" (starting with the entry dated January 7); the day lost was due to the overnight trip from Jaffa. See the next discussion (and the Chronology, pp. 382–83) for M's further errors.

80.4 *Jan 19th*] Error for January 18; through the twentieth M is one day ahead in his dating; thereafter through the twenty-seventh he is two days ahead. He evidently recognized the error on January 26 when he corrected the date that he originally gave as January 28.

80.5 Abdallah] Doubtless the model for the striking Druse guide in *Clarel*, especially 2.7, 3.5, and 3.15. The Druse, a restless, handsome, warlike, and fiercely secretive group, inhabited the mountain country behind Beirut. An offshoot of Islam with elements of Christianity, they often dissembled their real convictions. Lieutenant Schroeder wrote, "The Arabs of the hills, and mountaineers are always the nobler race. I thought some of these, magnificent fellows; full, piercing eyes, noble figures, well set off in their costumes and glittering arms" (*Shores of the Mediterranean*, I, 163).

80.6–7 Greek Patriarch] To stay at Greek hospices, as here or earlier at Mar Saba (see 84.4–18 and accompanying discussion), foreigners needed authorization from the resident patriarch in Jerusalem or one of his representatives.

80.8 tower of Ramlah] The White Mosque was ancient enough to have been restored by Saladin (1190); from the top of the later minaret, 120 steps, the view stretched from the sea to the eastern mountains.

80.9 *Jan 20th*] Error for January 19.

80.9 Lydda] Though off the main road, the town and Crusader church were recommended to travelers as Saint George's burial site. Lieutenant Schroeder describes at length the beauties of the Plain of Sharon in late summer, the splendid Arab horsemen, and their exhibitions of skill and mock jousting:

> [The Vale of Sharon] is an immense meadow, . . . an area of perhaps twenty miles square, of beautiful rich lowlands, planted, in many places, with olive and fig orchards, and grazing plats, upon which herds of goats and cattle were browsing. In all this beautiful valley there is not a single fence, . . . and the park-like effect of the groves and valleys is very lovely. . . . Several Arab villages of brown mud cottages, with tall date trees intermingling, and ruins of ancient elegance, as arches of aqueducts, fountains, and causeways, are scattered over the plain. . . .
>
> At a signal from the sheikh, one of his troop . . . spurred forth from the line, and turning his horse suddenly, shook his lance, . . . and seemed to defy an adversary. Another hint from the sheikh, and a great negro, the most powerful of the band, sprang forward, poised his long lance, and approaching within a few yards of the other, seemed about to hurl it with unerring aim. (*Shores of the Mediterranean*, I, 193, 203)

80.13 Horsemen] Possibly "Horseman".

80.19 (Rose of Sharon?)] M's queried floral identification is mistaken; the rose of Sharon is either the althea, *Hibiscus syriacus*, a tall shrublike plant, or the evergreen shrub *Hypericum calycinum*, with yellow flowers; neither resembles "red poppies." The ride across the plain and the flower appear briefly in *Clarel* (1.1.35–42).

80.19 *Petra Party*] In *Clarel*, 2.30, "Of Petra," Rolfe, who has been with an exploring party, describes this once-lost fortress city, carved in a canyon wall in the fastness of southeastern Palestine. It was discovered by Johann Burckhardt in 1812.

80.22 *Jan 22*[d]] Error for January 20.

80.24 hotel] This "English Hotel," M. Blattner, proprietor, was described by a contemporary:

> We climbed into our hotel through a narrow *stone cylinder*, up which led a staircase, and, after being in these narrow quarters for some time, we emerged

> into a narrow, contracted court, in which were stable, kitchen, loafing-place for lazy Arabs, Greeks, and Turks, and grand receptacle for every species of filth. . . . Things were changed . . . when we entered the spacious dining-room. . . . The prospect from the window was superb; looking over the tops of the houses (for Blattner's was on the very summit of the high hill on which Jaffa is built). (William M. Turner, *El-Khuds the Holy* [Philadelphia: Challen, 1861], pp. 143–44)

By one estimate the town's population at mid-century was between five and seven thousand.

80.31 lovely] Possibly "lonely" (cf. the discussion at 99.29).

highest from the Ground of any. From the top of it, I see the Mediterranean, the Plain, the mountains of Ephraim. A lovely landscape. To the north the nearest spot

80.34 like Jonah] "But Jonah rose up to flee . . . from the presence of the Lord, and went down to Joppa. . . . But the Lord sent out a great wind into the sea, and there was a mighty tempest" (Jonah 1:3–4). When the sea in the roadstead was too rough, steamers did not stop at Jaffa at all but went on to Beirut to discharge passengers, hence M's long wait.

81.3 *Jan 23*[d]] Error for January 21.

81.5 Wrote] At this point M left four pages blank in notebook D and began his memorandum labeled "From Jerusalem to Dead Sea &c" on the fifth page. Thus this lengthy passage (82.27–94.38) which comes between the entries for January 26 and 27 was actually begun on January 23, covers January 6-18 (about Jerusalem) and January 23-25 (about the missionaries in Jaffa), and was finished on January 26, when he met Wood in Beirut.

81.6–7 American Missionary] Charles (1811–76) and Martha (1813–83) Saunders, from Westerly, Rhode Island, were sent in 1854 by the Seventh-Day Baptists as lay "agricultural" missionaries, to work jointly with another ministerial family. (In the general millenarian fervor for converting Jews, the Seventh-Day Baptists believed they would have special access to and affinity with Jews because of their Sabbatarian convictions.) Saunders had earlier been in the California gold rush, and both he and his wife learned Arabic while she studied medicine for "mental improvement" as well as ministry to the natives. In a letter to the church organ, the *Sabbath Recorder* (July 19, 1855), Charles wrote they had finally settled in a house about five minutes' walk from town. They, too, had both been to the Dead Sea earlier in the spring of 1856, and Charles had just returned from Jerusalem. He was ill for protracted periods, was blamed—with others—for some "mismanagement," ultimately had a rancorous disagreement with the other missionary, but also lacked financial support, and was recalled at the end of 1859. (Rev. Oscar Uberto Whitford, "The Seventh Day Baptist Missionary Society," in *Seventh Day Baptists in Europe and America*, 2 vols. [Plainfield, N.J.: The American Sabbath Tract Society, 1910], I, 348–49; Abram H. Lewis, *A Seventh-Day Baptist Hand-book* [Alfred Centre, N.Y.: The American Sabbath Tract Society, 1887], p. 44; *The Annual Report of the Seventh-Day Baptist Missionary Society* [New York, 1860], pp. 10, 14, 15; files of the *Sabbath Recorder*.)

81.12 "Book of Female Heroines,"] There were various books on the subject; this was probably one of the several versions of a collection by Daniel C. Eddy, which piously described the lives of eleven to thirteen notable women missionaries—e.g., *Heroines of the Missionary Enterprise* (Boston: Ticknor, Reed, & Fields, 1850).

81.15–16 Miss Williams] "Sister" Williams had moved from England to Philadelphia, then to Bethlehem, then to Jaffa with Mrs. Clorinda S. Minor (see 92.31–93.2 and accompanying discussion), with whom the Saunderses also stayed until her death. Afterwards Miss Williams lived with the Saunderses. Mrs. Sarah Barclay Johnson wrote of her, in Bethlehem, as "estimable and devoted, . . . engaged in teaching a group of bright-looking Arab children, who progress rapidly under their experienced and indefatigable teacher" (*Hadji in Syria; or, Three Years in Jerusalem* [Philadelphia: Challen & Sons, 1858], pp. 150-51). In Jaffa, she was teaching from a rabbi's house.

81.18 *Jan 24th*] Error for January 22.

81.21 Byron] John Galt's *Life of Lord Byron* (Philadelphia: Littell, 1830) reports that, voyaging from Constantinople to Greece, Byron "as he was walking the quarter-deck . . . lifted an ataghan . . . and unsheathing it, said . . . 'I should like to know how a person feels after committing murder' " (p. 113).

81.22 Joppa] The town appears in Egyptian records at least as early as the fifteenth century B.C. M uses indifferently either "Jaffa" or the older form "Joppa."

81.24 house of Simon] Of several reputed sites, M visited the most probable one, which was near the tanyards, southwest of town; one room had been converted to mosque use, and a small lighthouse stood atop the flat roof. Acts 10:1–23 gives the account of Saint Peter's residence and the vision that led him to preach to the Gentiles.

81.29 my chamber] Perhaps the same room described by another mid-century traveler:

> At Jaffa we found a clean, cool hotel, kept by a German Jew. Inserted into the lintel of one of the doors was a little glass cylinder, enclosing a parchment roll, on which was left visible, in Hebrew, the name of God revealed to Abraham (Shaddai),—the Almighty. . . . [The host] said it was a Jewish custom to remind those who entered the house of the presence of God. . . . Frenchmen, who did not read the Bible, sometimes mocked at it, and this led to angry discussion, so that from many of the doors it was now removed. . . . The entrance was by a narrow flight of stone steps into a court-yard, then up another flight of exterior stone steps to a platform, which was the roof of one room and the entrance to two others. (Mrs. Elizabeth [Rundle] Charles, *Wanderings over Bible Lands and Seas* [New York: Carter & Brothers, 1866], pp. 49–50)

The vial, the controversy with mocking Gentiles, and the Jewish hotel-keeper are used by M as in Jerusalem in *Clarel* (1.2.1–90), while the beam is used in Nehemiah's dwelling (1.22.29–30).

81.34 *Jan 25th*] Error for January 23.

82.1 "Diamond Necklace"] *Le collier de la reine* (1849–50), by the elder Alexandre Dumas (1802–70); by "opening chapter" M probably means its prologue, which establishes the setting.

82.3 Dickson's] See the passage beginning at 93.3 and accompanying discussion.

82.4 *Jan 26th*] Error for January 24.

82.7–8 I see . . . Hermon] M decided otherwise later and added a penciled note: "(Not so — a mistake)". (See the textual note at this point.)

82.27 *From . . . Sea &c*] For when this passage (through 94.38) was written, see the discussion at 81.5. The grand excursion made by nearly every traveler, if no other: Nazareth and Galilee were more distant from Jerusalem (though sometimes included if, like Twain's party, one started from Beirut). The customary route (or its reverse), just as M describes it, required three days, tents near Jericho, and permission from the Greek patriarch to stay overnight at the convent of Mar Saba. Travelers in a group had to buy the protection of an escort, for four or five shillings each. In M's probable group, with Cunningham and his dragoman, his share of costs would have been about a pound and a half. Parts 2, 3, and 4 of *Clarel* center respectively on the three stages of the journey.

JERUSALEM, FROM THE MOUNT OF OLIVES.

82.28 to Bethany] St. Stephen's Gate, just north of the Temple site (now occupied by the great Mosque of Omar), was the principal eastern exit from Jerusalem, from which led the road to Bethany, upwards of two miles away. Taylor also thought the hillside village a "miserable cluster of Arab huts"; he added, "the Grotto of Lazarus is here shown. . . . It belongs to an old Mussulman, who came out of his house with a piece of waxed rope, to light us down. An aperture opens from the roadside into the hill. . . . Descending about twenty steps at a sharp angle, we landed in a small, damp vault, with an opening in the floor" (*Lands of the Saracen*, p. 62).

Brook Kedron forms the Valley of Jehoshaphat running south along the east wall of the city, but that ravine continues southeast past Mar Saba to the Dead Sea—see M's attempt at that point in the journey to rationalize his error by writing of "two branches" (84.4). The gorge being followed here toward Jericho was sometimes identified as the Brook Kerith. Taylor and many others noted that from any height around Jerusalem one seems to look directly down into the Jordan Valley and the Dead Sea, nearly thirty-seven hundred feet below the city (see the illustration above, from Bartlett's *Walks*, facing p. 108). Traveling that route in the opposite direction of M's journey, he describes the "wilderness we now entered" as "fully as barren, but less rugged than that through which we passed yesterday [i.e., near Mar Saba]. The path ascended along the brink of a deep gorge, at the bottom of which a little stream foamed over the rocks" (*Lands of the Saracen*, p. 70).

82.32 Plain of Jericho] Taylor described the plain near the Dead Sea as "covered with a white, saline incrustation" and gradually changing, as one moved north up the valley of the Jordan, from a barren, gray, salt waste to soil covered with grass and herbs, the winding river-course itself marked by a green line of ash, poplar, willow, and tamarisk trees (*Lands of the Saracen*, pp. 65–67).

82.33 apple of Sodom] A frequent reference in nineteenth-century literature. The shrub M saw here was variously identified by Dead Sea travelers, but Warburton denies it that name: "One of the shrubs bore a small golden fruit, about the size of a walnut, that hung temptingly on its bending branches; within, it was full of a black dust. . . . The Arabs called it . . . *Lot's sea orange*: but this is not the true apple of Sodom, which I have seen elsewhere [in Nubia, I, 194–95]. . . . That is much larger, very fragile, and is full of cindrous-looking grains and a silken fibre" (*The Crescent and the Cross*, II, 108–9).

82.33–34 P. of J. . . . P. of S.] I.e., Plain of Jericho and Plain of Sharon.

82.34–35 Mount of Temptation] Twelfth-century Crusaders placed the scene of Jesus' forty-day fast and temptations on Mt. Quarantania, rising above the downward road from Jerusalem. Ruins remained of the Crusader fortresses guarding this strategic route, and Taylor speaks of a Roman tower on the first crest above the Jordan Valley (*Lands of the Saracen*, p. 70). M used Quarantania and the temptation in *Clarel* (2.14.54–58, 94–100, and 2.18.63–145). Earlier, the temptation scene figured in his penciled notes (1849–51) in Volume VII of his *Dramatic Works of William Shakspeare* (Sealts 460); see the NN *Moby-Dick*, pp. 958, 968–69, for this note and for the reproduction of M's markings and annotations near the end of the temptation in *Paradise Regained* (IV, 197, 220–21) in his copy of Milton's *Poetical Works* (Sealts 358b).

83.4 village of Jericho] This contemporary squalid village of a few mud huts and no accommodations was twenty miles and six hours from Jerusalem. Joshua's city was probably farther north, and Herod's city (bought by him from Cleopatra after Antony gave it to her), the one known by Jesus, was probably at the edge of the plain.

83.7 Marsada] M probably meant "Masada," the great fortress of the Maccabees looming over the Dead Sea to the south. He would not see the Greek convent of Mar Saba until late the next day (January 19; see the discussions at 81.5 and 84.4).

83.14 yellow stream] According to Taylor (in May, 1852), "It is almost impossible to reach the water at any other point than the Ford of the

Pilgrims," a considerable distance above the mouth. "The Jordan at this point will not average more than ten yards in breadth. It flows at the bottom of a gully about fifteen feet deep. . . . The water has a white, clayey hue, and is very swift. The changes of current have formed islands and beds of soil here and there, which are covered with a dense growth" (*Lands of the Saracen*, pp. 68, 67).

83.17–18 tother side] Possibly M meant to write "both sides" (H); but if the first word is "both", the second, which is clearly "side", is miswritten (lacking the terminal *s*). The first word, however, since its initial letter is crossed, appears to be "tother", in which case "side" is correct, and M's intended phrase is "tother side". Either phrase is geographically correct. The reading "tother side" is supported by M's use of the same colloquial locution ("t'other") at 59.28.

83.18 Lake George] In the past August, M and his brother Allan had visited this New York lake (see also 65.6 above). At some later time M, in pencil, changed "George" to "Como" (visible in the reproduction just above), presumably after he had visited Lake Como (121.31)—the comparison he used in *Clarel*, 2.29.1–19, with other details from this passage.

83.19 bitter . . . water] Mark Twain describes the terrain: "Salt crystals glitter in the sun about the shores of the lake. In places they coat the ground like a brilliant crust of ice" (*Innocents Abroad*, p. 596). Most travelers noted the bleakness of the landscape, the bleached tree-skeletons washed down by the river, and the leprotic vegetation; opinions varied on the taste of the water. To Warburton, "the water was so acrid, that when a drop touched the inside lip, . . . it seemed to burn like vitriol" (*The Crescent and the Cross*, II, 107); but to Taylor, "the taste of the water is salty and pungent, and stings the tongue like saltpetre. . . . Yet [after bathing] I experienced very little of that discomfort which most travellers have remarked" (*Lands of the Saracen*, p. 66); and Mark Twain claimed he spent over an hour in it (*Innocents Abroad*, chap. 55, p. 596). The water is about twenty-five percent salt—half sodium chloride, the rest magnesium chloride (the cause of its bitterness) and calcium chloride (the cause of its soapy feeling and frothy ripples).

83.22–23 Rainbow . . . against it.] The rainbow's meaning is diverse to the pilgrims in *Clarel*, 2.29.116–58, and it reappears as a "fog-bow" at the burial of Nehemiah in 2.39.148–61.

83.29 *Judea*] Taylor's description of the barren, tortured mountain region east and south of Jerusalem is representative: "The mountains were grim, bare, and frightfully rugged. The scanty grass, coaxed into life by the winter rains, was already scorched out of all greenness; . . . the glens and gorges . . . sank on either hand to a dizzy depth below, and were so steep as to be almost inaccessible. The region is so scarred, gashed and torn, that no work of man's hand can save it from perpetual desolation. It is a wilderness more hopeless than the Desert. If I were left alone in the midst of it, I should lie down and await death" (*Lands of the Saracen*, pp. 63–64).

83.38 ashes] A conjectural reading. See *Clarel*, 3.1.118–32.

So rubbishy, that no chiffonier could find any thing all in it. — No moss as in the Ruins — no grace of decay — no ivy — The unleavened nakedness of desolation — whitish ashes — — lime-kilns

83.38 lime kilns] M's added notations at this point (see the textual note) about "Port Esquiline"—an ancient Roman gate—and the samphire-gatherers of *King Lear* (VI, vi) were later incorporated in *Clarel* at 1.24.21 and 3.9.41 respectively.

84.1 tracks] Preceding verb lacking (presumably "leave").

84.4 *St. Saba*] The Great Laura of Mar Saba, founded by the ascetic Saint Sabas (439–532), became a famous community of contemplative monks, the prototype of Eastern Orthodox monasticism. The monastery, hung below the cliff-top path on the precipitous walls of the lower Kedron gorge, was a major tourist and pilgrim hospice on this route to or from the Dead Sea, and most writers describe what Warburton called the "fearful chasms," the battlemented walls, the steep path winding down to the gate, the labyrinthine passages and stairs, the comfortable travelers' quarters, the silent monks gliding about the innumerable terraces and gardens, and the "beautiful church, dimly lighted by two silver lamps, kept ever burning before pictures of the Saviour and the Virgin" (*The Crescent and the Cross*, II, 104–5; see also Browne, *Yusef*, pp. 372–73; even Mark Twain was impressed despite his dismay with the rigorous asceticism, *Innocents Abroad*, chap. 55, pp. 597–600). Women were prohibited, entrance required permission of the Jerusalem patriarch, and lodging cost two or three shillings a person, with extra for servants and porters.

84.10 "*racka*"] Arak or raki, a strong brandy—in Syria and Palestine generally prepared from raisins. (An editorial note to Lord Carlisle's *Diary*, p. 48, explains that raki is acceptable in the Levant because it was unknown in Mohammed's time and therefore not expressly prohibited in the Koran.) It figures prominently in *Clarel*, 3.11–14, as the pilgrims carouse in the monastery.

84.18 *Date Palm*] Reputedly planted by the Christian Palestinian monk, Saint Sabas (see the discussion at 84.4). In *Clarel*, 3.25–30, it prompts meditations by various pilgrims (as the doubloon does in *Moby-Dick*, chap. 99). An imaginative large watercolor of the palm, painted by M's friend Peter Toft, "In memoriam of Herman Melville" and probably given to his widow in 1892, is now in the Berkshire Athenaeum, Pittsfield, Massachusetts.

84.19 to Bethalem] Bethlehem—distant nine miles, a two-and-a-half-hour ride out of the Kedron gorge onto high land, with Jerusalem visible another six miles to the north. M made a later penciled reference to this distant view at the journal notebook's end (153.10) and devoted parts of two cantos to it in *Clarel* (4.1 and 2). Unlike M's party, Clarel and his companions stay over at the Capuchin hospice in Bethlehem (4.7 and 16); the ironic reference to the praying Moslem is used in 4.10.51–64. In contrast to the terrible bleakness of the wilderness, the hills and ravines around Bethlehem were comparatively fertile. A young ministerial candidate, with much pious commentary, described the approach—

> from that extinguished Phlegethon of the Mar Saba . . . amid horrid grotesque rocks and awful shadows. . . . The first part of our journey from the Greek Convent, was threading slowly the defiles of knife-edged volcanic rocks without a tree or shrub, and now and then from some higher point catching a glimpse of the Dead Sea far below us shining dull. . . . We at length reached a somewhat opener country, where the hills grew faintly greener. . . .
>
> After some hours, across a deep and wide valley, far off, on the very climax of the rising hill region towards the north, Jerusalem appeared before us. . . .
>
> As one approaches the immediate neighborhood of Bethlehem the thin vegetation brightens and in the number of dark-leaved fig trees, silver olives, palms, glossy vineyards, and gardens fenced with the curling speckled monster cactus, David's town yet preserves its ancient fame, of the fruitful. At length Bethlehem itself was directly before us, a wedge-shaped mass of square, white, glistening stone houses, rising step-like one above another, . . . the whole compact diminutive town standing upon the rising crest of a hill. (James Mason Hoppin, *Notes of a Theological Student* [New York: Appleton, 1854], pp. 198, 200, 203)

84.22 In chapel] The tone of contemporary descriptions ranges from pious tolerance to Protestant outrage at the extravagant "pagan impostures" and violent bickering of the Greek, Armenian, and Roman monastics (see Mark Twain, *Innocents Abroad*, chap. 55, pp. 598–600, and Browne, *Yusef*, pp. 388–89). The enclosing church was thought to be perhaps the oldest in Palestine, erected by Constantine. The Chapel of the Nativity, in grottoes beneath the church, was lined with marble and adazzle with lamps. At a recessed altar, a silver star in the pavement marked the supposed place of birth—*Hic de Virgine Maria Jesus Christus natus est*—and contained six Greek lamps, five Armenian, and four Latin, while nearby the manger was represented in brown and white marble. Other chapels contained the tombs of St. Jerome and his two disciples, as well as altars to the Magi and the Slaughter of the Innocents.

84.28 rocks] M's later penciled notation at this point (see the textual note) reads: "See page 24 of Saunders for curious description of Jerusalem. (Jerusalem Cross 5 Wounds) P. 124." Robert S. Forsythe (in his review of Raymond Weaver's edition of this journal, *American Literature*, VIII [March, 1936], 93) rightly assumed that M refers to George Sandys (*A Relation of a Journey Begun An: Dom: 1610*), who in a description of monks in a Franciscan monastery indicates the function of the cross: "They bare five crosses gules, in form of that which is at this day called, the *Ierusalem* crosse; representing thereby the five wounds that violated the body of our Saviour" (London, 1652, fifth ed., p. 124). Whatever its medieval origins, many nineteenth-century pilgrims still sought the tattooing, as Thackeray noted (*From Cornhill to Grand Cairo*, chap. 13, pp. 213–14). In a Jerusalem cross, the two arms intersect at midpoint, and cross-bars terminate each end. The Timoneer in *Clarel*, 4.2.48–59, bears a tattoo containing such a cross. Perhaps M was first directed to Sandys by Taylor, who mentions him (*Lands of the Saracen*, p. 350) in his account of a sultan's tomb M had seen in Constantinople.

84.31 *Village of Lepers*] In the southwest quarter of Jerusalem; their usual station for begging was outside the Jaffa Gate. *Clarel*, 1.25 and 26, describes their plight, as does Browne:

> Dirt and disease go revoltingly together here; gaunt famine stalks through the streets; a constant moan of suffering swells upon the dead air. . . . Wasted forms sit in the doorways; faces covered with white scales and sightless eyes are turned upward; skeleton arms, distorted and fœtid with the ravages of leprosy, are outstretched from the foul moving mass; and a low howl is heard, the howl of the stricken for alms. . . . Look upon it and learn that there is a misery beyond all that you have conceived in your gloomiest hours . . . ; learn that even the Leper, with death gnawing at his vitals and unceasing tortures in

> his blood, cast out from the society of his fellow-man, forbidden to touch in friendship or affection the hand of the untainted, still struggles for life. (*Yusef*, pp. 363–64)

This part of Jerusalem occupies the eminence called Mt. Zion in the strictest sense, hence M's cryptic irony.

84.35 *Via Dolorosa*] This impressively gloomy, narrow street (so named only since the fourteenth century), from St. Stephen's Gate in the east wall (see the discussion at 87.14) toward the Church of the Holy Sepulchre, was much frequented by pilgrims as the supposed route where Jesus bore the cross.

84.37 *among the tombs*] Great graveyards occupied the Valley of Jehoshaphat (or Kedron) outside the east wall, and the lower Vale of Hinnom, which skirted Jerusalem from the west to the south, where it joined Jehoshaphat below the southeast Temple platform and walls (the illustration below is from Bartlett's *Walks*, facing p. 12). Devout Jews, Moslems, and

TOMBS IN THE VALLEY OF JEHOSHAPHAT

Christians alike desired to be near the traditional scene of the Last Judgment, based on Joel 3:2 and 12-14: "I will also gather all nations, and will bring them down into the valley of Jehoshaphat . . . , for there will I sit to judge all the heathen. . . . Multitudes, multitudes in the valley of decision." M again describes this site on the next leaf of his journal notebook (86.5–11; see the accompanying discussion at 86.11 for an account of the tombs of Absalom and Zachariah). This and other similarly monumental structures that M may have visited in and around Jerusalem figure prominently in *Clarel*. See 3.19, for Absalom's tomb; 4.30, for the "valley of decision"; and 1.28, for the Sepulcher of Kings.

85.4 *Church . . . Sepulchre*] M gives a more extensive account later (see 87.22–88.26 and accompanying discussion).

85.7 *Armenian Convent*] Located just southwest of M's hotel; it was large, wealthy, and reputed to have better members than most convents.

85.14–15 Chapel of the Ascension] On the central eminence of Olivet, across the Valley of Jehoshaphat from the eastern walls; Constantine erected a basilica here, and the Moslems, who also considered the place sacred, reerected a similar structure in 1834–35, though Luke 24:50 expressly states that Jesus and the disciples went out as far as Bethany. This whole passage on the indifference of nature is used in *Clarel*, 1.15.1–13.

85.16–17 Solomon's Temple] To provide a level platform, it was necessary to cut into the steep slope on the north and to fill in on the southeast behind great retaining walls; nineteenth-century excavations showed that the walls rose 160 feet from bedrock, of which only eighty remained visible above the accumulated debris of millennia. Phoenician markings on the lowest courses of stone were thought to be from Solomon's time. The accepted site for the Temple proper was toward the north end where the bedrock emerged through the artificial plateau; this site was claimed by the Moslems as that of Mohammed's ascent to heaven and was contained within the Mosque of Omar (the Dome of the Rock), second only to the Kaaba at Mecca in reverence. Despite relaxed restrictions on Christians after the Crimean War, permission to enter was almost impossible to obtain, and M seems not to have tried.

85.21 cheated in Jerusalem] Echoed but modified in *Clarel*, 2.8.18–37, where Rolfe confutes Derwent's meliorism by distinguishing between appearance and character, citing an experience of being cheated by a classically handsome Greek knave.

85.22 Connecticut man] Evidently the principal prototype for Nehemiah, Clarel's initial guide about the city (1.7–11). Walter E. Bezanson (in

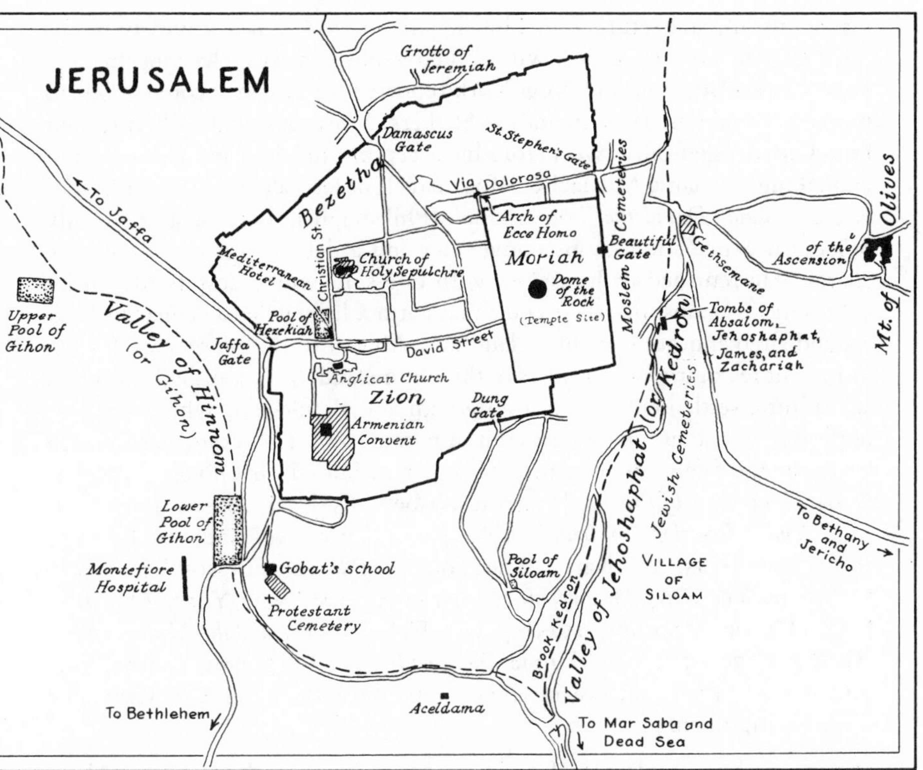

the NN edition of *Clarel* and earlier in his Hendricks House edition [New York, 1960], p. 544) cites an account of him by W. C. Prime: "An old gentleman, Mr. Roberts, an American, who has taken up his residence in Jerusalem, called to see us. . . . His business was independent Bible distribution. He is a New Englander who, without money or friends, has wandered . . . finally to Jerusalem . . . distributing the Bible, in the languages of the countries he visits" (*Tent Life in the Holy Land* [New York: Harper & Brothers, 1857], p. 317). *Clarel*, 1.22.36–65, with its metaphoric reference to Nehemiah's being fed by ravens, parallels another contemporary account: "Here we meet one of the Jerusalem celebrities. He has come, like the Jew, to die at the Holy City. But he is a Christian; has visions and revelations; believes himself the Elijah that was to come; has flags ready to deliver to the restored Jews . . . ; has doffed the Frank dress, and assumed the oriental costume" (Johnson, *Hadji in Syria*, p. 79).

85.26 Warder Crisson] Warder Cresson (1798–1860), from a well-to-do Quaker family, abandoned his first wife and six children in 1844, went to Jerusalem (where he was U.S. Consul for one month before a protest led to his dismissal), and returned to Philadelphia in 1848 to face a widely publicized lawsuit brought by his wife and covetous relatives, charging lunacy. Papers in Philadelphia and New York reported his previous conversions to five or six different sects, including Shakers, Mormons, and Millerites, but he acknowledged only two before his accepting Judaism and circumcision and taking the name Michael C. Boaz Israel, in Jerusalem in 1848. His *The Key of David. David the True Messiah* (Philadelphia, 1852) is a fanatically polemical explanation of his conversion and a defense against the lunacy charge. He returned to Jerusalem with one son, where despite his earlier exhortations against marriage and cohabitation, he married a Sephardic Jewess and sired another son and a daughter, Abigail Ruth. To prepare for the imminent restoration of the Jews to their homeland, he established a modern agricultural settlement between Jerusalem and Bethlehem, while violently opposing Christian missionaries with the same aim. He became a respected leader in the Sephardic community and was buried on Olivet. (Horatius Bonar, *The Land of Promise* [London: Nisbet, 1858], pp. 208–10; Jacob Raisin, *Gentile Reactions to Jewish Ideals* [New York: Philosophical Library, 1953], pp. 784–85; A. J. Karp, "The Zionism of Warder Cresson," in Isidore S. Meyer, *The Early History of Zionism in America* [New York: American Jewish Historical Society, 1945], p. 623; Field, *America and the Mediterranean World*, pp. 276–77, 279–80; Finnie, *Pioneers East*, p. 252.) Nathan, American-turned-Jew, father of Ruth in *Clarel*, 1.16–17, reflects some of Cresson's qualities and history.

86.5–6 (See over leaf)] I.e., his earlier remarks on the tombs of Absalom and Zachariah, at 85.3 (on the preceding leaf of the journal notebook).

86.11 Tomb] A monument with, as M notes, a large hole in its facade, standing slightly apart from the rocky ledge containing the tombs where Jehoshaphat, Zachariah (now commonly "Zechariah"), and Saint James were said to be buried. It was thought in the fourth century to be the monument Absalom had built for himself (II Samuel 18:18, M's apparent reference), but generally considered of later origin by biblical scholars of the nineteenth century (see John Kitto, *A Cyclopædia of Biblical Literature* [Edinburgh, 1845], I, 28; Bercaw 421). The tradition of throwing stones at Absalom's tomb had its origin in the story of Absalom's death—stones being cast out of hatred into the pit where Absalom's body was thrown (II Samuel 18:17). The tradition had evidently attached itself to this monument, as William M. Thomson, in *The Land and the Book, Southern Palestine and Jerusalem* (New York: Harper & Brothers, 1880), recorded: "Believing it to be Absalom's tomb, the Jews and natives throw stones against it and spit at it as they pass by" (I, 520). See *Clarel*, 3.19.148.

86.20 Beautiful . . . Gate] The alternate name "Golden" originated in a mistranslation from Greek into Latin; the actual biblical gate was probably located in the forecourt of the Temple (Acts 3:2), but the one M saw in the east wall of the city and mosque enclosure was in fact an early medieval structure. It was walled up by the Arabs because of the tradition M reports. Viewed from outside the wall, its fifty-five-foot length projecting outwards and roofed with low domes made a striking feature. M's later penciled notation "(Christ sitting in window)" (see the textual note at 86.17) may be his confused recollection of a Moslem tradition that on the Day of Judgment, Mohammed would sit on the Temple wall, Jesus opposite on Olivet, with a thread stretched between, over which according to their merits the judged would safely pass or fall into the hell-fire filling the valley.

86.34 Gihon] Alternative name for Hinnom, the valley skirting the city on the west and south. From the full name, Ge Bene Hinnom, came the corruption, Gehenna, and from the pagan burning of children as a sacrifice to Moloch in its southern reaches, the variant, Topheth.

86.38 unwholesome] The script seems to form "unhomlme", but the reading adopted here is probably the intended word. This whole page (D41, from "For" at 86.32 through 87.12), like many in this part of notebook D, is written in a very cramped hand and is heavily revised.

87.6–7 pool of Gihon] A reservoir constructed by the Teutonic Knights in the twelfth century, in the valley just south of the Jaffa Gate, and misidentified with the pool mentioned in Isaiah 22:9. North of the gate was the "Upper Pool," the basin to which M refers obliquely in the next clause: "And the king of Assyria sent . . . a great host against Jerusalem. . . . They came and stood by the conduit of the upper pool. . . . That night . . . the angel of the Lord . . . smote in the camp of the Assyrians a hundred fourscore and five thousand" (II Kings 18:17, 19:35).

87.11 Hill . . . villa] The Hill of Evil Counsel, a steep hill beyond the juncture of the vales of Gihon and Jehoshaphat south of the city; the field of Aceldama was currently identified as the north slope of this hill, though other sites had previously been so designated. M calls on both accounts of Judas's suicide. Acts 1:18–19: "Now this man purchased a field with the reward of iniquity; and falling headlong, he burst asunder in the midst, and all his bowels gushed out. And it was known unto all the dwellers at Jerusalem; insomuch as that field is called . . . Aceldama, that is to say, The field of blood." Matthew 27:3–8 asserts hanging. It was an unreliable medieval tradition that made the hilltop ruins those of the High Priest's villa and the scene of the Sanhedrin conspiracy. M's added marginal repetition, "Hill of Evil Council", in darker ink—see the textual note at 87.4–9—suggests a later date for this kind of addition. The same misuse of "Council" for "Counsel" ("the Crag of Evil Council") occurs in *Clarel*, 1.26.35.

87.14 St: Stephen's Gate] A sixteenth-century structure in the east wall; the pool to which M refers was probably the Pool of Bezetha, inside the gate (see *Clarel*, 1.28.113). Earlier, and more probably, the Damascus Gate in the north was considered the site of his martyrdom by stoning. The hill of Bezetha is the one north of the Temple site, but M conflates as "Zion" the other two on which the city was built: Zion, as noted earlier, was to the west; the adjoining slope to the south of Bezetha is Moriah.

87.22 Holy Sepulchre] To most Protestant visitors the uproar, the violent and even bloody sectarian quarrels, and what seemed to them the gaudy trumpery and imposture of most, if not all the enclosed sites, were scandalous, though even Mark Twain granted that the place might be the general location of the Crucifixion, and since the time of Constantine a church had stood here. Many biblical scholars, however, insisted that the true site must lie outside the city walls. The vast sprawling cathedral built by the Crusaders purportedly covered all the key points connected with the Crucifixion; partly destroyed by fire in 1808, it had been rebuilt, but was still in shabby disrepair because of the rivalry between the Greek and Latin factions. Bayard Taylor (*Lands of the Saracen*, esp. pp. 82–84) similarly describes the "confused labyrinth of chapels, choirs, shrines, staircases, and vaults" through which wandered streams of pilgrims and processions "of monks, with crosses, censers, and tapers, threading the shadowy passages, from shrine to shrine." The church was generally closed between 10:30 A.M. and 3:00 P.M., but one could get in then with a small bribe. Because of the vast pile's dark and gloomy character, however, morning was the recommended time for viewing.

Above this entry, M penciled in: "[No Jew allowed in Church of H. S.]" (see the textual note). This restriction was explained by Taylor: "A long time ago . . . the Sultan granted a firman, in answer to the application of both Jews and Christians, allowing . . . each sect to put to death any person belonging to the other sect, who should be found inside of their churches or synagogues. . . . In every place but Jerusalem it remains a dead letter. Here, although the Jews freely permit Christians to enter their synagogue, a Jew who should enter the Holy Sepulchre would be lucky if he escaped with his life" (p. 80). The story referred to in M's later red-pencil notation "*Greek tickets for heaven See Captain's story*" (see the textual note at 87.22–34) is told at 97.22–28.

88.5 church in a church] The Chapel of the Sepulchre proper, in the west apse, had been rebuilt after damage by the falling roof in the 1808 fire. It was a small building of white and yellow marble, whose inner sanctuary was about six feet square, dingy with the smoke of forty-three lamps—the gifts of devout princes and potentates—and half occupied by a marble slab, split and kiss-worn, covering the supposed tomb. It was the center of recurrent riots; in 1834, with a huge crowd waiting for the Greek "miracle" of the Holy Fire on Easter Eve, three hundred were suffocated or trampled to death.

88.25–26 Chapel . . . Cross] At the eastern end; twenty-nine steps led down to the Chapel of Helena (Constantine's mother), then thirteen more to the cave where she purportedly found the true cross and those of the two thieves (only here was native rock visible).

88.27 squalid alley] To Taylor, "Jerusalem, internally, gives no impression but that of filth, ruin, poverty, and degradation. . . . [Except for two or three streets on the west side] all the others, to the very gates of the Holy Sepulchre, are channels of pestilence" (*Lands of the Saracen*, pp. 77–78).

89.14 (Ecce Homo)] The arch, across the Via Dolorosa, was itself of the time of Hadrian (emperor A.D. 117–38) but traditionally marked the spot where Pilate presented Jesus to the crowd saying, "Ecce homo" ("Behold the man")—John 19:5 (Vulgate). See *Clarel*, 1.13, "The Arch."

89.22 Haddon Hall] In Derbyshire, once the seat of the dukes of Rutland, but uninhabited since the eighteenth century. Tradition held that Ann Radcliffe, struck with its Tudor baronial quality, used it as a model for the setting of her Gothic thriller *The Mysteries of Udolpho* (1794).

89.23–24 landscapes great part] Intervening word (presumably "a") lacking; the error occurred in the process of revision ("great part" was an insertion—see the textual note at 89.24).

89.34 Cave of Jeremiah] Actually underground quarries, just outside the Damascus Gate, but so-called since the fifteenth century. After paying a Moslem guard, one entered a small cave that led to a circular grotto about forty paces across.

90.6–7 *strata* . . . Jerusalem] Contemporary archaeologists distinguished such important "layers" as the cities of David and Solomon, of the Maccabees, of the Herods, of Hadrian, and of Constantine.

90.8 Stones of Judea] M developed this theme of stones in *Clarel*, 2.10.1–40, 61–74.

90.9 monuments & stumps of the memorials] Possibly "monuments stumps of them & memorials" (H).

[Stones of Judea. We read a good deal about stones in Scripture. Monuments & stumps of the memorials are set up of stones;

90.19 three] Possibly "there"; see *Clarel*, 2.10.193–94.

for [illegible] have to get them out of the way. But in vain; The removal of one stone only serves to reveal three stones still larger, below it. It is like mending the

90.32–33 Scotch Church] Isaiah 62:10: "Go through, go through the gates; prepare ye the way of the people; cast up, cast up the highway; gather out the stones; lift up a standard for the people." Such passages encouraged millenarian missionaries like those M refers to here and describes a little later. In 1839 the Scottish church sent four ministers to the East to determine the possibility of missionary work among the Jews in anticipation of the Second Coming. Their encounter with the London philanthropist Sir Moses Montefiore (see 94.19–25 and accompanying discussion) is mentioned in his diary entry for June 10, 1839 (*Diaries of Sir Moses and Lady Montefiore*, ed. Dr. L. Loewe, 2 vols. [London: Griffith, Farren, Okeden, & Welsh, 1890], I, 179). A book by two of them also reports it: after discussing the plight of impoverished Palestinian Jews, "Dr. Keith suggested that they might be employed in making roads through the land, as materials were abundant, and that it might be the beginning of the fulfilment of the prophecy" (Andrew A. Bonar and Robert M. M'Cheyne, *Narrative of a Mission of Inquiry to the Jews from the Church of Scotland in 1839*, third ed. [Philadelphia: Presbyterian Board of Publication, 1845], p. 143).

91.8 gloomy] Following noun lacking (presumably "caves").

91.12 Pool of Bethesda] An underground reservoir north of the Temple enclosure, so called because of its location near the present St. Stephen's Gate, itself once erroneously identified as the biblical "Sheep Gate" where the real Bezetha (also Bethesda) was located.

91.32 Church . . . Zion] The Anglican Christ Church, not far from M's hotel, was built in 1843–49 for resident Anglican bishops, though other

Protestants also conducted or attended services there. The seat was a joint venture initiated by Frederick IV of Prussia as a first step toward establishing an English style of church government. Bishops were to be nominated alternately by the two crowns, and the second, Samuel Gobat (1799–1879), was Frederick's nominee in 1846. He had been a missionary in the Near East (1829–32) and in Abyssinia (1834–37); the book M mentions is *Journal of a Three Years' Residence in Abyssinia* (London: Hatchard & Son, 1834; New York: Dodd, 1850). His *Samuel Gobat, Bishop of Jerusalem* (New York: Whittaker, 1885) is semi-autobiographical. Gobat's anomalous titular position gave him no real control over the independent English and Prussian missions, but he seems to have managed it skillfully. (On the establishment of the mission, see A. L. Tibawi, *British Interests in Palestine, 1800–1901* [Oxford: Clarendon Press, 1961], pp. 44–51.) M's account of Gobat's, as of other, missionary activities is biased by his own skepticism. This Jewish community, like others, resisted all proselytizing (except when starving), and Gobat tacitly redirected his schools throughout Palestine toward Arab Christian children, in part to counteract the influence of French Catholic schools (Tibawi, pp. 90–91), thereby antagonizing the Greek and Latin hierarchies. In 1853 he finished building an English school, which continued in use to 1948 (Tibawi, p. 110; see also chap. 4 and pp. 155–60). The considerable dissension in the Protestant Jerusalem colony centered in the hostile English consul, James Finn, and the conduct of the school was criticized—the ignorance of the headmaster and his assistant, for instance, and the seduction of younger boys by older native boys (Tibawi, pp. 133–38 and 117–21).

92.31 *Mrs Minot*] Clorinda S. Minor on her first impecunious, harebrained pilgrimage to the Holy Land in 1849 (as told in her *Meshullam! or, Tidings from Jerusalem* [Philadelphia: Minor, 1850]) met the converted London Jew John Meshullam during his attempt to introduce modern agricultural practices to a colony near Bethlehem. She later came back with followers to support Meshullam, then bought land at Jaffa in her own name against all Moslem custom and established a colony of American and German Sabbatarians. She helped the Dicksons and then the Saunderses to get settled. In 1854 Bishop Gobat deplored her colony: "In Jaffa there are already a few German and American families. The latter are handsomely subsidised from America, and by that means not only are they well off, but able to reduce the poor Germans to servitude; they make them work all Sunday, and keep Sabbath on the Saturday" (*Samuel Gobat*, p. 308). She wrote many letters and exhortations for support, to the *Sabbath Recorder* and other papers, with references to Miss Williams (see 81.15–17 and accompanying discussion) and to Lydia and Emma Neill, the sisters who lived with her. She died in November of 1855.

93.3 *Deacon Dickson*] Walter (1799–1860) and Sarah Eldredge (1800–1878) Dickson, with their son Henry and three daughters, came from Boston to Palestine in 1853 upon the death there of their son Philip, who had gone out in 1852 as an independent agricultural missionary. Like Mrs. Minor, Dickson bought land, a half hour's walk from town. The daughters Almira and Mary married John and Frederic Steinbeck of the small German colony, but in an 1858 Arab raid Frederic was killed, Walter wounded, and Sarah Dickson and Mary Steinbeck raped; the Dicksons thereupon returned home. Dickson's letters to the *Sabbath Recorder* display an argumentative and fanatical temperament. (S. A. Green, "Walter Dickson's Family," *Groton Historical Series*, II, no. vii [1888], 238–40; Field, *America and the Mediterranean World*, pp. 281, 284–85; G. W. Chamberlain, "A New England Crusade," *New England Magazine*, XXXVI [1907], 195–207.)

94.11 *English Consul*] As'ad Ya'qūb Khayyāt (or Kayat as he wrote it in English), born in Beirut to Greek Orthodox parents, was influenced by the American mission but remained Orthodox, aiming to reform the Eastern church from within. With a strong missionary impulse he founded a school, made three trips to England where he became a British citizen (1846), took a medical degree, then returned about 1849 to Jaffa as English consul. There he promoted agricultural improvements, notably the introduction of cotton (Tibawi, *British Interests*, pp. 142–44). Travel accounts are frequently commendatory, e.g., "Dr. K. has just claims to be considered a benefactor. . . . He has encouraged the culture of the vine; has introduced that of the mulberry and of the Irish potatoe. . . . In the court-yard we observed an English plough of an improved construction, imported by the consul" (Lt. William F. Lynch, *Narrative of the United States' Expedition to the River Jordan and the Dead Sea* [Philadelphia: Lee & Blanchard, 1849], pp. 450–51). The local American missionaries, especially those at Beirut, may have been jaundiced since they had expected to convert him to Protestantism.

94.19 *Montifiore*] Sir Moses (not Joseph—M's first reference, at 90.33, was correct) Montefiore (1784–1885) was the son of an Italian-Jewish London merchant. He made a stock-exchange fortune, retired in 1824, and devoted the rest of his long life and his wealth to his co-religionists. Altogether he made seven trips to Palestine, most recently in 1855, and again in 1857, with permission to build housing, a hospital, and a dispensary for Jews, lest they be tempted by Protestant medical help. Despite M's derogation, he was an able man, known to the czar, Napoleon III, and the sultan; obtaining permission to buy any land from Moslems (as for the hospital, outside the southwest walls) was otherwise almost impossible. The Montefiore *Diaries* (incomplete) are cited in the discussion at 90.32–33.

94.33 Wood] The Reverend Henry Wood (1806–73), former editor of the *Congregational Journal*, served as consul from 1854 to 1856. Thereafter he was a U.S. Navy chaplain and died as a captain in the Naval Home, Philadelphia. M's passport (in the Berkshire Athenaeum) bears his visa, "Good for Smyrna and Athens," dated January 28, 1857. Evidently he had heard of Mrs. Minor's implied break with John Meshullam at Bethlehem and her claim to the property bought with money sent from America in response to her praise and pleas for Meshullam's work. Dickson found her "rights" wholly justified, and the Reverend William Jones (the ordained associate of the Saunderses) defended her (letters to the *Sabbath Recorder*, May 4, and November 30, 1854). "L. Napier" conceivably refers to Lord Francis Napier (1819–98), secretary to the British embassy in Constantinople and occasional visitor to Palestine who had just been named minister to Washington (on January 21), but did not arrive in New York until March, 1857.

95.1 *Jan 27th*] Error for January 25.

95.1 "Acquila Imperiale"] An eleven-hundred-ton, four-hundred-horsepower steamer of the Austrian-Lloyd Co. (By sailing on this day, M missed a rather violent earthquake that night.)

95.5 Hotel] One of two by the name Belle Vue frequently mentioned by travelers, but identified here by its proprietor's having been "dragoman to Warburton"—without naming Bassoul, Warburton describes him as "a young Syrian Christian . . . very handsome, and dandified in proportion" (*The Crescent and the Cross*, II, 18). After distinguishing between the two hotels by location and clientele, James Lewis Farley names the proprietor of the one outside the walled town and near the tip of the promontory: "The proprietor of the latter, Nichola Bassoul, is a highly respectable Arab, and prides himself not a little on the support he receives from the Americans and English. . . . This hotel, although wanting in many of the comforts to which the English traveller is accustomed, is considered the best and cleanest in Syria. The charges are ten francs a-day. . . . It is beautifully situated, commanding an uninterrupted view of the sea; and on the right, looking from the balcony, over the town and St. George's bay there is a picture of surpassing loveliness" (*Two Years in Syria* [London: Saunders & Otley, 1858], pp. 54–55). Five years before, Bayard Taylor had also stayed here after release from quarantine (*Lands of the Saracen*, p. 30).

95.6 Warburton] Eliot Warburton (1810–52; his given name was Bartholomew Elliott) wrote *The Crescent and the Cross* after his wide-ranging trip in the Near East in 1843 (the American edition was published in Wiley & Putnam's Library of Choice Reading in 1852). It reads as the work of a rather priggish, pompous Englishman, pretentiously "literary" and given to shallow historical and religious meditations; it had at least seventeen editions in forty years. Restless and unsettled, he continued traveling until he died in the burning of the ship *Amazon* en route to Central America. M did not meet him in London, but seems to have read his book, perhaps prompted by conversation with Kinglake, fellow law student and parallel Levantine traveler (see 46.30 in the 1849 journal, and the discussion at 46.28).

95.6 Town] Writers as diverse as Warburton, Taylor, and J. Ross Browne gave enthusiastic descriptions of Beirut, on a promontory jutting west into the sea, with luxurious vegetation and snow-topped mountains to the east. So Warburton: "Beautiful Beyrout! It is not only now . . . that I yield to thee the palm over all the cities of the earth. . . . It is not only the magnificent scenery—the mountain, with its glens, like velvet folds, enclosing cascades like silver threads —the snowy peaks, the golden shore: nor the rich gardens that lie around the towered walls; the airy villages [perched on the mountain flanks] . . . ; the purple sea, and the rose-coloured sky—that invest the old Berytus with such a glory" (*The Crescent and the Cross*, II, 135). The town itself within its battered walls had been a squalid oriental village, but it was already on the way to becoming the commercial and educational center of the Levant.

95.15 *gate*] Possibly "*gale*".

& Pole brought into the house. The gale.
Tarter Couriers, dashing in with tidings
of war. — Quiet days — shell out

95.15–16 Tarter . . . war] Ethnically, the Tatars (or Tartars) were believed the ancestors of the Osmanli Turks, but Kinglake also gave a more narrow definition: "The Tatar, you know, is a government courier properly employed in carrying despatches, but also sent with travellers to speed them on their way" (*Eöthen*, p. 11). Syria seethed with unrest among the Moslem faithful over the postwar clemencies granted Christians, and among the mountain-dwelling Druse resentful of Turkish governance. Isolated outbreaks like the raid that killed Dickson's son-in-law broke into full-scale insurrection in 1860, leading to French intervention. Still other religious hostilities involved the Maronite Christians. Letters to the *Missionary Herald* throughout 1857, from Beirut and Syrian outposts, report unrest, hostility, violence, and the ineffectiveness of the local Turkish government.

95.18–19 Pasha's ball] Foreign travelers especially were almost always courteously received by the local pasha or governor. The name "Bashi Bazouck" (literally "crack-brained") designated irregular troops and mercenaries, particularly those recruited for the recent war. Commonly they had the reputation of being violent, undisciplined, and dangerous troublemakers. Mt. Sun Nin (modern Sannin) is the second highest peak (8,622 ft.) in the coast range, some twenty miles northeast of Beirut, but since it was accessible only by a roundabout trip, as was the mountain stream Adonis, it is unlikely that M visited either. The significance of these abrupt and repetitive notations is obscure.

95.24 "Smirne"] A small ship (860 tons, 160 horsepower); the cheating agent was presumably one G. Laurella. Accommodations on similar Austrian ships were described by Lieutenant Frederick Walpole six years before: "Fancy a narrow, long cabin, the bulkheads beautifully varnished, the sofas, etc. perfect; the skylights and all other air-holes carefully closed; the whole atmosphere redolent of bad tobacco smoke. Fifteen persons were seated at a table sufficient for eight. These consisted of eleven Greeks . . . (who used their forks like harpoons . . . and their knives as forks—save when they likewise performed the duty of saltspoons,) two officers, and ourselves. On the table were two plates of unripe oranges; two saucers of pickles; two ditto of salt Chilis; two wine-glasses of tooth-picks, two plates, with nine Sardines disposed star-ways in each" (*The Ansayrii*, 3 vols. [London: Bentley, 1851], I, 15–16). Taylor, however, recommended the Austrian-Lloyd line because while the French Messageries Imperiales (abbreviated M.I. at 96.13) had the better cuisine, their ships were more expensive, more crowded, and the servants "most uncivil" (*Lands of the Saracen*, p. 357).

95.33 Christ rose] Similarly Taylor wrote: "As I toiled up the Mount of Olives, in the very footsteps of Christ . . . I found it utterly impossible to conceive that the Deity, in human form, had walked there before me" (*Lands of the Saracen*, p. 84).

96.10 *Panurge*] Book 4, Chapter 18, of Rabelais's *Gargantua and Pantagruel* (trans. Urquhart & Motteux [London: Smith, Miller, 1844]) describes Panurge's seasickness and after as he "sat on the deck all in a heap, with his nose and arse together . . . moping and half dead; invoked and called to his assistance all the blessed he and she saints he could muster up; swore and vowed to confess in time and place convenient, and then bawled out frightfully." This is presumably the translation M borrowed from Evert Duyckinck in 1847–48 (Sealts 417, Bercaw 574).

96.18 few] Possibly "far". "Far" inland the whole island is mountainous, but only a "few" of the mountains are "lofty" ones.

Rhodes looked a large & high island with some few lofty mountains inland. Recent

96.19–20 "Street of the Chevaliers."] The Knights of St. John of Jerusalem retreated here after their expulsion from Palestine in 1308. Recently, an earthquake had badly shaken the fortifications, the Palace of the Grand Master, the church and the Street of the Knights, after which the powder magazine under the church exploded, destroying the palace, the church, and some six hundred people. Sir Henry Holland, Queen Victoria's physician whom M had met in London (see 26.4 and accompanying discussion), saw the ruins in 1857 and described the devastation as the most "striking" he had ever seen (*Recollections of Past Life*, p. 72).

96.29–30 bugs & fleas] M's lecture "Traveling" observed, "The minute discomforts, the afflictions of Egypt and Italy, in the shape of fleas and other insects, we will pass over lightly, though they by no means pass lightly over the traveler" (see the lecture as reconstructed in the NN *Piazza Tales* volume, p. 422).

97.16 Juan Fernandez] The four-year home of Robinson Crusoe's prototype, Alexander Selkirk; M saw these three lonely islands in November of 1843, four hundred miles off the coast of Chile, and had remembered them when writing the fourth sketch of "The Encantadas," first published in 1854 (see the NN *Piazza Tales* volume, pp. 137–39).

97.18 Niebuhr & Strauss] Barthold Niebuhr (1776–1831), German historian whose influential *Roman History* (1827–28, translated 1828–42) dissected myth and tradition to determine their core of ordinary fact. David Friedrich Strauss (1808–74), "higher critic" of the Bible, famous for his *Das Leben Jesu* (1835, translated by George Eliot, 1846) and his *Christliche Dogmatik* (1840–41), argued that except for skeletal biographical facts, the Christ of the Four Gospels was the wishful product of messianic expectations. The historian's and critic's influences are deplored by Rolfe in *Clarel*, 1.34:

> That stable proof which man would fold,
> How may it be derived from things
> Subject to change and vanishings?
> But let that pass. All now's revised:
> Zion, like Rome, is Niebuhrized.

97.29 Mike Walsh] Michael Walsh (ca. 1815–59), Irish-born New York editor, labor leader, politician, and foe of Tammany Hall. His paper

The Subterranean passionately advocated the cause of labor, and he was twice jailed for libel. (In the issue for January 24, 1846, he dubbed M's Tammany-allied brother, Gansevoort, "Gander-brained Melville"; see David S. Reynolds, *Beneath the American Renaissance* [New York: Knopf, 1988], p. 458.) After service in both the State Assembly and Congress, he was closely defeated (perhaps fraudulently) for reelection in 1854, then traveled abroad, became alcoholic, and was later found dead in a New York areaway, possibly murdered.

98.7 "Italia"] Another small ship, of 730 tons and 260 horsepower.

98.9 blades] At Smyrna, M probably had his first experience with the gondola, a low, double-ended craft propelled by a single oarsman who stood in the stern and sculled a single long oar. The back-and-forth motion of the oar may account for M's phrase "alternate blades of oars" in his description of midshipmen in these "queer little canoes" (to M, who had seen the huge war canoes of the South Pacific, even a moderate-sized double ender might seem little). Perhaps M noted the Austrian man-of-war because of a diplomatic incident involving one of them with an American warship in the same harbor in 1853. (Cf. Field, *America and the Mediterranean World*, pp. 234–37, and James Fenimore Cooper et al., *History of the Navy of the United States of America from 1815 to 1860* [New York: Oakley & Mason, 1866], III, 103.)

98.27–28 Acropolis . . . road] Travelers regularly remark this first view of the Acropolis six miles away in Athens. Mark Twain's account of a surreptitious expedition from his ship to it on a similar moonlit night is among the better-known ones (*Innocents Abroad*, chap. 32, pp. 341–53). Two of M's poems, "The Parthenon" and "The Apparition," make use of this distant glimpse; both in *Timoleon* (*Published Poems*, pp. 302–3, 313).

98.30 Santon] A wandering Moslem holy man; Warburton explains: "These santons are generally durweeshes who have become insane; their insanity passes for inspiration. . . . These ferocious fanatics wander about the country, committing all sorts of atrocities and indecencies, under the shelter of their sacred character" (*The Crescent and the Cross*, I, 194). The famous traveler John L. Stephens (alluded to in Chapter 1 of *Redburn*, p. 5) gives this description:

> I could not have believed . . . that anything so wretched . . . existed on the earth. . . . His face was dried, and seamed with the deep wrinkles of age and exposure; his beard long and white; and his body thin to emaciation. Over his shoulders and breast was a miserable covering of rags, but the rest of his body was perfectly naked; his skin was dry, horny, and covered with blotches resembling large scales, which, on his legs, and particularly over his knees, stood out like the greaves of an ancient coat of mail; and he looked like one who

literally crawled on his belly and licked the dust of the earth. (*Incidents of Travel in Egypt, Arabia Petræa, and the Holy Land*, 2 vols. [New York: Harper & Brothers, 1837], II, 21)

98.38 Hotel] The Hotel d'Angleterre was listed in Murray's guidebook to Greece as one of the three best in northwest Athens; charges, about ten francs a day. The guide, Alexander, also called one of the best, was a native of Corfu who spoke not only the usual French and Italian but also excellent English. "Boyd" is M's error for Sir George F. Bowen (1821–99), the "G. F. B." who wrote the 1854 Murray's *Greece*; he had come out as president of the university on Corfu (1847–51). His book *Ithaca in 1850* (London: Ridgway, 1851) convincingly identified the contemporary island as Odysseus's domain, and his *Mount Athos, Thessaly, and Epirus: A Diary of a Journey from Constantinople to Corfu* (London: Rivington, 1852) reported much of the personal experience lying behind the guidebook.

99.2 Wenham ice] From a pond in Wenham (north of Salem), Massachusetts, notable for the extraordinary purity and clarity of its ice shipped all over the world.

99.3 cross of Constantine] The simile is repeated in M's poem "The Apparition," referring to the miraculous appearance of the cross before a battle in the legend of Constantine's conversion (in *Timoleon*; *Published Poems*, p. 313).

99.4 Stirling] M had visited this famous Scottish stronghold sometime after leaving Glasgow; see p. 625.

99.5–6 Imperceptible . . . snow] See M's poem "Greek Masonry" (in *Timoleon*; *Published Poems*, p. 304):

> Joints were none that mortar sealed:
> Together, scarce with line revealed,
> The blocks in symmetry congealed.

Lieutenant Henry Wise had noticed this phenomenon: "The other matter I refer to, is a very singular cohesion which has taken place in the southwestern column of the Parthenon. Two of the sections of the shaft, a few feet from the base, have become absolutely joined together, either by some organic or atmospheric agency. . . . This phenomenon exists also, in two places in the steps to the portico, near the column" (*Scampavias from Gibel Tarek to Stamboul* [New York: Scribner, 1857], p. 101).

99.7 *Jupiter Olympus*] After centuries of pillaging, all that remained of the great temple (exceeded in size only by that of the Ephesian Diana) were 16 of its original 124 gigantic columns; but one of these was blown down in 1852. The western wall and attached columns of the Erechtheum also fell. Lieutenant Wise wrote: "The sections of the column with the capital fell in a straight line like a pile of bricks. There it lies now, grand even in death; with the private marks and chisellings of the ancient marble cutters as plainly visible on the intersections of the drums, as the hour they were cut" (*Scampavias*, pp. 227–28).

99.15 Marshall] Passport applications in the State Department archives indicate a great many Marshalls were in Europe in the 1850's; possibly this was the New York merchant John Rutgers Marshall, who had a New Orleans branch that suggests a potential interest in ice. Egypt, at least, was being supplied with ice by an American company by 1857 (David R. Serpell, "American Consular Activities in Egypt, 1849–63," *Journal of Modern History*, X [1938], 344–63; see p. 346).

99.17 Consul] Jonas King (1792–1869), the Presbyterian missionary, had been a storm center in Near East religious (and political) controversy because of his polemical attacks on other orthodoxies. He studied Arabic and other Levantine languages in Paris, went with other American missionaries to the Levant in 1824, in 1829 married into a Smyrniote Greek family, and in 1831 established a school in Athens. But he quickly lost Greek support by attacks on the Greek Church that led to his conviction for blasphemy. His acting consular appointment (1851–57) afforded him diplomatic protection from later harassment. His hospitable disposition drew praise from travelers; Stephen Larrabee (*Hellas Observed* [New York: New York University Press, 1957]) discusses King's activities (chap. 7) and quotes one visitor's description of him, "in a short rusty frock coat . . . carrying a blue cotton umbrella," and of his house crowded with stones from various antique sites (p. 197). (Finnie, *Pioneers East*, pictures him in his adopted Arabic dress, between pp. 18 and 19.) M's passport (in the Berkshire Athenaeum) bears his visa for Messina and Naples, dated February 10, 1857.

99.20 *Temple of Theseus*] Pentelic marble characteristically weathered to a golden yellow, and earthquakes had somewhat dislocated the drums of stone in its columns, but because of its early consecration as a church, the temple and tomb appeared very much as in the time of Pericles. The illustration on p. 450 is from the frontispiece (by J. M. W. Turner) to Volume VII of the *Works of Lord Byron* (London: Murray, 1832). While the Temple of Nike Apteros, the "Wingless Victory," had disappeared by the eighteenth century, in 1835 its fragments were discovered and almost

perfectly reconstituted the original. What M calls the "Genoese Tower," Murray's *Greece* (p. 157) calls only "mediæval"; though lofty, it was in ruinous state. Its walls incorporated two columns and part of a third from the classical Propylaea. (M's "Perysplea", a conjectural reading, probably refers to "Propylaea" or possibly to "Peristyle.")

Genoese Tower incorporating columns of Perysplea: — Pavement of Parthenon

99.28 Zephalonia] Cephalonia, the Ionian island, at that time part of the brief-lived "Septinsular" republic of the "United States of the Ionian Islands," established under British protection by the settlement of 1815 and finally ceded to Greece in 1864.

99.28 Lindy Foote's son] Unidentified. M's apparently familiar "Lindy" (possibly a misreading—see the reproduction) does not seem to fit either of two naval officers very likely known to him, and neither had a son of appropriate age to cause "a story." One was Sir Edward James Foote (1767–1833), who served in the Mediterranean under Nelson, and who captured the Maltese cannon noted by M in the Tower of London (15.31–32). The other was Andrew Hull Foote (1806–63), whose rise to admiral in the American navy was marked by his ardent opposition to both the slave trade and spiritous liquors. He had been associated in 1839 with Dr. Lockwood in Honolulu (see 73.8 and accompanying discussion); later, he was commandant of the Boston Navy Yard (1846–48), and his navy service in many respects paralleled that of M's troubled cousin, Guert Gansevoort.

Spent evening conversing with young
English officer from Zephalonia — Told
story of Lady Foote's son, &c. — Saw
the sunset from Lyccabacus. Lovely, divine.

99.29 *Lyccabacus*] Lycabettus, the nine-hundred-foot eminence a half-hour's walk northeast, gave the best view of city, plain, bay, and islands beyond.

99.29 Lovely] In the last line of the reproduction just above. The equally possible reading "Lonely" (H) would fit the landscape but seems less likely than "Lovely" if—as indicated by the order in which he reports the events—M had the company of the "young English officer" with whom he "spent evening conversing" (cf. the discussion at 80.31).

99.35 "Cydnus"] Recently built, its 1,196 tons and 370 horsepower put this ship in the class of the largest ones operated by the French Messageries Imperiales. Second-class fare, about 134 francs, plus 6 francs a day for meals. By reputation, the second-class cabins of the French line were the equal of first-class ones on the Austrian, so that many "discriminating" travelers took the cheaper accommodation. M, used to the discomforts of the Austrian ships, seems surprised by the number of passengers in this class.

100.2 Misseri] Mysseri was the guide and dragoman highly praised by M's London dinner acquaintance Alexander Kinglake, the author of *Eöthen* (see 46.30 and the discussion at 46.28). Mysseri and his English wife ran the best hotel in Constantinople according to such travelers or residents as Mrs.

Hornby. But Lieutenant Wise scoffed at both Kinglake and his dragoman: "This publican—from the prestige of his renown in a book entitled *Eothen*—assumes to be one of the most powerful Agas—Pashas even—in the Sultan's dominions. The way-worn traveller can behold him [in Pera] . . . attired in a profusion of rich furs and velvets. . . . We had reason to believe . . . that the sleek Sieur Mysseri was a sharper of eminence" (*Scampavias*, p. 268).

100.11 Hotel] Either the Victoria or La Trinacria, side by side on the main thoroughfare near the cathedral, the best available though "undesirable" for any lengthy stay; rates two and a half lira upward. The cathedral in Messina had been so damaged by earthquake and fire that repairs left but little of the original Norman structure. The whole city had been reduced by siege and plague to some ninety thousand people (according to Browne in 1851, *Yusef*, p. 81), and had been "entirely rebuilt since the famous earthquake of 1783." Aboard the *Constellation* fourteen years earlier, Lieutenant Schroeder found that "notwithstanding the fine effect from the strait, notwithstanding several wide streets, noble lava flag-stones, and substantial stone houses, the dirt and filth is terrible," also that there were "beggars in legions, and troops of lazaroni" (*Shores of the Mediterranean*, I, 75).

100.13 cafe near opera-house] The Caffè Veneziana was listed as "good"; both it and the handsome new Teatro Veneziana (1852) were but two blocks from the hotels.

100.16–17 Cap. Bell] Charles H. Bell (1798–1875), from New York, had been with Decatur in the Barbary wars, chased slavers on the African coast, and been promoted to captain in 1854; later he was commandant of the Brooklyn Navy Yard (1865–68). For the *Constellation*, see the discussion at 73.6. The origins of the other officers listed here were: William C. B. S. Porter, District of Columbia; John Pine Bankhead, Virginia; William F. Spicer, New York; Charles M. Fauntleroy, Virginia; and Thomas McKean Buchanan, Pennsylvania. The "Clerk" would appear to be a son of the captain. Of the two Virginians, Fauntleroy resigned (and was dismissed) on April 7, 1861, but Bankhead remained with the Union, was promoted to captain, and was the second commander of the *Monitor* when it sank off Cape Hatteras in the violent storm the night of December 30, 1862. (The first of M's two Civil War poems about the *Monitor*, "In the Turret" [in *Battle-Pieces*; *Published Poems*, pp. 39–40], concludes with a dirge for its sinking, but does not mention Bankhead.) See also the discussion at 124.23.

100.17 high hill] The Colle di San Rizzo (1,502 ft.), an hour's walk west. Lieutenant Schroeder described the view: "At our feet the solid city sat dipping almost in the blue waves, and but two or three miles beyond, the waving and broken hills of Calabria, dotted with white towns and the rich ripe crops of the season; the narrow pass of waters winding to the Rock of Scylla, which contrasted with the low jutting point of Pelorus. . . . On the left or west side, fruitful country valleys lay . . . , and at the south the mists of the valley shrouded the crest of Etna" (*Shores of the Mediterranean*, I, 77).

100.20 opera of Macbeth] According to Leyda (*Log*, II, 552–53 [Feb. 14, 1857]), Verdi himself conducted.

100.26 forts] The citizens of Messina were reputed the most restless in the repressive Kingdom of the Two Sicilies. After an uprising against the Spanish (1672–78), a large tract was cleared from before the Citadel (on the peninsula enclosing the harbor); in the uprisings of 1848, another large section in this vicinity had been leveled in a bombardment by the Neapolitans under King "Bomba" (see the discussion at 101.29).

100.31 Salvator Rosa] Rosa (1615–73) often used Calabrian scenery for his paintings of wild and desolate landscapes. M's "The Encantadas" was published in *Putnam's Monthly Magazine* (March–May, 1854) under the pseudonym "Salvator R. Tarnmoor" (see the NN *Piazza Tales* volume, pp. 600–601, and the discussion at 125.3 in that volume). See also the discussion below at 107.23.

100.32 Carnival] In 1857 Ash Wednesday fell on February 25, making this an early manifestation of the pre-Lenten Carnivale festivities.

101.2 cabin passage] Boats of the Vapori Siciliani Comp. Florio plied the route four or five times weekly, taking about thirty-eight hours with way stops. Reggio (the ancient Rhegium), across the straits, was a stopping place for Saint Paul on the way to Rome (Acts 28:13). Joachim Murat, installed by Napoleon as king of Naples, reigned briefly and was shot near the town of Pizzo on October 13, 1815, trying to recapture his kingdom. The third regular stop was the village of Paolo.

Wed. ~~Thursday~~, 18 Feb. Ere day break we passed
between Capri & Misenum & entered bay of Naples.
I was on deck. Dim mass of Vesuvius soon
in sight. Recognized it from picture of outline.
Soon, smelt the city. Brilliant lights.

101.11 outline] Possibly "mothers" (H)—at the end of line 3 above. Both of these possible readings are conjectural. The word "picture" is clear but may be either singular or plural; "outline" is given preference in the text

ITALY.

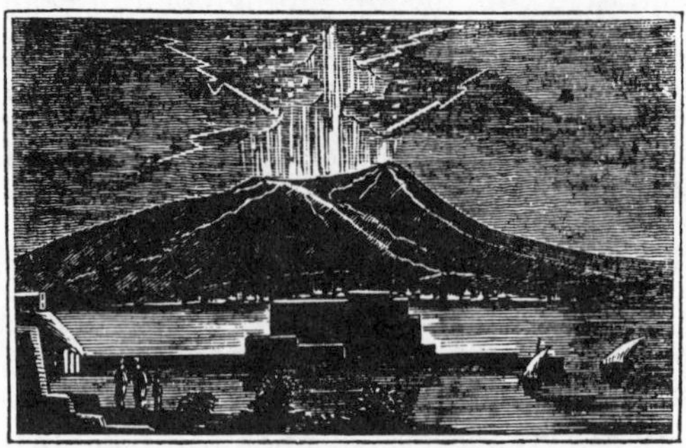

Eruption of Mount Vesuvius.

because it is safer to assume that M recognized the "dim mass" of Vesuvius from outline pictures (see above, from Olney's *Modern Geography*, p. 186; Sealts 390) than that he recognized it from "pictures of mothers" (the conjectural reading "mothers" would be taken to establish the "fact" that his mother—whom he elsewhere always called "Mama" [see e.g., p. 139 for three references to "Mama"]—owned one or more). We have no record of when M acquired the picture remembered by his granddaughter from her childhood in the 1880's as in his home then: "The white sails on the Bay of Naples, afloat in the front hall," the "coloured engraving of the Bay of Naples, its still blue dotted with tiny white sails" (Metcalf, *Herman Melville*, pp. 216, 282). "Vesuvius' plume of fire" is described in *Clarel* (1.35.84–87) as reddening the bay and tinging mast and spire—not as M saw it.

101.13 *Hotel de Geneve*] A second-class but comfortable inn just off the Piazza Medina near the harbor. (Gordon Poole, of the University of Naples, has located a picture of the building, reproduced in his "A Note on Herman Melville's Stay in Naples," *Melville Society Extracts*, No. 68 [November, 1986], 1.)

101.15 Rhinelander & Friedman] From State Department passport records, the likeliest candidates are Charles E. Rhinelander, aged twenty-six, of New York, who appears to have gone abroad early in 1857, and Arnold Friedman (aged thirty in 1855) also of New York. Friedman had applied in May, 1855, for the purposes of a "commercial tour." However, Poole (see the preceding discussion) could find no record of their names in the Neapolitan police archives, where M and his fellow passengers registered.

101.17 Pompeii] Excavations begun in the eighteenth century had by the mid-nineteenth cleared about a quarter of the area—the forum and an area to the west, the amphitheater, a few outlying streets, and the circuit of the walls. The "guards" were the government-appointed guides, and the one-piastre fee covered all sights, including the objects and pictures under lock. Thus the pious Samuel Prime and his party a few years earlier entered through the Street of Tombs, viewed the house of Diomede with the casts of the seventeen victims in its basement, other excavated shops and baths, the temples of Venus and Jupiter, a tavern, the houses of the "Cave Canem" sign, of Castor and Pollux, of Apollo, and of Sallust with its painting of Actaeon and Diana, and saw with disgust the lascivious paintings and phallic insignia (*Travels*, II, 164–68). (In a trial preface among the Burgundy Club manuscripts [left unpublished in his desk], M made an extended application of the "Cave Canem" sign; HCL-M; included in the NN volume *BILLY BUDD, SAILOR and Other Late Manuscripts*.) M may have known the detailed description of Pompeii and the artifacts in the museum in Naples found in James Jackson Jarves's *Italian Sights and Papal Principles* (New York: Harper & Brothers, 1855, chap. 8). (For M's interest in Jarves see the discussion at 106.30.) Along the coastal railroad, the three village stations mentioned were distant five, six, and seven miles respectively, Pompeii thirteen; trains left at seven, nine, and noon.

101.20 Vesuvius on horseback] Ascent usually commenced at Resina, but lava flows in the 1850's had made Torre dell'Annunziata (now Torre Annunziata), just outside Pompeii, the better starting point. A guide usually received four shillings, with two shillings for each horse, and the trip took about two and a half hours riding, another hour afoot climbing the last steep slopes—the tourist often assisted by the guide with a stout belt and rope. The prehistoric crater's broken walls partly surround at a distance the central cone of the great A.D. 79 eruption, which, when M saw it, was quiescent between the severe eruptions of 1855 and 1858. Hawthorne's friend G. S. Hillard had climbed the cone also, noting the "roaring and murmuring of the mountain—a heavy, sullen sound . . . recurring at brief and regular intervals" (*Six Months in Italy*, 2 vols. [Boston: Ticknor, Reed, & Fields, 1853], II, 148).

101.29 Noble street] The Strada di Toledo, now the Via Roma, Naples's principal north-south artery; the 418,000 inhabitants reportedly made it the noisiest in Europe. The Royal Palace at the harbor end was near the old fortress, the "Castel Nuovo," and its triumphal arch erected (1443) in honor of Alfonso of Aragon. The prevalence of troops, agents of the repressive policies of Ferdinand II ("King Bomba"), next-to-last of the corrupt and cruel Bourbons, had been augmented after the Sicilian revolt and Continental uprisings of 1848. A letter by Gladstone excoriating the abominable conditions of the tens of thousands of political prisoners, as well as repeated stories in London and New York papers, had recently made the king and the

Neapolitan government more notorious than ever. See the poems "At the Hostelry" and "Naples in the Time of Bomba" (both unpublished by M).

101.32 Capo di Monte] A lofty hill beyond the north end of the Strada di Toledo, site of the new royal suburban villa and gardens. The writer of Murray's *Southern Italy* and others did not share M's admiration for the vast, heavy, and graceless edifice of the villa. On the southwest slope was the eighth-century church of San Gennaro (Saint Januarius), whose tomb was beneath the high altar. Entrance to the three levels of the catacombs—with their long corridors lined by niches filled with skeletons—was only through the church.

101.34 bones] Possibly "tombs" or "times".

Bon. Catacombs — old man with lanthorn.—
Great extent. Old bones. Gloomy. Could'nt
get away. Thought crazy. — Walked about

101.35 Bought good coat] Apparently M lost one in Pompeii or on Vesuvius (see remark on "no coat," 101.26); later in Venice he bought still another (118.30).

101.37–102.1 Villa Real] The exclusive promenade along the shore, site of such expensive hotels as the Îles Britanniques, where M's dinner cost him between 2*s.* 8*d.* and 3*s.* 4*d.* Townsend's family were friends in Albany of M's relatives the Gansevoorts and the Lansings, and Howard in particular was a friend of M's sister Augusta. The police records show that the Townsends had arrived on February 7 (Poole, "A Note," p. 4).

102.3 San Carlo] After a fire in 1816 the Teatro Reale di San Carlo, next to the Royal Palace, had been completely rebuilt and refurbished into one of the largest and most splendid of the time.

102.5 letters] Among them, one to his family, dated the day before, reported his health much improved (Metcalf, *Herman Melville*, p. 163; No. 352 on the "Check List of Unlocated Letters," *Letters*, p. 314); it is not known what other letters M wrote at this time.

102.6 Posilipo] This excursion to the district west (not east, as M has it) of Naples was regularly recommended by the guidebooks. The carriage service in Naples was Italy's worst: a carriage (*vettura*) and driver (*vetturino*) would have cost about 8*d.* an hour, or a one-horse cabriolet, 5*s.* 4*d.* a day. Posilipo is the ridged promontory at the southwest edge of the city, between the harbor and the bay of Baia; the Strada Nuova di Posilipo more or less

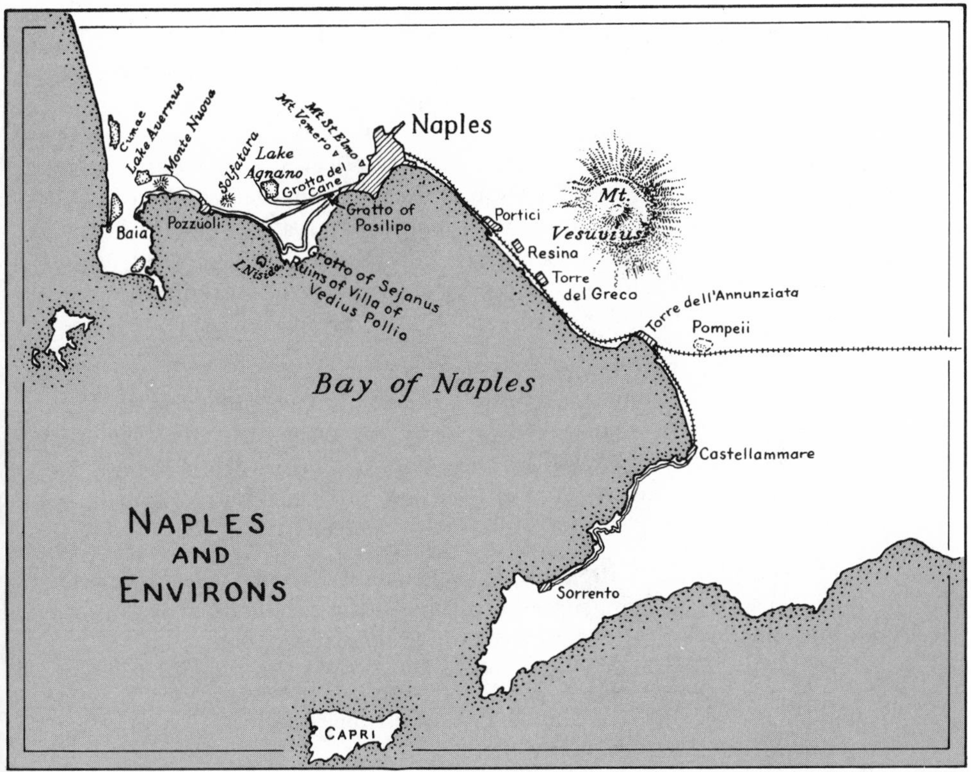

followed the coastline, commanding a succession of fine views. Pozzuoli (the ancient Puteoli) on the next embayment about six miles west of Naples has extensive Roman ruins, notably of the fabulous Augustan estate of Vedius Pollio, named by him Pausilypum (Greek for "end of care"), which came to designate the whole promontory. See M's poems "Pausilippo" (in *Timoleon*; *Published Poems*, pp. 297–99) and "Naples in the Time of Bomba" (unpublished by M), section 5. The tunnel of the Grotta di Seiano (Grotto of Sejanus), 2,755 feet long, was cut through the south end of the promontory, and beyond, the so-called Scuola di Virgilio (misnomer for a Temple of Fortune) occupied its tip. On the island of Nisida, just offshore, the remnant of an ancient crater, was a villa of Lucullus, associated with Cicero and Brutus. The village of Baia (the ancient Baiae) on the western shore was clearly visible from M's vantage; the area was celebrated alike for its beauty and Roman depravity. Caesar, Crassus, and Pompey had villas here, and here Hadrian committed suicide.

102.11 Solfatara] The region's beauty and latent volcanic activity suggested the sites of the Greek fables of Elysium, Hades, Tartarus, and the like.

The semi-dormant volcano Solfatara (outside Pozzuoli), for example, still emitted steam and noxious gases, mostly hydrogen sulfide. Returning to the city, M took the vehicular tunnel through the base of the promontory, the Grotto of Posilipo, 2,244 feet long. Constructed in Empire times, its axis was such that, at the equinoxes, the rising or setting sun shone through its length. In the Middle Ages it was believed to be Virgil's necromantic work and his tomb to be the fifteen-foot-square domed room on a precipice over its east entrance. Just north of the west tunnel portal lay the crater lake of Agnano, still exhaling poisonous vapors, on whose southeast shore was the small hillside Grotta del Cane, where for eight pence the custodian would place a dog on its floor to be overcome by the carbon dioxide constantly secreted from its walls.

102.22 Vomero Mount & Castle of Elmo] The two eminences on the southwest outskirts were occupied by many villas; the walls of the fourteenth-century castle high on Elmo were enormous. Just below were the fourteenth-century church of San Martino and adjoining Carmelite monastery.

102.24 Cafe] The Caffè d'Europe was one of the best, famous for its Neapolitan ices; a good dinner might cost two or three shillings. Jarves, too, singled it out for particular commendation (*Italian Sights*, p. 223).

102.32 Commissionaire] The exact form of M's word is unclear; the form given here occurs in a context also concerning passports in Murray's *France* (1848); see the discussion at 30.21.

Saturday 21st Feb. Upon going from
chamber in morning encountered by jabbering
man with document. Commissionaire. Into
breakfast room — people at table — "Do
any of you speak French?" Whereupon
Mr Rowse(?) spoke. Passport. &c.

102.34 Rowse(?)] Peter Warren Rousse (1832–87) was a New Jersey native and Rutgers graduate (1850), admitted to the New York bar in 1854, who spent 1854–57 traveling in Europe, before joining a brother-in-law, DeWitt C. Backus, in a law partnership, which he left after 1870 for a career in journalism (*Minutes of the Thirty-Second Annual Meeting of the Editorial Association of . . . New Jersey* [Camden, N.J., 1888], pp. 16–17). His sister,

Anna M. (Mrs. Backus?), on her passport application (received at the State Department, November 7, 1856) stated her age as thirty-one and her purpose, to join her brother. Rousse and his sister had arrived from Leghorn on February 13 and, like M, had declared to the police their intention to leave for Rome on February 24 (Poole, "A Note," p. 4). Though M saw much of the Rousses in Naples and Rome, he never learned to spell the name.

102.34 Passport] The Neapolitan kingdom's notorious bureaucracy is indicated by Murray's *Southern Italy*, pp. xliv–xlv:

> Before the traveller is allowed to enter the kingdom of the Two Sicilies, his passport must bear the visa of a . . . Neapolitan consul resident in the port of embarkation [M had complied in Athens]. . . . If he arrive by sea, he must present himself to the police of the port on landing, and take the usual receipt for his passport. No stranger is allowed to remain in Naples longer than a week who does not provide himself with a permission . . . granted for two months.

Exit was as tedious: "To go from Naples to Rome, after the signature of [his own minister or consul] the visa of the Papal nuncio is required; that of the police is then necessary; and, lastly, the signature of the minister of foreign affairs." M's trouble here is unclear—he had complied with all regulations, had been in Naples only three days, and had had no difficulty entering Messina. In any event, his passport (in the Berkshire Athenaeum) was visaed for Rome this day by the American consul, Alexander Hammett, whose fee was one dollar. This section of his passport displays the seals of four other authorities, all dated this same day. Poole notes that in the police register M—perhaps through a misunderstanding—declared his prospective lodging as the Albergo di Roma rather than the Genève; this discrepancy may have prompted official suspicion; the "Napoleon" he paid (103.32) may have been a hotel charge for taking care of passport matters (Poole, "A Note," pp. 2–3). Or it may have been a bribe—a practice which Jarves, for instance, bitterly described as necessary when dealing with Neapolitan officials (*Italian Sights*, pp. 312–13).

102.35 Museum] The Museo Borbonico, established in 1790 in a former cavalry barracks on the Strada di Toledo; in 1816 all the royal art treasures were deposited here, and new archaeological objects were commonly brought here. Usual hours were eight to two, and the fees numerous. In the Gallery of Bronzes, reputed the world's most extensive, the horse head survived from a colossal figure before a Naples Temple of Neptune, melted down by a cardinal for bells. In M's first lecture (1857), "Statues in Rome," all three busts mentioned here appear: Seneca likened to a pawnbroker, Nero a genteelly dissipated young man, and Plato a fastidious exquisite under the hands of his hairdresser (see the NN *Piazza Tales* volume, p. 401). The paintings were of secondary significance. The Raphael was probably the *Madonna col Divino Amore*, the infant Jesus on his mother's knee blessing St. John the Baptist; there were at least two Domenichinos, a *St. John Evangelist* and *The Guardian Angel Defending Innocence*. The Farnese Hercules and the Bull were brought to Rome by Caracalla to decorate his baths. The Hercules—the fatigued hero leaning on his club—was rediscovered in 1540 without its legs, which were not to be found for twenty more years; in the nineteenth century Prince Borghese brought the parts together for the king of Naples. In "Statues in Rome" M took up and developed his description (p. 406). Much later, in Chapter 2 of *Billy Budd, Sailor*, he described Billy's face as showing "that humane look of reposeful good nature which the Greek sculptor in some instances gave to his heroic strong man, Hercules"—originally "the Farnese Hercules" (Hayford-Sealts edition, pp. 51, 140–41).

103.17 St. Januarius] The thirteenth-century cathedral was nominally dedicated to the Virgin, but the Chapel of San Gennaro dominated, with its twice-yearly miracle of the liquefaction of the saint's blood, to the scandalized disapproval of Protestant onlookers.

103.17–25 Thence . . . driver] M elaborated this episode in his poem "Naples in the Time of Bomba" (unpublished by M).

103.27 Statue in net] In the Capella di San Severo, located in the older part of the town between the cathedral and M's hotel, among other allegorical statues stood *Vice Undeceived*, a figure attempting with an angel's aid to remove a meticulously carved rope net.

103.33 took train] The same train M had taken to Pompeii ran to Castellammare on the Sorrentine peninsula, an hour southeast of Naples. From there a winding nine-mile road swept along the cliffs to the resort town of Sorrento, with splendid views of bay and city. About half way a massive bridge on a double row of arches crossed a deep ravine; thereafter the road descended from its highest point by a series of terraces to the plain of the town. The house of Tasso's birth and later residence overlooked the sea from a three-hundred-foot precipice, but the present hotel, its rear constantly crumbling away as the sea undermined the cliff, could contain little of the original structure. Cooper and his family lived here for three months in 1829, while he wrote *The Water-Witch*. The "young Englishman" was presumably Edward Walter, aged twenty-seven, a resident of Messina who evidently arrived in Naples with M and also lodged at the Genève (Poole, "A Note," p. 3). (For *vetturino* see the discussion at 102.6 or 113.19.)

103.36 cock feathers] Both words conjectural.

Crowds of hackmen &c. Vehicles bargaining. Three horses, with cock feathers, all the way to Sorrento for about a dollar. — Grand drive. Road, windings

104.11 Lake Avernus] On this second visit M ventured farther west and north. The crater lake of Avernus had bubbled poisonous gases into the reign of Augustus. This region, including the nearby village of Cumae with its priestly oracles, is referred to in the *Odyssey* (bk. 11) and is famous for the visit of Aeneas (*Aeneid*, bk. 6). The little "temple" bearing the name of Apollo was in reality the ruins of a bath. The so-called Grotta della Sibilla on the south shore was not the true cave of the Cumaean Sibyl, discovered nearer Baiae in 1932. What M saw was the Augustan tunnel connecting Avernus with Baiae; it began at the lake's shore, with many adjacent chambers, now partly water-filled, and was long, dark, slimy, and crawling with reptiles. For eight pence, guides furnished four-foot torches of hemp, rosin, and tar. Lake Lucrinus, south of Avernus at the bay's edge, once furnished oysters to Roman voluptuaries; the ruins that M calls a "hotel" were of a bath. Monte Nuova at the edge of the bay was created by an eruption in 1538 after two years of violent earthquakes; from level ground the now cold and empty cone rose 440 feet. (M's quotation "secrets of his prison-house" is slightly modified from the speech of Hamlet's father's ghost to his son [I, v, 14].) M's Civil War poem "The Apparition (A Retrospect)" (in *Battle-Pieces*; *Published Poems*, p. 116) draws on this day's observations, particularly in the first and last stanzas.

104.34–35 *Venus* . . . Mercury] Of three larger ruins, these two were actually baths, misunderstood since the seventeenth century as "temples." That of "Venus" was externally octagonal, with a circular interior decorated rather magnificently, with stucco reliefs shocking to many. That of "Mercury," also circular with a vaulted ceiling, made an echo chamber or "whispering gallery."

105.2 momentoes] A conjectural reading. Possibly "monstrousness" (written "monstrues") (H).

[On the western shore of Italy, on a bay &c. — A living mountain — enumerate the momentoes of the monstrousness of Nature — ranges of [illegible] &c — Grand City.

105.19 towers] Possibly "bowers".

Wonderful old ruined palace at Pausilippo. Sea-palace. —
The road. Villas, grots, summer-houses —
ravines — towers, &c &c &c.

105.25 diligence from P.O] I.e., from the Post Office, a designation of the station of arrival and departure for the post vehicles, or diligences—the same as "Diligence office" above (105.15). Commercial diligences ran six days a week, leaving at eight in the morning and taking about twenty hours over the relatively good post road along the general route of the ancient Appian Way. Not all travelers, however, shared M's good opinion of the conveyances. Fondi, seventy-five miles from Naples, and Terracina, seventeen miles farther, a hundred miles from Rome, where the Volscian Mountains crowded the road along the coast, were on either side of the boundary of the Papal States with its suspicious customs officers. The Alban Hills bound the Campagna some twenty miles southeast of Rome. The Frenchman riding with M in the coupé was possibly Edmondo Paupert, a traveling salesman returning to France, who with M had arrived from Messina and expected to leave this day also for Rome (Poole, "A Note," p. 3). The Rousses may have also been in the diligence if they were still following their announced schedule. The illustration below of Rome from a distance north is from *Rome in the Nineteenth Century* by Charlotte A. Eaton (London: Bohn, 1852), facing p. 65.

ROME

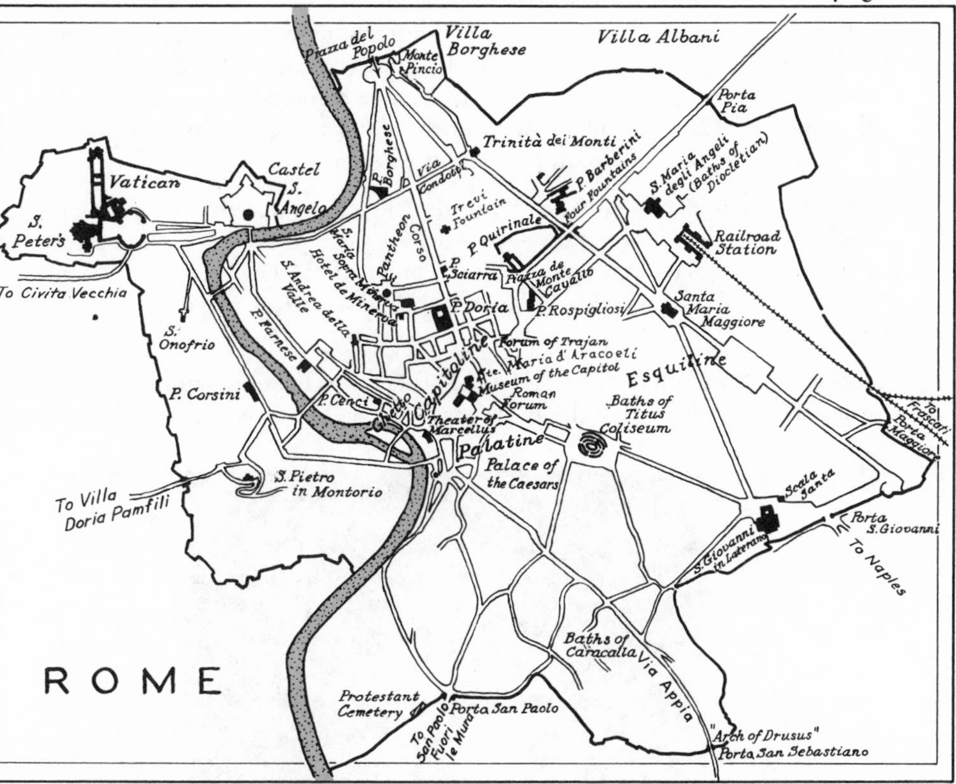

105.34–35 hotel de Minerva] On the piazza just southeast of the Pantheon; not fashionable but much frequented by the French. Rates were highest just before Easter but averaged one and a half to two shillings, exclusive of light and heat. In the piazza before the church of Santa Maria Sopra Minerva, Bernini erected (1667) a seventeen-foot obelisk on a marble elephant. In this same neighborhood Bayard Taylor had found lodging eleven years earlier (*Views A-Foot*, pp. 317, 330).

105.35 Capitol] The Capitoline Hill is less than half a mile from M's hotel, and Murray's *Rome* recommended an early visit for the view giving a general orientation to the city. The tower is part of the Palace of the Senators, the middle of the three buildings designed by Michelangelo around the three sides of the piazza.

106.5 Walked to St. Peters] By the most direct route, about one and a half miles. Initial disappointment was a familiar refrain in the writings of travelers; with each detail on so grand a scale, a sense of the huge proportions of the whole was slow to emerge.

106.9 S. Shaw] Samuel, younger half-brother of M's wife, Elizabeth, the youngest son (1833–1915) of Chief Justice Shaw; after finishing at Harvard in the spring of 1856, he sailed to Europe before M, traveled leisurely through Great Britain and northern Europe, and arrived in Rome just as M left (see 113.17–18 and accompanying discussion).

106.11 Hopper of Greylock] A glacial cirque—that is, a deep, steep-walled amphitheatrical hollow—on the west slope of the Berkshire mountain. M describes its appearance in the second part of "The Paradise of Bachelors and the Tartarus of Maids" (see the NN *Piazza Tales* volume, pp. 323–24).

106.12 Museum of Capitol] One of the three buildings atop the Capitoline Hill. In the Hall of the Emperors were eighty-three busts of Roman

Antinous (Capitoline Museum)

rulers and wives arranged chronologically; two were of Tiberius. In his lecture "Statues in Rome" (1857–58) M attributes the quoted remark about Tiberius's bust to a lady "in our hearing," with the comment, "Madam, thought I, if he had *looked* bad, he could not have been Tiberius"; see the NN *Piazza Tales* volume, p. 402. The Dying Gladiator (now called Dying Gaul) and the Antinous were together in a nearby hall, both objects of extravagant praise by nineteenth-century visitors. Bayard Taylor looked "on the Gladiator with a hushed breath and an awed spirit," declaring "that the rude, barbarian form has a soul, [which] may be read in his touchingly expressive countenance" (*Views A-Foot*, p. 335). And G. S. Hillard described the Antinous as "not merely beautiful" but "beauty itself" (*Six Months in Italy*, I, 290). In Naples M did not record seeing at the Museo Borbonico the most famous of many representations of Hadrian's favorite, but he seems to have viewed more than once the one here in the Capitoline Museum (illustrated opposite, from *University Prints*, ed. Edmund von Mach [Boston: University Prints, 1916], plate A415) and the one in the Villa Albani (see 107.18–20 and the discussion at 107.14–17). At some later time he acquired a more than life-sized copy bust of the boy, which two of his granddaughters recalled—see EMM, p. 136; Frances Osborne remembered it standing "on a tall white pedestal in the corner of the front parlor, draped with a . . . white veil to keep [off] the city dust" ("Herman Melville through a Child's Eyes," *Bulletin of the New York Public Library*, LXIX [December, 1965], 655–60; reprinted in Sealts, *Early Lives*, pp. 179–85). Hawthorne, on the other hand, barely glanced at the Antinous, but was deeply moved by the Dying Gladiator (*FINB*, p. 102); the Faun of Praxiteles, the inspiration for *The Marble Faun* (Boston: Ticknor & Fields, 1860), is also in this gallery.

106.16–17 barberousness . . . barberousness] Both occurrences possibly "barberisms" or "barbarians".

resentment. Soldier. — Dying Gladiator. Shows
That humanity existed amid the barberousness of the Roman
time, as it now among Christian barberousness. Antinous

106.18 Pincian hill] Its hilltop gardens, just inside the city's north wall, look down on the broad Piazza del Popolo; the wide paths and drives remained a fashionable promenade (see Henry James's *Daisy Miller*, 1878) for wealthy residents by the hundreds, strolling, riding horseback, or driving expensive cabriolets. On a Thursday like this, and Sundays, a military band played for two hours before sunset.

106.20 posturing] A conjectural reading. Possibly "touring" (H).

— Gardens & statuary — overlooking Piazza del Popolo. — Fashion & Rank — Promenaders posturing. modern statues; those of Antiquity. How little influence has taste on the world!— Fashion

106.24–25 Via Condotti] On this street leading west from the Piazza di Spagna and the Spanish Steps, the Caffè Greco still exists, but no longer as the haunt of bohemian artists of all nations, though many studios remain in nearby streets. (Margaret Thorp's *The Literary Sculptors* [Durham, N.C.: Duke University Press, 1965], chap. 2, describes the nineteenth-century café—its excellent coffee, its noise, smoke, untidiness, and camaraderie—and the general neighborhood milieu of would-be artists.)

106.27 Cenci] Probably an engraved copy of the once-famous *Beatrice Cenci* then attributed to Guido Reni; M saw the original five days later in the Palazzo Barberini (see the discussion at 108.31). In *Pierre* M had referred to "that sweetest, most touching, but most awful of all feminine heads—The Cenci of Guido" (bk. 26, chap. 1; p. 351). An engraved copy owned by M has survived; see reproduction, p. 474 (from *Log*, II, 556 [Feb. 26, 1857]).

106.30 *Feb 27th*] M wrote a (nonextant) letter home dated on this day that said he expected to return the next month (*Log*, II, 567 [April 7, 1857]; "Check List of Unlocated Letters," No. 353, *Letters*, p. 314).

106.30 A. Consul] The office of American consul was vacant for most of 1857, but M's passport (in the Berkshire Athenaeum) bears the visa of A. Ardisson, "Per il console," dated March 11, 1857.

106.30 Page, & Jarves] For the American painter William Page, see 111.20–21 and accompanying discussions and 112.1–2. James Jackson Jarves (1818–88), of a well-to-do Boston family, had been an editor and a traveler in California, Central America, and Hawaii, where he founded the newspaper *Polynesia* in 1840; he was not there when M was, in the summer of 1843. In 1848 he returned to America and Europe as diplomatic agent for the Hawaiians. M may have known his *History of the Hawaiian or Sandwich Islands* (1843, 1844), his frequent articles on art in *Harper's*, and his first book on art, *Art-Hints: Architecture, Sculpture and Painting* (1855); see also the discussion on the Sciarra Gallery, at 109.22. Despite Jarves's scoffing at Page's theories regarding Titian's coloring, they were friends, but it is not clear why M thought Jarves would be in Rome, since he had settled in Florence in

1852. Perhaps M expected him there because so much of Jarves's *Italian Sights and Papal Principles* was devoted to Protestant excoriation of papal Rome. (In 1871 M was given Jarves's *The Art-Idea*, 1864; now in the Gansevoort-Lansing Collection of the New York Public Library; Sealts 296.) Jarves's extraordinary collection of early Italian paintings is now in the Art Gallery of Yale University. M liked this early painting better than did Hawthorne and most other contemporaries. (For Jarves see Francis Steegmuller, *The Two Lives of James Jackson Jarves* [New Haven: Yale University Press, 1951].)

106.31–33 Baths . . . Shelley] Then only partly cleared and excavated, the vast Baths of Caracalla were, next to the Coliseum, the most impressive ruins in Rome. M may have read in Murray's *Rome* (p. 56): "These extensive ruins were the favourite haunt of the poet Shelley. In the preface to the 'Prometheus Unbound' he says, 'This poem was chiefly written upon the mountainous ruins of the baths of Caracalla, among the flowery glades and thickets of odoriferous blossoming trees which are extended in ever-winding labyrinths upon its immense platforms and dizzy arches suspended in the air. The bright blue sky of Rome, and the effect of the vigorous awakening spring in that divinest climate, and the new life with which it drenches the spirits even to intoxication, were the inspiration of the drama.' " M's probable early knowledge of Shelley is discussed by Merrell R. Davis in *Melville's MARDI*; M's treatment of the *Cenci* portrait in *Pierre* indicates knowledge of Shelley's tragedy, which he had mentioned in *White-Jacket* (chap. 89, p. 376). See M's poem "Shelley's Vision" in *Timoleon* (*Published Poems*, p. 283).

106.36 Protestant Burial Ground] The cemetery is about a half-mile west from the baths, just inside the south wall of the city. Its old and new parts were separated by a deep trench, with Keats in the old, Shelley in the new. Shelley's epitaph for Keats reads: "This grave contains all that was mortal of a young English poet, who, on his deathbed, in the bitterness of his heart at the malicious power of his enemies, desired these words to be engraven on his tombstone: 'Here lies one whose name was writ in water.' February 24, 1821." See the poem "Time's Betrayal" (unpublished by M), the last lines of which allude to "Keats, stabbed by the Muses." Looming outside the wall is the only pyramid in Rome, some 120 feet high, the monument of Caius Cestius (d. 12 B.C.); see the illustration by Turner on p. 468, from the title page to Volume XIII of the *Works of Lord Byron*.

107.3 Cenci Palace] There were two; M's return along the left bank to his hotel took him past the one near the bend of the river, where the Isle of Tiber is located, with a new suspension bridge just downstream. The immense gloomy pile, long uninhabited, had recently been partly converted

into a military school. In this general area along the river, south and west of the Capitoline, lay the walled ghetto, reputedly the city's filthiest district. Here also on the west slope are the remains of the theater, the second built in Rome, finished by Augustus; only twelve arches in its two lower tiers remained. The Orsini Palace, not otherwise remarkable, was built on the ruins. Near here also had stood the Portico of Octavia, built by Augustus to shelter theater patrons, from which remained a large brick arch, possibly the one M remarks. (Albert Bierstadt's 1858 painting of it is in the Boston Athenæum.) The guidebook descriptions of the Farnese Palace, still farther north and west and also near the left bank, provided M's judgment of its superlative quality (due to Michelangelo), with its great rusticated blocks of travertine rifled from the Coliseum; the whole superb Farnese collection of marbles had been transferred to Naples, where M had seen them (103.13–15).

107.14–17 Lost . . . Albani] The seventeenth-century Villa Borghese and its extensive grounds just outside the city walls on the north was open to the public only on Saturdays, hence M's concern for the time lost that morning "going after Consul &c." to get the required authorization to visit the nearby eighteenth-century Villa Albani (now Villa Torlonia), a little farther east. Their once-great collections had been plundered for the French; what remained at the Borghese (after Pauline Bonaparte's husband, Prince Camillo Borghese, sent France more than 200 pieces of antique sculpture) was the splendor of its grounds and villa, but the Albani, despite Napoleon's carrying off 294 sculptural pieces, was still the third most important gallery in Rome (M made a second visit on March 14—see 112.3–5 and the discussion at 112.4). A year later Hawthorne found the Borghese's gallery hall more magnificent than he would have imagined (*FINB*, p. 174). The "Venus & Cupid" noted there by M was probably either a bas-relief by Vincenzo Pacetti or an unattributed sculpture now in Room I.

At the Villa Albani the celebrated bas-relief of Antinous (found at Hadrian's Tivoli villa) had been returned from France; unlike M, Hawthorne was unappreciative: "A colossal bas-relief of Antinous, crowned with flowers, and holding flowers in his hand . . . is said to be the finest relic of antiquity, next to the Apollo and the Laocöon, but, I could not feel it to be so—partly, I suppose, because the features of Antinous do not seem to me beautiful in themselves; and that heavy, downward look is repeated till I am more weary of it than of anything else in sculpture" (*FINB*, pp. 210–11); the

Antinous (Villa Albani)

Athena (Villa Albani)

claim had been made by Johann Joachim Winckelmann, curator for Cardinal Albani. In his lecture "Statues in Rome" (NN *Piazza Tales* volume, p. 407) M speaks of the "medallion of Antinous with his eye reposing on a lotus of admirable design which he holds in his hand." The "bronze Apollo" M noted, the Sauroctonos half-life-sized, was attributed to Praxiteles by Winckelmann. Most of the pictures had been recently brought from the Albani city palace, including one of many versions of Raphael's *La Fornarina* (M's "Italian lady"?). The conclusion of M's poem "After the Pleasure Party," in *Timoleon* (*Published Poems*, pp. 259–64), juxtaposes a "helmeted" and "armed" colossal statue of the virgin Athena at the Villa Albani with a picture of the Virgin Mary as alternative models for its sexually harried intellectual heroine. The illustrations here of works in the Villa Albani are reproduced from *University Prints*, plates A417 and A102. For the Antinous in the Capitoline Museum, see the discussion at 106.12.

107.23 Thence . . . Moses] The Porta Pia, designed by Michelangelo but only recently completed, was the nearest way back through the city wall from the northeast. M's "fountain of Moses" is the Fontana dell'Acqua Felice (near the central station) with its colossal statue of Moses striking water from the rock, flanked by Aaron and Gideon. The Baths of Diocletian close by, the "most splendid of the ancient world," were early consecrated because traditionally built by the forced labor of forty thousand Christians; Michelangelo turned the great hall of the frigidarium into the church of Santa Maria degli Angeli. The grave of Salvator Rosa (see the discussion at 100.31) is in what is now the circular vestibule (the former tepidarium) while in the transept (formerly Michelangelo's nave) stand eight monolithic columns of pink Egyptian granite, sixteen feet in circumference and forty-five feet high.

107.26 four fountains] The Quattro Fontane occupy the corners of the intersection at the east angle of the Quirinal Palace grounds. When M returned the next day, he noted the planned vistas from this point: to the Porta Pia on the northeast, southeast to the obelisk in the Piazza della Santa Maria Maggiore, southwest to the obelisk before the Quirinal Palace, and northwest to the obelisk in the Piazza della Trinità dei Monti, above the Spanish Steps. This palace on Monte Cavallo (see the discussion at 110.2) was still a summer residence of the pope; in the plaza fronting it, the so-called Dioscuri, gigantic paired statues reining in rearing horses, had come from the Baths of Constantine, the huge basin of the fountain from the Forum, and the red granite obelisk surmounting it from the Mausoleum of Augustus. Next day M's notes continued the meditation on gigantic Rome (interposing his notion of peopling the Baths of Caracalla with these giant statues) that he adapted in his lecture "Statues in Rome." On the lower slopes of the Quirinal, leading down to the Roman Forum, M could see as much of Trajan's Forum as had been cleared by the French in 1812, but most was still covered by a clutter of huddled buildings. The base of the great column of Trajan, however, had been excavated in the sixteenth century.

107.30 Extent . . . Rome] At the city's greatest extent under the Antonines, the enclosing walls protected an estimated 1.5 million inhabitants; in the nineteenth century, most of its 178,000 residents crowded into a small area toward the northwest and St. Peter's, leaving the rest of the Imperial City with great deserted spaces.

108.1 old palaces] Many private palaces, like the Barberini, Albani, and Rospigliosi, had been built on the slopes of the Quirinal, up from the miasmal damps of the valley. Early in his Roman sojourn Hawthorne described walking these streets: "Indescribably ugly and disagreeable they are. . . . Ever and anon, even in the meanest streets . . . we pass a palace, extending far along the narrow way . . . distinguished by its architectural windows, iron-barred on the basement story, and by its portal arch through which we have glimpses sometimes of a filthy courtyard, or perhaps an ornamented one, with trees, a colonnade, a fountain and a statue in the vista" (*FINB*, p. 56). His descriptions of the Rospigliosi garden (noted later by M, 109.31–34) and of the Quirinal gardens suggest what M had seen:

"Pieces of marble sculpture, much weather-stained, and generally broken-nosed, stood along these stately walks; there were many fountains gushing up into the sunshine" (p. 163).

108.4 San Maria Maggore] Santa Maria Maggiore, the third-ranking basilica in Rome, on the summit of the Esquiline some blocks east of the Quirinal. Despite many alterations since its founding in A.D. 352, it preserved with unmatched faithfulness the characteristics of a Roman basilica. Its coffered ceiling is ornamented with the first of Pizarro's Peruvian gold, presented by Ferdinand and Isabella. The ruins of a reservoir, miscalled the Trophies of Marius, are nearby, while a mile farther southeast the Porta Maggiore is formed by two arches of the Claudian aqueduct. M echoes Murray in calling this the "finest ancient gate in Rome." The tomb of the baker Marcus Vergilius Eurysaces, dating from the end of the Republic, is unique in its decoration with stone mortars used for kneading dough and with bas-reliefs of domestic life.

108.7 St: John Lateran] Walking west along the wall, M would have reached the Porta San Giovanni, through which he entered the city from Naples. The basilica of San Giovanni in Laterano (St. John Lateran), seat of the pope as bishop of Rome, is next in importance only to St. Peter's; its most "elegant" chapel is that of the Corsini, containing the eighteenth-century tomb of Clement XII. Students of Bernini sculpted the twelve gigantic statues in niches along the nave, whose elaborate drapery was often criticized, e.g., by Sir Joshua Reynolds, quoted in Murray (*Rome*, p. 105). On a second trip (March 3, 108.36–38; see also the accompanying discussion), M saw in a nearby building the Scala Santa (Holy Stairs), supposed to be the twenty-eight steps from Pilate's house in Jerusalem; he alludes to them in *Clarel*, 1.5.58–63. In his lecture on "Statues in Rome" M began with those seen as one enters Rome from Naples (as he did)—the exterior group of colossal figures above the portal of this basilica.

108.10–15 Walk . . . tomb] M's mile and a half walk west along the Aurelian Wall from the Porta San Giovanni to the Porta San Sebastiano (where the ancient Appian Way began) first passed the Porta Asinaria by which the Ostrogoth Totila was treacherously admitted (A.D. 546), then the Metronia and the Latina. The "Arch of Drusus," just inside the Porta San Sebastiano, was then believed to be the most ancient of triumphal arches, but more probably dated from Trajan's reign (the base of the true Arch of Drusus, A.D. 19, is in the Forum area). This arch, together with the view it framed of the gate beyond, was a favorite subject of painters. The Appian Way, inside or outside the gate, is lined by many sepulchers and columbaria—structures with niches resembling pigeonholes for cinerary urns. The tomb of the Scipios, dating from 312 B.C., a series of excavated chambers just inside the gate, was discovered under a vineyard in 1780, but the sarcophagus of the founder had been removed to the Vatican. (Hawthorne described this area and nearby columbaria, *FINB*, pp. 107–8, 119–23.)

108.16 Palace] Returning past the Baths of Caracalla, previously visited, M passed to the south of the Palatine Hill, where it overlooks the Circus Maximus, covered by masses of ruins of the palaces of the emperors from Augustus on. G. S. Hillard described the area: "Imagine a hill, upwards of a mile in circuit, and less than two hundred feet high, strewn with shapeless ruins and yawning with excavations . . . ; intersperse it with kitchen gardens for the growing of such matter-of-fact vegetables, as cauliflower, artichokes, and lettuce; throw in occasionally the vine, the laurel, the cypress, and the ivy; overshadow it with here and there a stately oak; and crown the whole with a smart, modern villa; and you will have some notion of the Palace of the Cæsars. . . . One hardly knows whether to call the scene a landscape or a ruin. It is a labyrinth of vaults, arches, broken walls, and fragments of columns: a mighty maze of desolation without a plan" (*Six Months in Italy*, I, 299–300). (Systematic excavation did not begin until 1861, when Napoleon III bought a large part of the crest.) The Arch of Janus Quadrifons, a third- or fourth-century structure bisected in both directions, is near the river, beyond the end of the Circus Maximus; and at the riverbank the ancient Etruscan sewer, draining the marsh of the Forum area, empties into the river.

108.21 Vatican Day] Monday was the usual visiting day, but entrance was possible almost any time with a gratuity to the custodian. In the second story of the once-open colonnade ("the Loggie") connecting the original Vatican with the Villa Belvedere are frescoes after Raphael's designs; four scenes show Adam and Eve. Open to the weather until 1813, the frescoes were much damaged, some even obliterated. Michelangelo's frescoes in the Sistine Chapel had suffered much from damp, smoke, and repainting. (In "Statues in Rome," M spoke of the Vatican sculptures next after those at St. John Lateran and later of "the crowning glory" of the Vatican, the Apollo Belvedere, unmentioned here; see the NN *Piazza Tales* volume, pp. 399–404.) The collection of animal sculptures in a hall at the north end of the galleries was said to be the finest of its sort; a wolf and sheep group was not mentioned by either Murray or the later Baedeker, but intrigued M enough for a second notice (110.27–30).

108.30 Mosaic Museum] Located near the main entrance to the Vatican proper, this *atelier* was founded in 1782 to make mosaic reproductions of papal portraits and such famous works as Raphael's Madonnas, destined, as M notes, for the basilica of St. Paul's Outside the Walls (see the discussion at 111.26).

108.31 Palazzo Barberini] On the Quirinal, just north of the papal palace. The small art collection, open to the public daily from one to four, was famous for the extravagantly admired supposed portrait of Beatrice Cenci (illustrated above, from *Log*, II, 556), which, tradition said, Guido Reni painted either on the night before, or from memory after, her hanging for killing her incestuous father. (In fact Reni did not arrive in Rome until 1601, two years later, and in any case many now believe the painting was perhaps by Francesco Albani, or merely a Sibyl by Reni's pupil Guido Cagnacci, sometimes known as Canlassi.)

The painting's vogue seems due to Shelley's effusive admiration of it in the preface to his verse tragedy *The Cenci* (1819). Hawthorne, on his first visit, wrote, "It is the most profoundly wrought picture in the world," and on his third and last, "The picture is quite indescribable, inconceivable, and unaccountable in its effect. . . . The mouth is beyond measure touching; the lips apart, looking as innocent as a baby's after it has been crying. The picture never can be copied. . . . The copyists get all sorts of expression . . . , but nobody ever did catch, or ever will, the vanishing charm of that sorrow" (*FINB*, pp. 92–93, 520–21; M did not mark either passage in his copy of the 1872 abridged edition, Sealts 252). This observation had often been made, by, among others, Hawthorne's friend Hillard, who added that for years no copy had been allowed from the original, only from other copies (*Six Months*, I, 368). In *Clarel* (3.7.16–24) the character Vine (now commonly thought to be modeled on Hawthorne) in an unguarded moment,

> . . . wore that nameless look
> About the mouth—so hard to brook—
> Which in the Cenci portrait shows,
> Lost in each copy, oil or print;

Lost, or else slurred, as 'twere a hint
Which if received, few might sustain:
A trembling over of small throes
In weak swoll'n lips, which to restrain
Desire is none, nor any rein.

108.33–35 Galatea . . . Holbein] The *Galatea with Tritons* was attributed to Albani, especially admired for his mythological subjects. The collection's famous painting by Holbein the Younger is one of his portraits of Henry VIII, at portly full length and dressed for his wedding to Anne of Cleves. The *Disputation* (1506) is the one Dürer boasted to have completed in six days.

108.36 Corsini chapel] Remarked by M on his earlier visit to St. John Lateran ("Splendor of private tomb there," 108.8–9); see also the discussion at 108.7. Hawthorne: "We went into one of the chapels, and found it very rich in colored marbles, and going down a winding staircase, found ourselves among the tombs and sarcophagi of the Corsini family, and in presence of a marble Pieta . . . very beautifully sculptured" [by Antonio Montauti] (*FINB*, p. 74). Only on pious knees could one ascend the plank-protected Scala Santa (illustrated below, from Prime, *Travels*, II, 139). In a

THE HOLY STAIRS.

particularly scornful description, Jarves pointed out that "at the bottom there is always on duty a monk, who demands alms, and at the top a contribution plate beside a crucifix, into which the pilgrims deposit their offerings" (*Italian Sights*, p. 294).

109.1 Trevi Fountain] A two-mile walk to the site just west of the Quirinal, a fountain famous for its size, its great Neptune figure, and the tradition that those who throw coins into its basin will surely return.

109.4 St. Peters] The day before, it seems, M arrived after 11 A.M., the closing hour. Ascent to the main roof of St. Peter's, some 150 feet above the ground, was made easy by a spiraling incline, but thereafter the steep and narrow stairs winding between the dome's inner and outer shells took one some 300 feet higher, and finally a perpendicular ladder allowed one to enter the copper ball surmounting the dome. Hawthorne's full description reads in part: "The esplanade of the roof is of course very extensive; and along the front of it are ranged the statues which we see from below, and which, on nearer examination, prove to be roughly hewn giants. There is a small house on the roof, where, probably, the custodes of this part of the edifice reside; and there is a fountain gushing abundantly into a stone trough" (*FINB*, pp. 184–85). (Perhaps M's "M^{r} & Mrs C." stands for the Frederick Cunninghams; M had first encountered him in Jerusalem—see 79.32 and accompanying discussion.)

109.6 Corsini Palace] On the right bank, a mile south of St. Peter's. The gallery, open from ten to two except Sundays, had works of varying merit: "Holbein's Luther & wife" were separate portraits in the same room; Carlo Dolci's *Magdalen* was considered "inferior," and of Salvator Rosa's many paintings at least three could be called battle scenes.

109.8–9 St. Pietro in Montorio] St. Peter's in Montorio, legendary site of Saint Peter's crucifixion, another half-mile walk farther south of St. Peter's than the Corsini Palace and up the Janiculum slope. According to Giorgio Vasari, Sebastiano del Piombo painted the *Flagellation* from a drawing by Michelangelo, in a collaboration designed to counter Raphael's growing reputation. Guidebooks then and now commend the view of Rome from the piazza as the finest and most comprehensive; nearly as good is that from farther up the slope at the Acqua Paolo, a fountain not the largest in structure but the most copious in its supply of water.

109.11 Bridge . . . Valle] The bridge was the modern Ponte Sisto, on the ruins of the ancient Pons Janiculensis. The special feature of the church of Sant'Andrea della Valle (on the route to M's lodgings from the bridge) was the paintings on its interior walls, especially the *Glory of Paradise*, by Giovanni Lanfranco, inside the dome.

109.13 Villa . . . arches] On the south and east Palatine slopes successive emperors built huge arching substructures to support level terraces and buildings atop the hill. A convent building, later a Renaissance villa, had been established in the central ruins; in the early nineteenth century Sir Charles Mills "restored" the villa in "Tudor" style (for a reference to this villa by G. S. Hillard, see the discussion at 108.16).

109.15 Wolf] The famous Etruscan bronze with the suckling infant twins, Romulus and Remus, added in the Renaissance; not in the Capitoline Museum, but in the Palazzo dei Conservatori across the piazza.

109.15 Borghese Gallery] The gallery in the family's city palace near the left bank and west of the Spanish Steps (open to the public free daily except weekends): its eight to nine hundred paintings (according to Hawthorne) had been amassed by the family, a collection in Rome second only to the Vatican's. Hawthorne in a characteristically dyspeptic mood describes the faded magnificence of the interminable, bitterly cold twelve rooms, but names only one Italian painter (*FINB*, pp. 109–12). M's "C[aesar]. Borgia" was catalogued as by Raphael, but Hillard, with a rather naive notion of evil's appearance, disputed the attribution: "A remarkable portrait, representing a handsome man in the bloom of early manhood . . . ; probably the artist and subject are both misnomers. It is certainly not in Raphael's usual style, nor does the face respond to our conceptions of the monster Borgia. It is the face of a handsome, smiling, seductive, unscrupulous man . . . , reckless, pleasurable, and inventive . . . , but not absolutely a devil incarnate" (*Six Months*, I, 366–67). The well-known *Danaë* of Correggio, after traveling from owner to owner all over Europe, had been bought in England by Prince Borghese in 1824. (Like the others, it was transferred to the Villa Borghese at the end of the century.)

109.19 Pope] Pius IX had begun some well-meant governmental reforms in the Papal States, but had returned from his 1849 exile during the short-lived Roman Republic a bitter reactionary whose repressive measures earned him the punning name "Pio Nono"; among Protestants he was notorious for the dogma of the Immaculate Conception (1854—the doctrine of Papal Infallibility came later). Hawthorne saw him as "a stout old man, with a white scull-cap over his grey hair, a scarlet, gold-embroidered cape falling over his shoulders, and a white silk robe. . . . He walked slowly, with a sort of dignified waddle, stepping out broadly, and planting his feet . . . flat upon the pavement, as if he were not much accustomed to locomotion, and perhaps had known a twinge of the gout. His face seemed kindly, and venerable, but was not particularly impressive" (*FINB*, p. 150). French soldiers, sent by Louis Napoleon to return the Papal States to the pope in 1850, were still everywhere in Rome.

109.22 *Sciarra Gallery*] Baedeker later called the Palazzo Sciarra, near M's lodging, the handsomest one on the Via del Corso (but see M's similar praise for the Doria-Pamfili below, 111.5–6). Hawthorne too noticed its small "balcony" and made a similar one the setting for Hilda's climactic return in *The Marble Faun* (II, chap. 24, "A Frolic of the Carnival"; p. 272). Open only on Saturdays, "it has (Heaven be praised) but four rooms of pictures, among which, however, are several very celebrated ones" (*FINB*, p. 124). Because its collection was later sold off, identification of some pictures M saw is uncertain. The painting variously known as *The Cheating Gamblers, The Card Players*, etc., and commonly attributed to Caravaggio as one of his finest, disappeared after its sale (1899) but has since been identified (1955) with a damaged painting in the hands of a New York dealer (who sold it in 1987 to the Kimbell Museum, Fort Worth, Texas, for fifteen million dollars). The Claude painting M noticed was probably the one described as a landscape and sunset, though there were others in the same room. A number of "Holy Families" were there by such painters as Andrea del Sarto and Lucas Cranach, but Murray mentioned none by Dürer—only a *Death of the Virgin* (possibly one of the woodcuts for his series *Life of the Virgin*). The painting famous in the nineteenth century as Titian's *Bella Donna*—the only one Hawthorne thought worthy of his fame—appears now to be Palma Vecchio's *La Bella* in the collection of Baron Thyssen in Switzerland. M's parenthetical allusion to "Danae" may refer either to Titian's *Danaë* (if he saw it in Naples) or to the Correggio he saw the day before. Conceivably, he knew about the recent controversy over the *Danaë and the Shower of Gold* that James Jackson Jarves sold in Boston (1855) as by Titian, an attribution that America's only art magazine, the *Crayon*, scornfully refuted. The affair was to cost Jarves dearly in reputation; see Steegmuller, *The Two Lives of James Jackson Jarves*, pp. 139, 147–50, 152–53, 189–92; also the discussion at 106.30.

109.31 *Rospigliosi gallery*] The Casino in the gardens of the palace (built originally by a Borghese in 1603, over the Baths of Constantine on the Quirinal slope) was and is the great attraction, holding Guido Reni's masterpiece, the ceiling fresco of Aurora strewing flowers before the chariot of the Sun. Hawthorne found the picture "as fresh and brilliant as if he had painted it with the morning sunshine. . . . The alacrity and movement, briskness, and morning stir and glow, of the picture, are wonderful" (*FINB*, p. 94). At the end opposite the entrance a large mirror made viewing the ceiling easier. In an adjoining room hung *Death of Samson* by one of the Carracci, and nearby rested the twenty-four-pound shot from a French battery that had struck the Casino during the suppression of the 1848 uprising. The bas-reliefs M noted were probably the ancient sarcophagus reliefs built into the east wall.

A year later Hawthorne described the famous gardens: "We ascended a beautiful stone staircase, with a carved balustrade, bearing many marks of time and weather. Reaching the garden-level, we found it laid out in walks, bordered with box and ornamental shrubbery, amid which were lemon-trees, and one large old tree, an exotic from some distant clime. In the centre of the garden, surrounded by a stone balustrade like that of the staircase, was a fish-pond, into which several jets of water were continually spouting. . . . There was a pleasant sunshine in the garden, and a springlike, or rather a genial autumnal atmosphere, though elsewhere it was a day of poisonous Roman chill" (*FINB*, pp. 93–94).

110.2 *Quirinale Palace*] Now the official residence of the president of the Republic; it was begun in 1574 as a summer residence for the pontiff high above the malarial valley (see the discussion at 107.26). By permit one could enter any day from noon to four. Hawthorne's reaction was like M's: "A vast hall [150 feet long] . . . and an interminable suite of rooms, cased with marble . . . floored with marble, or mosaics, or inlaid wood, adorned with frescoes on the vaulted cielings. . . . I did not see a single nook or corner where anybody could have dreamed of being comfortable." The Gobelin tapestries, however, he found not "woefully faded . . . , but brilliant as pictures" (*FINB*, p. 162). Subjects were various: the marriage of Louis XIV, Jesus washing the feet of the Apostles, the miraculous draft of fishes, and so on. A large piece of the Sèvres on display was a vase given by Napoleon to Pius VII. Guido Reni's *Annunciation* was the private chapel's altarpiece; M's parenthetical reference to Raphael may be to his *Annunciation*, part of the predella with the early *Coronation of the Virgin* (if he had already noticed it in the Vatican, as he did on his next visit there, 110.31–32). The adjoining formal Italian gardens (open in the morning by permit) had concealed water jets that surprised the unwary, a water organ, and in a grotto a marble group representing Vulcan at his forge.

110.9 bases] Possibly "vases".

<u>The Gardens</u> — A Paradise without the fig —
freshness & aspiration of endless health — Shrewdness in
gardener — As stone is sculptured into forms of foliage,
so here foliage trained into forms of sculpture — walls,
niches, arches, casements, columns, bases, chambers

110.11 *Church out of Bath*] Santa Maria degli Angeli, previously visited by M (see 107.24–25 and the discussions at 107.23 and 112.6); the modified Greek-cross arrangement of nave and transept that Michelangelo created from the ancient hall was used to argue how much St. Peter's had lost by departure from that form.

110.12–13 church . . . Porta Pia] The church of Sant'Andrea al Quirinale, designed by Bernini, was described similarly by Hawthorne: "Methinks this little church (it is not more than fifty or sixty feet across) has a more perfect and gem-like beauty than any I have seen" (*FINB*, p. 95). He noted its elliptical shape, the cherubs and angels in white marble wreathed around its oval dome, its precious red-veined marble walls and white pilasters, and in one side chapel "the Great Carbuncle—at any rate, a bright, fiery gem, as big as a turkey's egg" (p. 96).

110.14 Lepri's] A bohemian restaurant frequented by impecunious artists, across the Via Condotti from the Caffè Greco; another American traveler described it as a "typical" Roman restaurant: "The Trattoria of Lepra . . . is among the best in Rome, and probably the worst in Europe! The entrance, through that squalid entry, the halt, and the maimed, and the blind beggars that thrust their greasy hats at you, as you pass that doorway, the dark and dirty stairway as you go up to the eating-room above, are enough to deprive the sturdiest of their appetites. . . . We . . . get our places, as we best may, in the crowd that frequents the establishment, dispose of our unintelligible meal, from off a soiled table-cloth, covering a table still more soiled . . . and hasten away" (Orville Horwitz, *Brushwood, Picked Up on the Continent* [Philadelphia: Lippincott, Grambo, 1854], pp. 126–28).

110.17 Jesuits Church] Il Gesù, principal church of the Jesuit order, is just north of the Capitoline. Santa Maria d'Aracoeli, built over the site of the ancient Temple of Juno on the north Capitoline crest, used for its interior twenty-two massive but unmatched columns from ancient buildings. M could have read about Gibbon in Murray's *Rome*: "It was in this ch., as he himself tells us, 'on the 15th day of October, 1764,' as he sat 'musing amidst the ruins of the Capitol, while the barefooted friars were singing vespers, that the idea of writing the Decline and Fall of the city first started to his mind' " (p. 121).

110.19 Baths of Titus] Little, if anything, remained of these baths built over the remains of Nero's Golden House, just north of the Coliseum, and superseded by the once-magnificent Baths of Trajan. What M saw were essentially the nearly buried remains of the Neronian structure, like the long corridor beautifully frescoed and known to Renaissance artists, but later partly filled with earth to deny shelter to brigands. Farther up the Esquiline slope is the church of San Pietro in Vincoli (St. Peter in Chains), where M probably saw Michelangelo's *Moses*, to which he refers in his lecture "Statues in Rome" (NN *Piazza Tales* volume, p. 406).

110.20–21 Mamertine . . . Tarpean] M either recorded this sequence of sites out of order or else unnecessarily backtracked a good deal. The Mamertine Prison on the lower north Capitoline slope, next to the Forum, was originally a cistern, then the infamous prison of Rome's enemies, including, by tradition, Saint Peter under Nero. The precipice on the southern Capitoline crest is called the Tarpeian Rock, the site of the central murder in Hawthorne's *The Marble Faun* (I, chap. 18); in the mid-nineteenth century, however, it was covered by mean buildings and its visible height was reduced to about seventy feet by accumulated debris at its base.

110.23 Stuarts' tomb] On the left, next after the baptismal font inside the entrance; the monument to James Stuart, the "Old Pretender," and his sons Charles and Henry was commissioned by George IV (as Prince Regent in 1819); that to James's wife Maria Sobieski is opposite. In his prose supplement to *Battle-Pieces* (1866), his Civil War poems, M used George's act as an example of generous forgiving (*Published Poems*, p. 182).

110.23 monuments] A conjectural reading. Around the sides of the transepts and nave of St. Peter's were the sepulchral monuments and tombs of many of the pontiffs.

[illegible]. — To St Peter — Tour of interior
— Stuarts' tomb. The Popes monuments. To

110.34 St. Onofrio] On the Janiculum slope, a short half-mile's walk south of St. Peter's. In the recently restored convent cell where Tasso died (1595) there was a bust of the poet in wax modeled after his death mask. His tomb in the first chapel on the left was just then being completed by a statue commissioned by Pius IX. (Miss Rousse could not have gone inside the monastery: women were excluded except on April 25, the anniversary of Tasso's death.)

111.5 Doria Pamfili palace] On the Corso, near M's lodging; it had a collection of nearly eight hundred pictures. Hawthorne, too, calls it "the most splendid in Rome," but writes only about the chill of fifteen unheated rooms and the dull appearance of its paintings (*FINB*, pp. 125–27). The double portrait then thought Raphael's original, of the jurist Bartolo and his pupil Baldo, is now considered a copy, probably Venetian, of the Venetian writers Andrea Navagero and Agostino Beazzano. The *Magdalen* is a copy of the Titian in the Pitti Palace, Florence; the *Machiavelli*, said by Murray to be by Andrea del Sarto, has now been attributed to Bronzino or the Florentine school. Of several mythological and scriptural landscapes by Claude, M does not mention the best known, *The Mill* and the *Temple of Apollo*. Brueghel the Elder's *Elements* were four paintings allegorically representing earth, air, fire, and water. The *Lucrezia Borgia* then attributed to Veronese has disappeared as such from later listings. (M did not note Velázquez's remarkable portrait of the Pamfili pope, Innocent X.)

111.16 Gibson] John Gibson (1790–1866), though a student of the neoclassic sculptors Canova and Thorwaldsen, imitated ancient Greek practice in coloring his marble. Gibson's address, near the Piazza del Popolo, headed the list of studios that Murray highly recommended visiting. Models of all his finished works were there, but most of the works themselves were in his native England. Hawthorne described Gibson in 1858 as unusually youthful looking, quiet, self-contained, and not especially vivid in dinner-table conversation. He found the famous *Tinted Venus* embarrassing in its relatively lifelike appearance; Gibson had applied a pale pink wash to the marble, colored the hair blond, gilded the apple in her hand, and ornamented both the head-fillet and robe hem in blue and gold (*FINB*, pp. 131–32, 293). (M's allusion to the seven-branched candlestick may refer to the one in the bas-relief of the sack of Jerusalem on the Arch of Titus; see also his reference to it among the miscellaneous entries in this notebook, 158.18.)

111.19 Bartholomew's] Edward Bartholomew (1822–58) began as a painter, discovered his color blindness, and turned to sculpture. He came to Rome in 1850 and gradually won recognition for scriptural works such as *Eve Repentant*, but like most sculptors of the period he preferred the "classical." He was shy by nature and now both crippled and in chronic ill health from smallpox. A visit to his studio provoked one of Hawthorne's notebook denunciations of the nude: "We saw several pretty statues and busts, and among them an Eve, after the fall, with her wreath of fig-leaves lying across her poor nudity; pretty in some points, but with an awful volume of thighs and calves. I do not altogether see the necessity of ever sculpturing another nakedness. Man is no longer a naked animal; his clothes are as natural to him as his skin" (*FINB*, p. 177). M's parenthetic "(Edition)" coupled with "Bust of young Augustus" suggests that Bartholomew had been commissioned to make copies, a frequent practice.

111.20 Page's] William Page (1811–85), whom M had sought on February 27 (106.30), was then the leading American portraitist, though his reputation faded later. In Boston he had painted John Quincy Adams,

Charles Sumner, James Russell Lowell, Wendell Phillips, and other worthies; in New York, Charles F. Briggs, William Cullen Bryant, and Evert Duyckinck's young son. His many friends, including Lowell and the Brownings, admired not only his painting but his nobility of mind and bearing. He was strikingly handsome and loved to recite poetry in his melodious voice. He shared with Elizabeth Barrett Browning a deep interest in Swedenborgian ideas and spiritualism. For the last eight of his eleven years in Italy (1849–60) he lived in Rome and pursued his preoccupation with Titian-like coloring. At the period of M's visit he was working on successive versions of a nude Venus, the first of which had just been exhibited in a scandalized Boston. Recently deserted by his second wife, financially hard pressed to keep a home with the three daughters by his first one, he was consternating his friends by his close attachment to the intelligent young widow (the bookseller Henry Stevens's sister) who became his third in 1857. Possibly M had met Page earlier in his Albany or Boston period or had entrée to him now via a mutual friend such as Charles F. Briggs (editor of *Putnam's Monthly Magazine*), Evert Duyckinck, or Henry Stevens (see the discussion at 27.3).

Page's studio was first at 39 Via del Babuino, opening out of the Piazza di Spagna, and later on the Via Gregoriana, opening off the top of the Spanish Steps. His biographer (Joshua C. Taylor, *William Page, The American Titian* [Chicago: University of Chicago Press, 1957]) informed Howard C. Horsford that he found no mention of M in the Page papers and no explanation for M's repeated enigmatic reference to "thin socks" (see the following discussion).

111.20 Thin socks] In his edition of this journal (New York: The Colophon, 1935) Raymond Weaver annotated this phrase, "I cannot convince myself the reading is not correct, but I have no idea of Melville's intention" (p. 141); but Forsythe's review of Weaver's edition (cited in the discussion at 84.38) found "no difficulty": M had "merely noted—gleefully, I fancy—that the season had advanced sufficiently for him to brave cold stone floors in cotton socks, discarding those heavy woolen footcoverings, perhaps knit by a female relative, in which he had tramped the streets of Jerusalem and in which he had stood before the Farnese Hercules at Naples. But be that as it may, I hardly think the words deserve a note." However, M calls his footcoverings "stockings" not "socks" (60.31, 140.11), and most likely, since he recorded the phrase in his summary of Page's discourses both times he saw Page (March 10 and 13—see 112.2) but nowhere else, the "thin socks" were not items of his own or of Page's dress but occurred in the discourses. As reported by Joshua C. Taylor (in his biography of Page cited in the preceding discussion), Page for many years developed, practiced, and compulsively expounded "far-reaching theories of painting," particularly of rendering

—To the studios. The English sculptor, Gibson. His colored Venus. Talk with him. The 7 branched candlestick &c. Art perfect among Greeks. Limits to human power,—perfection.—To Bartholomew's. His Eve. Bust of young Angelo—(Edition). To Page's. Thin socks. Titian—kneading of flesh—middle tint. Long lecture.—Home, dinner, bed.

flesh as he believed Titian had done. The method included beginning with a "middle tint," adding a full-bodied red and other strong colors, and then applying light layers of glazing through which these colors would show. Perhaps Page in his two discourses to M used the analogy of "thin socks" both times for these see-through layers (cf. M's phrase "middle tint" at 113.15). Taylor remarks that, with his Swedenborgianism, Page "could not talk of painting without discussing religion, or discuss religion without becoming involved in the technique of painting" (see pp. 175–77).

111.22 Appian Way] The ancient road entered the city through the Porta San Sebastiano, which M had already seen (108.12–13). Much of the modern road he had taken from Naples closely paralleled the ancient one. (By "Milton's Way" M presumably contrasts the narrow Appian and the broad and easy causeway constructed by Sin and Death after Satan's success, in *Paradise Lost*, X, 282ff.) Sections of the original roadway had recently (1850–53) been excavated as far as the eleventh milestone. Ruins of tombs on both sides became numerous after two miles, most of them overgrown, but at the sixth milestone the largest, the Casale Rotondo (352 ft. in diameter), provided room for a small farmstead. (As in Constantinople—see 62.1 and the discussion at 61.38—M here parodies Saint Paul, I Corinthians 15:42.) Somewhat to the left of the road, not far out of the city, a vaulted chamber with a copious water flow was once misidentified as the Grotto of Egeria, source of the Vestal Virgins' purificatory water. A small oak grove on a nearby hill was called the Sacred Grove.

111.24 Same] A conjectural reading.

Tomb with olive trees on it. Tomb in cellar, ruined in ruins. Same day, Grotto of Egeria.

111.26 St. Pauls] On the Ostia road, the ancient basilica of San Paolo Fuori le Mura, or St. Paul's Outside the Walls, extensively burned in 1823, had been almost rebuilt by Pius IX when M saw it. Because it was a mile out on the Campagna, its Benedictine monks were forced to vacate every summer by the increasingly prevalent malaria. Many catacombs, ancient tufa quarries, lie hereabouts south of the city walls; that of Saint Calixtus, near the Appian Way, had just been discovered (1854), with tombs of many early popes or bishops.

111.30 Coliseum] The idea of repeopling its ruins provides a central image in M's lecture "Statues in Rome" (see also 158.14–16, and the NN *Piazza Tales* volume, p. 404). M's brief phrase "The arch" perhaps refers to the nearby Arch of Constantine.

111.35 "Glitter . . . grows] M transposes and slightly misquotes phrases from Carlyle's translation (revised edition, 1839) of Goethe's poem "Kennst du das Land" in Book 3, Chapter 1 of *Wilhelm Meister's Apprenticeship:* "Know'st thou the land where lemon-trees do bloom, / . . . / The myrtle thick, and high the laurel grows? / . . . / Know'st thou the house, its porch with pillars tall? / The rooms do glitter, glitters bright the hall." As early as 1850 M had borrowed a translation of the novel from Evert Duyckinck (Sealts 230, Bercaw 304), but the edition is not known.

112.3 Trinita di Monte] Trinità dei Monti, at the top of the Spanish Steps. Hawthorne thought this church pleasant but not "very splendid," though unusually clean and neat because kept by a cloister of nuns (*FINB*, p. 81).

112.4 Caryatide] Centered in the entrance of the Casino of the Villa Albani. The statue was found in 1766 near the Appian Way; on its back were the names of the Athenian sculptors Kriton and Nikolaos. Later listings call it a Bacchante with a head from a caryatide. The grounds and buildings of the villa were commissioned (1758) of Carlo Marchionne by Cardinal Albani (for M's first visit, see 107.17 and accompanying discussion). "Father Murphy" and "Mrs. S", apparently other visitors to the villa, are unidentified.

112.6 B. of Diocletian church] I.e., Santa Maria degli Angeli. See the discussions at 107.23 and 110.11.

112.6 Simon Magus] The painting by Pompeo Batoni of the Samaritan sorcerer who tried to buy miraculous power from the Apostles (Acts 8:9–24); in *Clarel*, 2.37.76–81, a point on the Dead Sea is designated as the one where he flung away his book of magic. The meridian line of Rome was traced on the pavement of Santa Maria degli Angeli in 1701. (Perhaps M's cryptic word "transverse" refers to the double irony of a pagan bath converted to a great Christian church, and the great Christian church of St. Sophia to a mosque. Or perhaps he merely has in mind the eighteenth-century alteration of Michelangelo's design, which converted his long nave into a transept and shifted the portal from the end to the side.)

112.14 Frascati] Near the ancient Tusculum, Cicero's favorite residence in the Alban Hills twelve miles south of Rome. Its healthful air made it a favorite summer resort, and the railway had been opened in 1856, the first in the Papal States. The Villa Aldobrandini on the southern outskirts with its great park was one of the most magnificent in the vicinity. The maps in the Casino showed the manorial lands of the Borghese who now owned the estate.

112.23 Breakfasted] The Caffè Nuovo, on the Corso, some blocks from M's lodging, was an extensive, well-known establishment with a garden, billiard tables, and other amusements.

112.24 Torlonia Villa] Outside the walls to the northeast, open on Wednesdays, eleven to four. Torlonia was a newly rich banker whose "tasteless extravagance" was often deplored.

112.27 Crawfords studio] Thomas Crawford (1813–57) had come to Italy in 1835 with prodigious energy and rather grandiose ideas about monumental sculpture. He quickly established a reputation for his anecdotal and allegorical figures; his commissions included the statue of Washington in Richmond, and in Washington the *Armed Liberty* to top the Capitol's dome and the *America* pedimental group for its Senate wing, depicting the emergence of civilized white dominion over the Indians. At the time of M's visit he was absent and fatally ill, and he died in London later that year. Meanwhile his extensive studios in grounds among ruins of the Baths of Diocletian were kept open, with models of his completed and uncompleted works. (Just a year later Hawthorne unsympathetically viewed the "several great rooms," plaster casts, and marbles, *FINB*, pp. 129–31.)

112.30 Villa Doria Pamfili] The most extensive villa (four miles in circuit) outside the city walls, on the west side. Its splendid gardens, avenues, and parterres with towering stone pines were open at all times. Its terrace afforded an unobstructed view of St. Peter's a mile to the north. (Hawthorne's description of early spring here a year later is extensive, *FINB*, pp. 144–46.)

112.33–113.1 flourishes . . . chromoplates] Both words conjectural. The script of the first word seems clear enough, but the word given here for the second is a conjectural coinage; the technical process of chromolithogra-

The cedars & pines. Avenue of olives. View of St. Peters. The terrace gardens — the form of the parterres — flourishes of [illegible].

phy was still very new in the 1850's and the vocabulary not yet settled. It is possible M had seen such a word as the one postulated here though it never found permanent acceptance, or perhaps he coined it to describe the particular vividness and brillance of this "picturesque" scene.

113.4–5 Fountain . . . candlestick] La Fontana di Piazza Giudea, two concentric basins, one above the other on a pillar with distinctive Hebrew candelabra carved on its overflow conduits.

113.10 Tivoli] At the edge of the Sabine Hills some twenty miles east of Rome, four hours by carriage. Lake Tartarus, along the way, was rapidly disappearing because its calcium salts were constantly depositing on its margin as travertine rock. When Hadrian built the greatest villa of his empire on the slopes below the village early in the second century, its nearly ten-mile circuit included reproductions of the most interesting and beautiful things seen in his travels. Its enormous ruins had been long pillaged, countless art treasures had disappeared into medieval lime kilns, but many others were now in the great Roman collections. Perhaps the ruins here, if not those at Posilipo near Naples, suggested M's poem "The Ravaged Villa," in *Timoleon* (*Published Poems*, p. 266). He cites Plutarch's life of Hadrian in *White-Jacket* (chap. 85, p. 356).

The village, even more ancient than Rome, retained its attraction as a high, salubrious resort with a view across the Campagna to the city. The Anio (now Aniene) River, falling here some 350 feet, is mostly conducted through two tunnel galleries (1834) in the mountain's shoulder to prevent seasonal flooding of the village. A footpath gallery was cut into the gorge's wall. On the precipice above the gorge, the little circular so-called Temple of the Sibyl (or Vesta) with its ten remaining columns, has been the subject of innumerable paintings (though the painter Claude—mentioned later in this entry—does not seem especially connected with Tivoli, much as such scenery attracted him). The nearby extensive ruins, miscalled the Villa of Maecenas, were converted to an iron manufactury by Lucien Bonaparte. (For M's marginal note here on the Villa d'Este see the discussion at 155.1–6.)

113.17 *vises*] Murray's 1856 *Rome* advised, "Before leaving Rome all passports must be signed by the police, by the minister of the country to which the traveller is proceeding . . . , and [for U.S. citizens] by the American Minister, who makes no charge" (p. viii; Murray's 1858 *Rome*, however, does list a charge for the American minister [p. x], which must have already gone into effect in 1857 since M's visa [in the Berkshire Athenaeum], made out for Florence and Venice, bears the notation, "Paid $1"). Murray's *Central Italy* (I, 2) particularly warned, regarding visas, "Those of Austria and Tuscany should on no account be omitted."

113.17 Sam] The family had hoped M and his wife's younger half-brother, Samuel Shaw, could join up sooner to travel together. Sam's letter to his father dated March 24 describes the meeting: "I have seen Herman. When I arrived I learned he was at the Hotel de Minerve, and the first thing I did was to call there, but he was out. Returning to my own hotel . . . I found that he had been there and left a note for me stating that all his arrangements were made to leave for Florence in the afternoon and that I must see him between 3 and 4 or not at all. Accordingly I went and saw him off. He has been almost entirely alone but has found traveling companions. . . . Although his general health is much improved, yet at Rome, the climate and the dampness have affected him somewhat. He is considerably sunburnt and is stout as usual" (Metcalf, *Herman Melville*, p. 163).

113.19 started in veturino] M's efforts to engage a seat in the scheduled public conveyance failing (112.11–12), he and the Rousses evidently hired a private carriage (*vettura*—the *vetturino* is its driver); these could be had from stables near the Ponte San Angelo, at about seven shillings for the fifty-five-mile trip, without change of horses. There was a two-hour rest-halt at the coastal village of Palo, with a wretched inn and exorbitant prices. This mode took about half again as long as the eight or nine hours by the more comfortable government post. Cività Vecchia was the principal papal port for Mediterranean passenger steamers. A year later Hawthorne with his family and a mountain of luggage found the town and the same trip (in reverse) not only dreary but potentially dangerous from uncontrolled banditti (*FINB*, pp. 51–52). The illustration here is from *Rollo's Tour in Europe* by Jacob Abbott (Boston: Brown, Taggard, & Chase, 1862), p. 44.

113.25 French steamer] The *Aventine*, a small but new French-line ship; it regularly arrived Sunday morning from Naples and the east, and left in the afternoon for Leghorn. M seems to have traveled third or fourth class; if so he paid ten to sixteen francs and bought any meals separately.

113.33 Duomo &c] The four buildings—Cathedral (Duomo), Baptistery, Campanile, and Campo Santo—are grouped in a large open space in the northwest quarter of the town, then largely unpopulated. The masterpiece in the circular Baptistery is the thirteenth-century hexagonal pulpit by Niccolò Pisano, supported by seven pillars, the central one pedestaled on a crouching human figure, the others on animals. (The cupola of the Baptistery had just been restored, in 1855.) The famous Leaning Tower (Campanile) was then some fourteen feet out of plumb (see M's poem "Pisa's Leaning Tower" in *Timoleon*; *Published Poems*, p. 294). The Campo Santo (from which other burial places in Italy took their name) is a rectangular cloister (badly damaged in World War II), whose center is, according to legend, fifty-three shiploads of earth brought from Palestine when Saladin ejected the Crusaders; reputedly the soil reduced bodies to dust in twenty-four hours. The medieval frescoes in the surrounding cloister galleries had been damaged by damp, but even in the nineteenth century were famous. The ones M singles out seem to be those in the south gallery by the "Master of the Triumph of Death," including *Hell* and *Triumph of Death*. In the latter, "at the bottom, St. Macarius is demonstrating the fragility of life to a group of princes by taking the example of the three kings whose bodies are shown in various stages of decomposition" (Mario Bucci, in *Pisa Monumental Cemetery* [Pisa: Opera della Primaziale Pisana, 1960]). Vasari's original attribution to Andrea Orcagna has been replaced by a host of other candidates. In the Cathedral, M saw Andrea del Sarto's *St. Agnes*, one of his most admired works. The bronze doors of the Cathedral, which replaced the originals destroyed by fire in the sixteenth century, were designed by Giovanni di Bologna, and depicted in a number of panels the history of the Virgin and scenes from the life of Christ.

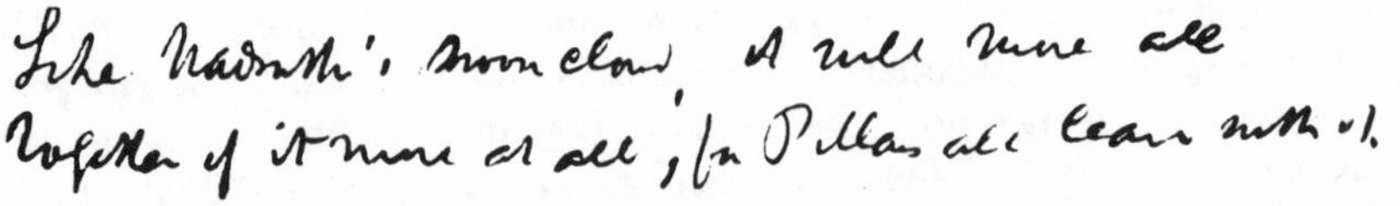

114.2–3 Wordsworth's moore cloud] Possibly "moon" (H), though no moon is alluded to in "Resolution and Independence," lines 74–77:

> Upon the margin of that moorish flood
> Motionless as a cloud the old Man stood,
> That heareth not the loud winds when they call;
> And moveth all together, if it move at all.

Melville had parodied lines from this poem in his story "Cock-A-Doodle-Doo!" (see the NN *Piazza Tales* volume, p. 272; Bercaw 766).

114.7 Impudent] Possibly "Impatient".

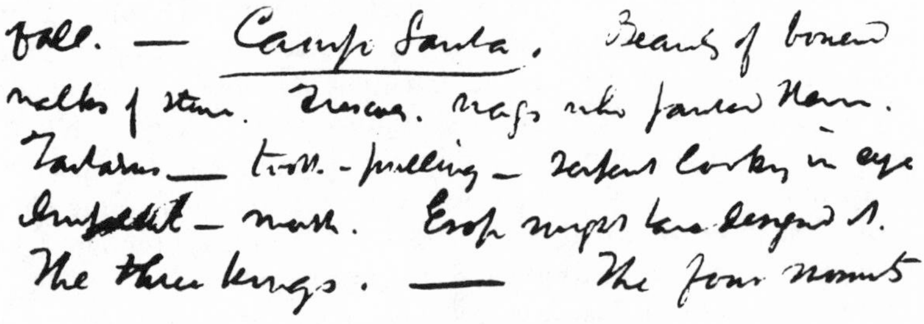

114.12 Sea-chapel] Santa Maria della Spina, built in 1230 on the south bank of the Arno during Pisa's great prosperity for the convenience of its mariners, was named after its once most famous relic, a fragment of the Crown of Thorns. A little upstream on the same side, the Loggia dei Banchi was notable for its long colonnade of open arches.

114.14–15 Hotel du Nord] In the center of Florence (Via Strozzi, just off the present Piazza della Repubblica), it was recommended as comfortable, moderately priced, and well conducted by an English-speaking proprietor; daily costs would have averaged five or six shillings. Breakfast could be had for eleven cents in American coinage, a good dinner for thirty-three or, at a hotel, fifty-five—according to Jarves (*Italian Sights*, p. 41). The Doney was (and still is) nearby on the Via Tornabuoni; its smoking room, like the Greco in Rome, was a gathering place for English and American artists; its main café was fashionable for pastries and ices.

114.16 Pitti Palace] Both the Pitti and the Uffizi were open free daily, except Sundays and holidays, until three in the afternoon. The Pitti was then still the Grand Ducal residence, magnificently furnished and well warmed; the Uffizi, on the north bank of the Arno and connected to the Pitti by an arcade over the Ponte Vecchio, vied with it in comfort and provision for the best display of their world-famous collections. M saw Cellini's models for his *Perseus* in the Uffizi's Cabinet of Modern Bronzes, one in bronze, one in wax (now in the National Museum in the Bargello). The completed sculpture now stands outside in the Loggia dei Lanzi. It is mentioned in M's lecture "Statues in Rome" along with Michelangelo's *Moses* as examples of large sculptures (NN *Piazza Tales* volume, p. 406), but curiously, not Michelangelo's gigantic *David*, of which the original (now in the Accademia delle Belle Arti) then still stood nearby outside the Palazzo Vecchio, as a copy now does.

114.22 Duomo] Though the original, unfinished facade of the cathedral of Santa Maria del Fiore had long since been removed but not yet replaced, Hawthorne, too, was overwhelmed by the beauty of Giotto's campanile and by the cathedral, its stained-glass windows, and its spaciousness, the whole "greatly more satisfactory than St. Peter's" (*FINB*, p. 286; cf. also 288--89).

114.23 fine] Possibly "five".

Magnificent. Could not enter. Bought fine mosaics for one Napoleon. — Breakfasted today at Caffe Doney.

114.25 Festa] Festival of the Annunciation of the Virgin Mary. In his strolling about, however, M could not have avoided what Jarves described as "streets—even those pretending to rank among the best . . . almost impassable on account of their filthy condition. This arises from the neglect of providing in their houses what in England and America are considered indispensable adjuncts of even the meanest of habitations" (*Italian Sights*, pp. 38–39).

114.26 Boboli] The Grand Ducal gardens stretching up the southern hillside behind and beyond the Pitti Palace. Hawthorne was not as enthusiastic about the view: "We had a good view of Florence, with the bare, brown ridges on the northern side . . . and glimpses of the river itself . . . between two rows of palaces. . . . The city does not present a particularly splendid aspect; though its great Duomo was seen in the middle distance . . . but the general picture was of a contiguity of red earthen roofs, filling a not very broad or extensive valley, among dry and ridgy hills" (*FINB*, p. 331). The illustration below of Florence from this viewpoint is from the frontispiece to Volume XII of the *Works of Lord Byron*.

114.27 Santa Croce] Some distance east of the Uffizi, erected for the Franciscans and largest of mendicant-order churches. "This vast church, naked, gloomy, severe, lighted by superb Gothic windows of stained glass, filled with illustrious tombs, has been justly entitled the Pantheon of Florence" ([Antoine Claude Pasquin] Valery, *Historical, Literary, and Artistical Travels in Italy,* trans. from second ed. by C. E. Clifton [Paris: Baudry, 1852], p. 353; M's copy of this edition, apparently bought in Florence, and annotated, is preserved in the Gansevoort-Lansing Collection of the New York Public Library [Sealts 533]). M does not mention Galileo's tomb in the left aisle, but those he notes are, in order from the entrance to the right aisle: first, the tomb of Michelangelo; second, an elaborate monument to Dante (his tomb is in Ravenna) erected as recently as 1829; then the "vast mausoleum" (Valery, p. 354) of the poet Vittorio Alfieri, commissioned of Antonio Canova by the countess of Albany (wife of Charles Stuart the Young Pretender and mistress of the poet); and last the tomb of Machiavelli, between the third and fourth side altars; and at the pillar opposite, one of the marble pulpits. (M perhaps mistook the adjoining cloisters of a convent for a Campo Santo like that at Pisa.) See an allusion in *Clarel,* 1.12.120–25.

114.30 Annunziata] The church of La Santissima Annunziata, a walk of some distance to the north and east of the Duomo; in the anterior cloister of the adjoining old Servite monastery, Andrea del Sarto painted his noteworthy frescoes, later protected from weather by glass panels. The one singled out by M was the second of five from the life of Saint Philip Benizzi. Hawthorne's friend Hillard had noticed this one: "One of them is a curious instance of the power of religious bigotry to destroy the simplest elements of Christian morality. The saint is walking in the country. Some gay young men, playing at cards under a tree, laugh at his uncouth appearance; whereupon, he prays to Heaven, and the young men are struck with lightning" (*Six Months*, I, 142).

114.32 Bellesgardo] The Porta Romana in the old city walls is at the head of the street leading from the Arno past the Pitti Palace to the main road to Rome. Outside, to the west and south the hill of Bellosguardo overlooking the city and lower Arno Valley was the site of numerous villas, among them the one Hawthorne rented in the later part of the summer of 1858. Murray's *Northern Italy*, II, 533, strongly recommended the view from here.

115.4 Venus] Into the Tribune of the Uffizi were then crowded its most admired treasures. The *Venus de' Medici*, found in Rome in the sixteenth century, was badly shattered but rather easily reassembled. Hawthorne at first was unusually moved:

> I could not quite believe that I was not to find the Venus de Medici; and still, as I passed from one room to another, my breath rose and fell a little, with the half-hope, half-fear. . . . At last . . . I caught a glimpse of her, through the door of the next room. It is the best room of the whole series, octagonal in shape, and hung with red damask. . . . The Venus stands somewhat aside from the centre of the room, and is surrounded by an iron-railing. . . . She is very beautiful; very satisfactory; and has a fresh and new charm. . . . The hue of the marble is just so much mellowed by time as to do for her all that Gibson tries . . . to do for his statues by color. (*FINB*, pp. 297–98)

Later, influenced by Hiram Powers's disparagements (see the discussion at 116.1), Hawthorne's enthusiasm waned. M in his lecture "Statues in Rome" softened his dispraise here of this sculpture in comparing it with the Vatican Apollo yet still found it not supernally ideal, but merely beautiful woman idealized (NN *Piazza Tales* volume, p. 403). The bronze *Wrestlers*, like the Venus, were found much broken, but had not been well restored; the heads in particular are not considered authentic. (Howard, in *Herman Melville: A Biography*, p. 251, mistakes these wrestlers for a different Uffizi sculpture in which one wrestler clutches the genitals of the other, who is about to throw him.) Of the two paintings of a reclining Venus by Titian (now in another room), the more famous is the one known as *The Venus of Urbino;* the other, with a Cupid, is generally considered a minor work finished by assistants.

Murray's *Northern Italy* remarks that the first is "Venus, so called, but supposed by some to be the portrait of a mistress of one of the Dukes of Urbino. In her rt. hand are flowers, at her feet a little dog," and that the second is "considered as inferior to the first" (p. 581). But since each loosely holds a bouquet (and holds a little dog), it is not altogether clear which one Valery means to commend—though probably the first—when he says both "are admirable; especially the one holding flowers, which is truly sublime in colouring: the voluptuous languor of her features wonderfully expresses the vague passions of a young woman" (p. 326). That he probably means the first is shown by his adding that the figure is "a portrait . . . that of the duke d'Urbino's mistress." Valery is possibly one source for the passage in *Clarel* (4.26.228–35) where the first is described by a Jewish character:

> Earth's best,
> Earth's loveliest portrait, daintiest,
> Reveals Judæan grace and form:
> Urbino's ducal mistress fair—
> Ay, Titian's Venus, golden-warm.
> Her lineage languishes in air
> Mysterious as the unfathomed sea:
> That grave, deep Hebrew Coquetry!

Of one or the other Titian Venus, Hawthorne merely remarks, "naked and lustful" (p. 299). In another group of rooms was an unusual collection (now rearranged) of (mostly) self-portraits, many by the greatest painters.

115.6 Accademia] Northeast of the Duomo, on the Via Ricasoli off the Piazza San Marco, the Accademia delle Belle Arti was founded in 1784 to bring together examples for students of Tuscan art from Cimabue and Giotto to Fra Bartolommeo. Many of the best paintings M saw there have since been transferred to the Uffizi. Among the Giottos were a series from the life of Saint Francis, a Madonna, and a series from the life of Christ. Murray quotes a certain "T. P." in praise of Fra Angelico, and singles out a Last Judgment in which "the figure of our Saviour is surrounded by glory and angels, and accompanied by the Virgin and Saints, and Apostles arranged precisely in the manner, and the same materials are employed, as by Raffaelle in the Dispute of the Sacrament . . . I should think there could be no doubt that Raffaelle . . . drew largely upon his works" (*Northern Italy*, II, 524–25; M would have seen the Raphael fresco in the Vatican). M alludes to Fra Angelico in *Clarel*, 1.18.29, in *Billy Budd, Sailor*, chap. 24, and in "At the Hostelry" (unpublished by M). A statue here that M does not name in his journal was Michelangelo's unfinished *St. Matthew*.

115.23 flower-girls] These Florentine vendors offered, even forced, bouquets on the traveler, hoping to secure his patronage throughout his stay and a present at his departure. A four-stanza song in *Clarel* was "something good" that M wrote, about such a "flower-girl of Florence," who, as such a blithe young man sings, "button-holes me with a rose" for which "I grudge to pay, but pay I must, / Then dine on half a dinner!" (2.5.54–69). Hillard (*Six Months*, I, 109–10) found these girls hard and intrusive, but the Reverend Daniel C. Eddy did not: "The flower girls meet you in every street; especially on the morning of the Sabbath are they out by hundreds, with their white arms and necks shaded by the wide hat. . . . These flower girls are modest and pretty. They do not often try to sell you flowers, but force them into your hand, and turn away as if they were indifferent about the pay" (*Europa* [Boston: Higgins & Bradley, 1852], pp. 430–31).

115.23 Museum of Natural History] Near the Pitti Palace, housing the various collections of the Medici; the mineralogical and botanical series (the latter, wax reproductions by Giovanni Battista Amici) were notable. Hawthorne was more philosophical than Valery regarding the reproductions of interior human anatomy, but found the representations of plague-stricken corpses morbid: "Under glass cases, there were some singular and horribly truthful representations, in small wax figures, of a time of pestilence; the hasty burial, or tossing into one common sepulchre, of discolored corpses; a very ugly piece of work indeed" (*FINB*, p. 309). The Sicilian, Zummo (Clemente Susini, 1697–1780), had created the display for Cosimo III.

115.24 dragons] A conjectural reading. Possibly "flagons" (H).

Not "Newly" & the flower-girls. — To the
Museum of Natural History. Immense collection.
Lapis Lazuli — chrystal vessels, dragons, perfumers
&c &c. Wax plants seed & germinations.

115.24 perfumers] A conjectural reading (at the end of line 3 above).

116.1 The 3 Fates] Current studies of Michelangelo do not even mention the painting, but a catalogue of the gallery (Giovanni Niccolai, *Pitti Palace* [Florence: Ramella, 1957], p. 28) attributes it firmly to Francesco Salviati, a painter profoundly influenced by Michelangelo. Its strong impression on M is indicated by his twice recurring to it in his jottings at the journal notebook's end, both times in a simile for the cypresses at the Villa d'Este, Tivoli; see 155.2–3 and 158.6–8. Hawthorne also wrote twice about the picture: "Three very grim and pitiless old women, who respectively spin, hold, and cut, the thread of human destiny, all in a mood of sombre gloom, but with no more sympathy than if they had nothing to do with us. . . . [A] terrible, stern, passionless severity, neither loving us nor hating us, . . . characterizes these ugly old women. If they were angry, or had the least spite against humankind, it would render them the more tolerable." And again, "One of them—she who holds the distaff—has her mouth open. . . . The second, who holds the thread, has a pensive air, but is still, I think, pitiless at heart. The third sister looks closely and coldly into the eyes of the last-mentioned, meanwhile cutting the thread with a pair of shears" (*FINB*, pp. 306, 334). In the same hall then were Salvator Rosa's often-mentioned *Battle Piece* and *Conspiracy of Catiline*, and two rooms beyond, his self-portrait (attribution now disputed). Hillard described the ornate tables: "There are also some twenty or thirty tables of Florentine mosaic, in themselves works of art, representing fruits, flowers, animals, landscapes; and I remember one imitating a breakfast service in the natural disorder of a half-finished meal" (*Six Months*, I, 156–57).

116.5 Powers' studio] Hiram Powers (1805–73), probably the most famous of American sculptors in his time; his demurely naked *Greek Slave* (1843), about which Elizabeth Barrett Browning wrote a sonnet, was the sensation of the Crystal Palace exhibition, and often copied (it is pictured in Thorp, *Literary Sculptors*, plate 10). After a jack-of-all-trades youth, including work in a clock factory, an organ factory, and a wax museum, he came to Florence in 1837, where he spent the rest of his life in a wide and admiring circle of noteworthy friends. Travelers made a point of talking with him, fascinated by his blunt common sense and intelligent grasp of a wide range of topics. Hawthorne sought him out repeatedly, and summarized his conversations at length (cf. an account of an evening in late June of 1858: "I have hardly ever before felt an impulse to write down a man's conversation, as I do that of Mr. Powers. The chief reason is, probably, that it is so possible to do it, his ideas being square, solid, and tangible, and therefore readily grasped and retained," *FINB*, p. 337; also p. 314). Still earlier, Hawthorne wrote of seeing in Powers's studio "a marble copy of the fisher-boy, holding a shell to his ear, and . . . casts of most of the ideal statues and portrait-busts which he has executed" (p. 279); at a different time, Powers showed him another model, "of Melancholy, or rather of Contemplation, from Milton's Penseroso; a female figure, with uplifted face and 'rapt look commercing with the skies'" (p. 313); and just before leaving Florence, he saw the *America* (1854): "It is a female figure, youthful, vigorous, beautiful, planting its foot lightly on a broken chain, and pointing upward. . . . The form, nude to the middle, has all the charms of womanhood" (p. 436). When he first saw Powers in June, 1858, he described him as "a plain, homely personage, characterized by strong simplicity and warm kindliness with an impending brow, and large, light eyes, which kindle as he speaks. He is gray and slightly bald, but does not seem elderly" (p. 279). Powers's extensive studio (Via la Fornace) a little north of the Pitti was just across the street from the Hawthornes' first residence in Florence.

116.6 Apron] Possibly "Open" (H). An apron was evidently Hiram Powers's usual occupational garb, as recorded both in a photograph taken by Longworth about 1861 (see Richard P. Wunder, *Hiram Powers: Vermont Sculptor* [Taftsville, Vt.: Countryman Press, 1974]) and in an engraving by Perine and Giles (reproduced below, from Hayward and Blanche Cirker, eds., *Dictionary of American Portraits* [New York: Dover, 1967]).

Hiram Powers

116.7 Cascine] The elegant, parklike Grand Ducal dairies along the northwest bank of the river, the fashionable afternoon place to walk or ride, to see and be seen. Hillard, in noting the predominance of foreigners, especially the English in carriages, added, "Smiles and greetings are interchanged, and even the solitary stranger cannot fail to catch something of that genial sunshine, which is diffused over a company of well-dressed and well-mannered persons" (*Six Months*, I, 109). The Luna, where M dined, was a not very good restaurant on the Grand Ducal square, the Piazza della Signoria.

116.12 dome] Brunelleschi's great dome is older and higher than that of St. Peter's but sits on a lower base. From a door in the left aisle M ascended 463 steps within its double shell to its upper gallery; by a ladder of 57 more steps he could have reached the cross on the summit. Vasari designed the frescoes, which included portrayals of Paradise, prophets, angels, saints, and the punishment of the condemned in gigantic bold figures—which according to Hawthorne were but dimly visible from the floor in the dusky light.

116.13 Fiesole] Ancient Etruscan hilltop town three miles north of Florence. The great blocks in its northern wall best showed its Etruscan origin. Near the Franciscan church and convent on the site of the ancient acropolis is a terrace commanding a southward view of Florence and the Arno Valley nearly a thousand feet below. At the Villa Palmieri (or dei tre Visi), near the steep road (Via di Giovanni Boccaccio) between Florence and San Domenico, on the way to Fiesole, Boccaccio located the storytellers of his *Decameron*, who fled the plague in the city; higher up, under the slopes of Fiesole, is the Villa Mozzi, a favorite retreat of Lorenzo the Magnificent and his philosophical companions.

116.17 *April*] Error for March.

116.17 Diligence] The conveyance to Bologna left at 4 A.M. three times a week and covered the seventy or so miles by 8 P.M.; coupé fare, about twenty shillings. Some peaks along this route reach four thousand feet, but the two highest passes are around three thousand; in winter and early spring, however, extra teams were required to manage the snow, especially the very steep approach to the Futa Pass. Just before the pass, carriages stopped at the hamlet of Monte Carelli (about eighteen miles), with a small, isolated roadside inn, perhaps where M had breakfast. M would have disagreed with most of Valery's disdainful comparison of the Apennines with the Alps: "They neither resound with the roar of torrents or cascades, nor the crashing of the avalanche; no majestic rivers or limpid streams originate there; the vegetation is colourless and scrubby, while instead of the bold precipitous peaks of the Alps darting straight upwards to the skies, the Apennines resemble a pile of hills heaped on each other" (*Travels in Italy*, p. 312). The diligence on this route (probably like most that M rode in the absence of railroads) was described by the Reverend Daniel Eddy as "a long, cumbersome vehicle . . . divided into different compartments. The cabriolet is an open sort of chaise on top; the coupe is the forward apartment, will hold four or five persons, and is considered as the best place for observation and ease; the interno, or interior, is an apartment with two seats opposite . . . , and is in the middle. . . . The baggage is put upon the top of the crazy carriage, and is liable every moment to fall through on to your head" (*Europa*, p. 444).

116.23 decorous] Possibly "decent".

in places. Lonely houses. Villages.
Mixed decorous people: Breakfast on
the route. Nothing of talk in the coupe:
But much smoking:

116.25 "Three Moors."] I Tre Mori, a second-rate inn. The inclinations of Bologna's two early twelfth-century towers, near the marketplace, are slight; the taller, over 300 feet, is only 4 feet off perpendicular, the other, unfinished between 150 and 160 feet, leaned by some 8 feet.

116.27 Gallery] The picture gallery, the Reale Pinacoteca, just beyond the university (see the discussion at 116.31) in the northeast quarter, was notable for its examples of the seventeenth-century Bolognese school, especially the Carracci and Guido Reni. Raphael's *St. Cecilia in Ecstasy* was the most important work. There were at least two Madonnas of the Rosary, one now attributed to Lodovico Carracci, the other by Zampieri Domenichino (praised by Valery). M understandably mistook Reni's *Samson Victorious over the Philistines* (also praised by Valery) for David. *La Maga Circe* is by Lorenzo Garbieri.

116.28–29 Campo . . . arcades] Outside the west gates, an extensive Carthusian monastery converted to a cemetery (Campo Santo) in 1801 by order of Napoleon; it and the church of the Madonna di San Luca, high on a hill to the southwest, were connected to the city by a continuous arcade of over six hundred arches.

116.31 University] Famous originally for law, then medicine, it was moved in 1803 to the old but commodious Palazzo Celesi; the coats of arms in the splendid courtyard are of the professors, not students. Bologna was famous for many "learned ladies"; among those memorialized in sculpture were Laura Bassi and Clotilde Tambroni, professors of mathematics and of Greek, respectively.

117.5 Ferrara] After Bologna, at the northeastern foot of the Apennines, M's route north-northeast crossed the level Lombardy plain of the Po Valley. Ferrara, once the magnificent seat of the Este family, was more than half deserted when M saw it, with grass growing in the streets. Various parts of the facade of the cathedral, San Giorgio, date from the twelfth, thirteenth, and fourteenth centuries (the uninjured bas-relief of the Last Judgment was one of a number depicting the life of Jesus; inside there was also a fresco of the Last Judgment by a pupil of Michelangelo). The Campanile had reached its fourth story by the end of the sixteenth century, when construction ceased.

117.12 old palace] Valery, after remarking the town's generally dreary atmosphere, described the fourteenth- to sixteenth-century Castello in the center "with its bridges, towers, and elegant balustrades, [retaining] in its exterior a fairylike air in accordance with its poetical recollections" (*Travels in Italy*, p. 218). On the walls of the cell in the Arcispedale Sant'Anna (down the street from the Castello), where, it was said, Tasso was imprisoned (1579–86), were the names of Byron and Delavigne and verses by Lamartine.

117.21–23 Rovigo . . . Padua] M crossed the Po (boundary between the Papal States and Austrian Venetia) shortly after leaving Ferrara, with all of the usual tediousness at the customs. Rovigo at twenty miles and Padua at twenty-seven more are in country marked by hot mud, sulfur springs, and numerous health spas. "Star of the East" appears to be M's mistranslation of La Stella d'Oro [gold], recommended as a clean, comfortable inn near the center.

117.24–27 famous caffe . . . town hall] The internationally famous Caffè Pedrocchi near M's inn in Padua, built in 1831 with a gambling fortune, was reputedly the largest and most luxurious in Europe. Almost next door is the Palazzo della Ragione, a vast thirteenth-century building whose upper floor is all one room, 262 by 88 feet; its great roof, supposed the largest of its kind unsupported by pillars, was believed the design of Fra Giovanni, an Augustinian friar who had seen a similar construction in India.

117.28 "Satan . . . host."] A six-foot sculpture of the Fall of Lucifer by Agostino Fasolata in the Palazzo Papafava, sixty figures carved in one block of marble. (Valery calls it "a horrible group . . . whimsically imagined and . . . admirable for its mechanism and workmanship," *Travels in Italy*, p. 213.) In his "Statues in Rome" lecture (NN *Piazza Tales* volume, p. 403), and perhaps here, M seems to have confused one of the angels with the figure of Satan, in actuality represented as an infernal monster at the bottom of the pile; see Henry F. Pommer, *Milton and Melville* (Pittsburgh: University of Pittsburgh Press, 1950), p. 138, n. 15; the statue is illustrated, facing p. 31.

117.29 Church . . . Shrine] In the southeast quarter, the thirteenth-century basilica of the city's patron saint. His particular shrine, elaborately wrought in marble and gold, illuminated night and day with golden lamps and silver candelabra, occupies the north transept. Twelve bronze Old Testament bas-reliefs decorated the choir, but M appears to have noted a Goliath and David by Andrea Riccio in the presbytery.

117.30–31 Promenade] The Madonna dell'Arena, also called the Prato della Valle, near St. Anthony's; a grassy, oval dale surrounded by a canal, a favored place for walking.

117.32 Giotto's chapel] Santa Maria dell'Arena, designed and painted by Giotto at the height of his abilities (1305) for Enrico Scrovegni; it is part of the castle made out of a first-century Roman arena at the north edge of Padua. The lowest of the quadruple row of frescoes illustrates allegorically the Vices on one side, the Virtues on the other. (M would have seen these singled out by Valery and described as "strange"—*Travels in Italy*, p. 204.) The upper three rows illustrate the Gospels and the life of Mary. Also adjoining the ancient arena is the thirteenth-century church of the Eremitani, with a three-hundred-foot nave and the important frescoes by Andrea Mantegna, seriously damaged in World War II and now partially restored.

117.35–36 Approaching Venice] The last four thousand or so yards of the twenty-six miles of railway crossed the lagoon on the bridge built in

Venice

1845, ending at the northwest termination of the Grand Canal. (The swampy tidal flats M refers to, along the Charles River at Boston, were about to disappear: the filling of the Back Bay was authorized in 1857.) The Hotel Luna was between the southwest angle of the Piazza San Marco and the Grand Canal; it charged from three francs upward for a room, one-and-a-half to two francs for breakfast, and three or four for dinner. Jarves particularly remarked on the cheapness of gondolas—"less than seventy-five cents per day for the best" (*Italian Sights*, p. 365). The illustration above, by J. M. W. Turner, is from Samuel Rogers's *Italy: A Poem* (London: Caddell, Moxon, Jennings, & Chaplin, 1830), p. 47 (for Rogers, whom M had met in 1849, see the discussion at 44.29).

118.1 Florian's] Internationally famous café, on the south side of the Piazza San Marco. The Palazzo Ducale, the Palace of the Doges next to the cathedral at the east end, was open from nine to four daily.

118.3 Bell Tower] M doubtless means the Campanile of St. Mark's, though he is naming these tourist attractions out of geographical order; the modern one is an exact replica of the original, which collapsed in 1902. It was 325 feet high and could be climbed by an inclined ramp circling the interior.

118.4 Guidecca] Giudecca, the name both of the small, closely connected island group to the south (the old Jewish section) and the broad canal separating it from the city's main part. Such a tour, along the great reverse S-curve of the Grand Canal, around the city by the northwest, and back by the Giudecca to the landings at St. Mark's, was recommended by guidebooks as imperative.

118.6–7 Ladies . . . outside] The cafés around the piazza were sharply separated between Austrian and Venetian patronage; Murray said, "Italian ladies rarely enter the cafés; they take their refreshment—ice or coffee—outside" (*Northern Italy*, I, 309). Their male counterparts, so Howells observed a few years later (when he was Lincoln's consul in Venice), were "all well-dressed, handsome men, with beards carefully cut, brilliant hats and boots, and conspicuously clean linen. I used to wonder . . . whether they . . . had never any thing else but lounging at Florian's to do. . . . Some men in Venice spend their noble, useful lives in this way, and it was the proud reply of a Venetian father, when asked of what profession his son was, '*È in Piazza!*' That was, he bore a cane, wore light gloves, and stared from Florian's windows at the ladies who went by" (*Venetian Life*, rev. ed. [Boston: Osgood, 1872], p. 59).

118.11 bead manufactury] M will visit the great Venetian glassworks on the island of Murano the next day, but there were small branches within the city, like that of the Murano Company near the mouth of the Grand Canal. Gold jewelry, like glass, remained a major Venetian craft in the city's decline and Howells describes such a shop as M saw:

> In the Ruga Vecchia at Rialto they yet make the famous Venetian gold chain, which few visitors to the city can have failed to notice hanging in strands and wound upon spools, in the shop windows. . . . It is wrought of all degrees of fineness, and is always so flexile that it may be folded and wound in any shape. . . . Formerly, in the luxurious days of the Republic, it is said the chain was made as fine as sewing-silk. . . . It had then a cruel interest from the fact that its manufacture . . . cost the artisans their eyesight. . . . I do not hope to describe the chain, except by saying that the links are horseshoe and oval shaped, and are connected by twos,—an oval being welded crosswise into a horseshoe and so on, each two being linked loosely into the next. (*Venetian Life*, pp. 249–50)

118.13–14 To Church] Santi Giovanni e Paolo: toward the northeast edge of the islands, and second in importance only to St. Mark's; the conspicuous tombs of many doges line the nave and chapels. Of the many bas-reliefs in the church, that noticed by M was probably one of the celebrated marble carvings in the Chapel of the Rosary, depicting scenes from the lives of the Virgin and Christ. In this chapel M would also have seen Titian's masterpiece, the *Martyrdom of St. Peter*, which was destroyed in a fire ten years later.

118.15 Aresenl] Arsenal: at the city's east end; by the nineteenth century but a moldering shell of its former greatness, vandalized by the French in 1797. In the armory the standard of the Turkish admiral, a red and yellow silk banner captured at Lepanto, was displayed.

118.16–17 Othello's house & statue] Guides sometimes pointed to a Palazzo Moro on the Grand Canal's west bank as the residence of Cristoforo Moro, supposed prototype of Othello, and they offered a time-blackened, fifteenth-century statue on the corner as proof. Tradition had fixed on no single residence for Shylock, but M's guide Antonio—or the gondolier—presumably designated some house in a newer Jewish section in the northwest quarter. Byron lived off and on (1818–19) in the middle of three Palazzi Mocenigos, on the Grand Canal's east bank just past the first great curve beyond St. Mark's (Howells called it one of the ugliest). The Foscari Palace is on the west bank, at the head of that curve, with a view along both reaches. (These palaces and Venice as a whole are recalled in the poem "Venice," in *Timoleon*; *Published Poems*, p. 291.)

118.20 Murano] Center of glass manufacture since the thirteenth century, on five islands three-quarters of a mile to the north of Venice proper. The "cemetery" M saw was on the small island of San Michele, off the north shore of Venice, where a former convent had been made into a cemetery, as were many others in the Napoleonic era (cf. the discussion at 116.28–29). The oldest church on Murano, Santi Maria e Donato, dated from the tenth century and was largely rebuilt in the twelfth.

118.21 Jesuit church] I Gesuati, near the landing on the north side. Its eighteenth-century ornateness was generally despised; Howells called it the "coldest" of many Venetian churches: "Those who have seen it will remember . . . its famous marble drapery. This base, mechanical surprise . . . is effected by inlaying the white marble of column and pulpits and altars with a certain pattern of verd-antique. . . . Even where the marble is carven in vast and heavy folds over a pulpit . . . or wrought in figures on the steps of the high-altar to represent a carpet, it has no richness of effect, but a poverty, a coldness, a harshness indescribably table-clothy" (*Venetian Life*, p. 46). Valery, however, considered it "splendid" (*Travels in Italy*, p. 184).

118.23 House of Gold] The Ca' d'Oro, named for the original gilding on its facade, on the north side of the Grand Canal just beyond the second great curve, was one of the most elegant of fifteenth-century Venetian Gothic palaces. Its owner at the time was Mlle. Taglioni, the famous dancer. The residence of the duke of Bordeaux was the Palazzo Cavalli-Franchetti, on the north side of the southern reach, just before the bridge that now crosses to the Galleria dell'Accademia. Near the north end of the canal, the duchess of Berry occupied the Palazzo Vendramin-Calergi, one of the very finest (Wagner died there). The Hôtel de Ville ("excellent hotel," *Northern Italy*, p. 309) was formerly the twelfth-century Palazzo Loredan (on the south bank of the middle reach), which, though not "conspicuous," Ruskin called "the most beautiful palace in the whole extent of the Grand Canal" (*The Stones of Venice* [London: Smith, Elder, 1853], II, 390).

118.26 Gallery] The Galleria dell'Accademia, a converted (1807) convent on the south bank of the canal, was open every day from noon to three. The masterpiece in its collection, Titian's *Assumption of the Virgin*, had been "discovered" (according to Valery, p. 167) behind a coat of smoky grime above the high altar of the church I Frari (to which it has since been returned). When M saw it, it was hung in a lower place and brighter light than that for which Titian designed it, and some observers complained that its coloring was too vivid, its figures too animated. Next, M may refer to either of two Tintorettos, *Rescue of a Slave from Torture* or *Rescuing a Saracen*, in a series on the miracles of Saint Mark that first made the painter famous. M's "Venetian noble" might be any of a number of such paintings, perhaps one by Titian or the one by Giorgione so titled in Murray. Among the most interesting of Venetian scenes is Gentile Bellini's *Procession on the Piazza of St. Mark* (1496). The huge canvas of the *Presentation of the Child Mary in the Temple* is a painting of Titian's maturity in the middle 1530's.

118.30 monsters] Doubtless one of those Ruskin called "Grotesque Renaissance"; he describes a similar figure: "A head,—huge, inhuman, and monstrous,—leering in bestial degradation, too foul to be either pictured or described. . . . This head [from a tower dedicated to St. Mary the Beautiful] is one of many hundreds which disgrace the latest buildings of the city, all more or less agreeing in their expression of sneering mockery, in most cases enhanced by thrusting out the tongue" (*Stones of Venice*, III, 121).

118.33 three masts] Those opposite St. Mark's that once flew the banners of the long-lost three dependencies, Candia, Cyprus, and the Morea. Seized by Napoleon in 1797, Venetian territory then passed back and forth between Austria and Italy, and finally to Austria in the settlement of 1814; in the Revolutions of 1848, Venetians declared themselves a republic but were reconquered by Austria in 1849. Howells's *Venetian Life* depicts the open hostility between citizen and soldier, and the consequent difficulties of his own Civil War consulship.

119.2–3 garden . . . Napoleon] The public promenade, at the eastern extremity of Venice, was little patronized because of its distance; it afforded fine views of the southern lagoon and the Lido beach beyond, the long, narrow, sandy—then largely deserted—littoral separating the lagoon from the open Adriatic. A gondola to the Lido took about forty-five minutes, and two gondoliers were recommended.

119.7 Armenian Convent] A community of Mechitarist monks, on the island of San Lazzaro, just inside the Lido, three-quarters of a mile southeast of Venice. Perhaps M was attracted to these out-of-the-way excursions because Byron often rode on the Lido sands and for a while studied Armenian at the convent. An anonymous Charleston traveler described the convent as covering scarcely "more than an acre of ground, but . . . securely and neatly walled around, in the midst of which stands the neat little church of the convent. Its walls are surmounted by a Turkish minaret, and surrounded by an extended colonnade, on either side of which may be seen numerous fruit trees and flowering shrubs, presenting the appearance of a little paradise. There are about fifty monks" (*A Summer's Tour in Europe, in 1851* [Charleston, S.C.: Walker & James, 1852], p. 95). Its printing facilities handling twenty-four languages made it the center of Armenian proselytizing and scholarly literature.

119.20 Malamocco Passage] The central channel leading from the sea, past the Lido, into the lagoon.

119.21 church . . . Octagonal] Santa Maria della Salute, on the south bank of the St. Mark's entrance to the Grand Canal, erected in 1631 in thanksgiving for the cessation of a disastrous plague. San Giorgio Maggiore, a major Palladian church on a nearby island south of St. Mark's, has forty-eight baroque choir stalls carved with scenes from the life of Saint Benedict.

119.23 Bridge of Sighs] Across a narrow side canal, connecting the rear of the Palace of the Doges, where prisoners received their sentences, with the public prison; the prison's severely plain facade next the palace was gloomy enough, and two great fires gutting the palace (1547 and 1577) blackened both buildings. In *Clarel* (4.5.76–77) M calls the winter of 1860, when young men were forced to choose North or South, the "True Bridge of Sighs" between two eras of American history.

119.28 from nature, after all] M's concessive observation about Titian's brown flesh colors may reflect a recollection of the two discourses on painting that William Page had recently delivered to him in Florence. In such discourses Page consistently defended his view (now only partially vindicated) that the low flesh tones of Titian's pictures were painted as we see them and were not the accidental result of darkening over time. (See Joshua Taylor, *William Page*, pp. 83, 137, and 168, and the discussion at 106.30 and the two at 111.20.)

119.29–30 vision . . . passage] Probably the source of M's poem "In a Bye-Canal" in *Timoleon* (*Published Poems*, pp. 292–93); see this passage:

A languid impulse from the oar
Plied by my indolent gondolier
Tinkles against a palace hoar,
    And, hark, response I hear!
A lattice clicks; and, lo, I see,
Between the slats, mute summoning me,
What loveliest eyes of scintillation,
What basilisk glance of conjuration!

119.37–38 Foscari palace] See the discussion at 118.16–17. Near here authorities used to build the temporary reviewing stands for the regattas because the site commanded such excellent views. The Austrian military seized the palace from the municipal government for a barracks because of its strategic location. Howells's description of his adjoining residence built by the same architects, added in the 1872 edition of *Venetian Life* (pp. 405–7), perhaps gives an idea of what M saw, especially the great painted ceiling timbers.

120.7 precious] A conjectural reading (in line 2 opposite), called in question if the following stroke is a comma; see the textual note.

120.8 mosaic] Word incomplete, written either "mosa" (for "mosaic") or "mura" (for "mural").

120.17 shake] Possibly "stake" (in the sense of "to support financially"). Much of the handwriting on this page (119) of notebook D (see the reproduction, on p. 508—this word is in line 3) is more than usually scrawled in haste; see also the readings discussed at 120.25, 28, and 30 below.

120.24 Byron] Elements of the episode are clear from Byron's letter, written "past two in the morning," to John Murray, May 18, 1819:

> In going, about an hour and a half ago, to a rendezvous with a Venetian Girl (unmarried and the daughter of one of their nobles), I tumbled into the Grand Canal. . . . My foot slipped in getting into my Gondola to set out (owing to the cursed slippery steps of their palaces) and in I flounced like a Carp—and went dripping like a Triton to my Sea-nymph—and had to scramble up to a Grated window "Fenced with iron within and without / Lest the Lover get in, or the Lady get out." . . . I have undergone some trouble on her account—for last winter the truculent tyrant her flinty-hearted father—having been informed by an infernal German Countess Vorsperg (their next neighbour) of our meetings—they sent a priest to me—and a Commissary of police—and they locked the Girl up. . . . We have lately been able to recommence. (*Byron's Letters and Journals*, 12 vols. [London: Murray, 1976], VI, 133)

120.25 cavalier sends] Both words conjectural (see line 16 in the reproduction of page D119, p. 508).

120.27–28 Whether . . . not] Possibly M did see Archduke Ferdinand Maximilian, brother of Franz Joseph (and later, briefly, emperor of Mexico until executed); he was appointed governor of the Italian provinces at the end of February, to reside alternately in Venice and Milan, and he did not leave Venice until April 19, 1857.

120.28 Boys] Possibly "Bangs" (see line 20 in the reproduction of page D119, p. 508).

How you do, Antonio—hope you very well, Antonio—Poor Antonio no money, Antonio no comfort. Get out of de way Antonio. Go to the devil, Antonio. Antonio you go shake yourself. ~~Look de rich m~~ You know dat Sir, dat to be de rich man, de poor man laugh always de bad smell? (For Con. Man) You know dat Sir?

Yes, Antonio, I am well aware of that. Charming disposition. Old blind man, give sixpence, & God will bless you [Will give, but dont like the blessing]. [Antonio good character for Con. Man] Did not want to die. Heaven. You believe dat? I go dere, see how I like it first.—This rich anecdote. Byron money etc every money to visit a lady in palace opposite. The Prussian countess, candle seen. Very wicked lady but very happy.—Floating atlas philosophy with Antonio the Mony. Ah, it was Pausillippo.—Whether was the brother of E. of Austria or not.—Leary old parasol. Burgs. Tulle lace. Anxious to settle it; hurry my boy, for I consider that one of the fine democracy would not look with disrespect upon the man who had &c &c.

April 6th. Left Venice at 5½ A M for Milan. Through Padua & Vicenza to Verona, where before you enter the cars, Between

Notebook D, page 119; NN120.14–120.34.

120.30 feirce] Possibly "free" (see line 22 in the reproduction of page D119, p. 508).

120.32 Left . . . for Milan] The new railroad still only reached Coccaglio, short of Milan by twenty-three miles. After following along the Po Valley, beyond Vicenza the route began skirting the foothills of the Italian Alps, and some miles beyond Verona it provided the first view of Lago di Garda while passing across a long viaduct over a deep valley.

120.37 continually] Possibly "constantly".

temples. Passed for the rest continually, the first tiers of the Alps. R.R. on dead level of Lombardy plain. Rich cultivation.

120.38 first tiers] Both words conjectural (in line 2 above). Possibly "front view" (H), "front tiers", "first view", or "first series".

121.2–3 Napoleon's campaigns] M probably read in Murray's *Northern Italy* (I, 255) that around Brescia, Napoleon had some of his most spectacular early triumphs, Lonato and Castiglione, on August 3 and 5, 1796, that "sealed the fate of the Austrians in Italy."

121.5 Hotel] Hôtel de la Ville (an inn): in the center of the city, a short distance from the cathedral. Murray: "The best situation in Milan, open and airy, . . . an excellent house, . . . and handsomely fitted up. . . . An excellent table-d'hôte at 4 francs; coffee and reading room, master and waiters speaking English; and baths in the house" (*Northern Italy*, I, 150).

121.8 Gallery] The picture gallery of the Brera, open daily from nine to three, was established in 1809–10 in a seventeenth-century Jesuit foundation; at this time, however, "of a multitude of pictures here, few make much impression. Those which are good must be picked out from a monotonous waste of mediocrity" (Hillard, *Six Months*, I, 18). The *Martyrdom of St. Catherine* that M noticed may be the one by Gaudenzio Ferrari, a Milanese painter mentioned favorably by Valery, who also particularly admired Gentile Bellini's very large *St. Mark Preaching in the Square of Alexandria (Travels in Italy*, p. 60).

121.10 expressions] A conjectural reading.

St. Catherine's Martyrdom. St. Mark at Alexandria is admirable for a variety of outlandish costume & expression. To the

121.11 Camp d'Armo] Piazza d'Armi: the large interior court of the Castello, which was rebuilt by the Sforzas in the fifteenth century and was being used as a barracks by the Austrian occupiers. Farther northwest, at the far edge of the original pleasure grounds adjoining the Castello Sforzesco (now a public park), Napoleon commissioned the white marble triumphal Arco della Pace (begun 1806, completed by the Austrians) as part of the expansive Foro Bonaparte he envisaged.

121.11 Leonardo] The abbey church of Santa Maria delle Grazie and the adjoining monastery with Leonardo's *Last Supper* (1495–97) are about a half mile southwest of the Castello. The church is fifteenth-century Lombard Gothic in brick, with elaborate external decorations in terra cotta around the lower part. The Dominican monastery had been used as military barracks since the French occupation of 1796, the refectory itself as a stable and granary for a period, a misuse that contributed to the painting's deplorable condition. But it had already badly peeled by the middle of the sixteenth century because Leonardo experimented with tempera on a dry wall. The *Crucifixion* on the opposite wall was painted by Giovanni Montorfano about the same time. M's parenthetical reference to Wordsworth is not clear; he may have been reminded of Wordsworth by Murray's quoting his profound admiration of the painting (*Northern Italy*, I, 174).

121.19 betray] As written, apparently "bely" (H), but M evidently intended to quote Jesus' word "betray" (Matthew 26:21).

(Photograph copy of it I saw) — Significance of the Last Supper. The joys of the banquet soon depart. One shall bely me, one of you — man so false — the glow of sociality is so evanescent, selfishness, so lasting. —

121.19 man] Possibly "men" (in line 4 above).

121.22 the cathedral] Begun in the fourteenth century, this was for a long time the largest church in the world. Its facade was not completed until Napoleon ordered it, and if M is speaking of later afternoon, the window he notes would be one of the three Gothic windows inserted at that time. The ascent to the roof began in the south transept, 158 steps, but from there, steps on the flying buttresses afforded M egress to other levels; 177 more steps would take him to the platform of the tower, and 193 more to the highest gallery of the spire. These outer staircases rose spirally in stonework of open tracery. By 1857 more than three thousand of the white marble statues intended for the pinnacles were in place (M's poem "Milan Cathedral" in *Timoleon* dwells chiefly on this aspect [*Published Poems*, p. 296]); M's enthusiasm differs from Valery's condescension in *Travels in Italy*. With a clear atmosphere (perhaps not likely in late afternoon) the view extends across the Lombardy plains to the Apennines in one direction and in the other to the French and Swiss Alps—Mont Blanc, Monte Rosa, and the Bernese Alps.

121.31 Lake Como] The twenty-eight-mile railroad ran to Camerlatta, and then an omnibus descended the last steep mile to the shore. The steamboat took six hours to traverse the length of the lake to Colico and back, passing the village of Bellagio at the point between the two southern arms of the inverted Y-shaped lake, bounded by precipitous shores rising to 7,400 feet. (Lake George, New York, was fresh in M's mind from a visit in August, 1856; in rereading his journal M substituted Como for George in a comparison of natural scenery; see 83.18 and accompanying discussion.) The illustration above by Turner is from Samuel Rogers's *Italy*, p. 32.

121.35 windrows] I.e., heaped rows of rocks; possibly "windows" (H).

122.11 Ticino] The river, twenty miles west of Milan, draining Lago Maggiore, was the boundary between Austrian Lombardy and the kingdom of Sardinia until 1859. The eleven-arched Ponte Nuovo across the wide gravelly bed was started by the French; Valery calls it "magnificent" (*Travels in Italy*, p. 35), but calls Novara "an old dirty Spanish town" (p. 33)—from the Spanish occupation of the sixteenth century—with some "rich and beautiful churches." The promenades were on the old Spanish fortifications. Rebuilding of the eleventh-century cathedral began in 1831; its portico was a kind of museum of ancient altars, funerary urns and inscriptions, and across the courtyard was the ancient baptistery, in whose circular interior stood life-size wax figures representing events of the Passion. The angels mentioned by M adorned the high altar, the church's chief monument. The pasteboard tableau he recalled was doubtless an Easter representation, equivalent of the elaborately staged Twelfth Night representation Hillard saw at Santa Maria d'Aracoeli in Rome (*Six Months*, I, 340–41).

122.18 Hotel] Hôtel de l'Europe: described as one of the best in Turin, it was on the piazza fronting the old Castello, across town from the train station.

122.23 Via di Po] A handsome street bordered by arcades, running southeast from the Piazza Castello to the now-named Piazza Vittorio Veneto at the river. On the other side rises a range of hills, then with many fine villas.

122.24 Gallery] The revolutionary French army carried off much of the royal collection, but the remainder was in the Palazzo Madama (the more modern additions to the ancient Castello) until 1865. The gallery was open daily, though committee meetings of the Sardinian Senate sometimes blocked particular rooms. Giuseppe Crespi painted the queen of Bohemia confessing to Saint Giovanni Nepomuceno, and the four allegorical paintings noted by M appear to be those of Francesco Albani, using Venus to represent Fire, Juno as Air, Galatea as Water, and Cybele as Earth. Besides Titian's *St. Jerome*, the collection also had a version of his *Pope Paul III*, like the one in the Naples gallery. The considerable holdings of Netherlands artists originated in the collection of Prince Eugene of Savoy. Besides Van Dyck's *Children of Charles I* (of England), there were six portraits of various young royal Savoyards; also, the several Brueghels and David Teniers the Younger were extensively represented.

122.33 Philadelphia] The street plan of Turin still tended to follow the ancient Roman encampment's geometric layout. With the kings of Sardinia restored to this capital after Napoleon's defeat, its population nearly doubled. Valery found it coldly regular "without magnificence" (*Travels in*

Italy, p. 694); Murray claimed, "At least one fourth of the city has been erected since the restoration of the royal family, and of later years nearly one third has been added to it on the S. side. . . . The streets . . . are all in straight lines, intersecting each other at right angles. . . . The houses are of brick intended for stucco" (*Northern Italy*, I, 13–14). A state official supervised all new building, reinforcing the uniformity.

122.36 Mount Rosa] 15,217 feet high, on the Swiss-Italian border, slightly east of north from the city; Murray's nineteenth-century map of the city, however, showed the Via di Grossa running northwest, in which direction the highest peak would be the Gran Paradiso (13,324 ft.).

123.4–5 Po . . . church] Presumably the new Gran Madre di Dio (1818–31) across the river, built on the model of the Roman Pantheon to commemorate the monarch's return after Napoleon's defeat.

123.8 cars for Genoa] Most of the one-hundred-odd miles is in the Po Valley through a fine vineyard area, but climbing through the coastal range to reach the seaport, the roadbed traversed deep cuts, hairpin turns, and eleven tunnels, the longest of which, the Galleria dei Giovi, pierced the mountains for 3,470 yards.

123.14 Kate's affairs] Most likely fragile gifts purchased for M's sister Catherine (1825–1905), who married John C. Hoadley in 1853. Conceivably, however, M may refer to his seventeen- or eighteen-year-old first cousin Catherine Gansevoort, his kindly uncle Peter Gansevoort's daughter, who became quite close to the family.

123.15 Feder] A good hotel in the former Admiralty Palace, but like most in Genoa, near the noisy Custom House, the Free Port, and the railway freight station. Lieutenant Wise had stayed there a few years before and found it expensive: "The Feder was kept by Madame Feder—or rather it kept her, and very handsomely, too, I should judge, from the charges she made. The article of wood alone, drove us to the verge of bankruptcy. . . . Our breakfasts were not bountiful, though palatable. . . . When we dined at *table d'hôte* . . . we made a rule to destroy all we could not eat. There was something revengefully consoling in the act, and compensated us for the money we spent" (*Scampavias*, pp. 326–27).

123.15–16 Strada Nuovo] Strada Nuova, now the Via Garibaldi, a street (with its continuations under other names) leading from near the harbor toward the center, lined with many of Genoa's great palaces, a highly recommended tourist attraction. M appears to be remembering Chapter 28 of *The Prince* (1532), "In What Manner Princes Ought to Keep Their Words," which outlines the advantages of the *appearance* of virtue, and the possible disadvantages of actual virtue. Mark Twain and his fellow Innocents also visited the palaces: "The huge palaces . . . are each supposed to be occupied by one family, but they could accommodate a hundred. . . . These houses, solid marble palaces . . . are, in many cases, of a dull pinkish color, outside, and from pavement to eaves are pictured with Genoese battle-scenes, with monstrous Jupiters and Cupids and with familiar illustrations from Grecian mythology. Where the paint has yielded to age and exposure and is peeling off in flakes and patches, the effect is not happy" (*Innocents Abroad*, chap. 17, pp. 166–67).

123.23 pavilion] Possibly "promenade" or "parterre".

Palaces. In evng walked on pavilion nigh port. Lofty hotels. Hotel of the Cross of Malta. View of hills in distance.

123.23 pavilion nigh port] The Porticata alla Piazza (or Portici di Sottorípa), an arcade once extending from Genoa's Free Port to the Arsenal; underneath were shops, on top a long terraced walk. Howells described it as a "certain cavernous arcade which curves round the water with the flection of the shore, and makes itself a twilight at noonday. Under it are clangorous shops of iron-smiths, and sizzling shops of marine cooks, and, looking down its dim perspective, one beholds chiefly sea-legs, . . . more or less affected by strong waters, . . . sailors from all parts of the world" (*Italian Journeys* [New York: Hurd & Houghton, 1867], p. 56). Across the street facing the harbor were the Feder and several other hotels, many stories tall (Lt. Wise counted 149 steps up to his Feder room); among them, the Hotel Croce di Malta occupied a building that once belonged to the knights of that order—Mark Twain and his fellows encamped here.

123.26 promenade on ramparts] The Spianata del Acquasola, a park laid out on the superseded old eastern inner ramparts.

123.27 Cathedral] San Lorenzo shows architectural elements from early twelfth-century Romanesque through French Gothic to the Renaissance. The common symbol of Saint Lawrence, the gridiron on which according to legend he was martyred in the third century, was of course prominent. Two towers were planned for the church, but only the south one was ever completed.

123.28–29 Ducal Palace] Adjacent to the cathedral, and seat of both the governor and the local senate; now the Palace of Justice.

WOMEN OF GENOA.

123.29–30 head dress] Most visitors commented on this fashion. Mark Twain: "There may be prettier women in Europe, but I doubt it. . . . Two-thirds [of the population] are women, I think, and at least two-thirds of the women are beautiful. . . . Most of the young demoiselles are robed in a cloud of white from head to foot. . . . Nine-tenths of them wear nothing on their heads but a filmy sort of veil, which falls down their backs like a white mist" (*Innocents Abroad*, chap. 17, p. 160; the illustration above is from p. 161). "Undine" is a capricious water sylph in the fairy romance of that name (1811) by Baron de la Motte-Fouqué (Sealts 319; Bercaw 432). The subtitle of Sir Walter Scott's *Anne of Geierstein* (1829) was *The Maiden of the Mist.* This day was Easter Sunday, hence the crowds on display.

123.32 Light house] On the promontory bounding the old harbor on the west; the structure itself is 230 feet high (353 steps) and stands nearly 400 feet above the sea.

123.33 forts] Genoa, in a coastal-mountain amphitheater, was guarded by successively extended rings of fortifications second only to those of Paris. At the high point (1690 ft.), the great citadel of Il Sperone dominated the city and harbor, while other forts commanded all approaches. The circuit inside the wall was some twenty miles. M by mistake apparently wound up at the park on the abandoned inner ramparts he had seen before. If so, the little church he passed was either San Stefano before the park, or Santa Maria Immacolata uphill to the northeast, or most likely San Bartolomeo degli Armeni near the upper walls. (Henry Pommer, *Milton and Melville*, p. 66, suggests M's reference to Satan derives from his memory of *Paradise Lost*, especially passages in Books I and II.)

124.14 Doria palace] Presented (1522) to the famous admiral Andrea Doria (1468?-1560), the city's most splendid palace stands toward the old harbor's western curve; now surrounded by rail lines, it was then surrounded by extensive gardens.

124.18 *April 14th*] Error for April 13. From here to the end of this journal M's dates or days are often wrong. On April 24 he noticed the error which started at this point and made a second entry (126.34) with the remark "(Mistake of a day before)." But two days later in London he called April 26 "Monday" when both calendar and context call for Sunday, and this discrepancy also appeared in the entry for April 29 through May 1, which were Wednesday through Friday (127.33). Finally, the entry for the following Sunday should be May 3, not 2 (128.13), an error which persisted through the entry for May 5 (actually May 6, 129.26). It also appears that at times a sleepless night merged memory of one day into the next, and that at others his first jotting notes in some memo book for later transfer to this one may have confused days and dates. See the double account of Oxford, at 128.13–129.6 and 156.1–38.

124.19 palaces] The Roman palace's characteristic inner court was not open to street view, unlike those of Genoa (Murray quotes a description to which M evidently refers): "The usual disposition exhibits a large hall . . . leading to a court surrounded by arcades. . . . Beyond this court is the great staircase . . . , and further still is frequently a small garden, shaded with oranges. . . . It is invariably open to public view; and the long perspective of halls, courts, columns, arches, and flights of steps, produces a most magnificent effect" (*Northern Italy*, I, 97). The Palazzo Rosso belonged to the Brignole Sale family and was called "Red" as distinguished from the "White" of the Palazzo Bianco on the opposite side of the Strada Nuova. Considered the street's most magnificent palace, it certainly had the greatest collection of paintings—including examples by Van Dyck, Rubens, Giorgione, Veronese, Tintoretto, and Titian. (Both palaces, with their collections, were later bequeathed to the city.) Customs still occupied the lower floor of the Palazzo San Giorgio, edifice of the once powerful but now suppressed Banco di San Giorgio; over its main entrance, until Italy's reunification, hung links of the great chain that had closed the port of Pisa before it was carried off in 1290 by the victorious Genoese.

124.23 Constitution] A slip—in fact the *Constellation* (see the discussions at 73.6 and 100.16–17), whose officers M would encounter all the way to Switzerland. Its purser was Irish-born Lieutenant John Johnson, who entered the navy from North Carolina in 1850.

124.24 *Ap 15th*] Error for April 14; see the discussion at 124.18.

124.24 Lake Maggiore] The new (1855) railroad from Genoa to the lake (111 mi.) had the advantage of evading tedious Austrian customs. As far as Alessandria, it followed the tramontane route that M had traversed a few days earlier; thereafter it crossed the Po Valley northward through Novara to Arona on the lake. The excellent Sardinian government steamer then plied the narrowing, precipitously bordered lake to Magadino, fifty-six miles away in the Swiss Alps; along the way it passed Count Borromeo's Isola Bella, a once low, barren, rocky island transformed into splendid terraced gardens of subtropical luxuriance, about which both Murray and Hillard waxed rhapsodical.

124.29 Bellinzona] Magadino was a small malarial village in the floodplain of the upper Ticino River; nine miles farther up the valley, at Bellinzona, the steep ascent of the San Gotthard Pass began. The road was reconstructed in 1832 in an attempt to regain for the route the commercial importance it had lost to Napoleon's great road through the Simplon, the next pass on the west. From June through the summer it was easily passable by carriage, but in winter and early spring only by one-horse sledges across the summit, and after a storm it was impassable for as much as a week.

124.32 *April 16*] Error for April 15; see the discussion at 124.18

124.34 Airolo] A small village at the entrance to the pass proper, thirty-six miles from Bellinzona, altitude, 3,794 feet. Mr. Abbott may be of the family M had met in Greece, but since M later calls him Dr. Abbott, he may be Dr. Henry Abbott (1812–59), English physician in Cairo, and close friend of the American consul Edwin De Leon, who spoke of him as a frequenter of Shepherd's Hotel, where M and Dr. Lockwood had stayed (De Leon, *Thirty Years*, I, 178–80). Dr. Abbott had earlier brought his notable collection of Egyptian antiquities to New York for exhibition and sale (eventually sold to the New-York Historical Society), but had returned to Cairo in 1855. (He is mentioned by other travelers in Egypt; Walt Whitman's newspaper account, "One of the Lessons Bordering Broadway; The Egyptian Museum" [1855], is reprinted in *New York Dissected*, ed. Emory Holloway and Ralph Adimari [New York: Rufus Rockwell Wilson, 1936], pp. 30–40; a portrait of Abbott in oriental dress faces p. 32.)

125.1 warehouse] Reached by twenty-eight switchbacks, the high point of the pass is nearly seven thousand feet above sea level; it is a saddle between eight-to-ten-thousand-foot peaks and a scene of sterile desolation. The main hospice, maintained by the canton, was a massive building with attached warehouses and fifteen beds; intermediate shelters mitigated the hazards of forty-foot drifts and numerous avalanches.

125.5 Andermatt] A small village at 4,450-foot elevation, eighteen miles from Airolo, its counterpart on the south side. From here the Reuss River cuts through a short, treeless plain and falls into the lower gorge by a great cataract; below, the Devil's Bridge spanned it amid the route's most sternly grand scenery. Goethe's *Autobiography*, which M bought in London in 1849 (see 144.30; Sealts 228), gives a highly colored description of this route to the summit, the limit of his youthful journey; M presumably also had read Bayard Taylor's rather overwrought account of walking through here to Italy, in *Views A-Foot* (chap. 30). Altorf (or Altdorf), legendary scene of Tell and the apple, thirty-three miles farther, is also a small village; then Fluelen is only two miles away, on the Bay of Uri, the southeast arm of Lake Lucerne. The Tellen-Platte, a narrow shelf between the precipice and the water with Tell's chapel, about a third of the distance along the east shore, marks the traditional spot of the patriot's escape from Gessler's boat.

125.7 April 17] Error for April 16; see the discussion at 124.18.

125.11 Thorswalden's lion] Carved in the sandstone bluff above the road to Zurich by Bertel Thorwaldsen (1768–1844); the famous monument commemorating the Swiss Guards who fell defending the Tuileries in 1792 was, when M saw it, still guarded by a red-uniformed old survivor. The three "Old Bridges" across the lake's outlet were notable, especially the Mill Bridge, with a famous though faded medieval painting of the Dance of Death.

125.13 *April 18*] Error for April 17; see the discussion at 124.18.

125.16 "The Crown."] A clean, comfortable, first-rate inn, according to Murray. The high, tree-shaded terrace behind the fifteenth-century Gothic minster afforded one of the best views of the towering peaks to the southeast, notably of the Jungfrau, the Finsteraarhorn, and the Aletschhorn, and also down into the gorge of the Aar River encircling the city on three sides.

125.18 *April 19th*] Error for April 18; see the discussion at 124.18.

125.19 Fay] Theodore Sedgwick Fay (1807–98), first U.S. Minister Resident to Switzerland (1853), was a popular essayist and novelist, and had been an associate of N. P. Willis; Poe's scathing review of his *Norman Leslie* (1835) opened the war between Poe and the New York literary establishment. (M's passport [in the Berkshire Athenaeum] bears Fay's visa for France and England, dated this day, April 18.)

125.20 Rail Road] The Berne-Basle line was completed except for a tunnel under the Ober-Hauenstein, finished the next year. From Soleure (or Solothurn) twenty-one miles north of Berne, a good new road wound up through a great cleft formerly so steep that wagons had to be hauled up and let down by rope and windlass. Among the old castles M could have seen were such well-known ones as Bipp, Blauenstein, and Falkenstein. The illustration above, by J. M. W. Turner, is from the title page to Volume XI of the *Works of Lord Byron*.

125.21 *April 20th*] Error for April 19; see the discussion at 124.18.

125.22 Smyth] Henry A. Smythe (b. 1817) had come to Europe in March; subsequently he founded the successful New York firm of Smythe, Sprague, & Cooper, and became president of the Central National Bank. From this casual encounter, after Smythe's appointment in 1866 by President Johnson as Collector of Customs for the Port of New York, came M's appointment by Smythe as inspector in November, 1866. See Harrison Hayford and Merrell R. Davis, "Herman Melville as Office-Seeker," *Modern Language Quarterly*, X (June–September, 1949), 168–83, 377–88, and especially p. 386, for a fuller account of Smythe's influence.

125.25 Saddle Back] An alternative name for Mt. Greylock, the highest peak in the Berkshires, visible from Arrowhead, M's Pittsfield residence.

125.27 L——] Liesthal, eight miles from Basle, where the new railroad awaited completion of its great tunnel (in which a collapse just a month later on May 28 killed sixty-three laborers).

125.27 "The Wild Man"] Le Sauvage, or Wilder Mann, on Freie Strasse near the marketplace, was a good, quiet commercial inn with moderate charges.

125.29 *April 21*] Error for April 20; see the discussion at 124.18.

125.30 Cathedral] The one completed spire of the two projected for the Strasbourg cathedral was the highest in Europe, 474 feet; admission, fifteen centimes. A series of detached arcades and pillars of very hard but delicately wrought stone gave the impression of a screen over the main structure. Among signatures inscribed in the spire's open stonework M could have seen Goethe's and Herder's. If his train was on time, just before noon, he could also have seen the famous clock, in the south transept, showing at noon not only the hour, day of the week and month, the year and epoch, but a complicated assemblage of puppets in motion.

125.34 Passports] Neither the French nor Baden inspectors were particularly strict, but it was advisable to have visas in order. Frequent omnibuses traversed the four miles between Strasbourg and Kehl; the French station was on an island in midstream, the German in Kehl.

125.34 Heidleburgh] Heidelberg; this "-burgh" ending (also at 126.1) occurs repeatedly in *Moby-Dick* (see the discussion at 339.2 in the NN edition).

126.2 Hotel Adler] In the marketplace, recommended as clean, comfortable, and moderate in its charges.

126.3 *April 22*] Error for April 21; see the discussion at 124.18.

126.3 Castle] The ancient residence of the Electors Palatine, high on a bluff above Heidelberg and the Neckar Valley, had been devastated by warring armies and finally by fire in 1764; what M saw was a vast assemblage of red stone, roofless walls, and towers. On the northeast corner was the Gesprengte Thurm (Cleft or Rent Tower), eighty-seven feet in diameter with walls twenty-one feet thick. It figures prominently in Longfellow's *Hyperion* (1839), of which later illustrated editions showed sketches of the tower with linden trees growing atop, where the grieving hero liked to sit (reproduced here from the 1853 Bogue edition). A vault below the castle held the great (49,000 gal.) Heidelberg Tun, celebrated in Chapter 77 of *Moby-Dick*, but not mentioned here.

THE RENT TOWER.

126.5 University] The oldest (1386) in Germany; when M saw it, best known for medicine and law, with some seven hundred students. It was housed in a plain building in the center of town.

126.11 Goethe's statue] Then in the Goethe Platz, a tree-shaded promenade adjoining the old Rossmarkt in the western part of Frankfurt; badly damaged in World War II, it was later moved to Taunus Park. It was described as a bronze figure holding a laurel wreath, with half-reliefs on its pedestal depicting allegories of his several interests and figures such as Faust from his literary works.

126.11–13 Cathedral . . . &c.] The Catholic Cathedral of St. Bartholomew, near the river, had a plain whitewashed interior but was the scene of the election and coronation of the Holy Roman Emperors. Just east of the church a bust of Luther marked the supposed house from which he addressed the crowd on his way to Worms. The Judengasse, an ancient narrow street northeast of the cathedral, still retained something of the filth and squalor of an enforced ghetto. Murray's guide to the *Continent* (1856)—i.e., north Germany and the Lowlands—commented that the Jews formed "no inconsiderable portion" of Frankfurt's population, other observers estimating as much as a tenth of the total. The birthplace of Meyer Anselm Bauer (Rothschild) was in the Judengasse, but though the small moneylending business which he had begun at the "Sign of the Red Shield" had expanded into the worldwide bank managed by his five sons, headquarters still remained in Frankfurt.

126.14 *Apl 23*] Error for April 22; see the discussion at 124.18.

126.18 Faust's statue] M may be referring again to the Goethe statue or to the as-yet-incomplete group in the adjacent Rossmarkt honoring Gutenberg, which had as a subordinate figure his creditor Fust, whose lawsuit confiscated his nearly complete Bible and left him penniless.

126.18 "Ariadne"] *Ariadne on the Panther.* M's "H——" seems to indicate uncertainty as to the sculptor's name, actually Johann Heinrich von Dannecker (1758–1841), a friend of Goethe's in Rome; it was his most popular statue, in the neoclassic mode of Canova. Murray called it "the great boast of Frankfurt" (*Continent*, p. 500). Moritz von Bethman had a special circular museum built for it on the grounds of his villa just outside the old northeast city gate. In Samuel S. Cox's description: "It represents her at the culminating point of her history, when deserted by Theseus. . . . She has been wedded to immortality in the person of the God of the Vineyard. She is seated upon the leopard of Bacchus, with proud and beautiful mien, conscious of the celestial ichor . . . in her veins!" (*A Buckeye Abroad* [New York: Putnam, 1852], pp. 334–35).

126.19–20 Wiesbaden] One of Germany's ranking spas, twenty-six miles west of Frankfurt; perhaps it interested M because of its social scene. Murray's *Continent* devoted several pages to its description and called it the most frequented of all German baths—twenty thousand visitors annually—though perhaps not the most aristocratic in the region. It was on a branch line of the railroad, and M evidently got off too soon.

126.20 Mayence] Mainz: M seems to follow Murray in using the French name. Anciently the chief Roman fortification of the Rhine, and later the seat of the ranking Elector of the Empire, its principal attraction now was its vast ninth- and tenth-century cathedral of red sandstone, much damaged and much repaired. Steamboats left frequently from the quay for Coblenz and Cologne.

126.22 Hock-land] Across from Mainz, the Main River enters the Rhine from the east; here the Rhine also turns west for several miles past the "Rheingau" to skirt the Taunus Hills. The south-facing slopes above both rivers produce the best of the Rhenish wines, improperly called "Hock" in England (according to Murray). True Hock comes from the vineyards below Hochheim, along the Main just east of the Rhine, the railroad route M had just traveled. M had sampled the famous wines of the Rheingau on his 1849 trip (see 36.19–20, 37.1, 37.23, and 38.11–17), but had come upriver only to Coblenz. Now he had the chance to see the best of Rhine scenery, especially the section where the river turns north again, cutting a deep gorge through the encroaching heights. The time downriver to Coblenz, five hours, gave him spring daylight for much or all of this section, though the weather was cold and rainy.

126.24–25 Hotel de Cologne] Close to the landing and familiar to M from his 1849 trip (see the entries for December 8 and 9, 35.18–20 and 35.36–36.2, and the discussion at 35.18).

126.26 *April 24th*] Error for April 23; see the discussion at 124.18.

126.27 Amsterdam] By way of Utrecht, about 140 miles along the right bank; Murray recommended the recently completed line since the lower Rhine was "a most uninteresting river" (p. 80). Near Utrecht, ice had broken the river dikes in 1855, flooding the railway and devastating large tracts of land.

126.32 "Old Bible"] Not listed by Murray, but a later Baedeker rated it "one star," patronized by English and American travelers (*Belgium and Holland* [Boston: Osgood, 1874]). It was in the center of town, on the Warmoestraat, a street at a right angle to the harbor, one of two with the finest shops.

127.1 Picture Gallery] The Trippenhuis, a collection almost exclusively of Dutch painters (now incorporated in the Rijksmuseum); open free Thursdays and Fridays, ten to three. Paul Potter's *Bear Hunt* (now at The Hague), a popular rarity with figures life-sized, was partly damaged by peeling. *The Keel Hauling*, by the seventeenth-century Lieve Verschuier, reputedly depicted the punishment of a surgeon who attempted to poison Admiral van Nes. The famous *Night Watch* of Rembrandt—more properly *The Company of Captain Frans Banning Cocq and Lieutenant Willem van Ruytenburch*—has more recently been cleaned and shown not to be a night scene; *The Syndics* depicted the sampling officials of the Drapers' Guild (both paintings have been on permanent loan from the city since 1818). If the painting M calls "Portrait of a painter & his wife" is the one formerly considered a self-portrait by Frans Hals, it had just been purchased (1851), but it is now known as *The Marriage of Isaac Abrahamsz Massa and Beatrix van der Laen*. Among a great number of Dutch genre paintings, none are identifiable as the specific ones M noted of peddlers and of household or tavern scenes. At least four paintings by Teniers the Younger were in the collection (besides a *Temptation of St. Anthony*, three others depicting soldiers at leisure in a guardroom, a bricklayer smoking, and an old beer drinker), and three landscapes by Brueghel the Elder. (M's poems "The Bench of Boors," in *Timoleon* [*Published Poems*, p. 278], and "At the Hostelry" [unpublished by M] show his interest in such paintings.)

127.9 "Plantation."] The "Plantaadje" and adjacent Zoological Gardens in Amsterdam's southeast quarter, at some distance from M's lodgings, and across many canals and bridges. The palace (formerly the Stadhuis, 1648–55), was in the city's center. Murray recommended its cupola as "the best place to obtain a tolerably correct idea of this wonderful city" and the flat landscape, east to Utrecht, west to Haarlem (*Continent*, p. 50).

127.12 Broeck] A few miles north of Amsterdam, a village of eight hundred—including many wealthy retired merchants—frequently celebrated as the world's cleanest village. M may have remembered Washington Irving's sketch "Broek; or, The Dutch Paradise" in *Wolfert's Roost* (1855).

127.13 galliot] See *Redburn* (chap. 35): "The Dutch galliot, an old-fashioned looking gentleman, with hollow waist, high prow and stern" (p. 174).

127.15 "Colonie"] Once a separate village at the north edge of Albany, seat of the great Rensselaer patroon, with mills, offices, and residences of his managers, gardeners, and other dependents. Its southern boundary, Patroon Street (now Clinton Avenue), is adjacent to Clinton Square, where M had lived (1834–38) at No. 3 with his widowed mother and her other children.

127.16–17 Dance Houses] Perhaps included in Murray's paragraph: "In the suburbs are many places of entertainment, with *Gardens*, not unlike the tea-gardens in England, except that some of them are frequented by the higher classes of citizens. . . . Here are found billiard and ball rooms, skittle-grounds, refreshments of various kinds, and much smoking" (*Continent*, p. 27).

127.18 decorum] Possibly "decorousness" (compressed).

Three of them. Striking & pathetic sight. The promenading girls — music — their reserve & decorum. — Villany of the guide. To bed by 9 1/2.

127.20 cathedral] The Groot Kerk, a brick structure of the fifteenth century, notable for its splendid new (1840) organ, rivaled only by that at Haarlem. (M's parenthetical reference to the Amsterdam church seems to be to the Nieuwe Kerk—as distinct from the Oud or Old—next the palace, with its chief feature a great sounding board and the pulpit carved by Albert

Vincken Brinck in 1649.) Murray recommended the Rotterdam view from the tower over the flat, watery countryside. The house in which Erasmus was born (1467), on the street leading to the church, had become a gin shop, though bearing a small statue of the scholar and a Latin inscription.

127.23 steamer for London] Rotterdam is inland some twenty-five miles on the Maas estuary; steamers to and from London plied every Wednesday and Saturday, taking twenty-four to thirty hours.

127.26 *Monday*] Error for Sunday; see the discussion at 124.18.

127.27–28 "Great Eastern"] The steamer, at this time nearly completed in the yards on the Isle of Dogs, Millwall, was Isambard Kingdom Brunel's most ambitious project (629 ft. long, 19,000 tons), so huge that she had to be launched sideways in January of 1858, more than two years late. M's pessimistic prediction below proved right: no available steam engine could drive her efficiently; after money-losing years on the North Atlantic, she was converted into a cable-layer, then a floating billboard and amusement hall, and then scrap (1887).

127.28–29 Tavistock Hotel] In Covent Garden, described by Murray's writer (and M's dinner acquaintance) Peter Cunningham, as one of the less expensive ones, frequented chiefly by bachelors (*London in 1856* [London: Murray, [1856]], p. xxxvi). M had known the general address from his previous trip to London: John Miller, the dispatch agent for the American legation who had handled M's earlier manuscripts when Gansevoort was trying to place them, had a Tavistock address (see 45.17 and accompanying discussion). For the pall of Victorian Sundays in London, see the entry for November 18, 1849, the discussion at 21.6, and *Clarel*, 2.5.25–26 ("dumpish days, like Sundays dull . . . in London").

127.31 Longman's] The Longman firm in Paternoster Row (to which M had offered *White-Jacket* in 1849—see 21.26 and accompanying discussion). They had just published *The Confidence-Man* (probably on April 3), the contract for which Hawthorne had signed as M's agent on March 20, though neither Hawthorne nor M mentions the matter in known surviving documents. This cryptic note, however, reveals M's awareness of the transaction, and on this visit he probably secured one or more copies of the book in their edition.

127.32 Madam Tussaud's] The famous Waxworks museum of Madame Tussaud (1761–1850), in the Baker Street Bazaar, Portman Square; admission, one shilling, plus sixpence for the Chamber of Horrors. The representations of the Mannings, whom he saw hanged at the time of his earlier visit (see 17.18–19 and accompanying discussion), may have intrigued him.

127.33 *Thursday, Friday & Saturday*] Errors for Wednesday, Thursday, and Friday; see the discussion at 124.18.

127.34 "Cock"] For M's visits to this famous tavern in 1849 see 19.31–33 and accompanying discussion and 41.18–19.

128.1 Chrystal Palace] The original Crystal Palace from the 1851 exhibition had been reconstructed (with modifications) in 1853–54 at Sydenham, a south London suburb beyond Dulwich; enough of its original exhibits remained on display to justify M's remark "digest of universe." His disparagement of its glass architecture is repeated in his lecture "Statues in Rome," where he contrasts its durability to that of the Coliseum (see the NN *Piazza Tales* volume, p. 409). Trains to it left from London Bridge and took twenty minutes; round trip (including admission), two shillings for second class, or one and sixpence for third class (three times higher on Saturdays); open from ten to sunset. The Alhambra Court simulated the Court of Lions and two other parts of the Moorish-Spanish original. The Pompeian Court, though only a generalized Pompeian house, apparently reminded M of the House of Pansa, which he had presumably seen in February though he did not mention it in his journal. (He had mentioned both the Alhambra and the House of Pansa in earlier works; see *Mardi*, chap. 75, p. 229, and *Redburn*, chap. 46, p. 230.) The Egyptian Court suggested a generalized temple; it displayed a scaled-down model of the temple at "Aboo Simbel" with two statues of Ramses the Great on that temple's facade. Some distance away at the end of the north transept of the palace were full-scale figures from the temple of Ramses, "towering to the roof of the Transept" (Samuel Phillips, *Guide to the Crystal Palace and Park* [London: Bradbury & Evans, 1856], p. 151). The palace terrace commanded an extensive view over the gardens, the Surrey-Kent countryside, and north over the city. The illustration here is from the frontispiece to Volume II of *Tallis's Illustrated London*.

128.7 Thames Tunnel] The visits to the tunnel (shown on p. 278 above), suburban Richmond, and Hyde Park repeat excursions M had made in 1849 (see the entries for November 10 and 11 and the discussions at 15.37, 16.9, and 16.12).

128.10 Vernon & Turner galleries] Both collections were at this time housed in the National Gallery on Trafalgar Square; the former (given in 1847 by Robert Vernon), which M had visited in 1849 (see 43.1 and accompanying discussion), included some 160 examples of English painters, especially Hogarth, Reynolds, Gainsborough, Constable, Turner, and Landseer, while the remainder of the Turners were the artist's bequest (1851) to the nation. Turner's *The Fighting Temeraire* inspired M's poem "The Temeraire" in *Battle-Pieces*, as his note to it says (*Published Poems*, pp. 41–43, 174).

128.13 *May 2[d]*] Error for May 3; see the discussion at 124.18.

128.13 for Oxford] M visited Windsor Castle, nineteen miles from London, in November of 1849 (see the entry for November 22 and the discussion at 24.21); the route of the London and Great Western Railway up the Thames Valley passed some miles east of it on the other side of the river. The account of Oxford here is apparently a development or rewriting of hasty jottings made originally in a pocket notebook—see 156.3. The pulpit M noticed is in St. John's Quadrangle of Magdalen College, whose deer park adjoins on the north and east.

128.29 Fell's avenue] The elm-lined Broad Walk across Christ Church Meadow along the Thames, laid out by Dean Fell in 1670.

128.33 Stair case] In the fan-vaulted entrance leading to Christ Church's great hall. The Paris chapel with a single central pillar is that of the Hôtel de Cluny, which M saw in 1849; see the discussion at 33.19.

129.2–3 Knights . . . gentleman] This comparison is modified in the characterization of Derwent, *Clarel*, 2.1.29–33:

> A priest he was—though but in part;
> For as the Templar old combined
> The cavalier and monk in one;
> In Derwent likewise might you find
> The secular and cleric tone.

129.6 "Mitre"] On High Street; listed, like all the inns, as bad but expensive.

129.7 *May 3^d*] Error for May 4; see the discussion at 124.18.

129.8 "Red Horse."] Washington Irving's lodging where, by his own account, he wrote the *Sketch Book* chapter on Stratford. "Geoffrey Crayon's" chair and poker were still shown.

129.8–9 Shakspere's home] On this spelling, see the discussion at 43.6. The birthplace, purchased in 1847 by subscription, was currently being repaired and restored, but autographs, including those of Kean, Scott, Thackeray, Dickens, Carlyle, Byron, and Tennyson, still adorned its walls, ceilings, and windowpanes. Of New Place, the big house Shakespeare purchased upon his retirement and died in, only the foundations remained. In *Clarel* (4.7.53–65) Rolfe and Derwent discuss the way "Shakespeare's house in Stratford town" is "Set . . . apart in reverence due: / A shrine to which the pilgrim's won."

129.14 Edge Hill] If M's stage followed the left bank of the Avon instead of the direct route, he would have passed Charlecote Park (where according to legend Shakespeare was caught poaching). There Charles I and his army encamped the night before the battle of Edge Hill (October 23, 1642), about ten miles to the southeast, the first battle of the civil war. The imposing fourteenth-century Warwick Castle, which withstood the Royalist forces in 1642, overlooks the Avon in the south part of the town.

129.18 Parthenon] The new City Hall (1834–50), with forty Corinthian columns, was modeled on the Temple of Jupiter Stator in Rome, not the Parthenon.

129.19 *May 4th*] Error for May 5; see the discussion at 124.18.

129.20 burnt district] Henry Adams remembered his youthful passage through this Black District in late 1858, from Liverpool to London by way of Birmingham: "The plunge into darkness lurid with flames; the sense of unknown horror in this weird gloom which then existed nowhere else, and never had existed before, except in volcanic craters; the violent contrast between this dense, smoky, impenetrable darkness, and the soft green charm that one glided into, as one emerged—the revelation of an unknown society of the pit—made a boy uncomfortable, though he had no idea that Karl Marx was standing there waiting for him" (*Education*, chap. 5, p. 72).

129.22–23 "City of Manchester"] An iron screw-steamer, 2,109 tons, Captain P. C. Petrie; it departed on May 6 and arrived off Sandy Hook on May 19 in late evening. Its first-class passengers, including "Mr. Melville," are listed in the *New-York Times*, May 21, 1857.

129.23–24 Brown . . . Co.] The highly prosperous mercantile firm of transplanted Americans, agent in Liverpool for the New-York and Liverpool United States Mail Steamers.

129.24 saw Hawthorne] This was their last known meeting. Hawthorne's notebooks do not record it; between April 19 and May 10 there is no entry. For Mr. Bright, see 51.14 and accompanying discussion. M had left his trunk at the consulate (see the discussion at 51.19).

129.25 *"Grecian"*] There was a Liverpool hotel with this name, but the entry may refer to a sister-ship of the *Egyptian*, in which M had sailed to Constantinople.

129.26 *May 5th*] Error for May 6; see the discussion at 124.18.

JOURNAL 1860

131.6 Tom . . . Griggs] Tom was Captain Thomas Melville (1830–84), youngest of M's three brothers (see p. 197). Fanny was their youngest sister, Frances Priscilla (1827–85), who lived with their mother in Gansevoort, New York, but may have been in Boston to see Tom. George Griggs was the husband (m. 1854) of their older sister Helen Maria (1817–88). M's granddaughter characterizes him at a later date as a "gruff, parsimonious husband" (Metcalf, *Herman Melville*, p. 214). Mr. S. Endicott Peabody, of the Boston firm of [Francis] Curtis & Peabody, 40 India Wharf, was an owner of the *Meteor;* he lived in Salem.

131.16 this] No noun follows.

132.1 *June 11th Saturday*] Since Saturday did not fall on June 11 (but on the ninth) in 1860, either the date or the weekday is incorrect. More likely M mistook the date not the day, and the correct date was June 9. Likewise, he misdated the next three entries: presumably he wrote June 12 for 10, June 20 for 18, and June 27 for 25. (This day the ship was some fourteen hundred miles east of Bermuda.)

132.5 an English brig] The *Elizabeth Baxter*, according to Leyda (*Log*, II, 619 [June 9, 1860]).

132.18 *June 12th*] Error for June 10.

132.20 *June 20th*] Error for June 18.

132.25 "Quarterlies"] Perhaps M means "Quarterlies" literally, i.e., such ones as the *Quarterly Review* or the *North American Review*, though more likely he means magazines in general, including monthlies like *Harper's*, to which he had subscribed until the spring of 1859 (Sealts 240). In his letter to Evert Duyckinck written aboard ship just before sailing (May 28, quoted on p. 635 below), M added at the end, "I have a good lot of books with me—such as they are;—plenty of old periodicals—lazy reading for lazy latitudes" (*Letters*, p. 200).

133.3 A comet] A contemporary astronomer, George F. Chambers, briefly described a comet of "considerable brilliancy" that suddenly appeared in the north on June 19, 1860, and was visible for eight weeks (*Descriptive Astronomy* [Oxford: Clarendon Press, 1867], pp. 297, 432; plate XIV, p. [295], illustrates it with drawings made in Rome). It was named the "Great Comet," catalogue number "1860 III," and was visible in both hemispheres. (This day the ship was about 350 miles off the central Brazilian coast, nearly 700 miles east-northeast of Rio de Janeiro.)

133.10 *Sunday July 21*] Again the date and weekday do not match, and the correct date was July 22. This day, the ship was about 750 miles northeast of the Falkland Islands, headed for the Straits of Le Maire, between Tierra del Fuego and Staten Island. The next entry, too, is incorrectly dated: August 8 for the correct 6 (a Monday—note the correctly dated entry August 7 for the following Tuesday).

Although M does not mention it, in the preceding days or weeks he had been reading Hawthorne's recent book *The Marble Faun* (1860); it had been given him by his Pittsfield neighbor Sarah Morewood, probably in May just before he left, though he misleadingly wrote in it "Pittsfield. June" (Sealts 534). That he had been reading it for some time is indicated by a marginal notation in Volume II, early in Chapter 9: "(Lat. 41° South Atlantic)".

133.11 haglets] A small species of sea gull; a kittiwake. M wrote at some unknown time a poem "The Haglets" (in *John Marr and Other Sailors* [1888; *Published Poems*, pp. 218–25]) based on an earlier, much shorter poem left in manuscript, "The Admiral of the White," which turns on a story he heard on his Mediterranean trip: a ship's compass fatally deflected by the steel in a store of arms (see the discussion at 56.9–10). This earlier version involves only English and French combatants, with no mention of birds. ESM's penciled annotation on the manuscript leaf reports, "Herman gave this to Tom."—i.e., Thomas Melville. In "The Haglets" the instrumentality of the compass is obscured but still present, while the conflict is between the English and the great Spanish Plate Fleet transporting its cargo of American gold and silver across these Atlantic waters, and the birds appear as prominently ominous portents of disaster (as well, the concluding stanza is an elaborate allusion to meteors). W. H. Shurr gives an account of the poems, including two newspaper versions published simultaneously in 1885 and the final version of 1888 (*The Mystery of Iniquity* [Lexington: University Press of Kentucky, 1972], pp. 130–31). Whether M was working on any of these poems on this voyage is not known, but that he was thinking of some of his poems then is indicated by a letter to Tom two years later (May 25, 1862): "You remember the romantic moonlight night, when the conceited donkey repeated to you about three cables' length of his verses" (see p. 645).

133.12 hard] If the curved stroke before the *h* is not superfluous but an *s*, the intended word may be "sharp" (miswritten "shard").

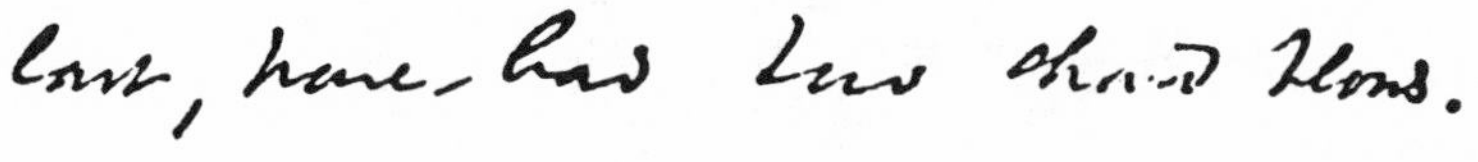

133.15 *Aug 8*] Error for August 6.

133.16 gales] On M's forty-first birthday, August 1, the ship had crossed 50 degrees south, beyond which the most fiercely persistent gales could be expected. In M's long letter to his son Malcolm, from the Pacific side, he said they had had "forty or fifty" days of such weather (see below, p. 636). The first gale of three days, according to the report on the *Meteor* in the San Francisco *Daily Evening Bulletin*, sprang up suddenly on August 2, just after they had crossed 50 degrees (*Log*, II, 621 [Aug. 1]).

133.32 "Black Prince"] A new ship (1856), of almost the same tonnage as the *Meteor*, owned by the Boston firm of Bush & Wildes. It once rivaled the *Meteor* in a record run of thirty-eight days from San Francisco to Hong Kong, but generally it had bad luck. On this passage under Captain Charles H. Brown it had left New York five days before the *Meteor* left Boston, but it arrived in San Francisco seven days later, having lost its jibboom, cutwater, and figurehead. Yet this was its fastest run on this route. It once had a mutiny, and in 1865 it disappeared in the North Atlantic with all its crew (Octavius T. Howe and Frederick C. Matthews, *American Clipper Ships, 1835–1858*, 2 vols. [Salem: Marine Research Society, 1926–27], I, 42–43; Carl C. Cutler, *Greyhounds of the Sea* [New York: Putnam's, 1930], pp. 444, 505, 510, 518).

The unnamed one of the "two ships" M mentions above was presumably the *Derby*, whose name he noted inside the front cover of *The Iliads of Homer*, vol. II (Sealts 277): "Cape Horn. 2. 'Meteor' & 'Derby' ". The *Derby* was a medium clipper, about the same size as the *Meteor* and *Black Prince*, launched in 1855 for an association of Salem owners. Under a Captain Hutchinson, she had an even worse time than the *Black Prince*; she had left New York still earlier, May 15, and did not reach San Francisco until October 19, 155 days later.

134.4 Cape Horn] M's letter to Malcolm described this passage and, in some detail, the fatal accident the next morning. See below, pp. 635–36. In *Clarel* (3.29.9–23) M describes Rolfe far below the others at Mar Saba:

> Far down see Rolfe there, hidden low
> By ledges slant. Small does he show
> (If eagles eye), small and far off
> As Mother-Cary's bird in den
> Of Cape Horn's hollowing billow-trough,
> When from the rail where lashed they bide
> The sweep of overcurling tide,—
> Down, down, in bonds the seamen gaze
> Upon that flutterer in glen
> Of waters where it sheltered plays,
> While, over it, each briny hight
> Is torn with bubbling torrents white
> In slant foam tumbling from the snow
> Upon the crest; and far as eye
> Can range through mist and scud which fly,
> Peak behind peak the liquid summits grow.

M's 1860 passage of Cape Horn was his most likely source of these vivid lines, though he had made two previous passages (1841, 1844), both reported in *White-Jacket* (chap. 28, p. 116; chap. 26, pp. 104–9). In *Mardi* M gave a description of his fictional characters' east-to-west rounding of the "Stormy Cape of Capes" (chap. 165, pp. 543–44), followed by a lurid account of San Francisco and its disillusioned starving gold-hunters (chap. 166, pp. 545–48). See also *Clarel*, 1.21.14–15.

134.11 Ray] Ray's first name was "Benjamin," and in his letter to Malcolm M wrote that the accident had happened off "the very *pitch* of the Cape," just after Tom had had to order the topsails furled in a gale of sleet and hail. After describing the brief prayer service and burial, M added that Ray and Fisher had meant to settle in California (pp. 635–36, below). ("Fisher" is a later correction: it was inserted above the line, and the wet ink blotted across on the next page.)

134.25–26 Russia caps] M described to his son Malcolm the one he himself wore, "a very thick leather cap, so called by sailors" (p. 635, below).

135.3 heart] Possibly "head".

MISCELLANEOUS ENTRIES

139.1–20 *Allan* . . . 60] Erasures make most of the entries on this paste-down unusually problematic (see also the following discussion). As a consequence the following words are all uncertain readings: in line 1, *"Mama"*; 2, "Mal"; 3, "Change" and "Stan"; 5, "(Albany"; 10, "For Mama"; 13, "Carriage"; 15, "from Albany"; 18, "fare"; and 19, "Ferry". Many, if not all of the entries, appear to fall between the time M moved his family back to New York City in 1863—particularly after his brother Thomas's appointment in 1867 as governor of Sailors' Snug Harbor, Staten Island—and the deaths of his mother and brother Allan, both in 1872. But also, if the names at the upper right edge are indeed "Mal" and "Stan" (for his sons Malcolm and Stanwix), they at least would seem to have been written before Malcolm's death in 1867. "Greenwood" is possibly the fashionable cemetery in Brooklyn. "Augusta" is M's next younger, unmarried sister (1821–76). "Lathers" is no doubt Richard Lathers (1820–1903), the wealthy brother-in-law of Allan Melville's first wife; at the time of Malcolm's death, Lathers was his employer at the Atlantic & Great Western Insurance Company. See the discussion at 37.24.

140.3 Gabriel] Because of the erasures on this page, the conjectured G is not visible and "North" (line 5) and "laundry" (line 15) are uncertain readings.

140.7 Edinburgh] After leaving Glasgow in late October or early November, 1856, M went on to Edinburgh where he spent "five days, I think" before going to Liverpool (letter to his brother Allan, written in Liverpool, November 10–14, 1856; see p. 625, below).

141.1–7 Captain . . . Mate] Officers and ships of M's 1849–50 trip to Europe and back—see the discussions at 3.6, 10.33, and 42.27.

141.6 the Colonel] In M's letter (November 10–14, 1856) to his brother Allan from Liverpool (pp. 624–25), he mentioned "an officer" who had "interested me considerably," a "good deal of a philosopher" who had been all over the world, including service with native troops in India. On a passenger list of the *Glasgow* is "G. C. Rankin" from Toronto (*New York Journal of Commerce*, October 15, 1856). This was George Campbell Rankin (1801–80), who had been surgeon with the Twenty-fifth Regiment of Native Infantry, at the end of 1849 stationed at Hajipur, the Punjab. (M added this address, in pencil, at the end of the list of English addresses from the 1849 trip to London; 148.28–29.) Rankin's stations had also included China and Canada, but in 1852 he had retired and settled in London. (A London address, East India United Service Club, 14 St. James's Square, is the last item at the end of the 1856–57 journal—159.12–14; this may imply that M looked him up when he returned to London at the end of April, 1857.) Under only the initials G. R., his book, *What Is Truth? or, Revelation Its Own Nemesis*, was originally published in London in 1854 and in an enlarged second edition in 1856, both issued by John Chapman. The nature of the book and of Rankin's interest for M is indicated in the prefatory note to the first edition: "Its internal discrepancies, and unpropitious results, seeming clearly to indicate that Christianity, at least, is not Truth; the following casually preserved fragments of desultory correspondence on the subject, may, it is hoped, from their very lameness, provoke abler intelligences and defter pens to take up, on behalf of betrayed humanity, the cause of natural religion against conventional usurpation." It is heavily and sarcastically anticlerical in an elaborately learned style, with much quoting from Latin, French, Arabic, Italian, and other works, church commentators, ecclesiastics, writers including Dante, Goethe, Locke, and Dickens, with references to Indian mythology and digressions on the rights of women, sexual freedom, and the evils of laissez-faire enterprise.

141.8 fixed fate &c.] The phrase is from the discourse of the fallen angels, *Paradise Lost*, II, 555–61. The notation shows that on this 1856 crossing M fell in with a congenial companion for such conversations, as he had with Adler on the 1849 crossing, and would take Hawthorne to be on the Southport sands (see the preceding discussion and the one at 4.34–35; also Hawthorne's journal entry, pp. 627–33 below).

141.10–12 The . . . shame."] It is unclear what the allusion to "The Perjurer" refers to. The source of the quotation is Ben Jonson's *Every Man out of His Humour*, to which M makes penciled allusions two pages later (he had bought the 1692 folio in London—see 18.11–12 and 144.3); in V, x the vain wife quotes these lines to the affected courtier after attributing them to Lyly's Euphues. Actually, they are an adaptation of the opening lines of the letter that Philautus, Euphues's sometime friend, writes to his newest passion, Camilla, in *Euphues and His England* (1580): "Hard is the choice, fair lady, when one is compelled either by silence to die with grief or by writing to live with shame" (quoted here from *Euphues: The Anatomy of Wit; Euphues*

& his England, by John Lyly, ed. Morris Croll and Harry Clemons [London: Routledge, 1916], p. 340).

142.13 "crocodile"] In De Quincey's *Confessions of an English Opium-Eater* (see 46.11–13 and accompanying discussion), the short original version concludes with the section, "The Pains of Opium"; in it De Quincey recounts his horrible fantasies and dreams: under the notation "*May* 1818," he describes the throngs of tropical, oriental, and Egyptian images haunting him, notably being "kissed, with cancerous kisses, by crocodiles," and again, "the main agents were ugly birds, or snakes, or crocodiles; especially the last, . . . the object of more horror than almost all the rest. . . . All the feet of the tables, sofas, &c. soon became instinct with life: the abominable head of the crocodile, and his leering eyes, looked out at me, multiplied into a thousand repetitions" (pp. 171–73).

142.15 Rousseau] M bought the *Confessions* in London; see 40.20 and accompanying discussion and 144.15. (When Rousseau was a tutor in the family of M. de Mably, his mood varied from enthusiasm to murderous rage according to the children's behavior.)

142.17 Dr Johnson] For M's purchase of Boswell's *Johnson*, see 44.14 and accompanying discussion and 144.7. As "usher" (i.e., assistant teacher) in a school at Market Bosworth, Johnson felt he was treated with "intolerable" harshness by his patron. On p. 220 of the third volume, Goldsmith has been telling his dinner companions about his living with a farmer to avoid distraction while he wrote his *Natural History*; the farmer's family thought him eccentric, a "Gentleman." Thereafter, on this page, the conversation turns to ghosts. Perhaps Boswell's interjected allusion to W. J. Mickle, a translator (1776) of Camoëns's *Lusiads* (1572), caught M's attention; in *White-Jacket*, Jack Chase declaims from his translation and shows knowledge of his life (chap. 65, p. 270, also chaps. 74 and 93).

142.27 "Vulgar Errors"] At the same time he bought the Boswell, M bought the 1686 folio of *The Works of the Learned Sr Thomas Brown, Kt.* [ed. Archbishop Tenison] for sixteen shillings (see 44.13 and accompanying discussion and 144.8). In this collection, "Enquiries into Vulgar and Common Errors" comes first, and on p. 17 (in bk. 1, chap. 6) there is the printed marginal note "Eating of Man's Flesh" (most of the marginal notes were not originally Browne's, however). What this note refers to is not cannibalism but the ancient myths of Actaeon eaten by his dogs and of Diomedes by his horses, which among other fables Browne is explaining away on rational, skeptical grounds as examples of the ways such myths perpetuate "vulgar" misunderstanding. It is possible, too, that M is remembering Montaigne's famous essay on cannibals; he, or his brother Allan, had bought an edition of Montaigne in 1848, probably the *Complete Works*, edited by William Hazlitt (London: Templeman, 1842 or 1845; Sealts 366, Bercaw 502).

142.35 Jonson] For M's purchase of the 1692 folio *Works* see 18.11–12 and accompanying discussion and 144.3. In this folio, pp. 25–60 are occupied by the satiric comedy *Every Man out of His Humour*, displaying absurd character behavior and affectations. All three passages on pp. 51, 54, and 57 that M cites are marked in the margins of his copy now at the New-York Historical Society. In V, v, in a dispute over the merits of pork, the scurrilous jester, Carlo Buffone, responds to the envious scholar, Macilente, "Marry, I say, nothing resembling Man more than Swine, it follows, nothing can be more nourishing: for indeed (but that it abhors from our nice Nature) if we fed upon one another, we should shoot up a great deal faster, and thrive much better: I refer me to your usurous *Cannibals*, or such like: but since it is so contrary, Pork, Pork, is your only feed."

The reference to "clothes" comes from IV, vi, where the affected courtier, Fastidius Brisk, gives a long account of a duel he fought, an account mostly occupied by a description of various parts of his extravagant apparel slashed or pierced in the rapier exchanges before his opponent fled. The quotation about "folly" is a loose paraphrase of the envious scholar, Macilente, to the would-be gentleman, Sogliardo, tricking him into making a fool of himself before a lady at court: ". . . you must talk forward (though it be without sense, so it be without blushing) 'tis most Court-like, and well" (V, i).

144.1 Books . . . London] Those mentioned in the daily entries of the main text, obtained in Paris and Cologne as well as London, have been noted there (see the discussions at 18.11, 20.28, 23.3, 24.6, 40.21, 43.6,15–16,18–19, 44.13,14,33, 46.12, and 47.18); Sealts, *Melville's Reading*, gives all the rest of the known information. The four century dates were inserted later in pencil. Eleanor Melville Metcalf thought M gave his mother in January, 1850, one of the copies of the English edition of *Redburn* (EMM, p. 172); it is now in the Berg Collection of the New York Public Library. The other, she thought, M gave to his friend and sometimes family doctor, Dr. Augustus Kinsley Gardner; his accompanying letter (February 4 or 11, 1850) reads: "Will you do me the favor to accept the accompanying set of 'Redburn' as a slight token of my having remembered you while away. — I lodged with Madame Capelle in Paris & will tell you what I saw in that gay city, when I am so happy as to see you again" (*Letters*, p. 105). M gave one copy of the English edition of *Mardi* to his brother Allan, another to Evert Duyckinck (see M's letter of February 2, 1850 [*Log*, I, 364; *Letters*, pp. 101–2]).

146.13 Medal] Either this medal (for 5 or .5 francs) or the one listed in the next line (for 1 franc) was probably sent to George Duyckinck, enclosed with the letter (February 2, 1850) to Evert accompanying the gifts of his own *Mardi* and Samuel Butler's *Hudibras:* "It comes from a mountainous defile of a narrow street in the Latin Quarter of Paris, where I disinterred it from an old antiquary's cellar" (*Letters*, p. 103). One of the Cologne stoppers was meant for Evert—see the discussion at 38.20. And in Cologne, M seems to have bought one or more other medals; he sent one to his wife's half-brother Lemuel Shaw, Jr. (see *Letters*, p. 104 [No. 72], and the discussion at 35.26–27).

147.1–9 *Root . . . Marett*] This list of names may be connected with the renewed attempt in 1861 to secure a consulship for M from the new Republican administration in Washington. Excepting the two names with addresses, all were Pittsfield neighbors, and three (Campbell, Colt, and Rockwell) were among those signing a joint letter (March 14) to Lincoln recommending M. In addition, Rockwell wrote a separate letter (March 25) to Senator Sumner, claiming acquaintance with Lincoln and calling M "my neighbor & friend" (*Log*, II, 634, 638).

Julius S. Rockwell (1805–88) had an eminent public career—in the state legislature, in the House of Representatives, and as the appointed successor to Edward Everett in the Senate; he had been appointed to the superior court in 1859. There are two known letters from M to Rockwell, the first dated March 20, 1861, requesting his support, and the second, from Washington, March 27, thanking him and Colt as well as other signers of the petition (*Log*, II, 1969 issue, 944–45).

James D. Colt (b. 1819; since James D. Colt, Jr., was this Colt's grandfather, "Jr." seems to be a slip on M's part), a nephew of Dr. Campbell (see below), had studied law with Rockwell and then entered into partnership with him (in the manuscript, the word "Lawyer" has been canceled before the firm name); he also served in the legislature and in 1865 was appointed a justice of the supreme judicial court.

Dr. Robert Campbell (1796–1866), a physician, was described by J. E. A. Smith, Pittsfield historian, M's acquaintance and biographer, as unexcelled in "mental power or in liberal culture," an "excellent connoisseur in the fine arts," and a man of the highest personal and professional integrity.

Dr. Oliver S. Root (1799–1870) was the physician who attended M when he broke his shoulder in a wagon accident moving furniture into Pittsfield in November, 1862.

George S. Willis (b. 1810) was a neighbor—the one who after that accident helped M into his nearby farm home; it was Willis who in 1856 bought the western half of M's farm (*Log*, II, 655 [Nov. 7, 1862], 516 [June 28, 1856]; J. E. A. Smith, *The History of Pittsfield* [Springfield, Mass.: Bryan, 1876], pp. 595–96, 411–12, 352–53).

The Reverend George R. Entler's known connection to M is less close—but he was in the party with M in the noisy expedition to the top of Greylock in August of 1851 (*Log*, I, 423–25 [Aug. 11]). Philip Marett was married to Elizabeth Shaw Melville's maternal aunt; as a junior officer of the New England Bank, Boston, he had been involved in the settlement of the will of M's grandfather, Major Thomas Melvill; later as president of the bank he misused its funds and resigned (*Log*, I, 57 [Nov. 8, 1842], 245 [May 22, 1847]). Marett's fortune nevertheless ultimately benefited Elizabeth and Herman through generous bequests from both Mrs. Marett in 1878 and their daughter Ellen Marett Gifford in 1889 (*Log*, II, 769 [Sept. 13, 1879], 823 [March 5, 1890]).

148.1–28 *Tupper* . . . Rankin] All individuals named on this list are mentioned at one or more points in the journals and in the discussions. See the index.

150.6 Sn] Possibly "Sw".

150.8 Jock] Possibly "luck" (H). M's *J* often resembles his initial *l*. Compare the initial letter of this word (in line 1) and the *J* in "Jugglers" (in line 12) in the reproduction of manuscript page C43 on p. 151.

150.18 Taylor's offer] This may be the Taylor, an English engineer, who operated the sultan's mint—perhaps M met him at the hotel. Or more likely, perhaps, it is Dr. Franklin Taylor, cousin of Bayard Taylor and M's fellow passenger on the ship to England in 1849 when M enthusiastically sketched plans with him to go on to the Levant (see the discussion at 4.18). In London, Taylor may have offered himself as a guide ("cicerone") to two ladies on a European tour; see 17.30–33 and accompanying discussion.

152.5 Sanders] Charles Saunders, the American missionary in Jaffa; see 81.6–7 and accompanying discussion.

153.3–6 Pera . . . knaves] From the years immediately preceding the Crimean War, there is this contemporary diplomat's account: "Constantinople has, of late years, become a theatre of incessant intrigue between the leading states of Europe, through their envoys at that capital. The Ottoman cabinet is always constructed in a French, Russian, or English sense; and is swayed by the outside influences of the representatives of those powers" (Alfred de Bessé, *The Turkish Empire*, trans. from the German by Edward J. Morris [Philadelphia: Lindsay & Blakiston, 1854], p. 22).

153.12 (Inscription . . . Cheops)] Herodotus wrote about the Great Pyramid: "Upon the outside were inscribed, in Egyptian characters, the various sums of money expended in the process of the work, for the radishes, onions, and garlic consumed by the artificers." Murray's *Egypt* quotes Herodotus (e.g., p. 174, 1847 edition); as well, M in 1849 had bought the thirty-seven volumes of Harper's Classical Library, including the Reverend William Beloe's translation of Herodotus (Sealts 147).

153.13 the "Bible"] M's inn in Amsterdam; see 126.32–33 and accompanying discussion.

154.1–16 Frescoes . . . *Nant.*] The variety of the media and handwritings on this page suggests jottings for different uses at different times, possibly from the late 1850's when M was preparing lectures and writing poetry, to the early 1870's when he was working on *Clarel*. See the HISTORICAL NOTE, pp. 189–90.

154.4 Haydon] Doubtless Benjamin Robert Haydon (1786–1846), the English historical painter. In 1854 M bought the posthumously published *Life . . . from His Autobiography and Journals*, 2 vols. (New York: Harper, 1853; Sealts 262), whose editor, Tom Taylor, M had met in London in 1849 (see 24.9–10 and accompanying discussion). Leyda (*Log*, I, 486 [April 7, 1854]) points out that M used a passage from this work (I, 54–55) in *Israel Potter* (chap. 23, p. 157). M also sooner or later owned *Painting and the Fine Arts* (Edinburgh: Black, 1838), reprinted from the articles Haydon and William Hazlitt had contributed to the seventh edition of the *Encyclopædia Britannica* (Sealts 263).

154.6 J. C. . . . Taheiti] In *Clarel*, 4.18.39–45, Rolfe, talking with Vine, Ungar, and Derwent on a hillside above Bethlehem, finds his thoughts wandering to Tahiti,

> That vine-wreathed urn of Ver, in sea
> Of halcyons, where no tides do flow
> Or ebb, but waves bide peacefully
> At brim, by beach where palm trees grow
> That sheltered Omai's olive race—
> Tahiti should have been the place
> For Christ in advent.

154.11–13 Spinoza . . . (Note)] These penciled jottings appear to be developing associations: of eminent Jews, memory of the Rothschild countinghouse M had seen in Frankfurt (with its casks and bales, 126.12–17), the depositories in Constantinople mosques he had remarked (66.10–12); his wry recollection of the verse "Lay not up for yourselves treasures upon earth" (Matthew 6:19); and the passage he cites here in Maccabees (see the following discussion) describing a similar safekeeping practice in the Jerusalem Temple.

A. P. Stanley's *Sinai and Palestine* (which M bought in 1870) further associates Maccabees, Temple, and grapes in remarking, "The 'vine' was the emblem of the nation on the coins of the Maccabees, and in the colossal cluster of golden grapes which overhung the porch of the second Temple" ([New York: Redfield, 1857], pp. 162–63; Sealts 488). Stanley's calling Judah the "true climate of the vine" is then echoed by the young Lyonese (*Clarel*, 4.26.153–65) in calling Judah "The true wine-zone of Noah" with which "agrees / The ducat of the Maccabees." The postdiluvian scene in Genesis where the drunken Noah shames his sons and curses Canaan seems M's later association, added in ink. (Here and elsewhere in the poem Walter E. Bezanson identifies the Stanley sources in the NN edition of *Clarel*.)

154.13 M. 2B. 3C.] In Chapter 3 of the second book of Maccabees in the Apocrypha, Apollonius, governor of the northern provinces, hearing that there was much treasure in the Jerusalem Temple, sent a messenger to confiscate it, but the high priest Onias explained that the treasure was deposits of widows and orphans, and others, and that it was altogether impossible to wrong those who had put trust in the holy place.

154.14 *Eclipse*] Presumably the name of a ship. There was an extreme clipper with that name, but she was destroyed on the west coast of Mexico in 1853. Two others, one registered from Barnstable and the other from New Bedford, Massachusetts, were located by William H. Tripp, curator of the Old Dartmouth Historical Society and Whaling Museum of New Bedford, but nothing seems to suggest a connection with Captain Pollard below.

154.15 Pollard] George Pollard (d. 1870 at age eighty-one), captain of the *Essex* which was sunk by an enraged whale in 1820, a disaster well known to readers of *Moby-Dick*. While M mistakenly thought that a whaling captain he saw in 1842 on his own Pacific voyage was Owen Chase, the mate of that ship, he had in fact soon after talked with his son, who lent him Chase's *Narrative*; in 1851 he had received a copy from Chief Justice Shaw (Sealts 134) and in 1852 had met Pollard, living quietly as a night watchman on Nantucket. In *Clarel*, 1.37.11–108, the figure of Nehemiah reminds Rolfe of a sailor whose story, somewhat fictionalized and transposed, is that of Pollard, spoken of as now "gone home at last / Into the green land of the dead." M's own manuscript memorandum about Chase is reproduced and transcribed in the NN *Moby-Dick*, pp. 971–95, and in Thomas Farel Heffernan, *Stove by a Whale: Owen Chase and the Essex* (Middletown, Conn.: Wesleyan University Press, 1981). Henry F. Pommer gives a detailed account of M's use of Pollard's career, in "Herman Melville and the Wake of the 'Essex,'" *American Literature*, XX (November, 1948), 290–304.

155.1–6 *Subjects* . . . portrait] These lines in pencil also appear to be trial possibilities for use in lectures or poems and in two respects appear to reflect a recent rereading of entries devoted to his last days in Rome (March 19–21) and then in Florence (March 27–28). At the time of his excursion to Tivoli (March 20), he did not mention the Villa d'Este there. The sixteenth-century villa, with its elaborate fountains, terraces descending down the slope toward the gorge, and the reputedly tallest cypresses in Italy, is at the west edge of Tivoli. A few years before, however, Hillard described the building, the terraced gardens, and elaborate waterworks in their state of neglect: "a building which, from its formal and elaborate magnificence, might stand as a representative of its whole class. . . . It is now uninhabited and falling to decay; but the garden—with its pines, cypresses, and avenues of box, left by their unpruned growth to form an 'obsolete prolixity of shade'—still retains a melancholy charm" (*Six Months*, II, 219). Along the margin of the entry for March 20, 1857, briefly noting the ride past Lake Tartarus to Tivoli, M penciled in the same phrase that appears in line 4 here: "From *Tartarus to Tivoli*" (see the textual note at 113.10). The *Three Fates* painting supposed to be by Michelangelo he had noted a few days later in the Pitti Palace, Florence (March 27, 116.1–3). See also, near the end of this notebook (158.1–8), four lines in pencil, three of which could relate to his lecture "Statues in Rome," and then in ink the Villa d'Este comparison repeated.

158.9–11 [Seeing . . . good] These first three lines (in ink) appear to be related to the last lines on D230, mentioned in the preceding discussion. The remainder of this page and the next (in pencil), with respect to the Coliseum at least, anticipate M's lecture "Statues in Rome."

158.27–28 arabesques] Possibly "antiques".

159.2 distant cheerless] Both words conjectural.

159.6 carriages] Possibly "caring".

159.9 De Leon] For De Leon, see the discussion at 73.4; for Wood, the discussion at 94.33.

159.11 McCartan] M's connection with this man is not known. The list of deaths, Poughkeepsie, N.Y., *Daily Press*, April 30, 1858, reports: "In this city, last evening, Daniel McCartan, formerly of New York City, in the 37th year of his age." City directories from mid-century indicate that he was a painter living at 21 (or 22) Smith St., and that his presumable widow, Mary, and son, Daniel, continued to live there (information in a letter from Amy VerNooy, Local History Librarian, Adriance Memorial Library, Poughkeepsie).

159.12 Rankin] See the discussion at 141.6.

Textual Notes

FOR explanation of the features of the manuscripts recorded in these notes, see the NOTE ON THE TEXT, p. 243 above. After the closing bracket, all words in italics are editorial, and all in roman are authorial (unless labeled *ESM*). The following symbols and abbreviations are used:

A, B, C, D, E	the five manuscript notebooks
(*H*)	reading preferred by Howard C. Horsford
ESM	Elizabeth Shaw Melville, wife of Herman Melville
/	end of line
//	divides words or phrases successively canceled
?word	prefixed question mark indicates conjectural reading
xx	undeciphered letters (number of x's approximates number of letters involved)

JOURNAL 1849–50

3.2 Journal] *A1; above this word, notation in pencil by ESM:* Herman Melville's

3.3 detention] *miswritten* dentention

3.4 passengers] *before canceled* we

3.11 As] *A2; after redundant* Thursday Oct 11th *(fenced)*

3.12 thinking] *written over* the

4.6 *Friday*] *A3*

4.6 *Oct* 12th] *underlined twice*

4.7 played till] *intervening wavy line in two-cm space between these words*

4.7 of] *inserted above caret*

4.9 to recall] *intervening comma canceled*

4.18 Taylor] *A4; after redundant* (Oct 12) *inserted in top margin without caret*

4.32 *Saturday*] *A5*

4.32 *Oct 13*] *underlined twice*

5.8 gymnastics] *A6; after redundant* Saturday Oct 13 *(month and date underlined)*

5.12 close] *inserted with caret, above canceled* double

5.22 within a] *rewritten*

5.22 or] *A7*

5.26 about] *written over rubbed-out* the

5.31 last] *miswritten* lasted

5.36 he] *A8; after redundant* Saturday Oct 13 *(fenced)*

6.10 as] *A9; after redundant* Saturday *(fenced)*

6.24 I] *A10; after redundant* Sunday *(underlined)*

6.38 would] *A11*

7.14 thence] *A12; after redundant* Monday Oct 15 *(fenced)*

7.28 ague] *after canceled* geue

7.28 little] *A13*

7.31 Barney] *underlined in pencil with* Macky *inserted above also in pencil without caret, both by ESM*

7.31 Orianna] *underlined in pencil by ESM with the added notation:* Lizzie

8.7 *Friday*] *A14*

8.7 *Oct 19*] *underlined twice*

8.9 *Oct 20*] *underlined twice*

8.19 Orianna] *above this word, notation in pencil inserted without caret by ESM:* Lizzie

8.19 Barney] *above this word, notation in pencil inserted without caret by ESM:* Macky
8.22 *Sunday*] *A15*

9.1 *Tuesday*] *A16*
9.1 *Oct 23*] *underlined twice*
9.2 stiff] *written over* still
9.15 McCurdy] *A17*
9.18 *Oct 26*] *underlined twice*
9.22 Oriental] O *written over* o
9.27 get to London.] *inserted in bottom margin without caret*
9.28 *Saturday*] *A18*
9.28 *Oct 27.*] *underlined twice*
9.30 &] *rewritten*

10.1 *Oct 28*] *underlined twice*
10.3 ("Where . . . man?")] *above this phrase, notation by ESM in pencil:* Macky's baby words
10.6 afternoon] *A19*
10.11 Stout] S *written over* s
10.14 *Oct 30*] *underlined twice*
10.15 ("Where . . . man?)] *a small crosshatch in pencil inserted without caret above this phrase by ESM with matching crosshatch before her penciled note in right margin:* Macky's baby talk —
10.17 Channel] C *written over* c
10.17 Scilly] *miswritten* Sclliy
10.19 superb] *original* supurb *altered to* superb
10.19 near] *A20*
10.23 *Oct 31*] *underlined twice*
10.29 *Nov 1st*] *underlined twice;* N *written over rubbed-out* O
10.33 civilities] *A21*

11.5 *Nov 2^{d}*] *underlined twice*
11.11 my] *A22*
11.12 6] *written over* 2
11.18 X X X X] *first three X's added in right margin; the fourth added in left margin before next line*
11.24 Determined] *A23*
11.30 Isle] I *written over* i
11.34 passed] *after canceled* made

12.1 Cathedral] *A24*

12.5 dissappointments] *miswritten* dissappoints
12.11–12 ("Where . . . books?)"] *beneath this phrase, notation in pencil by ESM:* (First words of baby Malcolm's)
12.13 I commence] *B3; after blank page B2 (for B1 see p. 140); at top of B3, notation in pencil by ESM:* For the Journal of voyage out, see the small paper book
12.29 — one] *B4*

13.13 evening] *B5*
13.15 All] *after canceled* Early
13.16 6] *written over* 7
13.31 published] *B6*
13.32 guinea] *written over rubbed-out* hal

14.11 to] *B7*
14.24 Westminster] West/minster *without line-end hyphen*
14.31 Stopped] *B8*

15.7 guided] *miswritten* guidedd
15.11 London] *after canceled* the
15.14 person] *B9*
15.23 fowls] *after canceled* Tu
15.24 that] *initial* t *written over* g
15.26 be] b *written over* m
15.26 made] d *written over* t
15.27 foreign] *miswritten* forigen
15.29 thence] t *rewritten*
15.29 Fish] F *written over* ?d
15.32 The] *B10*

16.12 at] *B11*
16.32 anxiety] *B12*

17.5 dozing] *altered from* dozey
17.10 A regular Yankee.] *deleted later by lining and cross-marking*
17.11 with the] *B13*
17.12 McCurdy] *beginning here the usual brownish-black ink replaced by blue (see the textual note at 21.9)*
17.29 *Wednesday*] *B14*

18.9 to] *B15*
18.29 looked] *B16*

19.11 his] *inserted above caret*
19.12 he] *B17*
19.32 and] *B18*
19.32 Stout] *after canceled* Porter

20.12 towards] *inserted above caret*
20.15 Street] *B19*
20.26 adjoining] *miswritten* adjoinging
20.29 St: Giles] S *written over* G
20.36 the] *B20*

21.5 Apothecaries] *rewritten and blurred*
21.9 Lizzie] *in blue ink; brownish-black ink resumes thereafter*
21.14 unasked] u *written over another letter*
21.22 reception] *B21*

22.8 Wrote] *B22*
22.13 Did'nt] 'nt *added*
22.14 Iago] *miswritten* Iiago
22.22 the] *inserted above caret*
22.27 of] *written over* in
22.29 Belgrave] *B23*

23.10 fried sole.] *in blue ink*
23.11 called] *B24*
23.14–24 But . . . things.] *passage deleted later by lining and cross-marking; see the discussion at 23.11–12 and the* NOTE ON THE TEXT, *p. 219*
23.26 took] *B25*
23.36 Delf's] *canceled, then restored by dashed underlining*

24.6 in] *B26*
24.23 state] *B27*
24.23 damnatory] atory *written over* ed
24.32 prince] nce *written over* ce
24.34 America] *miswritten* Americca
24.36 Mr &] Mr *added in right margin*; & *added in left margin*

25.2 the] *B28*
25.20 *Friday*] *B29*
25.36 proved] *B30; this word inserted above caret*

26.1–4 At . . . by] *passage deleted later by lining and cross-marking; see p. 219*
26.4 conversing] *later overwritten by* Conversed *to begin new sentence after preceding cancellation*
26.14–15 Such . . . it.] *canceled with several strokes in darker ink*
26.15–16 Conventionalism] C *written over* c
26.16 now] *B31*
26.32 H. G. Bohn's] *B32*
26.35 *Midnight.*] *dashed underlining, double-dashed under* night.

27.12 vestibule] *B33*
27.19 was] *before canceled* a
27.26–28 a . . . night.] *passage deleted later by lining and cross-marking; see p. 219*
27.28 last] *B34*
27.28 fat, ugly,] *deleted later by lining and cross-marking; see p. 219*

28.1 to town] to *miswritten* to to
28.5 end] *B35*
28.5 told] *written over* s
28.24 Came] *B36*
28.26–27 & very] *ampersand added in left margin before* Very *(vestigial capital)*

29.3–4 time, on Sunday.] *comma converted from period;* on Sunday. *inserted above and connected to caret*
29.4 Newton] *B37*
29.6 Sam] *miswritten* Same
29.13 Bonne] ne *added*
29.20 my] *B38*
29.26 Found . . . &] *lined through once with nearly empty pen*
29.27–28 Mrs. . . . before.] *deleted later by lining and cross-marking; see the discussion at 29.26 and p. 219*
29.37 At] *B39*

30.17 &] *miswritten* & & *(the second ampersand begins B40)*
30.17 then] *B40*
30.32 not] *B41*
30.35 *Thursday 29th Nov*] *underlining dashed*

31.11 Next day,] *added in bottom margin with line indicating connection to entry at top of following page*

31.11 *Friday.*] *B42; this word inserted in top margin above caret*
31.19–20 Restaurant] R *written over* C
31.26 Was] *B43*
31.31 *Saturday Dec 1st.*] *originally* Friday, 30th Nov. *(underlined), then* Fri *canceled and* Satur *added in left margin with connecting line to remaining syllable* day *then all this canceled and corrected date inserted above without caret*

32.6 Home] *B44*
32.15 school] *miswritten* shool
32.18 sculpture] *after canceled* sclu
32.20 Middle-Age] *altered from* middle-age
32.20 to] *B45*
32.27 sixth] *miswritten* sixt
32.30 Guide] *originally* Gudle *then* i *added with* l *uncanceled*
32.35 five] *B46*

33.10 Adler] ler *written over* lr
33.11 to dinner] *B47*
33.25 And] *B48*
33.27 He invited] He *inserted above caret before* Invited *(vestigial capital)*
33.28 to dine] *after canceled* home
33.35 incredible] *B49*

34.2 Back] B *written over* T
34.6 Parisian] *miswritten* Pariasin
34.8 *Friday*] *after canceled* Thu
34.11 Off] *B50*
34.22 phlegmatic] h *written over* l
34.24 a fine] *B51*
34.26,29 revelry] *both occurrences originally* revellry *then second* l *canceled*
34.32 up] *after canceled* dow
34.37 a] *B52*

35.9 Liege] *after canceled* Leige
35.12 Prussian] *B53*
35.23 I] *B54*
35.31 in] *B55*

36.3 We] *B56*
36.12 *Schefferen*] en *indistincly altered or canceled in pencil*

36.12 St] *B57*
36.18 & an] a *written over a second* &
36.18 between] *after canceled* beth
36.21 &] *B58*
36.28 from] *B59*
36.37 and] *B60*
36.38 castles] *miswritten* castels

37.1 When] *after an X added in left margin*
37.8 At] *B61*
37.10 Ehrbrincedstein] h *written over* ri
37.11 superb] *original* supurb *altered to* superb
37.17 right] *B62*
37.26 travelling] *B63*
37.28 imbibe] *miswritten* imbible
37.35 X X X] *B64*

38.3 Cunard] n *rewritten*
38.12 Drachenfells] Dra- *at end of B64;* chenfells *at top of B65*
38.24 *Wednesday Dec 12*] *inserted above caret*
38.26 in] *B66*
38.39 a little] *B67*

39.7 *Thursday 13th Dec*] *inserted above caret*
39.12 Took] *B68*
39.25 had] *B69*
39.33 Both] *miswritten* Bothe
39.38 so] *B70*

40.12 to a] *B71*
40.23 at] *B72*
40.32 shall] *miswritten* sahal
40.36 for] *B73*

41.5 sort] *after canceled* a
41.9 was] *B74*
41.24 Church] *B75*
41.25 The] T *written over* t
41.37 aristocracy] *miswritten* artistocracy
41.38 And] *B76*

42.1 with] *after canceled* w

42.9 ½ *past 6. P.M.*] *underlining dashed*
42.12 go] *B77*
42.25 Took] *B78*
42.38 Saints] *B79*

43.12 *Tuesday*] *B80*
43.14 Great] *after canceled* Little
43.24 receipt] *B81*
43.24 dies] s *mended*
43.36 *Wednesday*] *B82*
43.36 '49] 9 *written over* 8

44.8 a] *B83*
44.18 & so] *B84*
44.19 apothecary.] *before canceled* about
44.22 Last night dined] Last night *added before* Dined *(vestigial capital)*
44.25 comical] *word deleted by lining and cross-marking; see the* NOTE ON THE TEXT, *p. 219*
44.29 This] *B85*
44.37 Privy] P *written over* T

45.2 Tenniel] *B86*
45.13 night] *B87*
45.14 Barney] *underlined and marked by ESM with a crosshatch in pencil; a matching crosshatch in right margin precedes her underlined words also in pencil:* Baby boy
45.21 Last night dined] Last night *inserted above caret before* Dined *(vestigial capital)*
45.25 left] *B88*
45.33 an] *miswritten* and
45.37 Dock] *B89*
45.37 the Wharves] t *written over an earlier* W

46.10 Sailed] led *written over* ls
46.11 Thence] *B90*
46.21 author] *B91*
46.32 3] *B92*

47.12 for] *B93*
47.25 *Tuesday*] *B94*
47.27 short] *miswritten* shrort

47.36 out] *B95*

48.8 12.M.] *end of B95; for B96 see p. 141*

JOURNAL 1856–57

49.2 Sailed] *B97*
49.2 1856] *56 written over 57 in ink; tail of 7 erased; in right margin, notation in pencil added, then erased:* (1856)
49.11 Next] *B98*

50.1 *Next*] *B99*
50.9 village —] *last word on B99; at foot of page, notation in pencil by ESM:* Continued in small mem. book — marked "Journal up the Straits" — Sailed from Liverpool to Constantinople Nov. 18 — 1856 *Pages B100–269 blank; for pages B270–284 see pp. 141–49*
50.10 Memorandum . . . Liverpool] *C1; beside this heading, notation added in pencil:* Began and continued at sea, which accounts for the part of the writing.
50.21 bounty] *C2*
50.33 steamers] *C3*

51.10 *Thursday*] *C4*
51.21 but] *C5*
51.22 disappointment] *miswritten* disappoint
51.25 *Voyage . . . Constantinople.*] *underlined twice*

52.6 Entered] *C6*
52.20 *Wednesday*] *C7*
52.23 passages] *written over* the
52.24 town] *miswritten* twon
52.26 it] *written over* in
52.33 *Friday*] *C8*
52.33 *29th*] *marked by an X, with corresponding X in top margin before underlined notation:* one day error in date *(see the discussion at this point)*

53.12 of] *C9*
53.12 Matapan.] *before rubbed-out* I
53.14 islands] ands *corrected*

53.25 &c] *C10*
53.25–26 &c — picking . . . &c —] *first* &c *added in left margin, before dash;* picking . . . &c — *inserted in top margin, half-circled and connected to caret*
53.26 port] *written over rubbed-out* seaport
53.34 m'cadamized] *after canceled* grave

54.3 of] *C11*
54.4 & poverty] *after canceled* manliness & *with new ampersand inserted above, circled and connected to caret*
54.4 Town.] *before rubbed-out* Ma
54.9 ermine] *written over rubbed-out* wh
54.10 suggested] *after canceled* to be em
54.15 opera] *written over rubbed-out* top
54.18 red] *C12*
54.20 Few] *after canceled* No one
54.33 Saw] *C13*

55.10 Greek] *C14*
55.23 Three] *C15*
55.23 months] *written again, above, in pencil, not necessarily by M*
55.30 whortleberrying] *written over rubbed-out* hunt
55.32 Abbotts] *final* tts *written over* ts
55.37 Abbots] bots *written over rubbed-out* bts
55.37 enclosed] *C16*

56.6 Saw] *written over* M
56.11 *Monday Dec 8th.*] *underlined twice*
56.12 from] *C17*
56.18–19 all colors] *after canceled* & these rags of *with new ampersand added in right margin after* nations,
56.19 mob] *before canceled* of struggling creatures
56.20 gesturing] *after canceled* and
56.25 taken] *C18*
56.25 down] *written over rubbed-out* aft
56.25–26 down . . . discharged] *above this phrase, notation in top margin in pencil:* Cap. T's story of arms.
56.31 Beautiful] *miswritten* Beautif
56.32 is this.] *added in right margin after preceding period changed to comma*
56.33 Tuesday] *miswritten* Tueasday
56.36 Tom] *inserted above caret*

57.2 When] *C19*
57.12 aspect . . . continents.] *above this phrase, notation in pencil inserted without caret:* For Asia here see 2d book (Lion) *(68.35; see also the textual note at that point)*
57.17 then] *C20*
57.25 his] *written over rubbed-out* the
57.32 as near] *C21*

58.2 bark] *miswritten* barks
58.5–6 before . . . breeze.] *inserted above, circled and connected to caret*
58.9 by] *C22*
58.12 boy] *miswritten* bog
58.20 Magic] *written over rubbed-out* Saw
58.23 (like] *C23*
58.30 *Burnt Districts*] *added and boxed*
58.33–59.1 terrible . . . among] *passage to end of page marked in left margin by single pencil line and in right margin by double pencil line, also by an asterisk in right margin after* terrible
58.35 Pocket-compass.] *inserted above caret*

59.2 the] *C24*
59.5–17 Saw . . . off.] *passage marked in red pencil by a large asterisk before* Saw *and in left margin by a single line to bottom of page*
59.11–12 Roman . . . whole.] *marked by large asterisk in red pencil in right margin*
59.12 To the Hippodrome] *marked by asterisk in red pencil in left margin*
59.14 Nothing] *after pencil check mark in left margin; above this word, notation inserted in pencil above caret and partly circled:* like light-houses.
59.17 Also] *C25*
59.22 soaring] *after canceled* isolated
59.23–33 Then . . . and] *passage marked in left margin by a single line in ink to bottom of page*
59.25 go] *after canceled* ent
59.27 marble] *after canceled* pill
59.33 wandering] *C26*
59.38 arms] *written over rubbed-out* m
59.39 everything] *before this word, notation added in right margin in pencil:* (Cairo)

60.1 Georgians] *inserted above, circled and connected to caret*

60.10 the] *C27*
60.10 Pigeon] *above this word in red pencil in top margin a large X*
60.14 off] *miswritten* of
60.15–16 Went . . . Sulyman.] *marked by large asterisk in red pencil in right margin*
60.16 third one] *after and above these words in right margin a check mark in pencil*
60.17 a] *after canceled* like
60.23 below] *after canceled* in the
60.26 as] *added*
60.26 in . . . car,] *C28; this passage inserted in top margin, with connecting line (when* as *was added after semicolon at end of last line of preceding page)*
60.30 Natural rock.] *inserted above, circled and connected to caret*
60.33–34 arches . . . &c.] *line marked by pencil check mark in left margin; above this line, inserted without caret in pencil a boxed notation:* Begin here
60.33–34 small . . . &c.] *underlined in red pencil*
60.34 &c &c &c.] *word inserted above without caret in pencil:* cupolas
60.36 elastic] *inserted in left margin above caret*
60.36–37 atmosphere . . . American] *lined through in pencil by single zigzag line*
60.37 cooled &] *inserted above caret*
60.37 sherbet-like] *inserted above without caret*

61.1 coins . . . circulate] *underlined in pencil*
61.1–4 Placards . . . nations.] *marked in right margin by a wavy line in pencil*
61.2–3 [(Turkish . . . Lottery.]] *inserted above caret*
61.3–4 You . . . nations.] *underlined in pencil; added in bottom margin in faint pencil:* I feel among the nations.
61.4–6 Sultans . . . crowds &c.] *phrases written along left margin in two groups, with a slash between; both passages placed here editorially; in bottom third of left margin:* Sultan's . . . flags. — *lined through in pencil; in upper two-thirds of left margin:* No wonder . . . crowds &c.
61.6 able] *C29*
61.7 *(Ruffians of Galata)*] *inserted without caret in center of top margin; placed here editorially*
61.8–14 The horrible . . . conjurers. —] *passage marked along right margin by line in red pencil with an asterisk at the beginning in pencil and another at the end in red pencil*

61.22 *Sunday*] *C30*
61.22 Sundays] *canceled; large X and* Sabbaths *inserted above without caret, all in red pencil*
61.23 Romanists] *after canceled* Christians
61.38 fell] *C31*

62.3–5 The walls . . . dead. ——] *in right margin, this passage marked in pencil by inverted brace with the notation:* cemetery
62.3 walls] *after canceled* haggard
62.4 inexorable] *after canceled* stern
62.15 towers] *written over* vi
62.16 Immensely] *C32*
62.16–17 Immensely . . . streets.] *passage marked in left margin by a curving line in ink, and above in top margin by a large asterisk in pencil*
62.19 disdain] *written over* dist
62.23 in] *written over rubbed-out* of
62.25 Armenian funerals] Armenian *added in left margin before* Funerals *(vestigial capital)*
62.25–28 Armenian . . . lanes.] *passage underlined; before it in right margin a large circle with dot in center, all in red pencil*
62.32 as if] *C33*
62.34 Ah, speak] *intervening* I *canceled*
62.36 ¶] *added in left margin*
62.37 rare] *after lined out* a

63.1–2 Wretched . . . girls.] *passage marked in ink in right margin by boxed notation:* For Note
63.1–10 Wretched . . . these.] *passage marked in pencil in right margin by an asterisk and wavy line*
63.1 Tokens] *inserted without caret above canceled* Signs
63.1–3 Tokens . . . flower-pots.] *passage intermittently underlined in red pencil*
63.3 lillies] *after canceled* beaut
63.10 Bridge] *miswritten* Brigde
63.10 darting] *C34*
63.10–15 darting . . . them] *passage marked by dashed line in red pencil along left margin*
63.15–18 Viewed . . . tent.] *passage marked with an X at beginning, boxed, and lightly slashed through with four diagonal strokes, all in red pencil*
63.17 domed] *inserted above caret*

63.21 60] *written over* 600
63.24 minaret] *C35*
63.32 Way . . . mosque.] *sentence marked by an X in heavy red pencil in left margin and an asterisk in heavy red pencil above*
63.32 surrounding mosque] *inserted without caret above and after this phrase, the underlined notation in red pencil:* Mosque bazarr
63.34–35 From . . . tiles.] *passage underlined in both black pencil and dashed red pencil, with red-pencil notation* fields of clover *inserted without caret above first line*

64.1 with] *C36*
64.1–2 with . . . nuts] *beside this phrase, notation added in pencil in right margin:* (Cairo)
64.3 P.] *added in left margin to replace canceled* £
64.3–8 boy . . . Armenian] *passage marked by a single pencil line in left margin*
64.5 I could] I *added in left margin before* Could *(vestigial capital)*
64.14 (chissled)] *inserted above caret*
64.15–18 Gilded . . . bazaar.] *passage marked by dashed lines in red pencil in margins*
64.15 carriages] *C37*
64.16–18 Yellow . . . bazaar.] *passage marked by intermittent underlining in black and red pencil*
64.16 boots] *added in right margin, to replace canceled* slippers
64.22 robbers. &c.] *after this phrase, notation added in pencil:* (The Bosphorous)
64.24–30 Magnificent! . . . evergreens.] *passage marked in left margin by a single pencil line*
64.25 challenge] *inserted without caret above canceled* rivalry
64.26 successively] *inserted above caret*
64.28 thereupon] *after canceled* though
64.32 The] *C38*

65.6 wonder] *C39*
65.7 have] ve *written over* d
65.13–14 The daisies . . . has] *lightly lined through in pencil*
65.13–14 a crimson] *after canceled* the
65.14 from they spring] *inserted above caret*
65.15 quite such a filigree] *inserted above without caret*
65.21 [[Curious] *C40*
65.21–23 [[Curious . . . religion. —] *passage followed by notation in brown ink inserted without caret above the dash:* (Note)

65.21–22 some of whom seem] *inserted in top margin, circled and connected to caret*

65.22–23 with one consent] *inserted above, circled and connected to caret after canceled* all

65.27–28 chain of malefactors] *marked through or underlined in red pencil*

65.28 about their necks] *marked through or underlined in red pencil*

65.28 file] *marked through or underlined in red pencil*

65.31 running] *inserted above caret*

65.32–33 Horses . . . passengers.] *underlined in pencil*

65.34 Splendid . . . arches.] *beside this phrase, notation in left margin in brown ink:* ant-hill of caiques

65.36 servant] *C41*

65.36–37 A . . . state.] *inserted without caret in top margin*

65.37 Sherbet . . . bridge-side.] *above this phrase, notation in pencil inserted without caret:* Negro Mosslem &c (caparisons)

65.38 Or a Georgian.] *above this phrase, notation in brown ink inserted without caret:* with tall cap.

65.38–66.1 The droves . . . advance.] *underlined in pencil*

66.5–6 Road . . . court.] *next line begins .8 cm below; in red pencil in intervening space, a dashed line across the page and a large X centered*

66.10 & mosaic] *inserted above, circled and connected to caret*

66.11 bales, with marks.] *inserted above, circled and connected to caret*

66.14 penstocks] *C42*

66.19 about] *below this word, notation in pencil by ESM:* Continued in leather covered book "bought in Constantinople" — Dec 16 — 1856 — *For C43 and C44, see pp. 150–52*

66.20 *Constantinople*] *D1; this word inserted above without caret and underlined twice*

66.20 *Tuesday, Dec 16*] *below this date, notation in pencil possibly by ESM:* 1856 *and opposite this date, notation in upper right margin:* [Continued from Small Journal]

66.36 the] *D2*

67.3 with a flourish] *inserted above caret*

67.6 *Wednesday Dec 17*] *entry marked by a large asterisk in red pencil below* 17

67.7 peculiar] *miswritten* peculair

67.9 You . . . enter] *inserted above, circled and connected to caret*

67.10 crown of] *inserted above caret*

67.12 A . . . masonry.] *added three lines below, before* — In the part *(at 67.16–17) circled and connected to caret*

67.12–15 It . . . caves)] *written in left margin, marked for insertion by an X with dots in interstices in left margin beside* Within . . . board. *(at 67.11–12) and by an X after* caves)
67.15 a] *rewritten*
67.18 quaint] *after canceled* old
67.19 tall] *added in left margin*
67.19 Seraglio] *D3*
67.20 (proper)] *after canceled* (prpper *now partly obliterated by manuscript deterioration*
67.25 (Silence . . . prayer.)] *written along upper half of left margin, unmarked for insertion; placed here editorially*
67.27 None . . . Nomadic] *inserted above, circled and connected to caret*
67.31 See] *marked by a faint curved line in red pencil in left margin*
67.34 not] *inserted above caret*
67.35–68.2 Ladies . . . foliage.] *passage marked by red-pencil line in left margin*

68.3 *Thursday*] *D4*
68.5 Kauck] *written over* Cai
68.8 Seraglio] S *written over* G
68.8–9 As . . . world.] *passage underlined in ink with notation in left margin* For Note *over a division mark*
68.10 Cemeteries] *notation on this word written in ink along left half of bottom margin:* Turks want to be buried in Asia *above division mark*
68.11 through] *miswritten* throught
68.14–16 Unlike . . . . fathers.] *passage marked in right margin with wavy red-pencil line*
68.15 dispersed] *written over* na
68.18 ere] *miswritten* are
68.19 heights] *D5*
68.20 air.] *whole word present in 1950 Houghton Library photostat, but only letter* a *remains after top right corner of page was later broken off*
68.35 Asia] *miswritten* Asaia
68.35 Asia . . . menageries] *underlined in pencil*

69.1 in] *D6*
69.13 where] *after canceled* from
69.18 Spent] *D7*
69.21 cowhide] *canceled and* riding whip *inserted above without caret, all in pencil*
69.22 Went] *written over* Thence

69.25 A] *written over rubbed-out* Some
69.36–70.5 Carries . . . Coals.] *six passages written in both margins, unmarked for insertion; placed here editorially*
69.36–37 Carries . . . him.] *written along lower left margin*
69.37–38 Has . . . together.] *written along upper left margin*
69.38–70.2 Camel . . . here.] *written along upper right margin*

70.2–3 [A . . . heigth.] *written along lower right margin*
70.3–4 [Motion . . . ship.] *written along middle of lower right margin*
70.4–5 [Camel . . . Coals.] *written along right margin of preceding page D6 to face other insertions*
70.4 like pancakes] *inserted above, circled and connected to caret*
70.6 interesting] *D8*
70.7 broken] *after canceled* tom
70.8 dilapidated] *inserted above caret*
70.27 England] *D9*

71.6 fable] *above this word, notation in pencil inserted without caret:* but desolate in fact.
71.9 but] *D10*
71.18 Came] C *written over rubbed-out* A
71.22 *Christmas.*] *underlined twice*
71.29 But] *D11*
71.31 curious] *after canceled* a

72.1 the flesh] *after canceled* goat
72.1 grape.] *added in left margin before canceled* vine.
72.9 new] *written over blotted* ol
72.11 got] *D12*
72.17 meagre] *inserted without caret above canceled* ?tame *or* ?lean
72.19 &] *after canceled* & Patmos
72.22–23 Many . . . statues.] *written along left margin; placed here editorially*
72.26–27 [Passed . . . sight.]] *written in bottom margin and marked for insertion by paired X's with dots in interstices*
72.34 *Sunday*] *D13*

73.12 *Thursday . . . 1857.*] *underlined three times*
73.12 *Jan*] *written over rubbed-out* Dec
73.14 *2[d]*] *before rubbed-out* 18
73.16 *Saturday*] *D14*
73.18 these] *converted from* this

73.25 orchestras] as *written over single letter*
73.25 organs,] *inserted with caret above canceled* boxes
73.33–74.2 [Streets . . . Quarters]] *written in left margin, marked for insertion by red-pencil asterisk and connecting line*

74.2 Quarters] Q *written over another letter*
74.3 Their] *after uncanceled false-start* A
74.3 cadaverous] *after rubbed-out* l
74.3 ogerish] *after canceled* look
74.4 Haunted] *after canceled* Hunt
74.4 Cock] *D15*
74.7 (rubbish)] *inserted above caret*
74.8 thoroughfares] t *written over* s
74.11–14 [Flies . . . it.] *written below after* Grave & tranquil. *marked for transposition by paired X's with dots in interstices in the left margin*
74.13 gayety;] *before rubbed-out* ru
74.17 bamboos] *after canceled* sta
74.24 [Streets . . . beard.] *written along left margin; placed here editorially*
74.25 Thing] g *written over* k
74.26 (black)] *inserted above caret*
74.28 *View*] *D16*
74.32 gleam] *inserted without caret above canceled* are
74.33 solid] *miswritten* soild
74.33 wall] wa *written over* fo
74.34 fortresses] sses *written over* ss

75.3 *Pyramids.*] *underlined twice*
75.6 Isle] *miswritten* Ise
75.11 adhering] *blotted and rewritten*
75.12 midway] *D17*
75.13 hillock] *after canceled* a heap of
75.15 cross] *miswritten* corss
75.24 out] *after rubbed-out* h
75.29–30 [At . . . &c.] *written in left margin; placed here editorially*
75.32 Egyptians.] *before canceled* Moses
75.34 Egyptians] *D18*
75.36–37 giddiness &] *inserted above caret*

76.10 These . . . at.] *written along middle of left margin; placed here editorially*

76.11 as line] *canceled and* than that *added in right margin, all in pencil*

76.12 the two] *canceled and* alien *added in right margin, all in pencil*

76.20 black] *D19*

76.25 acacais; locusts &c] *original period altered to semicolon and* locusts &c *added*

76.30 fresh] *written over rubbed-out* da

76.39 In] *after canceled* At

77.5 *Account*] *D20*

77.9 honesty of] of *written over* &

77.15 reign] *miswritten* regin

77.16 tranquility] *miswritten* tranquily

77.20 beaver-dams.] *inserted above caret*

77.21 [No fences.]] *inserted above in left margin without caret*

77.25 of] *D21*

77.26–27 Canal . . . sand-hills.] *written seven lines below, on new line after* Smoking *(at 77.31) marked for transposition by paired X's with dots in interstices in left margin*

77.30 baggage] *miswritten* baggae

77.31–32 Cross . . . Machines] *added*

77.32 (1st class)] *inserted above caret*

77.35 pulverised] *canceled in pencil*

78.6 strokes.] *followed in bottom margin by notation in pencil:* A daub of Prussian Blue.

78.7 *The*] *D22*

78.7 stone] ne *rewritten*

78.7 do not seem] *canceled and* look less *inserted above without caret, all in pencil*

78.8 but] *canceled and* than *inserted above caret, all in pencil*

78.10–11 part to part.] *inserted above without caret; sentence originally continued:* column to capital & capital to pediment & pediment to dome. *then* column *canceled, with* shaft *inserted above without caret, then* shaft *also canceled along with original remainder of sentence*

78.11 stay] *before canceled* is stopping place

78.12 heigth] *before canceled* that *with succeeding* th *rubbed out; then notation in pencil inserted above without caret:* or breadth or length or depth that is stirred

78.12 immensity] *inserted without caret above canceled* magnitude

78.15 would] *written over another word*

78.15 impression] *initial* i *written over rubbed-out* &
78.15 of it] *canceled in pencil*
78.15 with] *after canceled* in
78.17 month] *written over rubbed-out* da
78.17–18 Its . . . you.] *inserted above caret*
78.18–20 Finding . . . stones.] *originally last sentence, in ink, on next page but marked for transposition by paired X's with dots at interstices; placed here editorially*
78.19 measures] *after canceled* computes t
78.21 adequately] *after canceled* com
78.23 one whit] *canceled in pencil*
78.24 from the] the *canceled with* its *inserted above without caret, all in pencil*
78.24 of the pyramid] *canceled in pencil; period added before* of
78.25 just] *canceled in pencil*
78.26 in impressiveness] *added in bottom margin*
78.26 as the] *D23*
78.27 unfurrowed] *after successively canceled* becalmed *and* unbroken
78.27 A] *inserted without caret above canceled* That
78.27–28 magestically] *inserted with caret above canceled* enhance &
78.28 it.] *before canceled* as
78.28 in panegyric] *inserted, circled and connected to caret; miswritten* panyegric
78.28 extraordinary] *inserted above caret*
78.29 affect] *after canceled* convey idea
78.30 Man] *after canceled* To *with* To the imagination *inserted in pencil above without caret*
78.31–32 It . . . priest.] *inserted without caret above successively canceled* But one // They who // named // The supernatural is someway involved with the pyramids.
78.31 that] *after canceled* the priest
78.32–33 inventors] *added in right margin before canceled* beings *in next line*
78.33 Egyptian] *before canceled* priests. *then(?)* s *added to make* Egyptians *then(?)* wise men. *inserted without caret above canceled* priests. *leaving vestigial plural* Egyptians
78.35 transcendent] *inserted without caret above canceled* wonderful *then canceled in pencil, then restored by dashed underlining*
78.35 mass & symmetry] *canceled in pencil*
78.35 & unity] *canceled, then restored by dashed underlining*
78.35 out] *after canceled* by

78.36 insignificant] *inserted above, circled and connected to caret after canceled earlier insertion* common

78.37 could] *above this word, phrase in pencil inserted without caret:* by an analogous art

78.37 rear] *after canceled* frame the

78.37 transcendent] *inserted without caret above canceled* sublime

78.37 conception] *after canceled* not

78.37 a God] *after successively canceled* religion. // a God. And religion

78.38 the pyramid founded.] *canceled, then restored by dashed underlining; then* Nature often violated in her mines *added, then canceled*

78.38 founded.] *after this word, notation in pencil at bottom of page:* [Casts no shadow great part of day. Explorers ?commencing out 30 miles in Desert.

79.1 *January*] *D24*

79.2 Many deck] *each word rewritten over itself*

79.4–8 *Jan* . . . Jerusalem. —] *passage marked by three pencil lines in right margin, one pencil curving line in left margin, and three X's in red pencil above its first line*

79.18 name] *D25*

79.19 Pool of] *at this point a large crosshatch in red pencil*

79.32 Frederick] Fre *written over* Cu

80.2 Spent] *after canceled* From

80.2 18th] 8 *written over* 7

80.2 city] *D26*

80.11 A] *after canceled* An

80.16 a] *after canceled* the

80.18 across] *miswritten* acorss

80.19 In the] *written over rubbed-out* Jan 21st

80.20 Meditterranean] *D27*

80.22 *Jan 22d*] *entry marked in red pencil by six X's above its first line, also by large asterisk in right margin in black pencil after first line, and five X's in red pencil at its end after* groves. *on next page (D28) at 81.17*

80.25 —Jaffa] *dash added in left margin;* Jaffa *written over* Th

81.5 Wrote] *D28*

81.29 crossing] *after canceled* in

81.29 overhead] *D29*

81.31 some] *after canceled* a

82.7–8 I see Leabanon — Mt Hermon] *underlined, with an X below each name and notation inserted above without caret:* X (Not so — a mistake) *all in pencil*

82.11–12 solemn] *D30*

82.12 ☞ (Jonah's pier)] *inserted above without caret; placed here editorially*

82.23 resigned] *inserted above caret*

82.26 like] *after canceled* so

82.26 Prussian] *after canceled* blue

82.26 Blue.] *followed by blank page D31; see the discussion at 81.5*

82.27 *From . . . &c*] *D32; this heading underlined twice*

82.33 green,] *after this word, notation inserted in pencil above caret:* (part of it)

82.34 Mount] *inserted above canceled* Hill *with connecting line to caret*

83.3 Hell] *after canceled* Tophet.

83.7 Marsada] *D33*

83.9 mouldy] *underlined in pencil*

83.10 every] *written over rubbed-out* or

83.10 escort] *after rubbed-out* gu

83.16 Robbers] *after canceled* Ride over

83.18 George] *canceled with* Como *and* (over leaf) *inserted above caret, all in pencil*

83.22–23 Rainbow . . . it. —] *written along right margin, unmarked for insertion; placed here editorially*

83.24–25 bitumen] *partly written over rubbed-out* as

83.25 washed] w *written over* &

83.26 as] *after canceled* a

83.26 for] *D34*

83.34–35 So . . . it. —] *originally written after* man. — *(at 83.36) but marked for transposition by connecting line*

83.36–38 No . . . desolation] *underlined in red pencil*

83.37–38 unleavened] *after canceled* nak

83.38 lime-kilns] *below this word, two notations in pencil in bottom margin:* Port Esquiline of the Universe. (For Note) / St. Saba — Samphire gatherers — monks *with* dreadful trade. *written below* Samphire gathers

84.1 Crossed] *D35*
84.1 with . . . over] *underlined in pencil*
84.3–4 two . . . hearses] *circled in pencil*
84.4 zig-zag] *second* z *written over rubbed-out* g
84.5 sepulchral ravine] *circled in pencil*
84.5 ravine] *after canceled* hollo
84.5 smoked . . . fire] *circled in pencil*
84.5–6 caves . . . the depth] *underlined in pencil*
84.5 &] *miswritten* & &
84.13–14 sides . . . recluses] *underlined in red pencil*
84.14–15 stone eyries] *underlined in red pencil*
84.16 little hermitages] *underlined in red pencil*
84.16–17 balustrade . . . monks] *underlined in red pencil*
84.17 black-birds] *D36; this word underlined in red pencil*
84.17 with bread] *underlined in red pencil*
84.17–18 terraces . . . precipice] *underlined in red pencil*
84.26–28 — On . . . rocks.] *passage boxed in heavy red pencil*
84.28 rocks.] *after this word, notation in black pencil at bottom of page:* See page 124 of Saunders for curious description of Jerusalem. *with* 124 *underlined once and* Saunders *twice in red pencil; also in red pencil at lower left corner of the page, fistnote before the phrase:* (Jerusalem Cross 5 Wounds) P. 124.
84.29 Jerusalem] *D37; after this heading a crosshatch added in red pencil*
84.35–36 *Thoughts* . . . faces.] *marked through with a wavy line in pencil*

85.2 (tradition . . . scripture)] *inserted above without caret; placed here editorially*
85.4–6 *Church* . . . resting] *passage marked through by four diagonal pencil strokes*
85.4 Anointing stone] *inserted above, circled and connected to caret*
85.6 Pilgrims . . . resting] *interlined*
85.8 Hill-side] *D38*
85.8–9 Hill-side . . . carts.] *above this entry, three X's in red pencil centered in top margin*
85.10–15 [The mind . . . Ascension.] *above this entry, six X's in red pencil; entry also lined through diagonally both ways in black pencil*
85.10 sadly & suggestively] *inserted without caret above canceled* strangely
85.11 & Man] *inserted above caret*
85.11 to the] *after canceled* in a
85.12 Zion;] *before successively canceled* in the // the shadows of // upon the hill-side, // minaret and // mosque & church are

85.12 side by side in] *originally followed by* the *canceled; all inserted without caret above canceled* church are
85.12 impartial] *originally* impartially *then* ly *canceled*
85.13 equality] *inserted above caret*
85.13 on Olivet] *inserted above caret*
85.14 Chapel] C *written over* c
85.16–20 [The South . . . &c.] *above this entry, a large crosshatch in red pencil*
85.17 Omar] *inserted without caret above canceled* the Saracen
85.17 upon] *before canceled* triumphing over
85.17 foundation] *inserted with caret above canceled* huge
85.18 that] *after successively canceled* the very // the
85.18–20 the . . . &c.] *canceled in pencil, then above this passage, the penciled notation:* the relationship of the two faiths
85.19 religion] *inserted without caret above canceled* faith
85.21 [How . . . Jerusalem.] *above this passage a dividing line in red pencil; this passage also canceled in black pencil*
85.25 proving] *D39*
85.26 Philadelphia] *miswritten* Philadlephia
85.28–29 [The . . . way.] *centered above this entry a crosshatch in red pencil*
85.31 occupying] *after canceled* terraced, and
85.32 perpendicular] *after canceled* living

86.1 [In Jehosophat] *centered above this entry four X's in red pencil*
86.1 grave] *originally* graves like *then* like *canceled leaving vestigial plural*
86.10 maledictory] *after canceled* sullen
86.11 amusements] ts *rewritten*
86.11 Tomb)] *D40*
86.12–19 — The . . . dead.] *vertical pencil mark through this passage*
86.12 project] *after canceled* pr
86.14 The] *written over rubbed-out* All
86.17 Beautiful] *miswritten* Beautif
86.17 Gate] *above this word, notation in pencil:* (Christ sitting in window)
86.18–19 The . . . dead.] *passage marked out by incomplete wavy pencil line*
86.19 — cemeteries all round. —] *inserted below without caret*
86.22 & also] *after canceled* supposed to be that
86.28 the saturation of] *originally* thoroughly to saturate *then* thoroughly to *canceled,* the *inserted above caret,* saturate *changed to* saturation *and* of *inserted, circled and connected to caret*
86.29 subject,] *before canceled* to its *then comma added*

86.30 its] *after canceled* its
86.30 weird] *inserted without caret above canceled* melancholy
86.30 at] *after canceled* ea
86.31 walked] *after canceled* s *and before canceled* out
86.31 walls.] *originally* walls, *with following* glad to escape // to escape the pent-up air within. *successively canceled*
86.31–32 so . . . concerned] *written below, circled and inserted with arrow*
86.32 here.] *added after canceled* in this taste.
86.32 For] *D41*
86.32 could] *after canceled* was
86.33 clusters] *after canceled* or l
86.33–34 along . . . near] *inserted without caret above successively canceled* alo // about
86.34 Jaffa] *after canceled* gates
86.35 groups] *inserted without caret below canceled* troups of people
86.35 always] *inserted without caret above canceled* perpetually
86.35 fountains, vales &] *inserted above caret*
86.36 so small] *after successively canceled* an atm // a city
86.37 lofty] *added after canceled* massive *inserted above caret*
86.37 obstructing] *after successively canceled* keeping out // preventing
86.37 ventilation,] *before successively canceled* & making twilight before its time // abridging the sunlight
86.38 hasting] *after canceled* abridging the
86.38 unwholesome] *miswritten* unhomlme *after canceled* twil
86.38 And they] And *inserted above without caret before* They *(vestigial capital)*
86.38 share] *after canceled* feel *and before canceled* that the

87.1 were it only] *inserted above caret*
87.1 arbitrary] *after canceled* prescription of and lim
87.3 tomb] *miswritten* tombs
87.3 hostile] *inserted above without caret*
87.4–9 I . . . Sennacherib.] *beside this passage, notation written later in ink in right margin:* Hill of Evil Council
87.4 hill] *after canceled* valley
87.5 watched] *after canceled* saw
87.5 precipitation] *inserted without caret above the second of the successively canceled phrases* decrease of the // growth & the decay
87.5 solemn] *inserted above caret following inserted, then canceled* vast
87.6 far] *inserted above without caret*

87.6 haunted] *inserted without caret below canceled* jagged *with* & // arid // dry *successively inserted above without caret then canceled*
87.6 hid] *originally* hid deep *inserted above caret, then canceled;* black *added then canceled following* deep *then* hid *restored by dashed underlining*
87.7 darkened] *after canceled* valley
87.8 cliff-girt] *inserted without caret above canceled* horrid *with following* basin of *also canceled and* silent *inserted above without caret, then canceled*
87.8 riven] *after successively canceled* old oli // old
87.9 army] *inserted without caret above canceled* encamped host
87.9 Sennacherib.] *before canceled* A
87.9–10 I saw] *inserted above caret*
87.10 reddish] *after canceled* loam
87.10 soil] *inserted without caret above canceled* earth
87.10 confessing] *after canceled* took on
87.10 inexpiable] *inserted above caret*
87.10 guilt by] *before canceled* still deeper dyes *with* scarlet *inserted without caret above that phrase, then canceled*
87.11 deeper] *added before canceled* glowing
87.11 dyes.] *before successively canceled* And that other feild // I saw the silent
87.11 I saw] *inserted above caret*
87.11 ruined] *after canceled* vi
87.13 the feild] *D42*
87.14–20 [And . . . &c.] *marked through by three diagonal pencil strokes*
87.16 slowly] *after canceled* gli
87.17 after] *after canceled* slowly creeping
87.19–20 entering . . . &c.] *underlined in both black and red pencil*
87.20 &c.] *miswritten* &c..
87.22 [The Holy Sepulchre] *in space above this entry, notation in pencil:* [No Jew allowed in Church of H. S.]
87.22–34 [The . . . is a] *passage to the end of the page marked through by diagonal pencil strokes; also two underlined phrases in red pencil written vertically along lower half of right margin:* Greek tickets for heaven / See Captain's story
87.23 Laberithys] *after canceled* a laberyth
87.23 mouldy] *inserted above caret*
87.24–25 in . . . wall] *inserted above caret*
87.28 Christ] *after canceled* the
87.28 veined] *after canceled* looks like
87.28 streaks] *after canceled* red &

87.28 mouldy] *after canceled* soiled
87.29 slab] *inserted without caret above canceled* counter
87.29 Near] *after successively canceled* I often stoo // There
87.29 blind] *inserted without caret above canceled* marble
87.29 of worn marble,] *inserted above caret*
87.30 the reputed] *inserted above caret*
87.30 among] *after canceled* they
87.30–31 the showman point] *inserted above caret before* they show you *with only* they *canceled leaving vestigial* show
87.31 smoky] *inserted above caret*
87.32 hole] *written over rubbed-out* cr
87.32 fixed] *originally* fixed & *before canceled* the rent in the rock. *leaving vestigial* &
87.33 cellar] *inserted without caret above canceled* hole
87.34 On] *after canceled* Near
87.34–88.16 kind . . . own] *entire page D43 marked through in pencil by one diagonal stroke*
87.34 railed with] *inserted without caret above canceled* of
87.35 overlooking] *miswritten* ovrelooking
87.36 spectacle] *miswritten* specatle
87.38 grated] *inserted above caret*

88.1 it.] *before canceled* with *period then inserted*
88.2 lofty] *after canceled* dome; a
88.2 & ruinous] *inserted above caret*
88.2–3 whose . . . laths] *originally written two lines below, circled and inserted with arrow*
88.2 fallen] *after canceled* li
88.3 a sort] *after canceled* ben *with* beneath, the painted walls are cracked & mildewed. *inserted above caret, then canceled*
88.3 plague-stricken] *inserted without caret below canceled* dusty
88.4 reigns] *before successively canceled* beneath // around. // the ru // the much painted & mildewed walls
88.4 around.] *before canceled* In the middle *also, above in right margin, an X in red pencil*
88.5 church in] *after canceled* small
88.5 It] *before canceled* bears the aspect of age
88.5 marbles] *after canceled* precious
88.6 faded] *inserted above caret*
88.6 porch] *after successively canceled* porch // little

88.7 issues a garish] issues a *miswritten* issue a *inserted without caret above* stream a // a *successively canceled; with* soft // mellow *inserted without caret after* issue a *also successively canceled, then* garish *finally added after* mellow
88.7 upon] *after* soft & golden *inserted above caret then canceled*
88.7 faces] *after successively canceled* faces of // eager
88.9 First] *after canceled* You enter, first
88.9 wee] *inserted above caret*
88.10 enter the] the *inserted without caret above canceled* this
88.10 tomb] *after successively canceled* Aladdin-like // golden
88.10–11 It . . . lanthorn.] *inserted without caret above second line of the successive cancellations:* Your eyes // Wedged // in the narrow space, // in *(inserted above without caret)* // into the contracted space, you are dazzled by the sepulchre lamp In the // & da
88.11 half-] *inserted above without caret*
88.11 stare] *inserted without caret above canceled* look
88.12 ineloquence] *after canceled* ineloquent stone
88.12 wipe] *after canceled* ask yourself
88.13 as from] *after canceled* the
88.14 countenances] *at this point an X in red pencil in right margin*
88.15 tacitly] *inserted above caret*
88.16 your own.] *before canceled* After coming from
88.16 After] *D44; after canceled* the Sepulchre, they wander off listlessly, & sit down upon some of the many steps around
88.16–20 After . . . day.] *sentence marked in red pencil in right margin by two X's, one beneath the other*
88.16–26 After . . . &c.] *passage marked through with one diagonal pencil stroke*
88.16 while in] *before canceled* the place,
88.17 going] *after canceled* & be
88.17 rapid] *after canceled* ro
88.17 chapels] *after canceled* shrines
88.17 either] *inserted without caret above canceled* sit down in melan
88.18 listless] *inserted without caret above successively canceled* stupid // melancholy
88.18 disappointment,] *miswritten* disappoint, *before canceled* & melancholy
88.18 seat themselves] *inserted without caret above canceled* collect
88.18 huddles] *after canceled* little *with* seated *inserted above without caret, then canceled*
88.19 indifferently] *after successively canceled* carrying on a melancholy gossip // gossipping

88.19 sectarian] *inserted above caret*

88.20 The] *after canceled* In this respect *with* the *then capitalized*

88.20 thronged] *inserted above without caret*

88.21 & theological] *inserted without caret above successively canceled* & exchange of // &

88.21 and still] *after successively canceled* where the // an idea not

88.22 the special] *after successively canceled* not bigger than // the

88.22 sects] *miswritten* scets

88.23 the Copts] the *inserted above without caret*

88.23 the Syrians] the *inserted above caret*

88.24 much] *inserted without caret above canceled* just

88.24 boxes] *after canceled* stock

88.25 commercial] *after canceled* other Ex

88.27 squalid alley] *inserted without caret above successively canceled* Via Doloroso // street

88.28 long] *inserted without caret above canceled* lofty

88.28 old] d *rewritten*

88.28 wall] *after canceled* wall

88.29 every] *inserted above caret after canceled* the

88.29 at their base,] *inserted above caret, before successively canceled* is accumulated every description of // reeks an accumulation of piles of cont

88.29–30 in open exposure] *inserted above caret*

88.30 last] *originally* worst & last *canceled, with* last *restored by dashed underlining*

88.30 & least nameable] *inserted above without caret*

88.30 city] *after caret and connecting line to circled notation in pencil above and in right margin:* barbarous

88.32 apparent] *inserted above caret*

88.32 (by . . . hoped)] *originally* by the Turks, *then* only . . . hoped *added in right margin and parentheses added*

88.32–33 a main] *inserted above canceled* the one

88.33 containing] *after canceled* wh

88.33 supposed] *canceled in pencil*

88.33 tomb of] *before successively canceled* Christ. // God.

88.34 This] *D45; after successively canceled* This // This wall behind

88.34–89.10 This . . . work.] *passage marked through by one diagonal pencil stroke*

88.35 wynd] *after canceled* lane,

88.35 a space] *after canceled* a more

88.36 where] *after canceled* whe

88.37 with . . . gate,] *inserted without caret above canceled* so low that

88.37 & grimy enough] *inserted above caret*
88.38 immediate] *after canceled* vic
88.38–89.1 masonry-locked] *inserted above caret*

89.1 church] *final* ch *rewritten*
89.2 upon] *after successively canceled* upon wh // covered with
89.3 Dead] *at this point in right margin a small x in red pencil*
89.4 made] *inserted above caret*
89.5 irregular,] *before canceled* & is lapped over by porches
89.5 careless] *added in right margin*
89.5 lapping over] *before canceled* upon the original erection *with* edif // pile *successively inserted without caret, then canceled, above* erection
89.6 & venerable] *inserted above caret*
89.6 tower,] *before canceled* extremely old,
89.7 barked . . . &] *inserted above caret*
89.8 sculpture] *before canceled* graced
89.8 graced] *before canceled* the facade; but Time
89.11 *Interior of Jerusalem.]* *underlined twice*
89.11 Gate] *before canceled* to
89.11–12 Calvary] *after canceled* Latin con
89.12–13 Silence . . . &c.] *marked in red pencil in right margin by a large crosshatch*
89.14 (Ecce Homo)] *underlined twice in pencil*
89.16 *Talk*] *D46*
89.18 just] *after canceled* a little
89.18 sold] *after canceled* th
89.20 peculiar] *inserted above without caret*
89.20 associations] *after canceled* and potent theological
89.20–21 by its extraordinary] *after* from its wh // extraordinary *successively canceled and* more peculiar *inserted above without caret, then canceled, with* extraordinary *restored by dashed underlining*
89.21 evoke] *after canceled* be enhanced to our admiration & wonder. *and before canceled* very
89.22 haunted] *inserted without caret above canceled* old
89.23 curdling] *after canceled* horrific
89.23 diabolical] *initially canceled;* horrible *inserted above caret, then canceled;* haunted *inserted above without caret, then canceled;* diabolical *restored by dashed underlining*
89.24 great part] *inserted without caret above and in left margin*

89.25 their terrific] *originally* their diabolical *with* diabolical *canceled; then* terrible *inserted above without caret and canceled; then caret added after* their *and* terrific *inserted above; then in pencil* ghastly *inserted above caret before* theology *and* terrific *canceled in pencil*
89.29–32 [The . . . in] *passage marked in red pencil in left margin by a pair of dashed lines*
89.32 (sober & penitent)] *inserted above caret*
89.33 Jerusalem] Je *written over* the
89.34 the] *D47*
89.34–35 The . . . Lamentations] *passage marked through in pencil by short diagonal strokes*
89.35 lamentable] *inserted above caret*
89.35 Lamentations] L *written over* l

90.1–2 [Inside . . . cactus.] *underlined with dashes in red pencil*
90.3–5 [The . . . morning.] *sentence marked through in pencil by four short diagonal strokes; in red pencil, in right margin an inverted brace marking sentence, also a small x outside*
90.3–4 & . . . man,] *inserted above, circled and connected to caret*
90.8–23 [Stones . . . stone;] *passage to the end of page D47 marked through by diagonal strokes in pencil*
90.9 stumps of the] *inserted above without caret*
90.9 men] *after canceled* St. Stephen was
90.10 death;] *before canceled* for a penalty; *with semicolon added after* death
90.13 stony walls & stony feilds,] *inserted above caret*
90.14 stony eyes & stony hearts] *canceled, then restored with dashed underlining*
90.14 Before] *after canceled* If you look to
90.14 & behind you] *ampersand inserted above without caret; comma after* you *canceled*
90.20 an] *written over* th
90.21 one's] *miswritten* one
90.22 or] *miswritten* of
90.23 but] *D48*
90.23–91.9 but . . . anchorites.] *marked through by two diagonal strokes*
90.23 to] *inserted above caret*
90.24 worn] *after canceled* smooth
90.26 that] *miswritten* than
90.26 whimsical] *inserted with caret above canceled* great
90.27 entered] *after canceled* contracted with
90.29 there] *miswritten* they

90.31–36	[There . . . way.] *originally last two lines on D49 (after* skull. *at 91.28) and all of D50 (beginning with* and *at 90.32); transposition indicated by asterisk with dots in interstices on D48 and an X with dots in interstices on D49; passage then marked through by three diagonal pencil strokes on each page*
90.32	"Deputation] *written over rubbed-out* Jewish
91.8	the gloomy] *inserted with caret above canceled* it
91.9	gloomy] *inserted above caret*
91.10–12	[There . . . smell.] *these two sentences boxed in red pencil*
91.13	[Three] *D49*
91.15	(Saturday — the Jews)] *before canceled* — but on different *all written below, with place for insertion indicated by two X's*
91.16–18	[The . . . faiths.] *marked through by four short diagonal strokes in pencil*
91.17	divergent] *inserted above caret*
91.23	Palestine] P *written over* Ju
91.26	Hapless] H *written over* The
91.27–28	[In . . . skull.] *marked through by wavy line in pencil*
91.27	emigrant] *after canceled* Jews are
91.29	Christian] *D52; after blank page D51 (for D50 see the note at 90.31–36)*
92.1	man] m *written over* &
92.11	School] *D53*
92.20	Rhode-Island] Rh *written over* Con
92.27	the Lord's] *D54*
92.35	America] *miswritten* Amecan
93.3	*Deacon*] *after canceled* M[r] Dick
93.5	about] *D55*
93.19	comfortless,] *indeterminate brief stroke, interpreted here as comma, but possibly hyphen or dash (H)*
93.26	*Mrs. D*] *D56*
93.34–35	The fact] *after rubbed-out quotation marks*
93.37	Mr] M *written over* our
93.39	basicly] ly *written over original* basicy
94.5	They] *D57*
94.14	not] *inserted above caret*
94.16	any] a *written over* t
94.19	Croesus] *rewritten*

94.20 A] *D58*

94.27 place] *miswritten* places

94.36–38 Mr Wood . . . &c] *D59; below this passage, notation in pencil:* (Arch of Ecce Homo)

95.1 *Jan*] *D61; after blank page D60*

95.6 tongue] *miswritten* tonuge

95.8–10 Town . . . reef.] *underlined in pencil*

95.11 *(26)*th] (26) *inserted (not underlined) without caret above (underlined) canceled* 28

95.11–12 Lazy . . . rocks.] *underlined in pencil*

95.14 *27,*] *inserted above caret*

95.14–15 snow . . . horizon] *intermittently underlined in pencil and marked by three X's after* snow *one above and two below*

95.15 &] *D62*

95.18–22 Orientalls . . . Judges.] *written in pencil, possibly because of faulty pen or ink, for when M tries to resume in ink the script is very scratchy*

95.22 the Consul.] *below this phrase, an* S *as if new line were begun and abandoned; next dated entry begins one cm below*

95.23 *Sunday . . . 1857.*] *underlined twice*

95.28 been] *D63*

95.32 realize] *miswritten* relaize

95.34 Cypruss] y *written over* i

96.11 Scene] *D64*

96.29 to] *D65*

97.1–8 All . . . distances.] *this passage marked by a line in heavy red pencil in right margin*

97.10 and] *miswritten* and & *(ampersand begins D66)*

97.10 Patmos] *D66*

97.15–18 Could . . . barreness.] *opposite this passage, notation written in ink in right margin, after fistnote symbol:* The Icarian Sea. &c.

97.18 Niebuhr] *after canceled* that

97.21 countries] ries *rewritten in pencil*

97.24–26 Priest . . . plan] *passage to end of page D66 marked in heavy red pencil in left and right margins; in right margin a broad parallel pencil stroke in black, also across bottom of page dashed line in red pencil*

97.26 of] *D67*

97.32 of] *miswritten* of of

98.4 waiter] *D68*
98.8 Austrian] *miswritten* Austrais
98.15 (Little present)] *added*
98.17 Third] *D69*
98.18 (Feb 8th Sunday)] *written at bottom of page, with insertion indicated by paired X's with dots in interstices*
98.29 Trying] *D70*
98.31 gravity] *miswritten* graivty
98.35 saint though thou art] *canceled, then restored by dashed underlining*
98.35 though thou] *miswritten* though though

99.5 Imperceptible] *D71*
99.16 Meditterranean] *written over* the
99.20 *Feb*] *D72*
99.25 (frozen together.)] *inserted without caret above* blocks *placed here editorially*
99.29 *Lyccabacus.*] *underlined three times*
99.32–33 covered] *D73*

100.7 Calabria] *written over rubbed-out* It
100.13 *Feb*] *D74*
100.22–25 Captain . . . Spicer] *a vertical wavy line separates the two columns of officers' names*
100.31 look] *D75*

101.1 *& Tuesday*] *inserted above caret*
101.1 *& 17*] *inserted above caret*
101.3 till] *written over rubbed-out* ?a
101.9 *Wed. 18*] Wed. *added in left margin to replace underlined* Thursday *canceled;* 8 *written over canceled* 7
101.15 Rhinelander] *D76*
101.17 Resino] *blotted*
101.18 whether] *miswritten* weather
101.22 abandoned] *written over* qu
101.23 slagmass] g *inserted in original* slamass
101.24 liquorice] *after canceled* ligor
101.27 Ate] A *written over rubbed-out* C

101.28 *Thursday Feb 19th*] Thursday *(not underlined) inserted with caret above (underlined)* Wednesday *canceled;* 9 *written over* 8
101.31 Royal] *D77*

102.8 school] *miswritten* schoof

102.10–11 the Solfatara] *D78*

102.16 keeled] *miswritten* kelld

102.26 in] *D79*

102.33 French] *written over* En

103.6 horse — colossal] *D80*

103.16 — Had] *dash added in left margin*

103.22 most] *D81*

103.34 Brunswick] *after canceled* New

104.1 broad] *D82*

104.13 Long] *D83*

104.24 (parvenue)] *inserted above caret*

104.25 not] *miswritten* no

104.26 secrets] *D84*

104.31–32 Singular . . . vigor.] *underlined in pencil and marked by large check mark in left margin*

104.32 Ruins . . . . rocks.] *underlined in pencil*

104.34 *Temple*] *after rubbed-out* Th

105.1 mountain] *miswritten* mountains

105.3–9 Solfatara . . . past.] *passage marked in pencil first by a line down left margin to bottom of page D84 and then in right margin of next page (D85)*

105.4 sober] *D85*

105.8 one] *after canceled* from

105.11 its] *miswritten* it

105.17 Rome] *in double-size letters*

105.18–19 The . . . &c.] *in bottom margin*

105.19 road] *after canceled* rodd

105.20 Such] *D86*

105.24 young] y *written over* l

105.24 cap on.] *after these words, notation in pencil:* (Sentencing cap)

105.25 *Tuesday Feb* 24th] *beside this entry along middle of right margin, notation in pencil underlined and preceded by a fistnote:* For Rome / See page at end of book [*D233; p. 159*]

105.33 *Wednesday Feb* 25th] *originally after* home. *(at 105.34) on new line, then marked with line and caret for insertion above*

105.35 elephant.] *inserted with caret above canceled* hippottamus.

105.35 Capitol] C *written over* c

106.1 come] *miswritten* coming
106.2 mood] *D87*
106.7 Sophia's] S *written over tail of* J
106.13 so] *after canceled* wicked at all
106.14 manliness] *after canceled* manhood
106.17 Christian] *miswritten* Christinan
106.19 (Music on Pincian)] *written in bottom margin in ink; placed here editorially*
106.22 place] *D88*
106.35 trouble] *miswritten* troubles

107.5 above] *D89*
107.10 Bridge] *miswritten* Brigde
107.15 Italian] *miswritten* Itialn
107.17 along the walls —] *words inserted above, with connecting line to caret and dash added in left margin before* Antinous
107.19 mantle] *miswritten* mantilla
107.25 The] *D90*
107.28 gigantic] *miswritten* gilgantic

108.5 Porta] *after canceled* Gate
108.6 ancient] c *converted from* t
108.6 gate] *D91*
108.7–10 To . . . &c] *written four lines below after* Arch of *(at 108.13) circled and directed by arrow for insertion*
108.15 Scipio's] *written over* Ci
108.17 stairs] *miswritten* stiars
108.22 visiting] *D92*

109.1 Walked] *D93*
109.15 To Pincian] *D94*
109.19 — Pincian] *dash written over* in
109.22 *To Sciarra Gallery*.] Schiarra *with* h *canceled; dashed underlining*
109.23 Cheating] *inserted with caret above canceled* Three
109.29 Titian] *after canceled* Tith
109.31 *To . . . gallery*] *dashed underlining*
109.31 *Rospiglioso*] *D95*

110.2 *To . . . Pope*.] *dashed underlining*
110.11 *To . . . Bath*] *dashed underlining*
110.12 church] *D96*
110.18 rifled] *miswritten* rifleld

110.27 tongue] *miswritten* tonuge
110.29 show] *D97*

111.3 one] *inserted above caret*
111.9 portrait] *D98*
111.25 Nothing] *D99*

112.5 landscape] *D100*
112.8 Attacked] *after canceled* To St. Peters. To the Pincian
112.8 singular] *miswritten* singluar
112.11 16th] 16 *miswritten* i6
112.13 haze . . . limbs.] Sixtine . . . limbs. *added, then* haze *inserted above caret*
112.19 Maps] *D101*
112.23 16] *miswritten* i6
112.23 Caffe] *miswritten* Cafffe
112.28 Backwoodsman] *miswritten* Backswoodsman

113.1 Finer] *D102*
113.3 alley] *after canceled* st
113.10 *Friday March 20th.*] *beside this entry, notation in right margin in pencil, with decorative underlining:* From Tartarus to Tivoli.
113.16 the] *D103*
113.32 Nothing] *D104*
113.33 car] *after rubbed-out* f

114.12 Collonaded] *miswritten* Collondaed
114.14 Hotel] *miswritten* Hote
114.15 Nord] *D105*
114.23 mosaics] *after canceled* camoes (*possibly* carven)
114.31 of] *D106*
114.32 Bellesgardo] *after canceled* Bllo
114.34 lane] *after rubbed-out* g

115.1 *Thursday*] *inserted (not underlined) without caret above canceled* Friday *(underlined)*
115.12 more] *D107*
115.15 massive] *written over* co
115.20 *Friday*] *inserted (not underlined) without caret above canceled* Saturday *(underlined)*
115.24 &c.] *miswritten* &cc.
115.28 among bones] *inserted with line connected to caret*

115.30 *N°*] *D108*
115.34 In] *after canceled* Supe
115.35 Pope's] *after successively canceled* Pope // the antique-

116.11 five] *D109*
116.21 New England] *intervening pen mark*
116.25 *Monday*] *D110*
116.32–34 First . . . Peters.] *added in two squeezed lines in space at original end of entry*

117.5 came] *D111*
117.11 attitudes] *miswritten* attudes
117.19 quite] *D112*
117.22 there; dismantled] *semicolon written over period before* Dismantled *(vestigial capital)*
117.24 *Wednesday*] *inserted (not underlined) without caret above canceled* Tuesday *(underlined)*
117.30–31 Promenade] *D113*
117.32 Giotto's] *after canceled* Go
117.35–36 Approaching] *after canceled* Entering Venice

118.1 *Thursday*] *inserted (not underlined) without caret above canceled* Wednesday *(underlined)*
118.1 Ducal Palace] *placed here editorially; inserted above, circled and connected to caret, misplaced after* Mark's *(at 118.2) though the following description refers to* St. Mark's *not* Ducal Palace
118.5 Mark's] k *written over* co
118.5 enjoyment] *D114*
118.6 Public] *miswritten* Publlic
118.9 affable] *miswritten* affablle
118.13 qualities] *miswritten* qualtities
118.14 chapel] *written over rubbed-out syllable*
118.19 *Saturday*] *inserted above caret, not underlined*
118.21 Back] *D115*
118.32 *Sunday*] *inserted above caret*
118.32 Breakfast] *after canceled* Took gondola.
118.33 basilica] *miswritten* balsilica
118.34 breakfast] *miswritten* breksfast

119.1 the flags] *D116*
119.1 shadow] s *written over another letter*

119.1 bell-tower] *after this word, notation above caret inserted in pencil:* walking in it.
119.2 Pigeons] *miswritten* Pigoens
119.5 the] t *written over* D
119.13 blended] b *written over rubbed-out* l
119.15 silks] *initial* s *rewritten*
119.18 old] *D117*
119.21 Octagonal] *after canceled* Series of carvings, very fine
119.23 black] *miswritten* blacks
119.25 promenading] *miswritten* promendaing
119.28 (Titian . . . Venetian)] *inserted above and connected to caret*
119.30 end] *written over rubbed-out* pas
119.35 in] *after canceled* like
119.36 for] *D118*

120.7 precious] *followed by a stroke, possibly a comma*
120.9 old] *inserted above without caret*
120.9 refectories] *inserted without caret above canceled* eating-houses
120.9 old] *inserted above caret*
120.14 How] *D119*
120.14–19 How . . . Sir?] *after this passage, in space remaining at end of paragraph, notation in pencil:* (For Con. Man)
120.14–15 do, Antonio] Antonio *miswritten* Anatonio
120.17 yourself.] *before canceled* For to de rich m
120.18 always] *inserted above caret*
120.20 not] *written over* aw
120.29 &] *written over rubbed-out* fav
120.34 Verona] *D120*
120.36 between] *after canceled* btw
120.37 on] *written over rubbed-out* to

121.2 Napoleon's] N *written over* n
121.10 expressions] *miswritten* expresssions
121.12 Curious] *D121*
121.22 than] *miswritten* that
121.28 Dined] *D122*

122.6 *Thursday*] *D123*
122.12 Remained] *after rubbed-out* 4
122.20 figures] *D124*
122.23 Via] V *written over* N
122.29 deforming] *after canceled* distor

122.31 Interesting] *after canceled* The ci
122.35 paid] *D125*

123.11 Road] *D126*
123.17 reality] *miswritten* realtiy
123.20 reality] *miswritten* realtiy
123.25 *Sunday*] *D127*
123.34 heigth] *miswritten* heigith
123.37 Took] *D128*

124.10 Loneliness] *miswritten* Lonleness
124.12 glen] *D129*
124.13 by] *blotted*
124.15 at] *written over rubbed-out* fo
124.26 At] *D130*
124.32 from] *written over rubbed-out* Sim
124.32 *April 16*] *inserted above caret and underlined*

125.1 Scene] *D131*
125.7 April 17] *inserted above without caret*
125.14 only] *D132*
125.26 Ride] *D133*
125.26 across] *miswritten* acorss
125.28 Deep, broad, rapid.] *added*
125.30 To] *after canceled* Crossed the
125.31 asparagus] *inserted above caret before* what *as answer to the question; placed here editorially*

126.5 The University] *D134*
126.5 ruin] *at this point in upper right corner of page the notation:* 29
126.15–17 Went . . . porters.] *passage marked by wavy vertical line down left margin*
126.19–20 Wiesbaden] W *written over* Fr
126.20 but] *D135*
126.34 *April*] *D136*

127.2 Dutch] *miswritten* Ductch
127.17 three] *D137*
127.32 *April*] *D138*

128.10 Vernon] *D139*
128.13 *Sunday*] *D140*

128.13 *May*] *written over* April *in heavier ink*
128.15 Reading] ing *rewritten*
128.24 Grotesque] *D141*
128.26 wholesome] *miswritten* ?wholesem
128.37 beautiful] *D142*
128.37 ranting] *after* presumptuous *added in pencil in left margin above caret*

129.5 pitcher] *miswritten* picture
129.10 Tomb] *D143*
129.13 Warwick] k *corrected in pencil*
129.13 Wonderfully] *miswritten* wonderlly *with stroke for* f *added over* ly
129.22 Arrived] *D144*
129.25 *The "Grecian"*] *written in right margin; placed here editorially*

JOURNAL 1860

131.2 Journal] *E1*
131.4 Herman Melville, Passenger.] *below this line, notation in ink by ESM:* Summer of 1860
131.5 *1860*] *E2*
131.11 handkerchiefs] *miswritten* handercheifs

132.8 were] *E3*
132.17 than] *miswritten* that
132.22 Southern] S *written over* N
132.23 sensibly] bly *rewritten*
132.23 sinking] g *rewritten*
132.28 *Wednesday*] *E4*
132.34 *Crossed the Line*] *written twice normal size*

133.1 S] *written over* N
133.6 were born] w *written over* s
133.9 breeze] *rewritten*
133.13 Put] *E5; across top of page, notation in pencil by ESM identifying page:* From a journal on the "Meteor" commanded by Capt. Thomas Melville, bound for San Francisco
133.15 *Monday*] *above this word, notation in pencil by ESM:* 1860
133.19 boy] y *rewritten*
133.22 getting] ge *rewritten*

133.24 staysail] il *written over* le
133.32 Prince] nce *rewritten*

134.1 *Wednesday*] *E6*
134.3 Just] J *written over* A
134.6 within] *miswritten* with
134.14 head-foremost] *after canceled* his
134.15 Macey] *after canceled* Cha
134.15 (Fisher)] *inserted above without caret (possibly later) in ink (which blotted facing page)*
134.21 sharp] r *added*
134.21 Tom] *E7*
134.28 aloft.] *added after* activity. *without deleting original period*
134.28 ship's] s *written over* in *with apostrophe added*
134.33 which] *terminal* h *rewritten*
134.36 if nothing] f *rewritten*
134.37 King] K *rewritten*

Report of Line-End Hyphenation

THE FIRST LIST below records the forms adopted in the present edition (NN) for compound words that were hyphenated at line-ends in the manuscript and that the editors had to decide whether to print as single-word compounds without hyphens or as hyphenated compounds. The second list enables one to determine the reading present in the manuscript of compounds that happen to be hyphenated at the ends of lines in NN; any word hyphenated at the end of a line in NN should be transcribed as one unhyphenated word unless it appears in this list. A slash (/) indicates the line-end break in the manuscript in a word that might possibly be hyphenated in more than one place. For further comment on these lists, see pp. 243–44.

I. NN *forms of compounds that were hyphenated at manuscript line-ends*

3.9	oyster-man	12.22	boatmen
4.34	foreknowledge	14.24	Westminster
5.20	tackle-fall	18.21	Thanksgiving
8.23	somehow	20.37	White-Friars
9.3	double-reefed	21.20	Paternoster
12.17	midnight	35.33	Middle-Age

43.25	good-hearted	86.15	midway
68.9	pleasure-grounds	92.9	ward-meeting
70.2	saw-buck	98.8	man-of-/war
73.27	Lattice-work	98.34	stumbling-block
75.4	donkey-boys	129.17	Newcastle-upon-/Tyne

II. *Compounds containing line-end hyphens in* NN *that should be retained in transcription*

4.9	mast-head	86.12	side-hill
4.29	middle-aged	87.27	anointing-stone
12.17	state-room	88.38	masonry-locked
16.25	St Martin's-In-the-Feilds	97.30	beer-shop
20.1	Denmark-Hill	100.18	ward-room
49.2	screw-steamer	126.15	hard-ware
77.18	Barn-yard	132.23	flying-jib-boom
82.16	dirt-heaps	133.19	pig-pen
84.2	Arab-Bedouin		

Melville's Agricultural Tour Memorandum (1850)

EXCEPTING Melville's journal notebooks, none in which he made literary memoranda has survived. In lieu of notebooks, he seems often to have used any paper at hand for his notes, including the endpapers of books (whether or not the notes related to them) and even the back of a map. For this reason the document presented here and the one on pp. 599–607 are included in this volume of his journals, though their content relates to works in other volumes. Even when elliptical or cryptic, his notes are revealing both in themselves and for the glimpse they give of his note-making habits.

In July of 1850 Melville accompanied his cousin Robert Melvill, chairman of the committee on crops of the Berkshire Agricultural Society, on an inspection tour in the south-central part of the county. He wrote this two-page tour memorandum in pencil on the verso of the front free endpaper and the facing recto of a binder's leaf in *A History of the County of Berkshire, Massachusetts* (Pittsfield: Bush,

1829), edited by David Dudley Field.[1] His dated signature in ink, "H Melville. / Pittsfield July 16. 1850", indicates that he acquired the book there two days before starting the tour on July 18 from the old family mansion run by Robert as a boardinghouse, where Melville was a paying summer guest. The eighteenth was the same day whose date he wrote, with his signature and "from Aunt Mary", in Hawthorne's *Mosses from an Old Manse* (see p. 599 below); and if that was in fact the day and date of the gift, from Robert's mother, the widow of Major Thomas Melvill, she must have presented him the book, perhaps for travel reading, before eight o'clock in the morning, the hour when he and Robert set out. The subject of the Berkshire *History*, and its folding map of the county (see p. 598), made it a likely book to take along, if not quite a guidebook, and some of Melville's notes in it may have been set down on the trip, as none of those in *Mosses* seem to have been (see pp. 599–600 and p. 603 below).

The continuous cast of Melville's two-page record, without a separately dated entry for each of the three days—Thursday the eighteenth, Friday the nineteenth, and Saturday the twentieth, shows that it is a later memorandum not, strictly speaking, a diary.[2] Its recall of specific detail, however, shows that Melville wrote it soon after the tour. The reason why Melville used for it the two blank page-surfaces

1. The book is now in the Melville Collection of the Berkshire Athenaeum, Pittsfield, Massachusetts, the gift of Agnes Morewood, granddaughter of the brother to whom he inscribed it (in pencil) below his own signature: "to Allan Melville / 1868" (see Merton M. Sealts, Jr., *Melville's Reading: A Check-List of Books Owned and Borrowed* [Columbia: University of South Carolina Press, 1988], no. 216). The notes are reproduced here (at approximately original size), by permission of the Berkshire Athenaeum and with the kind assistance of Ruth T. Degenhardt, Kathleen Reilly, and Richard Leab of its staff. The transcription was made from the original memorandum by Jay Leyda, who first published it in "White Elephant vs. White Whale," *Town and Country*, CI (August, 1947), 69, and then in the *Melville Log* (New York: Harcourt, Brace, 1951), I, 379–80; it was verified and corrected from an independent transcription (1989) from the original by Hershel Parker. Melville's additional notes are reported below, pp. 591–92. A copy of the book annotated by Jay Leyda (1947) to show Melville's notes and markings, and soon given to Harrison Hayford, is now in the Melville Collection of The Newberry Library (Melville 67–1599–17). Leyda's transcription of Melville's additional notes is the basis, corrected by the Northwestern-Newberry editors, of those given on pp. 591–92 below.

2. In the article cited in footnote 1 above, Jay Leyda miscalled it a "diary" (p. 69) and so misdated its writing in the *Log,* placing it under July 18 with the heading, "Melville begins . . . his record of 'the rambling expedition'."

he did, the third and fourth, was probably that he had already used the two preceding blanks (the front pastedown and the recto of its conjugate front endpaper) for a clipping from the *Pittsfield Sun* for July 4 that he labeled "Revolutionary Reminiscences." The same paper on July 18 announced the coming agricultural tour:

> The Committee of the Agricultural Society, ON CROPS, will commence the discharge of their duties on THURSDAY of the present week. They will go down from Lenox on the western side of the County, and return on the eastern during this week. On MONDAY next, they will go from Pittsfield through the eastern towns to the north, and return by Lanesborough.

There is no evidence whether Melville went on the second week's northeastern swing. Jay Leyda discovered all the documents of this first tour and Melville's part in it, as cited in footnote 1 above; also in Leyda's article was his discovery of Melville's ghosting some of his cousin's subsequent "Report of the Committee on Agriculture" (see the article, which reprints the "Report" and two local newspaper take-offs on it). The "Report" is included among Attributed Pieces in the Northwestern-Newberry *Piazza Tales* volume, pp. 449–51, 788–91.

Why Melville made this tour memorandum is not clear. Although he was in the midst of writing *Moby-Dick*, but probably just then at a pause, a passage in his 1849 London journal shows that he had already entertained the idea that he might "serve up the Revolutionary narrative of the beggar"—the work that became *Israel Potter* in 1855, six years later (see 43.15–17 and accompanying discussion). Into that work went other notes he made in the *History*, probably later, as well as passages from it, as indicated in the following paragraph.

Melville's additional notes on the blank rear leaves and endpapers of the *History* (but not his marginalia in it) are reported here. On p. 468, in the space below the end of the index, he penciled a five-line note: "Roots of a tree is the stem inverted. By experiment, the plum, cherry, &c have proved it.—"; additional words are erased but leaving the words ". . . from me they . . ." still decipherable. On the top half of blank page [470] he listed six items in column that interested him on certain pages of the book: "Table Bug — Block bug 39"; "Autumnal tint — hectic"; "Variety of Apples 87"; "Old Man — soldier 118"; "Jonathan Edwards 254"; "Brainard, 242". His note on "Table Bug" points to a possible source for his tale "The Apple-Tree

Table" (1856); see the Northwestern-Newberry *Piazza Tales* volume, p. 722. His note on "Old Man — soldier" refers to a passage about Colonel John Patterson's local regiment in the Revolution that Melville used in *Israel Potter*; see the Northwestern-Newberry edition, p. 187, n. 12. Five items in column at the top of blank page [472] are names of varieties of grass: "Redtop"; "Ribbon Grass"; "Finger Grass"; "Orchard Grass"; "Hair Grass". A final item is seven lines of poetry, the last two of them erased and undeciphered, that Melville wrote boldly in ink that sank in and spread like that of his signature at the front. He wrote them probably about the same time as his signature, before those in pencil just listed. Holding the book open sideways, Melville wrote these lines on the rear pastedown one after the other from the outer edge inwards:

"Let them talk of Blue Ridges
  And Natural Bridges,
But give me the Valley of Berks: —
  There the hill-horse neighs,
  There wind the purple ways,
[*two lines rubbed out except their terminal* !"]
— Shaker Poet.
[*erasure after* x]

This poem is not in the *History*, and the "Shaker Poet" has not been identified.

In the agricultural tour memorandum, Jay Leyda (*Log*, I, 379–80) identified the given names of the five men named there without them, and supplied one corrected surname: Eleazer Williams (line 12), Caleb Smith (line 17), Nelson Joyner (for Melville's "Joiner", line 26), John L. Cooper (line 29), and Luther Hinckley (line 32).

The Northwestern-Newberry [hereafter NN] transcription follows the principles stated for the journals; see pp. 236–42 above.[3] No words of Melville's are clearly misspelled except the proper name "Joiner's" (line 26); "waggon" (line 3) was listed as a variant spelling by Worcester (1855) and as "falling into disuse" by Webster (1859). Two words in which Melville elided letters are transcribed in stan-

3. For convenient reference, the lines in transcriptions are numbered, and individual words may be referred to by both line and word count—e.g., on the front free endpaper, verso, of the *History*, 10.5 is "took" (division marks and rules are not numbered or counted as lines in these transcriptions). Words or letters inside angle brackets were canceled; italicized words inside square brackets are editorial.

dard spelling: "Glorious" (line 18) and "Detained" (line 19). Four of Leyda's readings are corrected: "chairman" to NN "Chairman" (line 7); "in" to NN "at the" (line 9); "From thence" to NN "Thence" (line 21); and NN reports the comma Leyda omitted after "Housatonic" (line 22).

The dark background of the reproductions is unavoidably so because the paper has browned considerably, and many of the words are indistinct because Melville's penciled writing does not contrast strongly with it, even on the original pages. Note the heavy show-through, in reverse, of his signature on the second reproduced page. The map (p. 598) is a segment reproduced (in original size) from the folding "Map of Berkshire County, Mass." bound into the *History of Berkshire* before the title page. Though it was somewhat out of date by 1850, it will help readers in following Melville's agricultural tour.

[*on verso of front free endpaper*]

On Thursday July 18, 1850,
at 8. A.M. started with
Robert in his waggon on a
tour of the Southern part of the
County of Berkshire, to view the
state of the crops — he being
Chairman of the "Viewing Committee"
of the Berkshire Agricultural Society.
— Arrived at the Lenox Meeting
house on the hill, took a round
turn into the hollow — thence [*altered from* hence]
to Richmond, dining at Williams'
nigh to R.R. Depot. Went
to a high hill in Richmond to see
a crop of rye on a mountain.
Fine prospect. Put up for the night
at old Cap. Smith's in Lenox,
near the Pond. Glorious place, &
fine old fellow. Detained there
till next day at noon by a
severe storm. <From> Thence went
to Stockbridge, & across the Housatonic,

On Thursday, July 18. 1850,
at 8. A.M. started with
Robert in his "waggon" on a
tour of the Southern part of the
County of Berkshire, to view the
state of the Crops — he being
Chairman of the "Viewing Committee"
of the Berkshire Agricultural Society
— stopped at the Lenox Meeting
House on the hill, took a second
turn into the Churchyard — thence
to Richmond dining at Williams's
near the R.R. Depot. Thence
to a big hill in Richmond to see
a crop of rye on a mountain top —
Fine prospect. Put up for the night
at old Capt. Smith's in [illegible],
by the [illegible]. Glorious place, &
fine old fellow. Started the[illegible]
hill next day at noon by [illegible]
[illegible] — thence next
by [illegible], & [illegible]

[*on recto of binder's leaf*]

over "the plains," & by Monument mountain, thro' Barrington to Egremont, where we put up at a Mr Joiner's for the night. After breakfast, next day, went into Sheffield, & dined at Mr Cooper's. Thence thro' the two villages of Sheffield to Stockbridge, & *teaed* with Mr Hinckley in the village. And home on Saturday night by R.R. to Pittsfield.

over the [illegible] by the [illegible]

mountain, [illegible] to

Egremont, where we put up at a Mr Joyner's for the night. After breakfast next day, went into Sheffield, & dined at Mr Coopers. Thence thro' the two villages of Sheffield to Stockbridge, & took tea with Mr [illegible] in the village. Arrived home on Saturday night by R.R. to Pittsfield.

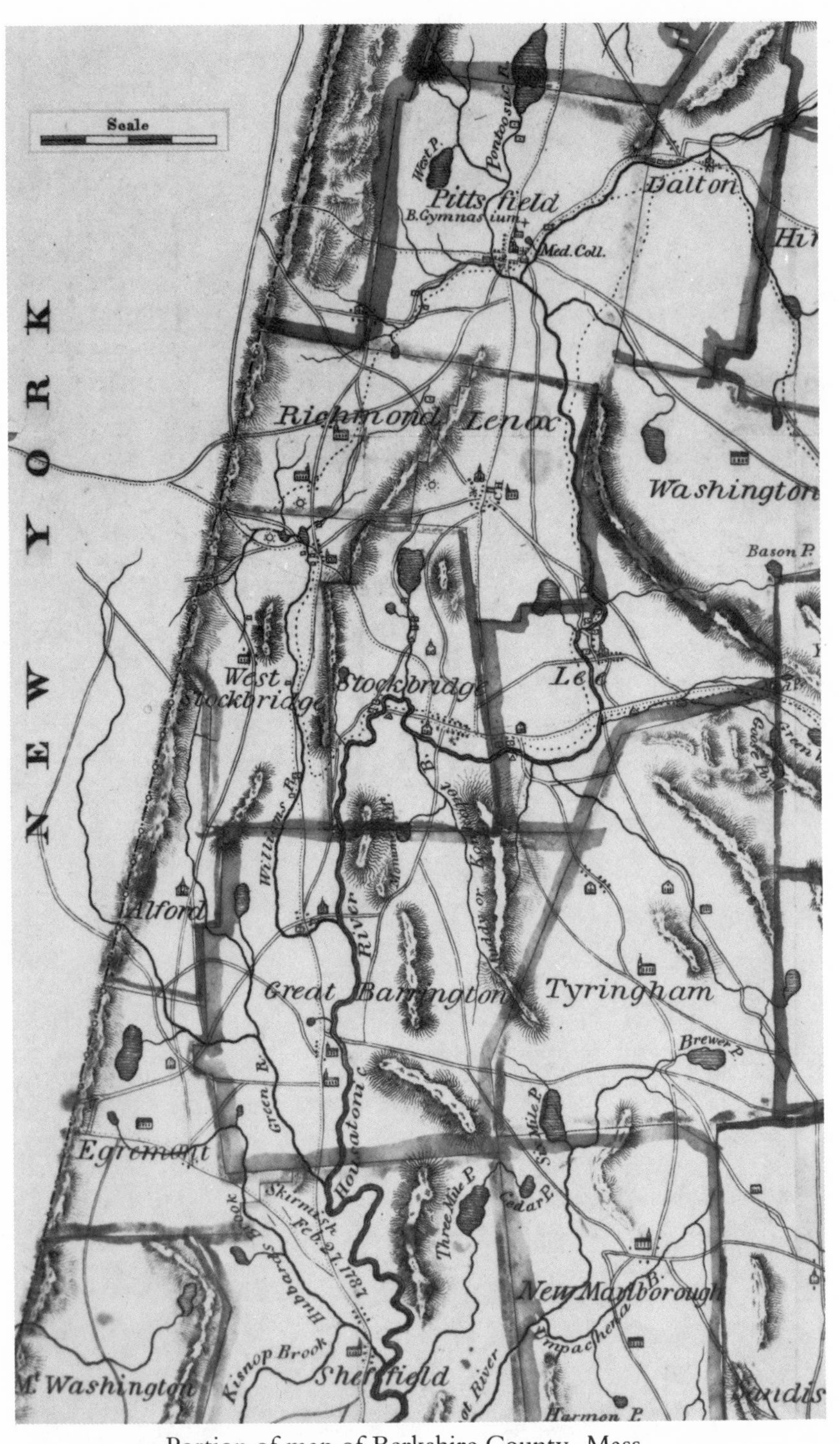

Portion of map of Berkshire County, Mass.

Melville's Notes in Hawthorne's Mosses *(1850?)*

MELVILLE WROTE the ensuing notes, all in pencil, on the rear endpapers of Hawthorne's *Mosses from an Old Manse* (New York: Wiley & Putnam, two parts in one volume, 1846). At the front of this book he wrote "H. Melville. from Aunt Mary. Pittsfield. July 18. 1850". That morning he set off on the agricultural tour that occasioned the memorandum presented above, pp. 589–98. After meeting Hawthorne on August 5, he took up the book again, jotted in it at least some of the notes presented here, and wrote his now famous enthusiastic essay about it, "Hawthorne and His Mosses."[1] Although the notes may be classified as marginalia, Mel-

1. The book is now in the Melville Collection of the Houghton Library of Harvard University, with the call number *AC85.M4977.Zz846h, the gift in 1937 of his granddaughter Eleanor Melville Metcalf (see Merton M. Sealts, Jr., *Melville's Reading: A Check-List of Books Owned and Borrowed* [Columbia: University of South Carolina Press, 1988], no. 249). It is described in the Northwestern-Newberry *Piazza Tales* volume, pp. 654–55, 663–64. The notes are reproduced here (at approximately original size) by permission of the Houghton Library, Harvard University.

ville did not make them simply in response to particular passages in the book. They should be recognized as memoranda, some or all of which he recorded for possible future literary use.[2]

Dating seems certain only for the two cryptic phrases Melville wrote near the top of the rear pastedown (line 1). Their content shows they were memos he worked up in the *Mosses* essay he composed on August 9–10, 1850. He must therefore have made these memos just before or while writing it.[3] In the phrases "Developable parts" and "Secret properties" (both in line 1) he noted down the cues for ideas he developed in the essay's next-to-last paragraph, in which three of those four words reappear (italicized here):

> For there is a sure, though a *secret* sign in some works which prove the culmination of the powers (only the *developable* ones, however) that produced them. . . . I somehow cling to the strange fancy, that, in all men, hiddenly reside certain wondrous, occult *properties* . . . which . . . may chance to be called forth. . . . (p. 253)

Moreover, a little earlier in the essay the sense, though not the exact wording, of his note "I had formerly read 'Twice Told Tales'" (line 2) also reappears: "I have thus far omitted all mention of his 'Twice Told Tales', and 'Scarlet Letter'. Both are excellent" (p. 249). So the anonymous writer of the essay has "formerly read" both works (an admission incidentally undercutting his claim all along in it that he has just discovered Hawthorne's writings).[4]

Below the two notes just discussed Melville drew a long rule, in

---

This transcription by Harrison Hayford (1942) was verified by Robert C. Ryan (1989), both reading from the manuscript notes. An inaccurate and incomplete transcription with a reproduction was included by Wilson Walker Cowen in his 1965 Harvard dissertation, "Melville's Marginalia" (published in photoreproduction, New York: Garland, 1988), pp. [v]–[vi], 418–19.

2. See the HISTORICAL NOTE, p. 164, footnote 2.

3. For Melville's essay see the Northwestern-Newberry *Piazza Tales* volume, pp. 239–53; for its dating see that volume as cited above in footnote 1, and also the Northwestern-Newberry *Moby-Dick*, pp. 612–14. Unless otherwise noted, quotations and page references here are from the Northwestern-Newberry [hereafter NN] editions.

4. The verb form "had read" may indicate that Melville added the sentence later. In 1849 Melville borrowed *Twice-Told Tales* from Evert Duyckinck, in *White-Jacket* (chap. 68, p. 283) complimented "A Rill from the Town Pump," a sketch in the book, and in a letter to Duyckinck, February 12, 1851, declared that he "hadnt read but a few" of the *Twice-Told Tales* (1837) before then (*Letters of Herman Melville*,

line 2 wrote several more words, and beneath them drew another long rule. Possibly these words in line 2 were further cues for his essay. They are now lost to us because someone later partly erased all of them (as well as the long rule below them), and because at some time between 1942 (when Hayford's transcription noted their erasure) and 1965 a Houghton Library label (shown in Cowen's 1965 reproduction) was placed on the rear pastedown, its top edge covering all but the first two (possibly more) of them, which may still prove recoverable. (Not shown in the reproduction are the initials "E.M.M.", penciled in the lower right corner, those of Eleanor Melville Metcalf, to whom ownership of the book had descended through her mother and her grandmother, Elizabeth Shaw Melville.)

Across from the pastedown, on the verso side of its conjugate free endpaper, Melville wrote three sets of notes. While there seems to be no way to tell for sure when he did so, the internal evidence indicates that he made the first two sets just before he wrote his *Mosses* essay. But one of his marginalia, which he dated, should warn us that he marked and wrote in this copy of *Mosses* over the years: "Nothing can be finer than this. / May 1865" (below a marked passage in "The Celestial Railroad" [pt. I, p. 189]).

The three sets of notes on this free endpaper are separated from each other by two of Melville's characteristic broken division-rules (with internal vertical strokes), one of them below the words in line 1 and another below those in lines 2–4. (His continuous rule below the words in line 5 marks a less strong division.)

In the first set, in the top line, the only note is: "Shenstone's Schoolmistress p. 207." For some reason Melville made it when he read a sentence in the sketch "A Virtuoso's Collection" (*Mosses*, pt. II, p. 207): "A bundle of birch rods, which had been used by Shenstone's schoolmistress, were tied up with the Countess of Salisbury's garter." The fact that Melville capitalized the word "Schoolmistress" (Hawthorne did not) as if in a title suggests that he was familiar with the poem Hawthorne alludes to, "The School-Mistress" (1743, 1748), a Spenserian imitation by William Shenstone (1714–63). In it the bucolic schoolmarm alternately birches her naughty boys and feeds them cakes, and her birch-rod discipline is mock-seriously

ed. Merrell R. Davis and William H. Gilman [New Haven: Yale University Press, 1960], p. 121).

commended as the right way to train up bishops, chancellors, and bards. There is no record whether Melville owned in 1850 the copy of Shenstone's *Poetical Works* (Cooke's edition, London: Cooke, 17—) that he gave to his sister Fanny in 1862 (Sealts 490). We can only speculate why he singled out an allusion to Shenstone's poem from the whole of *Mosses* and from the dozens of items in "A Virtuoso's Collection," a sketch he did not mention in his essay though he marked in it.[5]

5. Two related reasons may be suggested, both implying literary use (but neither requiring familiarity with the poem beyond Hawthorne's allusion to the schoolmistress, though that would have quickened both). A first possible reason for Melville's note on Shenstone's schoolmistress, as for his 1849–50 journal notes on Rousseau and Dr. Johnson as schoolmasters (see p. 142 above), could have been some idea he had of writing about schoolmastering, perhaps including his own experience at it (1837–38, 1839), of which he had not made literary use. If he did have that idea no such set piece ever came of it as his chapter of the year before, "A Man-of-war College" in *White-Jacket*, ridiculing the pedantic "professor" (chap. 83, pp. 345–49). But in *Moby-Dick* he touched on schoolmasters several times, in pathetic or comic tone. He attributed "Etymology" to "the Late Consumptive Usher to a Grammar School." As an unloved boy, Ishmael had a "stepmother who, somehow or other, was all the time whipping [him] or sending [him] to bed supperless"; but next he lorded it himself as a country schoolmaster and made "the tallest boys stand in awe" of him; and then he endured the keen "transition from a schoolmaster to a sailor," a victim once more, whom "old sea-captains" would "thump and punch" about. Again, Melville had fun in his gamy chapter about lordly "schoolmaster" whales presiding over their female "schools" like bashaws over harems, and with sexual innuendo he cited the *Memoirs* of Vidocq as to "what sort of a country-schoolmaster that famous Frenchman was in his younger days, and what was the nature of those occult lessons he inculcated into some of his pupils" ("Etymology," p. xv; chap. 4, p. 25; chap. 1, p. 6; chap. 88, p. 393). A second, more naked reason for Melville's interest in Shenstone's schoolmistress could have been her birch rods. Corporal punishment, especially flagellation, was a sore theme with him, though from early to late in his writings he revealed ambivalent feelings about it, as about all kinds of inflicted authority. In *Omoo* (1847) he treated the routine flogging of navy boys comically and without "applauding" that disciplinary system conceded that "there is no substitute for it" (chap. 29, p. 108). In *White-Jacket* (1849) he erupted into passionate denunciation of official flogging in the U.S. Navy and proclaimed his own horror of the lash and near escape from it as an enlisted man. Throughout *Moby-Dick* (1851) he expanded his theme of shipboard and universal thumps, kicks, and mutilation by unjust superiors. Yet in a jocular letter of 1862 (excerpted below, p. 645) he encouraged his sea-captain brother Tom to keep on "strapping" his young sailors and adapted some lines from Byron whose severe "spare the rod, spoil the child" moral resembled Shenstone's approval of birchrodding "Bum y-galled"

Melville's second set of notes on the free endpaper verso (lines 2–4) lists details about a house and its natural setting. These details were very likely his working notes for the first paragraph of his *Mosses* essay, which he drew from the old Melvill house in Pittsfield where he wrote it:

> . . . a fine *old* farm-*house* . . . dipped to the *eaves* in foliage—surrounded by mountains, *old* woods, and *Indian* ponds . . . [with] larch *trees* at my window. (p. 239)

(Five different words identical in his notes and his essay are italicized here.) A "house" with "eaves" (overrun by vines or dipped in foliage) is present both in the notes and in the essay but is not "Angular" but "old" in the essay; it has something "Indian" about it in both, but in the essay nearby "ponds" not "loop-holes"; and it has "trees" around it in both, but they are "old Locust trees" in the notes and "old woods" and "larch trees" in the essay. The repetition of words is striking, and, with allowance for the omission of other words and for the shifts normal in writing from such sparse hints, the evidence may be thought convincing that the notes were cues for the opening paragraph of his essay. If they were, Melville must have made them on or just before August 9, 1850, when he began the essay. In that case, he must have made his "Shenstone's Schoolmistress" note at least a little earlier, since it occupies the space just above them.

Melville's third set of notes on the free endpaper (lines 5–14) is unrelated to anything in Hawthorne's *Mosses*. Some printed work, perhaps a serial publication, with the (possibly approximate) title "Masonic Mirror & Symbolical Chart" (line 5) was apparently his source for the notes he made below in two stages (lines 6–8; then 9–14, circled for transposition to follow line 5). All of these notes pertain to Masonic ritual and objects that the Order interprets as "symbolical." These would have appeared in any such work, and some or all of them would have been pictured in any "Symbolical Chart" of the sort regularly used in Masonic instruction. Every Masonic temple offers a representation of "Solomon's temple," though with a separa-

---

schoolboys. Resuming the theme in *Billy Budd, Sailor* (c. 1885–91) he made Billy feel his own earlier horror of the lash, and in the soup-spilling episode had Billy get "playfully tapped from behind" with the "official rattan" of the master-at-arms, who then fetched a heedless drummer-boy "a sharp cut" with it (chap. 10; Hayford-Sealts edition [Chicago: University of Chicago Press, 1962], pp. 72–73).

tion of its outer and its more secret inner shrine, the "Holy of Holies," that Melville's description (lines 6–8) seems not to observe, just as it jumbles emblems pertaining to different degrees of Masonry.[6] The past tense in his phrase "looked like a pantry" seems to indicate that at least lines 6–8 may describe an actual Masonic temple, not a picture, that Melville had viewed, since with a picture still in view he would probably write that it "looks" rather than "looked" like a pantry. More likely, however, since he would not have been allowed to see the inner shrine, these lines are his first formulation of a description to be worked up further in a literary piece, as indicated both by the past tense and by their ending with "& &c &c"—a way he often broke off such sentence starts.[7]

6. Although no work with this title has been located, enough others have titles containing the words "Mirror," "Hieroglyphical," and "Chart" to make its existence appear likely. Serials with *Masonic Mirror* in their titles were published in various cities, including Boston, Philadelphia and New York, London, and San Francisco, from the 1820's into the 1850's (though apparently not in 1850). Numerous works, some sympathetic and some hostile, were available that gave accounts of Freemasonry and its rituals and of the items Melville notes. His earlier acquaintance with such a book may be reflected by his references in *White-Jacket* to the frigate's signal-book as containing "the Masonic signs and tokens of the navy," and to an officer's saluting with his sword "as if making masonic signs" (chap. 46, p. 194; chap. 39, p. 163). So may his later recollection of it in his references in *Moby-Dick* to the whale's "secret inner chamber and sanctum sanctorum" and its "mystic gestures . . . akin to Free-Mason signs and symbols" (chap. 78, p. 344, and chap. 86, pp. 378–79). Thanks to the Scottish Rite Cathedral Assoc., Chicago.

7. See p. 187 above, and the notes reproduced in *Moby-Dick*, p. 969, lines 16, 18, 20, and 21b. Melville's reading and thoughts betokened by these Masonic notes may have found outlet in *Moby-Dick*. It was well under way when he got the *Mosses* volume in July, 1850, and nearing its end in April of 1851 when he told Hawthorne in a letter that he was inclined "to think that the Problem of the Universe is like the Freemason's mighty secret, so terrible to all children. It turns out, at last, to consist in a triangle, a mallet, and an apron,—nothing more!" (*Letters*, p. 125). Without knowing about the notes in *Mosses*, Harold Beaver, in his annotations to *Moby-Dick* (Penguin: Harmondsworth, 1972), pointed out "a whole underworld of Masonic allusions" in it. Beaver pressed, no doubt too far, his "decoding" of "this rogue masterpiece" as an "elaborate hoax" using Masonic rituals to celebrate the homosexual brotherhood or "order" of whalemen. (See especially his notes to his pp. 99, 212, 226, 472, 487, 559–62, 576, 616.) Among other allusions Beaver picked up Stubb's sentence about the Order of the Garter ("In old England the greatest lords think it great glory to be slapped by a queen, and made garter-knights of," chap. 31, NN p. 132). Quoting from Masonic ritual he associated this Garter ritual with "The mason's investiture with his apron 'more honourable than the Garter or any other Order

The NN transcription follows the principles stated for the journals, pp. 236–42. For line numbering and symbols used see p. 592, footnote 3 above. Several words, all on the rear free endpaper, verso, need comment. A single word is transcribed as clearly misspelled: "compases" (9.7). Three words with elided letters are transcribed in standard spelling: "Schoolmistress" (1.2), "overrunning" (4.2), and "Symbolical" (5.4). Cowen (cited in footnote 1 above) reads "covering" for NN "overrunning" (4.2), "loop holes" for NN "loopholes" (2.4–3.1), "chart" for NN "Chart" (5.5), and "triangle" (a possibly correct reading) for NN "trough" (8.6); he finds "illegible" the third and fourth words in line 1 on the rear pastedown, NN "Secret properties".

One item may be glossed: "Ruth . . . *Shoe*" (9.1–5). The candidate for the first of the three degrees of Masonry (Entered Apprentice) in the Blue Lodge is conducted around the temple missing one shoe (or both). One theory finds the origin of the shoe symbolism in Jewish tradition and points to the Book of Ruth, 4:7–9. Bernard E. Jones explains that there "we learn that to unloose and give it to another person was a gesture of sincerity, of honest intention, a confirmation of a contract" (*Freemason's Guide and Compendium* [London: Harrap, 1950], pp. 268–69). In this work Jones, himself a Mason, examines the lodges, symbolic rites, and objects of Freemasonry historically, including most of those listed by Melville.

---

in existence, being the badge of innocence and the bond of friendship'" (Beaver's note to his p. 226), and also with Ishmael's argument that "we harpooneers of Nantucket should be enrolled in the most noble order of St. George" (chap. 82, NN p. 362). Stubb's allusion to "garter-knights" may indeed point to a link between Melville's note at the top of the page on Shenstone's *Schoolmistress* and those below on Freemasonry. Although it was not the "Countess of Salisbury's garter" in Hawthorne's sentence that Melville noted, he presumably caught and perhaps held in mind this reference to her legendary loss of a garter as the occasion for the founding of the Order of the Garter (by Edward III in the mid-fourteenth century). Stubb's allusion to ceremonial slaps by the queen (Victoria) shows an out-of-character knowledge more likely for Ishmael (see the NN discussion at 103.39). Melville's familiar use of passages from the *Chronicles* of "my glorious old gossiping ancestor, Froissart" in *Mardi* (chap. 24, p. 78), *White-Jacket* (chap. 68, p. 284, lines 19–20), and *Moby-Dick* (chap. 42, p. 191, and chap. 60, p. 280, lines 28–29) suggests his familiarity also with Froissart's account of the unrequited love of Edward III for the persistently virtuous Countess and of his instituting the Order, though not because of her lost garter (bk. I, chaps. 77, 89, 100 in either the Berners or the Johnes translation; no copy used by Melville is known).

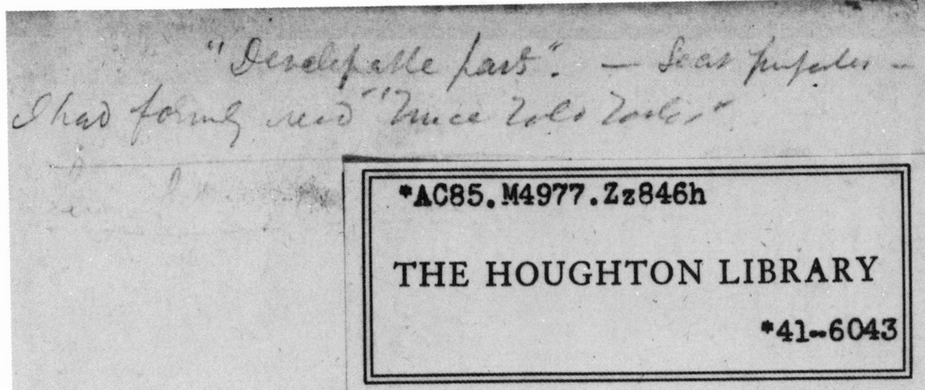

[*on rear pastedown, reproduced above*]

1 "Developable parts". — Secret properties —
2 I had formerly read "Twice Told Tales".

———————————

3 [*two or more undeciphered erased words (and others covered by the Houghton Library label), with an erased rule below them*]

[*on verso of rear free endpaper, reproduced opposite*]

1 Shenstone's Schoolmistress p. 207.

——— " ——— " ———

2 Angular house, Indian loop-
3 holes. — Old <l>Locust trees.
4 vines overrunning the eaves & gutters,

——— " ——— " ———

5 "Masonic Mirror & Symbolical Chart."

———————————

6 "Solomon's temple" Interior of the Holy of
7 Holies — looked like a pantry.
8 The brazier of brass — big trough. &c &c &c

9 Ruth iv & vii —— *Shoe* — Squares, compases,
10 levels, trowels, hammers, aprons, hour-glasses,
11 bee-hives, spades, swords, books, joined hands, [*add* keys,
12 pens, chisels, candlesticks.]
13 — Compas[*add* s] & square crossed upon an open
14 book — [*lines 9–14 circled, with guideline for their insertion following line 5*]

Shenstone's "Schoolmistress" p. 207.

Angular House, Indian Cup-boards. — Old Locust trees.
Vines rattling the eaves & gutters,

"Masonic Mirror & Symbolical Chart."
"Solomon's temple" Interior of the Holy of Holies — looked like a pantry.
The Graves of [illegible] — big trough. &c &c.

Ruth. IV § VII — Shoe — Squares, compasses, levels, trowels, hammers, aprons, hour-glasses, bee-hives, spades, swords, books, joined hands, keys, pens, chisels, candlesticks.
— Compass & square crossed upon an open book —

Melville Abroad: Further Records (1849–60)

THESE RECORDS closely related to Melville's trips abroad supplement his own journal accounts. They are grouped in three sections corresponding to the three trips recorded in his journals, 1849–50, 1856–57, and 1860, and each section is provided with an explanatory headnote, including cross references to documents quoted or cited in the HISTORICAL NOTE and DISCUSSIONS. The three documentary records not previously edited are discussed in separate headnotes and are shown in photoreproductions. Further contextual documents will be found in the *Letters of Herman Melville*, ed. Merrell R. Davis and William H. Gilman (New Haven: Yale University Press, 1960), Jay Leyda's *Melville Log* (New York: Harcourt, Brace, 1951; rev. ed., New York: Gordian Press, 1969), and Eleanor Melville Metcalf's *Herman Melville: Cycle and Epicycle* (Cambridge: Harvard University Press, 1953), pp. 64–78.

1849–50

THE RECORDS in this section fall into two groups. The first group includes three letters of introduction written for Melville by Edward Everett and one written by Richard H. Dana, Jr., with three letters about securing them (by Everett, Samuel Shaw, and Melville) and two more by Melville expressing thanks for them.[1]

Melville's own letters in all three sections of Further Records are reprinted from the Davis-Gilman *Letters*, without following the form of his datelines, and without the full annotations. See also p. 175 above and the discussion at 21.33 (about Everett's letters); the discussion at 22.2 (about N. P. Willis's letter of introduction); and pp. 174–75 and the discussion at 23.3 (about Dana's letter and Melville's visit to Moxon).

The second group of records here sheds further light on Melville and his activities in Paris and London: passages from two of Melville's own letters, a fragment of a map he bought at Galignani's Reading Room in Paris (endorsed with his notation to that effect and other memoranda), a passage about Melville in a letter by George Adler, and a list titled "London" that Melville drew up later of things to see and do there. Further references are made on p. 173 and in discussions at 20.28, 21.19, 21.20, 23.3, 38.20, 40.5, 146.13 (all relating to Evert and George Duyckinck), and at 30.7 and 46.6–7 (for Davidson's letter about Melville in London), and 144.1 (for Melville's letter referring to his stay in Paris).

Draft letter: Edward Everett to R. Monckton Milnes, Cambridge, September 3, 1849.

My dear Milnes,

I have been requested by my much valued friend the Chief Justice of Massachusetts to ask the favor of your personal acquaintance for his

1. The following letters, transcribed by Robert C. Ryan (1989), are reprinted by permission of the Massachusetts Historical Society: Edward Everett's four unsigned draft letters, from microfilm of his letterbooks; and Samuel Shaw's letter to Richard H. Dana, Jr., in the Dana Family Papers. Since the draft letter of Richard H. Dana, Jr., to Edward Moxon, also in the Dana Family Papers, and George Adler's letter to George Duyckinck, in the Duyckinck Collection of the New York Public Library, were not available for transcription, Eleanor Melville Metcalf's transcriptions are reprinted here from *Herman Melville,* pp. 66 and 73.

son-in-law, Mr. Herman Melville. I have not the advantage of knowing this gentleman personally; but he is well known to the whole reading world, as the author of some of the most striking & original productions of the day; I refer to "Typee" & "Omoo". His character and connections are such that I may safely commend him to your friendly *accueil*; his literary merit needs no praise of mine. I think you saw his brother, who was U. States' Secretary of legation in Mr. McLane's time. Mr. Herman Melville is well worthy of your kind notice on his own account & if you will permit me to think that I have any interest in your good offices, I beg to avail myself of it in his favor.

Bancroft sent me some time ago a copy of your letter on Foreign Affairs to Lord Lansdowne. He did not tell me that it was *hommage de l'Auteur*; but my vanity led me to hope it might be; and in fact I should take it ill of you to write any thing so liberal, clever, & seasonable & not send me a copy. At any rate whether I am under obligations to you or not for the pamphlet, I certainly am for much satisfaction in its perusal.

Not doubting that you will own that I have repaid the obligation, by giving you an opportunity to make Mr. Melville's acquaintance, I remain my dear Milnes, as ever Sincerely Yrs

P.S. My wife & daughter if they knew I was writing to you would command their kind remembrance.

Draft letter: Edward Everett to Samuel Rogers, Cambridge, September 3, 1849.

My dear Mr Rogers,

It is such an age since I have written to you, that I am really under obligations to my honored friend the Chief Justice of Mass[ts]. who has asked of me for his son-in-law Mr. Melville, the favor of one or two letters to London. This gentleman (I am sorry to say) is not known to me personally. He is known to you and the entire reading world by his "Typee" & "Omoo" & another work of the same class which I have not yet seen. I understand Mr. Melville's character to be altogether such as to warrant me in commending him to your kind notice. His brother who was Secretary of Legation under Mr. McLane was I think known to you. Few of our writers have been so successful at home as Mr. Herman Melville & I am happy to perceive that his productions are well known on your side of the water.

Mr. Melville is going to pass a few months in England & France; & while he is in London, I want him to see a few of those choicest spirits, who even at the present day increase the pride which *we* feel in speaking the language of Shakespeare & Milton. In a word, my dear friend, I want you to admit him to the freedom of N°. 22 St. James' Place.

I need not tell you how constantly we think of you;—how often we speak of you;—how regularly we do the honors of your portrait to all who come to us. I should be delighted to have under your hand & seal, the confirmation of the good accounts I have of you from others; & I pray you to believe me, my dear Mr. Rogers, with the strongest Attachment sincerely Yours

Draft letter: Edward Everett to M. [Gustave] de Beaumont, Cambridge, September 3, 1849.

My dear M. de Beaumont

This note will be handed to you by my ingenious countryman Mr. Herman Melville, the author of "Typee", "Omoo" & another work of the same class, which I have not yet read;—publications which have had great success both in Europe & America; & rank with the most original & *picquant* of the day. They have, if I mistake not lately been made the subject of an elaborate criticism in the *Revue des deux mondes.*

Mr Herman Melville is about to visit London & Paris. I have not the advantage of knowing him personally. We live as far apart as Paris & Lyons, & you know we have no Paris or London in the U. States, which for some portion at least of the year, gathers all into its net. But I have been requested by my much honored friend, the Chief justice of the Commonwealth,—the father-in-law of Mr Melville,—to procure for him the advantage of making the acquaintance of some of those persons in Europe, whom an intellectual American is most desirous of knowing. You must not allow yourself to wonder that I have thought of you; & I beg to assure you that I shall regard any kindness shewn to Mr. Melville as doubly shewn to myself. Desiring my kindest remembrance to all the family of Lafayette I remain, my dear M. de Beaumont, ever Sincerely Yours

Draft letter: Edward Everett to Chief Justice Shaw, Cambridge, September 3, 1849.

My dear Sir,

Your letter of the 31 Augt. was handed to me on Saturday Ev'g.

I am obliged as a general rule to decline giving letters of Introduction to my friends abroad, for several reasons which will occur to you. I am however always happy to have it in my power to make exceptions, though I do it but rarely. The extraordinary literary merit of Mr Melville warrants me in doing so, in his case, and a desire to meet any wish of yours furnishes me a strong additional motive.

Lemuel Shaw, Chief Justice of Massachusetts, 1851. Courtesy of the New York Public Library, Gansevoort-Lansing Collection.

I enclose you for Mr. Melville a letter to Mr. Monckton Milnes, a [young] gentleman of Fortune;—An M.P.; A Cambridge man of Trinity College;—A poet of considerable ability;—A very companionable person in the highest society; And another to Mr. Nestor [*canceled*] Rogers, the Nestor of English poets now I think in his 87th year, whose table has been for years the centre of the best society in London.

M. de Beaumont is the grandson-in-law of Lafayette; he travelled in this country in 1833 with M. de Tocqueville to examine our penitentiaries;—he has written an ante-slavery novel called *Marie ou l'esclavage* & a work on Ireland. He was sent last year by the Provisional government of France as Minister to England, where he staid five months only.

They have no Society in Paris like that in London; or if they have I do not know it. But I know no one better able to introduce Mr. Melville to men of education & position, than M. de Beaumont. In sending these letters to Mr Melville, I must ask you to request him, not to mention that he has received any letters of introduction from me. I am so often applied to & so often have to refuse, that it is quite desirable to me, when I do it, that it should not be known.

Wishing Mr Melville an agreeable visit to Europe & the full enjoyment of his reputation, I remain, my dear Sir, as ever with the highest respect, faithfully Yours

Samuel Shaw to Richard H. Dana, Jr., Boston, September 5, 1849.

Dear Sir, Our friend Mr. Herman Melville is about going to Europe, & I am desirous of procuring for him a few good letters of introduction. I have already obtained some of the first quality. It occurred that you might aid him, in this matter, either personally & through someone else, & I cannot doubt, that you would be happy to do so.

If you find that you can furnish me with a letter or two for Mr Melville, I shall feel quite obliged by it, & as I am going to N.Y. in a few days, I shall be happy to be the bearer.

Respectfully & very truly
yours, Samuel Shaw

Excerpt: Melville to Lemuel Shaw, New York, September 10, 1849.

My Dear Sir—In writing you the other day concerning the letters of introduction, I forgot to say, that could you conveniently procure me one from M[r] Emerson to M[r] Carlyle, I should be obliged to you. . . . If, besides a letter to M[r] Carlyle, M[r] Emerson could give you *other* letters, I should be pleased.

Draft letter: Richard H. Dana, Jr., to Edward Moxon, Boston, September 12, 1849.

My dear Sir, Allow me to introduce to you my friend, Mr. Herman Melville, of New York. Mr. Melville is the Author of those well known & popular narratives of adventures at sea & in the Pacific Islands, with which you are doubtless familiar. So many persons have affected to believe his a nom de guerre, that I am happy to learn his intention of visiting Europe in propria persona, so that his readers there may satisfy themselves not only that he is a veritable person, but a most agreeable gentleman of one of our best families. In some cases I might hesitate whether my relations with yourself would authorize me to introduce a friend to your attentions, but I am sure you will derive so much gratification from the acquaintance with Mr. Melville, that I feel as if I were only communicating to you a pleasure of my own.

I should like very much to have him see Capt. Jones, if he is in London.
Most sincerely yours Richard H. Dana, Jr.

Excerpt: Melville to Richard H. Dana, Jr., New York, October 6, 1849.

If I have till now deferred answering your very kind letter by Judge Shaw, it has been only, that I might give additional emphasis to my reply, by leaving it to the eve of my departure. Your letter to M[r] Moxon is most welcome. From his connection with Lamb, & what I have chanced to hear of his personal character, he must be a very desirable acquaintance.—

Excerpt: Melville to Lemuel Shaw, New York, October 6, 1849.

My Dear Sir—

On Monday or Tuesday next the ship is to sail, and I must bid you the last good-bye.

On looking over the letters of introduction again, I am more than ever pleased with them; & would again thank you for your kindness. A few days ago, by the way, I received a letter of introduction (thro' the post) from M[r] Baldwin to his son in Paris.

Lizzie is becoming more reconciled to the idea of my departure, especially as she will have Malcolm for company during my absence. And I have no

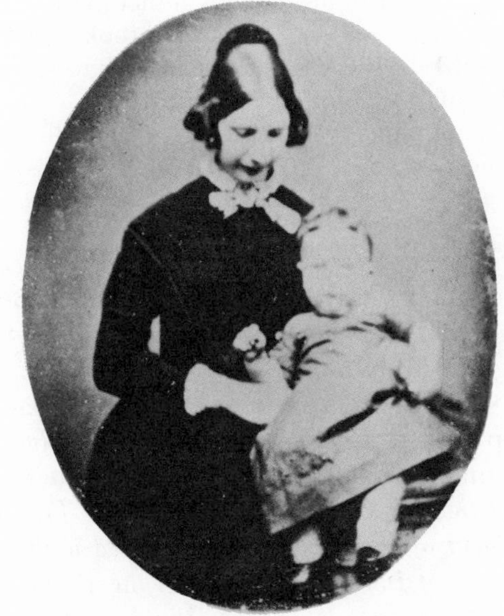

Elizabeth Shaw Melville and Malcolm, 1849. Courtesy of the Berkshire Athenaeum.

doubt, that when she finds herself surrounded by her old friends in Boston, she will bear the temporary separation with more philosophy than she has anticipated. At any rate, she will be ministered to by the best of friends.

It is uncertain, now, how long I may be absent; and, of course, my travels will have to be bounded by my purse & by prudential considerations. Economy, however, is my mottoe.

Excerpt: Melville to Evert A. Duyckinck, Paris, December 2, 1849.

My Dear Mr Duycknk,

I could almost whip myself that after receiving your most kind & friendly letter, I should suffer so long an interval to go by without answering it. But what can you expect of me? I have served persons the nearest to me in like manner. Traveling takes the ink out of one's pen as well as the cash out of one's purse.—Thank you for the papers you sent me.

—The other evening I went to see Rachel—& having taken my place in the "*que*" (how the devel do you spell it?) or tail—& having waited there for full an hour—upon at last arriving at the ticket-box—the woman there closed her little wicket in my face—& so the "tail" was cut off.

—Now my travelling "tail" has been cut off in like manner, by the confounded state of the Copyright question in England. It has prevented me from receiving an immediate supply of cash—I am going home within three weeks or so.—But I have not failed to enjoy myself & learn somewhat, notwithstanding.

Give my best remembrances to your brother. Tell him I stumbled upon an acquaintance of his—a book dealer in the Strand. Tell him that Davidson proved a good fellow, & that we took some punch together at the Blue Posts.—Mr Delf I was not so happy as to see when I called there.

But I may see him on my return.

My compliments to Mrs Duyckncк & all your pleasant family, & Beleive me Sincerely yours

H Melville.

Melville's map from Galignani's, Paris, December 3, 1849.

Melville's journal entry on this date reports, "Went to Galignani's after breakfast to get Continental Guide" (32.29–30). The only part of this guide known to survive is a fragment of a map. The Northwestern-Newberry editors have established that this fragment comes from a map entitled *Bradshaw's Map of the Railways, in Central Europe. 1849.* This map was sold as part of *Bradshaw's Continental Railway, Steam Navigation, & Conveyance Guide, and Traveller's Manual for the Whole Continent of Europe . . . Accompanied with a Well Executed Map of the Railways of Europe, and Also of the Rhine*, then a monthly 120-page publication priced at one shilling (see the discussion at 9.23–24). Since Melville mentions buying a "Continental Guide" he acquired the map not separately but by buying *Bradshaw's Continental Railway . . . Guide*—probably the latest number dated December (No. 31), because Galignani's, as the principal publisher listed on the title page (though it was printed by the Bradshaw firm in England), would have had it promptly available. (But numbers from the preceding months, and some of the early months of 1850, also had the 1849 map. Apparently no other Bradshaw publication would have had this map.)

The whole map (44.4 cm high by 60 cm wide) was folded into sixteenths then glued between the front wrapper and the title leaf of the *Guide*. It was so folded that the verso of the surviving fragment would have constituted part of the two outside surfaces of the folded map; the surface on which Melville wrote his name and made his notations would have been the one facing the title page.

The fragment (reproduced below, p. 619) shows, on its recto, parts of Holland, Belgium, and France.[2] At the top of the recto, parts of four numerals show, the last two identifiable as "4" and "9", evidently from "1849". On the verso, running lengthwise of the fragment, from its bottom to its top edge (where "49" appears on the recto), are Melville's signature and four additional lines of his notes:

2. This "Map with Melville Inscription" is now so listed in the Herman Melville Collection of the Clifton Waller Barrett Library, University of Virginia Library (accession number 6252–e). It is reproduced here, enlarged approximately ten percent from its original size and apparently for the first time, by permission of the Manuscripts Division, Special Collections Department. The fragment was received by the library on December 17, 1963, from Mr. Barrett, to whom it was sold by Goodspeed's Book Shop, Boston, in 1959. According to a letter of October 2, 1959, from Gordon T. Banks of Goodspeed's, the fragment was sold to the firm that day by "the granddaughter of Herman Melville"—whom he misidentified as "Frances Thomas" (Melville's daughter) but who was in fact her daughter Francis Thomas Osborne. According to Mr. Banks, she described "the Melville signature and inscription as having been cut from a guide book which he purchased in Paris." This information was kindly supplied to the Northwestern-Newberry editors by David Vander Meulen (April 24, 1989), along with a description of the fragment from which some details not apparent in the reproduction are extracted here. The approximately rectangular fragment of wove paper (no watermark, thickness .0025″), now browned, measures 11.4 × 4.9 cm (distance from "Rheims" to "Hague", 7.5 cm). The large dark area showing in the reproduction both recto and verso is caused by a large piece of cellotape (8.9 × 1.9 cm) that covers the right-hand third of the recto of the fragment discoloring the paper on both sides. Comments on the map and the *Guide* here are based on the holdings of the Parsons Collection of the New York Public Library.

Herman Melville
Bought at Galignani's, Paris,
Dec: 3d 1849. —— Restaurant
Anglais, Boulevard Italiens.
Chocolat.

This date and place of purchase correspond to those in Melville's journal entry. Comparison of the further notations with that entry (and the one for December 4) suggests that the "Restaurant Anglais" is the one he referred to in the entry as "Rosbeuf," while "Chocolat" refers not to a drink he had while he dined there but to the "cup of 'chocolat,' which was exquisite" that he had later in the evening at the "Cafe de Foy." Evidently these notations were memoranda that Melville jotted on the back of the map still later that evening to be written up in his journal—as they were, apparently on the following day. They furnish a slight surviving sample of the kind of memoranda he occasionally made on available paper to become journal entries (see his reference to a nonextant "smaller notebook" for his "Oxford" entry, 156.3, and p. 166, footnote 2 above).

Excerpt: George Adler to George Duyckinck, Paris, February 16, 1850.

Our friend Mr. Melville has, I hope, long ago reached his home again safely, and you will have gained from him an account of our voyage and peregrinations in England and London. I regretted his departure very much; but all I could do to check and fix his restless mind for a while at least was of no avail. His loyalty to his friends at home and the instinctive impulse of his imagination to assimilate and perhaps to work up into some beautiful chimaeras (which according to our eloquent lecturer on Plato here constitute the essence of poetry and fiction) the materials he has already gathered in his travels, would not allow him to prolong his stay.—

Excerpt: Melville to Nathaniel P. Willis, London, December 14, 1849.

I very much doubt whether Gabriel enters the portals of Heaven without a fee to Peter the porter—so impossible is it to travel without money. Some people (999 in 1000) are very unaccountably shy about confessing to a want of money, as the reason why they do not do this or that; but, for my part, I think it such a capital clincher of a reason for not doing a thing, that I out with it, at once—for, who can gainsay it? And, what more satisfactory or unanswerable reason can a body give, I should like to know? Besides—tho'

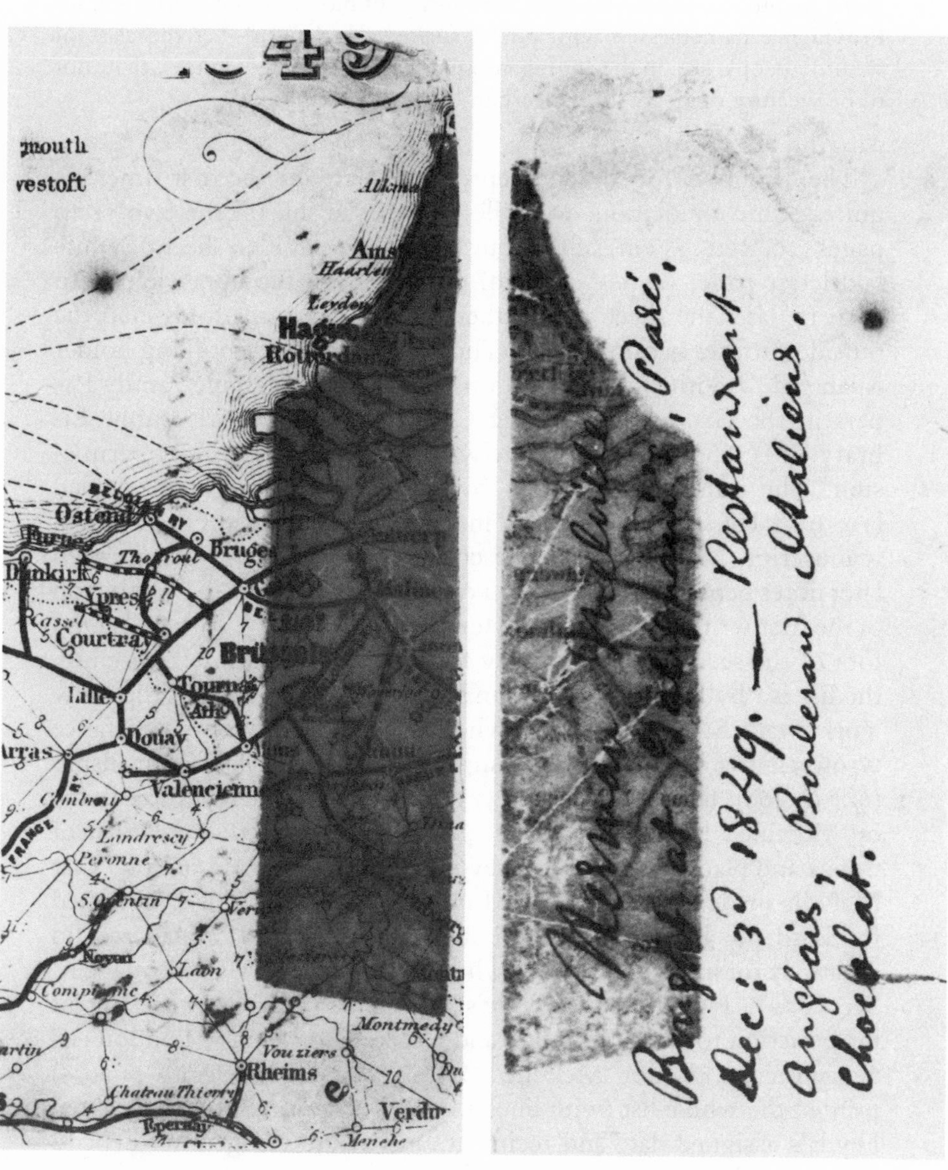

[recto] [verso]

Fragment of Melville's map from *Bradshaw's . . . Continental Guide*, bought at Galignani's, Paris. Courtesy of the Alderman Library, University of Virginia.

there are numbers of fine fellows, and hearts of blood, in the world, whom Providence hath blessed with purses furlongs in length—yet the class of wealthy people are, in the aggregate, such a mob of gilded dunces, that, not to be wealthy carries with it a certain distinction & nobility.

Melville's "London" (1853?)

The "London" document, reproduced here for the first time, requires some annotation. Melville wrote it in ink on the two recto pages (20 × 12.75 cm) of the four formed by a folded sheet of white laid letter paper (25.5 × 20 cm) embossed on the upper left recto corners; later the sheet was further folded with three folds, and the outside surfaces became soiled. The document's present filing holder is labeled "An itinerary of London," among the Melville Family Papers in the Gansevoort-Lansing Collection, New York Public Library. It is reproduced here (the writing in original size) by permission. The transcription (1989) by Harrison Hayford was verified (1989) by Hershel Parker, from independent readings of the original manuscript. Not shown on the cropped reproduced pages are two later notes penciled probably by a cataloguer: "[June 1853]" at the top of the first written page, and "[Memorandum by A. J. Parker]" at the foot of the second. No authority for either note is known; certainly the list is "by" Melville, not Amasa J. Parker, a justice of the New York State Supreme Court, who at Peter Gansevoort's instance wrote a letter (April 20, 1853) supporting Melville for a consulship (*Log*, I, 469). Jay Leyda (*Log*, I, 475) printed only the first three items on Melville's list, identifying it (presumably correctly) as "a list of things and places for Peter Gansevoort to see and do in London" that Melville made sometime before June 11, 1853, when this uncle sailed for England; Leyda gave its location as "NYPL:GL" but cited no authority for his assignment of when and for whom Melville made it. See *Log,* I, 476–77, for Melville's giving his uncle Peter a letter of introduction to Robert Cooke, and Cooke's consequent London entertainment. Eleanor Melville Metcalf (*Herman Melville*, p. 175) printed the whole list (with lines 12 and 13 transposed); she accepted Leyda's assigned date and recipient, and acknowledged her debt to him for a photostat.

In the present transcription, the same principles are followed as for the journals (see pp. 236–42 above; for line numbering and symbols used see p. 592, footnote 3 above). One word is transcribed as clearly misspelled: "Edinborough" (22.4). Six words with elided letters are transcribed in standard spelling: "pensioners" (6.7), "American" (7.4), "Negro" (7.5), "among" (8.1), "Greenwich" (9.1), and "emigrants" (11.1).

[*first page*]

London
— " —

Covent-Garden — before breakfast.
A sail in the Penny steamers on the river.
A Lounge on the bridges.
Go to Greenwich Hospital in the *morning* so as to see the pensioners at dinner. (An American negro is among them)
Greenwich Park, for the view.
Leicester Square — the French emigrants. Good breakfast there.
Seven Dials — Gin shops.
Judge & Jury — Drury Lane

[*second page*]

The Temple — Go to the Church on Sunday. (Templar's tombs)
—— Dining Halls & Desert Room & Kitchen on week days.
Lincoln's Inn Kitchen.
Reform Club
"Blue Posts" Cork Street near the Arcade — fine punch & dinners.
For fine ale — Edinborough Castle Strand —

London

Covent-Garden — before breakfast.

A sail in the Penny steamers on the river.

A Lounge on the bridges.

Go to Greenwich Hospital in the morning so as to see the pensioners at dinner. (An American nego is among them)

Greenwich Park, for the view.

Leicester Square — the French emigrants. Good breakfast there.

Seven Dials — Gin shops.

Lodge & Ivory — Drury Lane

The Temple — Go to the Church on Sunday. (Templars' tombs) — Dining Halls & Desert Room & Kitchen on week days.

Lincoln's Inn Kitchen.

Reform Club

"Blue Posts" Cork Street near the Arcade — fine punch & dinners.

For fine ale — Edinburgh Castle Strand —

[Memorandum by B. J. Parker]

1856–57

TWO ESPECIALLY valuable records supplement Melville's journal account of this trip, both dealing with only its early part. The first, by Melville himself, covers his voyage from New York to Glasgow and his movements in Scotland and England from October 26 to November 8—none of this covered by regular journal entries. It is given in a long letter to his brother Allan from Liverpool, November 10, 13, 14. See also p. 183 and the discussion at 50.12. The second record is Hawthorne's extended notebook entry of November 20, two days after Melville sailed for the Mediterranean. Its earliest published version, Mrs. Hawthorne's abridgment (rendered tantalizing and misleading by her ellipsis dots), is given here—minus her depersonalized rendering of the Chester passage—before the complete entry because it is the one Melville read in his copy of *Passages from the English Note-Books* (Boston: Fields, Osgood, 1870), II, 155–56 (Sealts 251). It was the only one available until the publication of its full transcription in *The English Notebooks of Nathaniel Hawthorne*, edited by Randall Stewart (New York: Modern Language Association of America, 1941), pp. 423–27, which is reprinted here by permission (as verified by G. Thomas Tanselle in 1989 from the original notebook in the Morgan Library). See other references to these documents in the HISTORICAL NOTE, pp. 183, 183, footnote 25, 184, and in the discussions from 50.29 through 51.19.

For Melville's subsequent travel, from his departure from Liverpool on November 18, 1856, to his arrival in New York on May 4, 1857, there are almost no known surviving documents supplementing his journal. The most interesting is Samuel Shaw's letter describing his meeting with Melville in Rome, March 21, 1857; it is excerpted in the discussion at 113.17.

Melville to Allan Melville, Liverpool, November 10, 13, 14, 1856.

My dear Allan—I have been ashore about two weeks, and as my plans of further travel are now beginning to mature, I proceed to write you. But first let me speak of my movements thus far.—As for the voyage over, it was upon the whole not disagreeable, though the passengers were not all of a desirable sort. There was, I think, but one American beside myself. The rest were mostly Scotch with a sprinkling of English. Among others there were some six or seven "commercial travellers," a hard set who did little but drink and gamble the whole way over. With these fellows of course I had precious little to do. But there was one man, who interested me considerably, one who had been an officer of the native troops in India, and besides was a good deal of a philosopher and had been all over the world. With him I had many long talks, and we so managed to kill time. The weather was pretty good with the exception of a gale which lasted about 36 hours, which obliged us to "lay to" about 18.—I staid in Glasgow three or four days. It is a very fine commercial city, with a great commerce, noble streets, and an interesting old cathedral. I went to Dumbarton Castle, some twenty miles distant and to Loch Lomond near by. From Glasgow I went to Edinburgh, remaining there five days, I think. I was much pleased there. I went to Abbottsford & Melrose. And I went to Perth & Stirling.—Of some Scotchmen on board the steamer, I enquired about "Scoonie" (How is it spelt?) and learned there was such a place, and that was all. I endeavored to find out more about it; but though I consulted the books containing lists of all the clergy in Scotland, I could find no clergyman or parish called "Scoonie." But even if I had learned more, I do not know as I would have sought out the place to make a personal call upon any one; because, unfortunately, the evening we arrived at Greenock I received an ugly hurt upon the bridge of my nose, which by no means improved my appearance. A sailor was lowering a boat by one of the tackles; the rope got foul; I jumped to clear it for him, when suddenly the tackle started, and a coil of the rope (new Manilla) flew up in my face with great violence, and for the moment, I thought my nose was ruined for life. But the wound has now healed, and I hope that in a few days little or no scar will remain.—But for the week succeeding the accident I presented the aspect of one who had been in a barroom fight.

—From Edinburgh I finally went to York, by way of Berwick & Newcastle, on the east coast, and after a day's stay in York to view the minster, I came here.—I have, with one small exception, travelled entirely in the "Parliamentary" trains, that is, the cheapest ones. Travelling any distance by the first class or even the second, is exceedingly dear. And yet it is not easy to travel in the "Parliamentary," because only one such train runs a day on any road, & [it] generally [usually?] starts before day-light in the morning; and the Parliamentary trains on different roads do not connect.—I propose calling to see Mr. Hawthorne here.

—About my further travel, at present I think that, if no obstacle interpose, I shall take a steamer to Constantinople from this port. I can go for $100; which is cheaper than the transatlantic steamers. The steamers hence for Constantinople touch at Gibraltar & Malta. If I go by this route to Constantinople, I shall save money. The only difficulty is about getting my passport in order for the various places afterwards. From Constantinople I should go to Alexandria by steamer, & so to Cairo, & from thence by steamer to Trieste, Venice, and bring up at Rome for a considerable stay. I may be mistaken, but I think that what funds I have, will enable me to accomplish this, though my absence from home will not probably be prolonged beyond March at the furthest. So at least I think now.—I have been ashore now two weeks, and spent in all about thirty five dollars. But this has been by the strictest economy, both in R.R. lodging, & eating.—Concerning my enjoyment of the thing, it is rather solitary business, poking about the world without a companion. Still, my health is benefited. My hip & back are better, & also my head. But I find that in walking I have pretty often to rest.—All this is about myself. How are you? And Sophia? and the small ones? I hope all goes well. I have written Mama.

—About the trunk, it is as I told you—I am going to store it here at Liverpool till I return from the continent. I shall take nothing but the carpet-bag.—Part of my tour in Scotland I had with me a Mr Willard of Troy (you remember the name at the steamer office) a theological student, very uninteresting, but better than nobody. He left me for London at York. I am now alone, & expect to be for some time.

—I shall write to Lizzie the day I leave here for good, (which will probably be in about a week, as no suitable steamer for the Mediterranean sails previous to then) and in that letter to her, I will endeavor to state, where letters from home will reach me; though I doubt whether I shall be in the way of getting any letters after quitting England.—Thinking that letters might have been sent for me to the care of Murray or Bentley at London, I have written to them to forward such letters to me at this place.

Thursday Nov. 13th
Evening.

Ere you get this you will have been pained to hear of the serious accident to George Duyckinck on one of the rail roads near London. I only heard of it day before yesterday from Mr Hawthorne in the cars as we were going out to his place. My first feeling was to go on at once to London to see Mr Duyckinck, thinking that possibly he might have no acquaintance near him; but Mr Hawthorne told me that upon reading an account of the affair in the paper (containing G. Duyckinck's name among others) he had at once written to a friend in London to interest himself in Mr Duyckinck's behalf; and had obtained a reply to the effect that no one was allowed to see him where he lay at St. Thomas' Hospital, I think. But this morning Mr H. received another letter saying, that Mr D. was getting on well, and had friends about him; which I was the more rejoiced to hear, since as matters have turned out, I could not have gone to London without the utmost disarrangement of my plans. Nevertheless, did I suppose that my presence would be particularly welcome to Mr Duyckinck, or give him ease, I would go on to see him as it is. But the extent of my acquaintance with him hardly justifies me in supposing that such would be the case. There are probably those about him now; whom he would rather have than me. May God grant him a speedy recovery. I have not written to him, thinking of course that letters he does not read.—

I have now as good as determined upon sailing hence in the screw-steamer "Egyptian" for Constantinople, on Monday next. I have been on board the ship. I think this voyage is the best thing I can do—it is certainly the cheapest way in which I can spend the coming 26 days—for such will be the length of the voyage, including stoppages. I shall miss much however in going at this season of the year—June is so much better. But that can't be helped.

By the way, you had better (after reading it) send this letter on to Lizzie, as it may contain items omitted in my letters to her. And Lizzie can send it to Helen &c, if it be worth while.

Li[ver]pool
Friday evening, 14th Nov.

The "Persia" sails tomorrow early. This will go in her. I am going to take the Mediterranean tour—will start on Monday early. You will not probably hear from me again in some time. But I will write when I can. God bless you,

My love to Sophia & kisses for children.

Affectionately Your Brother
Herman.

Saw Mr Hawthorne this morning—but heard nothing further of Mr G. Duyckinck. It is not improbable—, I suppose, that ere this reaches you his brother may have crossed the seas to him.

H^m.

Abridgment by Mrs. Hawthorne (with her ellipses) of Nathaniel Hawthorne's account of Melville in Liverpool and Chester.

November 20th. — A week ago last Monday, Herman Melville came to see me at the Consulate, looking much as he used to do, and with his characteristic gravity and reserve of manner. . . . . We soon found ourselves on pretty much our former terms of sociability and confidence. . . . . He is thus far on his way to Constantinople. I do not wonder that he found it necessary to take an airing through the world, after so many years of toilsome pen-labor, following upon so wild and adventurous a youth as his was. I invited him to come and stay with us at Southport, as long as he might remain in this vicinity, and accordingly he did come the next day. . . . . On Wednesday we took a pretty long walk together, and sat down in a hollow among the sand-hills, sheltering ourselves from the high cool wind. Melville, as he always does, began to reason of Providence and futurity, and of everything else that lies beyond human ken. . . . . He has a very high and noble nature, and is better worth immortality than the most of us. . . . . On Saturday we went to

Chester together. I love to take every opportunity of going to Chester; it being the one only place, within easy reach of Liverpool, which possesses any old English interest.

Hawthorne's complete account of Melville in Liverpool and Chester.

November 20th, Thursday. A week ago last Monday, Herman Melville came to see me at the Consulate, looking much as he used to do (a little paler, and perhaps a little sadder), in a rough outside coat, and with his characteristic gravity and reserve of manner. He had crossed from New York to Glasgow in a screw steamer, about a fortnight before, and had since been seeing Edinburgh and other interesting places. I felt rather awkward at first; because this is the first time I have met him since my ineffectual attempt to get him a consular appointment from General Pierce. However, I failed only from real lack of power to serve him; so there was no reason to be ashamed, and we soon found ourselves on pretty much our former terms of sociability and confidence. Melville has not been well, of late; he has been affected with neuralgic complaints in his head and limbs, and no doubt has suffered from too constant literary occupation, pursued without much success, latterly; and his writings, for a long while past, have indicated a morbid state of mind. So he left his place at Pittsfield, and has established his wife and family, I believe, with his father-in law in Boston, and is thus far on his way to Constantinople. I do not wonder that he found it necessary to take an airing through the world, after so many years of toilsome pen-labor and domestic life, following upon so wild and adventurous a youth as his was. I invited him to come and stay with us at Southport, as long as he might remain in this vicinity; and, accordingly, he did come, the next day, taking with him, by way of baggage, the least little bit of a bundle, which, he told me, contained a night shirt and a tooth-brush. He is a person of very gentlemanly instincts in every respect, save that he is a little heterodox in the matter of clean linen.

He stayed with us from Tuesday till Thursday; and, on the intervening day, we took a pretty long walk together, and sat down in a hollow among the sand hills (sheltering ourselves from the high, cool wind) and smoked a cigar. Melville, as he always does, began to reason of Providence and futurity, and of everything that lies beyond human ken, and informed me that he had "pretty much made up his mind to be annihilated"; but still he does not seem to rest in that anticipation; and, I think, will never rest until he gets hold of a definite belief. It is strange how he persists—and has persisted ever since I knew him, and probably long before—in wandering to-and fro over these deserts, as dismal and monotonous as the sand hills amid which we were sitting. He can neither believe, nor be comfortable in his unbelief; and he is too honest and courageous not to try to do one or the other. If he were a religious man, he would be one of the most truly religious and reverential; he has a very high and noble nature, and better worth immortality than most of us.

He went back with me to Liverpool, on Thursday; and, the next day, Henry Bright met him at my office, and showed him whatever was worth seeing in town. On Saturday, Melville and I went to Chester together. I love to take every opportunity of going to Chester; it being the one only place, within easy reach of Liverpool, which possesses any old English interest. It was a fitful and uncertain day; and began to shower just as we left the Landing Stage in crossing the Mersey; but, arriving at Chester, we had glimpses of sunshine, and walked round the wall with hardly a spatter of rain. Chester wall is as interesting a promenade as can be found in England. Starting from the East Gate, and turning to the left, we soon come to the old Cathedral, with its churchyard, its great tower, its buttresses, of red freestone, with patches of reparation that look square and angular, but generally with an aspect as if it were thawing, or as if it were a sugar toy, and had been sucked in a child's mouth; so much have the storms of ages worn away this soft material. Passing onward, we look down from the wall into a precipitous depth, at the bottom of which creeps a canal, with long and narrow canal-boats moored in it. A little further, stands the tower, uprising beside

Nathaniel Hawthorne, steel engraving, 1851, from the Cephas Thompson painting, 1850. A copy was presented to Melville by Sophia Hawthorne, 1851 (HCL-M).

the wall, from the top of which King Charles beheld his army defeated on Rowton Moor—which is now well covered with houses, and most unlike a battle field. Farther on, at an angle of the wall, is another tower, and a ruinous and ivy-grown outwork. From this part of the wall, we see the Welsh hills, blue in the distance; and the air from these hills comes freshly down upon Chester, making it a healthful place of residence, aged and mouldering though it be. Then comes the Roodee, the modern race-course, and which the Romans are supposed to have hollowed out and used for the same purpose; a green, circular space, outside of the wall, whence its whole circumference can be taken in. Within the wall, at nearly the same point, is the castle, almost entirely a modern structure, although there is one old tower, said to have been built by Julius Caesar, I believe—at all events, by the Romans. Here the wall makes another angle, and we come in sight of the Dee, which, just as we were passing along, had a bright silvery sheen of sunshine, and a breezy ripple. At this spot, the wall passes close beneath the castle, and beneath a prison which forms a part of it, and which is built of a cold, gray granite, most fit for prisons. Next we see an old bridge, with arches, and on the hither side, some tall, decayed edifices, with hundreds of broken windows, and all powdered duskily with flour; for these are ancient mills, and are still as busily employed as ever. The view across the Dee, and on the other side, is here very picturesque and beautiful; and the dam, stretching across the river, is almost a cascade. Adown the river, we see pleasure boats, some of them with awnings, and a small steamer. Turning another angle of the wall, we see orchards beneath us, on the outer side, the trees of which, though tall, do not reach up to a level with our feet; and gardens, cultivated close up to the old stone foundation; and all the domestic snugness of old established houses and grounds, that have been laid out within the centuries since Chester wall ceased to be a warlike rampart. On the city-side, the houses abut upon the wall, and rise directly up from it, with doors opening upon the walk; the other side of the house fronting upon one of the city-streets. It is very curious and pleasant to see how the city has swelled, and overflowed the girdle that once kept it in; although some of the exterior houses look almost as ancient as any of those within. Beyond the wall, too, we saw the tower of St John's church, with a statue in a niche over the door, looking (to repeat my simile of the Cathedral) like a sugar image which a child had sucked in its mouth; so much is it worn and defaced. And now, between edifices overtopping the wall, and shutting it in on either side, we come back to the East Gate, and descend by a stone staircase into the bustling street. The whole circuit of the wall is estimated at two miles, and there is a paved walk the whole way, broad enough for two to walk abreast, garded by a railing on the inside, and a parapet of stone externally. Of course, the upper portion has undergone many repairs; but the stones of the foundation were probably laid by Roman hands.

It being now one °clock, or thereabouts, we walked through some of the Rows, in quest of a dinner, and found one in a confectioner's shop; these establishments being a frequent resort of Englishmen—and especially of Englishwomen—for hasty refection, in preference to a hotel. We were shown upstairs, into an antique room fronting on the street, with cross-beams, panelled walls, a large table and some smaller ones, and a good fire. The waiting maid brought us some little veal-pies on a tray, and some damson tarts on another tray; and we had, besides, some Bass's ale, and made a very comfortable meal at the cost of a shilling and two-pence each. And then we went to the Cathedral, which I had occasion to describe, I think, or at least to talk about, several times before. Its gray nave seemed to impress me more than at any former visit. Passing into the cloisters, an attendant—he did not seem to be a verger, or other solemn personage, but was a very intelligent and ready-witted man—took possession of us, and showed us about the Cathedral.

Within the choir, there is a profusion of very rich oaken carving, both on the screen that separates it from the nave, and on the seats, and on the walls; very curious, and most elaborate, and lavished most wastefully, where nobody would think of looking for it—where, indeed, amid the dimness of the Cathedral, the exquisite detail of their elaboration could not possibly be seen. Our guide lighted some of the gas-burners (of which there are many hundreds in the Cathedral) to help us see them; but it required close scrutiny, even then. It must have been out of the question, when the whole means of illumination were a few smoky torches or candles. There was a row of niches, where the monks used to stand for four hours together, in the performance of some of their services; and to relieve them a little, they were allowed partially to sit on a projection of the seats, which were turned up in the niche for that purpose; but if they grew drowsy, so as to fail to balance themselves, the seat was so contrived as to slip down, thus bringing the monk to the floor. These projections on the seat are each and all of them carved with curious devices, no two alike. The guide showed us one, representing, apparently, the first quarrel of a new-married couple, wrought with wonderful expression. Indeed, the artist never failed to bring out his idea in the most striking manner; as for instance, Satan under the guise of a lion, devouring a sinner bodily, and again in the figure of a dragon, with a man half way down his gullet, the legs hanging out. The carver may not have seen anything grotesque in this, nor have intended it at all by way of joke; but certainly there would appear to be a sort of grim mirthfulness in some of the designs. One does not see why such fantasies should be strewn about the holy interior of a Cathedral, unless it were intended to contain everything that belongs to the heart of man, both upward and downward.

In a side aisle of the choir, we saw a tomb, said to be that of the Emperor Henry Fourth, of Germany, though on very indistinct authority. This is a square, oblong tomb, carved, and, on one side, painted with bright colors, and gilded. During a very long period, it was built and plastered into the wall of the Cathedral, and the exterior side was whitewashed; but, on being removed, the inner side was found to have been ornamented with gold and color, in the manner in which we now see it. If this was customary with tombs, it must have added vastly to the gorgeous magnificence to which the painted windows, and polished pillars, and ornamented cielings, contributed so much. In fact, a Cathedral in its fresh estate seems to have been like a pavilion of the sunset, all purple and gold; whereas now it more resembles deepest and grayest twilight.

Afterwards, we were shown into the ancient Refectory, which is now used as the city Grammar School, and was furnished with the usual desks and seats for the boys. In one corner of this large room was the sort of pulpit, or elevated seat, (with a broken staircase of stone ascending to it,) where one of the monks used to read to his brethren, while sitting at their meals. The desks were cut and carved with the scholars' knives, just as they used to be in the school-rooms where I was a scholar. Thence we passed into the Chapter House; but, before that, if I rightly remember, we went through a small room, in which Melville opened a cupboard and discovered a dozen or two of wine-bottles; but our guide told us that they were now empty, and never were meant for jollity, having held only sacramental wine. In the Chapter House we saw the library, some of the volumes of which were antique folios, though most of them might have fitted other shelves as well as these. There were two dusty and tattered banners hanging on the wall, belonging to a regiment that was raised in Cheshire; and the attendant promised to make us laugh by something that he would tell us about them. The joke was, that these two banners had been in the battle of Bunker Hill; and our countrymen, he said, always smiled at hearing this. He had discovered us to be Americans by the notice we took of a mural tablet in the choir, to the memory of a Lieutenant Governor Clarke, of New York, who died in Chester before the Revolution. From the Chapter House, he ushered us back into the Nave, ever and anon pointing out some portion of the edifice more ancient than the rest, and showing pillars, or pedestals, or parts of the walls, that varied several hundred years in antiquity from other parts close beside them. And when I asked him how he knew this, he said that he had learnt it from the Archaeologists, who could read off such things like a book. This guide was a lively, quick-witted man, and did his business less by rote, and more with a vivacious interest, than any guide I ever met.

After leaving the Cathedral, we sought out the Yacht Inn, near the Water Gate. This was, for a long period of time, the principal inn of Chester, and was the house at which Swift once put up, on his way to Holyhead, and where he invited the clergy of the Cathedral to come and sup with him. We sat down in a small snuggery, behind the bar, and smoked a cigar and drank some stout, conversing the while with the landlord. The Chester people, according to my experience, are very affable, and fond of talking with strangers about the antiquities and picturesque characteristics of their town. It partly lives, the landlord told us, by its visitors, and many people spend the summer here, on account of the antiquities and the good air. When our cigars were out, and our tumblers empty, he showed us a broad, balustraded staircase, into a large, comfortable, old fashioned parlor, with windows looking on the street, and on the Custom House that stood right opposite. This was the room where Swift expected to receive the clergy of Chester; and on one of the window-panes (about the size of eight inches by ten) were two acrid lines, written with the diamond of his ring, satirizing those reverend gentlemen, in revenge for their refusing his invitation. The first line begins rather indistinctly; but the writing grows fully legible as it proceeds. I have forgotten the purport—which is the less matter, as it is preserved in the guide books.

The Yacht Tavern is a very old house, in the gabled style. The landlord told us that the timbers and frame-work are still perfectly sound. In the same street is the Bishop's house (so called as having been the residence of a prelate, long ago) which is covered with curious sculptures, representing Scriptural scenes. And, I believe, in the same neighborhood is the County Court, accessible by an archway through which we penetrated, and found ourselves in a passage way, very ancient and dusky, overlooked from the upper story by a gallery, to which an antique staircase ascended, with balustrades, and square landing-places. A printer saw us here, and asked us into his printing-office, and talked very affably; indeed, he could hardly have been more civil, if he had known that both Melville and I have given a good deal of employment to the brethren of his craft.

We left Chester at about four °clock; and I took the rail for Southport at half-past six, parting from Melville at a street-corner in Liverpool, in the rainy evening. I saw him again on Monday, however. He said that he already felt much better than in America; but observed that he did not anticipate much pleasure in his rambles, for that the spirit of adventure is gone out of him. He certainly is much overshadowed since I saw him last; but I hope he will brighten as he goes onward. He sailed from Liverpool in a steamer on Tuesday, leaving his trunk behind him at my consulate, and taking only a carpet-bag to hold all his travelling-gear. This is the next best thing to going naked; and as he wears his beard and moustache, and so needs no dressing-case—nothing but a tooth-brush—I do not know a more independent personage. He learned his travelling habits by drifting about, all over the South Sea, with no other clothes or equipage than a red flannel shirt and a pair of duck trowsers. Yet we seldom see men of less criticizable manners than he.

1860

MELVILLE'S *Meteor* journal is supplemented here by four surviving records from his own hand while aboard during 1860: an excerpt from his letter to Evert Duyckinck on May 28, just before sailing; his letter to his eleven-year-old son Malcolm begun on September 1, 1860; another to his seven-year-old daughter Bessie on the next day; and his shipboard pencil drawing of "Arrowhead in the Olden Time A.D. 1860", apparently made in early October, with his later accompanying note about it. The letter to Bessie is reproduced (with the writing at true size), by permission, from the original in the Melville Collection of the Houghton Library of Harvard University.

Finally, two items written by Melville after his *Meteor* voyage are reprinted here. The first is an excerpt from his letter in 1862 of jocular advice and reminiscence for his brother Tom (by then captain of another ship). The second is the Christmas poem he addressed to Tom, probably in 1860 while Tom was still its captain (see p. 206 above; for its revised form see *Published Poems*, p. 228); the transcription was made by Robert C. Ryan (1989) from the manuscript in the Houghton Library of Harvard University and is printed by permission. These and a few other documents are referred to and quoted in the HISTORICAL NOTE, pp. 195, 197, 199–201, 203; in discussions at 132.35, 133.11, 133.16, 134.4, 134.25; and on p. 602 above. For Elizabeth Shaw Melville's much later brief memorandum of Melville's *Meteor* voyage, see Merton M. Sealts, Jr., *The Early Lives of Melville* (Madison: University of Wisconsin Press, 1974), p. 171.

Excerpt: Melville to Evert Duyckinck, Boston, May 28, 1860.

On board ship "Meteor"

My Dear Duyckinck: I am glad that the postponement of the ship's day of sailing gives me a chance to answer your letter, recev[d] in reply to mine, on the eve of my leaving Pittsfield. It was a very welcome one—quite a wind from the feilds of old times. . . .

I anticipate as much pleasure as, at the age of fourty, one temperately can, in the voyage I am going. I go under very happy auspices so far as ship & Captain is concerned. A noble ship and a nobler Captain—& he my brother. We have the breadth of both tropics before us, to sail over twice; & shall round the world. Our first port is San Francisco, which we shall probably make in 110 days from Boston. Thence we go to Manilla—& thence, I hardly know where.—I wish devoutly you were going along. I think it would agree with you. The prime requisite for enjoyment in sea voyages, for passengers, is 1st health—2[d] good-nature. Both first-rate things, but not universally to be found.—At sea a fellow comes out. Salt water is like wine, in that respect.

I have a good lot of books with me—such as they are;—plenty of old periodicals—lazy reading for lazy latitudes.—

Here I am called away, & must close.

Good bye to you
& God bless you
H Melville

Melville to Malcolm Melville, Pacific Ocean, September 1, 16, 1860.

(Off the coast of South America
On the Tropic of Capricorn)

Saturday September 1st 1860

My Dear Malcolm: It is now three months exactly since the ship "Meteor" sailed from Boston—a quarter of a year. During this long period, she has been continually moving, and has only seen land on two days. I suppose you have followed out on the map (or my *globe* were better—so you get Mama to clean it off for you) the route from Boston to San Francisco. The distance, by the straight track, is about 16000 miles; but the ship will have sailed before she gets there nearer 18 or 20000 miles. So you see it is further than from the apple-tree to the big rock. When we crossed the Line in the Atlantic Ocean it was very warm; & we had warm weather for some weeks; but as we kept getting to the Southward it began to grow less warm, and then coolish, and cold and colder, till at last it was winter. I wore two flannel shirts, and big mittens & overcoat, and a great Russia cap, a very thick leather cap, so called by sailors. At last we came in sight of land all covered with snow—uninhabited land, where no one ever lived, and no one ever will live—it is so barren, cold and desolate. This was Staten Land—an island. Near it, is the big island of Terra del Fuego. We passed through between these islands, and had a good view of both. There are some "wild people" living on Terra del Fuego; but it being the depth of winter there, I suppose they kept in their caves. At any rate we saw none of them. The next day we were off Cape Horn, the Southernmost point of all America. Now it was very bad weather, and was dark at about three o'clock in the afternoon. The wind blew terribly. We had hail-storms, and snow and sleet, and often the spray froze as it touched the deck. The ship rolled, and sometimes took in so much water on the deck as to wash people off their legs. Several sailors were washed along the deck this way, and came near getting washed overboard. And this reminds me of a very sad thing that happened the very morning we were off the Cape—I mean the very *pitch* of the Cape.—It was just about day-light; it was blowing a gale of wind; and Uncle Tom ordered the top-sails (big sails) to be furled. Whilst the sailors were aloft on one of the yards, the ship rolled and plunged terribly; and it blew with sleet and hail, and was very cold & biting. Well, all at once, Uncle Tom saw something falling through the air, and then heard a thump, and then,—looking before him, saw a poor sailor lying dead on the deck. He had fallen from the yard, and was killed instantly.—His shipmates picked him up, and carried him under cover. By and by, when time could be spared, the sailmaker sewed up the body in a peice of sail-cloth, putting some iron balls—cannon balls—at the foot of it. And, when all was ready, the body was put on a plank, and carried to the ship's side in the prescence of all hands. Then Uncle Tom, as Captain, read a prayer out of the prayer-book, and at a given word, the sailors who held the plank tipped it up, and immediately the body slipped into the stormy ocean, and we saw it no more.—Such is the way a poor sailor is buried at sea. This sailor's name was Ray. He had a friend among the crew; and they were both going to California, and thought of living there; but you see what happened.

We were in this stormy weather about forty or fifty days, dating from the beginning. But now at last we are in fine weather again, and the sun shines warm. (See page 5th)

Pacific Ocean

On the Line, Sept. 16th 1860

My Dear Malcolm: Since coming to the end of the fourth page, we have been sailing in fine weather, and it has continued quite warm.—The other day we saw a whale-ship; and I got into a boat and sailed over the ocean in it to the whale-ship, and stayed there about an hour. They had eight or ten of the "wild people" aboard. The Captain of the whale-ship had hired them at one of the islands called Roratonga. He wanted them to help pull in the whale-boat when they hunt the whale.—Uncle Tom's crew are now very busy making the ship look smart for San Francisco. They are tarring the rigging, and are going to paint the ship, & the masts and yards. She looks very rusty now, oweing to so much bad weather that we have been in.—When we get to San-Francisco, I shall put this letter in the post office there, and you will get it in about 25 days afterwards. It will go in a steamer to a place called Panama, on the Isthmus of Darien (get out your map, & find it) then it will cross the Isthmus by rail road to Aspinwall or Chagres on the Gulf of Mexico; there, another steamer will take it, which steamer, after touching at Havanna in Cuba for coals, will go direct to New York; and there, it will go to the Post Office, and so, get to Pittsfield.

I hope that, when it arrives, it will find you well, and all the family. And I hope that you have called to mind what I said to you about your behaviour previous to my going away. I hope that you have been obedient to your mother, and helped her all you could, & saved her trouble. Now is the time to show what you are—whether you are a good, honorable boy, or a good-for-nothing one. Any boy, of your age, who disobeys his mother, or worries her, or is disrespectful to her—such a boy is a poor shabby fellow; and if you know any such boys, you ought to cut their acquaintance.

(Continued from 6th page.)

Now, my Dear Malcolm, I must finish my letter to you. I think of you, and Stanwix & Bessie and Fanny very often; and often long to be with you. But it can not be, at present. The picture which I have of you & the rest, I look at sometimes, till the faces almost seem real.—Now, my Dear Boy, good bye, & God bless you

Your affectionate father
H Melville

I enclose a little baby flying-fish's wing
for Fanny
[*enclosure:"wing"*]

The Melville children, circa 1860: Stanwix, Frances (Fanny), Malcolm, and Elizabeth (Bessie). Courtesy of the Berkshire Athenaeum.

Melville to Elizabeth ("Bessie") Melville, Pacific Ocean, September 2, 1860.

My Dear Bessie: I thought I would send you a letter, that you could read yourself—at least a part of it. But here and there I propose to write in the usual manner, as I find the printing style comes rather awkwardly in a rolling ship. Mamma will read these parts to you. We have seen a good many sea-birds. Many have followed the ship day after day. I used to feed them with crumbs. But now it has got to be warm weather, the birds have left us. They we[re] about as big as chickens—they were all over speckled—and they would sometimes, during a calm, keep behind the ship, fluttering about in the water, with a mighty cackling, and whenever anything was thrown overboard they would hurry to get it. But they never would light on the ship—they kept all the time flying or else resting themselves by floating on the water like ducks in a pond. These birds have no home, unless it is some wild rocks in the middle of the ocean. They never see any orchards, and have a taste of the apples & cherries, like your gay little friend in Pittsfield Robin Red Breast Esq.

—I could tell you a good many more things about the sea, but I must defer the rest till I get home.

I hope you are a good girl; and give Mama no trouble. Do you help Mama keep house? That little bag you made for me, I use very often, and think of you every time.

I suppose you have had a good many walks on the hill, and picked the strawberries.

I hope you take good care of little

FANNY

and that when you go on the hill, you go this way:

[*see reproduction for Melville's drawing*]

that is to say, hand in hand.

By-by
Papa.

Pacific Ocean
Sep. 2d. 1860

My Dear Bessie: I thought I would send you a letter, that you could read yourself—at least a part of it. But here and there I purpose to write in the usual manner, as I find the printing style comes rather awkwardly in a rolling ship. Mamma will read those parts to you. We have seen a good many sea-birds. Many have followed the ship day after day. I used to feed them with crumbs. But now it has got to be warm weather, the birds have left us. They were about as big as chickens—They were all over speckled—and they would sometimes, during a calm, keep behind the ship, fluttering about on the water, with a mighty cackling, and whenever anything was thrown overboard they would hurry to get it. But they never would light on the ship — they kept all the time flying or else resting themselves by floating on the water like ducks in a pond. These birds have no home, unless it is some wild rocks in the middle of the ocean. They never see any orchards, and have a taste of the apples & cherries, like your gay little friend in Pittsfield Robin Red Breast Esq.

—— I could tell you a good many nice things about the sea, but I must defer the rest till I get home.

I hope you are a good girl; and give Mama no trouble. Do you help Mama keep house? . . .

That little bag you made for me, I use very often, and think of you every time.

I suppose you have had a good many walks on the hill, and picked the strawberries.

I hope you take good care of little

FANNY

and that when you go on the hill, you go this way:

That is to say, hand in hand.

By-by

Papa.

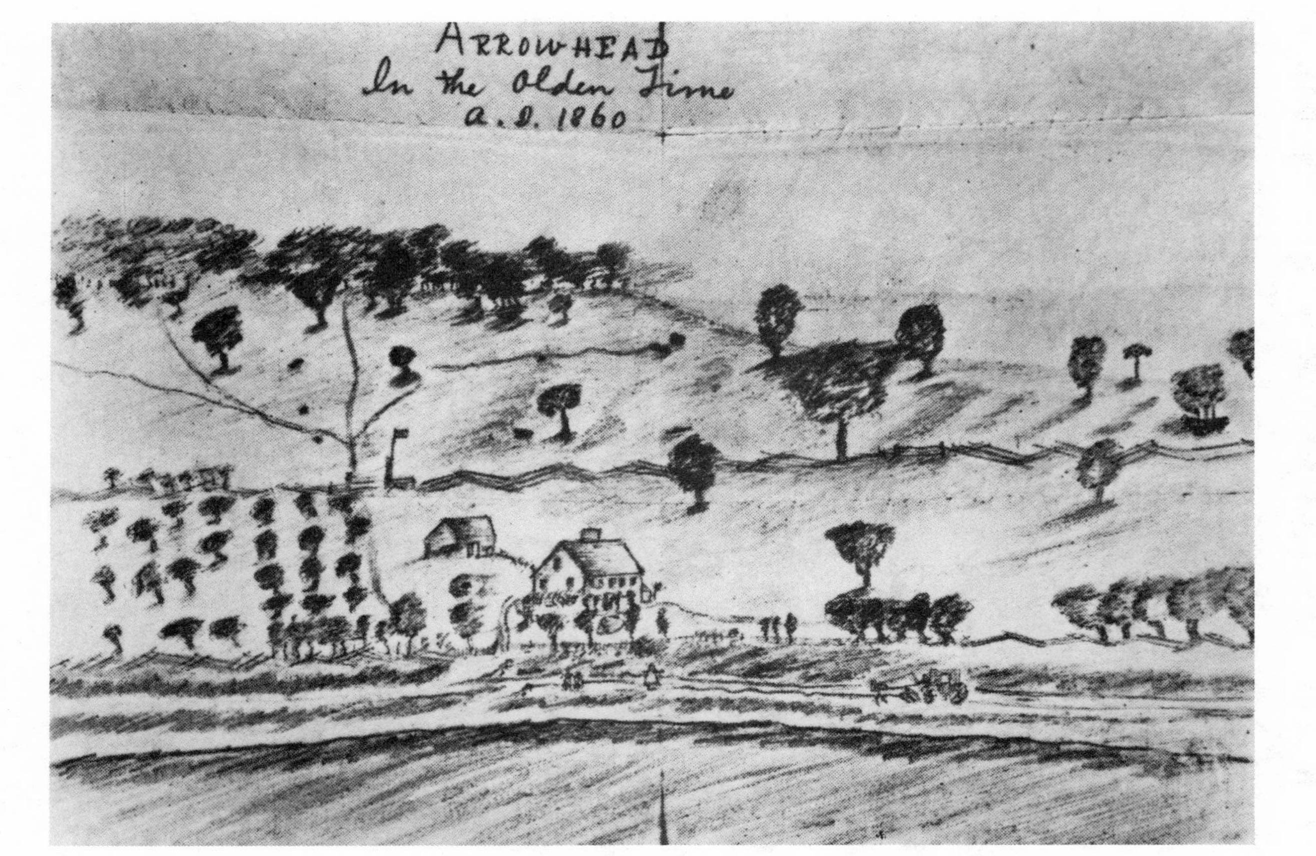
ARROWHEAD
In the Olden Time
A.D. 1860

Melville's drawing "Arrowhead in the Olden Time A.D. *1860", with his note about it.*

The original drawing and accompanying note, now lost, were lent by Eleanor Melville Metcalf to Raymond Weaver for reproduction in his biography and were not returned to her. See his *Herman Melville: Mystic and Mariner* (New York: Doran, 1921), where each is separately shown on the plate facing p. 368. There the drawing (10.1 x 7.3 cm) is placed above, with the caption "MELVILLE AS ARTIST", and the note (6.8 x 5.5 cm) below, uncaptioned. No further information is given on the plate or in the text. Study of Weaver's two reproductions shows that Melville made both the drawing (in pencil, with the heading possibly in ink) and the note (possibly in ink) on paper manufactured with lines, and that he worked both times across, not parallel, to the lines, which are faintly visible on the plate, running vertically at intervals of .5 cm. The original dimensions of both items remain conjectural, but to judge from the narrow .5 cm line intervals in Weaver's reproductions compared to the .8 cm ones in the paper of his 1860 journal and of page 7 of his letter to Malcolm, both were probably nearly two-thirds (60 percent) larger than shown on the plate. Both reproductions were obviously cropped: Melville is unlikely to have left no margins on his drawing or to have executed it—or his note—on the small scale shown (see, for example, how tiny the horse, carriage, and figures still are in the enlarged reproduction here). In 1951, Jay Leyda reproduced the drawing (enlarged to 15 x 11.4 cm) in the *Log* (II, Plate IX), necessarily from Weaver's plate since Leyda listed no source and reported the drawing and note as "unlocated." Leyda also gave there the first transcription of the note (II, 627), stating that it was "on reverse" of the ("unlocated") drawing without saying how he could know that, but probably by being told by Mrs. Metcalf or Weaver or both, from memory. In any case, the same spacing (.5 cm) between lines on both items on Weaver's plate indicates that the relative size of the drawing and the note was kept the same when they were reduced to fit on it. Here, both are reproduced from that plate, enlarged (by 60 percent) to 11.4 × 16 cm and 8.2 × 10.3 cm, to make them about the probable original size.

In Melville's caption, the phrase "In the Olden Time" dated "A.D. 1860"—the same year the drawing was made—may be taken as humorous or may indicate that the caption was added in after years. The accompanying note was written some while after the drawing was made, as shown by its first sentence, but before his return home, as indicated by its later ones.

The present transcription (by Jay Leyda, 1951, verified by Harrison Hayford, Lynn Horth, and Robert C. Ryan, 1989) follows the same principles as for the journals (see pp. 236–42; for line numbering and symbols used see p. 592, footnote 3). All words, many of them elided, are given in standard spelling. One word has a possible alternative reading: "cabin" (2.7) for NN "calm". Leyda read "Such" (4.1) for NN "such".

1 Drew this at sea one afternoon
2 on deck — & then in the calm. — Made
3 me feel as if I was there, almost ——
4 such is the magic power of a fine
5 Artist. —— Be it known I pride myself
6 particularly upon "Charlie" & the driver. —
7 It is to be supposed that I am in
8 the carriage; & the figures are
9 welcoming me.

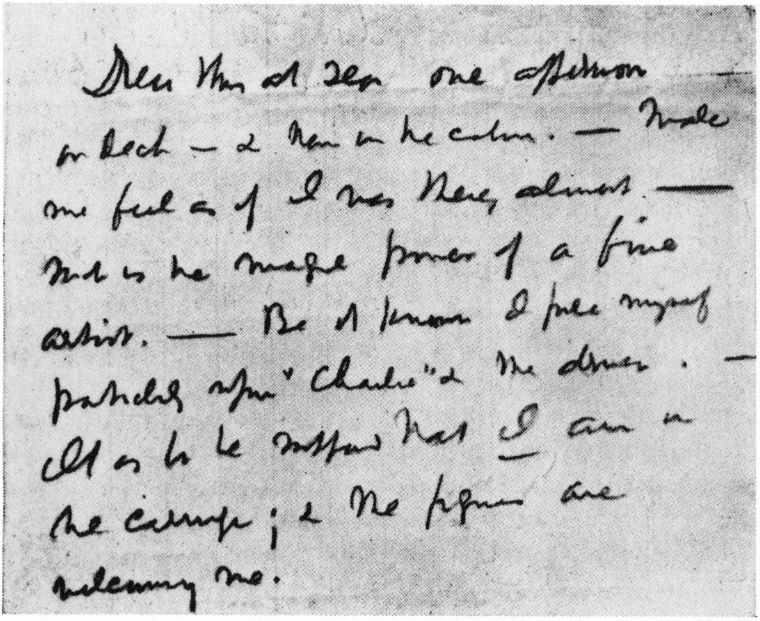

Advice and a reminiscence of the Meteor *voyage: excerpt from Melville to Captain Thomas Melville, May 25, 1862.*

—As for your treatment of those young ones, there I entirely commend you. Strap them, I beseech you. You remember what the Bible says:—

"Oh ye who teach the children of the nations,
  Holland, France, England, Germany or Spain,
I pray ye *strap* them upon all occasions,
  It mends their morals—never mind the pain"[3]

In another place the Bible says, you know, something about spareing the strap & spoiling the child.—Since I have quoted poetry above, it puts me in mind of my own doggerel. You will be pleased to learn that I have disposed of a lot of it at a great bargain. In fact, a trunk-maker took the whole stock off my hands at ten cents the pound. So, When you buy a new trunk again, just peep at the lining & perhaps you may be rewarded by some glorious stanza stareing you in the face & claiming admiration. If you were not such a devil of a ways off, I would send you a trunk, by way of presentation-copy. I cant help thinking what a luckless chap you were that voyage you had a poetaster with you. You remember the romantic moonlight night, when the conceited donkey repeated to you about three cables' length of his verses. But you bore it like a hero. I cant in fact recall so much as a single *wince*. To be sure, you went to bed immediately upon the conclusion of the entertainment; but this much I am sure of, whatere were your sufferings, you never gave them utterance. Tom, my boy, I admire you. I say again, you are a hero.—By the way, I hope in God's name that rumor which reached your owners (C & P.) a few weeks since—that dreadful rumor is not true. They heard that you had begun to take to ———drink?—Oh no, but worse——to sonnet-writing. That off Cape Horn instead of being on deck about your business, you devoted your time to writing a sonnet on your mistress' eye-brow, & another upon her "tourneur."—"I'll be damned" says Curtis (he was very profane) "if I'll have a sonneteer among my Captains."—"Well, if he has taken to poetizing," says Peabody—"God help the ship!"—I have written them contradicting the rumor in your name. What villian & secret enemy of yours set this cursed report afloat, I cant imagine.

3. The original lines, in Byron's *Don Juan*, II, 1–4, read:
Oh ye! who teach the ingenuous youth of nations
Holland, France, England, Germany or Spain,
I pray ye flog them upon all occasions,
It mends their morals,—never mind the pain.

Poem (1860?): Unpublished by Melville.

To Tom

Thou that dost thy Christmas keep
Lonesome on the torrid deep,
But in thy "Meteor" proudly sweep
O'er the waves that vainly comb—
Of thee we think,
To thee we drink,
And drain the glass, my gallant Tom!

Thou that, duty-led, dost roam
Far from thy shepherd-brother's home—
Shearer of the ocean-foam!
To whom one Christmas may not come,—
Of thee I think
Till on its brink
The glass shows tears, beloved Tom!

Index

PAGE NUMBERS 1–160 refer to pages in the journals themselves; all proper names on these pages are indexed. Numbers in bold indicate illustrations. Titles of books and works of art are indexed by the name of the author or artist, and also by title if the author or artist's name is not given with it by Melville. See under names of cities for streets, hotels, bridges, parks, sightseeing attractions, and so forth; major attractions are also listed separately. Since Melville's spellings and others then current often vary, spellings in the index follow now-standard forms adopted in the DISCUSSIONS.

JOURNALS

WORKS

COLOPHON

THE TEXT *of the Northwestern-Newberry Edition of* THE WRITINGS OF HERMAN MELVILLE *is set in eleven-point Bembo, two points leaded. This exceptionally handsome type face is a modern rendering of designs made by Francesco Griffo for the office of Aldus Manutius in Venice and first used for printing, in 1495, of the tract* De Aetna *by Cardinal Pietro Bembo. The display face is Bruce Rogers's Centaur, a twentieth-century design based on and reflective of the late-fifteenth-century Venetian models of Nicolas Jenson.*

This volume was set in type by Alexander Typesetting, Inc., of Indianapolis, Indiana. It was printed and bound in paper by Braun-Brumfield, Inc., of Ann Arbor, Michigan, and bound in cloth by John H. Dekker & Sons, Inc., of Grand Rapids, Michigan. The typography and binding design of the edition are by Paul Randall Mize.